1001 GUITARS
TO DREAM OF PLAYING BEFORE YOU DIE

1001 GUITARS

TO DREAM OF PLAYING BEFORE YOU DIE

GENERAL EDITOR
TERRY BURROWS

FOREWORD BY
DAVE GREGORY

UNIVERSE

A Quintessence Book

First published in the United States of America in 2013 by
UNIVERSE PUBLISHING
A Division of Rizzoli International Publications, Inc.
300 Park Avenue South
New York, NY 10010
www.rizzoliusa.com

2013 2014 2015 2016 / 10 9 8 7 6 5 4 3 2 1

ISBN: 978-0-7893-2701-7

Library of Congress Control Number: 2013933404

QSS.GUTR

This book was designed and produced by
Quintessence Editions Ltd.
230 City Road
London EC1V 2TT
www.1001beforeyoudie.com

Senior Editor Ruth Patrick
Editors Ruth Patrick, Henry Russell, Bruno MacDonald
Designer Tea Aganovic
Production Manager Anna Pauletti

Editorial Director Jane Laing
Publisher Mark Fletcher

Color reproduction by KHL Chromagraphics, Singapore
Printed in China by Midas Printing Ltd.

Contents

Foreword | Dave Gregory

It all began for me in England in the late 1950s. I would have been about seven years old when I asked my father what the instrument was I could hear playing on the radio. He grunted disapprovingly and said, "It sounds like an electric guitar." Electric guitar! Somehow those two words together had an immediate impact. I knew what a guitar was: a cute-looking box with a round hole favored by Spanish dance musicians. But an electric guitar? That sounded dangerous. And it sounded different; it had a distinctive twang to it, produced by means that were a mystery . . . how did it work?

Not long afterward, I saw a picture of an electric guitar in the embrace of one Hank B. Marvin of the then hugely successful Shadows. What I saw exceeded my wildest dreams: it was sleek and slender, had an odd metal bar attached to the bridge, some weird gadgetry on a white plate under the strings, and, best of all, it was the color of a fire engine, bright red! In Marvin's hands, it produced a vibrant sound that perfectly matched its glamorous looks. It was called a Fender Stratocaster—wow! I so wanted to learn more about it, hoping that one day I might actually get to *touch* one just like it.

It turned out that there was more to the sound than just the instrument. Apparently, you needed an amplifier to make it work as it had no acoustic properties to speak of. That's where the "electric" bit came in: the sound from the strings was carried electronically via special windings called "pick-ups," to which were attached controls to alter volume and tone. The signal would pass via a plug-in lead to the amplifier, which did exactly that, boosting the sound of the vibrating strings through a loud speaker. It was all too exciting for words.

The Shadows dominated the airwaves of BBC radio in the early 1960s, and I soon became hooked on this new musical phenomenon, which I later learned had its roots in American pop and rock 'n' roll. The Ventures and Duane Eddy were pioneers of instrumental guitar rock in the United States, together with one-offs like Link Wray's "Rumble" and Dick Dale's "Miserlou"; simple good-time party music aimed at teenagers. As intoxicating as this music was to me as a child, it was generally frowned upon by my parents, which served to add a rebellious aspect to it that I found appealing. And when birthdays and Christmases came around, at the top of my wish list was a guitar.

There was no chance of that! While The Beatles turned the world on its head with some of the greatest music ever heard, using electric guitars as a basis for their sound, I was packed off to piano lessons in order to learn about "serious" music. Just before Christmas of 1966, at the age of fourteen, I was finally allowed to purchase my first electric guitar, funded by money from a paper round and paid off in monthly installments. Within weeks of this event I was sacked by my piano teacher for "failing to practice"; this did not go down well with my parents! But one thing I could never have been accused of was failing to practice the guitar. Every waking moment would be spent grappling with chord shapes, with blisters and calluses on my fingers from forcing the steel strings down onto frets one-quarter of an inch below. I didn't even own an amplifier; that would have to wait. The most important thing was learning how the guitar worked as an instrument, and—equally importantly—how I looked with the thing slung across my shoulder.

And it's the romantic imagery that sets the electric guitar apart from almost every other musical instrument. As this book adequately demonstrates, it comes in all shapes, sizes, body styles, and colors, and all guitars have individual personalities that appeal to players of all musical genres. Not that it is necessary to be a player to appreciate them, either; they are, for the most part, beautiful objects to look at, and as time goes by, many are becoming valuable antiques. The quality of the raw materials and the designs and production methods used by the major American manufacturers like Gibson, Fender, and Gretsch in the 1950s and early 1960s have clearly stood the test of time; as a result, these are some of the most sought-after guitars today, often realizing astonishing sums at auction. But a glance through these pages reveals other treasures, perhaps not so obviously opulent, that have a nostalgic, kitsch, or sentimental value that are also a joy to behold.

Whatever reasons there might be for your attraction to the guitar, we hope you'll find this rich compilation as enjoyable to look at as we did to put together.

Dave Gregory

Introduction | Terry Burrows

In the summer of 2012, I signed up for what I thought sounded like the pleasant role of General Editor on a mighty new project, *1001 Guitars To Dream Of Playing Before You Die*. The content of the book was pretty self-explanatory—profiles and photographs of lots of guitars. Naturally, my first job was to select the instruments I wanted to include. When I mentioned this daunting task to friends—well-informed musicians included—they usually responded with the same question: "Are there 1001 such guitars?" As it happened, that turned out to be the least of my worries, as I struggled to establish a sane rationale for why most guitars had to be omitted. Eventually, in assessing many thousands of instruments, I sought a balance between those of historical and cultural significance, of classic production models, custom-built obscurities, interesting one-offs or oddities, guitars only affordable to merchant bankers and lottery winners, some nice (and nasty) cheapies . . . and I slipped in a handful just because I thought they looked pretty cool.

So what is this book about? A history of the guitar? A directory of the greatest guitars ever built? The world's most detailed compilation of guitar porn? I guess it's really a combination of all three. It certainly does contain some of the most notable guitars ever built. If you're a classical musician, for example, then dreaming of Segovia's 1937 Hauser is as close as you or anyone else will ever get to playing it—New York's Metropolitan Museum of Art will see to that. Or how about Jimi Hendrix's Olympic White Strat, the one used on his eloquent anti-Vietnam War protest "The Star-Spangled Banner" at the Woodstock Festival? What about The Beatles, that most regal of rock royalty? Unless you happen to be a close friend of Dahni Harrison you probably won't get your hands on "Rocky," a Strat hand-painted in vibrant psychedelic colors by his dad. And if you're a jazzer without the necessary several hundred thousand dollars in the bank to take to auction, then you're not going to get close to owning one of the beautiful archtops built by Jimmy D'Aquisto—venerated as perhaps the greatest guitar maker of the twentieth century since his untimely death in 1995.

Of course, for a book of this size and scope, a large number of the featured guitars will be production models. And I make no apologies for the volume of Stratocaster, Telecaster, and Les Paul variants on offer here; the continued dominance and influence of instruments designed during the first decade of the solidbody electric era makes this to some degree inevitable. Yet the reason for this unending popularity is not always easy to fathom, and may lead some to consider the guitar world as retro, conservative, resistant to change, or perhaps just easily influenced. At least some of this is attributable to the emergence of the "vintage" guitar market. At some point the 1970s, a viable industry appeared as certain guitars built nearly three decades earlier began selling for more than their brand-new equivalents. This phenomenon may have been to some extent attributable to a perceived drop in quality control by the leading manufacturers—

the most famous example being the great/tedious Fender pre-/post-CBS debate, where corporate streamlining that followed Leo Fender's 1965 company sale was seen as precipitating a decline in quality. Over time there can be little doubting that cost-cutting measures did have an impact on the consistency and earlier polish of Fender guitars, but the question of whether in practice this made them particularly "inferior" as musical instruments is harder to assess. After all, Jimi Hendrix frequently played post-CBS Strats; could his 1969 Woodstock appearance have been improved by playing a '54 Strat? Would he have sounded any less like the Hendrix we know wielding a cheap Squier "Hello Kitty" Strat… had they existed at the time?

Gradually, of course, the idea of buying old guitars for investment took hold, and basic laws of economics began to apply; potential investors were attracted in greater numbers, chasing an ever-dwindling supply of guitars, and prices began to inflate. So when there were no more bargains to be had among the rare or classic Fenders and Gibsons, the speculators moved onto other models or brands from the time . . . to a point where now nearly any guitar built before the mid-1970s is deemed to be in some way "collectible."

This has caused mirthful reflection among some older musicians. A few years ago I was lucky enough to be chatting with a guitarist (I won't name him here) active on the London music scene at the height of the psychedelic era—for someone like me this was the next best thing to jumping into a time machine set for "1967." At the time of our conversation he was well into his sixties, and talked enthusiastically about the groundbreaking music . . . not to mention the women and the drugs, all evidently in plentiful supply. And he laughed at my reaction as he told stories of crudely ripping humbuckers out of late-1950s Gibsons and replacing them with single-coils pulled out of early-1960s Strats, of chopping chunks out of bodies that were too heavy, and how on one occasion one of The Rolling Stones had given him an old Gibson that had been broken . . . so he took off the hardware and pick-ups . . . and left the rest in a rubbish bin in Soho! "Terry," he implored, "they were just tools to us—nobody knew they were going to be worth anything!"

And this is the crux of the issue, really. Is a guitar merely an artist's tool or is it something more?

Generation X-ers reading this might be able to recall learning their chops on Japanese plywood guitars built during the 1960s—at a time when, unlike today, there were few decent guitars coming out of the country. They were discovered rotting away in dusty old junk shops over the decades that followed, and cost us next to nothing. They were poorly constructed, the necks were prone to bowing and warping, the action was so high that many of us nearly gave up before we'd mastered our first barre chords, and they all seemed to come equipped with a vibrato arm that would sabotage the tuning if our hands went anywhere near to it. These (possibly exaggerated) recollections illustrate a modern generation gap of hefty proportions. For the past two decades, it hasn't really been possible to buy guitars that bad—they're simply not made. A modern-day $150 Chinese Squier Stratocaster may lack the finesse and bite of the "real" thing, but it's likely both to play and sound pretty reasonable. With that in mind, then, why would somebody pay ten times that amount for something broadly similar, straight off the production line, just because it has the word "Fender" written on the headstock? Or a hundred times that amount just because that Fender happened to have been built fifty years earlier? Are these instruments *so* significantly superior?

This seems to suggest that for many, a guitar is significantly more than just musical instrument—a personal statement, even. Why should this be? Perhaps it's about creating a connection to past era . . . or to an admired musician? As a youngster, the impetus to buy a Telecaster came entirely from seeing pictures of Syd Barrett. (A few days later I even stuck a bunch of little circular mirrors onto the body!) Or is it perhaps about buying into the iconography of the brand? Or are some trying to recapture the mojo of a long-lost youth? Is this a reason why even now the most popular electric guitars were designs created more than a half a century ago? Of course, one other possibility exists: that Leo Fender, Gibson's Ted McCarty, and other 1950s pioneers just got it right the first time.

But do other musicians have anything like the same depth of feeling about their instruments? I'm not so sure. I love my 1958 Gretsch Anniversary. It has a history that's tantalizing and unknowable. It's older than I am, and whenever I pick it up I feel I direct connection to that mysterious past—even though it's by no means a great instrument.

So given the retro mentality that plays such an important role in the modern guitar world, are we to suggest that to all intents and purposes, progress ceased around the end of the 1950s? Hardly. Granted, a time-traveling guitarist transplanted to a modern-day guitar store from that era would probably be more alienated by the shop assistant's clothes and haircut than any of the instruments on show. But perhaps subsequent developments have been overshadowed simply because the impact of the electric guitar itself has been so momentous on the musical landscape since that time. Indeed, if we take a look at the history of the guitar from its earliest days, we see a more measured evolution, with a small number of key milestones popping up along the way.

We can trace this broad flow of history if we view this book from cover to cover. In practice, our story begins with small-bodied five- and six-course Renaissance instruments and passes through to the recognizable six-string classical guitars that evolved during the mid-nineteenth century via innovations made by Spanish guitar makers such as Antonio de Torres Jurado. At the same time, across the Atlantic, we find the beginnings of an American tradition initiated by German émigré builders such as Christian Frederick Martin; toward the end of the century we find makers such as Orville Gibson and A. H. Merrill applying the design principles of the violin to the guitar, creating the first archtop models. At the beginning of the 1930s, we see the magnetic pick-up fitted to acoustic guitars, and in 1936 the appearance of the first significant electric guitar—the Gibson ES-150. And then, during the 1940s a number of individuals experimented with solidbody electric guitars, before Leo Fender's Broadcaster came off the production line in 1950—followed shortly after by the Precision, the first production-line bass guitar— effectively kicking off a revolution in music. Thereafter we see any number of interesting experiments and refinements, as makers dabbled with unusual materials, such as plastic bodies and aluminum necks. Not to mention the ways in which progressive thinkers of each generation have tried to second-guess the needs of the contemporary player: seven-and eight-string guitars; models with in-built synthesizers; guitars than can control external devices or computers—right up to the most contemporary "robot" models.

So what of the future? Does it lay with the likes of the Gibson Firebird X robot guitar with its impressive automated tuning system and in-built audio-processing software? Or perhaps a few decades from now that will just seem a bit silly. For some perspective, check out a 1967 clip from the U.S. panel quiz show *I've Got A Secret* (you can easily find it online). Host Steve Allen's blindfolded celebrity panelists listen to a piece of organ music, unaware that it is actually being played in the studio on a guitar—a Vox Guitar Organ. They fail to guess the secret, everyone is suitably amazed, and the English inventor, Dick Denning, is revealed. The host asks him why he did it: "The idea is to make a guitar sound like an organ," is Denning's deadpan reply. Sadly, as great as this technology was for its time, it transpired that hardly anybody did want to make their guitar sound like an organ.

So ten, twenty, or thirty years from now, will the Firebird X be remembered as a critical development? Or will it be the Vox Guitar Organ of the 2010s? Only time will tell. And what comes next? As natural resources become more scarce, perhaps more man-made solutions will have to appear; we already feature a guitar with a body created by a 3D printer (see page 920). Or perhaps, as digital sampling becomes ever more sophisticated and computer memory almost throwaway, we'll find guitars routinely kitted out with terabytes of onboard sample data. Wouldn't it be fun on stage to make a guitar sound like a cello, euphonium, or flock of geese at the flick of a switch, without also having to cart around a load of ancillary technology? Maybe not. Perhaps our grandchildren will instead get the same simple thrill we once had thrashing about in a garage with a guitar, a distorted amplifier, and a bunch of mates, succumbing to what Frank Zappa once famously described as "the single most blasphemous device on the face of the Earth—the disgusting stink of a too-loud electric guitar."

Index of Guitars by Manufacturer

Buscarino
Mira 901
Virtuoso 688

Byers
Classical 805

Campbell American
Space Biscuit 902
Transitone 806

Campellone
Special 694

Caparison
Angelus 838

Carrington
Classical Guitar 705

Carvin
2-MS 357
Brian Bromberg B24P 930
H2 706

Casio
MG-500/510 607

Catalina
Electric Guitar 316

Chapman
Stick 452

Charvel
Desolation Star DST-3 FR 1Hs
  903
Model 4 602
Surfcaster 658

Citron
AEG 863

Clearsound
Strat 500

Cole Clark
Violap 787

Collings
360 838
Lyle Lovett 744
MF5 Mandolin 863

Conklin
GT-4 732

Contreras
Carlevaro 567

Coral
3S18 Electric
  Sitar 370

Cort
GS Axe-2 905
Matthius Jabs
  Garage 2 885

Crafter
CTS 155C 756

Crown
Electric Guitar 291

D'Angelico
Teardrop 181

D'Aquisto
Archtop Electric 333
Archtop Mandolin 426
Avant Garde 617
Flat Top 568
Seven-string 445

D'Armond
M-75Ty 745

D'Angelico
Excel 99
New Yorker 101

Daemoness
Cimmerian 7 864

Daisy Rock
Heartbreaker 765

Dallas
Tuxedo 230

Danelectro
3412 Shorthorn 192
3923 Doubleneck 194
4123 Guitarlin 195
4623 Longhorn 191
5015 Convertible 230
"Baby" Sitar 387
Bellzouki 292
E2N4 Dane E 371
Hodad 745
Pro 1 292
U-2 172
UB-2 173

Daniel Friedrich
Classical Guitar 548

DBZ
Bolero AB Plus 906

De Aguilera
Six-course Guitar 31

Dean
Armott Tyrant 824

Dean
Dave Mustaine
  VMNT 814
Dave Mustaine
  Zero 930
Golden E'lite 531
Rusty Cooley 931
TonicS 766

Decibel
Javelin 7 885

Defil
Aster Rock 532
Kosmos 568
Jola 461

Deimel
Firestar 931

Ditson
Model 261 55

Dobro
Model 16 96
Model 55 72

Domingo Esteso
Flamenco Guitar 92

Domino
California Rebel 371

Doug Irwin
Tiger 513

Duesenberg
49er 839
Mike Campbell 825

Dupont
MD50 588

Dwight
Ephiphone
  SB533 275

Dyer
ASB-1 61

Earthwood
Acoustic Bass 514
Blue Moon
  Special 533
Wandré DLX 865

Eggle
Berlin 2 660

Egmond
Archtop Guitar 174
Model 3 334
Scout 334
Solid 7 293

Eko
700 255
BA4 500

Soloist 577
Warrior Pro 650

Jackson Corey
Beaulieu 941

James Ashborn
Parlor Guitar 41

James Tyler
Studio Elite 611

Jay Turser
JT-LTCRUSDLX 873

Jaydee
Mark King Bass 578

Jedson
Telecaster Bass 431

Jerry Jones
Master Sitar 651

Johann Stauffer
Acoustic Guitar 36

John Bailey
JBSG2 386

John Birch
AJS Custom 478

John Entwistle
Frankenstein 373

John Veleno
Veleno 443

Jolana
Alfa 348
Iris 455

Jose Oribe
Classical Guitar 351

José Ramírez
Classical Guitar 49

José Ramírez III
Classical Guitar 180

Jose Romanillos
La Buho 598

Joséf Benedid
Six-course Guitar 31

Joseph Bohmann
Harp Guitar 57

Joseph Di Mauro
Modèle Jazz 165

Julián Gomez Ramiréz
Steel-string Guitar 86

Kalamazoo
KG2A 349

Kapa
Continental 361

Karnak
Isis 594

Kawai
Concert 397
Teardrop 398

Kay
Barney Kessel Pro 186
Jazz II 268
K45 Travel Guitar 554
K5965 Pro Bass 236
LP Synth 554
Red Devil 283
Solo King 217

Ken Smith
BT Custom V 555

Kent
Polaris 324

King Blossom
RGM 2 916

Kinkade
Dave Gregory 579
Klein
Electric Harp
  Guitar 739

Klein/Taylor
Acoustic Bass 727

Knight
Mandola 603

Koontz
Custom Flat Top 504

Kramer
450G 479
650G 480
B3 Baretta 942
Ferrington 595
Floyd Rose Sustainer 635

Krawczak
Twin Soundboard 698

Kremona
Orpheus Valley 795

Krundaal
Bikini 284

Kubicki
Factor 4 Bass 635

Kustom
K200C 399

La Baye
2x4 380

Lacey
Artist Special 917

Lado
505-QS Bass 796

Lâg Tremontaine
T200 D12 758

Lakewood
Sungha Jung Signature 917

Lakland
Duck Dunn Signature Model 810

Landola
Double Neck 423

Larrivée
RS-4 874

Les Paul
Log 123

Letts
Fretless Bass 850

Levin
Goliath 325

Levin Orkestergitarr
De Luxe 110

Lindert
John Henry 750

Line 6
James Tyler Variax
  JTV-89US 875

Loog
II 943

Louis Panormo
Classical Guitar 38

Lowden
Richard Thompson 876

Luna
Andromeda 797

Lviv
Electric Guitar 432

Maccaferri
Islander 187

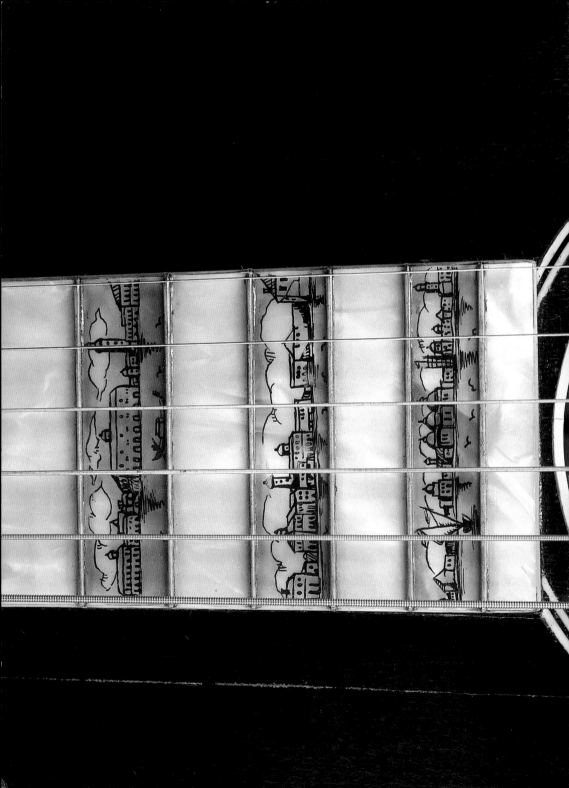

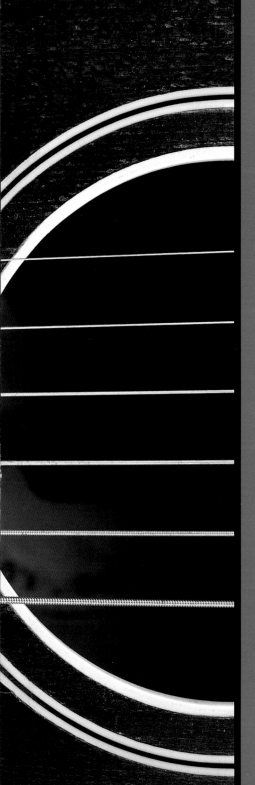

Pre-1930s

Guadalupe
Vihuela 1525

Type Six-course Spanish Renaissance vihuela
Body & neck Spruce top, flat back made from alternating strips of boxwood and kingwood in a radiating pattern
Other features Rosettes and inlaid mosaics on soundboard

In 1536, Luys Milan published a very large collection of compositions in tablature for vihuela called *El Maestro* in the Spanish city of Valencia. It was to be the first of seven important collections of music for the vihuela to be published by as many composers over a forty-year period, ending in 1576. Particularly notable are those by Luis de Narváez and Alonso Mudarra. The best of the fantasias, variations, songs, dances, and transcriptions of contrapuntal church music by these composers are arguably among the best music of the period for any instrument. Shortly after, with the arrival of early Baroque guitars, the vihuela became history.

There are only three known surviving vihuelas, though others are thought to have been converted to Baroque guitars. The "Guadalupe," now in the Musée Jacquemart-André in Paris, is the earliest and most elaborate, with an astonishing geometric pattern on the back that almost upstages the beauty of the front. The neck, heel, and peghead all are one integral piece made with sections of boxwood and kingwood, and its sides are made of interlocking panels of boxwood and kingwood. With a string length of 31⅜ in. (79.8 cm) it is an unusually large instrument, and not representative of most vihuelas of the time. The name GVADALVPE burned into the peghead is thought by some to indicate its maker as Joan de Guadalupe of Toledo. **GD**

Fantasias Musica de Vihuela (1998) features works by Luys Milan, Luis de Narváez, and Alonso Mudarra—three of the greatest composers for the vihuela—performed by virtuoso lutenist Hopkinson Smith on a modern reconstruction.

Belchior Dias
Five-course Guitar 1590

Type Five-course early Baroque guitar
Body & neck Fingerboard flush with soundboard, peghead
Other features Frets (originally gut) tied around the neck, 26¾ in. (68 cm) string length

This beautifully proportioned and decorated instrument is attributed to the Portuguese maker Belchior Dias, based on the similarity of construction and decoration details to a smaller 1581 guitar undoubtedly by Dias in the Royal College of Music, London. This example has had modifications and repairs over time, notably a replacement top in the twentieth century, but the laminated parchment rose is thought to be original.

The sixteenth century was a period of transition for the guitar on the Iberian Peninsula, from a smaller four-course instrument (also popular in France, Italy,

"Aristotle shows us how natural man delights in hearing music and poetry … and Spanish sensibility delights in nothing more than in the sound of the guitar."

JOAN CARLOS AMAT (1527–1642)

and England) with a history and repertoire running in parallel to the courtly six-course vihuela, a bigger guitar-shaped instrument. There was also a five-course vihuela, tuned to the same interval pattern as the modern guitar, for which blind vihuelist Miguel de Fuenllana published nine pieces in his *Orphenica Lyra* of 1554. This instrument may be what would become the five-course *guitarra española*, described by Joan Carlos Amat in 1596. As the Renaissance gave way to the early Baroque and intricate polyphonic music began to transition to a freer mode of musical expression, the guitar seems to have scaled up and the vihuela scaled down to meet the needs of musical fashion. **GD**

Giorgio Sellas
Chitarra Battente 1627

Type Five-course Baroque guitar
Body & neck Spruce top, mother-of-pearl fingerboard
Other features Mother-of-pearl panels on head, around sound hole, and on purfling; decorated body

From the late sixteenth century, Spain, Portugal, and Italy saw the earliest transition from a four-course to a five-course guitar. In Italy, the wealthy north, and in particular Venice, was a major center of a Baroque musical style as epitomized by Monteverdi, and was a magnet for musicians and luthiers. Italian guitarists developed a system of chord symbols called *alfabeto* with strumming patterns in the new *battente* (*rasgueado*) style for songs and dances of the time. Numerous publications emerged, starting with one from 1606 by Girolamo Montesardo. By 1630, Giovanni Paolo Foscarini

"Historically [the guitar] only had four courses, Maestro Espinel of Madrid added a fifth and that was the origin of its perfection."
GASPAR SANZ, *c.* 1640–1710

brought out a book of solos in mixed tablature, which notated the range of effects played on the five-course guitar, including melodic passages, rhythmic strumming, plucked chords, slurs, and ornaments.

Part of a dynasty of luthiers making bowed and plucked-string instruments, the German Giorgio Sellas (1585–1649) and his brother Matteo had workshops in Venice where they helped it become a major center of guitar construction. One of the more ornate examples, this *chitarra spagnola* (the Italian name for Spanish guitar) by Giorgio Sellas from 1627 was probably converted into a *chitarra battente* about a hundred years later (when these first appeared) by fitting a kind of tailpiece to take the extra strain of the wire strings that would also now have been fitted. **GD**

Portrait of the Artist as a Guitarist (1636) by Jean Daret.

Matteo Sellas
Five-course Guitar 1640

Type Five-course Baroque guitar
Body & neck Spruce top edged in fruitwood, back and sides in yew, black-stained walnut fingerboard
Other features Ebony bridge with mustache ends

A twelve-year-old Matteo Sellas (*c.* 1602–1654) left his native Fussen in southern Germany to find his fortune in Venice, where he started work as an apprentice in the workshop of his older brother Giorgio Sellas, who had made the same journey about fifteen years earlier. Matteo opened his own workshop in the 1620s and went on to have a very successful business with many apprentices and craftsmen in his employ.

This 1640 instrument, with its inlaid floral vinework, intricate single-tier parchment rose topped with pearwood, and walnut-veneered pine head is the least ornate of the Sellas guitars that have survived and has a simpler finish than most guitars of the time.

One of the very confusing complications at the time, and for interpreters today, is the various methods employed to tune the strings. There was the so-called re-entrant tuning: aa, d'd', gg, b'b', e'e', with the third course, "gg," giving the lowest note. Some guitarists favored the fourth high "d" string doubled with one an octave below it, and some also favored the fifth "a" string doubled with a lower octave.

By 1640, Francesco Corbetta (*c.* 1615–1681), playing guitars such as this, was establishing himself as western Europe's preeminent guitarist–composer, and would be so until the appearance of Gaspar Sanz and Robert de Visée a generation later. **GD**

Most Baroque guitars are too valuable and fragile to be taken out of museums, but a modern reproduction with gut strings will replicate their original sound. On *Corbetta: Guitar Music* (1996), Jakob Lindberg plays a selection of Corbetta's solo pieces and suites.

René Voboan
Five-course Guitar 1641

Type Five-course Baroque guitar
Body & neck Spruce top, tortoiseshell back and sides, ebony fingerboard
Other features Ebony and ivory inlays on back and sides

France's "Sun King" Louis XIV (1638–1715) was a keen guitarist, and had famous guitarists like Francesco Corbetta and Robert de Visée play for him at Versailles, where they were rubbing shoulders and performing with court musicians such as Jean-Baptiste Lully and François Couperin. Louis XIV may well have played a Voboam instrument.

René Voboam (*c.* 1606–*c.* 1671) was the head of a dynasty of Parisian guitar makers that made some of the finest instruments anywhere in Europe for over a hundred years, of which twenty-seven signed and

"One can find in France courtiers and ladies who try like monkeys to imitate the Spaniards ... and learn guitar playing."
PIERRE TRICHOT, 1640

dated instruments have survived. In all that time the basic model did not change much and remained largely influenced by Voboam's original design, as exemplified by this instrument of 1641.

This guitar, with its ebony and ivory purfling, bridge, sound hole, and fingerboard inlays, has René Voboam's name and the date of manufacture engraved on an ivory rectangle set in the headstock. The ebony and ivory inlays on the back and sides are set in an attractive herringbone pattern. The instrument's overall length is 37 in. (93.7 cm) and it has a depth of 2¾–3 in. (7–8 cm). Its string length is 27½ in. (69.6 cm). It is the only instrument that can safely be attributed to Voboam and perhaps the only one that has survived. **GD**

Antonio Stradivari
Five-course Guitar 1688

Salomon
Five-course Guitar 1760

Type Five-course Baroque guitar
Body & neck Spruce top, four-part back and sides in maple, head and neck of poplar or walnut, dark oak fingerboard
Other features Two transverse soundboard braces

Type Five-course guitar
Body & neck Spruce top, fingerboard flush with soundboard, peghead
Other features Strung with five double courses

This guitar, known as the "Hill" guitar, safely housed in the Ashmolean Museum in Oxford, has an amazing pedigree. Made by the Italian violin maker Antonio Stradivari (c. 1644–1737), whose instruments are valued in the millions of dollars, it is one of only two guitars by him that have survived largely intact, with fragments of three others also in existence. Simpler and more austere-looking than many of the opulently decorated guitars made in Venice or Paris for example, it nevertheless has Stradivarius trademarks like the choice of woods used and in its orange varnish—the same as his violins. It also has bone diamond-and-circle inlays around the sound hole and rose.

All of Stradivari's guitars have unfortunately been tampered with in one way or another (this one much less so than the others) either as restoration projects or to customize them according to changing fashion and requirements. One of them, the "Sabionari," was turned into a six-string guitar with shortened new neck and head in about 1800. **GD**

Paris in 1760 was one of the most important centers for music in Europe and the guitar was undergoing something of a revival there after several decades when it had fallen out of favor. The Paris workshop of Jean-Baptiste Dehaye (1713–1767), better known by his trade name Salomon, made instruments of the violin and viol families, along with harps and guitars.

The features of the Salomon guitar of 1760, like other French guitars made at the time, hardly differed from the five-course Baroque guitars made fifty or sixty years earlier: the fingerboards still lay flush with the soundboard; they had the same pegheads, the same five double courses, and the same gut frets tied around the neck. However, the ornate rose had given way to a sound hole and the styling was generally simpler, as befitted the aesthetic of the light, melodious, and fun new Italianate music style, Galant. At the time this was sweeping aside a late-Baroque style that had become increasingly flamboyant, complex, and unfashionable. **GD**

Joséf Benedid
Six-course Guitar 1787

De Aguilera
Six-course Guitar 1797

Type Six-course classical guitar
Body & neck Spruce top, maple back and sides, ebony fingerboard flush with soundboard, peghead, metal frets
Other features Strung with six double courses

Type Six-course classical guitar
Body & neck Spruce top, cypress back and sides, fingerboard flush with soundboard, peghead, gut frets
Other features Lower bout 10½ in. (26 cm)

A contemporary of the Pagés brothers and part of the Andalusian School of Cádiz, Joséf Benedid was, like them, a maker recommended by celebrated guitarist–composer Fernando Sor. An early adopter of fan bracing, Benedid used three braces under the bridge, generally simpler than the Pagés' bracing system. This guitar, with its elegant ornamentation in mahogany and mother-of-pearl inlays, has an aristocratic look, somewhere between the Pagés' humbler-looking 1804 model and more ornate examples of the period.

The final decades of the eighteenth century saw renewed interest among fashionable Spanish society, long mesmerized by foreign music, in its own national music and consequently its quintessential instrument, the guitar. Even the aristocracy, who typically had disdained the instrument, were now charmed by it. At this time, the market in Spain for six-course guitars and guitar music grew, but aspiring guitar virtuosi were following the money to culture capitals Paris, London, and Vienna—and playing single-stringed guitars. **GD**

Little is known of Madrid luthier Benito Sánchez de Aguilera. He was probably a minor maker in his day, one of many supplying a booming demand for guitars and guitar music toward the end of the eighteenth century. His renovated 1797 instrument strung with six double courses is basic and unfussy. We don't know if replacement parts matched the originals, but the guitar most likely had a simpler bridge than the fancy mustache bridge a twentieth-century restorer added to it. Few makers were using mustache bridges at that time, particularly such large ones.

The replacement head may also have been different, but this was a transitional period in guitar design, from stringing and bracing to shape and size. It was 200 years earlier when four-course guitars and six-course Renaissance vihuelas were transitioning to five-course Baroque guitars. About 150 years later, guitars would be electrified. With the guitar, history has shown us, perhaps more so than with any other instrument, that almost anything is possible. **GD**

Pagés
Six-course Guitar 1804

Type Six-course classical guitar
Body & neck Spruce top, fingerboard flush with soundboard, peghead
Other features Strung with six double courses, fan bracing

Brothers Joséf and Juan Pagés worked out of Cádiz from about 1770 to 1822 and were part of the Andalusian School that produced some of the finest instruments in Spain. In 1770, the six-course guitar had begun to supersede the five-course version in Spain. Six courses remained the standard there well into the 1800s, despite the fact that most Italian and some French makers were creating six single-string guitars from about 1785. Important innovations in music for the six-course guitar began appearing in Spain from 1780, notably by Antonio Ballesteros, Federico Moretti,

> *"Although I use a guitar of seven single strings, it seemed ... appropriate to accommodate these principles to six courses, that being what is generally played in Spain."*
> FEDERICO MORETTI, 1799

and Fernando Ferandiere. The music was in notation; tablature, in use for plucked instruments since the 1500s, had been virtually abandoned by 1750.

From the 1790s, Pagés guitars were among the very first classical guitars to be fan braced, a key feature of Spanish guitars and one that, through contact with composer and guitarist Fernando Sor, would come to influence Louis Panormo's instruments in England, and would later famously be developed by Antonio Torres during the late 1800s into the modern instrument we know today. Both Fernando Sor and Dionisio Aguado, the most famous Spanish guitarist–composers of the classical period, extolled the qualities of Pagés guitars. **GD**

Preston
English Guitar 1804

Type Six-course English guitar
Body & neck Spruce top; maple neck, head, back, sides
Other features Twelve brass frets, brass rosette, brass and ebony capo, ebony and ivory bridge, watch-key tuner

The popularity of the metal-strung English guitar, of which Preston of London was one of the better-known makers, relegated the five-course gut-strung guitar in England to oblivion from the 1750s until 1815. That was when Spanish guitarist–composer Fernando Sor established himself in London, bringing renewed interest in the Spanish instrument. The English guitar had reigned supreme, fashionable in particular with dilettantes and upper class ladies, for whom it was something of a fashion accessory. It had an ebony fingerboard covered with tortoiseshell and ebony,

"The guitar has a watch-key tuning device, which was better suited to the guitar's short metal strings."

NATIONAL MUSEUM OF AMERICAN HISTORY

and six courses of metal strings tuned to C major (c, e, gg, c′c′, e′e′, g′g′). Many ladies chose it above the spinet and harpsichord, but many considered it trivial and not worth bothering with. Consequently most repertoire written for it at the time is somewhat insignificant—a Bach sonata for violin and the English guitar being a notable exception.

The English guitar became a successful export to several other countries. In North America, it was a popular domestic instrument in the new republic: It was played by Benjamin Franklin and several were owned by Thomas Jefferson's family. It was introduced into Portugal in the 1750s and evolved into today's Portuguese guitar, its timbre an essential part of Lisbon's Fado music. **GD**

Amédée Thibout
Lyre Guitar 1805

Type French lyre guitar
Body & neck Spruce top, back and ribs of maple, sound holes edged with mother-of-pearl and ebony segments
Other features Pin bridge with ebony foliate mustaches

Very popular in the salons of Paris from the late 1700s to about 1830, the French lyre guitar at the hands of suitably clad, coiffured, and posed young ladies, evoked the aesthetics of a Neoclassicism inspired by ancient Greek and Roman history and antiquities that were influencing arts and fashion at the time. Painters like Ingres in France and Goya in Spain drew and painted women with lyre guitars. Marie-Antoinette is said to have played one. Guitarist–composers of the period like Ferdinando Carulli, Matteo Carcassi, Fernando Sor, and Mauro Giuliani published some

"A few words on the new French lyre … I can truly say that this lyre guitar is barely fit for strumming second-rate accompaniments."
THE MUSICAL TIMES OF GERMANY, 1801

music for it. Even a young Beethoven is seen with one in a painting of 1804 by W.J. Mahler. It was quite a fad.

The majority of lyre guitars, like this one by Amédée Thibout, luthier in Caen, were French, though Italy produced quality instruments too. Most lyre guitars are of a similar design with decorative variations—this one has an ebony fingerboard with twelve frets, its arms are surmounted by brass eagle heads, and it has a peg box with rear-facing pegs—they stand upright on a flat base integral to the body, and have hollow arms with a yoke or crossbar to which a six-string guitar neck of varying lengths is attached. They are attractive objects but compared to a regular guitar, they are ergonomically awkward to play and disappointing in sound quality. **GD**

A nineteenth-century French postcard depicting young ladies playing a lyre guitar. ➜

Johann Stauffer
Acoustic Guitar 1820

Type Hollow-body, figure-eight acoustic guitar
Body & neck Maple back and sides, spruce top, laminated neck
Fingerboard Rosewood

Although the classical guitar largely evolved in the Mediterranean regions of Europe, significant developments were taking place in Germany and Austria. Johann Georg Stauffer (1778–1853) was the most important luthier of the Vienna School. The design for which he is best remembered came about through a collaboration with the celebrated Italian concert guitarist and composer Luigi Legnani, who took a great interest in the design and construction of the instruments he played and who would later establish himself as a fine luthier in his own right.

Stauffer first built these guitars from around 1815. The body was relatively orthodox, the back and sides were crafted from maple, and the top from spruce with intricate rosewood binding. The veneered neck was, unusually, adjustable with a key. Most striking was the headstock, with its six-in-a-line tuners. This design quickly became influential in Northern Europe. It would also play a seminal role in the evolution of the guitar in the United States, through Stauffer's most celebrated apprentice, Christian Friedrich Martin.

Although Martin's history is patchy during this time, it seems likely that he joined Stauffer in around 1813. A skilled craftsman, shortly after the end of his training he became Stauffer's foreman in the workshop. He would later return to his hometown of Markneukirchen in Germany before migrating to the United States in 1933, where he founded C.F. Martin & Co., now the oldest guitar manufacturer in the world.

There is no evidence to suggest Martin worked on this 1820 guitar, but this Stauffer design would be a critical influence on his earliest American guitars. **TB**

René Lacote
Classical Guitar 1835

Type Classical guitar
Body & neck Spruce top, ebony fingerboard flush with top
Other features Transverse bracing, Italianate mustache
bridge, frets 13–17 attached directly to soundboard

René Lacote (1785–*c.* 1870) was the leading exponent
of the French school of guitar making in the first half
of the eighteenth century, with his guitars being
favored by major guitarist–composers including
Dionisio Aguado, Ferdinando Carulli, Fernando Sor,
and Napoléon Coste. His guitars had such a lasting
reputation that counterfeits with forged labels were
being made in around 1900.

Lacote guitars, prized for their bright sound and
quick response, are still played by period instrument
professionals and enthusiasts. They were made with
exceptional craftsmanship and a lot of attention was
paid to detail and external finish. As for the internals,
Lacote initially adopted the single transverse brace
system above the sound hole from his teacher César
Pons, but then improved on it by having a specially
shaped transverse brace under the bridge area and, in
models like this one from 1835 where the fingerboard
itself does not extend onto the soundboard, small
transverse braces in the area under the higher frets.

The Lacote workshops produced a wide range of
models with many patented innovations. In 1826,
Lacote collaborated with Carulli in designing a ten-
string guitar with frets for the top five strings and five
"floating" sub-basses. He went on to make further
nine- and ten-string variations. **TB**

Jerry Willard plays the same model of Lacote
guitar on his album *Night At The Opera*, which
features fantasies on well-known operas by
early Romantic guitar virtuosi Mauro Giuliani
(1781–1829) and Johann Kaspar Mertz
(1806–1856).

Louis Panormo
Classical Guitar 1836

Type Classical guitar
Body & neck Spruce top, rosewood back and sides, maple headstock, mahogany neck, ebony fingerboard
Other features Multiple purfling, six-pinned bridge

"Louis Panormo, the only maker of guitars in the Spanish style" is how Panormo advertised his guitars made in London in the period roughly between 1820 and 1850. In the early years of the nineteenth century, the English were largely unacquainted with the guitar until the Spanish guitarist and composer Fernando Sor gave concerts, taught, and lived in London between 1815 and 1823, causing a sensational rise in interest. It was at that time that the Panormo family's workshop, primarily making violins at the time, turned to making guitars guided by Sor. Unfortunately they

> *"Mr. J. Panormo made some guitars under my direction in London, as did Mr. Schroeder in St. Petersburg."*
>
> FERNANDO SOR, ON WORKING WITH LOUIS' BROTHER JOSEPH

were not among Sor's favorite instruments. By the 1830s, the guitar had become very popular in England and enjoyed considerable patronage. A large number of instruments was made at the Panormo workshop in London, many of which are still in circulation.

Panormo is not considered an innovator in that his designs were a consolidation of best practice and features from French and Spanish guitars. He used Spanish fan bracing, adopted from earlier Spanish guitars; the headstock design was used on French and Spanish guitars; the bridge design is French. But his guitars are distinctive and immediately recognizable as Panormos. They are generally much quieter and warmer-sounding than a modern classical guitar and are often reproduced by modern makers. **GD**

Martin
Acoustic Guitar 1838

Type Flat-top acoustic guitar
Body & neck Maple back and sides, spruce top, cedar neck
Fingerboard Ebony

C.F. Martin & Co., the world's oldest guitar manufacturer, was critical in the development of the American flat-top steel-string tradition. And yet the roots of the Martin story lay 4,000 miles to the east, in the Saxony town of Markneukirchen, where Johann Georg Martin ran a successful furniture-making business. The guitar was not a well-respected instrument at this time, and most were built by trained cabinetmakers rather than skilled luthiers. Born in 1776, Martin's son, Christian Friedrich, entered the family business as a boy, but showing exceptional promise, he was sent to Vienna where he was apprenticed to Johann Stauffer, one of the leading luthiers of the Austrian/German school.

In 1833, Martin and his young family emigrated to the United States. His earliest guitars were built in the Viennese style of his mentor. The model shown here resides at the Metropolitan Museum of Art, New York, and dates back to 1838. It was built at Martin's shop on Hudson Street in New York City, a year before he settled in Nazareth, Pennsylvania—an area he chose for its well-established ex-patriot German community.

There are clear similarities between this guitar and those produced by Stauffer in Vienna (see page 36), in particular the curled headstock with its unusual array of "six-in-a-line" tuning pegs. These were described in the company ledgers as "Vienna Screws" and were imported at great expense by Martin from Vienna.

The business thrived until his death in 1873. However it was when his grandson Frank Henry Martin took over in 1888 that it became synonymous with quality and innovation. To this day, the company remains in the hands of his descendants. **GD**

Martin & Schatz
Acoustic Guitar 1840

Type Viennese-style acoustic
Body & neck Mahogany, Stauffer-style headstock with six-in-a-line tuners
Fingerboard Ivory

Heinrich Schatz was a nineteenth-century luthier who was among the first to leave his native Germany for a new life in the United States. He was also a friend and associate of Christian Friedrich Martin.

In the early 1930s, having left the employ of Johann Stauffer in Vienna, Martin returned to Germany to find a trade war in full swing: the guild of cabinetmakers fought with the guild of violin makers for the exclusive legal right to build guitars. The cabinetmakers (of which Martin was a member) eventually won, but he found the guild system too restrictive. Encouraged by

"Martin & Schatz from Vienna, pupils of the celebrated Stauffer, guitar & violin manufacturers…"

FROM THE PAPER LABELS FIXED TO THE EARLY GUITARS

Schatz, who had successfully settled in the United States, Martin and his young family followed suit.

Martin was quickly able to plug into an existing network of Central European luthiers. Martin and Schatz ran separate workshops—Martin in New York; Schatz in Pennsylvania—but their business activities intersected frequently, with both working on instruments at separate locations and supplying materials to one another.

Built in 1840—by which time Martin had followed Schatz into Pennsylvania—this guitar has a Northern European–style body and Stauffer's unique headstock design. Indeed, the labeling of the guitar shows quite clearly that Martin was more than happy to trade on the reputation of his former employer. **TB**

James Ashborn
Parlor Guitar 1850

Type American parlor guitar
Body & neck Rosewood-veneered maple on back and sides, Indian rosewood-veneered chestnut neck
Fingerboard Rosewood

James Ashborn's significance in the history of the guitar is less down to quality than his manufacturing —he was arguably the first luthier to apply the principles of mass production to the guitar. At his workshop in Torrington, Connecticut, employees were engaged according to skill. One would machine the tuners, another would fret the fingerboards, and another would French polish the finished guitar.

Ashborn also took advantage of the sophisticated machinery being used by wagon builders—band saws, table saws, and routers, powered by the flow of

"He was able to create a factory environment where workers did what they were good at and … became very fast and consistent."
VINTAGE GUITAR MAGAZINE

water in the nearby Naugatuck River. With these radical new methods, Ashborn established himself as America's most prolific maker of guitars and banjos.

The guitars were unusual in design, combining the small-bodied English parlor tradition of Panormo with the interior fan-bracing found in Spanish classical instruments. Yet the way in which the neck was fixed to the body was highly unorthodox: the dovetail joint was replaced by the more complex—and reliable— butt joint. This could only have been achieved with ingenious technological thinking and advanced materials such as loops of cloth-backed sandpaper.

In spite of this mechanized manufacturing, Ashborn produced sophisticated instruments that required significant amounts of skilled handwork. **TB**

Torres
"First Epoch" 1858

Type Classical guitar
Body & neck Spruce top, Brazilian rosewood back and sides, cedar neck, ebony fingerboard
Other features Rosewood bridge with mother-of-pearl

Antonio de Torres Jurado (1817–1892) is arguably as towering a figure in the history of the guitar as Stradivari is in the history of the violin. This guitar is from his so-called "first epoch" (1850s to 1870) and was made when he worked out of Seville, Spain.

His instruments perfectly consolidated the best features of Spanish guitars made in the generation or two that preceded him, notably those of Pagés, Benediz, and Martinez. His most important contributions included increasing the size of the body by about 20 percent, introducing a new system of fan

> *"Tárrega soon realized that the existing repertoire for the guitar was inadequate for an instrument made by such a man."*
> JULIAN BREAM

bracing that used seven struts radiating from below the sound hole, fixing the string length to 25½ in. (65 cm), using a saddle on the bridge, redefining the body shape, and minimizing decoration to achieve an understated and timeless appearance. He was also an early adopter of mechanical machine heads in Spain.

A carpenter by trade, it was his long and close association with the Spanish guitarist–composer Julián Arcas that spurred him to become a luthier, building guitars with improved tone, volume, and projection that would be suitable for professional virtuosi. In 1869, a teenaged Francisco Tárrega traveled from one end of Spain to the other to acquire a guitar from him. A year later Torres moved to Almeria and, after a hiatus of several years, began his "second epoch." **GD**

Francisco Tárrega was one of the first celebrated virtuoso guitarists. →

Martin
1-28 1860

Type Flat-top acoustic guitar
Body & neck Ivory-bound body with red spruce top and Brazilian rosewood back and sides, rosewood neck
Fingerboard Ebony

By the 1850s, C.F. Martin had developed a style of his own. The former Stauffer influence began to diminish, and he began to adopt innovative approaches to the construction of his guitars. He's widely credited with developing the idea of X-bracing for the body of his instruments: this technique comprised a pair of wooden supports that formed an "X" shape across the soundboard below the top of the sound hole, the lower "arms" of the brace positioned to support either end of the bridge. By contrast, a fan shape of bracing is most commonly used on classical guitars. The practical differences are more in strength rather than sound—there are opposing views on the tonal benefits of either method. There is no documented proof that Martin invented X-bracing, but it certainly evolved from the close-knit community of German luthiers working in Pennsylvania. But there is no doubt that Martin was the first of the larger-scale guitar makers to adopt and popularize the system.

During this period, Martin also began to normalize the sizing of his guitars: "1" was the standard model; the smaller "2" was a small parlor size; "0" was a larger concert style; the largest was the grand concert "00." The two-digit suffix denoted the style of the guitar: the higher the number, the more costly and decoratively demanding the instrument. Style 28—like this 1860 model—was characterized by the heavy use of the ornate herringbone pattern of marquetry used on the tops, backs, and sides of the body, and of the five-nine-five band rosette around the sound hole. Until 1918, the tops and backs were bound with genuine elephant ivory. **TB**

Vicente Arias
Classical Guitar 1870

Type Classical guitar
Body & neck Spruce top, Brazilian rosewood back and sides, ebony fingerboard
Other features Torres-like fan bracing, unique rosette

Less than thirty of Vicente Arias' guitars are known to still exist, and this 1870 model is one of his earliest. These instruments are highly collectible, not only for their rarity but for their exceptional craftsmanship, rich tonal qualities, and uniqueness—no two guitars by this maker are the same. About half of these rare guitars were collected together for a conference celebrating Arias in Florence, Italy, in 2005.

Vicente Arias (1833–1914) was born in Ciudad Real, Spain, where he lived and worked until a move to Madrid in his later years. Arias adopted the innovations

"… Arias guitars are … highly regarded by collectors for conscientious craftsmanship, good tone, and … the beauty of the rosettes."
PAULINO BARNABE

in body shape and size, string length, and bracing famously credited to Torres and brought to the craft a supreme attention to materials and construction detail, including the designs of his rosettes, each of which is unique. There is an elegant classicism of design in this early guitar that is sustained throughout his output. His guitars are also light in relation to their size, even in larger, later models. Arias continued making guitars well into his sixties.

Anecdotal evidence suggests that in around 1878–1879, celebrated guitarist–composer Francisco Tárrega—considered the founder of modern classical guitar technique—ordered a custom instrument from Arias, small enough that he could easily carry it on his person and use it for practice on his travels. **GD**

Haynes
Parlor Guitar 1870

Martin
2-27 1874

Type American parlor guitar
Body & neck Spruce top, Brazilian rosewood back and sides, mahogany neck, ebony fingerboard
Other features Tilton patent tailpiece and floating bridge

Type American parlor guitar
Body & neck Brazilian rosewood back and sides, spruce top, cedar neck, herringbone and ivory binding
Fingerboard Ebony

This was a very popular American guitar design in the latter half of the eighteenth century, with roots in guitars made and played in Europe forty or fifty years earlier. Much of the music played on it would also have been in the European tradition and took place in the urban middle-class setting of the parlor, the American equivalent of the French salon. As early as the 1850s, guitars like these were also played in black minstrel groups that fused African and European music into a genre that would evolve into uniquely American ragtime and jazz. These guitars would have been gut-strung, with a mellow tone and somewhat small voice. From about 1890, steel-strung models appeared that would enable these guitars to compete with and be heard in larger ensembles. With steel strings enabling note "bending," it would see in the birth of the blues. This very high-quality instrument by John C. Haynes of Boston had X-bracing, a silver medallion in the sound hole, a silver-plated tailpiece, and Tilton-patented components. **GD**

Until the middle of the nineteenth century, there was a popular perception that the guitar was a women's instrument—especially the popular small-bodied "parlor" guitars.

The Martin 2-27 "ladies'-size" model was described in the company's first retail price list in 1874 as being "inlaid with pearl" and "ivory bound," making it "fancier" than the higher-numbered style 28. Retailing at a hefty $58.50—around $1,000 at today's prices—these models were intended for ladies of means. In fact, the most expensive models listed are all ornate "Ladies'" parlor guitars, hitting a peak with the "richly inlaid" 2-42, which cost a mighty $90.

The 2-27 was one of the most popular Martins of the nineteenth century, and remained in production until 1898. Surprisingly, perhaps, it was by no means the smallest body size available—Martin's size 5 was a "terz" guitar, its name taken from the German word for "third" and so-called because the tuning was raised by three half tones (a major third). **TB**

Torres
"Second Epoch" 1882

Martin
00021 1886

Type Flamenco guitar
Body & neck Spruce top, cypress body, cedar neck, ebony fingerboard
Other features Rosewood bridge, peghead facing, pegs

Type Double-neck harp guitar
Body & neck Spruce top, Brazilian rosewood back and sides, ebony fingerboard
Other features X-bracing, ivory nuts and saddles

Antonio de Torres Jurado gave up making his celebrated "first epoch" guitars in 1870, moved with his family from Seville to Almeria, and started running a china shop there. Conversely, guitarist–composer Francisco Tárrega (1852–1909), who had acquired his first Torres guitar in 1869, was just starting on a phenomenal career, developing repertoire and technique that would help make the classical guitar the serious concert instrument it is today. He played that first Torres guitar of his for twenty years until it literally started falling apart, and he continued to play and champion Torres guitars.

Torres started his "second epoch" in 1875, making guitars part-time, while also tending to the china shop and even taking in lodgers to make ends meet. Around the time this 1882 flamenco guitar was made, he started doubling his output to around twelve guitars a year, though in general these were much more modest instruments than those from the glorious "first epoch." Sadly, he died impoverished and in debt in 1892. **GD**

Harp guitars with free-floating strings, normally sub-basses, were popular from the end of the nineteenth century into the early twentieth century, with renewed interest over the past several decades by specialist harp guitar players. The instruments were configured in a bewildering number of ways, from having a single theorbo-like headstock to an additional neck—some attached, some unattached, as in this Martin model—to a hollow arm extension, as in the famed Knutsen-patented harp guitars made by Dyer, and many other curious and eye-catching variations. All important luthiers had a range of harp guitars in their catalogs.

With its gut stringing, still common at this time and for decades to come, and its eighteen strings—six fretted and twelve floating—this guitar would have sounded very harplike in the popular music groups, chamber ensembles, and mandolin orchestras of the time. In the late 1880s when this guitar was made, a third of Martin's output of some 330 instruments were in fact mandolins. **GD**

Washburn
Style 108 1892

Type American parlor guitar
Body & neck Spruce top, rosewood back and sides, ebony fingerboard
Other features Width of lower bout 12½ in. (31.75 cm)

Washburn was a brand established in 1885 by Chicago music publishers and instrument manufacturers Lyon & Healy for their range of parlor guitars, mandolins, banjos, and zithers. They also made woodwind, brass, and stringed instruments and world-class harps out of a large factory working on assembly-line principles. Chicago at the time was a major hub for guitar making and distribution, and Washburn competed there with the likes of the Larson brothers and Joseph Bohmann, among others. A major manufacturer, by 1916 Washburn reported having made over 20,000 guitars.

"The guitar, as a ladies' instrument ... is decidedly vulgar ... There is nothing graceful about a young lady playing a guitar."

S.S. STEWART (PREEMINENT BANJO MANUFACTURER), 1885

Featuring in the 1889 Washburn catalog, the small and pretty 108 model, with its top-of-the-line trims using highest-quality mother-of-pearl inlays on the fingerboard and headstock, marquetry, and celluloid, was an ideal ladies' guitar.

Washburn parlor guitars from the mid-1880s were fine ladder-braced instruments that came in four sizes with a rising scale of inlays and ornamentation. Not much changed until the First World War and the onset of the Jazz Age when demand declined for parlor guitars and their limited volume. In 1928, Washburn was sold to Regal Musical Instrument Co., which made Washburn guitars until the mid-1940s when the brand faded away—until its resurrection in the 1970s as part of U.S. Music Corp. **GD**

José Ramírez
Classical Guitar 1897

Type Classical guitar
Body & neck Spruce top, Spanish cypress back and sides, Brazilian rosewood fingerboard, American machine heads
Other features Rosette inlaid with mother-of-pearl

José Ramírez I (1858–1923) was the first in a dynasty of guitar makers that has made exceptional instruments for about 130 years—for most of that time out of the Madrid workshop he opened in 1890. The Ramírez brand is today held in the same esteem as Steinway is for pianos. His reputation rested primarily on his flamenco guitars, which were built larger than those of Torres, or Torres-inspired models like those of Vicente Arias. He is credited with creating the "tablao," a guitar with a large but shallow body that gave more volume and projection. This was particularly valued

> *"If a guitar maker did not die in a social welfare hospital, it was because he did not have the means to get there."*
>
> JOSÉ RAMÍREZ

by guitarists who needed to be heard above the singing, clapping, stamping of feet, castanets, and audience noises in flamenco bars. If this classical model is anything to go by, they were rustic in appearance with none of the timeless elegance of a Torres or an Arias guitar—but they got the job done.

José I introduced his younger brother Manuel to guitar making. Both sons of a well-off land owner, they could have chosen the secure life of ranching over a precarious living making guitars in what was at the time a small and declining market for the instruments. Then, through Manuel's association with a young Andrés Segovia, the Ramírez brand began achieving a level of international prestige and demand that José I could not have dreamed possible. **GD**

Gibson
Style O 1898

Type Acoustic guitar
Body & neck Walnut back and sides, spruce top
Fingerboard Walnut

Orville H. Gibson (1856–1918) invented the archtop guitar at the turn of the nineteenth century, and the company that bore his name took the ball and ran with it, ensuring the legacy of his inventions would influence guitar makers to the present day.

Born in Chateaugay, New York, as a young man he moved to Kalamazoo, Michigan, and from the mid-1880s he worked clerical jobs while combining his skills as a wood carver and his interest in music in a passion for instrument building. His early handmade creations included violins, mandolins, a ten-string

"The Gibson mandolins and guitars are recommended by the most expert players … Their volume and tone is not equaled by any other instruments."

LABEL ON THE INSIDE OF THE GUITAR

guitar–mandolin hybrid, an ornate harp guitar, and the Style O prototype archtop guitar we see here.

Orville's grasp of the principles of stringed instrument construction meant he was ideally placed to apply them to guitars. His most radical innovation was to carve the top, back, and sides from single pieces of wood, as he had with his groundbreaking mandolins in the 1880s. The pieces would be "tuned" to maximize their resonant properties, by tapping and carving the wood in a process resembling that of European violin makers. As with his mandolins, this Style O (for "oval") has a "Neapolitan"-style oval sound hole but no internal bracing or neck block, and is surprisingly lightweight. **OB**

Stewart & Bauer
100 1900

Type American parlor guitar
Body & neck Spruce top, Brazilian rosewood back and sides, mahogany neck
Other features Ebony bridge; ivory binding, nut, and saddle

This guitar was the top-of-the-line model that George Bauer made during the short 1898–1910 partnership of Stewart & Bauer in Philadelphia. It is one of the most beautiful, ornate, and highest-quality examples of so-called parlor guitars. It features decorative design details such as mother-of-pearl inlays on the convex ebony fingerboard with a tree-of-life inlay, and mother-of-pearl inlays on the head, around the front edge, and the sound hole.

At the time, the 100 A concert-size model sold for the princely sum of $110, with the default ladies' size

> *"The fingerboards had striking, exotic star-and-crescent inlays—very similar to the inlays on some high-end Stewart & Bauer banjos."*
>
> DAVID K. BRADFORD, 19THCENTURYGUITAR.COM

going for $100 and the 100 B extra-large concert size for $120. These ladder-braced, gut-strung guitars were distributed by Sears & Roebuck, who warned buyers against stringing these guitars with wire strings, an act that would make their warranty void.

At the end of the Civil War, the guitar's earlier popularity in East Coast middle-class America waned for decades until there was a resurgence of interest through the banjo, mandolin, and guitar (BMG) ensembles that emerged in the 1880s. Around 1900, on the concert stage and in society parlors, William Foden (1860–1947), the most famous American guitarist virtuoso of the time, would have been dazzling audiences with guitars of this caliber. **GD**

Gibson
Style O 1903

Type Archtop acoustic
Body & neck Birch back and sides, spruce top, mahogany neck
Fingerboard Ebony

When Orville Gibson formed the Gibson Mandolin-Guitar Company with a consortium of Kalamazoo businessmen in 1902, his direct involvement lessened. The company forged ahead with his designs and, buoyed by success with mandolins, began evolving its archtop guitars, dominating the market for decades. The Style O archtop represents two decades of refinement of Gibson's original concepts, and incorporates lasting milestones of guitar construction.

The Style O appeared in the 1903 Gibson catalog in three sizes, with three levels of ornamentation. The Style L was also available (with a conventional round sound hole) with similar specs. Alternate headstocks soon appeared, progressing from the early wide-ended "paddle" type, and including a slotted "transition" version. Then, in 1908, a giant leap toward what we have come to recognize as the look—and construction—of a modern archtop guitar was made with the debut of a redesigned Style O, later known as the Style O Artist. The brainchild of Gibson chief engineer George Laurian, it had a mandolin-style upper bout in the shape of a scroll, internal bracing, an asymmetric neck with an extended treble-side, a "trapeze"-style tailpiece, and, for the first time on any guitar, a cutaway on the lower bout to facilitate access to notes on the upper frets. **OB**

On the cover of Bob Dylan and the Band's album, *The Basement Tapes* (1975), guitarist Robbie Robertson clutches his 1920 Gibson Style O. He also famously played a Gibson Harp Guitar in the finale of Martin Scorsese's rockumentary, *The Last Waltz* (1978).

← Country blues musician and singer Big Bill Broonzy playing his Style O, *c.* 1935.

Vicente Arias
Classical Guitar 1906

Type Classical guitar
Body & neck Spruce top, extended ebony fingerboard
Other features Unique rosette design cast in epoxy block

Over three decades after making the 1870 guitar also featured in this book (see page 45), Vicente Arias was in his sixties and still building high-quality guitars of exceptional elegance and craftsmanship. The design of the earlier instrument can still be traced in the shape, size, and lightness of this guitar and especially the headstock, now looking even finer, as does the bridge. An important feature of this guitar is the fingerboard that extends the range from the usual top B, a half-step higher to a C. Although renowned for the beauty of his rosettes, each of which is unique, his

"The achievement of a beautiful sound from an Arias guitar results from constant attention."

RAPHAELLA SMITS

creativity did not end there: He made guitars with as few as four and as many as eleven braces, and some larger-sized guitars, like an 1899 example with eight strings from the collection of the late Narciso Yepes, which Belgian guitarist Raphaella Smits used to record the music of Antonio Jiménez Manjón (1866–1919).

When this guitar was made, the late Romantic period was coming to an end, as would, in 1909, the life of its most famous guitarist–composer, Francisco Tárrega. Modernism in music, as in art, was coming into fashion. Though Tárrega's disciples, notably Miguel Llobet and Emilio Pujol, were to take his legacy forward well into the twentieth century, it was the emergence of a young self-taught superstar called Andrés Segovia that would change everything. **GD**

Ditson
Model 261   1906

Type American parlor guitar
Body & neck Spruce top; rosewood back, sides, and neck
Other features Martin styling in body shape, head, and rosette; tailpiece to take steel strings

In the latter half of the nineteenth century, Oliver Ditson & Co. of Boston was one of the biggest music publishers of the northeastern United States with stores first in Philadelphia, then New York, and later Boston where Ditson also had its factory. Through subsidiaries and agents, Ditson became one of the biggest manufacturers of a wide range of musical instruments. In 1865, a Ditson & Co. partner, John Haynes, established John Haynes & Co. to make instruments, and it was Haynes who ran Ditson & Co. from 1888 until his death in 1907. That would make this

> *"That class of plunkers whose ideal guitarist is … armed with a steel-string jangle-trap …"*
> ANONYMOUS GUT STRING ADVOCATE, 1897

1906 parlor guitar one of the last made on his watch. A seemingly humbler instrument than those Haynes produced several decades earlier, the styling reflects the influence of C.F. Martin guitars. From about 1916, Ditson was one of Martin's largest customers, selling the "Ditson Model" Martins as well as a large number of regular models bearing the C.F. Martin stamp.

The year 1906 was still a transitional period for gut and silk versus steel strings. C.F. Martin and Gibson would not make flat-top guitars with steel strings until the 1920s, but Ditson had been doing so since the 1890s and it was steel that enabled the sound and playing techniques that gave birth to early blues, country, and jazz guitar styles in the first decades of the twentieth century. **GD**

Gibson
Style U1 1906

Type Harp guitar
Body & neck Convex ebonized spruce top, mahogany back and neck, mother-of-pearl inlays
Other features Ten sub-bass strings, stair bridge

The harp guitar, or plucked instruments like it, was not uncommon in Europe from early in the nineteenth century, but it was only in 1891, with a patent by Hansen, that an instrument with sub-basses emerged in the United States. Gibson began making them from 1903, offering four models on a rising scale of features and prices (Styles R, R1, U, and U1). Common to all models is an octagonal harp arm that runs beneath the soundboard to the rim at the end of the body, which is attached to the guitar waist with a small wood pyramid. Another reinforcement arm, symmetrical to the harp arm, on the treble side of the instrument, completes a frame inside the body. Gibson made sure this instrument was not about to collapse in on itself under the immense tension of the sub-basses. The pianolike frame contributes to the remarkable sustain of this instrument.

This Style U1 harp guitar was one of the more expensive Gibson models. It is a colossus of a guitar—21 in. (53.25 cm) wide and 48 in. (122 cm) long—originally designed to be played in a similar position to a cello, it came with a steel spike that extended from its base. Despite their extraordinary qualities and belle époque charms, these harp guitars remain museum and conversation pieces and are only rarely played today. **GD**

Champion of the Gibson Style U, Tom Shinness plays a 1913 model on *Translucent Harp* (2004), a selection of his compositions infused with new-age, jazz, and folk. Eight tracks are for solo harp guitar; others feature an eclectic range of other instruments.

Joseph Bohmann
Harp Guitar 1910

Type Harp guitar
Body & neck Convex top and back, double neck
Other features Seven internal sympathetic tunable
vibrating rods, damper pad, hand rest, double bridges

This freakish-looking instrument is one of three types
with sympathetic vibrating rods inside the body that
Bohmann made while in his sixties and still at the
height of his inventive powers as a manufacturer of
guitars, mandolins, and violins in Chicago. Taking the
double-neck innovation he developed over earlier
decades (one standard and one with twelve sub-bass
strings tuned chromatically) he patented several new
ones specific to this type of guitar, including the set of
vibrating rods and a convex top and back with sloped
shoulder design for easier access to the higher frets.

" … The World's Greatest Musical
Instrument Manufacturer."

JOSEPH BOHMANN

Bohmann's target market for his harp guitars had
included the mandolin orchestras popular at the time
in which, typically, one harp guitar would provide an
accompaniment for a flute, violin, two mandolins, and
two mandolas. There were also larger ensembles
like the Steinway Mandolin Orchestra with fifteen
instruments including three harp guitars, a harp,
a cello, and numerous mandolins.

Reputedly a bombastic, shamelessly self-
promoting megalomaniac, Bohmann's pride
may have been his downfall. Like Shelley's
Ozymandias, his legacy turned out to be
unloved, forgotten, and virtually lost to the march
of history. After his death his factory was shut down
and left virtually untouched for some forty years, with
finished and half-finished instruments still in it. **GD**

Enrique García
Classical Guitar 1912

Type Classical guitar
Body & neck Spruce top, Brazilian rosewood back and sides, ebony fingerboard
Other features Oval sound hole, innovative fan bracing

Considered the founder of the "Barcelona" or "Catalan" school of guitar makers from the time he opened a workshop there in 1895 (after serving an apprenticeship at Ramirez in Madrid), Enrique García (1868–1922) was probably the most internationally famous maker of classical guitars in the early twentieth century and a big influence on makers like Francisco and Miguel Simplicio and Ignacio Fleta. His style of construction includes an innovative fan bracing system that normally had eight braces (a system that would be developed by Fleta) instead of the more common Torres seven, and a creative approach to the appearance of the instrument, with models that could be very ornate, including features like inlays and his trademark carved heads. The unusual sound hole on this 1912 model is a case in point. Whether one likes it or not, it certainly makes a visual impact, though as to whether it makes any difference to the guitar's already exquisite sound properties is a moot point.

In the year this guitar was made, García started exporting guitars in significant numbers to Argentina, at the time one of the world's wealthiest countries and a major South American center of culture. Concerts by virtuosi like Domingo Prat, Miguel Llobet, and Emilio Pujol in Buenos Aires stirred thousands of guitarists—many eager to own one of García's guitars. **GD**

Marc Teicholz, first prizewinner of the 1989 International Guitar Foundation of America competition, plays a guitar from García's early tyears in Barcelona on *Valseana*, an album of waltzes that features eighteen guitars by many famous makers of the past 150 years.

Gibson
L-4 1912

Type Acoustic guitar
Body & neck Spruce top, maple back and sides, mahogany neck
Fingerboard Ebony

Gibson's L-4 debuted as a bigger and louder update of the L-1 and L-3 models, which Gibson initially designated a "grand concert" model on account of its larger size. Its 16-in. (40.5-cm) body (measured across the lower bout) certainly gave it plenty of oomph and bottom-end presence, and it quickly established itself as the guitar of choice among rhythm players in the emerging Dixieland and big band jazz trends of the era. The L-4 never really looked back, and enjoys the distinction of being Gibson's longest-running production model (the present-day version sports a Florentine cutaway and pick-ups; its production was interrupted in 1956, resuming in the late 1980s).

The 1912 model was carved by hand and shared the same woods as its smaller L-Series siblings, but had one extra fret (making twenty in total) and an ivoroid-bound oval sound hole. Cosmetic tinkering followed, including a round sound hole in 1928, until, in 1935, Lloyd Loar's f-holes (first seen on the L-5 model, see page 62) were finally added to aid sonic projection.

When the 1950s electrified the guitar world, Gibson based its ES-175 on the L-4's concept and construction, replacing the carved top with a laminated one. A cutaway was added to the original L-4, until the changes coalesced into the L-4 CES—Cutaway Electric Spanish—with various pick-up configurations. **OB**

The Quintessential Eddie Lang, 1925–1932 (1998) showcases the versatile jazz chops of this pioneering virtuoso on both his Gibson L-4 and, from 1928 onward, a Gibson L-5. Lang expanded the possibilities of the guitar as a recording and a solo instrument.

Manuel Ramírez
Flamenco Guitar 1913

J.F. Stetson
Parlor Guitar 1915

Type Flamenco guitar
Body & neck Spruce top, cypress back and sides, ebony fingerboard
Other features Golpeador, 26 in. (66 cm) scale length

Type American parlor guitar
Body & neck Spruce top, Brazilian rosewood back and sides, mahogany neck, ebony fingerboard
Other features X-bracing, inlays on fingerboard and head

It was a classical guitar made by Santos Hernandez, then an apprentice in the workshop of Manuel Ramírez (1864–1916), younger brother of José I, that the great virtuoso Andrés Segovia (1893–1987) played for the first twenty-five years of his brilliant career and that dazzled concert goers, musicians, and critics alike. Ramírez gave it to a young Segovia in around 1912 on hearing him play for the first time. It helped make all three of their reputations and inspired Hermann Hauser, whose guitars Segovia would later play before returning to Ramírez guitars again around 1960. The guitar is now in the Metropolitan Museum of Art in New York.

With flamenco guitars like this 1913 example, Manuel Ramírez transformed what came before him into a model that even today remains a benchmark to luthiers. Sadly, it seems José I never could forgive him the accolades and for opening a shop in Madrid, in direct competition with him. Manuel was teacher and mentor to guitar makers Santos Hernandez, Domingo Esteso, and Modesto Borreguero. **GD**

This parlor guitar was distributed by W.J. Dyer & Bro. of Minnesota and J.F. Stetson was Dyer's brand for its regular flat-top guitars. They were in fact manufactured by the Larson Brothers of Maurer & Co. of Chicago, who made a range of instruments for Dyer. Larson guitars like this were handmade to a very high standard, with only the best-quality woods, and are reputed to have superior sound quality and sustain, with a warm and rounded midrange and full-sounding upper register.

At the end of the nineteenth century and beginning of the twentieth, there was a lively, sometimes heated, debate about gut versus steel strings. The Larsons started introducing steel strings to their flat tops in 1904, twenty years before C.F. Martin did, so this guitar was made to be steel strung. In the United States in 1915, when this guitar was made, music that had been steeped in the European tradition throughout the nineteenth century had found a uniquely American voice, and its guitars a uniquely American style. **GD**

Dyer
ASB-1 1920

Oscar Schmidt
Hawaiian 1920

Type Harp guitar
Body & neck Spruce top; mahogany back, sides, and neck; ebony fingerboard and bridge
Other features Hollow arm with six sub-bass strings

Type Hawaiian steel-string guitar
Body & neck Koa top, back, and sides; mahogany neck; rosewood veneer headstock; ebony fingerboard
Other features Tree of life mother-of-pearl inlays

The Minnesota company W.J. Dyer & Bro., for a time during the early part of the twentieth century the largest distributor of musical instruments west of Chicago, started selling harp guitars from around 1904 as something of a sideline from its main business as purveyor of pianos, organs, and other instruments.

The Dyer harp guitar, today one of the most popular models with harp guitar players, is based on a design patented by Chris Knutsen in 1898. Dyer contracted the Larson Brothers of Chicago to manufacture them, initially under license until 1912, when Knutsen's patent expired. Sadly, the Larsons were not credited at the time as the makers of the instruments, though they made significant refinements and improved on the construction quality of Knutsen's originals. The distinctive sub-bass' headstock with its peghead inlays was a modification attributed to the Larsons. In 1919 Dyer stopped advertising harp guitars, making this near-top-of-the-line 1920 model one of the last of the line. **GD**

This type of guitar—its body made from fabulously exotic Hawaiian koa wood, the laptop position it was played in, the beguiling sound of a steel bar sliding over the strings, and the music of the Hawaiian islands played on it—caused a sensation when it first graced the American mainland in the hands of Hawaiian musicians at the 1915 Panama-Pacific International Exposition in San Francisco. Soon many makers set about satisfying the demand from clients stampeding to own this curious invention and its little cousin, the ukulele. It was easy. All they needed to do was customize their standard parlor guitars by using koa wood and by raising the nut a little.

The Oscar Schmidt Company, then of New Jersey, was one of the first to get in on the action. This eye-catching example from 1920, traditionally tuned to an A-major chord, is one of the more elaborate models from that period, with its mother-of-pearl inlays and twin-pyramid bridge design. It would have appealed to well-heeled aficionados of the new craze. **GD**

Gibson
L-5 1922

Type Acoustic guitar
Body & neck Spruce top, birch or maple back and sides, maple and mahogany neck
Fingerboard Ebony

Lloyd Loar (1886–1943), like Orville Gibson before him, combined engineering nous with musical expertise. During his five-year tenure between 1919 and 1924, he advanced many of the technical aspects of Gibson's designs. His masterpiece, however, was the Gibson L-5 archtop, released in 1922 and now regarded as one of the most important guitar designs of all time.

Competing with big-band brass sections was a challenge for 1920s guitarists. As on previous Gibson models, f-holes in place of round or oval sound holes improved projection and enabled the L-5 to make itself heard, as did the 16-in. (40.5-cm) body (boosted to 17 in. [43 cm] with 1934's "Advanced" model).

Gibson's flagship had fourteen frets clear of the body, a truss rod (patented by employee Thaddeus McHugh in 1921) to aid neck alignment, a height-adjustable bridge, and a celluloid pickguard to aid picking-hand stability and comfort. It had a warm, full-bodied tone that could as easily do the bidding of country stars like Mother Maybelle Carter as it would later deliver the punchy rock 'n' roll of Scotty Moore.

A cutaway model was introduced in 1939, followed in 1951 by a fully electrified version, the L-5 CES—the guitar Wes Montgomery turned into a jazz icon. Naturally, the L-5's phenomenal success has had a direct influence on countless designers since. **OB**

Smokin' At The Half Note (1965) features Wes Montgomery's dulcet L-5 tones. It was described as "the absolute best jazz guitar album ever made" by Pat Metheny, who recently bought Montgomery's L-5 from George Benson at auction.

Jazz guitarist Eddie Lang performs on stage with a Gibson L-5 guitar *c.* 1928 in Chicago.

Hernández
Flamenco Guitar 1925

Type Flamenco acoustic guitar
Body & neck Cypress back and sides, spruce top, mahogany neck
Fingerboard Ebony

Santos Hernández (1873–1943) was one of the twentieth century's most gifted luthiers. His work—along with Domingo Esteso (1882–1937)—helped define the character of the modern flamenco as being something distinct from its classical counterpart.

Hailed as "the Stradivari of flamenco," Hernández was born in Madrid, where he learned his craft under the watchful eye of master luthier José Ramírez, by whom he was employed for twenty-three years. When Ramírez died in 1923, Hernández set up on his own, and his workshop quickly became a popular meeting place for flamenco players of the day.

Reflecting the poverty of flamenco players, cheaper woods such as cypress were traditionally used for the instruments' backs and sides. Lighter than traditional rosewood, this also helped create the earthy percussive tone. Because of its stability, cypress can be worked very thin; combined with its light weight, this facilitates the biting flamenco tone. Spruce was used on the soundboard—as it is on most high-quality flamenco guitars—as it produces a clearer, more focused sound.

Hernández guitars were built in the tradition of Antonio Torres, designed for a strong attack and power. But Santos added an innovative harmonic downward-sloping bar beneath the soundboard, giving the treble a much firmer sound. **TB**

Sabicas was one of the most celebrated flamenco guitarists of the twentieth century. He used Hernández-built guitars throughout most of his career. Some of his finest playing can be heard on the album *Flamencan Guitar Solos* (2008).

Francisco Simplicio
Classical Guitar 1925

Type Classical guitar
Body & neck Spruce top, Cuban mahogany back and sides, ebony fingerboard
Other features García-like fan bracing system

Francisco Simplicio (1874–1932) was a cabinetmaker in Barcelona for about twenty years before starting to make guitars in 1919 for Enrique García, then probably the most in-demand classical guitar maker in the world. Simplicio took over García's shop when García died in 1922, and for years made guitars just like García's before introducing his own innovations, such as uniquely tapered braces and an experimental guitar with a double sound hole.

This model is pure García in size, appearance, weight, and fan bracing system with eight braces—now with Simplicio's tapering. Even the carved head is almost identical to García's. Until 1925, his labels indicated he was the "only disciple and student of Enrique García," which no doubt helped his sales and reputation. Like García, he became successful with exports to Argentina—which, in the early twentieth century, was experiencing an economic and cultural boom with an amazing interest in the guitar. He was helped by his son Miguel to make about thirty-five guitars a year from 1922 until his death ten years later.

Famous guitarists who played Simplicio guitars include José Rey de la Torre and Leo Brouwer. The very last guitar that he built before he died was owned by de la Torre. Miguel Simplicio allegedly had to finish it by adding the frets, tuning machines, and bridge. **GD**

Andrés Segovia And His Contemporaries Vol.10 (2005) includes the very first of José Rey de la Torres' recordings, playing the very last guitar that Francisco Simplicio made. In this 1946 recording, he and Segovia play music by Fernando Sor and Francisco Tárrega.

Washburn
Bell Style 1925

Type Flat-top gut-string acoustic guitar
Body & neck Mahogany back, sides, and neck;
spruce top
Fingerboard Rosewood

In the 1920s, the banjo was still king because its volume and sharp attack made it the rhythm instrument of choice for most big bands, but it was also a time of experimentation for some guitar makers. It just wasn't quite clear in which direction the guitar was to go. In 1925, instrument maker Lyon & Healy's Chicago factory tried this unusual bell-shaped body, selling it under its premier Washburn brand name and introducing serial numbers, with guitars all beginning with 52 and the other two digits being the model number.

The bell guitar was largely built of mahogany with a spruce top. It had a classical-style open headstock, normal fixed bridge, and simply decorated round sound hole. The only added glamour was an intricate floral gold-leaf decoration stenciled around the soundboard. At $165, including its custom-made case, the bell-shaped guitar was considered expensive at the time.

The bell guitar's most famous user was American poet and musician Carl Sandburg. Carl was a big guitar fan and collector. The "poet of the people" used the bell-shaped Washburn to accompany his verse. His Washburn can still be seen at his home in Flat Rock, North Carolina, a U.S. National Historic Site.

The bell-shaped body looks strange today, but at the time it was less so. Washburn also made pear-shaped tenor guitars and a bell-shaped ukelele. **SH**

The Great Carl Sandburg: Songs of America (1999) is a contemporary release of a mid-1950s recording. It is one of the rare albums on which the poet can be heard singing folk songs and playing his Washburn Bell Style guitar.

Weissenborn
Style C 1925

Type Hawaiian steel-string guitar
Body & neck Top, back, sides, V-shaped neck, and headstock in Hawaiian koa wood
Other features Ebony fingerboard, "bat-wing" bridge

Hermann C. Weissenborn was a maker of pianos and violins when he immigrated from Germany to the United States in 1902, setting up a workshop in Los Angeles in 1910 where his main activity appears to have been instrument repairs. In the early 1920s, he jumped on board the popular Hawaiian music bandwagon and began making ukuleles, Martin-style flat tops like this Style C (third in a line that went from Styles A to D) for "slack-key" finger-style playing, and the teardrop-shaped Hawaiian lap steel guitars with their hollow necks and sloping shoulders in Styles 1, 2, 3, and 4. It is

> "I'm drawn to its resonating sound. It is very expressive. I stick with the Weissenborn; it says something new to me every day."
> BEN HARPER

the latter group for which he is best known and which have undergone a revival in recent years as alternatives to National and Dobro guitars favored by players like Ben Harper, Bob Brozman, and David Lindley.

C.F. Martin's flat-top styling would have been the primary influence on the X-braced Weissenborn Style C. The other key influence, but primarily for his hollow-neck lap steel guitars, was Chris J. Knutsen, who is credited with originating the overall design. Now very collectible and valuable, in the 1920s Weissenborn's guitars sold from $40 up to $79, less so after the stock market crash of 1929. Weissenborn's fortunes during the 1920s, propelled by the Hawaiian music craze of that time, faded away through declining demand during the Depression years of the 1930s. **GD**

National
Tricone 1927

Type Acoustic resonator
Body & neck "German Silver" body with mahogany neck
Fingerboard Ebony

Before the development of the electric guitar, the major problem faced by any group player was one of volume. The 1920s saw a number of valiant efforts to deal with this issue, the most ingenious being the use of "mechanical" amplification.

At the request of guitarist George Beauchamp, during the mid-1920s John Dopyera produced the first "resonating" guitar. The principle was simple: a thin aluminum cone, rather like a loudspeaker, was fitted inside the body in direct contact with the bridge saddle. When the guitar strings were struck, the cone picked up the vibrations and amplified the sound.

The experiment was sufficiently successful that in 1927 Dopyera and Beauchamp founded the National String Instrument Corporation. The first instrument they produced was a metal-bodied guitar fitted with three conical aluminum resonators connected at the center by a T-shaped aluminum bridge on top of which was a maple bridge saddle. This system was called the Tricone. Most guitarists seem to agree that single cones provide greater volume and the Tricone system a better quality of sound and greater sustain.

National produced four Tricone models before Dopyera left to found the Dobro company. The models differ only in their etched body designs: the Style 4 shown here features a chrysanthemum engraving. **TB**

The compilation *Hula Blues: Vintage Steel Guitar Instrumentals From The '30s and '40s* (1974) contains recordings by some fine players, such as Jim Holstein of the duo The Genial Hawaiians who played his Tricone both in conventional style and in horizontal lap position.

Gibson
Nick Lucas 1928

Type Flat-top acoustic guitar
Body & neck Spruce top, mahogany back and sides
Fingerboard Rosewood

New Jersey–born "Crooning Troubadour" Nick Lucas (1897–1982) was at the peak of his popularity in the late 1920s when Gibson formalized his association with its guitars by releasing a number of Nick Lucas models. Lucas had made history in July 1922 when he committed the first solo jazz guitar instrumentals, *Pickin' the Guitar* and *Teasin' the Frets*, to record. As the Roaring Twenties came to a close, he was embarking on a career in musicals, selling millions of records to boot.

The 1928 Gibson Nick Lucas model (aka "Special") was Gibson's first artist-signature guitar endorsement,

> *"I wanted a wider neck, deeper sides, and a smaller body that would be more presentable on stage."*
>
> NICK LUCAS

and appeared in many permutations. Initially shaped like the L-1, one factor that remained constant throughout the six subsequent design tweaks—including the number of frets, materials, cosmetics, bridge type, and even body shape—was a deeper body, which had a marked effect on its tone. The "Florentine" banjo of 1927 provided the inspiration for this particular custom-order guitar's fingerboard adornments, which, strangely, depict scenes of Venice.

The most celebrated Nick Lucas user was none other than Bob Dylan. In his earlier days, Dylan had always used Martin or other Gibson acoustics, but in the final years of his acoustic period—before his controversial electric conversion in 1965—his instrument of choice was a Nick Lucas. **OB**

Epiphone
Recording D 1928

Type Archtop acoustic guitar
Body & neck Maple back and sides, spruce top, maple neck
Fingerboard Ebony

Long before the Epiphone brand became little more than a label slapped on cheap Gibsons produced in China, it was an independent guitar manufacturer of considerable standing. Indeed, throughout the 1930s, Epiphone and Gibson had fought a fierce commercial battle over production of archtop guitars.

The roots of the company dated back to 1873 in Smyrna in what was then the Ottoman Empire (now Izmir, Turkey), when Anastasios Stathopoulos began building and selling stringed instruments. He continued to build and sell his own instruments after he'd relocated to Long Island, New York, in 1903. Following his death in 1915, his son Epaminondas took control of the business, and began to produce banjos.

If the Gibson L-5 had kick-started the demise of the banjo in 1922, Stathopoulos' first guitars certainly didn't acknowledge this fact. Combining the owner's nickname "Epi" with "phone," from the Greek word for "sound," the brand made its debut in 1928 with the small-bodied "Recording" series. The model "D" had a maple back and sides and a hand-carved spruce flat top. The maple neck had a "V" profile and was topped with an ebony fingerboard. With more than a nod to Epi's previous instruments, the headstock was inlaid with pearloid and housed six banjo-style tuning pegs.

Like the other members of the Recording series (A to E) these guitars lacked the volume of the L-5 and were not hugely popular. Three years later production ended and the first range of Epiphone Masterbilts appeared: jazz players were quick to discover guitars like the Emperor and Deluxe models, now highly prized by collectors. **TB**

Epiphone
Recording E 1928

Type Flat-top acoustic guitar
Body & neck Single cutaway, spruce top, maple back and sides, set maple neck
Fingerboard Rosewood

It was small, sounded weedy, and no one famous played one. Yet this was the start of one of the great guitar dynasties—the first Epiphone. Epaminondas or "Epi" Stathopoulo, son of a Greek immigrant instrument maker, was a successful banjo maker, at the time the coolest instrument in the United States. Nevertheless in 1928, Epi started to branch out into guitars. Epiphone's Recording series was his first effort, designed to compete with the hottest ax of the time, Gibson's L-5.

The Recording came in five styles; A was the plainest and E the fanciest. All had the same sloping cutaway.

"The Recording guitars were not initially a success. One problem was a lack of celebrity endorsement. The other was a lack of volume."
EPIPHONE OFFICIAL HISTORY

At the top of the line was the $175 E. This had very fancy floral neck inlays and a lavishly carved and decorated headstock. The back was arched, the finish was a dark sunburst, and there was a black plastic floating pickguard stretching from the neck to the bridge. But the spruce and laminated maple bodies were smaller than Gibson's and sounded weak in comparison.

The L-5 was loud enough that its rhythmic chords could cut through the sound of a whole band. The Epiphone's didn't. The guitars seemed too small and ornate to some players. With no celebrity endorsements the Recording series was not the success Epi hoped for. Thankfully he was not deterred and soon launched a second and much-improved series of guitars—the Masterbilts. **SH**

Dobro
Model 55 1929

Type Acoustic resonator
Body & neck Walnut body and
mahogany neck
Fingerboard Rosewood

From the beginning of their business relationship as founders of National, George Beauchamp and John Dopyera had fought over fundamental issues of the resonator design, and both also felt they deserved principal credit for its development. Having created a single-cone resonator that was cheaper to produce than the National Tricone system, in 1928 Dopyera and his brothers Rudy, Emile, Robert, and Louis broke away to launch the Dobro Manufacturing Company.

The problem faced by the brothers was that National owned the patents on all of Dopyera's designs, so he was forced to come up with an ingenious variant. This involved inverting the cone, so that instead of the bridge resting its apex, it was fitted to a cast aluminum "spider" that had eight legs spanning the perimeter of a downward-pointing cone.

Although the word "resonator" conjures up the attractive brass or nickel-bodied Dobro and National models, all of the Dobro guitars until 1935 were built from wood but fitted with Dopyera's internal resonator, with its decorative metal covering and two circular metal ports in the upper bout. The Model 55, like most of those designated numbers lower than 100, was a lower-priced model, and usually featured neck binding, a very dark body finish, and an engraved coverplate. This model was discontinued in 1934. **TB**

Award-winning bluegrass player and master of the Dobro, Phil Leadbetter has been honored with his own signature model. He showcases his Dobro skills on his instrumental album *Philibuster!* (2000).

Martin
OM-28 1929

Type Acoustic guitar with mahogany blocks
Body & neck Solid Adirondack red spruce top, select hardwood neck
Fingerboard Solid black ebony

What's not to love about a Martin "Orchestra Model" OM-28 Marquis? Not only does it come with the enviable Martin pedigree, it has a sophisticated tone, heaps of overtones, and possesses fabulous fingerpicking clarity while its thick, strong neck and overall build—back and sides of East Indian rosewood, herringbone trim, ebony fingerboard, and nuts of fossilized ivory—give the impression it just might last forever. And of course add to that Martin's "Golden Era" appointments, including the Adirondack spruce top and scalloped braces—a timber barely used in guitars since the Second World War and which blossoms and reaches its full potential over time— and you have a vintage prewar sound without the expense of a trip to a custom shop.

Similar to the Eric Clapton 000-28EC model in scale and ornamentation, the OM-28 has greater string spacings at the bridge, wider nut spacing, and a longer scale. It is more balanced than the Martin D series, and you can strum it as hard as you like without any distortion. The largish 1¾ in.-wide (4.5 cm) modified V-neck, however, may take a little getting used to.

So is it any wonder that those few who admit to having possessed—and then sold—a Martin OM-28 refer to the point of sale as "a moment of lunacy"? Buy one, and it may well be the last guitar you ever need. **BS**

John Mayer is a well-known contemporary OM-28 player, who in 2006 was given his own signature model OM-28. His third album, *Continuum* (2006), showed a change of direction toward a new, more blues-oriented sound.

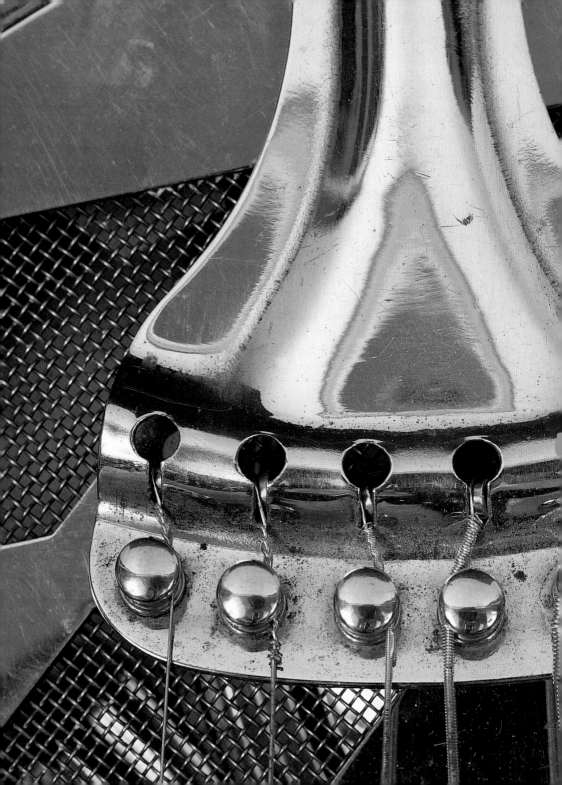

1930–1949

National
Style O 1930

Prairie State
Bass 1930

Type Acoustic resonator
Body & neck Nickel-plated (brass from 1932),
mahogany neck
Fingerboard Bound ebony

Type Acoustic bass guitar
Body & neck Spruce top, poplar back and sides,
mahogany neck
Fingerboard Ebony

When the single-cone Dobro resonators produced from 1928 by his former business partner John Dopyera were successful, George Beauchamp began producing National single-cone resonators using designs created by Dopyera before he and his brothers left the company.

The first such instrument to appear was the famous National Style O. The principle on which it was designed was much the same as that used on the Tricone models, except that the bridge was now fixed at the center of a single 9½-in. (24-cm) cone. These National resonators are referred to as "Biscuit Bridge" models. The size of the single cone provided greater volume, but a cruder tone.

Although the early resonators were popular with Hawaiian lap-style players, the Style O captured the imagination of many blues players of the period—names such as Reverend Gary Davis and Son House. The most celebrated modern exponent is Mark Knopfler, whose own vintage Style O was used to great effect on the Dire Straits hit "Romeo and Juliet." **TB**

An innovative instrument in the large-bodied Prairie State range from the Larson brothers of Maurer & Co. of Chicago that makes full use of their double-rod system, patented in 1930, to reinforce this huge acoustic bass guitar. It has nineteen frets meeting the soundboard at the twelfth, and an extending spike enables it to be played upright or between the knees in a cello position. Among the other Prairie State models the Larsons made at about this time is a six-string version of this acoustic bass guitar with virtually the same body and neck and another stocky super-jumbo-sized six-string guitar appropriately called the "Big Boy." With their Prairie State and Euphonon models the Larsons tried to address the problem of getting more volume out of the acoustic guitar. This acoustic bass guitar would have provided a robust bass range in larger ensembles, as did the harp guitars, mando cellos, and mando basses of the mandolin orchestras that had been around for some decades but whose popularity had by 1930 already begun to wane. **GD**

Serenader
Venetian 1930

William C. Stahl
Acoustic Guitar 1930

Type Venetian-style flat-top acoustic guitar
Body & neck Spruce top, maple back and sides,
V-shaped neck, pearloid fingerboard, rosewood bridge
Other features Venetian head and body styling

Type Flat-top acoustic guitar
Body & neck Spruce top, Brazilian rosewood back and
sides, mahogany neck, ebony fingerboard and bridge
Other features Larson-patented support rod system

The Chicago manufacturer Stromberg-Voisinet made this guitar—and many like it in different sizes and trim options—for Buegeleisen and Jacobson (B&J), long-established New York instrument vendors who, by the 1930s, had operations in Canada and even imported instruments from Europe. Serenader was their brand for a very wide range of guitars sourced from a number of manufacturers.

This so-called Venetian style of guitar was made from 1927. From about 1930 it evolved into an archtop Kay Kraft range of guitars popular with blues musicians that was made until 1934. The guitar's shape is similar to Venetian mandolins dating back to the nineteenth century. The unique design, with its ladder bracing and pickguard, has been attributed to Joseph Zorzi, an Italian-American luthier who started work as production manager at Stromberg-Voisinet in 1926, a year before these models first appeared. There was also a four-string tenor guitar version that looked very much like an elongated, supersized mandolin. **GD**

This is a handsome guitar made by the Larson brothers of Maurer & Co. of Chicago who, in addition to manufacturing guitars for their own Maurer, Prairie State, and Euphonon brands, also supplied guitars to William C. Stahl. A Milwaukee publisher of arrangements, methods, and music for the banjo, mandolin, and guitar, Stahl had expanded his business to sell instruments as well, and was probably the Larsons' most important client around the time this guitar was built.

The guitar, with its distinctive pickguard design also seen in the mandolins Stahl sold as far back as 1912, is the Larsons' Prairie State model—with Stahl's label on it taking the credit. It has laminated braces, an unusually shaped pickguard, and the trademark Larsen fingerboard inlay pattern. Only a few guitars with this exact specification are known to exist. It is a sturdy guitar, made with the double-rod system the Larsons patented in 1930. One rod enables adjustment of the neck, while the other (visible through the sound hole) reinforces the body against collapse. **GD**

Stromberg-Voisinet
No. 49 1930

Type Hawaiian guitar
Body & neck Spruce top, exotic hardwood back and sides, pearloid fingerboard
Other features V-shaped neck, tropical beach scene decal

When this model 49 Hawaiian guitar was made, the Depression had arrived with the catastrophic stock market crash of 1929; businesses collapsed, money was tight, and companies making affordable music instruments like Stromberg-Voisinet were perhaps in a better position to weather the storm than others.

This Chicago manufacturer started out in 1890 as the Groeschel Mandolin Company. It became Stromberg-Voisinet in 1921 and was renamed again as the Kay Musical Instrument Company in the 1930s. It has its place in the hall of fame not as a result of the quality of the instruments, which was average at best, but by its having made in 1928 one of the first electric guitars to be marketed, the Stromberg Electro. Stromberg-Voisinet is not to be confused with Stromberg, makers of superior archtop jazz guitars from the 1930s to the 1950s.

Until the advent of the pedal steel guitar in the 1940s, this was the type of instrument known as the Hawaiian guitar. Fundamentally a traditional steel-strung parlor guitar, it was played either on the lap with a specially raised nut and a sliding steel bar or with a normal nut in a normal position in the Hawaiian "slack-key" finger style. It was hugely popular on the American mainland from 1915 to the 1930s and continues to be so in Hawaii today, with slack-key guitar players winning Grammy Awards in recent years. **GD**

From these recordings of the 1940s, one senses how much of an antidote Hawaiian music must have been to the bleakness of the 1930s Depression. *The History Of Slack Key Guitar* (1997) includes performances by Gabby Pahinui, one of the instrument's most influential exponents.

Vega
Steel-string Guitar 1930

Type Archtop steel-string acoustic guitar
Body & neck Maple back and sides, spruce top, maple neck
Fingerboard Rosewood

Vega had been making instruments in Boston, Massachusetts, since the late nineteenth century but was best-known for banjos. Its Vegavox model was played by self-styled "King of the Banjo," Eddie Peabody.

The company had been making guitars too. Their quality was good, but they hadn't made big inroads into the market. As guitar sales in the United States began to rise in the late 1920s and early 1930s, Vega tried to take advantage with a new line of guitars.

Vega launched banjo-guitars, four-string tenor guitars, and strange "cylinder" guitars. These had a

> *"He (Joe Termini) coaxes some of the hottest jazz out his Vega guitar that audiences have ever heard."*
>
> CONTEMPORARY REVIEW

bulge right down the middle of the back and front, which was supposed to improve the tone and projection, but to the modern eye looks uncomfortable to hold and play.

The most popular contemporary Vega guitar, however, was the more conventional-looking steel-string acoustic with both an arched back and a top carved like a violin. This sunburst f-hole guitar had a trapeze-style tailpiece, floating scratchplate, bound body and headstock, and block-inlaid fingerboard.

Texas country-band leader Leo "Tex" Butler played one, as did music-hall star Joe Termini, and it would later become popular with jazz musicians. The model stayed in production and Vega later produced early electrified versions. **SH**

Epiphone
Broadway 1931

Type Archtop f-hole acoustic guitar
Body & neck Walnut arched back and sides, solid spruce top, dovetail mahogany neck
Fingerboard Ebony

New York instrument maker Epi Stathopoulo's first attempt to take on the dominant Gibson L-5 had failed. However, the young Greek immigrant learned fast. Within three years, he launched a far superior guitar.

The Epiphone Masterbilt series was an even bolder attack on the Gibson "Master Model" L-5. These seven carved-top f-hole archtops closely mimicked the Gibson's features. They also had floating scratchplates, and trapeze tailpieces.

The Broadway was in the middle of the line and at $175 was the best value. The guitar had a walnut back

"With the original Masterbilt line of 1931, Epiphone challenged Gibson for supremacy in the guitar world."

HENRY JUSZKIEWICZ

and sides, solid spruce top finished with a deep tobacco sunburst, ebony fretboard, and a patented "expansion rod," which was a version of the innovative truss rod Gibson had invented a decade before. The bridge was adjustable for height so players could alter the action of their guitar.

The decoration of the Recording series was toned down, although the headstock was still inlaid with floral patterns and scrolls, the fretboard had diamond inlays, and the body and fingerboard were neatly bound.

Most importantly the Masterbilts had the style, playability, and sound to be a success in a big band's rhythm section. Epiphone now had a guitar to take on Gibson and begin a sales battle that lasted for a quarter of a century. **SH**

Epiphone
Deluxe 1931

Type Archtop acoustic
Body & neck Maple back and sides, spruce top, maple neck
Fingerboard Rosewood

Anastasios Stathopoulo arrived in Long Island, New York, in 1903. A maker of ouds—an Arabic lute-style instrument—his son, Epaminondas (known as "Epi"), gradually shifted the emphasis of the family business toward banjos. The Epiphone name appeared in 1928, the same year as the company's first guitars. Throughout the 1930s, the brand was responsible for producing some of the finest archtop guitars in the United States, developing a fierce rivalry with the Gibson Corporation.

First built in 1931, the large-bodied Deluxe was a direct competitor to Gibson's L-5—itself considered revolutionary for its volume and projection. The Deluxe, however, was a considerably more attractive guitar.

The Deluxe featured a "Masterbilt" headstock with its beautifully ornate floral inlays. One of the most striking and interesting features of early Epiphone models is the famous "Frequensator" tailpiece, which enables bass and treble strings of different lengths to be used. Increasing the length of the bass strings causes greater tension, making the strings tighter; the shorter top strings have a looser tension, making it easier to bend notes and play solos in the upper register.

In 1941, the Zephyr Deluxe emerged, the first electric version of this model. The guitar shown here is a 1934 Deluxe, which has been customized with the addition of a pick-up—probably at some point during the 1940s. **TB**

One of the pioneers of cool jazz, Billy Bauer played an Epiphone Deluxe with pianist Lennie Tristano at the time of his seminal 1949 recording "Digression," one of the first examples of "free improvisation."

Martin
D-28 1931

Type Acoustic guitar
Body & neck Sitka spruce top, rosewood body and sides, mahogany neck
Fingerboard Solid black ebony

The D-28, Martin's much-copied Dreadnought, is the model against which all others are judged. Originally designed by Martin in 1916 and marketed under the brand Oliver Ditson, it was mostly, and still is—as implied by its name—larger, bolder, and louder than most other guitars, and by the 1950s had become the instrument of choice for folk singers across the United States and the standard-bearer of bluegrass music.

Martin-branded Dreadnoughts debuted in 1931. The D-28 had distinctive strips of herringbone marquetry around its top and a zipperlike strip of purfling bisecting its back. D-28s from the mid-1930s also had uniquely positioned scalloped cross-braces that were extremely close to the sound hole, which gave the top a unique kind of flex and maximized bass response and volume in nonamplified venues. This X-bracing and the tones it helped produce are the reason that many aficionados still claim the D-28s of the time represent the high-water mark of Martin craftsmanship (the bracing was discontinued in 1945).

Despite the ensuing decades of change, including the demise of tortoiseshell pickguards, horse-hide glues, and the switch from prized Brazilian rosewood in the back and sides to East Indian rosewood, all D-28s since have remained faithful to that very first Dreadnought, the "Holy Grail" of acoustic guitars. **BS**

Neil Young famously owns the 1941 Martin D-28 once belonging to country legend Hank Williams. He said: "I try to do the right thing with the guitar. You don't want to stink with Hank's guitar." It can be heard on, among others, his album *On The Beach* (1974).

← Neil Young plays his Martin D-28 in concert in 1973.

Rickenbacker
Frying Pan 1931

Type Lap steel guitar with circular body
Body & neck Production models built from aluminum
Fingerboard Maple
Pick-ups Horseshoe magnets

Behold, one of the most significant musical instruments of the twentieth century! According to some, the "Frying Pan" was the first electric guitar. Although not strictly true, in 1931 it became the first stringed instrument with a magnetic pick-up to go into production.

Guitarist George Beauchamp had previously made his name as the co-inventor of the principles of the cone resonator before he began experimenting with magnetic pick-ups, taking a single coil of wire and wrapping it around two large "horseshoe" magnets. Once tested, Beauchamp asked one of his colleagues at National to build him a maple body and neck: the instrument was quickly constructed and the electronics fitted. Beauchamp christened it the "Frying Pan."

At this time, there was a fashion in the United States for Hawaiian music—more so than for the guitar—and it made more sense to produce a Hawaiian lap steel. A small six-stringed instrument, the lap steel was played horizontally with pitch changes made by moving a small metal bar along the strings with one hand and picking with the other.

The earliest Frying Pans came in two models—the A-25 and shorter-scaled A-22—and were sold under the Rickenbacker brand with a small amplifier and speaker. Within two years, the principles were applied to the first Rickenbacker Electro Spanish guitars. **TB**

Alvino Rey was the first musician to popularize Rickenbacker's lap steel guitar. He was often billed as "Alvino Rey And His Singing Guitar." *Alvino Rey! His Greatest Hits* is a good starting point in exploring his guitar-playing talents.

Gibson
L-75 1932

Type Archtop acoustic guitar
Body & neck Mahogany back and sides, spruce top
Fingerboard Rosewood, pearl, celluloid

In 1932 Gibson added to its line of archtops two diminutive models: the f-hole-sporting L-75 and the round-sound-holed L-50. The L-75 model in particular went through no end of structural and cosmetic changes, and the model shown at right has a Dreadnought-esque body contour (see page 83) and an eye-catching fingerboard and headstock, fronted by celluloid with pearl diamond inlays mounted on rosewood. This "mother-of-toilet-seat" bling was inspired by an expo at the Chicago World's Fair, held in 1933 and 1934, for which Gibson (in nearby Kalamazoo, Michigan) created a new "Century of Progress" flat-top model with a similar neck, in order to capitalize on worldwide interest in the fair. Very few L-75s with this ornate styling were issued.

In its earliest incarnations, the L-75 was a very lightweight archtop, on account of its 14½-in. (36.8-cm) body. By 1935, its body had been lengthened, and widened to the 16-in. (40.5-cm) format shared by the L-5.

Perhaps one of Gibson's less-celebrated models, the L-75 was discontinued in 1939, and nowadays is considered a relatively rare bird by eagle-eyed collectors. As far as we can tell, the L-75 was not a particular favorite of any noted players, although Eric Clapton certainly had one in his extensive collection. He'd acquired his 1935 model in 1999 as a replacement for a charity-auctioned Gibson L-4 that he admitted he'd "found hard to part with." He sold it five years later at Christie's in New York, raising just under $10,000 for his Crossroads rehabilitation center in Antigua. **OB**

Julián Gomez Rámírez
Steel-string Guitar 1932

Type Steel-string acoustic
Body & neck Brazilian rosewood with softwood top, rosewood neck
Fingerboard Honduran mahogany

To enter into the brave new world of jazz, guitarists of the 1930s sought a revolutionary instrument that cut through the brash, loud voice of horn-led bands. Luthiers took a cue from the banjos used in some early Dixieland ensembles and added steel strings to guitars—often with catastrophic results, as the bodies were not always strong enough to handle the dramatically increased tension.

Spanish luthier Julián Gomez Rámírez found a solution. After an apprenticeship with José Ramírez I in Madrid, Rámírez set up shop in Paris in around 1914 at 38 rue Rodier in the Pigalle *quartier*. He was experienced in building steel-string mandolins and bandurrias, so adapted his interior bracing to craft a suitably strong jazz guitar. With two large sound holes, Rámírez's guitar projected its brash new voice loud and proud.

He made the body of Brazilian rosewood topped by a two-piece softwood soundboard, which created a warm sound. The guitar's neck joined the body at the twelfth fret, but the mahogany fretboard extended far into the body to a twenty-second fret, offering guitarists a wide palette of notes. The slotted headstock borrowed from classical guitar technology. The tailpiece and movable bridge followed mandolin practice, while the zero fret fine-tuned the intonation.

In Paris, Rámírez's guitars found fans with gypsy guitarists playing in orchestras, dance bands, and jazz bands. The guitar pictured here, serial number 695, was specially made for gypsy jazz maestro Pierre "Baro" Ferret, who often loaned it to his friend Django Reinhardt. Django used this guitar in his early days before adopting the Selmer Maccaferri jazz guitar. **MD**

Oscar Schmidt Co.
Stella 1932

Type Flat-top parlor guitar
Body & neck Solid birch top, back, and sides; poplar neck
Other features Ladder braced, floating bridge, black "satin" finish, decal ornamentation around and below sound hole

Looking like the kind of guitar a wandering Depression-era Mephistopheles might play to beguile his listeners into trading their souls for temporal gain, this instrument is part of a black range of guitars with decals, a feature the manufacturer called "decalomania." The pattern around the sound hole is identical to that on another model in the range with additional decals of playing cards known as "The Gambler," its appearance evoking an image of smoky Prohibition-era speakeasies and gambling dens. Stella was the brand name for these inexpensive, mass-produced instruments. But they had good tone and volume and were an attractive choice for poorer Americans and for blues musicians of the time, such as Charlie Patton, Leadbelly, and Blind Willie McTell, all of whom played Stellas.

Apart from Stella guitars, the Oscar Schmidt Company's other guitar brands included Sovereign and La Scala. Schmidt at its peak had three factories in the United States and four in Germany, making it one of the biggest manufacturers at that time. Oscar Schmidt died in 1929 and most of the company didn't survive the 1930s Depression. In 1939, the Stella, Sovereign, and La Scala brands were sold to the Harmony Company. The Oscar Schmidt name has been revived in recent decades by U.S. Music Corp. for a range of instruments marketed alongside its Washburn brand. **GD**

King Of The Georgia Blues (2007) is a six-CD collection of the work of American blues musician Blind Willie McTell. He can be seen playing a Stella guitar on the sleeve of this fine boxed set.

Selmer "Maccaferri" Orchestra 1932

Type Steel-string acoustic guitar with single cutaway
Body & neck Indian rosewood back and sides, French spruce top, walnut neck
Fingerboard Ebony

With its unique shape and sound, the Selmer guitar—more widely known as the Selmer Maccaferri—is uniquely associated with one figure: the incomparable Belgian-born, Romany guitarist Django Reinhardt.

The guitar was first produced in 1932 by the French Selmer company. The body of the guitar was crafted specifically to accommodate an internal resonator by the Italian guitarist and luthier Mario Maccaferri. The body of the Selmer is visually distinctive for two reasons: the unusual perpendicular cutaway that allowed easier access to the upper frets and the Art Nouveau styling of the D-shaped sound hole—often called *le grand bouche* ("the big mouth"). It was also one of the first guitars to use a metal-reinforced neck—or truss rod—to cope with the stress of steel strings.

Following a business dispute in 1933 with owner Henri Selmer, Maccaferri, who had overseen the production of the guitars, withdrew to resume his concert career. This resulted in a number of design changes. Most notably, the resonator unit, which had been designed to project a greater acoustic volume and even out the tone, was dropped. In fact, this had not been a universally popular innovation, with many early customers complaining of rattling and asking for the unit's removal. In 1936, further design changes led to its evolution into the Selmer Modèle Jazz. **TB**

Django Reinhardt used the Selmer guitar throughout most of his career until his death in 1953. *Django Reinhardt On Vogue Complete Edition (1934–1951)*, released in 2012, is an outstanding summary of his work.

Slingerland May Bell Cathedranola 1932

Type Acoustic steel-string resonator guitar
Body & neck Mahogany, koa, or birch body; spruce top; mahogany neck
Fingerboard Rosewood or gold pearloid

Those who know Slingerland as a Gibson-owned drum maker may be surprised to know that the original company made stringed instruments between the World Wars. Henry Slingerland was based in Chicago, selling ukelele lessons. With every twelve lessons, customers got a free uke, built by a German craftsman.

Demand grew until a factory was opened and the range extended to include banjos, mandolins, guitars, and eventually, drums. The guitar division created some pioneering early electric Spanish and laptop guitars before the Second World War, but these were never fully pursued.

One of their most sought-after guitars today is the striking Art Deco–styled Cathedranola acoustic. Guitar historians are unsure whether Slingerland built them in its own workshop or had them made by Regal or Harmony. The truth is probably that some were made at each location. This instrument was designed to compete with the popular Dobro and National resonators of the time, without infringing their patents.

Slingerland's resonator used a spruce disk under the metal cover that acted as a second sunken soundboard. Some experts refer to this as a "fake resonator," but although the Cathedranola wasn't as loud as its rivals, it was louder than a standard guitar and had a uniquely sweet tone.

The neck was rounded at the back, and there was also great variety between individual guitars—many different woods and decorations were used—although all have the two distinctive "cat's-eyes" sound holes. The guitars were sold in a chipboard case along with their standard guitar strap of the time—a length of rope. **SH**

Martin
D-45 1933

Type Dreadnought acoustic
Body & neck Rosewood back and sides, cedar neck
Fingerboard Ebony

At the elite end of the vintage guitar market exists a tiny, deep-pocketed group of cognoscenti, liable to view their objects of desire in the same light as a precious antique or work of art. In its original form, the prewar Martin D-45 exhibits what could be termed the guitar collector's "holy trinity": superlative quality as a musical instrument; looks of rare beauty; and, above all, immense rarity.

First introduced in the 1904 catalog, Style 45 was among the most elaborate designs created by C.F. Martin and Co., with its abalone pearl inlays that dazzle on practically every border of the body and the fabulously ornate fingerboard and headstock inlays.

Style 45 first appeared as a Dreadnought in 1933 when a custom one-off was built for Gene Autry—a hugely significant figure in the emergence of the guitar as a popular instrument in the United States. His priceless original is in Los Angeles' Autry National Center of the American West. Opulent both in looks and cost, the D-45 appeared in the catalog only between 1938 and 1942, by which time it found itself at odds with the austerity of the war years. Only ninety-one D-45s were built, and they are now among the most collectible "production" acoustic guitars, especially those with the snowflake fingerboard inlays built in 1938. C.F. Martin & Co. revived the D-45 in 1968. **TB**

Stephen Stills, who can be heard here on *Déja Vu* (1970), purportedly bought new D-45s in 1969 as a gift for the other members of Crosby, Stills, Nash, and Young. He famously owns an original 1939 model.

Rickenbacker
Electro Spanish 1933

Type Hollow body electric
Body & neck Mahogany body and neck
Fingerboard Hardwood
Pick-ups Horseshoe pick-up

Using the magnetic horseshoe pick-up developed by George Beauchamp, Adolph Rickenbacker's pioneering electric Ro-Pat-In Frying Pan model of 1931 appealed to Hawaiian-style players. Later that same year, they launched the Electro Spanish model, an acoustic guitar body fitted with the same pick-up. As the 1933 catalog pronounced, "Brother musician listen to a miracle!"

The debut version was offered from 1932–1935, featuring a body bought in from Harmony of Chicago. This was the same body used in National's Trojan resonator guitar, and featured f-holes in the upper body

> *"On the earliest Spanish models, they simply silk-screened the Electro name in gold onto the headstock."*
>
> RICHARD R. SMITH, *THE HISTORY OF RICKENBACKER GUITARS*

bouts and a nineteen-fret neck joined to body at the fourteenth fret. The horseshoe magnets were mounted at the bridge, and the strings ran through their center. The price, "complete with speaker," was $175. The "speaker" was a tiny amplifier, which was essential to the Electro Spanish not only for its amplification but also to control the volume. This issue was remedied in 1934 with the addition of a single volume control.

The Electro Spanish was offered with Rickenbacker's special vibrato tailpiece, and the Electro Mandolin and Electro Tenor were also produced. The Ken Roberts model was offered from 1935–1940, which boasted f-holes in the lower bouts and a twenty-two-fret neck. The Electro Spanish continued into the 1940s with the horseshoe pick-up mounted in an archtop body. **MD**

Domingo Esteso
Flamenco Guitar 1934

Type Classical guitar
Body & neck Indian rosewood back and sides, German spruce top
Fingerboard Rosewood

Domingo Esteso holds a unique position in the development and evolution of the flamenco guitar. Born in 1882, Esteso learned his trade in the Madrid workshop of the great Manuel Ramírez. Starting his apprenticeship in the late 1890s, Esteso worked for Ramírez until his mentor's death in 1916. In the Spanish tradition of the time, Esteso continued working for his widow, and for a short time afterward he and colleague Santos Hernández created instruments labeled *Viuda de Manuel Ramírez* ("Widow of Manuel Ramírez").

In 1917, Esteso opened his own shop in Madrid, where he concentrated largely on building flamenco guitars; his wife, Nicolasa Salamanca, was given the task of applying the finishing varnish. Many of Esteso's early guitars were exported to Argentina, and his connection to Ramírez enabled him to attract some important customers. Among them was Ramón Montoya, widely viewed as the father of modern flamenco, who prized the instrument's warm yet punchy percussive sound.

When Esteso died in 1937, his nephews Faustino, Mariano, and Julio continued building for his widow. Following her death in 1960, they renamed the workshop *Hermanos Conde, Sobrinos de Domingo Esteso* ("Conde Brothers, Nephews of Domingo Esteso") where they produced some of the finest flamenco guitars of their time. **TB**

Ramón Montoya was the first virtuoso flamenco guitarist, his work during the 1930s all but defining the genre. His immaculate technique can be heard on the album *El Genio De La Guitarra Flamenca* (2003).

Ramón Montoya: the father of modern flamenco. ➔

Gibson
Martelle Deluxe 1934

Type Flat-top acoustic
Body & neck Mahogany back, sides, and neck;
spruce top
Fingerboard Rosewood

Gibson adapted to the Great Depression by creating budget-brand versions of its high-quality instrument lines, keeping the production lines moving and supplying demand at lower price points. The company also sold bodies to companies such as National, and struck up distribution deals by supplying instruments to mail-order companies such as Montgomery Ward, who would promptly rebrand them or sell them to specialist music stores.

This scenario continued into the 1960s, and in the present the result is a range of tantalizingly familiar guitars appearing on auction sites for clued-up collectors to bid frantically upon and to debate on forums endlessly thereafter. This 1934 Gibson Martelle Deluxe is an example of one such brand, thought to have been created for Kalamazoo Musical Instrument Company co-owner Charles Martelle. The guitar is a version of the Roy Smeck Stage Deluxe, a Hawaiian flat-top model which, unusually for a prewar Gibson, was a tie-in with a star of the day, in this case, Roy Smeck, the multi-instrumental vaudeville performer "The Wizard of the Strings." The Martelle Deluxe was identical to its Gibson-branded counterpart with one critical exception: there was no adjustable truss rod.

House-brand Gibsons like the Roy Smeck were made available to instrument distributors from the early 1930s and played a key role in keeping Gibson in business until the end of the Second World War. Other examples were the Kel Kroyden brand, which sold Kalamazoo-produced flat-top guitars, banjos, and A-style mandolins, and Recording King, which sold its Ray Whitley models at less than half the price of a similar Gibson J-55. **OB**

Gibson
Super 400 1934

Type Archtop acoustic
Body & neck Maple back and sides, spruce top, set maple neck
Fingerboard Ebony

When archtops ruled the world back in the 1920s and 1930s, Gibson's phenomenally successful L-5 became the workhorse that had made its way onto practically every bandstand. However, in 1931, when the company's main rival Epiphone threw down the gauntlet with the nine-model Masterbilt range, Gibson had to react.

What it came up with, against the backdrop of a U.S. economy recovering from the Great Depression, was its most sumptuous, regal, and expensive model yet—the Super 400. It was the largest guitar Gibson had produced, with a body width of 18 in. (45.75 cm)

> *"The appearance of … the Super 400 had a symbolic quality … Because its mere invention argued for the importance of the guitar in jazz."*
> BRUCE NIXON

where most archtops, including the L-5 and the wider new Epiphones, measured around 16 in. (40.5 cm). The Super 400's non-cutaway chassis enabled projection, and it had a more rounded, sweet, and textured tone.

The Super 400 of 1934 was ostentatious but still retained its dignity; its tonewoods were premium, its inlays eye-catching yet elegant, and its tailpiece was engraved by hand. By 1939, it had gained a larger upper bout, different internal bracing, larger f-holes, a better tailpiece, and a cutaway version.

The original brochure for the Super 400 claimed it an "extraordinary guitar in every way—its price is a criterion of its quality." Present-day collectors agree: "Intro-model" and early Super 400s are rare and command a high price in the vintage guitar market. **OB**

Dobro
Model 16 1935

Type Acoustic resonator
Body & neck Nickel-plated "German Silver" body, mahogany neck
Fingerboard Bound ebony

From the late 1920s, the National and Dobro companies were engaged in a curious rivalry largely defined by personal animosities between owners George Beauchamp and John Dopyera. Both companies produced rival instruments of a similar quality, often using parts from the same source and—perhaps strangest of all—throughout this time the Dopyera brothers remained major shareholders in the National String Instrument Corporation. However, the period in which both companies were conceived was when the United States had the most perilous economy, and by

> *"Dobro amplifying guitars are … distinctive in design and appearance. Violin Edge construction eliminates all soldered joints."*
> **DOBRO ADVERTISING, 1935**

1932, in the depths of the Great Depression, both companies were struggling to survive. Following lengthy legal action, the Dopyera brothers gained control of both companies, and in 1934 they were merged into the National Dobro Corporation.

The Dobro brand would continue to produce predominantly wooden-bodied resonator guitars, although a small range of metal-bodied instruments would appear from 1934, such as the M-16. Metal-bodied Dobros from this period are visually distinctive because of the "fiddle-edge" construction, which eliminated the need for soldered joints between the top, back, and sides. The M-16 was known as the "Artist's Model" and featured a heavily engraved Dobro crest on the back of the body. **TB**

Martin
D-18 1935

Type Acoustic guitar
Body & neck Solid spruce top and mahogany neck
Fingerboard Rosewood

Prior to Elvis Presley's appearance in October 1954 on the *Louisiana Hayride* and the *Grand Ole Opry* shows in Shreveport, Louisiana, on which Hank Williams was discovered in 1948, the man who would be "The King" purchased an old Martin 000-18 from Sid Lapworth, an instrument manager at the O.K. Houck Piano Company in Memphis, Tennessee. Sid later recalled Elvis paid a $5 deposit, and paid the balance of the $79.50 purchase price over a number of installments.

Elvis' Martin 000-18 had a solid mahogany neck and a solid spruce top with a twenty-fret rosewood

> *"He'd break strings all the time. In the early days he'd just keep beatin' on it until we got through the set."*
>
> SCOTTY MOORE, ELVIS' GUITARIST

fingerboard. The guitar wasn't the fanciest of Martins, but it had a fabulous sound. The "0" prefix referred to the guitar's size, with "0" the smallest, up to the larger "000" and beyond to the largest: the D-18. The styling of Elvis' 000-18 Martin was typical of the majority of Martins since the 1880s.

As he did for all purchasers, Sid gave the young musician a choice of an extra set of strings, some picks, or some special stick-on letters made by the Chicago firm of David Wexler. Elvis chose the letters, and unlike most people, who tended to place them on the outside of their guitar cases, he chose to stick them horizontally across the guitar's face. When he was done, the letters spelled out unambiguously who the guitar now belonged to: "E-L-V-I-S." **BS**

Vivitone
AS9 1935

Type Electric archtop
Body & neck Spruce body, mahogany and rosewood neck
Fingerboard Ebony
Pick-ups Loar-patented Acousti-Lectric

Celebrated luthier Lloyd Loar, who had designed the all-conquering L-5 guitar, left Gibson to form his own company in 1934. Loar was a gifted musician and engineer with many ideas ahead of his time. As soon as he left Gibson, Loar patented an electric coil pick-up and set up Vivitone in Kalamazoo with former Gibson executive Lewis Williams. They began producing a range of stringed instruments using this pick-up.

This pioneering guitar was one of the first to use electronics. It gave players the option of engaging a pick-up mounted inside the body by lowering metal

> *"Knowing as I do Loar's innovations and how they have impacted my work … I hold this man's work in the highest regard."*

TERRY MCINTURFF, GUITAR MAKER

bars running through the bridge. These transferred vibrations downward. The bars could be adjusted to produce pure acoustic sound, pure electric sound, or a mix of both. Today the pick-up sounds more like an amplified resonator guitar.

This meticulously designed guitar had f-holes in the back and a small sound hole under the bridge on the top. Inside was a bracing system that transferred pressure from the top to the back, creating a second soundboard. The guitar also featured Grover machine heads, a mahogany bridge capped with ebony, and a Bakelite endpin. A wooden panel on the side of the guitar slid out like a drawer to allow access to the pick-up.

One of these groundbreaking guitars is kept at the U.S. National Music Museum in South Dakota. **SH**

D'Angelico
Excel 1936

Type Hollow body archtop with single Venetian cutaway
Body & neck European maple back and sides, book-matched spruce top, solid flame maple neck
Fingerboard Ebony

Arguably the greatest ever luthier of the United States, John D'Angelico perfected the archtop acoustic guitar style. Indeed, many experts would claim that the quality of his craftsmanship has only truly been rivaled by his apprentice, Jimmy D'Aquisto, who only began producing his own highly acclaimed guitars following the death of his mentor in 1964.

D'Angelico set up his guitar workshop in 1932 at 40 Kenmare Street in New York City. All D'Angelico instruments were strictly handmade in limited quantities: Even at their peak in the late 1930s, he and his tiny workforce were only able to produce thirty instruments per year. Yet D'Angelico guitars were no more costly than similar mass-produced Gibson and Epiphone models.

D'Angelico initially produced two guitars modeled on the revolutionary Gibson L-5 archtop, the 17-in. (43-cm) budget Style A and the more ornate Style B. In 1936, these designs were superseded by the Excel and New Yorker models, featuring such characteristic flourishes as the Art Deco "stair-step" tailpiece and matching raised pickguard, and pegheads inspired by the contours of New York's recently erected Empire State Building.

The Excel was particularly popular among jazz musicians, and was also used by no less a master player than Chet Atkins, prior to his sponsorship deal with Gretsch in 1954. **TB**

American swing jazz guitarist Oscar Moore played a D'Angelico Excel on many recordings during the 1940s. He can be heard on the album *The Complete Capitol Recordings Of The Nat King Cole Trio* (1991).

D'Angelico
New Yorker 1936

Type Archtop guitar
Body & neck European maple back and sides, spruce top
Fingerboard Ebony

John D'Angelico's New Yorker model was first produced in 1936. Like the noted Excel, it became extremely popular among jazz musicians of the period.

Unusually, perhaps, even though by the late 1940s D'Angelico's work was widely admired, his hand-built guitars were priced much the same as a high-end factory-built Gibson. By the time of his death in 1964, his workshop records show that 1,164 D'Angelico guitars had been built, his assistant Jimmy D'Aquisto completing the ten in progress at that time. He would eventually buy the workshop from D'Angelico's family and build his own equally revered archtops. The esteem in which he held his mentor was clear from the influence of D'Angelico's designs on his own work. Both luthiers were featured prominently in 2011's Guitar Heroes exhibition at New York's Museum of Modern Art.

The mixture of craftsmanship, design, and scarcity have made D'Angelicos highly desirable both to modern collectors and museum curators of Art Deco exhibitions. Recent auctions have seen D'Angelicos produced in the 1960s selling in excess of $50,000. The mystique surrounding these guitars is compounded by their individuality—since they tended to be custom built for specific clients there is a wide variation in specification.

The D'Angelico brand was revived in the twenty-first century by New-Jersey-based D'Angelico Guitars of America. Trading under the banner "A Legend Reborn," it has produced a number of high-quality U.S.-built reproductions as well as cheaper models from other parts of the world. Although these are decent enough instruments, they clearly would not be expected to bear any real comparison to the originals. **TB**

← Rhythm and blues player Steve Gibson with a D'Angelico New Yorker, c. 1955.

Epiphone
Emperor 1936

Type Acoustic archtop
Body & neck Maple back and sides, spruce top, maple and walnut neck
Fingerboard Ebony

Making its debut in 1936, the Emperor was the flagship model of the Stathopoulo-era Epiphone brand. With its 18½-in. (47-cm) beast of a body, it was the company's retort to Gibson's own 18-incher, the Super 400.

In production until 1954, the Emperor was a luxury instrument featuring a carved solid spruce top and back and sides cut from curly maple. The edges of the body were bound with seven-ply celluloid Pyralin. It had a 25½-in. (64.75 cm) scale length and a seven-piece maple and walnut neck. As might be expected of an instrument of this quality, the fingerboard was ebony with pearl V-block inlays. The hardware was gold-plated, and the raised, bound pickguard was tortoiseshell.

Responding to the demands of jazz musicians whose evolving single-note playing required greater access to the upper registers, in 1941 the Soloist Emperor made a very brief appearance, its single cutaway making it easy for the guitarist to play up to the twenty-second fret.

Many Emperors from this time were doctored with the addition of a pick-up. Epiphone responded in 1951 with the three-pick-up Zephyr Emperor Varitone, the mighty Zephyr Emperor Regent (1952–1953), and finally the Emperor Electric (1954–1957).

The most expensive archtop models the company made at the time, prewar Emperors are among the most collectible of all Epiphones. **TB**

Freddie Green is widely rated as one of the finest of all jazz rhythm guitarists. He used an Epiphone Emperor on most of his recordings in the late-1930s with Count Basie, which can be heard on *Verve's Choice: The Best Of Count Basie* (1964).

Gibson
Doubleneck L-10 1936

Type Archtop acoustic
Body & neck Maple back and sides, spruce top, maple
and mahogany neck
Fingerboard Rosewood

Thought to be the only archtop double-neck guitar
Gibson ever produced, this beguiling example was
commissioned by guitar player Art Pruneau (that's his
name on the headstock; it also appears on the truss-
rod cover). It's also likely the company's first f-hole
guitar with a natural finish. Four years earlier, Gibson
had built a one-off flat-top double-neck for celebrated
vaudeville guitarist Jack Penewell. His design had
been a "Twin-six" with different tunings adopted for
each neck. Since Penewell was well known, it's likely
that this was a direct influence on Pruneau's instrument.

> *"[I wanted] to get a wider range of harmony
> and chords, as you were very limited on only
> six strings no matter how you tuned it."*
> **JACK PENEWELL, ON INVENTING THE DOUBLE-NECK GUITAR**

The six-course guitar and four-course tenor necks
join to a 17 in. (43 cm)-wide, 3½ in. (9 cm)-deep body,
but the guitar still retains an elegant line, a tribute to
Gibson's skilled craftsmanship (the L-10 was originally
a 16-in. [40.5-cm] body, but was upsized in 1934).
Originally intended as a cheaper alternative to the
by-then ubiquitous L-5, it was more-or-less structurally
identical to that model, except for its black finish. After a
number of cosmetic changes involving the fingerboard
decoration and the introduction of a fancy headstock
design, it was eventually discontinued in 1939.

That relatively short production run ensures that
the guitar is one of the rarest of the prewar Gibson
archtops for collectors, making this particular double-
neck one of the most prized of them all. **OB**

Gibson
ES-150 1936

Type Hollow body electric
Body & neck Maple back/sides, spruce top, mahogany neck
Fingerboard Rosewood
Pick-ups One blade pick-up (replaced by P-90 in 1940)

Launched in 1936, the Gibson ES-150 was the first successful "Electric Spanish" guitar—the instrument that convinced many players that the electric guitar was, in fact, a serious proposition. Like many Gibson models of the time, the model's designation indicated its price—$150. For what was then a princely sum, you got a guitar, an EH-150 amplifier, and a guitar cable—everything you needed to get up and running.

Jazz guitarist Eddie Durham is widely thought to have performed the first recorded electric jazz solo—he used an ES-150 with the Kansas City Six in 1938. However it was one of Durham's converts, a young player named Charlie Christian, who popularized the instrument and the very idea of the virtuoso electric guitarist. The hexagonal blade pick-up used on the ES-150 even became known as the "Charlie Christian." In a brief career, his fluid solos and warm tone all but created the jazz guitar sound that we know today, and influenced every player of note who followed.

The ES-150 was a hugely significant instrument. Acoustic players simply were not loud enough to compete with horn sections in the popular jazz orchestras of the day—and amplifying an acoustic guitar with a microphone all to often ended in howling feedback. For the first time, the guitarist could step out and take that solo. **TB**

The brief career of Charlie Christian—he died of tuberculosis at twenty-five—was, thankfully, captured in recordings with Benny Goodman's ensembles. His finest work is captured on the compilation *Charlie Christian: The Genius Of The Electric Guitar* (1987).

Charlie Christian redefined the role of the guitarist in jazz with his ES-150. ➡

Oahu
Deluxe Jumbo 1936

Selmer
"Maccaferri" Jazz 1936

Type Flat top, steel-string acoustic guitar
Body & neck Body of various solid woods, mahogany neck
Fingerboard Ebony

Type Steel-string acoustic guitar
Body & neck Laminated rosewood back and sides, spruce top, walnut neck
Fingerboard Ebony

The Oahu Publishing Company from Cleveland in the Midwest was set up during a craze for Hawaiian guitar playing. They sold sheet music, gave lessons, and sold guitars.

Many were cheap and forgettable lap steel guitars . . . but the Deluxe Jumbo was a gem. "The Oahu Deluxe Jumbo is GUARANTEED to be the finest and best guitar ever manufactured by anyone," the company announced.

For once, the marketing spiel wasn't far off the mark. The Deluxe Jumbo was made by a team of highly skilled European immigrant luthiers at the Kay Custom Shop in Chicago. It was a superb music machine with a strikingly sweet and powerful sound and exquisitely finished looks.

The body was all solid wood—either maple or rosewood and spruce—with pearl binding. There was a beautifully bound headstock too, and an ebony fingerboard inlaid with a twisting mother-of-pearl vine. **SH**

The original Selmer Maccaferri (see page 87) was built with a wooden resonating chamber suspended within the lower bout. Not everyone liked the sound it made or the buzzing problems it caused, so many owners removed the resonator through the big D-shaped sound hole and used the guitar normally.

Maccaferri left Selmer after just eighteen months and the guitar was updated in 1936 without his input. This was called the Modèle Jazz in French—the Jazz Model in English. The sound hole was changed to a small oval, and there was revised ladder bracing and a longer neck. The resonator was ditched for good. But some of Maccaferri's most important innovations were retained, including the pioneering cutaway design, the sealed oil-bath machine heads, the slightly arched top, and the steel-reinforced neck.

The Selmer had the same appeal in Europe as the archtops did in the United States—its volume enabled acoustic guitarists to be heard over the sound of a contemporary dance band. **SH**

Telesforo Julve
Classical Guitar 1936

Busato
Modele Jazz 1937

Type Nylon-string acoustic guitar
Body & neck Spruce top, cypress back
and sides
Fingerboard Ebony

Type Steel-string acoustic guitar
Body & neck Rosewood with spruce top,
rosewood neck
Fingerboard Mahogany

Spanish guitar maker Telesforo Julve had a great reputation in his hometown of Valencia. He built classical and flamenco guitars in the traditional style or with a "tornavoz"—a wooden cylinder that fitted inside the sound hole that linked the front and back of the guitar and was thought to improve the tone. He also built exotic lyres and innovative cutaway Spanish guitars. Yet Julve had little international reputation when he died in 1949. His name might have been forgotten but for an unlikely connection with British guitar hero Bert Weedon.

The early exponent of electric guitar in the UK was also famous for writing a series of influential plectrum guitar tutor books. Weedon was also the first guitarist to have a British hit single with "Guitar Boogie Shuffle" —and behind his electric expertise was a solid musical training.

Bert was in fact an accomplished classical guitarist and away from the limelight he owned and played the 1936 Telesforo Julve pictured above. **SH**

The history of Busato is shrouded in mystery. Following the jazz guitars developed by Mario Maccaferri for the French Selmer company, Busato's instruments were beautifully crafted, light in weight, cutting-edge in design, and sometimes even better-sounding. These facts were not lost on Selmer's renowned endorser, Django Reinhardt, who also played a Busato.

Like Maccaferri, Bernabe Busato came from Italy to Paris, likely in the 1920s. His nickname, "Pablo," hints at time spent in Spain, where he may have studied with one of the masters.

Busato's guitars were copies of Selmers, but with unique features and innovations. Busato may have led the way with the small oval sound hole giving a more directed sound, and the neck joining the body at the fourteenth fret. It's possible that Busato inspired Selmer to update its own guitars with these features.

Busato built guitars until his death in the early 1950s, after which his rare instruments—such as this late-1940s model—have become legendary. **MD**

Hermann Hauser
Segovia's Guitar 1937

Type Classical guitar
Body & neck Spruce top, Brazilian rosewood back and sides, mahogany neck, ebony fingerboard
Other features Landstorfer tuning machines

Every so often, the trajectories of history and individuals converge and extraordinary things happen—things like this 1937 guitar. In 1924, Andrés Segovia had recognized Hermann Hauser (1882–1952) as a maker of note upon hearing his guitars in an ensemble concert in Munich. At the time Hauser was making guitars in the Germanic tradition with designs and construction principles that harked back to the Viennese Stauffer guitars made a hundred years earlier. Encouraged by Segovia, Hauser set about studying his 1912 Ramírez guitar, as well as guitarist Miguel Llobet's 1859 Torres, and embarked on a long journey of discovery, with Segovia a most demanding client.

For over ten years, guitars were evaluated and rejected by Segovia until in 1937 he was presented with this same guitar, which now sits in the Metropolitan Museum of Art in New York. The guitar consolidates features of Ramírez and Torres designs, both internally (notably the Torres-like bracing system) and externally (the head and rosette design), and introduces the fruits of Hauser's own research, like a soundboard that is domed and significantly thicker than normal. The sound properties of this guitar are legendary: it is strong, clear, rich, rounded, finely balanced, and ineffably beautiful. Segovia, then nearing the heights of his fame, said it was "the greatest guitar of our epoch." **GD**

Andrés Segovia, the most influential, and arguably the greatest, classical guitarist of the twentieth century, plays his 1937 Hauser on this set of recordings, most of them from the 1950s. Segovia was then at the height of his powers and a colossus on the world stage.

← Andrés Segovia playing his Hauser guitar.

Levin Orkestergitarr De Luxe 1937

Type Steel-string archtop acoustic
Body & neck Maple and spruce top, maple neck
Fingerboard Mahogany
Pick-ups Two PAF humbucking pick-ups

Levin of Sweden was one of the oldest, most revered guitar makers in the world, with a continuous history dating back to 1900. This Orkestergitarr De Luxe is not only the company's top-of-the-line model, but probably the most famous Levin of all time.

The company's founder began as a furniture maker. Herman Carlson Levin immigrated from Sweden to the United States in 1887, working as a carpenter before getting a job with an instrument maker. By 1890, he and two pals had an instrument repair and building shop in New York. He chose to immigrate back to Sweden, erecting his Levin Instrumentfabrik in Gothenburg in 1900. Levin's factory built everything from mandolins to lutes, harp guitars, and American-style archtops.

In 1937, Levin announced the Orkestergitarr De Luxe as its flagship model. It featured a hand-carved top and back, as on the finest D'Angelico of the day. The neck was bolstered by a non-adjustable T-shaped Duraluminum truss rod. Multiple bindings and mother-of-pearl inlays abounded and all hardware was gold-plated. During a 1939 tour of Scandinavia, Duke Ellington's guitarman, Fred Guy, fell in love with this De Luxe, which he played for much of his career. When Django Reinhardt toured the United States with Ellington's band, he borrowed this Levin for a photograph that appeared on the cover of *DownBeat* magazine and numerous LPs. **MD**

Fred Guy's playing on the Levin can be heard on the 1949 Norman Granz-released album, *The Jazz Scene* (repackaged and re-released in 1994). The album features tracks by jazz greats such as Duke Ellington, Coleman Hawkins, Lester Young, and Billy Strayhorn.

Django Reinhardt posing with the Levin pictured at left in 1946. →

Stromberg
G-1 1937

Type Archtop acoustic
Body & neck Pressed laminated hardwood back, spruce top, maple neck
Fingerboard Ebony

In the 1930s, guitar makers fought to build ever-louder guitars that could be heard over the sound of ever-grander bands and orchestras. Before electrical amplification, for acoustic guitars this meant three things: bodies that were large, larger, and even larger.

Charles Stromberg and his son Elmer of Boston initially offered their archtop G-1 in 1937 with a body that was a solid 16 in. (40.5 cm) wide. This was the company's least-expensive model, featuring a pressed laminated hardwood back and formed top. The interior included two parallel braces bolstered by three lateral

> *"If D'Angelico guitars are the Stradivarius of the guitar world, Stromberg is the Guarneri."*
>
> THE UNIQUE GUITAR BLOG

braces. The result was a fine, if basic, guitar. But the bar was soon raised. Gibson's flagship L-5 model went to 17 in. (43 cm) wide, and Stromberg was forced to follow suit. Then, Gibson increased its top-of-the-line body by a full inch, and the G-1 too was recast with an 18-in. (45.75-cm) body.

While National and Dobro offered resonator guitars and Rickenbacker tinkered with electro-magnetic pick-ups, Gibson, Epiphone, and D'Angelico battled for acoustic archtop volume. But in the end, Stromberg was the winner. The body of its monstrous Master 400 was 19 in. (48.25 cm) wide, large enough to be heard without amplification in a big-band setting. It was also so immense many players couldn't reach their arms comfortably around its gigantic body. **MD**

Tutmarc
Audiovox 736 1937

Type Solidbody fretted bass guitar
Body & neck Black walnut
Fingerboard Purpleheart
Pick-ups One single-coil pick-up

Leo Fender was a great innovator, worthy of his reputation as the most important figure in the evolution of the electric guitar. But he was rarely an originator. The mass production of the Fender Precision electric bass from 1951 would undoubtedly revolutionize the way music was performed, but he was by no means the inventor of the bass guitar. That accolade must go to Seattle-based musician and inventor Paul Tutmarc.

Experimenting with a reduction in size of the double bass, in 1935 he built an electric upright bass. But 1937 was Year Zero for the bass guitar, when he

"I personally played the electric bass in John Marshall Junior High School, here in Seattle, in 1937 and 1938."

PAUL H. "BUD" TUTMARC, JR.

developed the Audiovox Model 736 "Electronic Bass Fiddle." It was designed to be played in the horizontal position, and is therefore the first true electric bass guitar.

So why have Paul Tutmarc's achievements not been more widely appreciated? More than likely the age-old lament of the failed inventor: bad luck; bad timing. The Model 736 was not a commercial success. It cost a pretty penny, too: $65 for the bass and a further $75 for the matching Model 936 amplifier. It was not that well suited to the prevailing musical styles of the period, and it emerged only four years before the Second World War—a period during which guitar manufacture went into a state of limbo.

Paul Tutmarc's invention was, it seems, just a little too far ahead of its time. **TB**

Gibson
EH-150 1938

Type Twin eight-string-neck lap steel guitar
Body & neck Maple top
Fingerboard Rosewood
Pick-ups Two "Charlie Christian" hexagonal pick-ups

Nowadays, this EH-150 twin-neck lap steel guitar may seem a curio from a bygone age, but it was introduced at a watershed moment in the development of the electric guitar. Gibson was the market leader when, in 1935, it debuted its first electric guitar—the cast-aluminum E-150, a Hawaiian-style lap steel guitar with a single pick-up. By 1936, the body had changed to maple and the name to EH-150—also the designation of Gibson's 40-watt amp of the time. Recognizing that lap steel players frequently used different tunings, in 1938 the somewhat unwieldy double-neck EH-150D appeared, some models combining seven- and eight-string necks. The EH-150D was not a huge commercial success and was discontinued in 1939; the EH-150 ceased in 1943.

Both the EH and ES models were sold together with amplifiers, and this put the electric guitar at the forefront of catalog-scrutinizing guitarists of the time. One such player who opted for the ES-150-and-suitcase-amp package was Charlie Christian, who could play a bit: so much so, in fact, the model was later renamed after him, as was its hexagonal pick-up.

Alas, the EH-150 may not have played such a prominent role in rock 'n' roll as its illustrious sibling, but luminaries such as Steve Howe and David Gilmour have been known to own one and, respectively, play one live and on record. **OB**

David Gilmour has been using lap steels for his slide guitar playing since 1970. He used Fender and Jedson models at the peak of his popularity with Pink Floyd. He used a Gibson EH-150 during sessions for his solo album *On An Island* (2005).

Gibson
SJ-100 1938

Type Flat-top acoustic guitar
Body & neck Mahogany back and sides, spruce top, maple neck
Fingerboard Ebony

SJ stood for "Super Jumbo" and this classic Gibson flat-top acoustic had the big sound to match its name.

It was an underrated instrument though, whose loftier SJ-200 sibling was billed as the flagship of the line—"The King of Flat-tops." The 100 and 200 names referred directly to their price tags in dollars. The SJ-200 had a deeper body and more pearl decoration, and became a favorite of postwar cowboy movie stars, while the SJ-100 remains fairly obscure.

The SJ-100 was introduced in 1939, a year after its precursor the J-100, with a large mahogany body (17 in.

> *"The SJ-100 is one of Gibson's more obscure models ... in performance it should be ranked among Gibson's most noteworthy models."*
>
> VINTAGE GUITAR MAGAZINE, 2012

[43 cm] across the lower bout). The scratchplate had scalloped curves and the mustache-style bridge had individual height adjustments. There was thick three-ply binding at about ¼ in. (6 mm). The ebony fingerboard had pearl dot markers and there were Kluson tuners.

Within two years, the SJ-100's 26-in. (66-cm) scale was reduced by ½ in. (1 cm), the mustache bridge reverted to a normal design, and the headstock fell into line with other Gibson models. The guitar was discontinued when the United States entered the Second World War and Gibson switched production to war-related materials.

In the 1970s and again in the 1980s Gibson tried reintroducing the Jumbo, again called the J-100. It even included rare versions based on the original 1939 design, the J-100 XTRA and SJ-100 Centennial. **SH**

Gibson
SJ-200 1938

Type Flat-top acoustic guitar
Body & neck Spruce top, rosewood back and sides
(maple back and sides after 1947), mahogany neck
Fingerboard Single-bound ebony

When it came to the production of high-quality archtop acoustic guitars, Gibson was pretty well unrivaled—indeed, through Orville Gibson's work at the end of the nineteenth century, the company had all but invented the genre. But as far as flat-top steel-string guitars were concerned, even though the first Gibsons had appeared in 1926, Martin was the first port of call for most players.

In 1938, Gibson launched the "Super Jumbo" range of models, the flagship of which was the J-200 (shown at left). Designed in collaboration with singing cowboy Ray Whitley, it was aimed squarely at the professional player. Its name was derived from the massive 16⅞-in. (41.5-cm) body—the largest Gibson had produced. The Super Jumbo's most visually distinctive feature was its "mustache" bridge carved from ebony. The guitar retailed for a whacking $200, and for an extra $50 it was possible to order it with your name inlaid in the fingerboard. A year after it was launched, it was rechristened the SJ-200 . . . and then in 1955 it reverted to its original designation.

Given the precarious state of the U.S. economy prior to its entry into the Second World War, there was not a market for luxury guitars like the Super Jumbos and production quantities were low. Consequently, models from this period are now among the most highly collectable of acoustic guitars. **TB**

Elvis may not have been the most accomplished of musicians, but—as his guitarist Scotty Moore acknowledged—his aggressive strumming was a crucial element of his early Sun-era sound. Elvis would play "200s" throughout his performing career.

Blues players like Reverend Gary Davis often favored the loud, large-bodied SJ-200. ➡

Epiphone
Zephyr 1939

Type Hollow body electric
Body & neck Maple body, mahogany neck
Fingerboard Rosewood
Pick-ups One Epiphone Master

The 1930s was undoubtedly Epiphone's golden decade. It was a period that first saw the emergence of the Masterbilt models—archtop instruments produced to the highest possible standard—used by some of the most significant players of the day, like Les Paul and George Van Eps, for whom in 1939 Epiphone would build a seven-string guitar with a low "A" string. That same year would see the introduction of Epiphone's first dedicated electric guitars.

The Zephyr name was, in fact, applied to an entire range of instruments and amplification, including not only the single-pick-up archtop electric shown here, but a banjo, mandolin, and electric lapsteel. As with many early electric guitars, since there was no amplifier "culture," the Zephyr was offered as a "starter pack" containing guitar, amp, and cable—everything the fledgling electric player needed to get up and running. The amplifiers were available as AC or AC–DC models, with the complete packages coming in at around $200.

The Zephyr guitar has a distinctive "bikini" headstock plate and unique "notched" mother-of-pearl block finger inlays. The hollow body was constructed from maple with a set mahogany neck and bound rosewood fingerboard. A single-coil Epiphone Master pick-up was fitted in the bridge position. The Zephyr was produced until 1959, and the pick-up was located in varying positions in different periods: from 1942–1949 it was shifted along to the center position; in 1950 it was moved to the neck position, thus producing the mellow sound we now associate with classic jazz guitar. From 1950–1953 an Epiphone New York was used, which was changed to a DeArmond from 1954–1959. **TB**

Gretsch 6040
Synchromatic 400 1939

Type Archtop acoustic
Body & neck Spruce top, maple sides, five-piece laminated maple neck
Fingerboard Ebony

The Gretsch Company was founded in Brooklyn, New York, in 1883 by twenty-seven-year-old German-born immigrant Friedrich Gretsch, who manufactured banjos, drums, and tambourines at his small instrument store until his death in 1895. His son Fred continued with the family business and moved into a new ten-story building in Brooklyn in 1916, but didn't turn his attention to guitars until the late 1930s when the company introduced its first-ever electric guitar—the Electromatic. When the era of the big band saw archtop guitars supplant the banjo as the most popular

> *"My fingers seem to travel twice as fast on my new Synchromatic. The most amazing combination of … tone and playing ease."*
> HARRY VOLPE

stringed instrument of the day, Gretsch added to this shift with a new series they called the Synchromatics. It wouldn't be long until the musical world at last began to hear what it would call "That Great Gretsch Sound."

The Synchromatic was Gretsch's response to the dominance of Gibson. Instantly recognizable with their harp-shaped tailpieces, asymmetrical necks, "cat's-eyes" sound holes, and a remarkable stepped bridge that mimicked the Art Deco influences of the era, they started at the base 100 model all the way up to the top-of-the-line 400, made to compete with Gibson's Super 400. The Synchromatics, however, failed to put a dent in Gibson's acoustic monopoly, although today they are every bit as collectible. **BS**

Prairie State
Larson Custom 1939

Recording King
Ray Whitley 1939

Type Archtop acoustic guitar
Body & neck Solid spruce top, maple back and sides, maple neck
Fingerboard Ebony

Type Flat-top acoustic guitar
Body & neck Spruce top, rosewood or mahogany back, maple neck
Fingerboard Rosewood

Arched using their signature arching technique, the 1939 Larson Custom was a typically gorgeous Larson Brothers' creation with a solid headstock with pearl and abalone inlays, engraved inlays on the fingerboard, and its very square, slightly asymmetric body shape.

As beautiful as it is on the outside with its triple-bound sound holes, body of fiddleback maple, and ¼-in. (6-mm) mother-of-pearl trim, it's what's inside a Larson Custom that is most impressive: a unique pattern of ladder and three-ply X-braces, with the top brace typically a spruce/mahogany/spruce combination for greater strength that produces a bluesy sound uncommon among prewar acoustics. Sound-hole reinforcement braces and tone bars are solid spruce while its neck is connected to the endblock using a banjo-style metal rod to ease neck tension through the body. It was the exceptional bracing that set Larson guitars apart from the rest, built to last following the uncompromising principles of what the company called its "built-under-tension" approach to design. **BS**

Ray Whitley was a well-known singing cowboy during the 1930s. Whitley had played a critical role in the development of the Gibson J-200 Super Jumbo, and in 1939 he endorsed another Gibson guitar, this time one built exclusively for sale in the Montgomery Ward mail-order catalog. It was given the brand name Recording King and featured Ray Whitley's signature on the headstock. These fine instruments were marketed only in 1939 and produced in a very limited run. Some sources have suggested that only 470 original Recording Kings were built—235 in mahogany and 235 in rosewood—although Gibson shipping ledgers suggest that the real number may be a good deal lower. And they were something of bargain, retailing from $19.95–$29.95—half the price of the similarly proportioned Gibson J-55.

Celebrated eccentric folk guitarist John Fahey picked up a Recording King in 1969 and used it exclusively on his recordings until 1978, when it was smashed during a domestic quarrel. (It was lovingly repaired a quarter of a century later, after Fahey's death in 2001.) **TB**

Wilkanowski
Airway W2 1939

Type Archtop acoustic guitar
Body & neck Spruce top, poplar back and sides, ebony neck
Fingerboard Rosewood

Stand-alone classics of the archtop guitar era, the Wilkanowski series of acoustics were the creation of William Wilkanowski, a Polish violin maker who had immigrated to the United States in the early years of the twentieth century. He worked for the Fred Gretsch Company in Brooklyn before manufacturing his own guitars over a prolific four-year period from 1937 to 1941.

Conforming to a generalized size and shape, some came with the name AIRWAY and a W or W2 on the headstock. There were no serial numbers and they evolved with some rapidity, not unusual with handmade instruments. Only thirty or so were ever produced, all of them among the finest examples of the guitar as art. With hand-carved rosewood bridges, f-holes eerily reminiscent of those one would find on a violin, and wooden bindings instead of the plastic still found on even the finest guitars of the era, no two Wilkanowskis were alike and only a few have survived to the present day. **SB**

Euphonon
Dreadnought 1940

Type Jumbo-sized, pinched-waist dreadnought acoustic
Body & neck Spruce top, Brazilian rosewood back and sides, ebony fingerboard
Other features Transparent and decorated pickguards

The Larson Brothers of Maurer & Co. of Chicago made this 1940 pinched-waist dreadnought guitar as part of their Euphonon and Prairie State brands of larger-bodied instruments ranging from 15 in. (38 cm) to 27 in. (68.5 cm) body width. As well as making instruments for these two brands and those of their Maurer label, they manufactured for large distributors like W.C. Stahl of Milwaukee, Wisconsin, and W.J. Dyer & Bro. of St. Paul, Minnesota, who applied their own brand names to them. As the Larsons hardly ever put the Maurer name to these instruments, it is sometimes an exercise in forensics to determine provenance. The top-of-the-line Euphonon instruments like this one were of very high quality, often with innovations like laminated necks and braces and finished with wonderful ornamentation. The general opinion among collectors is that the exceptional craftsmanship and distinctive sound quality with great sustain and tonal balance of the best larger-bodied Larson guitars puts them on equal footing with the best of Martin and Gibson instruments. **GD**

Gibson
ES-300 1940

Type Electric archtop
Body & neck Spruce top, maple back/sides, mahogany neck
Fingerboard Rosewood
Pick-ups 7-in. (18-cm) slanted pick-up

The Gibson Guitar Company first began collaborating with the great jazz guitarist Les Paul in the mid-1930s, and in March 1939 delivered to him a 1936 L-7 with an experimental ES-300 pick-up. Paul began using the L-7 in some of his soon-to-be legendary collaborations with Fred Waring and his orchestra, but the pick-up would go on to create some history of its own.

The ES-300, released to the public in mid-1940, was electronically unlike other prewar electrics, distinguished by its unusually long, slanted pick-up but otherwise exhibiting many of the features of its predecessor, the

"When I got my first guitar, my fingers wouldn't go to the sixth string so I took off the big E and played with just five strings. I was only 6 or 7."

LES PAUL

ES-250: a 17 in. (43 cm)-wide body, curly maple back, and an L-5-styled tailpiece. The ES-300 was Gibson's premier prewar electric guitar and was debuted, in a beautiful blond finish, at the Chicago Musical Instrument Trade Show in July 1940, and began to reflect the changing attitudes toward electric guitars from mere background instruments to single-note lead instruments.

The secret to the ES-300 was its remarkable new pick-up. Designed by Walter Fuller using a new alloy, Alnico, for its magnets, he spent months experimenting with various positions in order to achieve a sound as close to an acoustic guitar as an electric could get by placing the pick-up diagonally away from the bridge on the bass side for a deeper tone and closer to the bridge on the treble side for the highs. **BS**

Les Paul
Log 1941

Type Electric guitar with solid central body
Body & neck Pine body, maple wings, mahogany neck
Fingerboard Rosewood
Pick-ups Home-built pick-ups

There was a great deal more to Les Paul than merely having given his name to one of the most famous ranges of electric guitars in history. A highly skilled jazz/country picker in his own right, Lester William Polsfuss was also a trailblazing music technologist.

The first electric guitars that appeared early in the 1930s were little more than acoustic instruments with pick-ups fitted. A routine problem for many early takers was the howling feedback that could occur at high volumes. This was the sound from the amplifier's loudspeakers causing the instrument's sound chamber to resonate, which in turn made the strings vibrate. Paul, among others at this time, realized that a solution lay in building a guitar with a solid body that would not be so prone to this phenomenon. Given workshop space during downtime at the Epiphone factory, in 1941 Paul built an instrument by fixing a stock Gibson neck to a 4 x 4 piece of pine, to which he fitted two home-built pick-ups. To make it look more like a conventional instrument, he fitted two "wings" from an Epiphone acoustic guitar. He called it "The Log."

Paul tried to interest Gibson executives in the idea, but they were unconvinced . . . until in 1950 Leo Fender successfully launched his own range of solid electric guitars. Paul was hastily recalled by Gibson. And the rest, as they say, is history. **TB**

Les Paul used his Log on many of the hit singles he recorded with his wife, singer Mary Ford, many of which can be heard on *Les Paul: The Absolutely Essential 3CD Collection* (2010).The original Log now resides in Nashville's Country Music Hall Of Fame.

Old Kraftsman Crown 1941

Type Steel-string acoustic guitar
Body & neck Spruce top, curly maple back and sides
Fingerboard Rosewood

Old Kraftsman guitars were made by Kay of Chicago for sale in America's *Spiegel* mail-order catalog. Kay used different brand names for the guitars it made specifically for each of the major catalog and store chains. Many of the guitars were budget models, but occasionally Kay would show its prowess with a really good instrument such as this.

The "Frankie Masters" Crown guitar model was a signature instrument for a popular swing band leader of the time, who sang and played guitar and had a number one hit with a song called "Scatterbrain" in 1939.

Kay's tribute to Masters had a sound hole cut in the shape of a crown and an elaborate series of finely worked inlays in the fretboard. There were gold inlays in the headstock and gold-plated tuners and a trapeze tailpiece too. Some models had a dark sunburst, others a natural finish—whichever you find, note that today the Frankie Masters Crown guitar has become extremely rare and collectible. **SH**

Ignacio Fleta "Guitarra Jaz" 1944

Type Acoustic archtop jazz guitar
Body & neck Carved spruce top with f- holes, mahogany body, ebony fingerboard with inlays, wooden bridge
Other features Sycamore bindings, metal tailpiece

Among the greatest makers of classical guitars, Ignacio Fleta (1897–1977) of Barcelona made mostly cellos, violins, some guitars, a harp, and even a lute before applying himself to making only guitars from the mid-1950s. Following the precedent of his older brother Francisco Manuel (who made a similarly dark-toned jazz guitar in 1943 among his output of mostly bowed string instruments), Ignacio made this unique jazz guitar in 1944 and recorded it in his journal as: "Guitarra Jaz [sic] no. 8, modelo especial."

Making the archtop was no particular challenge for Fleta, having carved many a cello soundboard before this project. A very unusual design feature of this guitar is the presence of a small circular sound hole in addition to the usual f-holes. Fleta's sons, Gabriel and Francisco, took over the making of Fleta guitars after his death in 1977. Gabriel Fleta said of his father's Jazz Guitar: "It was quite emotional to remember this instrument, which strangely enough we followed as children with great interest and enthusiasm." **GD**

Gibson
ES-140 1945

Type Archtop semi-acoustic single cutaway guitar
Body & neck Mahogany neck/sides, maple back/top
Fingerboard Rosewood
Pick-ups One P-90 pick-up

Gibson's complicated range of postwar ES guitars included this unique smaller design. The ES-140 was a three-quarter version of the ES-175 with a short-scale neck. In 1956, it was replaced with the thin-line ES-140T.

Guitar manufacturers of this era were experimenting to see which body style proved most popular—the ES-140's neck was 2 in. (5 cm) shorter than that of the 175. The pick-up was a P-90 single-coil with "dog-ear" attachments in the neck position. There was a tortoiseshell-grain floating pickguard, trapeze tailpiece, and the guitar was available in a sunburst or natural finish. Features included a rosewood compensated bridge and amber bonnet knobs.

The smaller body was more like a contemporary solid electric guitar in width and lighter than previous archtops. The guitar was more comfortable to play and its shorter neck made fast runs easier.

Harvey "The Snake" Mandel, who played with Canned Heat, The Rolling Stones and John Mayall, used an ES-140, and it was in production until 1968. **SH**

Martin
D-28 1946

Type Steel-string acoustic
Body & neck Indian rosewood back and sides, sitka spruce top
Fingerboard Ebony

The year 1946 saw changes in materials used in Martin guitars. The most striking change was a new wood for the soundboard. Prior to 1946 Adirondack spruce was considered the finest tonewood for guitars, and had been used on Martins for the previous century. A mixture of urban development and over-harvesting during the war had depleted the stocks of Adirondack, and prices consequently rocketed. It was replaced by the more readily available sitka (Alaskan) spruce.

Another change in 1946 was purely cosmetic and had no impact on the sound. The intricate herringbone marquetry found on the binding of Style 28 guitars had to be abandoned as the original stock came from Germany and was then almost impossible to procure. Experiments with alternative bindings were unsuccessful and in the end plastic was used.

The pre-1947 models are more desirable; the "post-herringbone" D-28 shown here is perhaps worth half the value to a modern-day collector. In 1976, herringbone was reintroduced on the HD-28 models. **TB**

Bigsby
Merle Travis 1947

Type Single cutaway solidbody electric guitar
Body & neck Maple straight-through neck with maple wings
Fingerboard Rosewood
Pick-ups One single-coil pick-up

Who is the "father" of the solidbody electric guitar? Popular perception would cite Leo Fender, although his role was more in bringing the idea to the market. In the 1940s, Les Paul and Paul Tutmarc made solidbody electrics, but both looked unorthodox. Arguably, the man who first produced an instrument that closely resembled those we know today was motorcycle engineer Paul Bigsby, who built a groundbreaking guitar conceived by country picker Merle Travis.

At the Crocker Motorcycle Company in L.A., Bigsby met motorcycle-enthusiast Travis. Experiencing tuning problems with the vibrato on his Gibson L-10, Travis thought Bigsby might offer a solution. But instead of repairing what he saw as a poor design, Bigsby came up with a new mechanism: the famous vibrato system with which he remains associated.

During a later meeting, Travis showed Bigsby a sketch of an idea for a single-cutaway electric guitar; Bigsby responded that, as an engineer, "I can make anything." Les Paul's crude, hacked-together Log may have been built several years earlier (see page 123), but Bigsby's result was a purpose-built solidbody electric guitar. Based in California, and an acquaintance of Leo Fender, it seems likely that the Bigsby Merle Travis influenced the early Fender production-line instruments. **TB**

Merle Travis introduced the influential "Travis Picking" technique that alternated bass notes picked with the thumb. *Guitar Rags And A Too Fast Past* (1994) is a five-CD collection of Travis' early work, some of which features Paul Bigsby's guitar.

Gibson
ES-350 1948

Type Hollow body electric
Body & neck Maple top, maple/mahogany neck
Fingerboard Rosewood
Pick-ups Two P-90 pick-ups

Keith Richards loves his Gibson ES-350, and he's careful about where he uses it: "It's too good to take on stage; I mean, I'd be afraid of breaking it or something, you know, by making a silly move. And it's a big guitar. I love it for the studio ... it's got such a beautiful all-round sound."

Unveiled in 1947 and launched a year later, the ES-350 (initially designated ES-350P—that's "P" for "premier") was a rounded cutaway version of the ES-300. As Keith rightly says, with its 17-in. (43-cm) body, it is a large guitar by modern standards. Although a small number of single-pick-up models were built at

> *"The electric guitar is a weird instrument really ... the best ones were built when they were first invented ... the Gibsons and Fenders ..."*
>
> KEITH RICHARDS, THE ROLLING STONES

the beginning of the run, it was kitted out with a pair of P-90 single-coils, each with a dedicated volume control on the lower treble bout and a master tone on the cutaway bout. These models had laminated maple tops. In 1952 the guitar's spec altered significantly, when the tonally superior spruce was used on the soundboard; at the same the electrics were redesigned to align with Gibson's standard control configuration— two-volume, two-tone, three-way pick-up selector switch. These models are deemed greatly more desirable, both to collectors and vintage guitar players.

The year 1956 was the end of production; ES-350s produced at this time were built with Ted McCarty's new Tune-o-matic adjustable bridge system. That year it was replaced by the slimmer-bodied ES-350T. **TB**

Paramount
Archtop 1948

Type Acoustic electric archtop jazz guitar
Body & neck Spruce top, maple back and sides, maple neck
Fingerboard Rosewood

New York manufacturer William M. Lange established the Paramount brand for high-quality banjos in the 1920s, and by 1930 had diversified into guitars. Among the first guitars to be marketed by Lange with the Paramount brand were four- and six-string resonator guitars made by C.F. Martin & Co., with a unique design using the Style 2 top on a special body that had a rim toward the back with small round sound holes. During the 1930s, Paramount was also making swing-era acoustic archtop guitars, some big and loud enough to be played in a big-band setting, though in the

> *"Guitarists should be able to pick up the guitar and play music on it for an hour, without a rhythm section or anything."*
>
> JOE PASS

1940s these came increasingly with pick-up systems so the problem of being heard effectively disappeared. Paramount changed hands in the early 1940s, becoming one of the lesser-known of Harmony's brands. The big-band style was falling out of favor in the 1940s, but Paramount's archtop guitars still had a role to play in jazz and popular music and would see in the beginnings of rock 'n' roll.

This 1948 example was one of Paramount's top-of-the-line archtops at the time, with its tortoiseshell pickguard, mother-of-pearl inlays, and pick-up base plates. In general design, it is not unlike a Gibson, Epiphone, or Stromberg archtop jazz guitar of the period, and it's a fine guitar, though in terms of quality, prestige, and desirability, it is not in the same league. **GD**

Stromberg
Ultra Deluxe 1948

Type Acoustic archtop jazz guitar
Body & neck Spruce top with f-holes, maple back and sides, maple neck and head with celluloid veneer
Fingerboard Ebony

Elmer Stromberg, the son in Stromberg & Son of Boston, was a maker of elite jazz guitars from the big-band era of the 1930s and into the 1950s, his best instruments rivaling those of his contemporary, John D'Angelico. Stromberg's earliest archtops, with a modest 16 in. (40.5 cm) body, date from the late 1920s. Taking Gibson's lead, he progressively increased the size of his guitars as the big-band era came into its own and more powerful instruments were required. By 1937, Stromberg launched the Master 300 and 400. With body sizes of 19 in. (48.25 cm) and amazing projection,

"One night … there he [Freddie Green] was with his [Stromberg] guitar and everything … he's been right there ever since."

COUNT BASIE

they were the biggest-sounding guitars available, boosting the rhythmic core of the jazz orchestra and able to be heard alongside its loudest instruments. Freddie Green played a Stromberg while contributing to probably the best rhythm section of the time, that of the Count Basie Orchestra; and in the hands of Freddy Guy to that of Duke Ellington's.

The Ultra Deluxe was Elmer Stromberg at his peak. From 1940, Stromberg guitars were of exceptional quality, made with carved, instead of pressed, arched tops and unique design features like a single diagonal brace on the top. It is a superb rhythm guitar that will punch through any jazz band or orchestra. Elmer and his father Charles both died in 1955, curiously within a few months of each other. **GD**

Gibson
ES-175 1949

Type Single cutaway hollow body electric
Body & neck Maple back and sides, maple laminate top
Fingerboard Rosewood
Pick-ups One P-90, two P-90s (1953), two humbuckers (1957)

Gibson had intended to set the benchmark for electric jazz guitarists in 1949 with the launch of its flagship "electro-Spanish" ES-5. Although a magnificent luxury instrument, it also sported a price tag to match, and many jazzers of the period looked to cheaper alternatives by Gibson and Epiphone. A clear winner would soon emerge in the shape of the cheaper ES-175. An electric counterpart to the popular L-4 acoustic guitar, the ES-175 is arguably the most famous jazz guitar, and remains a popular choice, both under the original Gibson and budget Epiphone brands.

The instrument's most striking visual characteristic is the "Florentine" cutaway: this was the first Gibson electric sporting such a feature. This offered the soloist—remember, use of electric guitar in jazz was still relatively new—greater access to the upper register, making playing above the eighteenth fret more comfortable.

Kitted out initially with one single-coil P-90 pick-up close to the neck, in 1953 the ES-175 was given a second P-90, this time alongside the bridge. Four years later, another seemingly small yet significant change took place when the P-90s were replaced with humbuckers. When played from the neck pick-up with a touch of treble rolled off, it is this incarnation of the 175 that was able to create the archetypal warm, smooth sound we now associate with classic jazz guitar. **TB**

The ES-175 has excelled outside of the jazz world: Steve Howe of prog-rockers Yes is so closely associated with the instrument that Gibson honored him with a signature model. A good example of his work can be heard on the classic album *Close To The Edge* (1972).

← Joe Pass, an influential exponent of unaccompanied jazz guitar.

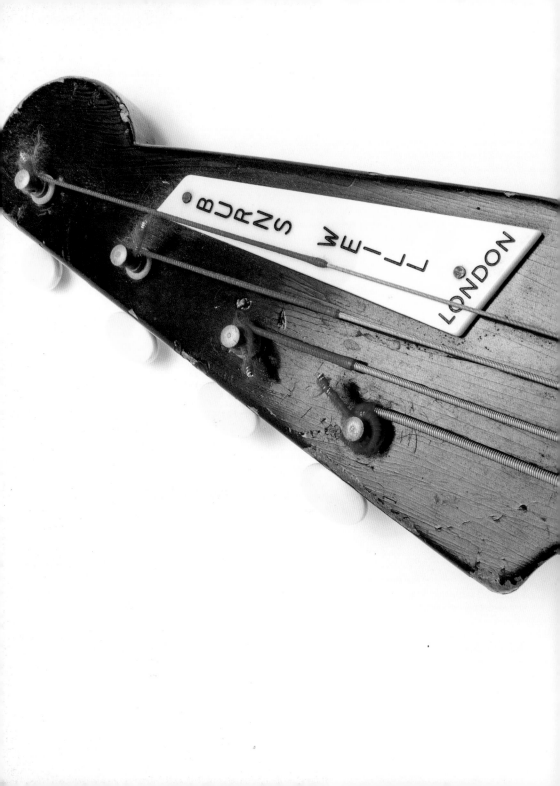

1950s

Fender
Broadcaster 1950

Type Solidbody electric
Body & neck Alder body, maple neck
Fingerboard Maple
Pick-ups Two single-coil (different windings and outputs)

It seems rather strange, given the influence he would have on the music produced during the second half of the twentieth century, that Clarence Leonidas (Leo) Fender had no musical grounding whatsoever. As a youngster his interests lay in electronics, and in his late 20s, with a loan of $600, Fender set up a radio repair shop in Fullerton, California. It was here that he first came face-to-face with musicians for whom he built amplifiers and P.A. systems, and became aware of the growing popularity of the amplified guitar.

Like Paul Bigsby and Les Paul before him, Fender and his colleagues sought the same solution to the inherent feedback problems of hollow body electric guitars, by creating an instrument from a denser material that would not resonate to the same degree. In 1948, Fender and one of his employees, George Fullerton, set about creating a production-line model. A year later, a small number of single-pick-up, single-cutaway designs, labeled "Esquire," were displayed at trade shows. After a year of solving basic design flaws—such as a lack of truss rod—and adding a second pick-up, the visually similar Fender Broadcaster came off the assembly line. A deliberately basic instrument, the Broadcaster was an affordable work-horse guitar aimed at the jobbing musician. And it was the first solidbody electric guitar to be mass-produced.

The Broadcaster turned out to have a very brief life: fearing an unintentional breach of copyright—the famous Fred Gretsch company was already marketing a range of "Broadkaster" drum kits—Fender chose to avoid a possible legal confrontation and so came up with a new name: the Telecaster. **TB**

A rare photograph of Jimmy Bryant playing one of the first Fender Broadcasters. ➡

Gibson
CF-100 1950

Type Electro-acoustic guitar
Body & neck Mahogany body and neck
Fingerboard Rosewood
Pick-ups One Gibson P-90 pick-up from 1951

The Gibson CF-100 first emerged in 1950 as a purely acoustic instrument—pick-ups and controls (and the "e" suffix) were added a year later.

This is a significant instrument, although surprisingly not that well known, as it was the first acoustic guitar to feature a built-in pick-up (a Gibson P-90) with adjustable pole pieces at the end of the fingerboard; this meant the sound hole had to be positioned farther back toward the bridge, and had volume and tone controls mounted onto the top of the body. Furthermore, a Florentine cutaway enabled the player full access to the upper frets. Prior to this, guitarists would have had to mount a floating pick-up in the sound hole of a regular acoustic guitar, which generally resulted in a poor amplified sound and—without the cutaway—limited playability.

The relatively small 14⅛ in. (37 cm) mahogany body had a depth of 4½ in. (12 cm) and a spruce top with scalloped X-bracing, which—in spite of its size—gave the guitar a loud and rich sound. The nineteen-fret bound fingerboard was cut from Brazilian rosewood and was one of the first Gibsons to feature the famed "Trapezoid" inlays found on Les Paul Standard guitars.

The guitar was discontinued in 1958 and is now deemed to be highly collectible. Gibson introduced a replacement, the J-160e, in 1954, but it failed to match the CF-100 for tone. Gibson reissued this fine instrument in 2010.

Bob Dylan played his CF-100, the guitar shown here, at a gig in New York City on October 15, 1990. Sadly, it now resides in a hamburger restaurant in Prague, complete with his set list taped to its side. **JB**

Sonora
Modèle Jazz 1950

Type Steel-string acoustic
Body & neck Laminated rosewood with spruce top, hardwood neck
Fingerboard Hardwood

New "brands" of guitars proliferated throughout France and Italy in the 1950s with lineages that were confused and mysterious—perhaps purposefully so. Legitimate dealers such as Paul Beuscher in Paris bought guitars from Bernabe Busato, Henri Miller, and others, relabeling them "Beuscher" guitars. Other makers produced copies of established classics, trading on their resemblance while skirting copyright laws and taxes. Some of these guitars were exquisite, bearing their original makers' construction qualities and tone. Others, much less so.

Sonora was one of these mystery brands. And one of the best, with a sound that makes these guitars sought after today. This Modèle Jazz is a typical example. Inside, the soundboard is supported by pointed bracework; the body has an arched "bombé" back and front; and the neck joins the body with a flat, rather than dovetailed, assembly—these were all standard features of the exceptional Busato guitars.

Sonora jazz guitars feature either a "grand bouche" sound hole as on this model, or a smaller, round hole. They originally bore "Sonora" decals on the headstock or upper body bout, but no label inside hinting at the workshop's location—ideal for confounding customs and tax agents. But as the decals tend to wear away over time, many of these mysterious Sonoras are today recognized only by their gorgeous tone. **MD**

Sonora guitars are beloved by many Gypsy jazzmen today, including Biréli Lagrène's rock-solid rhythm guitarist, Hono Winterstein, who can be heard on the album *Gipsy Project* (2001).

Fender
Precision 1951

Type Double cutaway solidbody electric bass
Body & neck Ash body, bolt-on maple neck
Fingerboard Maple (one piece, part of neck)
Pick-ups One single-coil pick-up

He may be widely viewed—rightly or wrongly—as the father of the solidbody electric guitar, but Leo Fender's place in music history doesn't end there. For more than half a century, the electric bass guitar has underpinned the sound in most genres of modern music. It is a role that, before the launch in 1951 of the Fender Precision bass guitar, was covered by the upright acoustic bass. Although by no means the first electric bass, the popularity and influence of the Precision brought an end to the long-standing problem of amplifying the bass in concert, and by fretting the fingerboard, it was possible to play bass parts with greater accuracy.

The original Precision was intended as a counterpart to the six-string Telecaster, and clearly shared a number of design features. The construction process was unashamedly simple—a slab of ash to which a neck was bolted—and the electrics were rudimentary, with the sound provided by a single-coil pick-up.

The Precision underwent a number of important revisions early in its life. In 1953, the body was given contoured edges, making it more comfortable to play, and in 1957 was dramatically restyled in line with Fender's successful "deluxe" guitar—the Stratocaster.

The Precision has never left the production line over the years, but has been offered in a variety of vintage reissued editions. **TB**

An early convert to the bass guitar, William "Monk" Montgomery was part of Lionel Hampton's ensemble. His Fender Precision, heard on the album *The Complete 1953 Paris Session* (1983), is one of the earliest notable uses of an electric bass guitar in jazz.

Bill Black, Elvis' bass player, was influential in the popularization of the electric bass. →

Fender
Telecaster 1951

Type Solidbody electric
Body & neck Alder body, maple neck
Fingerboard Maple
Pick-ups Two single-coil (different windings and outputs)

Fearing a copyright infringement of a range of Gretsch drum kits, Don Randall, who had handled Fender's early sales and distribution, was given the job of coming up with a new name for the Broadcaster guitar. He wanted something that reflected the technology of the new television era: thus it was rechristened the Telecaster. For the first half of 1951, however, Fender continued to use the same headstock decals, only with the removal of the original name. These instruments are now highly prized by collectors, and are referred to as "Nocasters."

The Telecaster was identical to its predecessor. Co-designer George Fullerton outlined his no-frills philosophy for a working musician's instrument: "You think of a cowboy and you think of Roy Rogers ... fancy hats and shirts and boots . . . but did you ever see a working cowboy? He's dirty and got rough boots on . . . we looked at guitar players as being working cowboys."

The first influential Telecaster player was Jimmy Bryant: the self-styled "Fastest Guitar in the Country" stoked up a good deal of interest when he was seen regularly playing his Tele in the early 1950s on the *Hometown Jamboree* TV show.

More than six decades after it first appeared, the Telecaster remains as popular as ever, and although perhaps best known as a "country" guitar, it has featured endlessly in all other types of music. **TB**

Dr. Feelgood's Wilko Johnson played his Telecaster without a pick, striking the strings with his fingernails. The band's top-selling album *Stupidity* (1976) is arguably one of the finest live albums ever recorded.

◄ Syd Barrett, founder member of Pink Floyd and pioneer of psychedelic guitar.

Gibson
L-5 CES 1951

Type Archtop electric guitar
Body & neck Solid spruce top, maple body and neck
Fingerboard Ebony
Pick-ups Twin P-90 single-coil pick-ups

The L-5 was already one of the world's most popular guitars and considered to be the classic blues/jazz archtop when Gibson made the decision to electrify it in 1951 and issue it as the L-5 CES. It wasn't the first to come up with the idea though. Django Reinhardt, for one, thought the L-5's electrification was long overdue.

Unveiled for the first time at the New York Gotham Hotel prior to the 1951 New York Trade Show, Gibson considered it its "commitment to the electric guitar" and it was first and foremost a jazz guitar, with its notes the product of its carved, solid spruce top and maple

> *"Wes Montgomery played impossible things on his guitar because it was never pointed out to him that they were impossible."*
> RONNIE SCOTT

back and rims that reflected its sound through its bridge and f-holes. It had a slightly thicker top than its acoustic counterparts and additional bracing to reduce vibration. The first thirty-one CESs to emerge from Gibson's factory came with rosewood bridges and twin P-90 pick-ups, and it was the pick-ups as much as anything that made this guitar a classic, the first-ever Gibson to sport what would become the company's classic two-pick-up circuitry, with two volumes, two tones, and a three-way selector switch, representing a great leap forward in pick-up design considering the technology in general was still in its early stages.

The legendary jazz recordings of Wes Montgomery in the late 1950s and early 1960s were produced using an L-5 CES. **BS**

Gibson
Super 400-CES 1951

Type Archtop hollow body semi-acoustic guitar
Body & neck Maple back/sides, spruce top, maple neck
Fingerboard Ebony
Pick-ups Two P-90 single-coil pick-ups, later two humbuckers

The original Gibson Super 400 was an influential prewar acoustic archtop guitar. This prestige instrument was first sold in 1934 and named for its enormous $400 price tag. After the war, a few Super 400s were custom ordered with pick-ups and Gibson realized the direction the guitar world was taking. It introduced the Super 400-CES (standing for "Cutaway Electric Spanish") in 1951. This was Gibson's first guitar with two pick-ups.

The body was much the same as the huge and lavishly appointed Super 400, but now with a cutaway and the addition of state-of-the-art electrics. In 1951, this meant a pair of P-90 single-coil pick-ups with a volume and tone control for each, plus a three-way toggle pick-up selector. The spruce top was slightly thicker to support the electronics and reduce feedback.

Guitar engineering was evolving quickly. Within two years, the P-90s were replaced by Gibson's new Alnico V pick-ups, with "staple" pole pieces instead of the P-90's screws. In 1953, the innovative Tune-o-matic bridge was added to the Super 400-CES, giving players far more control over string height and intonation. By 1957, pioneering Gibson humbuckers were installed.

Today, the Gibson Custom Shop still makes the 400-CES with much the same specification as it had in the late 1950s. The 400 name no longer describes its cost however ... the CES' retail price is around $17,000. **SH**

Scotty Moore recorded *The Guitar That Changed The World* (1964) on his new 1963 400-CES. Elvis used the same guitar in his famous 1968 comeback TV show. Images from the show of Elvis in black leather sitting on a stool playing the CES have become icons of the 1960s.

Bigsby
Grady Martin 1952

Type Double-neck solidbody guitar
Body & neck Maple body, guitar and mandolin necks
Fingerboard Rosewood
Pick-ups Four single-coil (three on guitar, one on mandolin)

Had Paul Bigsby exhibited the same commercial instincts as Leo Fender he may instead have become the household name: after all, he built a solidbody electric guitar a full three years before Fender. But Bigsby never seriously contemplated mass-manufacture of his guitars. Instead he attracted commissions from many of the leading country players of the day, such as Billy Byrd, Butterball Paige, and Grady Martin—for whom he produced this fascinating double-neck instrument that combines a standard six-string guitar with a mandolin.

With a small workshop built next to his home in Downey, California, Bigsby struggled to keep up with demand, and waiting lists grew to beyond two years. As his health floundered in the mid-1960s, Bigsby sold his business to former Gibson president Ted McCarty, who focused his attention on the Bigsby vibrato systems.

Bigsby kept no logbook or other records of his work, so it's impossible to say how many instruments he built: known to exist today are six standard guitars, one tenor, two double-necks, two mandolins and forty-seven steel guitars; they are rare and highly collectible.

Paul Bigsby could hardly be described as a forgotten man—the enduring popularity of his vibrato units, now produced by Gretsch, will see to that—but he certainly deserves greater recognition for his role in the evolution of the electric guitar. **TB**

Grady Martin was one of Nashville's "A-Team," an elite group of top session musicians who backed country's biggest stars from the mid-1950s. *Roughneck Blues 1949–1956* documents some of Martin's work with Buddy Holly, Johnny Burnette, Brenda Lee, and Red Sovine.

Grady Martin playing his specially commissioned Bigsby double-neck guitar. ➔

Epiphone Zephyr Emperor Regent 1952

Type Hollow body electric
Body & neck Maple back/sides, spruce top, maple neck
Fingerboard Rosewood
Pick-ups Three single-coil New York pick-ups

As far as archtop guitars were concerned, during the 1930s Epiphone had been a preeminent brand. But the war years were not kind. Struggling to maintain production during a period of austerity, Epi Stathopoulo, who founded the brand, died in 1943, and the company passed to his brothers. Although some excellent instruments emerged, the Epiphone brand was never fully able to recapture past glories.

The Emperor had been the company's most significant prewar archtop guitar. Launched in 1936, it was positioned in the market to compete directly with Gibson's flagship SJ-400. In 1950, it was offered with a Venetian cutaway—like similar models in the range, it was suffixed with the word "Regent." Two years later, an electric version of this model was launched: like all existing models that were electrified it took the "Zephyr" prefix.

The Zephyr Emperor Regent was the most luxurious electric guitar that the company would ever make. It enjoyed all the opulent features of its acoustic counterpart: seven-ply binding on the top and back, triple-ply binding around the f-holes, vine headstock inlay, and the gold-plated Frequensator tailpiece.

The electrics were also noteworthy: the three single-coil New York pick-ups were engaged by pressing the six button switches on the control panel—any combination of the three was possible, except, curiously, all three in simultaneous use.

The guitar emerged at a turbulent time: a labor dispute had broken out between the Stathopoulo family and the workers at their New York factory. It was the beginning of the end for Epiphone. **TB**

Gibson
ES-295 1952

Type Hollow body electric
Body & neck Maple back/sides/top, mahogany neck
Fingerboard Rosewood
Pick-ups Two P-90 single-coil pick-ups

Introduced in 1952, the ES-295 was launched as a high-end version of Gibson's ES-175, which—strange in hindsight given its perennial popularity—the company saw as a "value" instrument. In truth, there was not too much of a difference between the two guitars, but a shimmering gold finish with matching gold-plated hardware, ornate pickguard, and specially made white P-90 pick-up covers were enough to add a $120 price premium.

Like other electric archtops produced by Gibson during this period, the ES-295 had been aimed largely at the jazz market, but more often found itself in the hands of young rock 'n' rollers, the most celebrated of whom was Scotty Moore, whose ES-295 can be heard on the first dates of Elvis Presley's celebrated debut sessions for Sun Records in 1954—although shortly afterward he switched over to a Gibson L5-CES, which he thought was "probably the better guitar for our sort of music."

With its body shape and paint job, the ES-295 can be viewed as a hollow body partner to the Les Paul "Goldtop," which emerged the same year, but it would not enjoy a similar resurgence as its solidbody counterpart. Quietly dropped in 1959, it was briefly reissued more than three decades later as a signature model for its best-known patron. **TB**

Scotty Moore used his ES-295 on the first of the legendary *Sun Sessions* recordings (1976) with Elvis Presley, including such landmark recordings as "That's All Right" and "There's Good Rockin' Tonight."

Gibson Les Paul "Goldtop" 1952

Type Solidbody electric
Body & neck Mahogany body, maple top
Fingerboard Rosewood
Pick-ups Two P-90 single-coil pick-ups

Like America's other important guitar manufacturers, Gibson had adopted a position of curious onlooker when Leo Fender launched the Fender Telecaster—the world's first production-line solidbody electric guitar. In the mid-1940s, up-and-coming guitarist and inventor Les Paul had paid a visit to the Gibson factory to demonstrate his "Log," a a guitar with a solid body that would not feed back at high volumes. They were not impressed: "Gibson called me 'the character with the broomstick with the pick-ups on it,'" he recalled. But by the early 1950s, Paul had become America's best-known guitarist, scoring hit after hit with his wife, singer Mary Ford. With the Telecaster taking off, Paul was asked to put his name to Gibson's first solidbody.

What emerged was not exactly a radical departure for Gibson, the body contour clearly in the ES-175 lineage. Although Paul is popularly viewed as the guitar's "inventor," his role in its design is generally thought to have been limited to the one-piece trapeze bridge/tailpiece. In truth, Gibson was more likely to have sought his endorsement because of his growing popularity: by this time *The Les Paul Show* was being broadcast coast-to-coast by NBC.

Widely known as the "Goldtop," even after its legendary rehabilitation more than a decade later, the first Les Paul remained relatively unpopular. **TB**

Although he enjoyed only a brief career before his death in a motorcycle accident in 1973, Duane Allman remains a guitar legend. Probably the best-known "Goldtop," his Les Paul can be heard on Derek And The Dominos' *Layla And Other Love Songs* (1970).

← Duane Allman, one of the great guitar heroes of the early 1970s.

Gibson
Electric Bass 1953

Gretsch
6128 Duo Jet 1953

Type Solidbody electric bass
Body & neck Solid mahogany body, mahogany neck
Fingerboard Rosewood
Pick-ups One pick-up

Type Single cutaway chambered solidbody
Body & neck Mahogany body/neck, arched maple top
Fingerboard Ebony
Pick-ups Two DeArmond single coils (Filter'Trons from 1958)

Introduced in 1953, the Gibson Electric Bass represented the company's first foray into the world of the electric bass. Just as the Les Paul appeared in response to Leo Fender's Telecaster, the Electric Bass was created to stem the popularity of the Fender Precision: the first solidbody bass guitar.

Unlike the Precision—effectively a large electric guitar with longer and fatter strings—the Electric Bass was styled after an upright acoustic bass, with fake f-holes painted on the body. It was designed to be played both horizontally like a guitar, and vertically like an upright bass—this was achieved through the use of an ingenious telescopic endpin that extended the height of the body from the ground.

The single pick-up was fitted close to the neck, which ensured a deeper bass tone, but lacked the crisp definition possible on a Fender Precision. The Electric Bass—later known as the EB-1—was not popular; only 546 were built before it was discontinued in 1958. **TB**

The Fred Gretsch company had existed since the 1880s, but it wasn't until the late 1940s that the brand established itself as a maker of quality instruments. Like Gibson, the Gretsch board had been skeptical about the simplicity of Leo Fender's solidbody guitars, but their immediate success resulted in a rapid rethink. The result was the Duo Jet.

Not technically a solidbody guitar, the Duo Jet was built using separate pieces of mahogany with widely routed channels through which cables could be laid and electronic components fitted. A thin "lid" was then glued over the top of the arched body—on the earliest models, this was covered in a shiny black plastic layer used on Gretsch drum shells.

Although the Gretsch "solids" were not hugely popular at the time, they found one follower in the shape of a young George Harrison, whose Duo Jet can be heard on such Beatles hits as "I Want To Hold Your Hand"—some of the biggest selling singles of all time. **TB**

Guild Stuart X-500 1953

Albanus Seven-string Guitar 1954

Type Electric archtop, single Venetian cutaway
Body & neck Spruce top, maple body, 5-piece maple neck
Fingerboard Bound rosewood
Pick-ups Two P-90 single-coil pick-ups

Type Handmade seven-string archtop
Body & neck Various woods available
Fingerboard Ebony
Pick-ups Various Kent Armstrong and Gibson pick-ups

In the early 1950s, the fledgling company Guild, from its premises in Hoboken, New Jersey, built its hopes on the quality of its new range of acoustic archtops, the high-water mark of which was its Stuart X-500. It was introduced in 1953 and remained the pinnacle of the company's electric line for more than forty years. Similar in appearance and overall size to Epiphone's Zephyr Deluxe Regent and introduced to compete with Gibson's great L-5 CES, the X-500 was luxuriously appointed, sporting a bound tortoiseshell pickguard, V-wedge inserts of abalone, and mother-of-pearl inlays; initial examples incorporated beautifully bound rosewood fingerboards. Bridges were ebony, tailpieces in lyre style with a gold-plated engraved surface, and bodies were available in blond or sunburst.

The cutaway design made it popular, and it was available in an acoustic version with a solid spruce hand-carved top. It furthered Guild's already-impressive reputation for craftsmanship and today remains one of the company's most collectible instruments. **BS**

Swedish immigrant violin maker Carl Albanus Johnson learned to make guitars at the Stomberg factory in Boston. After working with his fellow Swede, he moved to Chicago in the 1950s and started building his own high-quality bespoke guitars.

The workmanship on these premium hand-made instruments was extraordinary. Albanus even machined his own tuners. The guitars varied widely but Albanus used many interesting features, including hand-carved quarter-sawn tops and a rare form of bracing with one single diagonal brace, resulting in the guitars becoming known for their bright, clear sound. Decoration was extensive, with seven-ply binding, beautifully bound f-holes, and hand-carved floating ebony pickguards with delicate binding.

This rare seven-string model includes many of Albanus' trademarks, including the hand-carved ebony tailpiece that reflected his violin-making roots. It's a two-pick-up electro-acoustic model with the controls mounted on the pickguard. **SH**

Marcelo Barbero
Flamenco Guitar 1954

Type Flamenco guitar
Body & neck Spruce top, cypress back and sides
Other features Traditional peghead, clear golpeador
(pickguard), ebony fingerboard

Born in Madrid, Spain, in 1904, Marcelo Barbero was a preeminent maker of flamenco and classical guitars who learned his craft while employed by Jose Ramírez II before setting up on his own in 1945, but not before a period of two to three years when he took over execution of back orders at the Santos Hernández workshop (when Hernández died in 1943) and whose designs influenced him greatly. His head design at this time is virtually identical to that of Santos Hernández. From about 1948 Barbero broke from the Santos model and started to develop instruments with sound properties equal to the demands of flamenco players who were playing solos alongside their traditional role of accompanying singers and dancers.

It is generally agreed that Barbero's best guitars were made between 1950 and his death in 1956. This guitar was made in 1954, at the peak of his capabilities, when he was experimenting with the bracing and wood thicknesses of his flamenco guitars to create a fuller- and warmer-sounding instrument, somewhat approaching the tone quality of a classical guitar.

Barbero has been spoken of as a "Stradivari" among guitar makers. His guitars were favored, among many others, by the legendary flamenco guitarist Sabicas, and can be heard on his seminal recordings of the early 1950s. **GD**

Sabicas (1912–1990), was one of the greatest flamenco guitarists and a major influence on arguably the greatest of them all: Paco de Lucía. The Barbero guitars Sabicas plays on the ten remarkable tracks of *Flamenco Puro* (1961) sound outstanding in his legendary hands.

Agustín Castellón Campos—Sabicas—was one of the first stars of flamenco. →

Fender
Stratocaster 1954

Type Double cutaway solidbody electric
Body & neck Ash or alder body, bolt-on maple neck
Fingerboard Maple or rosewood
Pick-ups Three single-coil pick-ups

1954 was an auspicious year in the evolution of the solidbody electric guitar, as Leo Fender unleashed the most famous electric guitar of them all: the mighty Stratocaster. Since then, pretty much every notable pop or rock guitarist has at some stage owned or played a Fender Stratocaster. Indeed, virtuoso players such as Eric Clapton, David Gilmour, and Yngwie Malmsteen seldom use any other model.

A number of factors lay behind the development of the Stratocaster, high among them being Fender's dedication to jobbing country players who had been using his Telecasters for the previous three years. A second factor was competition from upmarket brands such as Gretsch and Gibson—the latter hitting the solidbody market in 1952 with the Les Paul, a shiny, exotic beast that made the Tele seem crude by comparison.

Fender turned to Western swing guitarist Bill Carson, a musician with several years' experience of the Telecaster, who provided a wish list for his dream instrument. Features included individually adjustable saddles, three pick-ups, a versatile vibrato arm, and a body shape that could be played comfortably when both standing and sitting. Fender, along with George Fullerton and Freddie Tavares, united all of these features in an iconic design that would forever position itself at the very heart of popular music. **TB**

Deep Purple In Rock (1970) was the British band's international breakthrough album. Guitarist Ritchie Blackmore played his tasty, high-speed classically influenced licks on a Fender Stratocaster.

← Ritchie Blackmore live on stage with Deep Purple in 1991.

Gibson
Les Paul Custom 1954

Type Single cutaway solidbody electric
Body & neck Mahogany body and top, set mahogany neck
Fingerboard Ebony
Pick-ups Single-coil P-90 and single-coil Alnico 5 pick-ups

Two years after the launch of the Les Paul "Goldtop," Gibson revised the design, which largely consisted of refinements in hardware. Gibson also launched a second model, the all-black Custom, widely known as the "Black Beauty." The Custom saw the first appearance of the Tune-o-matic bridge and tailstop. Designed by Gibson president Ted McCarty, the bridge featured six saddles, adjustable lengthwise to enable precision intonation.

To differentiate the Custom from its predecessor, the body was given a mahogany top and an ebony fingerboard. However, the most significant difference was in the replacement on the Custom of the bridge P-90 with a high-output Alnico 5 magnet. This provided a good deal more attack than the P-90, which used Alnico 2 magnets.

In 1957, the Custom received a final reworking, when the single-coil pick-ups were replaced by a set of three of Gibson's new PAF ("Patent Applied For") humbuckers. The three-way switching of the previous models was retained, although in the central position both middle and bridge pick-ups became active: some late-Custom owners had their instruments rewired so that each position switched in just one pick-up.

The Goldtop was discontinued in 1958 and the Custom followed in 1961, as the Les Paul series morphed into the Solid Guitar—or "SG" as it became known. **TB**

Moving Waves (1971) by Dutch progressive rock band Focus, features the Les Paul Custom of Jan Akkerman, whose lightning-fast soloing can be heard on the hit "Hocus Pocus." Sadly, this is all-too-often overlooked in favor of the song's legendary yodelling.

Gibson
Les Paul Junior 1954

Type Single cutaway solidbody electric (original version)
Body & neck Mahogany body and neck
Fingerboard Rosewood
Pick-ups Single-coil P-90 pick-up

1954 was a significant year for the Gibson Les Paul. Not only was the Custom "Black Beauty" launched and the original Goldtop revamped, the Les Paul Junior was also released. The flagship models were expensive instruments; the rationale for the Junior was to create a high-quality instrument that would be affordable to youngsters and novices. To make this possible, the basic Les Paul was stripped of all its opulent trappings.

The Junior took the same body shape as its siblings, but instead of the carefully crafted arched top, it was cut from a flat, thin slab of mahogany. A single-coil P-90 pick-up was positioned alongside the bridge and the electrics comprised a single volume and tone control. The finishes were also basic: vintage sunburst or cherry red, with the mustard-colored TV version emerging two years later. In 1958, the Junior/TV range was given a cosmetic overhaul—the new twin cutaway proved to be a durable design, and twenty years later would provide a template for Paul Reed Smith's guitars.

The last original Juniors were produced in 1963, but they were reintroduced in 2001. A number of artist-edition models have since been released, among them Peter Frampton, Mick Jones (The Clash), Bob Marley, and a John Lennon version, with a Charlie Christian hexagon pick-up—reflecting a modification the ex-Beatle made to his Junior in the 1970s. **TB**

Mick Jones of The Clash used a Gibson Les Paul Junior on the band's legendary self-titled debut album of 1977. He purportedly chose a Junior because it was the guitar of choice of the New York Dolls/Heartbreakers icon Johnny Thunders.

Gretsch 6136 White Falcon 1954

Type Laminated hollow body electric
Body & neck Maple back/sides, spruce top, maple neck
Fingerboard Ebony
Pick-ups Two Dynasonics; two Filter'Trons (from 1958)

Arguably the most beautiful guitar to go into full-scale production, the Gretsch White Falcon was conceived in 1954 as an instrument capable of outperforming anything else on the market, most notably Gibson's wildly expensive flagship Super 400—for many players of that time, the ultimate impossible dream guitar.

Already close to a century old, the Fred Gretsch Company was a general producer of musical instruments, having played a significant role in the emergence of the modern-day drum kit. Some of the eye-catching visual features of the White Falcon undoubtedly betray this heritage, such as the thick sparkly gold plastic binding that covered the drum shells.

Gretsch marketing strategist Jimmie Webster had sought to create what he called "the Cadillac of guitars," but the White Falcon had not been designed with full-scale production in mind. Its first public appearance was as a one-off showpiece guitar at the 1954 NAMM trade show and was billed as "the guitar of the future." Yet such was the buzz surrounding this sumptuous vision that Gretsch had little choice but to offer the instrument to the world. With its unusually large body (17 in. [43 cm] wide by 2¾ in. [7 cm] deep) the White Falcon went on sale in 1955, presented as "the finest guitar we know how to make." It had a price to match: $600 is now the equivalent of well over $4,000. **TB**

Billy Duffy of The Cult is one of a long line of notable White Falcon users, among them Stephen Stills, Brian Setzer, and Dave Stewart. Duffy's versatile sound can be heard on most of The Cult's albums, including their breakthrough classic *Love* (1985).

Stephen Stills wields a White Falcon with his band Manassas. →

Gretsch
6022 Rancher 1954

Grimshaw
SS Deluxe 1954

Type Acoustic flat-top guitar
Body & neck Laminated spruce top, maple body, maple neck
Fingerboard Rosewood

Type Hollow body thinline archtop electric
Body & neck Laminated maple body, maple neck
Fingerboard Rosewood
Pick-ups Two single-coil pick-ups

In the early 1950s, big band and swing music were little more than a memory and the search was on for instruments that reflected the public's growing desire for a harder, more aggressive kind of sound. So in 1954 Gretsch did a little rebranding—it did away with the word "Synchromatic" and replaced it with "Town and Country," though the "new" series retained the body, back, sides, bracing, binding, frets, and block inlays of its twin.

It was, however, also given some very distinctive design elements found in the Jumbo Synchromatic, including a height-adjustable bridge; an elegantly sweeping pickguard; an angled, metal anchor plate; and a head-turning, distinctive triangular sound hole. The Town and Country had become the Rancher, and been given what many Gretsch aficionados still speak of disparagingly as the "cowboy treatment." The Rancher's heavy bracing meant using heavy strings and playing hard to achieve any real acoustic sound, and sold poorly until being discontinued in 1973. **BS**

After the Second World War, expensive American guitars were scarce in Europe because of austerity measures. This gave local manufacturers a chance, like the Grimshaws, a family firm from northern England that began making banjos in the 1930s.

In the 1950s, Grimshaw made archtop, acoustic, and electric guitars and sold them with varying degrees of success from their shop in London's Piccadilly. The SS (short-scale) Deluxe was the pick of the line. The body style was similar to a Gibson ES-335 but with unequal cutaways and "cat's-eyes" sound holes. Some had Grimshaw's own patented vibrato tailpiece system, some (labeled "Custom") had humbucker pick-ups.

Who guitarist Pete Townshend bought an SS Deluxe in the 1960s after he saw rock 'n' roll singer Joe Brown playing one. Gene Vincent, Joe Morreti of Johnny Kidd and The Pirates, and Bruce Welch of The Shadows also played the SS. Townshend confused guitar spotters when he played live—he added to his Grimshaw the headstock of a Rickenbacker he'd smashed up on stage. **SH**

Guild
"F" Series 1954

Höfner
Club 50 1954

Type Jumbo/Grand concert steel-string acoustic guitar
Body & neck Maple body, spruce top, walnut/mahogany neck
Fingerboard Rosewood
Pick-ups Three single-coil lipstick pick-ups

Type Thinline archtop electro-acoustic
Body & neck Maple
Fingerboard Rosewood
Pick-ups Two Höfner "black bar" single-coil pick-ups

The Guild Guitar Company was founded in 1952 in Manhattan, New York, and found a market producing high-quality archtop jazz guitars, both electric and acoustic. With the global expansion of the New York folk scene of the early 1960s, Guild began to focus on producing flat-top acoustic guitars that could vie with C.F. Martin for quality but were also competitively priced.

Guild's two most important acoustic ranges were the dreadnought "D" series (famously used by Richie Havens to open the 1969 Woodstock Festival) and the jumbo and grand concert "F" series. Guild's first flat-top acoustic series, the "F" line was introduced in 1954, but it was during the later blues and folk boom that it flourished. Prized both for its projection and deep, rich, clear tone, these guitars—such as the F-50 shown here—found particular favor among acoustic blues players such as Mississippi John Hurt.

The Guild brand was swallowed by the mighty Fender Corporation in 1995, but both the brand and the "F" series remain in production. **TB**

Höfner Club guitars were the cool starting point for many European guitarists who couldn't afford one of the big-name American imports. Players such as John Lennon, Paul McCartney, George Harrison, Ritchie Blackmore, Gordon Giltrap, Justin Haywood, and David Gilmour all went through a Höfner Club stage early in their careers.

This German-made line of archtops had a small hollow body that was 2 in. (5 cm) thick but didn't have a sound hole. It was given the name "Club" by British distributor Selmer only in the United Kingdom. The "40" had one pick-up and the "50" had two. Controls were mounted in a tortoiseshell panel, and there was a simple floating pickguard on the body.

The original pick-ups were single coils made by Fuma in Berlin. Höfner later introduced its own slimmer "black bar" pick-ups mounted on a rosewood base, then in 1960 they were replaced by a new pick-up with a slotted cover universally known as "the toaster." Finally in 1963, a Höfner humbucker was introduced. **SH**

Rickenbacker
Combo 600 1954

Type Double cutaway solidbody electric
Body & neck Birch body, maple neck
Fingerboard Rosewood
Pick-ups Single-coil horseshoe pick-up

In 1953, businessman Francis Hall bought Adolph Rickenbacker's Electro String Instrument Corporation. Hall had made his money selling Fenders. He renamed his new company after its founder and started work on new, modern Rickenbacker solidbodies: the "Combo" line. Hall was trying to update the company's appeal to the new generation of electric players. These modern-styled Combo guitars originally came with a blond finish, a big black scratchplate, and Rickenbacker's own hefty horseshoe pick-ups.

On the Combo 600, this was a single-coil unit that ran both above and below the strings. There was a volume and tone control plus a three-way preset tone selector switch.

On the Combo 800, the horseshoe had two coils. One was designed primarily for treble, the other for bass. The guitarist could switch both coils on to make it a full-sounding humbucker or select either a treble or bassy sound by choosing one coil over the other.

Although it was officially solidbodied, large chunks were hollowed out from the back of both the 600 and 800. This helped to reduce the weight of the 2 in. (5 cm)-thick body (plus the heavy pick-ups). These cavities were covered with metal plates.

Other features varied from year to year. Some have bolt-on necks, others are glued. Some have blue bodies, bigger pickguards, different-colored plastic parts, and different headstock logos. Vibrola tremolo arms were fitted in the late 1950s. The early Combos were quickly overtaken by more modern designs, but the Combo 600 wasn't officially dropped from the Rickenbacker lineup until 1969. **SH**

Supro
Dual Tone 1954

Type Solidbody single cutaway electric
Body & neck Basswood body, aluminum/wood/plastic neck
Fingerboard Rosewood
Pick-ups Two oversized single-coil pick-ups

To some players, the Dual Tone is one of the coolest-looking guitars of all time. David Bowie chose its classy retro looks to use on a world tour, and at times it has been the ax of choice for guitarists as varied as Dan White, Aerosmith's Joe Perry, Jimmy Page, and Link Wray—who was pictured playing one on the cover of his hit record "Rumble."

The design is as much a slice of 1950s America as drive-in movies and pink Cadillacs. Supro guitars were made in Chicago by manufacturer Valco, who also owned National. The Dual Tone got its name from

> *"Supros have fat necks, and for the uninitiated this can take some getting used to, but I find it's actually really fun to play."*
>
> **WILL RAY, FOUNDING MEMBER OF THE HELLECASTERS**

having a volume and tone control for each pick-up as well as a three-position selector, allowing players a wide variety of tones.

The design included a distinctive graduated tailpiece, a two-level pickguard, brass-plated hardware and large single-coil pick-ups that looked like humbuckers.

In the 1960s, Valco switched to using ultralight fiberglass bodies, but they originally used basswood covered with a wipe-clean plastic finish.

Their "Kord King" necks were an innovative design too: a sturdy aluminum tube was bolted to the body encased in wood and plastic with a rosewood fingerboard, like a giant truss rod. It feels quite bulky to play at first, but even very early examples often still have perfectly straight necks. **SH**

Fender
Champion 1955

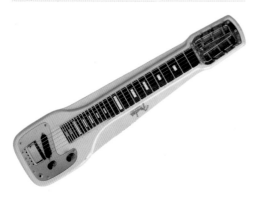

Gibson
Byrdland 1955

Type Six-string lap steel electric
Body & neck Perloid-covered hardwood, all-in-one body and neck, metal fingerboard
Pick-ups Single-coil Stratocaster pick-up

Type Hollow body electric
Body & neck Maple bottom and sides, spruce top
Fingerboard Ebony
Pick-ups Two Alnico single-coils (humbuckers after 1958)

Lap steel guitars were the first instruments produced by Leo Fender's new company in 1945. In some ways they were the forerunners of the company's pioneering electric guitars. The Champion was launched in 1949, originally as a six-string student model, with a wooden body covered in pearloid.

In 1955 Fender shortened the name of its lap steel guitar to Champ, and replaced the Telecaster-style pick-up with a Strat-style pick-up. Adjustable legs were available, but the body was now simply painted.

This model has since become one of the iconic lap steel guitars, mainly thanks to a brilliant clear sound, often likened to church bells. Other appealing features include the simple practical shape for comfortable playing, the high-quality Kluson tuners and full three-octave scale. Other manufacturers tried to alter their sound to match the Fender's, but it was generally too late—Fender, with the Telecaster twang and Champ's whine, had become THE sound of country music. **SH**

During his defining time as company president—a period that saw the launch of almost all of Gibson's enduring designs—Ted McCarty would often sound out practicing musicians for new ideas or refinements to current models. (Remember, some now-legendary Gibsons of the 1950s—like the Les Paul, Explorer, and Flying V—were dramatic failures at the time.) And even popular classics like Gibson's archtops, did not find universal favor. Suggestions by guitarists Billy Byrd and Hank Garland, both of whom liked the Gibson archtop sound but found them bulky to play, resulted in the birth of the company's first thinline model: the Byrdland.

Launched in 1955, the Gibson Byrdland was a slimmer take on the L-5CES, the electrified L-5 with a single cutaway: with a depth of 2¼ in. (5.5 cm), the Byrdland was thinner by more than an inch. The most striking aspect of the Byrdland's design is its scale length: at an unusually short 23½-in. (59.75 cm), it was specified to facilitate the frequent stretched chord voicings used by many jazz players. **TB**

Ignacio Fleta
Classical Guitar 1955

Joseph Di Mauro
Modèle Jazz 1955

Type Classical guitar
Body & neck Spruce top, Indian rosewood back and sides, cedar neck, ebony fingerboard
Other features Innovative bracing, trademark rosette

Type Steel-string acoustic
Body & neck Bird's-eye maple plywood with spruce top, maple neck
Fingerboard Softwood

For many years the instruments of choice of classical guitarist John Williams, and often played by Andrés Segovia and other top guitarists, Fleta guitars are renowned for their extraordinarily incisive power, brassy resonance, and no-nonsense sound properties. This was achieved by radically moving away from the lighter Torres design of old and increasing the mass and rigidity of the instrument by enlarging the bouts and adding bracing. His system evolved, with some variations, to nine fan braces and four harmonic bars, the lower one fitted diagonally.

Ignacio Fleta (1897–1977) had been building violins, cellos, and some guitars for around thirty years when (around the time he made this 1955 guitar) he heard Andrés Segovia play for the first time. From then on he decided to build only guitars. He made the first of three guitars for Segovia in 1957. But it was John Williams who is more closely associated with the guitars, playing and recording with them extensively during the 1960s and 1970s. **GD**

There were not one, not two, but three luthiers named Di Mauro crafting inexpensive yet exquisite-sounding guitars in Paris from the 1930s. Brothers Antoine and Joseph Di Mauro immigrated from Sicily to set up shop in the French capital. Here they crafted steel-string jazz guitars, inspired by Mario Maccaferri's Selmer guitars.

The Di Mauro brothers labored in a shared workshop, adding their own innovations to the Maccaferri formula, including f-holes, different woods, and later, electric pick-ups. While Antoine's instruments were best known, Joseph Di Mauro built this flagship model with a heart-shaped sound hole and upscale bird's-eye maple body. Antoine's son, also named Joseph, soon offered his own guitars, adding to the name confusion but keeping the family's workshop alive until 1993.

The Di Mauros were famed for their alchemy: their guitars were inexpensive instruments built on a budget, yet the sound was often lush and opulent, a rich tone admired by players then and now. **MD**

Gibson ES-5
Switchmaster 1955

Type Hollow body electric
Body & neck Maple body and neck
Fingerboard Rosewood
Pick-ups Three dog-ear P-90 single-coil pick-ups

First produced in 1922, Gibson's L-5 acoustic archtop had been hugely successful and influential—its design enabled guitarists to be heard when playing in concert with other musicians. In 1949, the ES-5 was Gibson's first electric model based on the L-5—in the words of Gibson's advertisement of the time, it was "the supreme electronic version." Aimed, like the L-5, at jazz music, it was armed with three pick-ups—the first Gibson to offer such a configuration. Gibson chose to omit switching, opting instead for four individual volume controls—one for each pick-up, and one overall control.

The ES-5 Switchmaster emerged in 1955, and although the guitar itself was unchanged, the electrics were given a complete overhaul. A four-way switch labeled "1-2-3-ALL" was inserted in the treble horn, and enabled each of the single-coil P-90 pick-ups to be selected, or, in the bottom position, all three to become active simultaneously. To give the player even more control, each pick-up was provided with a dedicated pair of volume and tone controls. In 1957, in keeping with other Gibsons in the "Electric Spanish" series, the P-90s were replaced with PAF humbuckers.

Eventually the ES-5 Switchmaster found its niche in the hands of rock 'n' rollers such as Carl Perkins, and remained in production until 1962. Gibson's Custom division has offered a reissue model since 1995. **TB**

Carl Perkins was one of Elvis Presley's biggest rivals during the 1950s, and "Matchbox"—as he was known—wrote such rockabilly classics as "Blue Suede Shoes." He and his Switchmaster can be heard on *The Essential Sun Collection* (1999).

Carl Perkins was one of the first stars of rockabilly in the mid-1950s. →

Gretsch
6120 Chet Atkins 1955

Type Single cutaway hollow body electric
Body & neck Maple body, set mahogany neck
Fingerboard Rosewood (ebony from 1958)
Pick-ups Two single-coil DeArmonds (Filter'Trons from 1958)

By the early 1950s, Gretsch was still better known as a manufacturer of high-quality drum kits, used by most of the top jazz players of the period. Much of the company's success in the guitar field was down to its association with an up-and-coming country picker, well known and admired in Nashville but yet to achieve nationwide fame. He was Chester "Chet" Burton Atkins.

Initially approached by Gretsch representative Jimmie Webster to endorse an existing design, Atkins had been unimpressed by the model on offer. After numerous further approaches, he relented only when Webster suggested that perhaps he should design a Gretsch guitar of his own.

In the end, the guitarist played only a limited role in the development of the 6120 Chet Atkins, fighting successfully against overused corny "cowboy" motifs. Much against Gretsch's wishes, he was also insistent that his model should be fitted with a Bigsby vibrato arm.

Of course, Atkins' fame soon spread and by the end of the decade he was widely acknowledged as one of the most technically accomplished players in any genre. And he was rarely filmed or photographed without a Gretsch guitar in his hand. And the otherwise modest Atkins would later claim, "The most important thing he [Webster] ever did was to sign me, because they started selling the hell out of guitars!" **TB**

Chet Atkins At Home (1957) was partly recorded in his own studio—he would take the backing tracks and spend time in his studio perfecting the guitar parts. He can be seen on the cover playing a Gretsch 6120, and heard playing his ingenious composition "Yankee Doodle Dixie."

← Chet Atkins at RCA Recording Studios, Nashville, Tennessee, in 1960.

Gretsch 6134 White Penguin 1955

Type Chambered solidbody single cutaway electric
Body & neck Mahogany body, maple top, mahogany neck
Fingerboard Ebony
Pick-ups Two DeArmond single-coil; (Filter'Trons from 1958)

Though visually stunning, Gretsch's great mystery guitar the White Penguin is not that special as an instrument, and yet auction prices—on the rare occasions that they come up—can approach $100,000. Its legendary status is due to the fact that nobody knows exactly how many originals were ever made. Although it's known to have been produced between 1955 and 1964, the White Penguin only appears in the 1959 Gretsch price list (at a hefty $490—over $3,000 in modern currency), and it's estimated that barely two dozen ever made it out of Gretsch's Brooklyn factory.

Based broadly on the Gretsch Duo Jet, the 6134 White Penguin appeared in a gorgeous snow-white finish with gold-sparkle trim and gold-plated hardware, and was clearly intended to be the solidbody partner to the more famous White Falcon (see page 158). According to veteran Gretsch employee Duke Kramer, it was named "because a penguin has a white front," and even featured a cartoon penguin waddling across the pickguard. **TB**

Gretsch 6199 Convertible 1955

Type Single cutaway hollow body electric
Body & neck Maple back/sides, spruce top, mahogany neck
Fingerboard Rosewood (ebony on the Sal Salvador)
Pick-ups DeArmond single-coil (Filter'Tron from 1958)

The Gretsch 6199 guitar was introduced in 1955. Initially known as the Convertible, three years later it was renamed after bebop jazz guitarist Sal Salvador, at that time widely admired for his work with Stan Kenton. The 6199 had a 17-in. (43-cm) maple body with "Copper Mist" back and sides; the carved spruce top featured two f-holes and was given a finish Gretsch termed "Lotus Ivory." It featured the brand's characteristic "G" tailpiece and gold hardware.

Sound came from a single floating DeArmond pick-up. The unusual volume and tone controls were mounted on a large pickguard, the knobs made using regular Gretsch strap buttons. This feature was not used on any other model. Since the pick-up and controls were mounted clear of the soundboard, the 6199 was louder and more resonant than other Gretsch models. The original Convertible had a bound rosewood fingerboard with "humptop" inlays (shown above); these were replaced on the Sal Salvador with an ebony fingerboard and characteristic "thumbnail" inlays. **JB**

Orpheum
Electric Guitar 1955

Stratosphere
Twin 1955

Type Hollow body electric
Body & neck Pressed archtop, laminated body, hardwood neck
Fingerboard Rosewood
Pick-ups Two single-coil pick-ups

Type Solidbody double-neck electric
Body & neck Sap gum body, two maple necks
Fingerboard Maple
Pick-ups Four single-coil pick-ups

There has always been a big market for low-budget instruments bought by students and struggling musicians, and in the right hands they can sometimes be made to sound outstanding. In the 1920s, Leadbelly and Blind Willie McTell made their reputations with low-cost Stella guitars. In 1955, Bo Diddley seemed to be playing a very similar guitar to this Orpheum on *The Ed Sullivan Show*, a popular television show.

The Orpheum brand was started around 1897 by William L. Lange of New York for a line of banjos, alongside his Paramount brand. He diversified into guitars in the 1930s but primarily with Paramount. Orpheum seems to have remained dormant until 1944 when Maurice Lipsky, a New York distributor, acquired the brand and in the 1950s went on to sell Orpheum electric archtops and hollow body electric archtops shaped like a Les Paul Standard, as this 1955 example is. In the 1960s cheap Orpheums were made first in Europe and then in Japan, and the brand died off by the end of that decade. **GD**

In 1952, Paul Bigsby built what is arguably the first double-neck electric guitar: it was a one-off job for country singer Grady Martin but never went into full-scale production. Two years later, virtuoso picker Jimmy Bryant was looking for a new instrument that would both provide him with new sounds and look good on stage. Russ Deaver, the owner of the Stratosphere Guitar Manufacturing Company in Springfield, Missouri, was able to provide Bryant with an ideal solution.

The Twin was the first double-neck electric to be produced in significant numbers. It featured twelve strings on the upper neck and six on the lower. Unusually, Stratosphere suggested that the individual pairs on the twelve-string be tuned, rather than in the more regular unison of octaves, to other pitch intervals; this would make it possible to play complex harmony lines (or very full chords). Unsurprisingly, it was difficult to use in practice. And if you doubt that, a quick listen to Bryant's own "Stratosphere Boogie"—recorded on the Twin—should put your mind at ease. **TB**

Danelectro
U-2 1956

Type Single cutaway hollow body
Body & neck Poplar edges, Masonite top/bottom, maple neck
Fingerboard Rosewood
Pick-ups Two single-coil Danelectro lipstick pick-ups

The year 1956 was an iconic one. Elvis Presley recorded "Heartbreak Hotel," the first hard disk was invented by IBM, and the electric guitar was soon to be at the forefront of popular music. Nathan Daniel, the founder of the Danelectro company, was also making a splash of his own in Red Bank, New Jersey, designing and building budget-conscious guitars—using a unique poplar frame and Masonite construction—by the truckload for outlets such as Sears & Roebuck. One of Danelectro's largest distributors, Sears sold instruments that were uniquely branded with the Silvertone name.

The U-2 first appeared in Danelectro catalogs circa 1956 and was available right through to 1958. The introductory price was $100 with an optional soft-shell case available for an additional $15. The classic single cutaway shape, dual lipstick pick-ups, flat fingerboard radius with larger fret wire, and overall light weight made it an instant Danelectro classic.

Early examples have a large "full bell" headstock, but this soon transitioned in late 1956 to one of the brand's instantly recognizable features—the classic "Coke-Bottle" profile. Subtle design changes and unique color options borrowed from the automotive industry included colors like Jade Green, Bermuda Coral, and Gleaming Black, all of which made the U-2 one of the more colorful examples produced by Danelectro.

The U-2 has continued to be a favorite among players and collectors. Joe Perry of Aerosmith is often seen warming up backstage with his original 1957 U-2. And Elvis Presley even played one during his stint in the armed forces. **DT**

Danelectro
UB-2 1956

Type Hollow body electric bass
Body & neck Pine frame, Masonite top/back, poplar neck
Fingerboard Brazilian rosewood
Pick-ups Two single-coil lipstick pick-ups

The Danelectro UB-2 has the distinction of being the first six-string bass designed and produced by any company. It produced such a defined, muted tone it earned the nickname "Tic-Tac" bass, which became an oft-used studio reference for that particular tone.

This classic "Tic-Tac" tone was mainly achieved by pairing the Danelectro UB-2 Baritone guitar with a Fender Deluxe reverb amp. Tunings vary, but the factory "B" tuning, along with the industry standard "E" tuning, were the most prevalent. The technique used to achieve the famous "Tic-Tac" sound is to double the bass not with an identical note, but a note a full octave above the original note. Danelectro excelled at achieving this particular sound while other manufacturers' instruments only shadowed it.

Andy Reiss of the Time Jumpers has two Danelectro Baritone guitars, one tuned to "B" and one tuned to "E." Harold Bradley was the most recorded Tic-Tac bass player in the industry. He toured with Ernest Tubb while still in high school, and was a busy studio musician playing on recordings by such esteemed artists as Patsy Cline and Elvis Presley. Tommy Allsup also did many sessions with the Danelectro UB-2—he was the guitarist for Buddy Holly and The Crickets. Other famous players who were known for their use of this sound were Leon Rhodes, Billy Sanford, Pete Wade, Jimmy Capps, and Spyder Wilson. In an interview, musician Marshall Crenshaw stated that in the intro to "La Bamba" by Ritchie Valens, a Fender Stratocaster and a Danelectro six-string bass were used to achieve the sound of that famous intro. **DT**

Egmond
Archtop Guitar 1956

Fender
Duo-Sonic 1956

Type Archtop acoustic guitar
Body & neck Laminated maple body, maple neck
Fingerboard Rosewood
Other features Floating pickguard

Type Solidbody twin cutaway electric guitar
Body & neck Ash, alder, or basswood body; maple neck
Fingerboard Maple
Pick-ups Two single-coil pick-ups

Egmond guitars were generally cheap beginner instruments built in a factory in Eindhoven, Holland. At first the Egmond family business sold guitars imported from Eastern Europe, but after the Second World War began making its own. By the 1960s, Egmond was Europe's largest guitar maker. Many were labeled differently, however, carrying names like Wilson, Rosetti, Vega, or Alpha. The brand later became famous after George Harrison, Paul McCartney, and Brian May revealed they had started playing on Egmonds.

These early acoustic archtops were sold at a fraction of the price of an imported American guitar. Yet the Egmond had all the features that would attract beginners—sunburst finish, simple body binding, floating pickguard, and stylized f-holes. With an adjustable bridge and a pair of three-a-side tuners this budget archtop was the starting point for many European players of the era but the cheapness of the wood and the lack of a truss rod meant that the majority haven't survived. **SH**

The original Duo-Sonic was launched in 1956 as a beginner's guitar. At its launch, the Duo-Sonic cost $149.50. It had the sturdy, practical Fender quality that made the Telecaster and Stratocaster such a success, including the bolt-on maple neck and fingerboard, and single-coil pick-ups (which could be selected individually or together as a humbucker).

The more budget-conscious features were a shorter-scale neck (22½ in. [57 cm] instead of 25½ in. [64.75 cm]) and a basic fixed bridge with no tremolo. The pick-up selector was a simple switch rather than the normal Fender "blade" system and the Duo-Sonic was only available in a light beige "Desert Sand" finish with a matching gold-colored scratchplate.

Four years later, Fender revamped the Duo-Sonic to virtually become a Mustang without a vibrato. In 1969, it was dropped because the majority of buyers bought the Mustang for its tremolo system. Ironically, today's collectors often prefer the Duo-Sonic because it lacks the Mustang's troublesome vibrato bridge. **SH**

Fender
Musicmaster 1956

Fernández
Classical Guitar 1956

Type Solidbody electric twin cutaway, three-quarter size
Body & neck Ash body, maple neck
Fingerboard Maple
Pick-ups One single-coil pick-up

Type Classical guitar
Body & neck Spruce top, rosewood back and sides
Fingerboard Ebony
Other features French polished, design by Manuel Barbero

In the mid-1950s, Fender decided to broaden the range of its solidbody electric guitars. The top-end Stratocaster and middle-market Telecaster were joined by a more budget-oriented series.

Fender launched the Musicmaster as its first three-quarter-scale solidbody electric for beginners and young players with smaller hands. Costs were kept low and Fender hoped these beginners would eventually progress from entry-level instruments to full-size Fenders.

The guitar itself was basic and functional, with one angled single-coil neck pick-up (from the Champ lap steel guitar) and no tremolo arm. The two-pick-up Duo-Sonic version followed a couple of months later.

As a cost-cutting exercise, Fender originally used the same ash body as the two-pick-up Duo-Sonic—with two cavities routed out but hidden by the aluminum scratchplate. They also shared the same shorter-scale one-piece maple neck, dull beige color scheme, six-in-line Kluson tuners with white plastic buttons, and a simple chrome-plated bridge with removable cover. **SH**

The names of Madrid luthiers Arcángel Fernández and his teacher, the legendary guitar maker Manuel Barbero, are inextricably linked, not least because Fernández was Barbero's only apprentice, taking over the running of his workshop for Barbero's widow in 1956 when Barbero died prematurely in his fifties. Over the decades that followed, Fernández kept pretty much to the design, styling, and construction of Barbero, from the woods used, to the bracing system, to the same headstock shape and rosette patterns as exemplified by this 1956 model, one of the first guitars made that bears his name. Barbero's son, also called Marcelo, was subsequently trained by Fernández and later shared the same workshop, but made guitars with his own label.

Fernández and Barbero are particularly renowned for their flamenco guitars. These have been played by such famous names as Sabicas, Carlos Montoya, and Tomatito. Interestingly, Fernández guitars have been highly sought after in Japan, and from the 1980s, most of what he produced was exported there. **GD**

Gibson
ES-135 1956

Type Semi-hollow body thinline electric
Body & neck Laminated maple
Fingerboard Rosewood
Pick-ups Two P-100 pick-ups

In 1956, the single Florentine cutaway of the ES-135 combined with a semi-hollow body was a first. Gibson had high hopes for it. Apart from the shape though, the ES-135 shared many of the ES-335's features—the thinline body and solid wood block down the middle of the body. What it didn't share was the 335's high price tag. The 135 was the cheapest ES you could buy.

Some of the features reflected this: the central wood block wasn't maple—it was balsa. Nevertheless it did the job of suppressing feedback. Likewise, the laminated maple neck wasn't bound, pick-up covers

"The result of an illicit liaison between an ES-175 and ES-335, this semi is an unsung hero. Go for the one with f-holes and P-100 pick-ups."
MUSICRADAR.COM, 50 GUITARS TO PLAY BEFORE YOU DIE (2011)

were plastic not chrome, and the rosewood fingerboard featured the simplest dot markings. Yet the construction, wood, and wiring were the same as the more expensive ES models. So the 135 was something of a bargain.

The floating trapeze tailpiece took the tension of the strings away from the top. Some say it added a bite to the sound. But buyers weren't in favor—it made changing strings more difficult and simply wasn't as cool.

The P-100 pick-ups look similar to P-90s, but they were in fact early Gibson humbucker designs. Their rounder tone wasn't loved by everyone—many players preferred the P-90's more biting sound. The humbuckers were soon dropped and P-90s hurriedly installed. Too late: The 135 was dropped after just three years. A more modern version reappeared in 1991. **SH**

Gibson
Les Paul TV 1956

Type Solid double or single cutaway electric
Body & neck Mahogany
Fingerboard Rosewood
Pick-ups One P-90 single-coil pick-up

The Les Paul Junior was launched as Gibson's budget line, with a slabby undecorated body and single-coil pick-up for just $99. But today a decent early example from the Junior range can fetch tens of thousands of dollars.

In the 1950s, the Les Paul Junior was targeted at beginners. It had a flat-topped body, in sunburst or cherry for the Junior and mustard yellow for the TV model. There was nothing fancy: simple dot markings on an unbound neck, single tone and volume control, and a stud-mounted tailpiece/bridge. The TV's finish was supposed to be Gibson's version of "natural," but was distinctively yellow with the wood grain visible, similar to Fender's popular butterscotch. The name meant that student guitarists could dream that their guitar was ideally suited to appearing before TV cameras: white would be too dazzling, yellow was just right.

From 1958, the Juniors were redesigned with a pioneering double cutaway body shape to allow easy access to the upper frets. At the same time a Les Paul Special range was evolving. This had a similar flat-top slabby body but two P-90s and four controls. Confusingly it was painted in what Gibson called "TV yellow," but was never officially called the Special TV.

Juniors have since become a popular professional guitar, especially among punk and rock players such as Johnny Thunders and Mick Jones. **SH**

Billie Joe Armstrong of Green Day bought a 1956 Les Paul Junior in 2000 that he has used ever since. He calls it "Floyd" and has since bought many others. Gibson has even released a signature Billie Joe Armstrong double cutaway Junior TV.

Höfner
500/1 1956

Type Semi-hollow electric bass
Body & neck Maple back/sides, spruce top, maple neck
Fingerboard Rosewood
Pick-ups Two 511B humbucker pick-ups

One of the most iconic guitars in pop history, the 1956 Höfner 500/1 "violin bass" was not an exceptional instrument. Indeed, it was not even the first bass guitar to feature such a body shape—Gibson's EB-1, although styled on an upright bass, had appeared three years earlier. Its status is simply down to its association with the biggest pop group of them all: The Beatles. Just as the patronage of John Lennon and George Harrison had turned Rickenbacker into a household name, Höfner would enjoy the Paul McCartney effect.

Founded in Schönbach, Germany, by Karl Höfner in 1887, the company managed to weather the Allied occupation at the end of the Second World War, by which time his son Walter—an innovative luthier and violin maker—was running the company. In 1955, he combined his expertise in these two fields to create the 500/1, a semi-hollow bass guitar with a violin-shaped body. It was a lightweight instrument with a rich tone driven by two powerful Höfner 511B humbucking pick-ups.

Paul McCartney's adoption of the 500/1 came about largely by accident: in 1961, while The Beatles were gigging in the nightclubs of Hamburg, McCartney took over bass duties from the original bass player Stu Sutcliffe. As a left-hander, all of the bass guitars he tried felt awkward when turned upside down, until he found the symmetrical 500/1. The rest, of course, is history. **TB**

Paul McCartney played his Höfner "violin bass" exclusively until 1965, after which he alternated with a Rickenbacker 4001. It can be heard on The Beatles' album *A Hard Day's Night* (1964).

Paul McCartney playing a left-hand Höfner 500/1 with The Beatles in 1965. ➡

Magna
Mark III Spanish 1956

José Ramírez III
Classical Guitar 1956

Type Electric guitar with chambered body
Body & neck Ash body and neck
Fingerboard Rosewood
Pick-ups One or two single-coil pick-ups

Type Classical guitar
Body & neck Spruce top, Brazilian rosewood back and sides, ebony fingerboard
Other features Longer strings, innovative bracing system

Magna Electronics of California already had a name for making Hawaiian guitars. After the Second World War, however, everyone's attention was shifting to the new king of pop instruments: the electric guitar.

Magna employed motorcycle builder Paul Bigsy to design its own line. Bigsby had already invented the hand vibrator lever system that still bears his name and had built a very early solidbody electric guitar for Merle Travis in 1947 (see page 126).

His Mark III Spanish was a small electric guitar with hollow chambers in the body, one or two single-coil pick-ups, and a unique tailpiece with a large cut-out "M." The whole top of the guitar was covered with a screw-on tortoiseshell Formica pickguard and there were two plastic knobs for volume and tone.

Prototype designs by Bigsby had a through-neck system, but production versions switched to a glued neck with a tongue of wood extending under the neck pick-up. They were advertised at the time as "the sound of true quality." **SH**

After the deaths of José I and Manuel Ramírez, José II took over the family business and developed the quality and brand recognition of Ramírez guitars, but it was his son José III (1922–1995) who took the firm into a glorious age when Ramírez guitars captured the interest of Segovia and became his favorite instruments from the 1960s to the 1980s. José III experimented to meet the exacting standards of players like Segovia, who spurred him on with constructive and even brutal criticism. Innovations he introduced include a new bracing system with extended struts and transverse support; the interior resonating chamber of his "De Cámara" guitars; cedar soundboards from 1965; a new varnish mix that improved protection and sound quality; and the use of a 26-in. (66-cm) string length to improve sound quality and projection. This 1956 model was made in the period between 1952, when José III first met Segovia, and 1960, when Segovia was sufficiently impressed to make Ramírez guitars his guitars of choice after playing Hausers for almost twenty-five years. **GD**

Rickenbacker
Combo 400 1956

D'Angelico
"Teardrop" 1957

Type Twin-cutaway solidbody electric
Body & neck Maple neck with maple "wings"
Fingerboard Rosewood
Pick-ups One single-coil pick-up

Type One-off custom acoustic archtop
Body & neck Maple back and sides, spruce top, maple neck
Fingerboard Ebony

Having created the first electric guitars in the early 1930s, the Rickenbacker name is, of course, etched firmly in the annals of guitar history. But by the beginning of the 1950s, it was a minor player, largely producing electric lap steel guitars. In 1953, former Fender salesman Francis C. Hall bought the company—his aim was to produce an electric guitar to compete with the Telecaster.

The first Rickenbacker solids had appeared in 1954; however it was the 1956 Combo 400 that would provide a design template for the company's guitars over the years to come. A budget "student" instrument, the Combo 400 was notable as the first Rickenbacker to be constructed using a straight-through neck. This production technique was based on a single cut of wood being used for both the center of the body and the neck; the "wings" were glued on separately. This expensive construction technique would become a standard feature on most Rickenbacker models thereafter. **TB**

In the middle of the twentieth century, guitar makers experimented with archtop designs—changing their shape, dimensions, and sound. But no one, at this time, went as far as New Yorker John D'Angelico.

D'Angelico made this one-off guitar for Pete Girardi from Atlantic City band The Teardrops, who wanted something distinctive and paid him $500. The teardrop guitar was based on D'Angelico's New Yorker but with dramatic changes to the body shape that enhanced the guitar both artistically and acoustically.

After years of neglect, Girardi took his old guitar to a White Plains guitar repairman in 1990 to see if it could be brought back to its previous glory. Luckily the repairman, Giuliano Balestra, had been head foreman at Gretsch in the early 1960s. After his expert restoration the Teardrop went on to change hands for increasingly large sums. It was later loaned to the Smithsonian Institution in Washington as an important American historic artifact. The insurers valued it at $500,000, making it one of the most valuable guitars in the world. **SH**

Fender
Precision 1957

Type Double cutaway solidbody electric bass
Body & neck Ash or alder body, bolt-on maple neck
Fingerboard Maple or rosewood
Pick-ups One split "P" pick-up wired as a humbucker

In the early years following its launch in 1951, the Fender Precision established itself as the leading light in a small but growing market. But as the 1950s progressed, competing products from its major competitors began to emerge: the Gibson Electric Bass (1953), the Danelectro UB-2 (1956), and the Rickenbacker 4000 (1957). Leo Fender decided in 1957 to give his bass a radical overhaul.

Several years earlier, the body edging had already gone from a squared Telecaster style to the smooth curve of Fender's popular "deluxe" Stratocaster; now the headstock design followed suit, the original slim line broadened in the manner of its most successful guitar. The pickguard was also styled on the Strat and cut from a single layer of gold anodized aluminum; in 1960 this was replaced with a multilayer celluloid design.

The original necks had been carved from a single piece of maple. These were replaced in 1959 by a rosewood fingerboard glued to the maple neck. This remained standard until the mid-1960s when a maple fingerboard was offered as an option. The original basic single-coil pick-up was replaced with a new split-coil version incorporating staggered pole pieces and wired, to all intents and purposes, as a humbucker.

The Fender Precision is without a doubt one of the most important instruments of the twentieth century and has remained in production ever since. **TB**

Jean-Jacques Burnel of The Stranglers created his unique sound by playing his Fender Precision using overdrive from a valve amplifier and picking the strings close to the bridge saddles; this effect can be heard on the album *Black And White* (1978).

John Deacon played a Fender Precision for much of his career with Queen. →

Gretsch 6122 Country Gentleman 1957

Type Hollow body electric
Body & neck Mahogany body and neck
Fingerboard Bound ebony
Pick-ups Two Filter'Tron humbuckers

The future of Gretsch guitars was set on a new track when Chet Atkins became involved in the development and launch of the 6120 model that bore his name. Although the affable Atkins was well known as "The Country Gentleman," his perfectionist tendencies led to disagreements with Gretsch in the early days of their relationship. He fought hard to tone down the "corny" country cactus-and-cattle décor, but once happy he became the perfect endorsee, rarely photographed without a 6120 in his hands.

The most pressing issue Atkins had with his signature guitar, however, was with the tone and sensitivity of the two DeArmond pick-ups, which he felt responded poorly to his celebrated picking style. Atkins turned to inventor Ray Butts, whom he had met selling amplifiers in Nashville. At the same time as the Gibson's famous PAF was being developed in Kalamazoo, Butts was developing his own twin-coil humbucking pick-up: the Filter'Tron.

The Filter'Tron appeared in 1957, and within a year would become standard on almost all of the Gretsch line. That same year, the 6122 Country Gentleman was added to the Chet Atkins line of models. Another high-end instrument, it featured a bound mahogany body with simulated f-holes and Gretsch's characteristic thumbnail inlays on the bound ebony fingerboard. **TB**

The Country Gentleman himself can be seen playing a Gretsch 6122 on the sleeve of his Top Ten album *Chet Atkins' Workshop* (1961) featuring pop and jazz material, which became the best-selling LP of his career.

Guyatone/Antoria
LG-50 1957

Type Double-cutaway solidbody electric
Body & neck Laminated body with maple top, maple neck
Fingerboard Rosewood
Pick-ups Two single-coil pick-ups

This guitar may not be too many people's idea of a dream instrument, but the Antoria LG-30—and its twin-pick-up sibling the LG-50—are curious relics from postwar Britain.

When rock 'n' roll crossed the Atlantic, there was scant choice for fledgling electric guitarists. An import embargo made top-end U.S. models extraordinarily expensive—if you were even lucky enough to find one. Stepping in to fill this void, a small UK company named J.T. Coppock based in Leeds began importing cheap guitars from the Guyatone factory in Japan. They were stock models, found around the world under an assortment of names, rebadged for the United Kingdom with the Antoria brand.

These were by no means carefully crafted instruments: the action was notoriously high and the sound somewhat thin. But they were available and affordable, and for many British teenagers of the 1950s, like the young Hank B. Marvin, were the only practical way of joining in with the rock 'n' roll revolution. Although Marvin would soon be envied as owning the first Stratocaster to enter the United Kingdom, and later endorsed his own signature Burns guitar, when his band The Drifters first backed Cliff Richard he was still playing his LG-50. The Drifters soon became The Shadows . . . and the rest is history. **TB**

Hank Marvin was still using his Antoria guitar when his band The Drifters backed Cliff Richard on his debut album, *Cliff* (1959). Richard established himself as the United Kingdom's first rock 'n' roll star with this album. It features a live version of the hit "Move It."

Harmony
Newport 1957

Kay
Barney Kessel Pro 1957

Type Solidbody electric
Body & neck One-piece plywood
Fingerboard Rosewood
Pick-ups One single-coil pick-up

Type Single cutaway archtop
Body & neck Maple ply body, spruce top, maple neck
Fingerboard Rosewood
Pick-ups One or two single-coil "Gold K" pick-ups

Harmony introduced the first Newport H42 Stratotone in 1955, when it joined the H44 in the range of solidbody "Electric Spanish" guitars that was its answer to the Fender Stratocaster. Marketed as being "more colorful, lighter to handle, and thinner, too" than the H44, it had stack-mounted Bakelite tone and volume controls (the lower one was the volume) and a simpler one-piece bridge, without the tailpiece, but still no way of adjusting the intonation. The only other control was a slide switch for "bass or treble emphasis." It also had what Harmony described as "chrome-like Harmometal wide edge bindings, with resilient black fluted plastic insert for smartness and protection." (As far as anyone can tell, "Harmometal" is aluminum.)

It came in a choice of two "Colorama colors"— Sunshine Yellow (that was the H42/1) and Metallic Green (the H42/2). In 1957 it retailed for $69.95 plus an extra $8.50 for the C44 carrying case. The same guitar was also marketed with a Silvertone badge. **AJ**

From the 1930s for three decades, Kay built cheap guitars sold in department stores or budget guitars for other manufacturers. But it also made a few high-end instruments. The Art Deco "Kelvinator" headstock was the clue that this was a different type of Kay—even if it was bizarrely named after a brand of refrigerator.

One of its finest was the line of archtops endorsed by jazz guitarist Barney Kessel, featuring his signature on the acrylic pickguard. Kessel, who played a mix of bebop and swing, was voted the world's number one guitarist in many magazine polls in the late 1950s.

The body featured an arched top and back but was made of laminated woods. It was available in sunburst or blond finish and featured either one or two Kay pick-ups, dubbed "Kleenex boxes" at the time, as they rather resembled tissue dispensers.

The Barney Kessel Pro was the smallest model in the line, followed by the Artist and the Jazz Special. At $170, it represented an affordable way into jazz archtops. **SH**

Maccaferri
Islander 1957

Type Six-steel-string acoustic guitar
Body & neck Plastic
Fingerboard Plastic with brass frets
Other features Intricate tuners with aluminum gears

Mario Maccaferri was a big fan of plastic. He had already invented a very usable plastic reed for woodwind instruments, which was endorsed by Benny Goodman. Having already built a range of commercially successful plastic ukuleles, he thought he might pull off the same trick with the guitar. Indeed, when he died he was working on a range of plastic violins, one of which was played at his funeral.

The Islander guitar was made by injecting plastic into a mold. The injection point was then covered with a medallion tailpiece. The neck joins the body in a proper dovetail joint and there are intricate tuners with aluminum gears within the headstock. The sound is thin but surprisingly pleasant.

These guitars are small—about the size of a parlor guitar—and yet despite the plastic neck and fingerboard, they were intended to be serious instruments. Unsurprisingly, the guitars were never much of a hit with professional players and so sales never took off. **SH**

Rickenbacker
Model 1000 1957

Type Solidbody electric
Body & neck Maple body, through-body neck
Fingerboard Rosewood
Pick-ups One single-coil pick-up

Rickenbacker's Model 1000 debuted in 1957 as a student variation of its Combo range, which arrived earlier in 1954. The Combos featured a carved-top semi-solidbody with a glued-in neck. The student version offered a less-expensive solution, but one that was no less complex. Its neck ran through the body, with maple "wings" glued to each side. The tulip-shaped body had stylish twin offset cutaways.

The Model 1000 boasted a single-coil pick-up mounted near the bridge—not the Combos' horseshoe pick-up, but a new, simpler single-coil unit. This was controlled by knobs for volume and tone plus a selector switch, all set on a gold-anodized pickguard.

The Model 1000 was the budget guitar in the Rickenbacker lineup, with a short-scale, eighteen-fret neck. It was joined by the Model 900 with a twenty-one-fret neck and the two-pick-up Model 950. Following a slight reshaping of the body later in 1957, the student guitars continued in production all the way through 1971. **MD**

Rickenbacker
Combo 850 1957

Type Semi-solidbody electric
Body & neck Carved-top maple body, through-body neck
Fingerboard Rosewood
Pick-ups Horseshoe bridge pick-up and "multiple-unit"

The lineage of Rickenbacker's stylish Combo guitar range of 1954 linked back to the pioneering solidbody Ro-Pat-In Frying Pan of 1932. But the Combos were in keeping with most modern electric guitars of the day, setting the direction for Rick over the next several decades.

The Combos were designed by Roger Rossmeisl, who had left Gibson for Rickenbacker in 1954. His inspiration in designing the new Rick electric was likely the new solidbody Gibson Les Paul, released in 1952.

Rickenbacker christened its range the "Combos," since they combined features of the Frying Pan solidbody and Electro Spanish in a new model. The first Combo 600 and 800 models featured an elegant carved-top semi-solidbody with a glued-in through neck. A horseshoe-shaped pick-up at the bridge provided Rickenbacker's characteristic amplified sound.

They were updated as the Combo 650 and 850 with a more graceful, tulip-shaped body in 1957. The 850 boasted a twenty-one-fret neck, and later in its debut year a second pick-up was added at the neck. This smaller pick-up was termed a "multiple-unit" pick-up in Rick catalogs and functioned similarly to later humbucking pick-ups. Controls included a volume and tone knob, and two three-way selector switches, all mounted on the golden plastic pickguard.

The Combo 850 remained in production only until 1959. The small-bodied instruments were soon eclipsed in Rickenbacker's lineup by the thin hollowbody Capri that would become the company's flagship and most famous "look" up until today. Still, the Combo 850's design inspired the Model 325, soon to become famous in John Lennon's hands. **MD**

Rickenbacker
4000 Bass 1957

Type Solidbody electric bass
Body & neck Mahogany body with straight-through neck
Fingerboard Rosewood
Pick-ups Single horseshoe pick-up

For the first six years after Leo Fender's triumphant 1951 launch of the Precision bass, the market he had created was untroubled by any serious competition, until Rickenbacker's 1957 launch of the 4000 bass.

Designed by classically trained luthier Roger Rossmeisl, the 4000 gave the first glimpse of a dramatic new body shape: The smooth contours of the so-called "cresting wave" are now immediately recognizable, but at the time they provided a futuristic contrast with the comparatively lackluster Precision.

The 4000 adopted Rickenbacker's newfound approach to construction, making use of a "straight-through" neck and body-center cut from a single piece of wood (varieties changed over the years), with the upper and lower "wings" fitted separately. This was intended to give the instrument greater levels of sustain than the "bolt-on" approach used by Fender—this is especially evident on the bottom E string. To provide support, the neck was built with a double truss rod.

Electronically, the 4000 was relatively simple, with a single horseshoe pick-up close to the bridge position and a single volume and tone control. The bridge coverplate had an inbuilt movable string mute: In the normal position the strings were able to ring; when moved forward they gave what company president Francis C. Hall described as a "bass viol effect." **TB**

Bassist/vocalist Fred Turner played a Rickenbacker 4000 on Bachman Turner Overdrive's album *Not Fragile* (1974), which featured the classic rock perennial "You Ain't Seen Nothing Yet."

Aldens/Harmony
9908 Tuxedo 1958

Type Hollow body electric
Body & neck Laminated body, hardwood neck
Fingerboard Ebonized maple
Pick-ups One single-coil pick-up

Aldens was a Chicago-based mail-order catalog retailer active from the 1950s until the early 1980s. Unlike Sears Roebuck and other catalog companies that sold guitars, Aldens did not use a specific brand name—the guitars were either unmarked or featured a headstock logo or floral design based around the letter "A." Most Aldens guitars were simply existing stock models produced primarily at the Harmony factory, also in Chicago.

The model shown here was sold in the Aldens catalog as the 9908 Tuxedo. It was built by Harmony, which sold many, many more of this model as the H45 Stratotone Mars. A single-pick-up guitar, it made its first appearance in 1958 and was in production until around 1965. In spite of its appearance, it's not a solidbody instrument but features what the catalog called a "hollow tone chamber construction." It featured an "ebonized maple" fingerboard and a "straight-line hardwood neck with built-in steel reinforcing rod." On the Harmony-branded models, the single tone and volume controls were fitted to the lower part of the body; the Aldens version fits the electrics into the pickguard, and they are rather awkwardly located close to the bridge. The toggle switch mounted alongside the controls allowed the player to flick between "rhythm" and "solo" playing—this was achieved by overriding the tone potentiometer.

This guitar was a notch up from some of the cheap-and-cheerful models found in catalogs at the time, and retailed at $72—an extra $10 getting you a matching carrying case. As an Aldens model, it is rarer and more collectable than its Harmony counterparts. **TB**

Danelectro 4623
Longhorn 1958

Type Hollow body electric bass
Body & neck Pine frame, Masonite top/back, poplar neck
Fingerboard Brazilian rosewood with 30-in. (76-cm) scale
Pick-ups Two single-coil lipstick pick-ups

The Danelectro Longhorn is arguably one of the most unique-looking instruments ever designed by an American guitar manufacturer. Since its introduction in 1958, it has remained among the most popular instruments in the Danelectro lineup. Link Wray was well known for having used the Longhorn. The Who's Pete Townshend played the related Guitarlin and was also an endorsee, making an appearance in the company's 1967 catalog. His bandmate John Entwistle had such difficulty finding replacement strings in the United Kingdom he had to purchase another Longhorn bass each time he broke a string! Entwistle famously used a Longhorn for the groundbreaking bass solo on The Who's classic hit, "My Generation."

There were three official variants of the double cutaway Danelectro Longhorn design offered in the decade it was in production. The 4423 four-string bass, the 4623 six-string bass, and the 4123 six-string Guitarlin with an extended-range thirty-one-fret neck. Other than pick-up spacing, the design of the guitar remained unchanged.

In 1967, Danelectro also produced a hollow-body Longhorn under the Coral brand name, but it is the bass, with its distinctive low-end thud, that remains a popular model in the modern-day Chinese-manufactured reissues. **DT**

John Entwistle famously used a Danelectro Longhorn for the groundbreaking bass solo on his band's debut hit single, "My Generation," featured on the album of the same name, released in 1965.

Danelectro
3412 Shorthorn 1958

Type Hollow body double cutaway electric
Body & neck Pine frame, Masonite top/back, poplar neck
Fingerboard Brazilian rosewood
Pick-ups One or two single-coil lipstick pick-ups

1958 was a transition year for Danelectro and the last year for single cutaway designs. It was also the year Danelectro owner Nathan Daniel met Vincent Bell at the 1958 NAMM trade show. At the time Vincent Bell was an in-demand studio guitarist and jingle writer from New Jersey, and a talented designer and inventor. The two met and discussed each other's designs and ideas. Bell was soon hired on as design consultant, and their business relationship lasted until 1969.

The entire lineup was revamped and the Shorthorn Standard guitar with the new double cutaway body styling made its debut. Retail price was $75 for the single pick-up model and $100 for the double pick-up model. Unlike its single cutaway counterparts, which were available in a variety of custom colors, the new Shorthorn models were available in only two basic colors: black and bronze. Single pick-up models had master volume and master tone controls, double pick-up models had stacked concentric controls. They are otherwise identical in features with a twenty-one-fret neck and 25 in. (63.5 cm) scale length.

Pink Floyd guitarist Syd Barrett often used his black Shorthorn Standard in early publicity photos. Jimi Hendrix owned a 1958 Danelectro Shorthorn he nicknamed "Betty Jean." It was the guitar he asked his father to send to him when he was in the army in 1960. **DT**

Blind Faith, the ill-fated "supergroup" made up of Eric Clapton, Steve Winwood, Ginger Baker, and Ric Grech, produced just one album before their dissolution: *Blind Faith* (1969). Clapton used a Danelectro Shorthorn during this period.

Jimmy Page used a six-string Shorthorn live with Led Zeppelin.

Danelectro
3923 Doubleneck 1958

Type Hollow body electric guitar and bass combination
Body & neck Pine frame, Masonite top/back, poplar necks
Fingerboard Brazilian rosewood
Pick-ups Two single-coil lipstick pick-ups (one for each neck)

The Danelectro 3923 Doubleneck guitar and bass combination is the company's only venture into multineck instruments. Double-necked instruments are nothing new, having been around for at least 200 years. The acoustic harp guitar was one of the earliest forms of multineck instruments. In the 1930s and 1940s, electric Hawaiian lap and pedal steel guitars were all the rage, with two, three, and more necks available. The music industry was blooming; musicians wanted more choices and more sounds to incorporate into their music, and instrument companies were listening.

"Immediately after he plugged it into his rig, he says the Doubleneck spoke to him like no other instrument he's played before or since."
CHRIS KIES OF PREMIERGUITAR.COM, ON GUS SEYFFERT

The 3923 was available through 1966, then it was dropped when MCA took over the company in 1967. It is essentially an enlarged Shorthorn body fitted with both a 30 in. (76 cm)-scale four-string bass neck and a 25 in. (63.5 cm)-scale six-string guitar neck. It was available in Copper Burst and retailed at $175. The hollow body construction resulted in a well-balanced and lightweight instrument. The typical solidbody double-neck can weigh two to three times as much as the Danelectro Doubleneck, which made this a desirable instrument among working musicians. From 1950s recording artists Stan & Dan to Jimmy Page, the Danelectro Doubleneck has made a lasting impression on many. **DT**

Danelectro
4123 Guitarlin 1958

Type Hollow body electric
Body & neck Pine frame, Masonite top/back, poplar neck
Fingerboard Brazilian rosewood
Pick-ups Two single-coil lipstick pick-ups

The first instrument of its type, the Danelectro 4123 Guitarlin stood out uniquely from its counterparts— the Longhorn four- and six-string basses—by virtue of the subtle addition of an extended-range fingerboard: the seven additional frets made the Guitarlin an extraordinary thirty-one-fret instrument. This enabled the player to mimic the sound of a mandolin in the upper range, as well as a double-octave guitar between the first and the twenty-fourth frets. No manufacturer prior to the Guitarlin's introduction had offered such a unique development in design. As always, value was a big consideration in Nathan Daniel's sales philosophy, and the Guitarlin, he suggested, was like getting two instruments in one.

There were several differences in specifications. The pick-up spacing between all three Longhorn variants differed slightly, but they were otherwise almost identical, including the unique bronze and white Sunburst finish, dual concentric controls, a pair of lipstick pick-ups, and the classic "Coke-bottle" headstock profile.

Oddly, this version of the Longhorn series (1958– 1966) did not include a regular six-string guitar, although a few one-off models were produced. In 1967, following MCA's revamp of Danelectro, a Coral-branded Longhorn appeared, although by this time the bodies were hollow with binding and imported from Kawai in Japan.

Pete Townshend of The Who was often seen playing Corals and Danelectros, including the Guitarlin, which he used on stage as well as in the studio— including an early appearance in August 1965 on the seminal British pop TV show *Ready Steady Go!*. Link Wray was another well-known Guitarlin owner and player. **DT**

Epiphone
Crestwood 1958

Type Solidbody electric
Body & neck Mahogany body and neck
Fingerboard Rosewood
Pick-ups Two single-coils (mini-humbuckers after 1961)

When Gibson acquired the Epiphone brand in 1958, the first batch of new models produced were broadly equivalent to those produced by Gibson, only kitted out with what remained of Epiphone's stock of pick-ups and hardware. The solidbody Crestwood stands out as an original design; by this time Gibson had not produced a double cutaway solidbody electric, and the SG—perhaps its closest relative—was still three years away. The Crestwood was the brand's flagship solid—Epiphone's Les Paul, if you will.

Built at Gibson's Kalamazoo factory from similarly sourced materials as Les Pauls, the Crestwood was an outstanding instrument. With its elegant symmetrical cutaway horns and twin New York single-coil pick-ups, the Crestwood looked cool and had a sound to match.

The original Crestwood was only produced until 1959, replaced by the Crestwood Custom. By 1961, the stock of New York pick-ups and their matching "NY" control knobs had been exhausted; in their place were Gibson mini-humbuckers and "reflector" knobs. After 1962, the body shape was reconsidered, with the horns now subtly asymmetrical. A year later, the Crestwood Deluxe appeared, the horns now heavily offset.

As top-of-the-line guitars, the Crestwoods were not cheap to buy. A 1966 price list shows that a Deluxe retailed at $455; the same price as a Gibson SG Custom.

In 2012, Epiphone marked this underrated guitar by issuing a Fiftieth Anniversary Crestwood Custom, an exact replica of the 1962 model—in a limited edition of 1,962. It retailed at under $600—a bargain when you think that a decent original might set you back ten times that amount. **TB**

Vigilante Carlstroem of Swedish garage rock band The Hives sports an original Epiphone Crestwood. →

Epiphone
Sheraton 1958

Type Twin cutaway semi-hollow body
Body & neck Maple center block/wings, set mahogany neck
Fingerboard Rosewood
Pick-ups Two New Yorker humbuckers

The 1950s was a turbulent decade for Epiphone. Once Gibson's bitter rival, whose guitars were among the finest produced in the United States, the long-established family company began to lose its way with Second World War production cutbacks and then the death in 1943 of its driving force Epi Stathopoulo. Taking the helm, his brother Frixo oversaw the creation of the first generation of fine Epiphone electrics, but the company never regained its former position in the market. Compounded by a disastrous workers' dispute, Frixo's death in 1957 spelled the end for Epiphone.

In a twist of fate that would have had Epi turning in his grave, the company was bought out by Gibson, who continued production of some of the more prestigious models, while adding lower-cost versions of existing Gibson designs. This was the case with the Sheraton, which bore a close resemblance to the Gibson ES-335.

Gibson's Epiphones retained some of the brand's characteristic features, such as the Frequensator tailpiece and the New York humbuckers, but as stocks diminished these were gradually replaced by standard Gibson parts, such as Gibson Mini humbuckers.

Production of the Sheraton was discontinued in 1970, but later resumed in the Far East as the identity of the Epiphone brand was increasingly neutered as it became Gibson's de facto diffusion line. **TB**

Ivy Leaguers Vampire Weekend burst onto the global music scene with their debut album *Vampire Weekend* (2008); guitarist Ezra Koenig uses a modern Epiphone Sheraton and his "high-life"-influenced guitar work is central to the band's sound.

Ezra Koenig of New York indie rockers, Vampire Weekend. →

Fender
Jazzmaster 1958

Type Solidbody electric
Body & neck Alder body on original, maple neck
Fingerboard Rosewood
Pick-ups Two single-coil pick-ups

As the 1950s progressed, the rivalry between Fender and Gibson began to heat up. Although Fender's Telecaster and Stratocaster models were dominant of their type, Gibson's hollow body ES range had the jazz market sewn up. The 1958 NAMM trade show saw the launch of a new luxury flagship guitar—the Jazzmaster.

Whatever Fender had intended, this new model was a relatively standard solidbody electric guitar, and certainly unlike the instruments being used by most jazz players. The Jazzmaster was the first Fender designed with an "offset waist" body: unlike guitars such as the Stratocaster, the curves at the waist were not in horizontal alignment, giving the guitar a more modern, streamlined look. Other touches included a floating vibrato with locking mechanism and an overlong arm.

As far as the tone of the guitar was concerned, the newly designed pick-ups created a very un-Fender-like sound. Instead of the single-coils found on Strats and Teles, the Jazzmaster's soapbar pick-ups were wound flat and wide. This enabled a range of sounds from classic single-coil to Gibson-style warmth, to the pianolike mellow tones popular with jazz players. Although Joe Pass had a brief fling, the Jazzmaster almost completely failed to reach its target audience, but instead found a home among the emerging guitar instrumental and surf bands. **TB**

On most of The Cure's early work, like the band's debut *Three Imaginary Boys* (1979), frontman Robert Smith played one of his two Fender Jazzmasters; he named them "Black Torty" and "White Torty."

J. Mascis of Dinosaur Jr.—a big Jazzmaster fan. ➡

Gibson
EB-2 1958

Type Semi-hollow double cutaway four-string bass
Body & neck Laminated maple body, mahogany neck
Fingerboard Rosewood
Pick-ups One single-coil pick-up (humbucker from 1959)

The EB-2 was Gibson's bass version of the ES-335 six-string, with a similar semi-hollow body. It also featured a short-scale neck and was available at first only in sunburst or cherry red. There was only one pick-up with a volume and tone control.

The bass was improved after its launch. Within a year, a "choke" switch was added, which boosted or cut the bass frequencies. Also, in 1959, the original single-coil pick-up was replaced with a fat "Sidewinder" humbucker and in 1966, a smaller humbucker was added in the bridge position for the EB-2D model.

Over time, the brown plastic pick-up cover became black, then chrome; the banjo-style machine tuning pegs were replaced by proper Kluson machine heads; and the simple nonadjustable bridge was replaced with a fully adjustable one. But the appeal of the guitar remained—it was lightweight compared to solid basses and the short-scale neck was easier for fast runs.

The EB series soon became popular with professional bassists. Jimmy Page played one with The Yardbirds, Brian Cole of the Californian folk-rock group The Association used an EB-2 at the Monterey Pop Festival in 1967, and other users included Bob Lang of the British pop group The Mindbenders, pop star Suzi Quatro, Jethro Tull's Glenn Cornick, and Robert Levon Been of west-coast rockers Black Rebel Motorcycle Club. **SH**

Chas Chandler of The Animals, who later discovered Jimi Hendrix and was Slade's producer, used an EB-2 throughout most of his bass-playing career, including using one on the worldwide hit "The House Of The Rising Sun" from *The Animals* (1964).

British 1960s beat group The Animals, with Chas Chandler on Gibson EB-2 bass. ➡

Gibson
ES-335 1958

Type Semi-hollow electric
Body & neck Maple body, mahogany neck
Fingerboard Rosewood
Pick-ups Two humbuckers

During the 1940s, it was the drive to eliminate the feedback problems of amplified acoustic guitars that led Paul Bigsby, Les Paul, and Leo Fender down the path of creating electric instruments with solid hardwood bodies. Some players felt that these guitars lacked the warmth of tone traditionally associated with hollow-body instruments. Presiding over the Gibson corporation from 1950 to 1966—without doubt the company's golden age—one of Ted McCarty's many enduring legacies was an attempt to find a middle ground: the solution was the ES-335.

Launched in 1958, the Gibson ES-335 was an important landmark in guitar body design, although one that perhaps harks back to Les Paul's Log (see page 121). It was neither hollow nor solid: running through the center of the body was a solid maple block, with a pair of hollow maple side "wings" attached. The maple laminate top features two f-holes opening out of each of the hollow chambers. The unusually slim body was complemented by a comfortable neck and a cutaway that gave easy access to the twenty-second fret.

Introduced at a time when Gibson's electric guitars were struggling in the market, the ES-335 became a major seller. It has been in continuous production ever since, proving to be a versatile instrument at home in any musical scenario, from jazz and blues to heavy rock. **TB**

Roy Orbison was one of the ES-335's earliest takers, and the instrument was used on many of his peerless hit records of the 1950s and 1960s. Every home should own one of Orbison's many *Greatest Hits* collections, such as the one at left.

← Noel Gallagher of Oasis wields his ES-335.

Gibson
ES-345 1958

Type Semi-solid electric
Body & neck Maple body, mahogany/maple neck
Fingerboard Rosewood with double parallelogram inlays
Pick-ups Two Gibson humbucker pick-ups

The Gibson ES-345 and ES-355 were both introduced in 1958 as deluxe versions of the hit ES-335 model. The ES-345 was the first Gibson to feature a Stereo-Varitone switch—located just above the lead tone and volume knobs. This six-position switch was designed by Gibson's Walter Fuller.

The first commercial stereo records were also released in 1958—Gretsch's response was the "Project-O-Sonic"—its Country Club model with split Filter'Tron pick-ups. Gretsch split its pick-ups into bass and treble sides that could be placed in a stereo image via two

> *"It was an actual tone control circuit that removed certain frequencies from the pick-ups, and it could be any of the pick-ups."*
>
> **GIBSON'S WALTER FULLER ON HIS SIX-POSITION SWITCH**

amps, but the Gibson system used on the 345 was simpler, using a special Y lead to send the output of the neck humbucker to one amp and the bridge humbucker to another. Other differences between the ES-345 and ES-355 included a small crown headstock inlay instead of the split-diamond on the 355 and double Parallelogram instead of block position markers.

The ES-345 remained in Gibson's catalog until 1981 when it was effectively superseded by the Lucille model. During this time it went through various changes. In 1965, its stud tailpiece was changed to a trapeze tailpiece; an optional vibrato—either a Bigsby or Gibson Deluxe Vibrola, which was standard on the ES-355—was also an option. The ES-345 is currently available once again (msrp: $5,410). **DB/AJ**

Gibson
ES-355 1958

Type Semi-hollow electric
Body & neck Maple body, mahogany neck
Fingerboard Ebony
Pick-ups Two humbucker pick-ups

Two months after the launch of the celebrated ES-335 came its high-performance counterpart, the ES-355. It was, proclaimed Gibson, their "wonder-thin silhouette."

The best-known version of this model was the ES-355TDSV which featured stereo circuitry and a six-way "Varitone" control—a sophisticated piece of passive circuitry that enabled six different preset notch filters to be switched in. The ES-355 had the same construction as the 335, yet the advanced electrics and sumptuous gold-plated hardware made it substantially more costly.

During Gibson's so-called "Golden Age" of the late 1950s, products often seemed to miss their intended markets: the new thinline ES models were described in Gibson advertising as jazz guitars, but were rarely used as such; and, of course, it would be another decade before the solidbody instruments they produced in the late 1950s would start to interest young rock musicians.

The ES-355 is best known for its use by electric bluesmen, and in particular B.B. King, whose legendary black guitar he christened "Lucille." As with any relationship, there were teething problems: as much as he loved the sound and feel of his guitar, it was prone to feedback on stage. His solution was to deaden the sound box by stuffing a towel into the f-hole. In 1968, as a tribute to King, Gibson launched the Lucille model with, at King's request, the f-holes removed! **TB**

One of the most celebrated marriages in guitar history, B.B. King so loved his ES-355 that he named his 1968 album *Lucille* in her honor. The album begins with the title track, a ten-minute spoken word ode to his famous guitar.

Gibson
Explorer 1958

Type Solidbody electric
Body & neck Single cutaway korina body, set korina neck
Fingerboard Rosewood
Pick-ups Two PAF humbucker pick-ups

Ted McCarty presided over Gibson during what would be the most innovative and exciting period in the company's history—a time that saw the introduction of many models for which the Gibson brand is rightly revered. The Explorer was the second of McCarty's bold new "modernistic" designs, a brother to the Flying V and Moderne designs—guitars intended to dispel Gibson's slightly conservative image.

Unlike any preceding guitar, the Futura featured a dramatic angular body shape, its heavily extended treble horn counterbalanced by a similar protrusion at the opposite corner of the body. The headstock design was also unusual, its V-shape housing three tuners on each "leg." The sound came from a pair of PAF (Patent Applied For) pick-ups designed in-house in 1955 by Seth Lover—these were the first humbucking pick-ups. Shortly before the Futura went into production in 1958, McCarty—who had designed the new shapes—rechristened it the Explorer, and the headstock was quickly replaced by a drooping "hockey stick" design that would strongly influence the 1980s Superstrats.

McCarty's new line was a spectacular failure. The Moderne never reached production and the Explorer and Flying V were discontinued within a year. Although Gibson's production records are sketchy, it's estimated that less than fifty original Explorers were built. **TB**

Original Explorers are so rare and valuable that they are seldom used in performance. The most high-profile player is The Edge (David Evans) of U2; much of the 2000 album *All That You Can't Leave Behind* features the sounds of a Gibson Explorer.

U2's The Edge onstage with his Explorer in 2001. →

Gibson
Flying V 1958

Type Solidbody electric
Body & neck Korina body, korina/mahogany neck
Fingerboard Rosewood or ebony
Pick-ups Two humbucker pick-ups

As the 1950s progressed, it was becoming increasingly clear that as far as solidbody electric guitars were concerned, the venerable Gibson corporation was perceived to be falling behind the young upstarts at Fender—a company barely a decade old. The Gibson Les Paul may now be viewed as one of the iconic electric guitars, but when it first appeared it struggled to find a place in this newly evolving market. Company president Ted McCarty responded by developing a series of conspicuously modern instruments, and in 1957 filed patents for three unusual new designs: the Moderne, the Flying V, and the Futura.

The Flying V, with its space-age looks, was the first of McCarty's new "modernist" line of instruments. He certainly succeeded in producing a distinctive, futuristic guitar, the likes of which had not been seen.

The body of the Flying V prototype had been built from mahogany. This was not only very heavy and poorly balanced but expensive to produce. Instead, the lighter and more readily available korina was used.

It was a design too far ahead of its time; demand for the initial Flying Vs was poor, with dealer orders of less than 100 during 1958. It lasted barely a year in production. And yet the Flying V enjoyed a renaissance in the 1960s, and was played by the likes of Jimi Hendrix and The Kinks. Production resumed in 1967. **TB**

Bluesman Albert King, a major influence on Stevie Ray Vaughan, was the only notable guitarist to adopt the Flying V when it was launched. It can be heard to spectacular effect on his debut album *The Big Blues* (1962).

Gibson
Les Paul Junior 1958

Type Solidbody electric
Body & neck Mahogany body, mahogany neck
Fingerboard Rosewood
Pick-ups One single-coil P-90 pick-up

After four years as the most successful of Gibson's single cutaway Les Pauls, the budget student model was given a cosmetic overhaul. All of a sudden, it was made visually very distinct from the rest of the range, with a cutaway horn on the bass bout.

The rest of the guitar remained unchanged: mahogany body and set mahogany neck with a rosewood fingerboard. Still in place was the single P-90 "dog-ear" pick-up with a single volume and tone control, as were the standard colors: Sunburst, Ebony, TV Yellow, White, and Red. Also unchanged was the basic wraparound bridge with its limited adjustability.

The "double cut" Les Paul Junior has never exactly been fashionable but has remained a popular model. It certainly captured the imagination of a young Paul Reed Smith when he was designing his early PRS guitars: "It took me two years to draw that body shape, which is somewhere between a Strat and a Les Paul Junior, if you look at it really ... It's like, when you're in a band the first thing you do is cover songs, and then eventually you write your own music. It's the same thing ... this [the PRS guitar] is a song."

In 2012, Gibson produced a signature "double cut" Les Paul Junior for Billie Joe Armstrong of Green Day, complete with a skull and crossbones decal on the scratchplate. **TB**

Martin Barre used a 1958 Les Paul Junior on much of Jethro Tull's album *Aqualung* (1971)—a classic of British progressive rock—and is referenced by Ron Burgundy during his infamous "jazz flute" solo in the film *Anchorman* (2004).

Gibson
Les Paul Standard 1958

Type Solidbody electric
Body & neck Mahogany body/neck, maple top
Fingerboard Rosewood
Pick-ups Two Gibson PAF humbucker pick-ups

The Gibson Les Paul was a guitar born out of necessity. The company had first sent Les Paul packing when he tried to interest them in the potential of his solidbody Log guitar: "They laughed me out of the place," he later said. They were equally dismissive of the first Fenders, reputedly claiming that "anyone with a buzz saw" could build one. But when appreciation of the Telecaster began to gather momentum, they felt compelled to respond: in 1952, the sparkling gold Les Paul appeared. But after six years of production and several makeovers, the Les Paul had still not gained much of a foothold in the market. There was one final revamp in 1958, when a more sober sunburst Les Paul appeared. Produced until 1960, only around 1,700 of these Standards were built before it was abandoned to make way for the twin cutaway Les Paul—shortly afterward rechristened the SG.

Of course, this turned out to be far from the end of the story. During the 1960s, a new generation of young electric blues musicians began to discover the potential of the Les Paul, and prices for secondhand Standards began to rise. In 1968, Gibson revived the Les Paul and it has since become nothing less than an iconic instrument.

Original Les Paul Standards have since taken on a mythological status, and, on the rare occasions they come up for auction, they will inevitably sell for six-figure sums. **TB**

The guitar shown here was played by Peter Green during his early days with UK blues/rock pioneers Fleetwood Mac. The instrument can be heard on their acclaimed debut album *Fleetwood Mac* (1968).

← Peter Green of Fleetwood Mac playing his Les Paul in 1968.

Gretsch 6118 Anniversary 1958

Type Single cutaway hollow body electric
Body & neck Laminated maple body, maple neck
Fingerboard Bound ebony, rosewood after 1960
Pick-ups Twin-coil Filter'Trons (HiLo'Trons from 1960)

To mark the seventy-fifth birthday of the Fred Gretsch Music Company, in 1958 a budget model was launched. Taking the 6120 Chet Atkins shape, the appropriately monikered Anniversary models were available with one or two pick-ups, and offered either in a sunburst finish or a gorgeous two-tone "Smoke Green."

Although a good deal lower in price than the 6120 models, the early Anniversaries were not vastly different in tone or playability from their better-known siblings. The range was, however, severely downgraded during 1960 when the classic Gretsch humbucking Filter'Tron pick-ups were replaced with cheaper single-coil HiLo'Trons. Shortly afterward, the unbound ebony fingerboard was replaced with cheaper rosewood. The Anniversary remained in production until 1975.

In 1990, a year after the Gretsch name was reacquired by the family, a new twin-pick-up Smoke Green Anniversary was launched, this time a high-end Japanese-built instrument with a price tag pushing $3,000. **TB**

Gretsch 6193 Country Club Stereo 1958

Type Hollow body archtop electric
Body & neck Maple body, spruce top, maple neck
Fingerboard Ebony
Pick-ups Two "stereo" Filter'Tron pick-ups

"Stereophonic" was a magic word in the 1950s, offering a vision of a brave new world of binaural sound. Gretsch led the way among guitar makers in developing a stereo guitar, thanks to the Brooklyn company's chief "idea man," guitarist Jimmie Webster.

Webster easily adapted the Filter'Tron humbucking pick-ups created by Ray Butts, splitting the windings in half so there were two sets of windings per pick-up. The "stereo" sound here thus was simply a splitting of the guitar's signal: the top three strings' sound came out of one speaker, the bottom three strings' out of another.

Gretsch proudly promoted its pioneering stereo function as the grandly titled Project-O-Sonic system. It was offered on the firm's flagship models, the Country Club and White Falcon, with ads proclaiming that the "guitars open up a whole new world of sound!"

It was a sonic world that Gibson and Rickenbacker both rushed to catch up with, but stereo guitars were a fad that soon faded. **MD**

Hagstrom
P46 Deluxe 1958

Hagstrom/Goya
"Sparkle" Bass 1958

Type Single cutaway solidbody
Body & neck Birch celluloid-covered body, birch neck
Fingerboard Pearloid
Pick-ups Four single-coil pick-ups grouped into pairs

Type Single cutaway electric four-string bass
Body & neck Birch celluloid-covered body
Fingerboard Pearloid
Pick-ups Two Hagstrom pick-ups

By the time this beautifully kitsch P46 Deluxe emerged in 1958, the Swedish Hagstrom company was already well established as one of the first large-scale producers of electric guitars outside the United States.

Based in the town of Älvdalen, Albin Hagstrom opened his factory in 1933, quickly gaining a name across Europe for producing high-quality accordions. This heritage is very apparent on the early Deluxe models, which feature the same distinctive sparkle and pearloid celluloid finish that was used to decorate his accordions.

Clearly modeled on the Gibson Les Paul, the most remarkable feature of the top-of-the-line P46 Deluxe was its unorthodox pick-up assembly. Among the earliest production-line guitars to sport four pick-ups, the complex switching system gave the P46 an unusual degree of sonic versatility, with selection achieved through the six push-button switches, providing numerous combinations of the four single-coil pick-ups. **TB**

The Goya name on a headstock was used by a number of different manufacturers over the years, all hoping to make their instruments sound more exotic.

This bass comes from the era when Goya was a name given to models made by the Swedish Hagstrom company. Previous Goyas had been made by Levin and later in Italy, Korea, and Japan, and some Goyas were labeled "Futurama" for sale in the United Kingdom.

Hagstrom had found that the expertise acquired through building accordions (their original main line) was easily and effectively transferable to the construction of electric guitars.

This was Hagstrom's first attempt at a bass guitar. The plastic-coated guitar used a short-scale neck with Hagstrom's "Speed-O-Matic" fretboard (covered with decorative Plexiglas). The neck was strengthened by the unique Hagstrom H-shaped truss rod.

U.S. importers Hershman thought buyers would be deterred by the name Hagstrom so labeled most of them Goya instead. **SH**

Harmony
H71 Meteor 1958

Type Thin hollow body electric
Body & neck Laminated maple body, maple neck
Fingerboard Hardwood
Pick-ups Two DeArmond pick-ups

In the 1910s and 1920s, Harmony of Chicago was the king of American guitar makers, accounting for more than half of all instruments produced and sold. By the 1950s and 1960s, it was producing instruments for numerous other makers as well as mail-order giant Sears Roebuck. At its peak in the mid-1960s, Harmony sold almost 1,000 budget and student guitars a day.

At the top of the Harmony line was the Meteor. The thin hollow body electric was a solid guitar with all the required features of the day, although lacking the cachet of the better-known prestige brands.

"Here you have a top of the line …
The ultra-thin Meteor electric [is] the
most comfortable-playing 'big guitar' yet."
1958 HARMONY CATALOG DESCRIPTION

The first version featured a single cutaway body highlighted by two stylish f-holes. The neck joined the body at the fourteenth fret, and boasted a full twenty-one frets. There were two DeArmond pick-ups controlled by a volume and tone knob. As Harmony's catalog promised, these guitars had "Maximum Electronics."

The Meteor was initially offered in two models. The H71 was natural-finish whereas the H70 wore a sunburst scheme. The Meteor line changed with the times, and the first versions were followed by a double cutaway model with a body mimicking the outline of Gibson's famed ES-335. The H71 double-cut came with a vibrato while the H61 had a solid tailpiece. The H75 and H77 were three-pick-up variants. Similar Meteors were sold by Sears as Silvertone models. **MD**

Kay
Solo King 1958

Type Solidbody electric
Body & neck Masonite body, maple neck
Fingerboard Rosewood
Pick-ups One or two single-coil pick-ups

In the period before electric guitars really took off, manufacturers were very experimental in their designs. Kay was responsible for more than its fair share of strange guitars at this time.

Universally known as "The State of Ohio Guitar," the Kay Solo King is many players' nomination for the ugliest instrument ever made. And the body shape not only mimics the mapped shape of the American state, it is cut from Masonite, a pressure-molded wood-fiber composite board. It's a lightweight, cheap material that was also used on some early Danelectro

> "The guitar has a nice, fat tone that's perfect for blues and quirky rock projects … it's such a trip to look at."
>
> **WILL RAY, FOUNDING MEMBER OF THE HELLECASTERS**

guitars, but is nevertheless considered an economy too far by most players.

The very thick-set neck has brass frets but no truss rod so the only way of adjusting the action is the simple archtop-style bridge, which raises and lowers but has no way of fine-tuning the intonation. There are two controls—volume and tone—in the speckled formica pickguard and one or two single-coil "pancake" pick-ups. The one pick-up version sold for $75; the two pick-up model for $95.

Kay built the guitar for two years, but it was sometimes sold under the name "Old Kraftsman." Whatever brand it sold under, the Solo King was regarded as a beginners' guitar and disappeared by 1960. Only recently has it begun to be prized by collectors. **SH**

Resonet/Futurama
Grazioso 1958

Type Solidbody electric
Body & neck Beech body, beech neck
Fingerboard No separate fingerboard
Pick-ups Three single-coil pick-ups

A semi-autonomous branch of the Henri Selmer company of Paris, Selmer UK was founded in 1928 and by the end of the 1930s it had become Britain's largest music company. The emerging popularity of skiffle and then rock 'n' roll during the mid-1950s suggested a business opportunity importing cheap electric guitars and basses into the UK and rebadging them as one of Selmer's own brands. The Futurama name was applied to many such instruments obtained from Europe and the Far East. The Resonet launched the range.

The Resonet hailed from the city of Blatná in Czechoslovakia. The state-owned Drevokov Cooperative mainly produced furniture, but in 1955 was also instructed to produce guitars. Although electric guitars produced in the Eastern Bloc were generally of poor quality, the Resonet Grazioso—as it was named at the factory—was no such thing. Dismantling a Fender Stratocaster, the aim was to "design" an instrument that featured certain improvements—this was surely true of the re-engineered vibrato system, which was more advanced and reliable than those found on Fenders at that time. At a time when trade embargoes effectively prevented the sale of the classic American models, the Resonet retailed at £55—the equivalent of around $1,000 in today's currency—making it then one of the most expensive guitars on the UK market. **TB**

George Harrison's first electric guitar was a Resonet, and he used it on his debut recording sessions, including on Tony Sheridan's "My Bonnie" (1961), the single that brought The Beatles to the attention of future manager Brian Epstein.

A seventeen-year-old George Harrison (right) on stage during The Beatles' Hamburg period. →

Rickenbacker
325 1958

Type Solidbody electric
Body & neck Mahogany body, set mahogany neck
Fingerboard Ebony fingerboard
Pick-ups Three PAF humbucker pick-ups

The first of the 1958 Capri range, the Rickenbacker 325 is a small-bodied, semi-hollow instrument with a three-quarter-scale length. It was designed by Roger Rossmeisl, a guitar craftsman from a family of German instrument makers. It would have remained a minor instrument in history were it not for John Lennon. During one of The Beatles' club residencies in Germany, he bought the 325 from a Hamburg music store, then played it almost exclusively during the heady days of Beatlemania.

Lennon's 325 was one of the first to come off the production line in early 1958—one of only four exported to Germany—and was something of a rarity. At first, Lennon's guitar had no sound hole; this feature was added to production models to indicate that it was not a cheaper solidbody instrument. It also had double the number of volume and tone controls found on subsequent models. Lennon's original 325 had a number of adjustments, including a black paint job applied by British guitar manufacturing legend Jim Burns in 1962, and a rewiring that disconnected the center pick-up so that the central position on the selector switch would blend the two active pick-ups.

Lennon eventually owned four 325s and was partly responsible for Rickenbacker's elevation to one of the most desirable guitar brands of the 1960s. **TB**

Until 1965, and the recording of the *Rubber Soul* album, John Lennon had used the Rickenbacker 325 on virtually all of the band's recordings; he would later become more closely associated with the Epiphone Casino.

← In 1964, at the height of Beatlemania, John Lennon takes to the stage with his modified 325.

Rickenbacker
450 1958

Type Solidbody electric
Body & neck Maple body, straight-through maple neck
Fingerboard Rosewood
Pick-ups Two single-coil pick-ups

Rickenbacker had debuted with its solids in 1954: these were the first instruments to feature the "swoosh" logo on the truss-rod plate—a design created by the wife of company president Francis C. Hall.

In 1958, a new Rickenbacker body design appeared: gone were the distinctive "tulip" cutaways of guitars like the Combo 450; in their place was a new body shape that came to be known as the "Cresting Wave." The single-pick-up model 425 was launched at the same time as its upmarket, twin-pick-up counterpart, the 450.

The 450 was Rickenbacker's first real solidbody hit, and went through a number of changes until its eventual discontinuation in 1984. Three years after its launch it was given a slimmer body, and a year later, the metal pickguard that covered much of the body was replaced with thick white plastic, which became an important part of the Rickenbacker look in the 1960s.

Throughout the mid-1960s Rickenbacker offered twelve-string versions of many of its models, and in 1964, the 450-12, shown here, appeared. Produced in very small quantities it is somewhat rarer than the classic 360-12, although not deemed as desirable by collectors.

In 1968, the 450-12 could optionally be fitted with Rickenbacker's crazy "comb," which at the push of a lever disengaged one of each of the pairs of strings so it could be used as a six-string guitar. It didn't really work. **TB**

Curiously, Fred "Sonic" Smith of the U.S. agitprop band the MC5 used a Rickenbacker 450-12, but set up as a standard six-string guitar. It can be heard on *The Big Bang: The Best Of The MC5* (2000).

Fred "Sonic" Smith of the MC5 with his "six-string" 450-12. →

Supersound Short-Scale Standard 1958

Type Solidbody electric
Body & neck Pine body, mahogany set neck
Fingerboard Rosewood
Pick-ups Two Supersound Hi-Fi single-coil pick-ups

In 1958, British amplifier maker Supersound decided to explore the idea of making solidbody electric guitars, which were still very scarce in the United Kingdom. Jim Burns had already built some six-strings of this type, so Supersound boss Alan Wootton enlisted his services to help with design and handle the woodworking side, while the company completed the production process. One of Burns' earlier efforts would become the Supersound Ike Isaacs Short-Scale model, but this was preceded by the more basic Short-Scale Standard solidbody, with both instruments employing a compact and jazz-friendly 23-in. (58.4-cm) scale length.

Supersound chose pine for the Standard's slim-depth body and this boasted a larger, less curvy single cutaway outline than the Ike Isaacs model, featuring unusual, flat-bottomed lower bouts that would resurface on some later Burns designs. The end result was quite chunky, although front and back contouring increased the creature-comfort quota, with this shaping again being similar to that seen on certain subsequent Burns models. The guitar featured two single-coil Hi-Fi pick-ups, while other hardware was equally own-made, such as a basic bar bridge and an even simpler tailpiece.

Although crude in comparison to well-established American equivalents of the era, the Supersound Short-Scale Standard was still an adventurous six-string, being the United Kingdom's first production solidbody electric. That said, few were made before those involved went their separate ways and, obtained via the family of the late Alan Wootton, this one is the only known, fully functioning survivor from those trail-blazing times, adding rarity value to historical importance. **PD**

Supersound Single-cutaway Bass 1958

Type Solidbody electric bass
Body & neck Mahogany body, mahogany set neck
Fingerboard Rosewood
Pick-ups One Supersound Hi-Fi single-coil pick-up

Having commenced construction of solidbody electric guitars in 1958, UK company Supersound went a step further by adding four-string equivalents that same year. This was an even bolder move, because although semi-acoustic basses were already on sale, the solid version was then almost unheard of in the United Kingdom. Knowledge was limited, but Supersound's Alan Wootton and Jim Burns came up with the design by studying a borrowed Fender Precision bass—a virtually unknown and unavailable instrument in the United Kingdom, as the postwar import embargo on American products was still being enforced.

The result actually bore little resemblance to Leo Fender's famous four-stringer. Instead it partnered a shorter-scale (30½-in./77.5-cm) set neck with a quite conventional, single cutaway body—although the lower body adopted a distinctive flattened outline. These features remained on subsequent examples, but a more curvy, sharply pointed horn hinted at some later Burns designs. The revised design still employed a traditional headstock with standard guitar tuners, but to obviate any doubt, a confirmatory "Bass Guitar" logo adorned the black scratchplate. The latter carried one single-coil, sited in the same position as the Precision's pick-up and, in terms of this location, the SCB was arguably the only four-string to follow Fender's lead at that time. The same didn't apply to other hardware, because a simple, single-bar bridge accompanied an equally basic, block-type tailpiece.

Despite its deficiencies, the Supersound SCB was a very important and innovative instrument from the formative era of the modern UK music industry. **PD**

Vega
SE385 1958

Type Solidbody electric
Body & neck Spruce and maple body, mahogany neck
Fingerboard Rosewood
Pick-ups Two single-coil pick-ups

The Vega Company dates back to the 1880s in Boston, Massachusetts, where it first built guitars and brass instruments. In the 1930s, it made decent-quality archtop guitars that were highly rated by jazz guitarists, but by the 1960s was mainly known for its long-necked five-string banjos. After it was taken over by C.F. Martin & Co. a decade later, Vega guitars were produced in Holland for a while.

The Vega SE385 is a successor to the mid-1950s E-400/401. The 400 had the same trapezoid tailpiece but, like many of the earlier Vega guitars that used the

> *"The only guitar that will give you full tone two ways—with or without the amplifier."*
>
> **VEGA BROCHURE**

unique "Duo-Tron" floating pick-up system, the volume and tone knobs were sitting on top of it. On the SE385 there is a volume and tone control for each pick-up in a more conventional position on the scratchplate. The pick-ups are covered by oblong metal plates, superficially resembling the appearance of humbuckers, but there are actually large single-coil pick-ups underneath.

The SE385 retains the odd-looking lyre-shaped metal bars that run between the tailpiece and the bridge pick-up—there are then two straight bars connecting the two pick-ups, and the neck pick-up is suspended just short of the neck. The Duo-Tron system keeps the pick-ups out of contact with the top of the body, both maintaining the purity of the signal and not interfering with the acoustic sound of the instrument. **AJ**

Watkins
Rapier 1958

Type Double cutaway solidbody electric
Body & neck Jelutong body, teal neck
Fingerboard Rosewood
Pick-ups Three single-coil pick-ups

It was 1957 when Charlie Watkins' brother Reg—after both had spent years developing and manufacturing amps with names such as Clubman and Dominator—suddenly decided, according to Charlie, that he "fancied having a go at making guitars." So they got busy in their workshop in Chertsey, Surrey, producing what would be the United Kingdom's second solidbody guitar (beaten into second place by just a few weeks by the Dallas Tuxedo). Then came the revolutionary Copicat Echo Unit, which sold hundreds of thousands, and in 1967 the first Watkins Electric Music P.A. system.

> *"My mum bought me my first guitar, which was a Rapier 33, which I still own to this day. I'll never part with it."*
>
> MICK HERBERT, RAPIER OWNER

These developments in sound technology made WEM an enormous force on the British music scene.

Rapier electrics debuted in 1958 and continued in production until the late 1970s. The Rapier Deluxe (1958–59) had an almost symmetrical body, predating the characteristic Strat shape to come. The Rapier 33 was first released in 1963 with beefy, slanted middle pick-ups, four-positioned selectors, and red paint right up to the headstock. Some were white, but these have tended to go cream with age, and the polyester is prone to cracking, although the necks have aged well thanks to metallic internal bracing. Reg Watkins sympathized with "lefties" and about 10 percent of Rapiers—the so-called "poor-man's Strat"—were made for left-handers. **BS**

Broadway
BW2 1959

Burns Short-Scale
Deluxe 1959

Type Solidbody electric
Body & neck Mahogany body and neck
Fingerboard Rosewood
Pick-ups Two Henry Weill pick-ups

Type Solidbody electric
Body & neck Mahogany body, oak top; mahogany neck
Fingerboard Rosewood
Pick-ups Two Besson Electone single-coil pick-ups

Broadway was a brand name used by British guitar dealer Rose-Morris, usually on imported instruments. But this distinctive solid electric from around 1960 was actually built in London.

It was rather a primitive attempt—the body was a crudely shaped plank of solid wood, usually with a sunburst finish and cream pearloid scratchplate. Some models had a split scratchplate featuring a turquoise section housing the volume and tone controls. The BW1 had one pick-up; this BW2 had two. These pick-ups were made by German immigrant Henry Weill in the basement of his London house.

Unusually, the name Broadway was stenciled across the upper bout of the body while the headstock was left blank.

This particular model was fitted with a Framus engraved tailpiece that allowed players the chance to add vibrato by pressing the plate with their palm. Like many unusual vibrato systems, this one was equally adept at putting the guitar out of tune. **SH**

This was one of the earliest instruments built by Jim Burns and among the first solid six-string guitars made in the United Kingdom. It was similar to the short-lived Supersound "Ike Isaacs Short-Scale" model introduced in late 1958. By then Supersound had severed connections with both endorsee Isaacs and Burns, but undeterred, the latter independently produced around twenty guitars based on his previous design.

However, the split from Supersound forced a few changes, plus some necessary improvisation. The circuitry was simplified, while the pick-ups that replaced Supersound's single-coils were actually intended for archtop acoustic guitars—likewise the wooden bridge and metal tailpiece. Other features stayed the same, such as the semi-solidbody, complete with carved oak top and a cream plastic panel forming the back.

This guitar confirms Burns' position as the pioneer of the British solidbody, because the market for such electrics didn't exist in the United Kingdom at the time, and no other maker had considered catering for it. **PD**

Burns-Weill Fenton Bass 1959

Burns-Weill Super Streamline Bass 1959

Type Solidbody electric bass
Body & neck Mahogany body, mahogany set neck
Fingerboard Rosewood
Pick-ups Two Weill single-coil pick-ups

Type Solidbody electric bass
Body & neck Sycamore body, sycamore set neck
Fingerboard Rosewood
Pick-ups Two Weill single-coil pick-ups

Although Supersound had terminated his employment, Jim Burns continued to pursue his guitar-building career. A search for suitable pick-ups brought him into contact with Henry Weill, who ran a London-based electronics business and also manufactured amplifiers. The two men accordingly established a partnership early in 1959 and soon produced electric instruments bearing the Burns-Weill brand name.

The Fenton was the least-expensive model, with styling that imitated popular solids being imported from the Far East at that time. The six-string Fenton was similarly small-sized, but the bass boasted a bigger body to partner a short-scale (29½ in./75 cm) set neck. The example shown features a rare rosewood fingerboard, since most Fentons employed lacquered sycamore, plus red position dots made from knitting needles! Along with the necessary pick-ups and controls, the scratchplate carried a contrasting-color mini pickguard and this became a cosmetic trademark of many instruments made by both Burns and Weill. **PD**

The partnership between Jim Burns and Henry Weill led to a line of guitars and basses being launched in May 1959, under the appropriate Burns-Weill banner. Most models in this new range employed radical body styling that evoked instant love-or-loathe reaction, with the latter opinion soon earning them the nickname "Martian Cricket Bats." Despite this somewhat derisive description, the basses in particular proved popular with players, perhaps because solid four-stringers were still quite thin on the ground in the United Kingdom in 1959.

Like its six-string stablemate, the angular Super Streamline bass employed an almost Art Deco-design headstock. This topped Burns' preferred short-scale (29½ in./75 cm) set neck, while fingerboard timber was either sycamore or rosewood, with the former featuring knitting-needle-derived red position dots. The body's geometric shape was complemented by an equally non-curvy scratchplate and this carried twin single-coil pick-ups, governed by a comprehensive array of controls that included a bass boost/cut slide switch. **PD**

Dallas
Tuxedo 1959

Danelectro 5015
Convertible 1959

Type Single cutaway solidbody electric
Body & neck Mahogany body and neck
Fingerboard Rosewood
Pick-ups One or two Henry Weill pick-ups

Type Hollow body acoustic/electric
Body & neck Pine frame, Masonite top/back, poplar neck
Fingerboard Brazilian rosewood
Pick-ups Optional individual single-coil lipstick pick-ups

The first mass-produced solidbody electric in the United Kingdom was designed by Dick Sadlier, who was well known at the time for writing instrument tuition books.

Unusually, the pickguard was clear plastic, sprayed black on the underside. Other features include the solid one-piece mahogany body turned out by a furniture factory and electrics made by German Henry Weill in his London basement.

One of these crude-looking guitars was found in the attic of John Lennon's home in Liverpool after he left. No one has been able to confirm that it was actually John's guitar, but it seems likely that it was his.

It may even have been the guitar that it is rumored he stole from another band at a Carroll Levis talent contest in Manchester. Whatever the history of this guitar, the Tuxedo was later exhibited in The Beatles Story museum in Liverpool, United Kingdom, and then auctioned in 2012 at Bonhams. The Tuxedo, plus two old banjo magazines and part of Lennon's childhood tree house, fetched £4,375. **SH**

The ultimate in versatility, the idea behind Danelectro's Convertible was to offer the novice student the option of an amplified model (#5005) or acoustic model (#5015) in the same instrument. Students could purchase the acoustic version and later upgrade to the amplified version by purchasing the optional owner-installed pick-up kit for an additional $20.

Early production Convertibles had a slightly thicker body and a single screw holding down the tailpiece. That quickly transitioned to a two-screw tailpiece mount and a slightly thinner body thickness. From 1959 until 1967 the double cutaway Convertible featured Danelectro's characteristic three-on-a-side "Coke Bottle" style headstock with vertical decal logo. From 1967 until production ceased in 1969, there were a number of notable changes including new color choices (red and blue) and a six-in-line headstock layout with a raised faux-chrome plastic "Danelectro" script logo. Nathan Daniel wanted to provide beginning students a low-cost alternative, and the Convertible was exactly that. **DT**

Epiphone
Rivoli 1959

Framus
Hollywood 1959

Type Semi-hollow short-scale bass
Body & neck Maple body, mahogany neck
Fingerboard Rosewood
Pick-ups One single-coil/humbucker pick-up

Type Semi-solid electric
Body & neck Semi-solid maple body, set maple neck
Fingerboard Bound rosewood
Pick-ups One, two, or three Framus single-coil pick-ups

Gibson bought out the Epiphone company in 1957 and the Rivoli bass of 1959 was the first instrument to set the pattern of the new relationship between the two brands. It was almost identical to the Gibson EB-2 bass—a short-scale, semi-hollow bass that was a four-string match for the ES-335 guitar.

Like the Gibson equivalent, the Rivoli started with one single-coil pick-up but quickly evolved into having a humbucker, then two humbuckers. It was available in natural or sunburst, then later in cherry red. Likewise, the simple banjo-style tuners became standard open-back machine heads and the bridge became more sophisticated over the years. Like the Gibson, the Rivoli featured a switch to boost or cut the bass frequencies.

The Rivoli was a cheaper alternative to the Gibson and became more popular in Europe than the United States. Chas Chandler of The Animals played one, as well as his EB-2, and Rivolis saw service in bands such as The Tremeloes, The Who, Herman's Hermits, Freddie and the Dreamers, The Yardbirds, and The Walker Brothers. **SH**

Framus began building solidbody electrics in 1958 with the Hollywood range. Like other European brands, the guitars looked solid but were in fact of semi-hollow construction—true solidbody versions came later in the 1960s, by which time the Framus factory, split over two sites in Bubenreuth and Pretzfeld, Germany, was considered the largest in Europe.

Both single and double cutaway versions were produced. The single cutaway aped the outline of the Gibson Les Paul; the symmetrical double-cutaway guitar's "flat" horns gave it a Melody Maker vibe. Either one, two, or three Framus pick-ups were offered, often with some unusual control switches, and various bridge styles and vibrato-equipped models were produced.

One of Framus' high-profile endorsees was German jazz guitarist Billy Lorento. He became known, after moving to the United States, as Bill Lawrence—one of the world's most respected pick-up makers. Both the Hollywood and the Billy Lorento model have recently been reintroduced by Framus. **DB**

Framus
Star Bass 1959

Type Solidbody electric
Body & neck Mahogany top/back, maple sides/neck
Fingerboard Bound rosewood
Pick-ups Two four-pole pick-ups on a metal scratchplate

In the 1950s, bass guitars were still largely the province of American manufacturers, in particular Fender and its iconic Precision model. As the Precision was too expensive for many budding bassists, there was a clear demand for a cheaper model, and at the end of the decade, the German manufacturer Framus came into the British market to supply that demand.

Its Star Bass might not have made more than a minor impact, however, had it not been for the rise of rock 'n' roll and R&B, and in particular the emergence into the public eye of The Rolling Stones. Their bassist Bill Wyman endorsed the Star Bass for three years from 1964, a period in which the impact of "beat" music resounded throughout the Western world. Exposure for the Framus brand was immense thanks to the huge amount of TV airtime afforded to the Stones and other Star Bass users such as Jet Harris, Brian Locking, and Heinz Burt. A hollow-bodied bass with an extremely narrow neck (a mere 1¼ in. [3 cm] at the nut!), the Star Bass also featured a short-scale 30½-in. (77.5-cm) neck and weighed only five pounds.

American endorsers included Charlie Mingus and Jim Hall, but the Star Bass made its home primarily in the United Kingdom and Europe, although by the end of the 1960s its future was in doubt thanks to extensive competition and the fortunes of the parent company. **JM**

Heinz Burt of The Tornados was an early user of the Star Bass, and can be heard on *Ridin' The Wind: The Anthology* (2002). Under the guidance of producer Joe Meek, Burt relaunched his career as a pop singer, enjoying modest success in the early 1960s.

Brian Jones and Bill Wyman of The Rolling Stones relax ahead of a 1964 TV recording.

Gibson
ES-330 1959

Type Thinline hollow body electric
Body & neck Maple/rosewood body, set mahogany neck
Fingerboard Rosewood
Pick-ups Two P-90 single-coil pick-ups

After the successful launch of the ES-335 family of thinline semi-acoustics in 1958, Gibson introduced a cheaper alternative in the form of the ES-330 the following year. With the neck set deeper into the body (joining it at the sixteenth fret), it lacked the solid maple internal center block and was supplied with two single-coil pick-ups. A single-pick-up model, the ES-330T, was also available until discontinuation in 1963.

Like its big brother the ES-335, the earliest ES-330s featured pearl dot fingerboard inlays, replaced with rectangular pearl blocks mid-1962. The pick-ups initially had black plastic covers but by the end of 1962 had been replaced with nickel-plated metal ones, remaining until production ceased in 1972. Most were supplied in Gibson's sunburst finish, though natural finish was offered until 1962 when a cherry alternative replaced it. In common with all Gibson semi-acoustics, a factory-fitted Bigsby vibrato unit was also available at extra cost.

Late in 1963, the body pattern of Gibson's thinlines altered slightly, with the rounded "Micky Mouse ears" double cutaway now being slightly more pointed in appearance. Not that this affected sales; the ES-330 proved hugely popular with musicians and artists across the entire musical spectrum of the 1960s, from jazz to folk, pop, and beat, and the only drawbacks from a playing point of view were limited access to the upper frets, and a tendency to feed back even at moderate playing levels. But its twin sister, the Gibson-manufactured Epiphone E-230T Casino—identical in construction and wiring—found favor with The Beatles and The Rolling Stones' Keith Richards, exemplifying the sound of the pre-Hendrix "Beat Boom" as a result. **DG**

Gibson Les Paul Melody Maker 1959

Type Solidbody electric
Body & neck Mahogany body, set mahogany neck
Fingerboard Rosewood
Pick-ups Two single-coil pick-ups with plain plastic covers

Gibson launched the Melody Maker in 1959, aimed at beginners and priced accordingly. Similar in appearance to the Les Paul Junior but less deep and with a thinner headstock, it featured a single pick-up, with input socket, tone, and volume controls mounted on a black plastic plate carrying the name "Melody Maker" in white print. It was also available with a shorter, three-quarter-length scale. It was an immediate success, and in its first year of production, over 3,000 guitars were shipped.

The following year saw some changes, including the introduction of the two-pick-up Melody Maker D, the pick-up being redesigned with a narrower bobbin. In 1961, the body shape changed to a double cutaway, and in 1962 the layout of the controls was rearranged in a diamond pattern. A Maestro vibrato unit was also offered as an option; note the model pictured—from March 1963—features an early version of Gibson's improved Vibrola unit, complete with Epiphone arm, and set farther behind the bridge than is usually seen.

The following year, the body was again slightly altered, retaining its shape until 1966 when the model was completely revamped in the popular chamfered SG style. Offered in a choice of colors, with a third pick-up option and even a twelve-string version available, it continued to appear in the catalogs until 1971, when it was replaced by the SG-100 family of electrics.

The Equals' rhythm guitarist Pat Lloyd was seldom seen without his D in the 1960s, though despite huge production numbers, the Melody Maker enjoyed few professional endorsements. Pat Travers and Joan Jett also favored mid-1960s models, albeit hot-rodded with humbucking pick-ups. **DG**

Kay
K5965 Pro Bass 1959

Magnatone
Mark V 1959

Type Semi-hollow electric bass
Body & neck Laminated maple body, set neck
Fingerboard Rosewood
Pick-ups One single-coil pick-up

Type Semi-hollow electric
Body & neck Maple
Fingerboard Rosewood
Pick-ups Two Alnico VI single-coil pick-ups

Advertised as an all-new "electronic" bass, the Kay Pro originally debuted as model K-162 in the 1952 Kay catalog, a companion to the model K-161 Thin Twin guitar. Despite its rather old-fashioned appearance, this was a very innovative model when originally introduced: aside from the totally obscure Paul Tutmarc's Audiovox bass and the upstart Fender, which debuted its Precision model a year earlier (in 1951), this Kay was the very first electric bass guitar offered by a major American manufacturer.

It featured an unusual semi-hollow construction without f-holes and had the same blade-style single-coil pick-up that was used on the Thin Twin guitar. One famous early user was Andrew "Blueblood" McMahon, who played bass with Howlin' Wolf. Because of this, the Kay Pro bass is sometimes also called the "Howlin' Wolf" model. The K-162 was renumbered in 1959, to K5965. The pictured example is an early K5965 from 1959 and has a non-original bridge and knobs. **EP**

Paul Bigsby was a rather cool 1950s dude who designed motorcycles for Crocker and posed for photos on his bike looking like an extra from a James Dean movie. He was also into guitars and helped build some of the earliest electric guitars, which were conceptualized by Merle Travis. Bigsby also designed the first vibrato unit that still bears his name.

Amplifier makers Magnatone hired him to design guitars for them in California, too. The top of this line was this Mark V, a classic piece of styling of the era. The solid body had routed chambers, but the central spine ran from the set neck right through the body, giving great stability and rigidity. The two new clean and bright Alnico pick-ups and Bigsby's own tremolo system made this a superbly specified guitar that was aimed purely at professional players.

The rarity, style, and history of the Mark V have made it one of the great treasures of the guitar world with today's collectors paying up to $10,000 for a good example. **SH**

Marma Solidbody Electric 1959

Type Solidbody electric
Body & neck Hardwood body, set neck
Fingerboard Ebony
Pick-ups Two Relogg pick-ups

When this Marma guitar was designed, few people in Germany had any set ideas about what a solidbody electric guitar should look like. The earliest electrics were introduced in Germany only about a decade earlier, when Wenzel Rossmeisl exhibited his pick-ups at the Leipzig Fair (c.1947).

Hollow body guitar production was well established in Germany, and most early electrics produced there in the 1950s tended to be electrified archtops. It is hard to imagine today just how bizarre and futuristic the modern solidbody "planks" would have appeared to traditional guitarists. This Marma—an acronym for "Musikhaus am Rhein in Mainz"—still appears rather bizarre and retro-futuristic. The guitar sports a bright, flashy red finish, large block fingerboard markers, a set neck, a simple floating wooden bridge, and multilayered binding. Controls are simple and logical: master volume, master tone, and a four-way rotary selector (bridge, bridge + neck, neck, and off). The fanciful shape, of course, is the instrument's most unique feature. **EP**

Vega 1200 Stereo 1959

Type Electric acoustic archtop
Body & neck Spruce top, maple back/sides, mahogany neck
Fingerboard Rosewood
Pick-ups Six treble-string pick-ups, six bass-string pick-ups

Vega was not the only maker to have split pick-ups in order to capture a stereo sound, but with its twelve pick-ups, the 1200 Stereo model was perhaps the most audacious. This is one of the most curious pick-up configurations one is likely to come across. There are six round treble-string pick-ups meant to be served by one amplifier and six round bass-string pick-ups meant to be served by a second amplifier. Apart from this curiosity, there is nothing specifically to commend this guitar over many other midrange archtop guitars of the period, and certainly not its looks—with that cluster of pick-ups and its ungainly pickguards, it is something of an ugly duckling.

Since the late 1800s, Vega was best known for its banjos. It also made a wide range of guitars and some very fine acoustic archtop guitars during the 1930s, but the quality of its instruments progressively declined from the 1940s until 1970 when it was bought by C.F. Martin & Co. with the intention of producing banjos. It didn't last long: by 1979, Martin had sold the brand. **GD**

1960s

Burns
Vibra Artist 1960

Type Solidbody twin cutaway
Body & neck Mahogany body, set maple neck
Fingerboard Rosewood
Pick-ups Three single-coil Tri-Sonic pick-ups

In 1959 the Burns-Weill company had produced two guitars: the Guyatone-inspired Fenton and the bizarrely shaped Super Streamline. But the working relationship between Jim Burns and Henry Weill floundered swiftly and both embarked on their own paths.

Burns quickly regrouped, launching in 1960 his own line of guitars beginning with three models: the Sonic, the twin-pick-up Artist, and this flagship design, the Vibra Artist. Visually speaking, the Vibra Artist was something of an oddity, its small twin cutaway body featuring a pair of curiously asymmetrical horns. Most

"The Vibra Artist's attributes were reflected in an asking price of £78, which was about a third more than that of the earlier Artist."
GUY MACKENZIE, THEGUITARCOLLECTION.ORG.UK

striking, however, was the appearance of what could be argued as the first two-octave fingerboard to be found on a production guitar; the treble cutaway gave very easy access right up to the twenty-fourth fret.

This first Burns line also saw the first appearance of the Tri-Sonic pick-up. These were unique in that the coils were held rigidly in position, making them less prone to feedback. There were three Tri-Sonics fitted to the Vibra Artist with multiple switching and dedicated volume and tone controls for each one, providing plenty of scope for creating very specific tones.

Burns guitars were not exactly in competition with their American counterparts, and retailing at £78, the Vibra Artist would have represented a considerable investment for most young musicians. **TB**

Epiphone
Sorrento E452TD 1960

Type Thinline hollow body archtop cutaway electric
Body & neck Maple top, back, and sides; mahogany neck
Fingerboard Rosewood fingerboard, pearloid oval inlays
Pick-ups Two PAF mini-humbucker pick-ups

The Epiphone-built Sorrento E452TD, modeled on the Gibson equivalent ES-125TDC, was manufactured between 1960 and 1969, generating modest sales and never coming close to the popularity of other Epiphone thinline models, such as the Casino or Sheraton. It was reissued with P90 pick-ups and some other modifications as the Sorrento ES-930J in 1993 and ran until 1997. In 2012, the Sorrento E45TDN, now equipped with a pair of Gibson USA mini-humbuckers, was one of three guitars reissued in Epiphone's 1962 50th Anniversary Collection.

> *"Even if this … archtop wasn't named after one of the most beautiful towns in the world, it would still be a guitar of exceptional allure."*
> WUNJOGUITARS.COM

The Sorrento's specification is superior to Gibson's ES-125TDC, coming with mini-humbuckers, individual Kluson Deluxe tuners, fancy fingerboard markers, and a Tune-o-matic bridge. The cherry finish of this example was an option from 1967. The Sorrento had its best sales from launch to 1966. Sales fell sharply afterward. It was the same story for most other Epiphone guitars, as cheaper foreign-made copies made big inroads into the market, taking over 40 percent of market share. The Sorrento was one of the casualties of this market war when Gibson moved Epiphone production to Japan in 1970.

Original Epiphone Sorrento models are now something of a rarity; only 2,631 were built during the decade in which they were produced. **GD**

Fender
Jazz 1960

Type Solidbody bass
Body & neck Ash or alder body, maple neck
Fingerboard Rosewood or maple on original
Pick-ups Two single-coil pick-ups

Leo Fender created a gradual musical revolution when he introduced the Precision bass in 1951; by the end of the 1950s, the electric bass guitar was a standard component of any rock 'n' roll band. The Precision may have been ubiquitous, but as the decade progressed, a number of challengers emerged with an eye on Fender's corner of the market. The most notable of these was the Rickenbacker 4000, with its bright, versatile sound, and a design and construction that made the Precision seem rather crude.

In 1960, Fender launched a deluxe bass; and just as the Precision had been modeled on the Telecaster (and after the 1957 redesign, the Stratocaster), sporting an elegant offset-waist body shape, the Jazz partnered Fender's new flagship model, the Jazzmaster.

As far as playing was concerned, the biggest difference between the Jazz and its precursor was the narrow width of its neck, which Leo Fender believed would appeal to jazz players, who at this time were still largely tied to their upright "bull fiddles." The Jazz featured a pair of newly designed single-coil pick-ups, each with two pole pieces per string. This produced a stronger treble, richer midrange, and tighter bass sound.

The Jazz has been in production ever since, and, along with its elder sibling, it remains one of the most popular bass guitars ever built. **TB**

Flea of the Red Hot Chili Peppers has been a frequent user of Fender Jazz bass guitars since the mid-1980s. *Californication* (1999) is the band's biggest-selling album, shifting 16 million units worldwide.

Flea of the Red Hot Chili Peppers on stage in 2004 at the Take Back the Senate concert. →

Galanti
Grand Prix 1960

Gibson
Hummingbird 1960

Type Solid-frame electric bass
Body & neck Mahogany body, maple neck
Fingerboard Rosewood
Pick-ups Two or three single-coil pick-ups

Type Dreadnought-style steel-string acoustic
Body & neck Mahogany back and sides, sitka spruce top, mahogany neck
Fingerboard Ebony

In the 1950s, the popular fashion for accordions started to fade as people switched to the exciting new electric guitar, so many accordion manufacturers started making guitars instead.

In Chicago, Frank Galanti started importing electric guitars made in his family's accordion factory in Italy. The construction quality was very good and the electrics used push-buttons like an accordion to vary the sound using different pick-up combinations.

With no sparkly pearloid in sight, the Galanti's looks were less accordionlike than some of its rivals'. The Grand Prix was considered a professional-quality guitar, especially in Italy.

The twin cutaway body was carved mahogany; the bolt-on neck maple with a curved two-piece matched rosewood fingerboard. Individual enclosed tuners were by Van Ghent, but the bridge and tremolo were Galanti's own design with wheels and screws for fine adjustment. One unusual feature was an "off" button, which killed the output of all the pick-ups. **SH**

It was Gibson's main rival in the acoustic guitar market, C.F. Martin and Co., who introduced the first Dreadnought model in 1916. Named after a famously oversized British battleship, the term described a guitar with a larger and deeper body shape than usual.

Introduced in 1960, the Hummingbird was Gibson's first Dreadnought designed in a "square-shouldered" style—with a horizontal upper bout that joined the neck at a perpendicular angle.

A typically high-end Gibson instrument—only the J-200 had a higher price—the back and sides of the original models were constructed from mahogany, typically giving off a warmer tone than the maple used on cheaper models; like many expensive acoustic guitars, the top was carved from sitka spruce.

The Hummingbird has remained in production but has seen many fundamental modifications, in materials used, internal bracing, and in recent years, an electro-acoustic option. However, models produced before 1968 are held in the highest regard by collectors. **TB**

Guild
DE-500 1960

Type Hollow body electric
Body & neck Maple/spruce body, mahogany/walnut neck
Fingerboard Ebony
Pick-ups Two DeArmond humbucker pick-ups

Forget about Andrés Segovia or Chet Atkins. At the turn of the 1960s, if you were to ask anyone to name the world's best-known guitarist, there would have been only one answer: Duane Eddy. As a player he was nothing special, and yet he enjoyed a string of worldwide hit records that all followed the same simple formula—a catchy melody played on a twangy guitar.

In 1960, Duane Eddy became the first rock 'n' roll musician to be honored with a signature guitar. Guild produced two Duane Eddy models, the DE-400 and the upscale DE-500. Both were luxury instruments crafted from the finest woods and kitted out with gold-plated hardware and a pair of specially built DeArmond humbuckers, designed to re-create Eddy's hallmark clean tone, which had previously been achieved using Gretsch and Danelectro models.

Better known for its flat-top acoustics, Guild struggled after the end of the 1960s folk boom. In 1995, the Guild brand was brought under the wing of the mighty Fender corporation. **TB**

Guild
Starfire III 1960

Type Hollowbody electric
Body & neck Mahogany or maple body, mahogany neck
Fingerboard Bound rosewood
Pick-ups Two DeArmond single-coil pick-ups

An upmarket development of the 1958 T-100D "Slim Jim" model, Guild introduced its Starfire range in 1960 with three variants: single pick-up I, two pick-up II, and two pick-up with "Bigsby True Vibrato" III. Like all of the company's electrics of the period, they were aimed at the jazz market, but would find favor with many pop musicians throughout the 1960s.

The guitars were manufactured with either maple or mahogany laminated bodies, with most of the latter finished in dark cherry. Many of these featured a top veneer of sapele, which had a striped appearance. There was no binding on the back of the body until mid-1962.

Guild initially fitted a unique DeArmond pick-up to the guitar, with adjustable screw pole pieces. By 1961, this had been replaced by DeArmond Dynasonics with white plastic tops, until 1963 when Guild's own chrome-covered humbucker was introduced. A Guild-branded Bigsby unit was introduced in 1961 to prevent unscrupulous dealers fitting their own Bigsby B3s to the cheaper Starfire II models and marking up the prices. **DG**

Harmony
Rocket H59 1960

Type Hollow body electric
Body & neck Maple/hardwood body, maple bolt-on neck
Fingerboard Rosewood
Pick-ups Three DeArmond single-coil pick-ups

Harmony's Rocket series comprised of three models; the single-pick-up H53 and two-pick-up H54 had already been in production for a year when the three-pick-up H59 "knobby special" arrived in 1960. The company's huge market base consisted mainly of beginners and students, lured by the "bang-for-buck" value of instruments delivering good looks, ease of playing, and a great sound.

Much of their sound lies in the DeArmond "Gold Tone Indox" pick-ups, top-quality windings made by Rowe Industries in Toledo, Ohio. Not designed to be overdriven, instead they produce a clear, well-defined, perfectly balanced signal that belies their flimsy appearance. Mounted on rosewood plinths of varying depth according to their location, the output wires run under the pickguard to a selector lever that activates each individually or all three simultaneously. A wide range of tones is available, from a warm jazz texture near the neck, to the general-purpose pop-and-roll of the center and the rockabilly twang by the bridge.

The neck incorporates a nonadjustable steel reinforcement rod, and feels very comfortable, though the frets are often uneven and not always finished well. The strings cross a floating rosewood bridge and are fixed at the rear to a tinny trapeze-style anchor. But at $140, the top-of-the-line H59 was still a bargain that today's collectors are discovering, if recent auction prices are anything to go by.

Though popular on the 1960s beat scene, the Rocket had few professional endorsers, the most notable being the teenage Steve Winwood during his early days with The Spencer Davis Group. **DG**

Steve Winwood playing his Rocket H59 in 1960. →

Höfner
Galaxie 1960

Type Solidbody electric
Body & neck Obeche body, maple neck
Fingerboard Rosewood
Pick-ups Three single-coil pick-ups

During the 1960s, Höfner was one of the largest manufacturers of electric guitars in Europe. These instruments hardly rivaled the big U.S. names in quality, but at a time when genuine Fenders were thin on the ground outside of the United States, models like the Höfner Galaxie provided a reasonable alternative, and were a notch above most of the Japanese imports.

Like many well-established European guitar makers, Höfner evolved from an altogether different instrument-making tradition. Karl Höfner was a violin maker who founded his company in Schönbach, Germany, in 1887. He established a reputation not only for craftsmanship but also innovation; later joined by his two sons, Josef and Walter, by the 1920s Höfner was the largest German manufacturer of stringed and fretted instruments.

Höfner's first efforts in the guitar market were low-key and aimed at providing low-cost models for students and children. It was not until the 1950s that any serious attempt was made at producing upmarket archtop acoustics and solidbody electric guitars and basses.

The early Höfner electric guitars were usually variations on twin-cutaway Fender themes—typically Strats and Jaguars—with the Galaxie range first appearing in 1960. The biggest departure from the American models, however, lay in an unusual array of controls. Eschewing the more usual single selector, the Galaxie featured three single-coil pick-ups, each with its own on/off switch and embedded rotary tone wheels. The overall sound was shaped by a single master volume and tone control. Some later Galaxies also featured "Rhythm"/"Solo" switching, enabling players to boost volume for playing lead parts. **TB**

← Johnny Hallyday pictured playing his Höfner Galaxie in 1964 during his military service.

Meinel and Herold
Solidbody Electric 1960

Roger
Model 54 1960

Type Twin cutaway electric
Body & neck Pearloid-covered body, mahogany neck
Fingerboard Rosewood
Pick-ups Two single-coil pick-ups

Type Thinline hollow body electric
Body & neck Solid top, back, and sides; set hardwood neck
Fingerboard Rosewood
Pick-ups Two single-coil pick-ups

Even behind the Iron Curtain, it seems as though every kid was strumming a guitar by the end of the 1950s. Importing a guitar from the West was generally out of the question, so some built their own (sometimes using parts from vandalized public phone boxes). The really lucky ones were able to afford one of the guitars built in the Soviet bloc.

This guitar emerged from the unlikely rock 'n' roll outpost of East Germany in 1960. The wooden body is completely covered in a pearloid plastic. The body is stenciled with the Meinel and Herold logo, although that company was the distributor for a group of manufacturers. This model most likely hails from an East German manufacturer like Musima or Migma, whose electric two-pick-up model it closely resembles.

These guitars featured a distinctive fretless section at the highest end of the fingerboard. Other features included the chunky bridge/tailpiece featuring a tremolo arm, a bare headstock, and plastic-covered pick-ups. **SH**

The Roger brand is by Wenzel Rossmeisl, a German maker of mostly high-quality archtop guitars from the 1940s, though by the mid-1950s he needed to diversify into instruments for a new musical era, as in this rare thinline hollow body Model 54, resembling a Fender Esquire but with softer curves. Economics of the time also dictated cheaper production methods. Gone is the "German Carve" archtop for which he and his son Roger are renowned, although it is suggested by the sunburst finish.

The years immediately following the Second World War were difficult for Germany and its businesses before the 1948 Marshall Plan to boost Western European economies. By 1950, the WR workshops were bankrupt. Roger left for the United States in 1953, taking with him skills from the rich German heritage of guitar making and also his father's formative influence, and would become a leading maker at Rickenbacker and Fender. Wenzel stayed in Germany and restarted the business in 1954, branding it Roger after his departed son. **GD**

Rosetti
Lucky Squire 1960

Type Electric acoustic archtop
Body & neck Laminated body, bolt-on neck
Fingerboard Rosewood finish
Pick-ups One single-coil pick-up

Most of us remember with fondness our first romances, our first cars, and—if guitarists—our first guitars, no matter whether they were pieces of junk or first-rate. The Lucky Squire, made by Egmond in the Netherlands and distributed in the United Kingdom with the Rosetti label was undoubtedly in the first category, but it enabled musicians like Gary Moore to get started. He called it "a horrible guitar" and he must never have tired of telling how its back fell off when playing it at one of his earliest gigs. George Harrison started out with the parlor-style Rosetti 276 from the Egmond Toledo series, then the cheapest guitar around. Thanks to the astronomic value of Beatles memorabilia, it was sold at auction in 2003 for £276,000. Brian May still has the Egmond Toledo he started with. Egmond also manufactured a cutaway version of the Lucky Squire with pickguard and two pick-ups called the Lucky 7. These guitars are today collectible as period pieces and by association with famous musicians, though it is hard to imagine anyone playing them seriously. **GD**

Silvertone
1444 1960

Type Hollow body electric bass
Body & neck Pine frame, Masonite top/back, poplar neck
Fingerboard Brazilian rosewood
Pick-ups One single-coil lipstick pick-up

Designed and built by Danelectro exclusively for Sears Roebuck, the Silvertone model #1444 bass was as "no frills" an instrument as you could get. Introduced in the company's 1959 Fall/Winter catalog, it was the first electric bass to be sold by Sears. It was priced at $79.95 with terms offered at $8 down and $8 a month. Keeping in line with the budget-conscious philosophy of both Sears and Danelectro, the 1444's features were a simple-but-elegant mixture that included a jet-black finish, a single cutaway hollow body, master volume and tone controls wired to a single chrome-encased lipstick pick-up, a clear Plexiglas pickguard with reverse-painted perimeter outline, and a horizontally placed raised faux-chrome plastic script logo. The Silvertone model has a four-in-line "Dolphin" shaped headstock, distinguishing it from the "Coke Bottle" headstock profile of the Danelectro branded instruments. The tuners varied between Kluson Ideal open-backs, Kluson Deluxe, or Skate-Key style on later instruments. **TD**

Robert Bouchet
Classical Guitar 1961

Type Classical guitar
Body & neck Spruce top, Brazilian rosewood back and sides, ebony fingerboard, domed soundboard
Other features Torres-like bracing system

First taking up guitar making in his late forties, painter, art professor, and amateur guitarist Robert Bouchet (1898–1986) made a total of some 150 guitars in his small apartment in Montmartre, Paris. His guitars soon became sought after by the world's greatest guitarists including Emilio Pujol, Alexandre Lagoya, Ida Presti, and famously, Julian Bream, who had three made for him. Bouchet guitars would also become extremely valuable: one of his guitars from 1964 sold at auction for $122,500 in 2009, a world record at the time.

Bouchet worked slowly and methodically, making some of his own tools and even his own French polish to improve the build process. He was a great admirer of the Spanish tradition of guitar making and in particular of Torres, from whom he initially adopted an identical seven fan braces system, later experimenting with five braces and other variations. An important innovation was a transverse bridge bar beneath the bridge and spanning the width of the guitar's lower bout. This is credited with enhancing the instrument's dynamic range and sustain, and also helps to reinforce the thin soundboards he preferred.

Julian Bream described the second guitar Bouchet made for him as "an absolute pearl. It had a beautiful sound, and a sustaining quality throughout its whole register rather like a small eighteenth-century organ." **GD**

On *Popular Classics For Spanish Guitar* (1964) Julian Bream plays ten well-known masterpieces of Spanish and Brazilian repertoire on Bouchet guitars. These are benchmark interpretations, imbued with total mastery of style, phrasing, articulation, and tone production.

Broadway
Plectric 1961

Type Solidbody electric
Body & neck Mahogany body and neck
Fingerboard Rosewood
Pick-ups One or two single-coil pick-ups

The Broadway Plectric was a product of the prolific Guyatone factory in Japan. British importers Rose Morris came up with the Western-friendly name "Broadway." The major British guitar retailer of the time was Bell of Surbiton, who produced catalogs allowing budding pop stars to buy instruments by mail order. It marketed the Plectric to a generation of guitar beginners at around £20.

There were two different models: the Plectric 1921 had one pick-up; the two-pick-up model was the 1922. Both were available with the basic Broadway tremolo

"A fine ... guitar beautifully finished in a deep maroon colour. High-fidelity single pick-up and controls ... Amazing value for such low cost."
BELL MUSICAL INSTRUMENTS CATALOG, 1963

arm as an option. This chrome-covered unit was made in the United Kingdom and fitted on the guitar's arrival.

Other budget features were the black Bakelite knobs, open-backed tuners with white plastic buttons, and a white plastic truss rod cover nailed in place ... because there was no truss rod underneath. The only way of adjusting playability was by raising or lowering the simple saddle bridge, which had a thumbwheel at either end. Yet the basics were good: the body and set neck were solid mahogany, there was a large Fender-style headstock, and the oversized single-coil pick-ups created a suitably 1960s jangly sound.

One Plectric oddity was that they were fitted with a mini jack socket; not the standard ¼-in. (6-mm) jack used by almost every other electric guitar on Earth! **SH**

Burns
Bison 1961

Type Solidbody electric
Body & neck Sycamore body, maple neck
Fingerboard Ebony
Pick-ups Four Ultra-Sonic single-coil pick-ups

Jim Burns is a legendary name in the British guitar-making world. A great innovator—he has been described as "The British Leo Fender"—he was simultaneously a terrible businessman—a man whose vision focused almost wholly on the product at the expense of balancing the books. How else can we account for the production in 1961 of a luxury instrument that cost £157 at a time when the average Briton earned under £10 a week—and the young men who might have wanted such a guitar, considerably less? With its striking body shape, the sharply pointed horns providing its name, the narrow six-in-line headstock with its unique underside "bat wing" profile, solid black paint job, and contrasting gold hardware, the Bison was a vision of opulence, appearing at a time when Britain was still feeling the pinch of postwar hardship.

The Bison certainly cut no corners as far as hardware was concerned. It was kitted out with four Ultra-Sonic pick-ups that Burns had commissioned from Goldring—a British company well-known for producing high-quality hi-fi cartridges; these were wired into Burns' versatile "Split Sound" circuitry. It also featured a custom-built "Boomerang" vibrato arm. And finally, playing adjustments could be made using Burns' "Gear Box" truss rod concealed in the neck heel.

Impractical to manufacture, just forty-nine examples of the original four-pick-up Bison were made before a successful cheaper, simplified redesign was introduced. But the original remains a legendary British guitar; indeed, a reasonable case could be made for claiming the Bison as the first truly great electric guitar to be produced outside of the United States. **TB**

Eko
700 1961

Type Solidbody electric
Body & neck Mahogany body, maple neck
Fingerboard Rosewood
Pick-ups Four single-coil pick-ups

Love them or hate them, the early Italian solids have a look all of their own. The shapes are sleek and sexy, the colors all vibrant sparkles, and the hardware and electrics often pretty unorthodox. OK, so they didn't sound so great and were hell to play, but does that matter so much when they look so cool?

Like Hagstrom in Sweden, the main Italian guitar manufacturers emerged from the world of the accordion. Almost entirely based around the Adriatic coastal town of Castelfidardo, Italy's accordion builders struggled first with the impact of the Second World War, and then a decade later with the advent of rock 'n' roll. Oliviero Pigini was the first of his peers to introduce guitars, taking over his uncle's accordion factory in 1959 and bringing experienced luthiers to the region. By the mid-1960s, his Eko was Italy's most significant guitar brand.

The 1960 Eko 400 Ekomaster was the first Italian electric guitar of any note and was used by many of Italy's fledgling rockers. A year later, this morphed into the 700 series—probably the single most celebrated electric guitar line produced in mainland Europe.

A unique vision, the 700 sported an unusual third cutaway at the bottom of the body, and had the sparkle finish used on accordions produced in the region. Pigini had developed a thick plastic coating for Eko guitars—although seemingly chiefly as a protective measure. **TB**

Adriano Celentano was one of Italy's first rock 'n' roll stars, often seen in the early 1960s playing Eko electric guitars. In a hugely successful career, he achieved international recognition in the 1970s with his "gibberish" song "Prisencolinensinainciusol."

Epiphone
Casino 1961

Type Hollow body electric
Body & neck Maple laminate body, mahogany neck
Fingerboard Rosewood
Pick-ups Two P-90 pick-ups

Another of the early Gibson/Epiphone "crossover" models, the 1961 Casino is a thinline, hollow body, twin-pick-up electric guitar—and essentially an Epiphone-branded version of the Gibson ES-330 that first appeared three years earlier. Curiously, the Casino has maintained a higher profile than its upmarket relative, and this is almost entirely through its association with The Beatles.

One might have thought that the most popular beat group in the world would play the most exclusive instruments, yet all three of the band's guitar players—George Harrison, John Lennon, and Paul McCartney—owned and played the relatively modest Casinos. McCartney set the trend, acquiring a three-year-old model in 1962; although he played bass on stage, he played his Casino on a number of Beatles recordings, most memorably the biting solo on George Harrison's song "Taxman"—one of the high points of the *Revolver* album. A year later, his colleagues bought 1965 models. It was John Lennon who would become most strongly associated with the guitar. His own Casino—shown here—became his principal instrument for the rest of his time with The Beatles.

The Casino is a very versatile instrument, and well suited to The Beatles' sound; it is equally capable of warm, jazzy tones and biting overdrive. **TB**

The Epiphone Casino features in The Beatles' film *Let It Be* (1970), and their accompanying album of the same name and year; Lennon plays his Casino on the famous live rooftop recording of the song "Get Back."

◄ Paul Weller onstage with his Sunburst Casino in 2011.

Fender
Bass VI 1961

Type Solidbody six-string bass
Body & neck Alder body, maple neck
Fingerboard Ebony
Pick-ups Three single-coil pick-ups

It wasn't exactly a bass, but neither was it really a guitar. When the curious Fender Bass VI first appeared in 1961 it left many players nonplussed. It wasn't, however, an original idea. Five years earlier, Nate Daniel had introduced his Danelectro six-string "tic tac" bass, which, like the Fender, was designed to be strung and tuned one octave lower than a regular guitar.

The Bass VI evolved from Fender's Jazzmaster guitar, although its body shape presages the Jaguar, which wouldn't go into production for another year. Unusually for a bass instrument, the Bass VI featured a tremolo arm, three pick-ups, and, a few years later, a bass cut switch. All of which suggested that it was designed to cater for the soloing bass guitarist—of which there were seemingly very few in the early 1960s.

The Bass VI was not a great commercial success, although it did find a niche among some surf and guitar instrumental bands. Some bass players might well have found the additional notes in the treble register liberating, although as many are likely to have struggled with the narrow string spacing that required a modification of playing technique and greater accuracy.

The Bass VI remained in small-scale production until 1975 and was made available as a vintage reissue in 1995. It remains a niche instrument with a fervent cult following. **TB**

The Bass VI was a demanding instrument for some players. It's not surprising to find that its two most noted exponents—Jack Bruce and John Entwistle of The Who—were both unusually nimble-fingered bass players. It can be heard on Cream's debut *Fresh Cream* (1966).

Fenton-Weill
Deluxe 1961

Type Solidbody electric
Body & neck Mahogany body, mahogany set neck
Fingerboard Sycamore
Pick-ups Two Weill single-coil pick-ups

By the end of 1959, the liaison between guitar maker Jim Burns and electronics expert Henry Weill had come to an end, with the former opting to establish his own Ormston-Burns company. Weill was far from happy with his erstwhile associate's unexpected and sudden departure, but decided to go it alone and maintain guitar manufacture. A new brand logo was naturally required, and for this Henry combined his surname with that of the least-expensive electric in the ongoing line, since he considered the Fenton-Weill title hinted at American (i.e. Fender-ish) associations.

Initially the range of guitars and basses continued unaltered, although the Fenton model was now called the Deluxe. But Weill soon decided to update Jim Burns' original designs, duly incorporating some curves into the previously angular Streamline models and giving the Deluxe an additional cutaway. The end results improved on their somewhat clumsy-looking predecessors and the Deluxe definitely benefited from this makeover. However, its small size remained, as did the scratchplate, although the latter was subsequently restyled to better match the revised body shape.

The pick-ups and control count remained further constant factors; likewise the long headstock and the red position dots down the fingerboard. Also ongoing was the basic bridge fitted to virtually every Burns-Weill and Fenton-Weill instrument. This two-piece, all-wood component was actually intended for acoustic guitars and adversely affected treble response, but Henry had bought a large quantity at little cost and thought it did a good enough job, which certainly indicated that UK electric design still had some way to go! **PD**

Futurama
III 1961

Futurama
Sophomore 1961

Type Solidbody electric
Body & neck Beech body, maple neck
Fingerboard Stained beech
Pick-ups Three single-coil pick-ups

Type Solidbody electric
Body & neck Laminated hardwood body, maple neck
Fingerboard Rosewood
Pick-ups Two single-coil pick-ups

Futurama guitars were originally manufactured in Czechoslovakia by Resonet, a division of the Drevokov co-operative, and designed by its managing director Josef Ruzicka. At this point the guitar was called a "Grazioso," but not long after Selmer began importing them into the United Kingdom in 1958, it decided that a "Futurama" would be easier to sell. Before Fender guitars became available in the United Kingdom, these guitars were very popular and were played by famous guitarists including George Harrison and Jimmy Page.

The Futurama III shown here is pretty similar to the original model except that the tremolo unit has been changed from a two-post system to a separate wood-mounted bridge unit, and the jack socket moved from the top to the side. In 1960, the headstock was changed from double- to single-sided. Probably because of the three eye-catching rocker switches that allowed every possible combination of pick-up selection, Selmer marketed the Futurama III as "the world's most advanced guitar." **AJ**

This was a budget-level electric guitar aimed at the new players who were joining the European rock 'n' roll craze every week. The Sophomore was built by Guyatone in Japan and imported into Britain in the 1960s. This guitar and its sister instrument, the Freshman, generally featured in the Selmer and Rose Morris catalogs at well under £20.

One such catalog called this "a fine double-cutaway guitar at a popular price." However, the Futuramas were usually seen by young players as cheap alternatives to the flagship Höfner guitars in the days before American guitars were imported. As soon as Fenders became widely available, Futuramas seemed to disappear.

The Sophomore featured two single-coil pick-ups with adjustable pole pieces for fine tuning the string responses. Other features were the three-way selector switch, adjustable bridge, tone and volume controls, and tremolo that allowed "variance of at least one full tone." It was, said the catalog, "an instrument you can really have fun with." **SH**

Gibson Barney Kessel Custom 1961

Gibson EB-3 1961

Type Hollow body archtop electric
Body & neck Spruce top; maple back, sides, and neck
Fingerboard Ebony
Pick-ups Two Gibson PAF humbucker pick-ups

Type Solidbody electric bass
Body & neck Mahogany body, set mahogany neck
Fingerboard Rosewood
Pick-ups Twin humbucker pick-ups

With two sharp Florentine cutaways, the Barney Kessel signature Gibson was a distinctive tribute to a top American jazz player of the 1950s.

The Custom—and the lesser Regular—were well-appointed big-bodied archtops with two humbuckers. The Custom featured Kessel's trademark bowtie as an inlaid mother-of-pearl position marker, had gold-plated hardware, a five-ply beveled pickguard, Grover tuners, and bound f-holes. The name "Barney Kessel" was marked out on a special badge on the tailpiece and the Tune-o-matic bridge sat on a rosewood plinth.

But the guitar's arrival coincided with the decline of jazz in the 1960s. The signature model stayed on the books for an incredible thirteen years, but sales were slow and Kessel's relationship with Gibson deteriorated fast.

For recording and live dates, Kessel usually played a 1940s Gibson ES-350 with a Charlie Christian pick-up, but, unwilling to be seen to endorse Gibson, the name on the headstock was often covered up with tape. **SH**

The Gibson EB-3, along with the single-pick-up EB-0 economy model (30 percent cheaper) and the single-pick-up six-string EB-6 (5 percent dearer) was launched in 1961. All had the popular Gibson SG body styling. Because of its greater tonal possibilities, major artists favored the EB-3 over the EB-0. The EB-6 never found favor and was discontinued in 1965.

With a scale of only 30½ in. (77.5 cm), the EB-3 was a small bass and, at only 8 lb. 3 oz. (3.7 kg), very light, making it a quick and easy-playing instrument. Its pick-ups produced, among the four distinct tones possible with its Varitone switch, a very deep and heavy sound sometimes described as "mud," and a built-in string mute enabled it to sound like an upright bass. About 13,000 units of the EB-3 were sold from launch in 1961 to 1979, its final year of production.

In the 1960s, the EB-3 was particularly popular with bassists in British bands, including Bill Wyman of The Rolling Stones, Jack Bruce of Cream, Andy Fraser of Free, and Glenn Cornick of Jethro Tull, among others. **GD**

Gibson
SG Custom 1961

Type Solidbody electric
Body & neck Mahogany body, set mahogany neck
Fingerboard Ebony
Pick-ups Three PAF humbucker pick-ups

The Les Paul had never been the popular hit that Gibson had wanted. At the turn of the decade, Gibson president Ted McCarty decided to give it a design overhaul. Gone was the thick mahogany archtop of the original, replaced by a simpler, flat-top body with a double cutaway. The neck became slimmer in profile and narrower at the nut. All that really remained of the original were the electrics. The naming of the new model remains a matter of conjecture. It has been said that Les Paul didn't like the look of the new guitar and asked for his name to be removed; sources at Gibson say that by 1961 a middle-of-the-road jazz guitarist like Les Paul was no longer a relevant endorsee. Whatever the truth, the new model was rechristened the "Solid Guitar"—or "SG" for short.

The SG came in four different flavors—the Standard, Special, Junior, and the flagship deluxe model, the Custom. Initially available only in shiny "Alpine White" (in spite of launch blurb offering a "Cherry Red" model), the opulent gold hardware mirrored another period classic—Gretsch's fabulous White Falcon.

From a sound perspective, the Custom differed from the other SG variants through the addition of an extra middle PAF humbucker; when the central position of the three-way-selector switch was chosen, both middle and bridge humbuckers were switched in. **TB**

One of Britain's greatest electric guitarists, the criminally neglected Ollie Halsall, is best known for his work with the bands Patto and Boxer. The track "Air Raid" from Patto's *Hold Your Fire* (1971) features some of the most astonishingly nimble rock guitar work ever committed to tape.

Sister Rosetta Tharpe performing for Granada TV's *Blues & Gospel Train* (1964).

Gibson
Johnny Smith 1961

Type Archtop hollowbody electric
Body & neck Maple body, carved spruce top, maple neck
Fingerboard Ebony
Pick-ups One or two suspended mini-humbuckers

"The King of Taste" was jazz guitarist Johnny Smith's nickname. Famed for his 1952 album *Moonlight In Vermont* featuring Stan Getz, and for composing the tune "Walk Don't Run," which subsequently became a hit for The Ventures, he won *DownBeat* magazine's poll for best guitarist of 1954 and 1955. It was little surprise that when Gibson revived its archtop line in 1960, the venerable guitar maker would seek his endorsement.

Ironically, Smith was not a Gibson player; he endorsed D'Angelico and then Guild—but as he didn't particularly like his Guild guitar, he was amenable to the idea of a Gibson signature model, provided they could make an instrument that he'd be prepared to use. The Johnny Smith model debuted in 1961 with a 17 in. (43 cm)-wide body and 25-in. (63.5-cm) scale length. But it was the pick-up arrangement that truly distinguished the guitar: Smith specified that the pick-ups be suspended and not screwed into the guitar body, allowing the carved-spruce top to resonate. To comply with this, Gibson used a mini-humbucker which had originally been designed by Seth Lover for Epiphone electrics. This was screwed to the bottom of the neck using a bracket soldered to its cover. The single volume control and output jack were fixed to the scratchplate to keep them out of direct contact with the body of the guitar. The original prototype had twenty-two frets, but apparently Smith didn't approve of this and asked Gibson to remove two of them.

The Johnny Smith was the most expensive of Gibson's Artist Models—and the most enduring, as well. It remained in the line until 1965 in both single- and double-pick-up form. **MD/AJ**

Gibson
SG Junior 1961

Type Solidbody electric
Body & neck Mahogany body, mahogany neck
Fingerboard Rosewood
Pick-ups One single-coil P-90 pick-up

Originally built until 1971, the SG Junior was a single-pick-up version of the SG Special (see page 266), launched in the same year. It featured one single-coil P-90 pick-up in the back position with a dedicated volume and tone control. The bridge was also the very basic stoptail, unlike the more sophisticated Tune-o-matics found on most other Gibsons by this time. This was superseded in 1965 by a vibrato bridge.

Like its earlier equivalent the Les Paul, the Junior was aimed at younger players or those wanting a genuine Gibson at a budget price. The guitar was initially branded "Les Paul Junior," silkscreened on the headstock, until 1963 when it was removed. In 1965, a number of design changes were implemented, including a new surround pickguard, a shift from nickel to chrome hardware, and new soap bar pick-ups replacing the original P-90s.

The launch of the Junior was accompanied by the SG TV Junior. Like the Les Paul TV, this was an identical guitar but finished in white or lime yellow, and was later sported on stage by Bon Jovi's Richie Sambora.

In the late 1990s, diffusion brand Epiphone issued its own SG Junior with a bolt-on neck, built at the Cort factory in Indonesia. Dirt cheap and aimed at beginners, these were excellent instruments for the fledgling hot-rodder—rip out and replace the pick-up, take some wire wool to the frets, and do some work on the set-up and you'll have learned something about the mechanics of the guitar and got a nice instrument in the process. [Note: hacking up guitars can be good fun ... but don't hold the writer responsible if you're left staring at a pile of broken wood, screws, and wires!] **TB**

Gibson
SG Special 1961

Type Solidbody electric
Body & neck Mahogany body, mahogany neck
Fingerboard Rosewood
Pick-ups Two single-coil P-90 pick-ups

Introduced at the same time as the SG Custom, Standard, and Junior models, the Special shared many of the features of the Standard, but was fitted instead with a pair of Gibson's high-output single-coil P-90 soap bar pick-ups. Prior to Seth Lover's development of the PAF humbucker in 1957, most of Gibson's electric guitars had been fitted with P-90s, at least since 1946 when they were introduced to replace the hexagonal "Charlie Christian" model. The very existence of the SG Special was clear recognition that many players (as evidenced by the enduring popularity of Fender guitars) continued to show a preference for the treble "bite" of a single coil.

The Special was issued with a fixed stoptail bridge, as shown in this example. This provided limited options for adjustment—just overall string height set by screws at either end of the saddle. From 1962, it became possible to order one with a Maestro vibrola fitted. The fingerboard on the Special featured simple dot inlays, unlike the trapezoid design found on the Standard and the rectangular inlays on the Custom models.

The SG Special in its original form was discontinued in 1971, replaced briefly by the SG Pro, which has a Tune-o-matic bridge and a Bigsby vibrato; a year later the Special resurfaced, but this time fitted with humbucker pick-ups. **TB**

Tony Iommi of Black Sabbath is one of the most influential figures in the development of metal guitar. The SG Special he christened "Monkey" can be heard on all of Sabbath's early albums, including their second effort, *Paranoid* (1970).

Gibson
SG Standard 1961

Type Solidbody electric
Body & neck Mahogany body, mahogany neck
Fingerboard Rosewood
Pick-ups Two PAF humbucker pick-ups

The slimmer body and neck designs of Gibson's SG line combined practical playing considerations with simple economy—they used considerably less wood, making them cheaper to produce. The old Les Pauls had been prohibitively expensive for many young players; lower production costs meant that SGs could be priced much closer to their cheaper Fender rivals.

From a playing perspective, the lower of the famous asymmetric cutaways offered easier access to the uppermost of the twenty-two frets; the neck of the Les Paul joined the body at the sixteenth fret whereas the SG joined at the nineteenth. Furthermore, the beveled edging made the SG more comfortable to play than the Les Paul, although the reduced body weight made it comparatively neck-heavy. Most players, though, saw the most immediate difference in the neck; it was slim in profile and narrower in width at the nut. Advertised by Gibson as "the fastest neck in the world," it's little wonder that the SG Standard, and its other variants, became so popular with the speedy soloing blues-rock guitarists of the next two decades.

Although the materials and electrics of the SG were the same as those found on the Les Paul, the reduced body mass of the SG resulted in a different sound, with less natural bass but more bite; it also made the SG more prone to feeding back. **TB**

Robby Krieger played a Gibson SG Standard throughout most of his time with The Doors. His powerful solo on the rock classic "Light My Fire" can be heard on the band's eponymous debut album of 1967.

Harmony
H22 Bass 1961

Kay
Jazz II 1961

Type Hollow body electric bass
Body & neck Laminated maple body; maple neck
Fingerboard "Ebonized" rosewood
Pick-ups One "Golden Tone" single-coil pick-up

Type Hollow body electric
Body & neck Laminated maple body; maple neck
Fingerboard Bound rosewood
Pick-ups Two "Gold-K" single-coil pick-ups

Harmony produced its first electric bass in 1961. With a single DeArmond pick-up, the H22 was intended to produce a sound that was a realistic substitute for the unwieldy upright double bass.

The body's top and back are flat, not carved like hollow body electrics, and bound with white celluloid. The neck is narrow but deep, with an adjustable truss rod, and topped with a large, spade-shaped headstock that houses cheap, two-on-a-plate, open-backed tuners. It has a medium scale-length of 30 in. (76 cm), though long-scale strings are necessary, because the wooden tail anchor sits 6 in. (15.25 cm) behind the floating, rosewood bridge. The pick-up delivers a strong, deep thud and can be switched into "baritone" mode by means of a toilet-flush lever near the volume and tone controls.

In 1964, the tailpiece was moved forward an inch (2.5 cm), and a different-shaped cover placed over it. Otherwise unaltered, the H22 was produced until 1969, when the double cutaway H22/1 replaced it. **DG**

The "Jazz II" was a double cutaway development of Kay's "Swingmaster" series, designed in the late 1950s in collaboration with jazz guitarist Barney Kessel. With maple veneers on the top, back, and sides, its flamboyant appearance was enhanced by a plastic headstock decoration, six two-piece pearl fingerboard inlays, and a wavy, silver-colored pickguard.

Oddly for guitars aimed at jazz players, all were supplied with Bigsby B3 vibrato units as standard. The pick-ups produce a rich, pure, distortion-free tone. The adjustable pole-pieces of the back pick-up were pitched wider than the front unit to allow for the course of the strings. The tuners were nickel-plated Grover Rotomatics, which were superior in quality to the Klusons used on most Kays (the guitar pictured has gold-plated Schaller replacements).

The Jazz II's Achilles' heel was the neck set, which rendered the break angle of the strings at the bridge virtually non-existent. But it still delivered tone and performance equal to some of the bigger brands. **DG**

Norma
Blue Sparkle 1961

Rickenbacker
460 1961

Type Solidbody double cutaway electric guitar
Body & neck Laminated hardwood body, maple neck
Fingerboard Rosewood
Pick-ups Two or three single-coil pick-ups

Type Solidbody electric
Body & neck Maple body and neck
Fingerboard Rosewood
Pick-ups Two Rickenbacker "toaster" single-coil pick-ups

Norma was a brand name invented by Strum 'n' Drum instrument importers and retailers in Chicago. The Norma guitars were actually built by Tombo in Japan, who were also building guitars labeled with names like Colombus, Angelica, and Condor at the time.

Tombo's specialty was copying 1960s Italian guitar designs. This rare six-string electric was inspired by Eko. It used a plastic finish that Tombo also used on its bass guitars—a blue sparkle with a red tortoiseshell pickguard. It was also available with a gold sparkle finish.

The guitar itself was a simple bolt-on neck design, laminated body with six-on-a-side tuners, tremolo tailpiece, and either two or three pick-ups, selected by an array of rocker switches.

The idea for a sparkly finish originated from accordions. It was first used on solid electric guitars by Italian manufacturers like Crucianelli, who switched from accordions to guitars as the fashions changed. Meanwhile, Tombo are still in business, but now concentrate on making harmonicas. **SH**

The first Rickenbacker 460 appeared in March 1961, and remained in production until 1985. Although not as highly regarded as the company's hollow-body models—such as the Capri series—which supposedly embodied the quintessential Rickenbacker sound, as found on Beatles' and Byrds' records—they still have their fans; early examples currently change hands for thousands of dollars.

The 460 was introduced as a deluxe version of the Combo 450, with neck and body binding, and triangle inlays on the fretboard. Like most solidbody Rickenbackers, it had a neck-through construction with glued-on body wings, and came in black, natural, or "fireglo." A "Rick-O-Sound" stereo output was added in 1962. The five knobs on the scratchplate are two volumes, two tone controls, and the smaller blend control—the 460 was the first Rickenbacker to get one.

The successors of the 460 were the 615 and 625, which were generally similar but had an additional tremolo mechanism. **AJ**

Rickenbacker
4001 Bass 1961

Type Solidbody electric bass
Body & neck Maple body, maple straight-through neck
Fingerboard Rosewood
Pick-ups Two horseshoe pick-ups

In response to Rickenbacker's 1957 "cresting wave" 4000 solidbody bass guitar—the first significant competition for the pioneering Fender Precision—in 1960 the Jazz was unleashed, its twin-pick-up arrangement enabling an increased tonal range. Rickenbacker added a second pick-up to the 4000 before, a year later, taking the decision to create a new model—the 4001.

Like all Rickenbackers, the 4001 was a high-end model constructed using the straight-through neck design. Not only was it kitted out with two pick-ups but other deluxe features, such as a binding on the body and neck as well as the characteristic Rickenbacker triangle inlays. At the time it represented a new gold standard for bass guitars, even if its relatively high cost was off-putting for some players.

The 4001 featured an interesting optional feature in that it could be wired for Rickenbacker's twin-output Rick-O-Sound system. A standard feature from 1971, this enabled separate audio signals to be taken from each pick-up. Players embracing the system could take a stereo cable from the 4001 and connect the two pick-ups to different amplifier channels or even separate amps.

A number of variants of the 4001 appeared over the years until a 1979 redesign resulted in the birth of the closely related 4003 model. The original 4001 was slowly phased out and production ended in 1986. **TB**

 A pioneering mix of heavy metal fused with punk attitude, Motörhead's 1977 eponymous debut album featured Lemmy on a Rickenbacker and introduced War-Pig, the fanged face that would become an icon of the band.

Vox
Apache 1961

Type Twin cutaway solidbody electric
Body & neck Mahogany body, maple neck
Fingerboard Beech
Pick-ups Three "maximum frequency" single-coil pick-ups

In July 1960, the British four-piece The Shadows reached No. 1 on the charts with a guitar instrumental tune called "Apache." Many bands, like The Shadows, used Vox's AC amplifiers. Vox had already started distributing cheap beginner guitars. After The Shadows topped the hit parade, the British manufacturer saw a chance to cash in on their success. Company boss Tom Jennings decided to commission his own line of electric instruments.

These were simple solidbody guitars with bolt-on necks in the Fender style. The Apache, Stroller, and Clubman were built by a cabinetmaker in Essex. The single-pick-up Stroller and twin-pick-up Clubman were more conventionally styled, but the Apache was a special lightweight electric guitar with a unique asymmetrical body shape. The Apache also used an unusual beech fingerboard and featured an unusual plug socket more like a TV aerial connector.

While the later Phantom Teardrop guitar went on to become a popular icon of the 1960s, the Apache was produced in limited numbers until it was discontinued in 1966. They have since become very sought after by collectors and prices today easily reach four figures.

Yet the guitar was originally a budget instrument. The specifications were pretty standard: three single-coil pick-ups with a selector switch, chrome hardware, a volume and two tone controls, Vox vibrato bridge system, and six-on-a-side tuners.

The name was revived in 2007 when Vox, now owned by Japanese electronics firm Korg, launched a new Apache. It was retro styled but very different—a travel guitar with built-in amp and speakers. **SH**

Vox
Stroller 1961

Type Solidbody electric
Body & neck Laminate body, sycamore bolt-on neck
Fingerboard Rosewood
Pick-ups One single-coil Vox V1 pick-up

Introduced in 1961—along with the Clubman, which was essentially a two-pick-up version with a Stratocaster-style body—the Stroller was one of the first two guitars to be mass produced by Vox. These were cheap entry-level instruments—in 1963, when it was discontinued, the Stroller retailed for £17. They were manufactured for Vox by Stuart Darkins & Co., a cabinetmaker in Shoeburyness, Essex. The construction was very basic: a bolt-on neck, floating wooden bridge, two knobs for volume and tone, a single pick-up and—unusually—a TV-type coaxial output socket. An

"Fine quality rhythm solid electric guitar. High grade VOX strings and single pick-up. Separate tone and volume controls…"
1964 VOX CATALOG

extremely light guitar, the Stroller weighed just 4½ lb (2 kg). The color range was also limited: either red or white.

At the time of its launch, British guitar instrumental band The Shadows—who famously endorsed Vox amplifiers—was enormously popular, so it's perhaps no coincidence that the Stroller's original body shape was based on the (albeit somewhat more ornate) Guyatone (also known as Antoria) LG50, Shadow Hank Marvin's favorite guitar at the time. The Japanese Guyatone—popular with many British guitarists in the early 1960s—was also the inspiration for the early Burns "Weill Fenton" model. After Marvin moved onto his famous red Fender Stratocaster, Vox redesigned the Stroller with a Fender-style double cutaway. The Stroller was superseded by the two-pick-up Shadow in 1963. **AJ**

Wandré
Rock Oval 1961

Type Solidbody electric
Body & neck Hardwood/fiberglass body, aluminum neck
Fingerboard Rosewood
Pick-ups Two single-coil pick-ups

Antonio Pioli is one of the most colorful characters in the history of the electric guitar. Born in 1926 in Cavriago, northern Italy, Pioli was a luthier, an anti-fascist partisan fighter, a conceptual artist, and a motorcycle aficionado. As wild as some of his guitar designs may have been, he was schooled in the most traditional of music craft skills in the workshop of his father, who was himself variously described as a luthier or a violin maker. Piolo Senior recognized the eccentricities of his son, giving him the nickname "Wandré"—local slang meaning "to go in reverse."

The Rock Oval was one of Antonio Pioli's most curious body shapes. Its extreme single cutaway was inspired by Salvador Dalí's 1931 painting, *The Persistence Of Memory*. Although a striking design, it was not entirely practical, being difficult to play in the sitting position. The large, trapezoid-shaped pick-ups were built by Athos Davoli, and featured stamped metal covers that read "Davoli/Made In Italy"; often this was the only mark on a Wandré guitar, leading to frequent misidentifications.

Not only did Pioli employ surreal body shapes, he also experimented with unorthodox materials, such as aluminum for the necks of his guitars. Italian woods were well known for their tonal qualities, but they lacked the strength of American maple, and were prone to warping. He was also the brain behind the motorbike-inspired Krundaal Bikini (see page 284).

Pioli continued to produce Wandré guitars until 1970, when he sold his factory to start a leather clothing business. A self-proclaimed *"artista della vita"* (artist of life), he died in 2004. **TB**

Bartolini
20-4V 1962

Type Solidbody electric
Body & neck Basswood body with maple neck
Fingerboard Pearloid
Pick-ups Four single-coil pick-ups

As far as the vintage guitar market was once concerned, Italian electric guitars from the 1960s held little more than kitsch value for most collectors; something colorful and sparkly to hang on a wall rather than plug in and play. But recent years have seen an increase in value of some of these once-unfashionable instruments.

In the early 1960s, rock 'n' roll began to catch on in Italy. Alvaro Bartolini, like many of the other accordion makers in Castelfidardo, responded by switching production to electric guitars. And in the sparkling body and pearloid fingerboard of the Bartolini 20-4V this heritage is abundantly plain. Indeed, most Italian models from this era looked rather similar, not only in their garish appearance but in the design of the electrics—four pick-ups on an electric guitar was common on these models, and yet rarely found on the American classics; similarly, they use giant rockers and transistor-radio-style rotary dials rather than flush-fitting knobs and selector switches. **TB**

Burns
Bison Bass 1962

Type Solidbody bass
Body & neck Sycamore body, maple neck
Fingerboard Ebony
Pick-ups Three single-coil pick-ups

The Burns company—or Ormston Burns as it was known on its formation—always blazed an individual trail when it came to the look, if not the function, of its guitars, and this was very true of the long-scale Bison Bass, a unique instrument when uniqueness was sadly lacking in the industry. You'll see Bisons pictured in a huge number of grainy, black-and-white live band photos of the day, bearing the large horns that gave them their name with pride. Session musicians were also keen on the Bison for its range of tones, at a time when a muffled thud was pretty much all that the pick-up and amplifier technology of the day could provide. While the instrument's heyday was definitely the 1960s, reissued Bisons from 1992 onward found a home in many modern rock bands, particularly in the United Kingdom. They could be seen adorning bass players in Britpop bands such as Oasis, whose admiration of 1960s artifacts was well-known, as well as later groups such as Kaiser Chiefs. Even sometime Megadeth bassist James Lomenzo plays one from time to time. **JM**

Burns Split Sound Baritone 1962

Dwight Epiphone SB533 1962

Type Solidbody electric
Body & neck Mahogany body, set mahogany neck
Fingerboard Ebony
Pick-ups Three PAF humbucker pick-ups

Type Solidbody electric
Body & neck Mahogany body, set mahogany neck
Fingerboard Rosewood
Pick-ups One single-coil P-90 pick-up

There was a glut of baritone designs in the 1960s as instrument manufacturers experimented, hoping to find the next big guitar craze. British guitar innovator Jim Burns created the Burns Split Sound Baritone—a six-string bass on a normal guitar body and neck.

A year later, Burns' baritone was very closely based on his Split Sonic six-string guitar. That meant it had a normal guitar's scale—24¾ in. (63 cm)—and a neck that was narrower than some conventional guitars. It was clearly designed for fast playing and chords, not for playing normal bass parts in a band. The baritone even had a tremolo arm. And like the Sonic, the Baritone's tone-control switch gave options of: "jazz," "treble," "split sound," or "wild dog."

Sadly the Burns Baritone didn't catch on with most buyers and became one of the rarest of all production Burns guitars—less than 200 were made. Nevertheless future Led Zeppelin bassist John Paul Jones played one early on in his career and always retained a liking for baritone guitars. **SH**

The Gibson-manufactured Dwight was a rebadged Epiphone Coronet, similar in every respect except for the headstock logo and a silver foil letter "D" replacing the traditional Epi "slashed C" emblem on the pickguard.

Little is known for certain about this short run of instruments, but received wisdom has it that the guitars were ordered by music dealer Dwight "Sonny" Shields in St. Louis, Missouri, who owned a store called Sonny's Music. Shields ran a guitar school as part of the business and had Gibson run up a batch of Coronets with his name on them that he would sell to his students. The first batch was shipped early in 1962, and though production figures are hard to ascertain it's thought that around eighty were produced in total.

Sonny's Music apparently suffered a serious fire in the 1970s, putting it out of business, an event that only adds to the mystery surrounding these guitars. The most visible professional endorser was Steve Marriot during his years with Humble Pie, though it's safe to assume he was not one of Shields' students! **DG**

Epiphone
E360TD Riviera 1962

Type Thinline semi-hollow body electric
Body & neck Maple body, set mahogany bound neck
Fingerboard Rosewood
Pick-ups Two mini-humbucker pick-ups

In 1960, a plant was constructed by Gibson specifically for the manufacture of Epiphone guitars, the company it had purchased in 1957. The Sheraton, the first thinline offered and modeled after Gibson's ES-355, had been in production elsewhere for two years before the Casino was introduced in 1961, based on Gibson's ES-330.

In 1962, the Riviera followed as an equivalent to the ES-335, complete with internal maple block and two mini-humbucking pick-ups, as used on the Sheraton. Most were offered in a honey-colored sunburst unique to Epiphone called Royal Tan (pictured), and in common with the Casino the pearl fingerboard inlays were single parallelograms. It also featured a two-piece Frequensator tailpiece—an Epiphone development dating back to the 1940s designed to provide more length to the three lower strings in an attempt to increase tone and sustain.

Though built to the same standards as Gibson's own models, the Riviera never really found favor with players to the same degree as the ES-335. Its smaller, brighter pick-ups give the guitar a warmer sound akin to a Stratocaster, not something Gibson players would usually seek out. While sales of the Casino soared, having been embraced by The Beatles among others, the more costly but less practical Riviera was produced in smaller quantities, and remains one of only a handful of bargains still to be found on the vintage guitar market. **DG**

The reviewer, Dave Gregory of XTC, played this guitar on a number of tracks, including "Grass" and "The Meeting Place" from the acclaimed album *Skylarking* (1986). The B-side of "Grass" was "Dear God," which was later added to the album after it became an unexpected hit.

Nick Valensi of The Strokes, the coolest band around at the start of the twenty-first century. →

Fender
Jaguar 1962

Type Solidbody electric
Body & neck Mahogany body, set mahogany neck
Fingerboard Ebony fingerboard
Pick-ups Three PAF humbucker pick-ups

The Jaguar was created with the popular surf guitar bands of the period in mind, many of whom had taken a liking to Fender's Jazzmaster. The guitars shared a number of features: the offset waist, floating tremolo bridge, and similar dual-circuit electrics.

The Jaguar was the first Fender to feature a twenty-two-fret fingerboard and with a 24-in. (61-cm) medium scale length, it was 1½ in. (4 cm) shorter than a full-scale Fender. It featured smaller single-coil pick-ups than its predecessor, and they were constructed with notched side plates to improve shielding and reduce both microphonic feedback and electrical interference.

An unusual feature of the Jaguar was the inclusion of a spring-loaded mute, which brought a set of rubber pads into contact with the strings. Deadening strings with the palm of the hand was a stock technique used by most surf and instrumental players, but was difficult to achieve with the Jaguar's floating bridge system. This mechanism was unpopular, however, and was removed by most players.

The Jaguar was never a mainstream hit, but it found its intended niche. By 1975, it was out of fashion and production ceased. More than a decade later, with secondhand prices still low, the Jaguar was discovered by a new generation of young musicians, and in 1999 it was relaunched. **TB**

My Bloody Valentine's 1991 album *Loveless* set a benchmark in the "shoegaze" genre. Kevin Shields' distinctive sound came from modifying the vibrato arm on his Jaguar, which he gently manipulated while playing chords.

Fenton-Weill
Dualtone 1962

Type Solidbody electric
Body & neck Ebony body and neck
Fingerboard Rosewood
Pick-ups Two Fenton-Weill single-coil pick-ups

Before he fell out with former partner Jim Burns, Henry Weill was the man who supplied the highly rated electronics for Burns-Weill guitars in the late 1950s. His own Fenton-Weill guitars were rather overshadowed by the success of Burns' designs during the 1960s.

The Dualtone was the successor of the Twinmaster and Triplemaster range, which merged with its Twistmaster guitars by 1962 (you could order a Triplemaster with a Twistmaster body by referring to it as a "Triple-twistmaster"). Of course these were discontinued by 1963—but that's what you get for naming a guitar after a dance craze.

According to the advertising literature, the Dualtone had "two high-gain pick-up units mounted on a laminated two colour assembly panel fitted with a selector switch, volume and tone controls giving powerful response and brilliant tonal quality…" and a "rosewood fingerboard; high gear ratio machine heads and ebony rocker-bridge ensure accuracy in both action and tuning." Furthermore it was "fitted with a super resilient 'Featherlite' vibrato"—(which Fenton-Weill was convinced "couldn't be improved in any way")—"and available in three standard colours—off white, leaf green and cherry red, all with blended-in black neck."

These guitars have a poor reputation for the quality of their fretwork but the pick-ups are more highly rated. Indeed, the Fenton-Weill pick-ups on this guitar were a precursor to the famous Burns Tri-Sonics and have a similarly rich tone while being built like a tank. Their trademark was later acquired by a company called Adeson, who continue to manufacture them. **AJ**

Gibson EBSF 1250 Double Bass 1962

Type Solidbody double-neck
Body & neck Mahogany body and neck
Fingerboard Rosewood
Pick-ups Two humbucker pick-ups (bass: two EB-3s)

If you were a guitar manufacturer in the mid-1960s, and you wanted a celebrity endorser for your product, you could do worse than pick Elvis Presley, the biggest solo artist there has ever been or is ever likely to be. The King was often seen playing a double-neck Gibson EBSF 1250, a beautiful guitar/bass combo that came in a variety of string configurations. While Elvis was hardly a master musician, and focused more on strumming simple guitar chords than tackling the four-string bass neck, the visual impact of this ambitious instrument was undeniable, and we imagine that Gibson's sales revenue didn't suffer from his patronage of their gear, either. The 1250 featured a bass neck copied from the 30½-in. (77.5-cm) scale of its successful EB-3 model and, rather curiously, also came with a built-in fuzztone derived from Gibson's FZ-1 pedal. In 1965, a six-string bass variant was added to the range, and the fuzz was dropped, along with the F in the model number. Elvis' model is now displayed in Graceland. **JM**

Gibson Everly Brothers 1962

Type Flat-top acoustic
Body & neck Maple back and sides, spruce top, mahogany neck
Fingerboard Rosewood

Phil and Don Everly dominated the airwaves of late-1950s America with such evergreen close-harmony hits as "All I Have To Do Is Dream" and "Cathy's Clown." In 1962, they were invited to collaborate with Gibson to produce their own signature guitar.

A slimmer-bodied version of the already narrow-waisted flat-top J-185, the most distinctive characteristic of the Gibson Everly Brothers was its unorthodox pickguard design. The soundboard was finished in black, with smart white binding around the sides; the double-grain tortoiseshell pickguard was—unusually—cut symmetrically to cover the area both below and above the sound hole. As attractive as this was visually, since the pickguard covered almost half the area of the soundboard, the natural vibration of the spruce was reduced. As a consequence, the guitar, although producing a beautiful tone, suffered a significant reduction in volume. Not that this deterred the likes of Paul McCartney, Bob Dylan, and Jimmy Page, all of whom have used this guitar on their recordings. **TB**

Hagstrom Futurama II 1962

Type Solidbody electric
Body & neck Birch body, bolt-on two-piece neck
Fingerboard Rosewood
Pick-ups Two single-coil pick-ups

Badged as Futurama by UK importers Selmer, the DeLuxe series was a replacement for an earlier Czech-manufactured range of the same name that had enjoyed popularity for some years among cash-strapped guitar students. Manufactured in Sweden by Hagstrom, the guitar was supplied with either two or three (III) pick-ups, and in a choice of colors: fire-truck red or sky blue.

The body of the guitar is formed from a composite of seven strips of wood 1⅞ in. (4.8 cm) wide by 1¼ in. (3 cm) deep, with a chamfer around the top and back similar to Gibson's SG range. The oblong pick-ups are wired to a plate of switches—on/off for each unit, a "Mute" switch that removes the high frequencies, and a "Tone" switch that reduces volume. A single volume pot controls the output.

The pick-ups are surprisingly strong, the neck unit in particular overcoming any woodwork issues and producing a rich tone. The slender neck—complete with adjustable "Kings Neck Expander Stretcher"—is easy to play on, particularly for those with small hands. **DG**

Hagstrom Futurama Coronado 1962

Type Solidbody electric
Body & neck Birch body; maple neck
Fingerboard Rosewood
Pick-ups Two single-coil pick-ups

This is a rather rare example of a guitar built specially to order by the Hagstrom company. In 1963, Ben and Lew Davis—former jazz musicians who had jointly set up Selmer UK more than thirty years earlier—ordered 200 guitars from the Swedish guitar manufacturer. Like other Selmer guitars, they were marketed under the Futurama brand, as can be gathered from the rather Fenderesque script on the headstock. These guitars had numerous interesting features, including an unusual acrylic fingerboard—"warp-proof and impervious to perspiration," according to the publicity—as well as sophisticated electrics that offered a wide array of tonal and volume control. This was no cheap guitar, retailing at over £80—at a time when the average weekly wage for most Britons was well under £10.

The Coronado Automatic was one of the last Futurama models to appear during the Davis Brothers' reign at Selmer—a year later, they sold up and spent the rest of their lives retired in the south of France. **TB**

Harvey Thomas
Custom Guitar 1962

Type Hollow body electric
Body & neck Carved maple hollow body, maple neck
Fingerboard Rosewood
Pick-ups Two single-coil pick-ups

Harvey Thomas was a colorful, eccentric guitar maker who created his instruments in a shed behind his ramshackle home in rural Washington. He collected Cadillacs and guitars, and performed locally as a one-man band using a guitar with frets wired up to also operate an electric organ.

His greatest legacy, however, was the unique collection of guitars he made. These included a triple-neck guitar, an "Iron Cross" guitar, and a guitar in the shape of a naked Polynesian woman. One of his creations was completely covered in real raccoon skin;

"The guy I sold it to took the scratchplate off and inside was Harvey Thomas' name . . . I'm going to try and get that guitar back one day!"
IAN HUNTER OF MOTT THE HOOPLE

another was in the shape of a swastika. There was a guitar that looked like a shotgun, one made from a toilet seat, and another in the shape of an ax—a real ax—that appeared in his catalog being held by a man in an ape costume, probably Thomas himself.

The guitar pictured here was fairly conventional by his standards—it was made in 1962 and is a dark-green hollow body archtop with an unusual body shape. Thomas ordered pick-ups and tuners from wholesalers, but usually made everything else himself.

Thomas' guitars sold from local guitar shops or his remote home (where he displayed them on an old pool table). His was a small-time operation with his creations costing from just $100. Now they have become highly collectible and change hands for up to $4,000 each. **SH**

Kay
Red Devil 1962

Type Hollow body electric
Body & neck Laminated maple body; mahogany neck
Fingerboard Bound rosewood
Pick-ups Two single-coil pick-ups

Kay never called this guitar the Red Devil: the name was coined by UK importers Höhner, who used it to great advantage in their marketing literature. The guitar presented a striking display of choice curly maple veneers covering the top and back, enhanced by a dark burgundy red lacquer.

Described by Kay simply as a "double cutaway with vibrato tailpiece," it was equipped with a chunky Art Deco-style tremolo unit, and a floating rosewood bridge. However, most of the exported examples featured Selmer's "Under License" Bigsby unit, complete with aluminum rocker bridge, the standard B3 Bigsby system eventually replacing the Kay device in the United States. The pick-ups were Kay's own single coils, later nicknamed "speed bumps," which were far from impressive. Six plectrum-shaped "pearlette" fingerboard inlays marked the fret positions, and its nineteen "nickel silver" frets appeared to be brass. Both top and back were bound in cream celluloid, four-ply on the top, with a cream plastic pickguard engraved with the "K" music-stand logo filled with black.

The neck, incorporating an adjustable steel truss rod, was fixed into its pocket with three bolts. That the neck angles were seldom set correctly did much to undermine Kay's reputation as an instrument maker—the company often relied on looks alone to sell its guitars, which it did very successfully. Thousands were supplied through mail order.

A hot looker but a poor performer, the K592 did not survive the decade, losing out to similarly priced but better designed instruments from the likes of Harmony, Hagstrom, and Höfner. **DG**

Krundaal
Bikini 1962

Type Hollow-body single cutaway electric
Body & neck Hardwood body, aluminum neck
Fingerboard Rosewood
Pick-ups Two single-coil Davoli pick-ups

When it comes to futuristic, unorthodox-looking guitars, few compare to the Krundaal Bikini, which is actually a product of Wandré Guitars and its eccentric owner, Antonio Pioli, whose approach to guitar design included stunning reverse bridges, combination aluminum/ wood headstocks, and sailing-mast-grade aluminum necks attached to bodies on adjustable hinges.

The Bikini's resemblance to a human ear—thanks to an egg-shaped, built-in amplifier attached to the underside of its body or, as the company liked to describe it, a "transistorized, electric strolling guitar-

> *"The Krundaal Bikini is a distinctive electric guitar, with an attached amplifier, shaped like a motorcycle tank and wheel."*
> GUITAR-LIST.COM

amp combo"—earned it the nickname "Buggerlugg." Not unlike other European integrated amp experiments of the early 1960s, such as the "Big Beat" by the Czech company Jolana, the Bikini was inspired by a motorcycle profile. It had a thinline body and two single-coil Davoli pick-ups, and a push-button pick-up selector switch system mounted on a very cool-looking rectangular control plate.

At first glance it might appear ungainly. But look again. Pioli's guitars were often referred to as "musical sculptures," and though it's tempting to deride designing guitars with motorcycles in mind, one should remember that Paul Bigsby, too, was a motorcycle enthusiast who designed his very own vibrato—using a spring from an old motorcycle. **BS**

Musima Otwin
Double Neck 1962

Type Solidbody electric
Body & neck Laminated hardwood and maple
Fingerboard Rosewood
Pick-ups Two single-coil pick-ups on guitar, one on bass

The Otwin guitar company was originally founded by Franz Otto Windisch in 1886. Based in Schoeneck, Germany (East Germany between 1949 and 1999) it employed between 70 and 120 people and made various kinds of stringed and fretted instruments. By the 1950s, it was mainly known for archtop acoustics. In the late 1950s, the brand was taken over by Musima—the former state-owned Musikinstrumentenbau Markneukirchen who also owned Meinel and Herold, and Migma—and they produced several original solidbody and semi-hollow body electric guitar designs during the late 1950s and 1960s. Some of these were exported to the United Kingdom under the Otwin and Rellog trademark, but most of them ended up being imported into the Soviet Union by Musima's Russian division.

The guitars most closely related to the Musima Otwin double-neck include the Musima Eterna—most solidbody Musimas featured the same body shape reminiscent of the English Burns design—this one is possibly best known for being played by Thurston Moore and Kim Gordon of Sonic Youth. It could also be a hybrid of the Musima I/2 Electric Guitar—described in Musima's catalog as a "fully electric, asymmetrical jazz guitar in Ruby Red and Black with high-gloss polished stiletto-neck trailer with steel truss rod"—and the V/2 Bass Guitar, which have the same slightly SG-like pointed horns and similar pick-up configurations. Migma also made a more flamboyant-looking double-neck that looks like a closer relative of the Musima Eterna. It's unlikely that either of these guitars ever existed in large numbers—possibly no larger than one. **AJ**

National
Studio 66 1962

Type Solidbody electric
Body & neck Res-O-Glas body; maple neck
Fingerboard Rosewood
Pick-ups One single-coil pick-up

The National brand holds an important place in the history and development of the acoustic guitar during the twentieth century. Yet, so closely is it associated with the beautiful metal resonators that first appeared in 1927, that it is easy to forget the company also made electric guitars.

The last of the original National resonators appeared in 1942, a year before three of the partners in the National Dobro Company—Victor Smith, Al Frost, and Louis Dopyera—created the new Valco company that produced large quantities of fretted instruments and amplifiers under a variety of brand names—among them Supro, Airline, and Oahu—but they always retained the National designation for their premium products.

The first National guitars were archtop acoustics. Some of these models used Gibson-built bodies, and these are now much sought after by collectors. They were followed by fine, hollow body electrics, such as the Debonaire jazz guitar.

During the early 1960s, Valco briefly produced a range of National solidbody guitars. These were unusually shaped instruments with a look that was futuristic, and yet simultaneously retro, with an Art Deco character. Cosmetics aside, the most unusual aspect of the design of this Studio 66 was the material used, a tough plastic that Valco termed "Res-O-Glas," and described as "polyester resins embedded with threads of pure gleaming glass." In a 1961 advert, it claimed that it was "a new, climatically immune, miracle material of the super space age . . . super durable . . . classically beautiful." **TB**

National
Westwood 77 1962

Type Semi-hollow body electric
Body & neck Mahogany/acrylic body; maple neck
Fingerboard Rosewood
Pick-ups One Silver Sound and two single-coil pick-ups

Valco produced National-branded solidbody electric guitars from around 1952 until they went out of business in 1968. Some of their instruments featured plastic bodies, which may have created the impression that they were after budget guitarists, but their instruments were by no means cheap.

Many National guitars of this period had extremely unusual body shapes—most famously the "Map of America" models, such as the Westwood and Glenwood ranges, with body contours seemingly inspired by the geographical outline of United States.

The semi-solid Westwood appeared in three different guises. At the top of the range, the cherry red Westwood 77 (shown here) boasted a pair of Vista Power pick-ups, labeled, curiously, as "Treble" and "Bass." These had been developed in 1952, and were used on most of National's top-end electric guitars.

There was an additional sound source: the Silver Sound bridge unit was designed to offer the player "perfect acoustic string tone reproduction." Although this seems to presage piezo/transducer bridge pick-ups, a brief look at the patent, filed in 1958, shows that it is essentially nothing more than a conventional electromagnetic pick-up. The Glenwood line was broadly similar, but with bodies constructed from National's Res-O-Glass plastic (see opposite).

Due to their unorthodox shapes, National solidbody guitars of the period are today highly collectable. Perhaps the most prominent fan of the body design was Bob Dylan, who used a white Res-O-Glas Westwood model as a slide guitar throughout his 1975 Rolling Thunder Revue tour. **TB**

Vox
Phantom 1962

Type Solidbody twelve-string electric
Body & neck Maple or ash body, maple neck
Fingerboard Rosewood
Pick-ups Two or three single-coil pick-ups

Formed after the end of the Second World War, the Jennings Organ Company made its name with the Univox, an electric keyboard similar to the more famous Clavioline (the "Telstar" instrument). The Vox brand name first appeared in 1958 with the hugely successful AC-15 amplifier. A year later, the iconic Vox AC-30 amp was joined by a range of low-price electric guitars, built by a cabinetmaking company in Essex, United Kingdom.

Founder Tom Jennings, however, had ambitions to produce something a little smarter and commissioned the London Design Centre to come up with a unique new shape. This curious pentagonal design was the result, which he christened the Phantom. The first models were built in the United Kingdom, but as demand rose, production shifted to the Eko factory in Italy.

The Phantom appeared in a number of different configurations, with two or three single-coil pick-ups, open-back tuners, and a bridge modeled on the Gibson Tune-o-matic. Optional extras included a Bigsby-style vibrato unit designed by Jennings. There was also an effect-laden stereo version—like the twelve-string model shown here—that allowed the guitar to be connected to two amps so complex panning effects could be used.

Among the early takers was Phil "Fang" Volk, who was seen on American TV playing a Phantom with Paul Revere & the Raiders. **TB**

Bernard Sumner used a Vox Phantom on early recordings with New Order, such as their debut album *Movement* (1981). It was the same guitar his former Joy Division bandmate Ian Curtis used before his death.

Joy Division's Ian Curtis, pictured on stage with a six-string Vox Phantom. ➡

Ampeg
Wild Dog 1963

Type Solidbody electric
Body & neck Sycamore and maple
Fingerboard Rosewood
Pick-ups Three Burns Split-Sonic pick-ups

Aside from the logo on the scratchplate, the Ampeg Wild Dog is identical to the British Burns "Jazz Split Sound" model. In the early 1960s, Ampeg attempted to establish a range that would compete with Gibson and Fender in the United States and also complement its own successful amplifiers—to this end, between 1963 and 1965, it imported UK-manufactured Burns guitars, and rebranded them as Wild Dogs. Ultimately this failed because they couldn't compete on price with guitars that were made in the United States, and consequently these guitars are now fairly rare.

The Burns Split-Sonic pick-ups are wired separately, divided between treble and bass, and this allowed for unusual combinations of pick-up selection—the "split-sound" setting uses the treble half of the bridge pick-up and the bass half of the neck pick-up. The pick-up selector has four options called "split-sound," "Jazz," "Treble," and "Wild Dog." It also has a Burns "Series II" tremolo system with a floating bridge that allows notes to be bent either up or down. **AJ**

Antoria
944 1963

Type Double cutaway solid electric
Body & neck Laminated hardwood body, maple neck
Fingerboard Rosewood
Pick-ups Two or four single-coil pick-ups

Antoria would much later become a Japanese brand famous for its copies of the main American guitars, but back in the early 1960s, the label was attached to this more quirky instrument.

The solid body was made from a thin slab of wood, but most of the hardware stood proud from the pearl-effect scratchplate so there was minimal routing in the body. The pick-ups in particular seem to stand right on top of the plate.

There appear to have been several varieties of 944 produced. It came with either two or four pick-ups, and the layout of switches and controls varied between guitars. Some had the name "Antoria" printed on the scratchplate instead of the headstock; others had the charming detail of the pick-up selector switches in the same color as the body. All had dot position markers, a Strat-style headstock, and covered bridges. The tailpiece served as a tremolo system, too.

In the United Kingdom the 944 was sold at £40 in the 1963 J.T. Coppock catalog. **SH**

Antoria
Bass 1963

Crown
Electric Guitar 1963

Type Solidbody bass
Body & neck Maple or alder body, maple neck
Fingerboard Rosewood
Pick-ups Two humbuckers, single coils or split coils

Type Solidbody electric
Body & neck Luan body, bolt-on neck
Fingerboard Rosewood
Pick-ups Two single-coil pick-ups

The explosion of pop music in the early 1960s led to a scramble for instruments across Europe and the United States. Instruments on both continents were highly expensive at the time, which led to the first wave of imitation imports from the factories of Japan. With bands springing up on a daily basis and money being tight in many households, and therefore putting Fender and Gibson instruments firmly out of reach for most players, the Japanese had a captive audience for their creations. Despite using Fender and Gibson instruments as templates, with a price tag around the £30 mark, it comes as no surprise that some of the guitars resembled little more than a painted plank of wood with basic hardware and pick-ups. Many instruments of the time were manufactured in the same factory but carried a different label on the headstock— these models were even found badged as Ibanez basses. J.T. Coppock (Leeds) Ltd imported the basses from companies such as Guyatone and Fujigen Gakki under the Antoria name. **JM**

By 1963, when this Crown guitar was built, Japanese manufacturers were enjoying all the benefits of the worldwide guitar boom. Demand for their six-stringed products was increasing every year, factories were increasing capacity, and new producers and distributors were getting into this hip and lucrative market seemingly every day. The mid-1960s truly was the golden age of Japanese guitar design.

This Crown has obviously been influenced by Fender's Jazzmaster and Jaguar models, right down to its pretty Sonic Blue "custom color." While it is often hard to determine the origins of obscure Japanese house brands, this particular model has an interesting pedigree. In 1962, Hoshino Gakki Ten began to produce its own guitars after originally marketing rebranded Guyatones. The model 882, along with its sisters, the 883 (three pick-ups) and 884 (four pick-ups) was one of these Hoshino instruments that found its way into early Ibanez catalogs and can sometimes be found with an Ibanez badge on the headstock. **EP**

Danelectro
Bellzouki 1963

Danelectro
Pro 1 1963

Type Hollow body bouzouki-style twelve-string electric
Body & neck Poplar frame, Masonite body, maple neck
Fingerboard Rosewood
Pick-ups Two single-coil lipstick pick-ups

Type Hollow body electric
Body & neck Pine frame, Masonite top/back, poplar neck
Fingerboard Brazilian rosewood
Pick-ups One single-coil lipstick pick-up

As founder of Danelectro guitars, Nate Daniel always had an eye for an innovative idea—and so much the better if it could be produced at a low cost. Vinnie Bell had been a top New York session player during the 1950s and also something of an inventor, and it was he who conceived of a hybrid of a traditional Greek bouzouki and a solidbody electric guitar with a bolt-on neck. The bouzouki has aa shorter scale than a standard guitar and features four paired courses of strings; Bell increased this to six and tuned it as a regular guitar.

Daniel was smitten with the idea and in 1961 the Bellzouki was launched. Like all Danelectros, while the body appears to be solid, it is in fact a poplar frame covered with Masonite.

Perhaps not the most radical development in the history of the guitar—the Bellzouki was effectively a variation on a twelve-string electric guitar—Bell would nonetheless continue his experimentation, and later developed the Coral electric sitar. **TB**

In both theory and appearance, the offset double cutaway Danelectro Pro 1 was quite an odd instrument. From a player's perspective, the eighteen-fret short-scale neck mated to a body joined at the thirteenth fret was hardly a design that encouraged playing the upper registers of the fretboard; perhaps that explains why it remained available for only one year—1963, the year of its introduction.

In practice, however, these odd traits combined with the most important element—Danelectro's characteristic lipstick pick-up—resulted in one of the mightiest slide guitars ever produced by an American guitar manufacturer. Retail price was $59.95, with an optional carrying bag costing an additional $10. Warren Haynes of The Allman Brothers Band and Gov't Mule has used his 1963 Pro 1 to great effect in and out of the studio. Its short scale, lightweight, small and uniquely angular body shape with that magical lipstick pick-up tone has made it a favorite studio tool of slide players around the globe. **DT**

Egmond
Solid 7 1963

Epiphone Crestwood
Deluxe 1963

Type Twin cutaway thinline hollow body electric
Body & neck Laminated hardwood body, maple neck
Fingerboard Wenge
Pick-ups One, two, or three single-coil pick-ups

Type Solidbody electric
Body & neck Mahogany body, set mahogany neck
Fingerboard Bound ebony fingerboard with block inlays
Pick-ups Three mini-humbucker pick-ups

Despite its name, this is a hollow body guitar made by Egmond in Holland. In the United Kingdom however, the Solid 7 was often branded by the importers as a Rosetti.

Like its fatter stablemate, the Lucky 7, this slim Egmond was designed with all the components on a "floating" platform—the pick-ups, scratchplate plus controls, and all the wiring including the jack socket and pick-up selector. This whole floating assembly could be bought separately to convert an acoustic archtop to a semi-acoustic.

There are plenty of clues that this was a low-price guitar. The headstock was bare. Instead the name "Solid 7" was stenciled on the upper bout. There was no neck pocket in the construction—the neck just screwed onto the body. There wasn't a truss rod either. And although the design featured six tuners along one side of the headstock, many Solid 7s featured two three-a-side tuners fitted end to end. Nevertheless, the Solid 7 later gained fame when it was revealed it was Paul McCartney's first electric guitar. **SH**

The rare and somewhat unloved Epiphone Crestwood Deluxe shares many features with its parent company's more popular Gibson SG Custom: both were made at Gibson's Kalamazoo factory with comparable components and construction quality and both sold for about the same price. Yet the Crestwood Deluxe sold little over 200 units during its 1963–1969 production period while the Gibson sold seven times as many.

This example in Cherry Red is at the high end of Epiphone's solidbody electric models from the 1960s, with the same body styling as other models in the range, including the Coronet, the Olympic, and the Wilshire that Jimi Hendrix played for a while from 1962. It features two volume and tone controls with a three-way selector switch, a Tune-o-matic bridge, and Tremotone vibrato—considered superior to devices Gibson used at the time. The six-a-side bat-wing headstock design was a feature that sought to capture some of the Fender Stratocaster's market share while differentiating it from Gibson models. **GD**

Epiphone
Professional 1963

Type Hollow body electric
Body & neck Mahogany body and neck
Fingerboard Rosewood
Pick-ups One mini humbucker pick-up

This must have seemed like an irresistible idea. Fed up with having to bend down to fiddle with your amp on stage? Don't want to turn your back on your audience? Why not have the controls for your amp built into the body of your guitar? An extra bit of reverb or tremolo? It's all here on the Epiphone Professional.

Close examination shows a rather lovely, Casino-style, hollow body electric, with a laminated mahogany body, a slim mahogany neck, and a twenty-two-fret rosewood fingerboard. Much of the body—including part of the f-hole—is covered by a scratchplate into which all of the guitar's electrics are fitted. This includes an intriguing selection of knobs and switches, lined up above the strings.

Where such a cool concept falls down is that it's designed to work properly with a specific Epiphone amplifier, one that came as part of the package: guitar and amp were connected via a unique multi-core cable. However, if you want to play the Professional through your Vox AC30, then it's back to the regular jack socket output (with which the Professional is also happily equipped). But when you do that, all of the pots on the top of the scratchplate are rendered useless.

The Professional also has an interesting selection of five "Tonexpressor" controls, each of which switches in a different EQ filter. Thankfully, these will work without the original amplifier.

The Professional is equipped with a single mini humbucker fitted at the neck. Many modern players would perhaps find this a limiting option, but, in the early 1960s, this was not an uncommon feature of electric guitars. **TB**

Fenton-Weill
Dualmaster 1963

Type Electric bass
Body & neck Mahogany body and neck
Fingerboard Rosewood
Pick-ups Two Weill single-coil pick-ups

By 1963, Fenton-Weill had moved to a small factory in Chelsea, South London, with a workforce of around fifteen people responsible for building and selling amplifiers and guitars, such as this fabulously stylish model, the Dualmaster. Built from parts largely imported from Germany, excepting the fine hand-built Weill single-coil pick-ups, it was available both as a guitar and bass and came in three standard colors: off-white, leaf green, and cherry red. Both body and neck were cut from mahogany and it featured a twenty-two-fret rosewood fingerboard. The model shown has been heavily customized and was originally owned and used by late-1960s pop star Keith West—best known as the singer on Mark Wirtz's "Excerpt From A Teenage Opera."

According to Fenton-Weill's 1963 advertising brochure, the twin cutaway Dualmaster incorporated "many of the features of the more expensive Fenton-Weill 'Twister' range." And it retailed for a very reasonable "34 guineas." (For anyone who is neither British nor under the age of about seventy years, a guinea was one pound and one shilling [£1.05].) The Dualmaster represented a bit of a bargain when you think that it was quarter of the price of a Burns Bison.

At this time, a young John Hornby Skewes joined Fenton-Weill—within a few years he would become a major British music retailer in his own right. Skewes would later recall that, like his former partner Jim Burns, Henry Weill was a great innovator but showed considerably less skill in his business dealings. In 1965, Fenton-Weill went bankrupt, and disappeared from the guitar world altogether, later emerging with a new business selling P.A.s and disco equipment. **TB**

Gibson
EDS-1275 1963

Type Solidbody twin-neck electric six- and twelve-string
Body & neck Mahogany body, two set maple necks
Fingerboard Rosewood
Pick-ups Four Alnico humbucker pick-ups

It's still one of the most famous—and most copied—guitar tracks of all time. Yet few of the millions who have played the iconic song "Stairway To Heaven" have played the guitar Jimmy Page used for its live performances.

The Led Zeppelin lead guitarist's instrument was a Gibson EDS-1275—which was basically a twin-necked SG. Page had to specially order his cherry-red model because Gibson wasn't producing it at the time.

The twin guitar allowed him to switch between six- and twelve-string guitar midsong. The six-string was used for the famous intro and solo of "Stairway"; the twelve-string for the rest of the song. Page's EDS-1275 was custom-made with a slightly different body shape and altered tailpieces to try to improve sustain. He replaced the Alnico pick-ups with T-top humbuckers.

Jazz rock fans also associate the Gibson twin-neck with another British virtuoso, John McLaughlin and his Mahavishnu Orchestra. Slash, James Hetfield, and Eddie Van Halen have also used the distinctive twin guitar. Even Elvis appeared with one in his 1966 movie *Spinout*.

The EDS-1275 had a shorter scale than the SG but was otherwise mostly standard Gibson fare, with mahogany throughout, Tune-o-matic bridges, and twin Alnico humbuckers on each set of strings. Today's version, however, is a Custom Shop Special and uses a maple neck. **SH**

Jimmy Page used his twin-necked EDS-1275 to play "Stairway To Heaven" live—it can be heard on the soundtrack album to the Led Zeppelin concert film *The Song Remains The Same* (1976).

John McLaughlin, star of the 1970s jazz/fusion scene, with his EDS-1275.

Gibson
Firebird I 1963

Type Solidbody electric
Body & neck Mahogany body center piece/sides/neck
Fingerboard Rosewood
Pick-ups One mini-humbucker pick-up

After attending a lecture in Kalamazoo, Michigan, given by retired auto coach-builder Ray Dietrich in 1963, Gibson president Ted McCarty approached him with a proposition to design a new guitar for the company. Dietrich gladly accepted, despite no prior experience in guitar design. Before the year was out, the Firebird range appeared on the scene, its outlandish looks turning many heads on its arrival.

Made entirely of mahogany, the neck and center section of the body were cut from a single length of timber, with "wings" attached to the sides. The headstock was carved to resemble a roosting bird and large-barreled "banjo" tuners were fitted, the tuning keys protruding to the rear. The cases in which the guitars were supplied did not take this into account, and many early Firebirds have suffered upper neck breaks as a result.

Weeks into production, the construction of the guitar's neck and center section was altered, adopting a laminate of nine strips of wood, a method still in use to this day. In addition, a red "flaming eagle" emblem was embossed into the white scratchplate.

The pick-up was designed to produce a bright, trebly sound, but the result was a raunchy screech that was not particularly practical or ear-friendly. Matched with the right amplifier, rolling the tone control around to 3 or 4 is usually sufficient to tame it. **DG**

Eric Clapton is the guitar's best-known endorsee, and his use of the Firebird I featured strongly in the last days of Cream, in particular the filmed performance in London on November 26, 1968: *Cream Farewell Concert*.

Gibson-honored blues legend Johnny Winter with his own signature Firebird. →

Gibson
Firebird VII 1963

Type Solidbody electric
Body & neck Mahogany body; mahogany/walnut neck
Fingerboard Bound ebony
Pick-ups Three mini humbucker pick-ups

When the Firebird first emerged in 1963, in addition to the single-pick-up I, Gibson introduced three further models. The III featured two pick-ups with the choice of a stud bridge or a Gibson Vibrola; the V came with the versatile Tune-o-matic bridge, a Maestro "Lyre" Vibrola, and trapezoid fingerboard inlays.

The flagship Firebird was the VII. It had all the trimmings of the Firebird V, with the addition of a third pick-up, a bound ebony fingerboard with block inlays, and striking gold-plated hardware—including the Maestro Vibrola, covers of the Gibson mini humbuckers and machine heads.

Gibson used the mini humbucker on all its "reverse" Firebirds. Its construction differed from its regular PAF humbuckers, providing a cleaner, brighter tone—one reason why Firebirds sound very distinct from the company's other solidbody electrics. The mini humbucker had originally been designed by Epiphone, and had come into Gibson's hands as a result of the company acquisition at the end of the 1950s.

The Firebird VII shown here is a 1963 model belonging to Phil Manzanera, guitarist with Roxy Music. Gibson production records show that only 20 VIIs were built that year—and probably no more than 250 were made in total before the body shape changed to the "non-reverse" style in 1965. **TB**

The Firebird VII has been Phil Manzanera's principal guitar since the early 1970s: in 2008, he even used the name as the title for a solo album. Its capabilities in his hands are showcased in Roxy Music's stunning second album, *For Your Pleasure* (1973).

Gibson
Thunderbird IV 1963

Type Solidbody electric bass
Body & neck Mahogany body; maple or mahogany neck
Fingerboard Ebony or rosewood
Pick-ups One or two bass humbucker pick-ups

In 1963, Gibson hired Ray Dietrich—who had previously worked for automobile makers Chrysler, Checker, and Lincoln—to develop a new look. He came up with the original "reverse" design for the Firebird guitar (see page 298). There was also an electric bass counterpart, the Thunderbird.

Gibson had achieved limited success in the bass guitar market. Its earlier models from the "EB" range had all featured 30½ in. (77.5 cm) scale lengths—3½ in. (8.8 cm) shorter than the full-scale-length Fenders preferred by most professional bass players. The Thunderbird bass drew on the construction style of the Rickenbacker 4001: it featured a 34 in. (86.3 cm) scale and a straight-through neck.

There were two Thunderbird models, and they slotted into the numbering system used by the Firebirds. The Thunderbird II was companion to the Firebird I, with a single pick-up, volume, and tone control; the Thunderbird IV (shown here) was the twin-pick-up counterpart to the Firebird III.

In 1966, following a legal claim by Fender that the body shape had copied its Jazzmaster guitar, Gibson changed the design of both "Birds" to the "non-reverse" body shape, where the lower extending horn was moved to the upper body. The non-reverse Thunderbird remained in production until 1969. **TB**

The Who's John Entwistle went through periods of exclusively playing one instrument—before moving on to something altogether different. He played a "reverse" Thunderbird during the second half of the 1960s, notably on *The Who Sell Out* (1967).

Gretsch
6070 Bass 1963

Type Hollow body electric bass
Body & neck Maple body and neck
Fingerboard Rosewood
Pick-ups One Filter'Tron pick-up

The 6070 was often referred to as the Country Gentleman, and it was Gretsch's most successful bass. This high-quality instrument had a long-scale neck and a hollow double cutaway body but was perfectly balanced for playing.

The 6070 was packed with interesting features: for example, those f-holes were purely cosmetic; they were painted on. This helped minimize feedback. There was a three-position tone switch, separate mute switch, two different finger rests, a "string-space-control" bridge, a single Filter'Tron bass pick-up near the bridge, and a tailpiece with a cut-out "G" decoration. There was even an extendable endpin that allowed the Gretsch to be played as upright bass.

The new hollow body bass was an immediate success. Who bassist John Entwistle played one in a summer 1965 *Ready Steady Go!* TV appearance. Soon there was a two-pick-up version—the 6072—then short-scale versions, which were famously played by Monkees bassist Peter Tork. **SH**

Gretsch
6109 Twist 1963

Type Solidbody electric
Body & neck Mahogany
Fingerboard Rosewood
Pick-ups One HiLo'Tron pick-up

Gretsch had decided to extend its appeal and create a guitar to compete with the successful Gibson Les Paul Junior. The Corvette solidbody range had a similar mahogany body for sustain, but the asymmetrical double cutaway design never really caught on.

The Twist model was a marketing-led special edition of the Corvette that had just a single bridge pick-up. It came with a yellow or red body, but its distinctive feature was a striped Lucite plastic pickguard. This was an attempt to join the contemporary craze for twisted peppermint candy in the United States.

The quality was high—with Kluson tuners, a nicely beveled body like an SG, and wooden-rimmed control knobs. Some were available with a Burns tremolo arm; others had Gretsch's unusual "Tone Twister" device. This was a primitive vibrato device fixed to the strings between the bridge and tailpiece. Sadly for Gretsch, it was hopeless at creating the fashionable tremolo sound of the time . . . but it was very effective in breaking strings. **SH**

Guild
Thunderbird 1963

Harmony H19 Holiday
Silhouette 1963

Type Solidbody electric
Body & neck Mahogany body, set neck
Fingerboard Bound rosewood, with block inlays
Pick-ups Two Guild humbucker pick-ups

Type Cutaway solidbody electric
Body & neck Maple, birch, or alder body; maple neck
Fingerboard Rosewood
Pick-ups One or two single-coil or humbucker pick-ups

When Guild introduced itself to the musical instrument business in 1953, it announced the manufacture of the still-embryonic solidbody electric guitar. In fact, it took Guild ten years to honor its promise: in its 1963 catalog, it showed three electric solidbodies—the Thunderbird S-200, the Polara S-100, and the Jet Star S-50.

The Thunderbird's original, quite conservative shape changed by 1964 into a more exaggerated asymmetrical design that blended elements of Gibson's SG and Fender's Jaguar—both in style and function—with three slide switches and a top-mounting vibrato. Uniquely, the Thunderbird and Polara featured a built-in stand that flipped out from the back of the guitar.

The Guild Anti-Hum humbucker became a favorite of many players, noted for its biting tonality. It seems the Thunderbird ceased production in 1968, although it still featured in Guild's literature. By the early 1970s, the trio of solidbodies had morphed into the more Gibson SG-like S-100 (with later S-90 and S-50 variants) and that built-in stand was consigned to guitar history. **DB**

Harmony's low-priced solid electric range of the mid-1960s rolled out of the Chicago factory between 1963 and 1967 in various versions, usually for different catalogs and department stores. The Silvertone 1478 was sold through Sears, the Holiday Silhouette was sold through the Aldens catalog, and the Harmony H-series guitars were put on general sale.

Among these guitars there were one- and two-pick-up versions and a confusing mix of various pieces of hardware and finishes. What they all shared was this simple lightweight asymmetrical body (vaguely inspired by Fender's Jaguar and Jazzmaster), a bright 1960s sound, and a low price tag, starting around $65.

Features included a vibrato tailpiece (for "Hawaiian guitar effects," according to the Sears catalog) and unshielded electrics, which meant the guitar gave off a distinctive hum when it was plugged in. The pick-ups, though, were one of the strong points—sometimes they were DeArmond "Gold Tone" humbuckers—although other pick-ups seem to have been fitted, too. **SH**

Hohner
Holborn 1963

Type Twin cutaway solidbody electric
Body & neck Beech body, maple neck
Fingerboard Rosewood
Pick-ups Two single-coil pick-ups

Matthias Hohner founded a company making musical instruments in southern Germany in 1857. He built the largest harmonica factory in the world and the company he launched still makes around a million harmonicas a year. In the 1960s, Hohner joined the latest global musical craze by launching its own electric guitars, which were low-cost rebranded instruments built for it by other manufacturers.

This early and rare Holborn electric was one of the first sold under the Hohner name. It was made in Britain, but guitar historians can't agree on who made it. In the

> *"This is the two-pick-up 'stablemate' of my Hohner Kingsway 111 and was described... as a 'solid guitar for the advanced player.'"*
> GUY MACKENZIE

murky mixed-up beginnings of the British guitar industry, the Holborn may have been built by Fenton Weill or Stuart Darkins' furniture workshop in Essex, which built early guitars for Vox and Dallas around the same time. The Holborn certainly looks similar to Vox's Ace produced at the same time. Or it could have used a combination of both Darkins' woodworking and Weill's electrics.

Whatever its provenance, the Holborn had a solid beech body topped by maple veneer. It had two chrome-covered pick-ups, a bolt-on neck, and a plastic scratchplate with "Holborn" printed vertically. The scratchplate was so thin you could clearly see the routed-out sections underneath it. This guitar belongs to British collector Guy Mackenzie and has had a nonstandard Broadway tremolo tailpiece added. **SH**

Hopf
Saturn 63 1963

Type Hollow body electric
Body & neck Maple/spruce body; maple neck
Fingerboard Rosewood
Pick-ups Two single-coil pick-ups

The Hopf family's involvement with the building of musical instruments in Germany dates back to the seventeenth century. The company that reached a peak of output in the early 1960s was founded in 1906 by Max Ernst Hopf. Initially, it produced classical guitars, but, in the 1950s, some attractive acoustic and electric archtop models started to appear—among them individualistic designs by luthier Gustav Glassl.

Until Hopf ceased trading in the mid-1980s, its best-selling model was the Saturn 63. Launched in 1963, it's certainly a significantly higher-quality electric than most guitars being produced outside of the United States at that time. The 16-in. (40.5-cm) hollow body was built from maple, with a spruce top; the bolt-on maple neck supported a twenty-fret rosewood fingerboard. Among other notable features is an unusually long 26-in. (66-cm) scale length—which is edging toward the lower reaches of the baritone range.

The lack of a clear influence found in a guitar like this is quite surprising: instead of a violin-style f-hole, cut into the top is a pair of unusual "cat's-eyes" sound holes. These, like the body itself, have a metal binding, which, along with the control panel, gives the guitar a rather futuristic look.

The electrics are simple but, again, unorthodox. The small octagonal knob is the master volume, and the two plastic-levered knobs look after the tone and pick-up switching. As on several German guitars of the period, the amplifier connection is via a DIN socket, rather than the standard jack socket. The single-coil pick-ups produce a pleasant Gretsch-like tone. **TB**

Brian May
Red Special 1963

Type Solidbody electric
Body & neck Oak body/neck, mahogany top/back
Fingerboard Painted oak
Pick-ups Three customized single-coil Burns Tri-Sonics

In an unusual route to stardom, Brian May abandoned a PhD in astrophysics to take a shot at the big time with his band, Queen. The instrument with which he would find fame was also curious. At a time when many parents saw the electric guitar as a gateway to a life of delinquency, aviation engineer Harold May embraced the idea of helping his sixteen-year-old son create an instrument from scratch.

Work began during May's school summer vacation in 1963. The wood derived from a reclaimed eighteenth-century oak mantelpiece. They carved a chambered body and covered it with two mahogany sheets to give the appearance of a solid piece of wood. The guitar's coloring was achieved using Rustin's plastic boat varnish.

The electrics of the Red Special were also unusual, featuring three Burns Tri-Sonic pick-ups, each customized in Araldite epoxy to prevent feedback. The guitar's unique sound was achieved by the unusual wiring of three pick-ups; they were connected in series, meaning the output from one pick-up is fed into the next. They also decided against using a selector switch, and each pick-up was given its own on/off and phase switches.

After thirty-five years of rock stardom, May ended what he called "the longest gap year ever," when in 2007 he finally submitted—successfully—his doctoral thesis to Imperial College, London. **TB**

Brian May's Red Special can be heard on all of Queen's albums, among them *A Night At The Opera* (1975), which contains the track "Bohemian Rhapsody," the United Kingdom's biggest-selling rock single of all time.

← Brian May used his home-built guitar throughout his time with Queen.

Mosrite
Mark 1 "Ventures" 1963

Type Solidbody electric
Body & neck Alder body, bolt-on maple neck
Fingerboard Rosewood
Pick-ups Two hand-wound single-coil pick-ups

The Mosrite brand first appeared in 1956, launched in California by Semie Moseley, a former Rickenbacker employee who had trained under both guitar pioneer Paul Bigsby and noted luthier Roger Rossmeisl, who would later create the classic Thinline series for Fender.

Mosrite's guitars were initially high-end custom-built instruments, but recognition came in 1963 when Moseley built a guitar for Nokie Edwards of The Ventures, at that time the most popular instrumental surf band in the United States. The Mosrite Ventures models created a visual template for which the brand would ultimately be remembered. The striking, characteristic body shape with its prominent treble horn is in essence a mirrored Fender Stratocaster. The feel of the body was enhanced with the use of the so-called "German Carve," a finely cut beveled edge that he learned from his years working with Rossmeisl.

Known later as the Mark 1, the guitar also incorporated Moseley's hardware, hand-wound pick-ups, and a vibrato arm, the Vibramute, designed with a mechanism that enabled the strings to be deadened.

Mosrite guitars were not cheap—a Mark 1 came in at twice the retail price of a Stratocaster. Curiously, however, it was in Japan that the brand flourished, a fact largely attributable to the fact that The Ventures were as popular as The Beatles in the Far East. **TB**

The Ventures in the United States and The Shadows in the United Kingdom remain the most successful guitar instrumental bands. Just as The Shadows all played specially created Burns guitars, The Ventures had their own "Mossies," which can be heard on *Ventures In Space* (1963).

Johnny Ramone was a noted Mosrite fan—he is seen here playing a Mark II. ➜

Mosrite Mark 1 "Ventures" Bass 1963

Type Solidbody electric bass
Body & neck Alder body; maple neck
Fingerboard Rosewood
Pick-ups One neck pick-up

Mosrite founder Semie Moseley established himself by creating the famous double-neck guitar played by Joe Maphis. The Mosrite name was a combination of the first part of his surname and the last part of that of the Reverend Ray Boatwright, his friend and financial backer. Success came with the Mark I "Ventures" models, built from 1963 to 1967—a range of guitars and basses endorsed and played by The Ventures, America's most popular instrumental band.

The Mark I bass has many of the same features as its six-string counterpart: the "reverse Stratocaster" body, and the sumptuous German Carve contours, as well as the short-scale 30-in. (76-cm) neck, with Mosrite's famously comfortable deep-set "speed frets." The single-neck pick-up is ideal for anyone looking for a 1960s-style "thump"—the kind of sound that Paul McCartney used to manage with his Höfner.

By 1964, The Ventures' twangy sound was losing its appeal, especially with the British Beat Invasion in full swing. Weirdly, however, they became increasingly successful in Japan, where Mosrite guitars suddenly became the hot new thing. But with Moseley unable to meet the new demand, numerous Mosrite-inspired instruments began to emerge, produced in large numbers by the likes of Yamaha, Ibanez, and Tokai.

After The Ventures' endorsement of Mosrite ended in 1968, Moseley struggled, and his factory closed down a year later. He would periodically attempt to revive the brand over the following two decades until his death in 1992. Even today, there are a surprising number of manufacturers producing replicas of the Mosrite Mark I. **TB**

National
Newport 84 1963

Type Hollow body electric
Body & neck Res-O-Glas and maple
Fingerboard Rosewood
Pick-ups One single-coil pick-up and one Piezo tranducer

Valco, the company responsible for the Newport 84, was created in 1943 by former partners of the National Dobro Company, best known for its resonator guitars. In 1961, it developed a method of molding guitar bodies out of polyester resin and glass threads, which it referred to as "Res-O-Glas." The guitar's finish was sprayed into a mold and this was sprayed with the material. The two pieces (front and back) were screwed together with five screws entering from the back and going into blocks of maple glued to the inside. As a result, the guitars weighed less than 8 lb. (3.5 kg).

The most visually striking feature of the Newport— like its sibling Glenwood range—was the body. Often now referred to as National's "map" guitar, the molded Res-O-Glas body is in the shape of the American map, with the upper pointed treble bout corresponding to the state of Florida when the guitar is held horizontally. The Newport was originally labeled "Val-Pro" and came in four models, the 82, 84, and 88 guitars, and the 85 bass. Each one included a three-way tone switch with volume knobs for the three positions plus a master volume control. The 88 was the luxury model. In 1964, the Newport was rebadged as a National guitar and given some minor changes, such as a pointed treble horn and vibrato tailpiece. The map guitar had one major drawback—there was no adjustable truss rod.

Valco guitars may have looked a little cheap and tacky back in the 1960s, but now they are insanely cool and have been used by stars such as David Bowie, The Cure, and The White Stripes. The Newport 84 has been reissued by Eastwood Guitars in recent years, although the body is now made of wood. **TB**

Rickenbacker
Astro Kit 1963

Voss
Electric Guitar 1963

Type Solidbody electric kit
Body & neck Pine and maple
Fingerboard Maple
Pick-ups One single-coil pick-up

Type Twin cutaway solidbody electric
Body & neck Laminated hardwood body, maple neck
Fingerboard Rosewood
Pick-ups Three single-coil pick-ups

While the more practical guitar players among us may have welcomed the concept of the build-it-yourself guitar kit, few name brands have ever produced one. But, as in many other areas, Rickenbacker is the exception.

Designed by Rickenbacker's Marvin Boyd, the Astro Kit guitar was a fully fledged twenty-five-part DIY project that came with unpainted body and neck and instructions. Rickenbacker claimed it was "ready to finish and assemble" and that "pliers and screwdriver" were the only tools needed. It was originally aimed at the 1963 Christmas market, by which time John Lennon had already been using his famous 325 for some time, and in a few short months a brand new twelve-string Rickenbacker would find its way into the hands of George Harrison and a guaranteed place in electric guitar folklore.

It was really quite a futuristic-looking design with a twenty-two-fret maple neck, a single pick-up with its volume and tone controls, plus an output jack placed on the offset, angular scratchplate. **DT**

The 1960s German guitar industry is as complicated to unravel as that of the United Kingdom and Japan. There was such a mix of old and new manufacturers and portable brand names that it makes the job of guitar historians almost impossible at times.

This asymmetrical double cutaway solidbody electric was labeled a Voss when it was built in 1963. Yet guitar collectors, like Britain's Guy McKenzie, who owns this example, believe it was built by the Klira company.

Klira had made stringed instruments in Germany since 1887, starting with violins and only embracing guitars as the trend took off in the 1950s. By the 1960s, it was an established guitar maker based in Bubenreuth in Bavaria. The name Voss was applied by the German distributors and exporters Voss Musik.

The actual guitar has a flat fingerboard, Fender-style headstock, and an impressive array of switches and buttons. The features are good quality for the era, with an adjustable bridge, truss rod, and tailpiece tremolo system. **SH**

Airline
Res-O-Glas 1964

Alamo
Fiesta 2568R 1964

Type Semi-hollow body electric
Body & neck Res-O-Glas body, maple neck
Fingerboard Rosewood
Pick-ups Two single-coil pick-ups

Type Double cutaway thinline hollow body electric
Body & neck Birch laminate body, maple neck
Fingerboard Rosewood
Pick-ups One, two, or three single-coil pick-ups

In the early days of the solidbody electric guitar, nobody would have imagined that, more than a half century later, Strats, Teles, and Les Pauls would be viewed as iconic designs, favored by successive generations of guitar royalty. In the early 1960s, some guitar makers tapped into the space-age mood of the time, producing models that appeared radically futuristic, but that now seem rather quaint—like this 1964 Airline Res-O-Glas.

Sold via mail-order catalog, the Res-O-Glas marks one of the earliest uses of composite materials in guitar manufacture. The body was made from glass fiber, although it was chosen less for its acoustic properties than its ability to withstand knocks. It comprised of two molded, chambered halves, the seam of which was then hidden with a strip of white vinyl binding around the edge.

For decades, the Res-O-Glas was little more than an obscure footnote in guitar history until its rediscovery in the late 1990s by Jack White of The White Stripes. **TB**

Vaguely inspired by Rickenbacker designs, this line of hollow body guitars was built by Alamo Electronics. Alamo was the brainchild of publisher Milton Fink who had employed Charles Eilenberg to start building amplifiers and lap steel guitars. By the early 1960s Alamo tried to join the growing electric guitar craze. Eilenberg created the Fiesta, a budget lightweight instrument that was aimed at the student/catalog market in the United States and sold from only $65.

Alamo had clearly studied the American budget guitar opposition. The pick-ups were single-coil units modeled on Kay's "speedbumps" and the "Acra-tune" bridge and tailpiece assembly were very similar to Danelectro's. It was just an angled piece of metal with six string holes and an adjustable saddle.

Different models had one, two, or three of the small but punchy single-coil pick-ups and some came with basic tremolo systems. Alamo's electronics background meant that it could offer beginners an amp-and-guitar package, with the Fiesta and an amp for $117.50. **SH**

Burns
Marvin 1964

Type Solidbody electric
Body & neck Honduras mahogany body, rock maple neck
Fingerboard Rosewood
Pick-ups Three Burns Rez-O-Matik single-coil pick-ups

After a couple of false starts, by 1964 Jim Burns was well established as one of the most significant makers of electric guitar outside of the United States. Burns models were not cheap copies of Fenders and Gibsons, but had a character and sound of their own. By this time Burns had managed to export guitars across the Atlantic, where they were badged and marketed by Ampeg.

It was a sign of Burns' success that he was able to attract as endorsees Britain's most popular band prior to The Beatles: The Shadows. Featuring Hank Marvin, The Shadows not only provided backing for singer Cliff Richard, but were also Britain's most popular guitar instrumental band. A typical Shadows record was free of flash or bluster—a catchy melody played cleanly with a touch of echo or reverb and gentle working of the vibrato arm. It was a simple recipe that provided sixty-nine hit singles, more than half of which were sans Cliff.

The Shadows' guitarists, Marvin and Bruce Welch, were the earliest British users of Fender Stratocasters. In 1963 they approached Burns to produce a new guitar, one that would maintain tuning better than their Fenders. What emerged was the Burns Marvin, a luxury three-pick-up model with an unusual scrolled headstock. Of greater significance, it also incorporated his Rez-O-Tube vibrato, which would enable Hank to twang away to his heart's content and stay in tune. **TB**

The Sound Of The Shadows (1965)—The Shadows' fourth album—features the band with their new Burns guitars. Only an estimated 300 original Marvins were built, making them highly collectible today.

It's Burns night! Hank Marvin in rehearsal with The Shadows in 1964. ➡

Catalina
Electric Guitar 1964

Type Solidbody electric
Body & neck Laminated body, bolt-on neck
Fingerboard Rosewood
Pick-ups One Rowe-DeArmond single-coil pick-up

The Kay Vanguard is a classic mid-1960s American student model, and has been a common flea-market and pawn-shop find for decades. These days, a nice example, while not exactly rare, is nevertheless an interesting enough prize, especially if it is a rather unusual variant that sports an obscure house brand and features a bright-red finish that rarely shows up in the standard Kay line.

During the mid-1960s guitar boom, one could buy such guitars everywhere. This example dates to 1964, which is easily evidenced by the date marked on the underside of its single Rowe-DeArmond pick-up. While indeed a simple budget model, the guitar nevertheless appears appropriately upscale thanks to its "custom color." It also originally housed a top-mounted Japanese vibrato that has since been removed on this example. Within a year or two, Japanese hardware would no longer be a novelty on American student models. By 1968, most such guitars would be wholly produced in Japan, and firms like Kay would be out of business. **EP**

Electro
ES-17 1964

Type Solidbody electric
Body & neck Maple body in Fireglo finish, set maple neck
Fingerboard Rosewood
Pick-ups One "Toaster Top" single-coil pick-up

Among the impressive range of guitars seen on tour in Tom Petty and the Heartbreakers' heyday was the seemingly humbler 1964 Electro ES-17. But for the differences in neck construction and the lesser quality of the finish, the Electro ES-17 is virtually identical to the higher-priced and more highly prized Rickenbacker 425 model. While the 425 has a neck-through-body construction, the ES-17 has a set neck. On the ES-17 the finish is thinner and not as smooth as the Rickenbacker. The body is thin and the guitar very light. Also light is its action, and it is considered easy to play. On the minus side, given its simple electronics, the tonal variety is limited and intonation can be a problem with the compensated metal bridge.

The ES-17 and its smaller sibling, the three-quarter-size ES-16, were part of a line of guitars produced by the Electro String Instrument Corporation, manufactured at the Rickenbacker plant and sold through a company called Radio-Tel, which also carried the same guitar with Ryder and Contello labels. **GD**

Fender Mustang 1964

Fender Stratocaster "Pre-CBS" 1964

Type Solidbody electric
Body & neck Poplar, alder, ash, basswood body; maple neck
Fingerboard Maple or rosewood
Pick-ups Two single-coil pick-ups

Type Solidbody electric
Body & neck Alder body; maple neck
Fingerboard Maple or rosewood
Pick-ups Three single-coil pick-ups

In the 1950s, Leo Fender pioneered "student" guitars: models such as the Musicmaster, and the Duo-Sonic, which were affordable, and had shorter necks that made it easier for underdeveloped fingers to make those difficult stretches.

The Mustang was in this tradition. With an offset-waisted body like a miniature Jazzmaster, it was available as a "three-quarter," 22½-in. (57-cm) scale length, twenty-one-fret model, or with a 24-in. (61-cm) scale length and twenty-two frets. Its electrics were a departure: both angled single-coil pick-ups had dedicated three-way switches operating in "on-off-on" mode, instead of a regular two-way selector, and the two "on" positions offered phase reversal. Also novel was the Dynamic Vibrato tailpiece, thought by many to be more sensitive and reliable than the Stratocaster's Synchronized Tremolo.

Fender continued producing the Mustang until 1982. Its later adoption by Sonic Youth, Nirvana, and The Melvins inspired the makers to reissue it in 1990. **TB**

By 1964, Fender was the most profitable musical instrument manufacturer in the United States, with annual sales of over $10 million. And business had now gone global: with a relaxing of import duties, American guitars had begun to hit Europe.

Leading the company during this time took its toll on founder Leo Fender. Early in 1964, thinking he was seriously ill, he agreed to sell his company for $13 million to the Columbia Broadcasting System (CBS).

Following the CBS takeover, the quality of Fender guitars declined greatly. The Stratocaster underwent a number of adverse changes: a new peghead; the body contouring was no longer sculpted and sleek; cheaper plastics were used on the pickguards; Indian rosewood replaced Brazilian rosewood on the fingerboards; polyurethane lacquer replaced nitrocellulose; and a new, one-piece die-cast bridge was hated by purists.

The Stratocaster remained a popular instrument, but it is only pre-CBS models that are now of interest to serious collectors. **TB**

Freshman
5800 1964

Type Solidbody electric
Body & neck Laminated hardwood body, maple neck
Fingerboard Rosewood
Pick-ups Two single-coil pick-ups

With its distinctive small body and sloping cutaway, the Freshman 5800 was branded a Selmer or Futurama when it went on sale in 1964. In reality, it was another example of a low-priced import from Japan. There was only one color scheme of red, white, and black. The word "Freshman" was written in a spaghetti-style script on the headstock, clearly meant to copy the Fender style. It seems this guitar was a close relative of an earlier Guyatone, but the history of Japanese guitars of this era is hard to untangle as various manufacturers used different names and even swapped parts between them. Importers then renamed them with any word they thought would catch the imagination of buyers.

The 1950s Guyatone version was a higher-quality guitar with a thicker body, set neck, and better pick-ups, while the Freshman was probably put together in the United Kingdom using the cheapest parts available. Photographs of Rory Storm and the Hurricanes (probably best remembered as Ringo's band before he joined The Beatles) in the late 1950s show Johnny "Guitar" Byrne holding the Guyatone—its cut-down body makes it look almost like a ukulele with a long neck.

The 5800, however, did have a rather nicely designed two-tone scratchplate housing its two "Freshman" pick-ups behind a wood-grain finish and with half mounts at either side. A sales catalog of the time called them "omni-directional response pick-ups." There was a "rhythm/solo" selector and three rotary controls. The neck, which was attached using just two screws, had no inlays or a truss rod and so tended to develop a warp that made it unplayable. **SH/AJ**

Gemelli
195/4/V 1964

Type Solidbody electric
Body & neck Hardwood body, maple neck
Fingerboard Acrylic
Pick-ups Four single-coil pick-ups

Hailing from the town of Recanti, twin brothers Umberto and Benito Cingolani had first worked on the designs of early models for Alvaro Bartolini. By 1963 they had struck out on their own creating the Gemelli brand—aptly enough, derived from the Italian word for twins.

Stylistically, the Gemelli models were very similar to those produced by Bartolini (see page 274), with sparkly plastic finishes well to the fore, and control panels featuring the same push-buttons and rocker switches found on Italian accordions.

"The guitar in constant demand … equipped with accessories of the highest precision … can be supplied with or without vibrator."
GEMELLI CATALOG, 1965

The four-pick-up 195/4/V was obviously derived from the juggernaut American guitars in body shape than many Italian guitars of the period, being squarely based on Fender Stratocaster/Jazzmaster styling. Of particular interest is the off-white acrylic fingerboard covering—an alternative take on the Hagstrom idea. This provided very effective protection—surviving Gemellis can often look like new … as long as the frets have not become dislodged.

Gemellis, like other 1960s Italian guitar brands, are now increasingly collectible. They can be beautiful guitars to have hanging on your wall as a talking point, or for posing with in a music video. But, in truth, as genuine musical instruments they leave more than a little to be desired. **TB**

Gibson SG Standard "The Fool" 1964

Type Solidbody electric
Body & neck Mahogany body, set mahogany neck
Fingerboard Rosewood
Pick-ups Two humbucker pick-ups

Young 1960s blues guitarist Eric Clapton had seen the work of the pair of Dutch psychedelic artists that called themselves "The Fool." They had painted the outside of The Beatles' Apple shop in London, decorated guitars and pianos for The Beatles, and designed clothes and album sleeves for top bands such as Procol Harum, The Hollies, and The Move.

In 1967, Clapton let the pair loose on his newly bought 1964 double cutaway cherry SG Standard. The two Dutch hippy artists, Simon Posthuma and Marijke Koger, promptly painted their 1960s-style image with oil paint over the whole guitar . . . even the back of the neck and fretboard. Clapton also hardtailed the SG by fixing the stock tremolo in place and switched the Kluson tuners for Grovers.

It's difficult to believe this paint-covered standard Gibson was the main instrument for Cream's lead guitarist for the next two years—probably their creative peak. It was used throughout the LP *Disraeli Gears* (1967) and appeared on *Wheels Of Fire* (1968), *Goodbye* (1969), and on two live albums. All the while, audiences reported seeing flakes of paint fall from the neck during Clapton's solos.

Eventually Clapton left the guitar with his friend George Harrison and it found its way to Todd Rundgren. The Fool became his main instrument in the 1970s. **SH**

Clapton used his customized "SG Fool" throughout Cream's second album *Disraeli Gears* (1967), which included the hit singles "Sunshine Of Your Love" and "Strange Brew." This was Cream's breakthrough recording, reaching No. 4 in the United States.

Clapton's colorful SG was eventually sold at auction for $500,000.

Gibson
Tal Farlow 1964

Type Electric hollow body archtop
Body & neck Maple top, back, and sides
Fingerboard Ebony
Pick-ups Two full-size humbucker pick-ups

Following Johnny Smith and Barney Kessel in Gibson's procession of signature jazz guitarists in the early 1960s was bebop guitar luminary Tal Farlow. Though highly respected among his peers in the jazz scene of the 1950s, and earning the nickname "The Gibson Boy" for his pioneering approach along the way, Gibson didn't actually sign him up for an Artist Model endorsement until 1962—by which time he'd settled into semiretirement from music, working as a sign writer in Sea Bright, New Jersey, for four years.

 He was closely involved with the signature model he designed, and the guitar was essentially a variation on his own personal ES-350. Like that guitar, it has a 17-in. (43-cm) body, a 25½-in. (64.75-cm) scale, a Venetian cutaway, and a maple top. Yet there are a number of cosmetic idiosyncrasies. There was the inlaid binding material in the lower bout, creating a scroll effect; a double-crown headstock inlay; a quirky pickguard; inverted J-200-style fingerboard inlays; a signature tailpiece with rosewood block; and a Viceroy Brown sunburst finish. Sonically, Farlow had suggested a sliding pick-up system, but settled instead for a pair of full-size humbuckers. The Tal Farlow is a much-coveted rarity, with only 215 being made between 1962 and 1969. Gibson reissued the model in the 1990s, in either sunburst or Viceroy Brown sunburst finishes. **OB**

The album *Chance Meeting* (1997) captures a joyous live performance from 1980 where virtuoso jazz guitarists Tal Farlow and Lenny Breau bridge the generation gap with sophisticated style. Farlow's signature guitar takes pride of place on the cover.

Gibson
Trini Lopez 1964

Type Hollow body electric
Body & neck Maple body, mahogany neck
Fingerboard Rosewood
Pick-ups Two humbucker pick-ups

Any youngster studying a list of classic Gibson signature models may find some of the names quite baffling. Tal Farlow? Jimmy Byrd? Barney Kessel? So who was Trini Lopez? Trini Lopez was America's first major Chicano popstar, who chalked up more than a dozen hit records, among them the folk song "If I Had A Hammer," which topped the charts in thirty-six countries in 1963. It was at this point that Gibson offered the young singer–guitarist his own signature model. This new instrument was, they stated boldly: "As exciting as the young performer who helped create it." In truth, it was a cosmetically modified ES-335.

Introduced in 1958, the ES-335 had been one of Gibson's great success stories. It was a guitar that, unlike a number of the company's other famous electrics, achieved immediate popularity. Gibson had already issued a number of variants before the Trini Lopez.

An undoubtedly attractive guitar, the Trini Lopez takes a diamond theme and runs with it. The violin-style f-holes are replaced with elongated diamond slits, and the fingerboard features matching split-diamond inlays. Perhaps the most curious difference is in the six-in-line headstock design, taken from the Gibson Firebird.

Enduringly popular, such high-profile players as Noel Gallagher from Oasis and Dave Grohl from Foo Fighters have been seen on stage sporting a "Trini." **TB**

He may have first found success as the drummer with Nirvana, but Dave Grohl played a Gibson Trini Lopez Standard throughout The Foo Fighters' 2005 double album *In Your Honor*.

Ibanez
1803 Bison 1964

Kent
Polaris 1964

Type Solidbody electric
Body & neck Mahogany body, maple neck
Fingerboard Rosewood
Pick-ups Three single-coil pick-ups

Type Solidbody double cutaway electric
Body & neck Mahogany body, maple neck
Fingerboard Rosewood
Pick-ups One, two, or three single-coil pick-ups

Now one of the largest Japanese guitar manufacturers in the world, Ibanez has a convoluted history dating back to 1870, when luthier Salvador Ibáñez built classical guitars that were exported to Japan. When the Ibáñez workshop was destroyed during the Spanish Civil War, the Hoshino Gakki company bought the rights from the family to produce Ibáñez-branded guitars in Japan.

Like other Japanese makers of the period, Hoshino responded to the "eleki" craze that saw Japanese youth forming electric-guitar-based beat groups, by building cheap copies of guitars from the West. The first Ibáñez electric guitars appeared in 1962, early catalogs showing a mixture of Japanese-styled designs and copies of U.S. and European models, among them, surprisingly, copies of models produced in the United Kingdom by Burns.

Although extremely well made, the model 1803 shown here is clearly more than "inspired" by the Burns Bison. Not only do we see the unique double cutaway horns, but even the unusually narrow six-in-a-line tuner arrangement on the headstock. **TB**

Back in 1964, the Polaris nuclear rocket was thought to be so cool that this Japanese import was named after it. The Polaris was a low-priced lightweight instrument, probably originally made by Guyatone but rebranded for American customers.

The quality of the Polaris was surprisingly good. It was made of solid wood, the fingerboard was good-quality rosewood, and the pick-ups had a well-rounded sound. Polaris I had one single-coil, Polaris II had two, and, not surprisingly, Polaris III had three pick-ups.

The basic guitar was promising, but there was no truss rod to adjust the neck and no way of adjusting the plastic bridge. The strings merely sat on metal rollers. Other cheaper details included six-in-a-line open-back tuners and the flimsy plastic control knobs and switches. Some guitars came with a basic tremolo system and a metal scratchplate.

Nevertheless, Lee Ranaldo from Sonic Youth used Polaris as a slide guitar and Bruce Springsteen is thought to have owned one early in his career. **SH**

Levin
Goliath 1964

National/Supro
Folkstar 1964

Type Dreadnought steel-string acoustic
Body & neck Maple back and sides, spruce top, bolt-on mahogany neck
Fingerboard Rosewood or ebony

Type Acoustic single cone resonator
Body & neck Fiberglass body, Kord-King neck
Other features Hardwood fingerboard, "Biscuit" bridge, aluminum tailpiece, Gumby head, Kluson butterfly tuners

Levin was a guitar manufacturer based in Gothenburg, Sweden. It sold guitars to the UK market under the name Levin and to the U.S. market under the name Goya.

By the mid-1960s, its Goliath guitars had a reputation in Europe as one of the best-value-for-sound acoustic guitars. Even at the height of the electric guitar craze, it was a big dreadnought-sized acoustic guitar made in the traditional way. The updated model of 1964 was officially called the Goya N-26 in the United States and the Levin LN-26 in Europe, although many simply called it the Goliath.

Levin were not trying to emulate the cool new electric guitars: the neck wasn't fashionably slim but a hefty piece of mahogany with an adjustable truss rod. The scale was slightly shorter than normal, but it felt cumbersome to players switching from solid electrics.

In the United Kingdom, famous users ranged from British home-grown country star Kelvin Henderson to Pete Townshend, who played a Goliath in his pre-Who days in The Detours. **SH**

Supro was a brand of guitars made by Valco from the 1930s. Valco, founded when the National and Dobro companies merged in 1935, manufactured acoustic guitars, metal-faced resonator guitars, electric lap steel guitars, and amplifiers with brand names that included Airline, Oahu, and National. It began producing solidbody electric guitars in the 1960s and in 1964 it launched the Folkstar, its first acoustic resonator guitar since the 1940s. It was hailed in the catalog as: "The most powerful non-electric guitar of them all! The original self-amplified guitar."

The Supro Folk Star came only in red and with a fiberglass body, which Valco called Res-O-Glas, though it was available in black from Airline. The model ran for about three years and was not a big seller, and the fact that it was a poor-sounding and projecting instrument did not help. The Folkstar's demise followed that of Valco, which became part of the Kay company in 1967 and, with a slump in the market, stopped trading altogether in 1968. **GD**

National
Varsity 66 1964

Type Single cutaway electric guitar
Body & neck Fiberglass body, maple neck
Fingerboard Rosewood
Pick-ups One Valco single-coil pick-up

The music of Californian punk-pop band The Muffs may not be to every guitarist's taste, but the frontwoman Kim Shattuck earned the respect of guitar fans everywhere when she started playing a black National Varsity.

This is a rare guitar. It was only produced for a year with the name Varsity. It was an evolution of a little-known National model called the Studio 66, which itself was a descendant of the Val Pro range of National's "map guitars." That was launched in 1961 with a bizarre raised Art Deco scratchplate molded from the Res-O-Glas body. The pick-up housing was curved to fit against the shape of the scratchplate, which swept underneath the strings above the pick-up, giving an unusual double-breasted lapel effect. John Entwistle owned one and Neil Young played one for a while, but it never really caught on.

The Studio lost its Art Deco styling in 1964 and became the Varsity. This model had an apostrophe-shaped scratchplate reminiscent of a Danelectro DC-59, and it lost the U-shaped lower cutout of the Val Pros in favor of a small vestigial horn, while at the same time growing a truncated upper horn that made it look almost like a Les Paul but not quite. In this respect, the design was a throwback to the Val Trol Custom that began the National range in 1959.

Apart from the fiberglass body, the spec of the guitar was simple: bolt-on neck, one single-coil pick-up with tone and volume controls, nickel floating tailpiece, rosewood bridge with thumbwheel height adjusters, and three-a-side plastic-buttoned Kluson tuners. **SH/AJ**

Rickenbacker
360/12 1964

Type Semi-hollow body electric twelve-string
Body & neck Maple body, three-piece maple/walnut neck
Fingerboard Rosewood
Pick-ups Two single-coil "Hi-gain" pick-ups

Rickenbacker introduced some changes to its hollow body range in the late 1960s, and although the 360/12 had been in production for five years, the company decided to upgrade its specifications to keep it in line with the musical trends of the period.

First to go was the metal "toaster" pick-up, somewhat volatile and feedback-prone when connected to a fuzz pedal or loud amplifier. In its place was the Hi-gain unit, developed for the top-of-the-line 381 model, which offered a strong output but lacked some of the chiming Rickenbacker sound. Shortly afterward, the neck was

> "I bought [the guitar pictured] used in 1981 and fell instantly in love with its jangly sound—despite finding it very difficult to play."
>
> DAVE GREGORY, XTC

extended to twenty-four frets and set deeper into the body, the front pick-up moved back by about an inch (2.5 cm). Sadly, nothing was done about the bridge and the string pairs were seated on six precast saddles, making accurate intonation an inexact procedure.

The guitar pictured is from 1976 and typical of the later style that remains virtually unchanged today. It could be challenging to play, however: the nut measured just 1½ in. (4 cm) wide—not a lot of space to accommodate twelve strings—and the stringing process is lengthy and tedious; the lovely "R" tailpiece being the principal source of frustration.

This writer used this guitar on XTC's *Mummer* (1983) and *English Settlement* (1982)—in particular on the hit single "Senses Working Overtime." **DG**

Rickenbacker
360/12 1964

Rickenbacker
370/12 1964

Type Semi-hollow body electric
Body & neck Maple body, maple and walnut neck
Fingerboard Rosewood
Pick-ups Two single-coil pick-ups

Type Semi-hollow body electric
Body & neck Maple body/neck with dual truss rod system
Fingerboard Rosewood
Pick-ups Three "Toaster Top" pick-ups

Rickenbacker's twelve-string version of its 360 has been in production ever since 1964 and has been used by many of the biggest names in rock 'n' roll including George Harrison, Pete Townshend, Brian Jones, Carl Wilson, and Roger McGuinn.

Initially popularized largely by Harrison, who used an early version in The Beatles' film *A Hard Day's Night* (1964), the first production models changed the square edges of the prototype to a rounded-off top and added white plastic binding to the sound hole—the "R" tailpiece was also introduced early on. The headstock had an innovative design in which the machine heads pointed alternately backward and outward, thereby saving space and making it easier to tune and, flying in the face of normal conventions, the strings with the split octaves are the high ones: a significant contributor to its legendary jangliness.

Rickenbacker supplied George Harrison with the new model in 1965 and he subsequently used it on the seminal *Rubber Soul* (1965) and *Revolver* (1966). **AJ**

In the mid-1960s, Los Angeles folk-rock band The Byrds shot to fame with "Mr. Tambourine Man," its frontman Roger McGuinn playing a modified version of the semi-hollow body electric twelve-string Rickenbacker 360/12 to produce the memorable and brassy jangle of the song's introduction and the band's distinctive signature sound. In choosing the Rickenbacker, McGuinn was inspired by The Beatles' George Harrison and his 360/12 with its unique sound from the movie *A Hard Day's Night* (1964). Soon after acquiring his 360/12, McGuinn had Rickenbacker install a third pick-up, effectively making it the prototype for the 370/12 model, which was yet to be marketed. The factory also added a compressor and reversed the configuration of the octave pairing of the strings so the downstroke hit the lower octave first. That guitar was stolen at a Byrds concert in 1966. McGuinn immediately ordered another identical one. In 1987 Rickenbacker took orders for a run of 1,000 units of the Roger McGuinn Limited Edition 370/12, introducing it as the "Secret Weapon of the 60s." **GD**

Selcol Beatles New Sound Guitar 1964

Teisco SS4L 1964

Type Ukulele
Body & neck Plastic
Fingerboard Plastic

Type Solidbody electric
Body & neck Laminated hardwood body, mahogany neck
Fingerboard Rosewood
Pick-ups Teisco gold-foil single-coil pick-ups

It's Christmas 1964. Little Beatles fans all over the United Kingdom are sitting around the tree opening their presents. What's this? "We knew you wanted to play guitar . . . like Paul McCartney," exclaims Dad, as a baffled child stares at the lump of off-white plastic with its crude cartoon faces of the Fab Four.

Selcol was an associate company of Selmer UK. It specialized in plastics. In addition to cheap garden furniture, Selcol also produced a range of plastic musical instruments aimed at the children's market. Biggest seller by far was the Beatles New Sound Guitar, which, in spite of its name, was a barely playable, four-string ukulele. Selcol gave other icons of pop culture similar treatment: Elvis, The Monkees, Tommy Steele.

Of course, anything from the 1960s with The Beatles' name attached is now hugely collectible. In mint condition, these babies can fetch upward of $600 at auction. And if you have one attached to its original backing card, then you can double that figure. **TB**

In the early 1960s, Teisco guitars began to be more influenced by George Jetson than Leo Fender. Exhibit A was the Japanese company's SS-4L.

This space oddity's most far-out feature is its control panel. By any standard, it's unconventional, not to mention inconveniently located above the strings. Thumb rollers for volume and tone sit among six rocker switches: one marked "R" (rhythm), another marked "S" (solo), and the rest dedicated to the SS-4L's four gold-foil pick-ups, thus allowing a ridiculous array of combinations.

The pick-up rockers are labeled "Mic 1," "Mic 2," etc., an acknowledgment (perhaps unintentional) of the pick-ups' microphonic properties, which make gold-foils coveted among slide players. And the gold-foils in the SS-4L are considered the holy grails of the type. Identifiable by their off-center pole screws, they feature Alnico magnets rather than the magnetized rubber used in many gold-foils. Ry Cooder famously employs Teisco gold-foils in two of his guitars. **DP**

Vox
Phantom Mark III 1964

Type Solidbody electric
Body & neck Single cutaway korina body, set korina neck
Fingerboard Rosewood
Pick-ups Three PAF humbucker pick-ups

The first of the curiously shaped Vox Phantoms (see page 288) quickly established themselves with British beat groups of the period, such as The Hollies and The Kinks. At the start of 1964, Vox followed up with a second unorthodox body shape. Broadly based on the appearance of a Renaissance lute, the Phantom Mark III (and its related models) would become known as the "Teardrop"—not only the most famous guitar in the Vox range but an iconic piece of 1960s design. Without question created for the prevailing musical mood of the period, the Phantom was designed with the new generation of stage-oriented beat groups in mind, the contours of its body making for an impractical or uncomfortable experience when playing in the sitting position.

Just as The Beatles established the Rickenbacker name with the general public, Brian Jones of The Rolling Stones had much the same impact on Vox guitars. The founder of the band, Jones used a prototype of the guitar until 1966: the Teardrop we see in period pictures of the Stones differs from those that went on sale in that it features a slightly elongated body.

The Vox brand would change hands many times over the next half-century, and although still active in guitar manufacture, the brand is best remembered for its seminal range of amplification. **SH**

The lead parts on The Rolling Stones' second UK album *The Rolling Stones No. 2* (1965) were played by Brian Jones on his Vox Phantom. The album features the same David Bailey cover shot used on the U.S. release *12 X 5* (1964).

Wandré
Twist 1964

Type Solidbody electric
Body & neck Hardwood body; aluminum neck
Fingerboard Rosewood
Pick-ups One or two single-coil pick-ups

Italian designer Antonio Pioli came up with some of the most curious guitars of the 1960s at his workshop in Cavriago. They appeal to modern collectors, not only because of the way they look, but also because of their quirky individuality: Wandré Guitars—named after Pioli's father's affectionate term for his eccentric tendencies as a teenager—can be difficult to identify and catalog, simply because there was no Wandré branding: some of the models were not given formal names, and within models there can be considerable differences from one example to the next. They were not, however, particularly obscure instruments: they were imported in reasonable numbers to the United States by Don Noble & Co., and to the United Kingdom by Jennings Musical Industries, makers of Vox guitars.

The model shown here has been named by a few sources as the Dura, but was, in fact, one of the Twist range of Wandrés. One of the more conventional body shapes, the Twist incorporated standard features, such as the "Duraluminum" neck, bulky, industrial pick-ups provided by his friend, Athos Davoli, a former aircraft engineer, and a variety of exotic finishes.

The Twist was available as a single, double, or triple cutaway: the last was especially curious, being little more than chunk "bitten" out of the bottom end of the body above the tailpiece. On the surface, this would seem to be a rather needless cosmetic effect, but in the wacky world of Wandré, who can truly tell what the maestro had in mind? After all, here was a man who, on another occasion, produced a guitar with a finish resembling a surrealist oil painting, gave it a nice rubber binding, and named it after Brigitte Bardot. **TB**

Burns-Baldwin
Double Six 1965

Type Twin cutaway solid electric twelve-string
Body & neck Solid alder body, maple neck
Fingerboard Rosewood
Pick-ups Three Tri-Sonic single-coil pick-ups

The sight of Elvis playing a Burns-Baldwin guitar should be enough to dispel any doubts that Burns instruments were ultracool in the mid-1960s. Elvis used his Double Six in two of his movies—and that wouldn't have happened unless the electric twelve-string looked like sex on legs.

The Double Six was basically a twelve-string version of Burns' Hank Marvin electric, named after one of the first British guitar heroes who led The Shadows. It had a few changes though: the three-piece, three-ply scratchplate was black not tortoiseshell, there were six-on-a-side Van Ghent enclosed tuners on the enlarged headstock, and three powerful slanted Tri-Sonic pick-ups. In place of the Marvin's tremolo system, the Double Six featured a simple metal bridge and separate fixed tailpiece. The Marvin was only available in white; the Double Six came in more exotic green or red sunbursts.

The bolt-on maple neck featured the usual Burns "gearbox" adjustment. It was favored by many players for being wider than the rival Rickenbacker twelve-string neck, giving more room for fingering. It was, however, an extremely heavy guitar to play standing up.

The clear, full, jangling sound of this electric twelve-string made a significant contribution to the sound of British pop bands of the era, including The Searchers, The Zombies, Easybeats, Troggs, and The Shadows. **SH**

Elvis Presley owned a green sunburst 1964 Double Six. He can be seen playing it in the first song in his MGM movie *Spinout* (1966), and it can also be seen in the last scene from *Easy Come, Easy Go* (1967). Today, it is on display at Graceland.

D'Aquisto
Archtop Electric 1965

Type Electric hollow body archtop
Body & neck Maple body; mahogany neck
Fingerboard Ebony
Pick-ups One Guild humbucker pick-up

By the time of his unexpected death in 1995, James L. D'Aquisto was widely viewed as the finest luthier working in America during the second half of the twentieth century. Indeed, vintage guitar guru George Gruhn described him as "a modern-day Stradivari . . . a genius at carving archtop guitars."

Of course, Jimmy D'Aquisto had the perfect background to succeed in the business: in 1953, as an aspiring seventeen-year-old jazz player, he began an apprenticeship with the legendary John D'Angelico, the New Yorker who built some of the greatest archtop guitars ever. When his employer died, eleven years later, D'Aquisto bought out the business.

Unsurprisingly, many of the guitars bearing the D'Aquisto name are visually reminiscent of those he had built for his mentor. However, he quickly evolved an experimental approach to his work. This was particularly true in the bridge construction, tailpiece (which he made adjustable), and sound hole designs, which shifted, first from the traditional "f"-shape to an elongated "S," and subsequently to even more unorthodox styles.

D'Aquisto was long established as one of the most important independent guitar makers of his time. His instruments were startlingly expensive. Yet, even though they were well beyond the pockets of all but the wealthiest musicians, at the time of his sudden death, there was a ten-year waiting list for new commissions. Their quality was matchless. But let's leave the last word to George Gruhn, who placed them "among an elite group of the finest fretted instruments ever made." **TB**

Egmond
Model 3 1965

Type Solidbody electric
Body & neck Laminated body, maple neck
Fingerboard Rosewood
Pick-ups Three single-coil pick-ups

The only well-known guitar brand to come from the Netherlands, Egmond—like Hagstrom in Sweden and Höfner and Framus in Germany—fed the demand for cheap guitars that mushroomed in the late 1950s. The company dated back to 1932, and grew out of a music shop in Eindhoven. Such was the demand for Egmond guitars during the rock 'n' roll boom that, in 1961, new, larger factory premises had to be found elsewhere.

Many fledgling British rockers cut their teeth on an Egmond, among them George Harrison, Brian May, and Rory Gallagher. However, these instruments rarely came into the United Kingdom with their own branding: they were more commonly sold to music distributors with their own brands—names such as Rossetti, Caledonie, Wilson, and Vega.

The Egmond Model 3 became available in around 1965. Its asymmetric waist is clearly modeled on that of the Fender Jazzmaster. Fender, however, never gave any of its instruments a finish like the sparkly plastic covering shown here. **TB**

Egmond
Scout 1965

Type Solidbody electric bass
Body & neck Solid wood unchamfered body, set neck
Fingerboard Rosewood
Pick-ups Pick guard with two integral pick-ups

The low-end Egmond Scout bass guitar, available also as a standard six-string electric, shared features with other Egmond models higher up the scale in terms of price and quality. It had the same body shape as the pricier Thunder and Typhoon models, as well as the top-of-the-line (for this large Dutch manufacturer, that is) Tempest, all of which replicated the Fender Jaguar and Jazzmaster in styling. It was equipped with a pickguard with an integral pick-up system as in the guitar played by an eighteen-year-old Paul McCartney in 1960. That was a Solid 7 model, branded Rosetti but nevertheless made by Egmond. McCartney said it was "a disastrous, cheap guitar" but good-looking. The same could be said about the Scout, perhaps more so. But, at a fraction of the cost of a Gibson or a Fender, Egmond guitars enabled many aspiring young musicians in the 1960s to easily get their hands on a guitar by saving their pocket money, working a paper route, or washing cars—and of course by asking mom and pop. **GD**

Elite/Crucianelli
40-V 1965

Favino
Modele Jazz 1965

Type Solidbody electric
Body & neck Plastic/hardwood body, maple neck
Fingerboard Rosewood
Pick-ups Four single-coil pick-ups

Type Steel-string acoustic
Body & neck Rosewood plywood body with spruce top, rosewood neck
Fingerboard Mahogany

By the mid-1960s, Oliviero Pigini's EKO—a company based in Castelfidardo—was Italy's top electric guitar exporter. In the same town, Crucianelli—accordion builders since 1888—had turned to guitar manufacture in the 1950s; its Elite range soon became Pigini's main competitor.

Outside influences are well in evidence on the Elite 40-V shown here, variations of which had been produced since 1962. There is the asymmetrical body styling of the Fender Jaguar/Jazzmaster, and the slim headstock echoes the Burns "batwing" style found on the Bison. Otherwise, the guitar exhibits many typical Italian accordion-style characteristics, such as the use of plastic, sparkling finishes, four-pick-up configurations, and push-button controls.

Crucianelli guitars were often exported with different badges, such as Ardsley, Baron, Crestone, Philharmonic, Reno, Supreme, and Sorrento. Like EKO, Crucianelli also made what some mistakenly regard as English guitars for the Vox company. **TB**

The history of great French jazz guitars was largely created by Italian luthiers who immigrated to Paris. Mario Maccaferri led the way in the 1930s, but it was Jacques Favino who, thirty years later, built some of the most enduring and beloved jazz instruments of all.

Favino apprenticed with Bartolo Busato building banjos, then made violins with Jean Chauvet. He began crafting his own American-style archtops in the 1950s.

Former Django Reinhardt sideman Matelo Ferret asked Favino to build jazz guitars to replace the now-old Selmers, and Favino started designing his own Gypsy guitars. His guitars featured larger, laminated bodies and a deeper, more resonant—and more modern—signature sound.

Jacques Favino was joined in his workshop by his son, Jean-Pierre, in 1973. When Jacques retired in 1979, J-P took over running the shop and still builds glorious Favino instruments from his atelier in the Pyrénées mountains today. The guitar shown dates from 1982, and was likely built by Favino father and son together. **MD**

Fender
Electric XII 1965

Type Solidbody electric twelve-string
Body & neck Alder body with bolt-on maple neck
Fingerboard Rosewood
Pick-ups Two split single-coil pick-ups

It was The Byrds' version of Bob Dylan's "Mr. Tambourine Man" that gave birth to the "folk-rock" genre. Mainly through association with George Harrison, Rickenbacker guitars quickly became de rigeur for those in search of the jangly folk-rock sound. Rickenbacker and other electric twelve-string manufacturers had done little more than add an extra set of machine heads and a new bridge to existing six-string designs. When Leo Fender decided to tap into what he thought would be a lucrative new market he took a different tack: going for a bottom-up purpose-built design.

The Electric XII took an offset Jazzmaster/Jaguar-style body and added a neck with a unique headstock, a downward-curving droop that quickly acquired the nickname "the hockey stick." The bridge was unique for its time in that it provided an individual saddle for each string, enabling extremely precise intonation. To increase sustain, the Electric XII retained the classic Telecaster's string-through-body design. The electrics were also unorthodox: a pair of split single-coil pick-ups were brought into action via a four-way selector switch. The two central positions offered—unusually—both pick-ups to be engaged, either in or out of phase.

The Electric XII had been discontinued by 1969; yet the guitar found high-profile fans: Pete Townshend of The Who and Led Zeppelin's Jimmy Page. **TB**

Although on stage he may have used the twin-neck Gibson EDS-1275, Jimmy Page used the 1965 Fender Electric XII on Led Zeppelin's seminal recording of "Stairway To Heaven," which can be heard on *Led Zeppelin IV* (1971).

One of Britain's greatest pop musicians, Roy Wood—then in The Move—tunes his Electric XII. ➡

Fender
V 1965

Fender
Villager 1965

Type Five-string bass guitar
Body & neck Alder body, maple neck
Fingerboard Rosewood
Pick-ups One split single-coil pick-up

Type Twelve-string acoustic guitar
Body & neck Two-piece spruce top, mahogany back and sides, one-piece maple bolt-on neck
Fingerboard Rosewood

The Fender V—named after its fifth string; it was the first electric bass guitar to possess such a thing—enjoyed only a brief period of popularity before being made obsolete. It was quirky, and a little unorthodox, but those qualities rarely translate into longevity, and thus the V was doomed to become a 1960s curio.

The guitar had its strengths, of course: despite possessing only fifteen frets, its high C string allowed players to access high-register notes with ease, and it was possible to hit a high E♭, well into the frequency range of a normal six-string guitar. However, its oddly narrow neck (Fender had not taken into account the need for a wider neck to accommodate the C string), and nondescript shape made it unpopular among the wider public. A few well-known players did own a V for a short while, most notably Jack Bruce of Cream. John Paul Jones began Led Zeppelin's 1973 tour using a Fender V, but by the end of it he had returned to four strings. In later interviews, he complained of the instrument's "dead" sound. **TB**

Following its acquisition of the Fender company in January 1965, the giant CBS corporation threw its weight behind getting the brand into as many musical areas as possible. The following spring was the genesis of the folk-rock boom, an opportunity seized upon by CBS to expand the line further into acoustic territory.

Four acoustic models were already in production at Fender when the takeover occurred, but former Rickenbacker luthier Roger Rossmeisl was put in charge of designing another four. Among these was the Villager, a twelve-string version of the Malibu, with a smaller 14½-in. (36.8-cm) body and full-scale neck. It included the Fender Truss Tension Tube, an internal aluminum rod intended to prevent warping, which also served as a mounting for the optional pick-up.

A new headstock was conceived to accommodate the twelve tuners, the upper edge curving to the right like an inverted hockey stick. This pattern was also used for the Shenandoah, Electric XII, and the Coronado XII that emerged the following year. **DG**

Framus 5/159
Strato Melodie 1965

Type Solidbody electric
Body & neck Maple body, maple neck
Fingerboard Rosewood
Pick-ups Two single-coil pick-ups

German guitar manufacturer Framus produced a few instruments with unusual string arrangements—including eight- and ten-string guitars—but the most unconventional was the 5/159 Strato Melodie nine-string guitar.

This was produced throughout the 1960s, but it appears that only about fifty of them were ever made. It had two oval, chrome single-coil pick-ups, a rosewood fingerboard, and was available in blue or red. The extra three strings doubled up the top three (G, B, and E), so it was like the top half of a normal twelve-string guitar.

It's difficult to identify many players who have actually used one of these, but they do include Terry Erickson of Neil Young's early band The Squires, and Reinhard Bock of a 1960s German beat group called The Tories. Bock didn't like his Strato Melodie very much—he found that if the action was set high enough to keep the strings from buzzing, they were almost impossible to hold down. **AJ**

Framus 5/168
Strato De Luxe 1965

Type Solidbody electric
Body & neck Maple body and neck
Fingerboard Rosewood
Pick-ups Three single-coil pick-ups

From 1946 to 1975, the Bavarian Framus company was among the largest guitar manufacturers in Europe. Framus guitars don't enjoy a particularly high reputation, but certainly have their place in history as affordable first guitars for many young musicians—among them Paul McCartney and John Lennon. Framus' best-known import to the United Kingdom was the Star bass, which Bill Wyman of The Rolling Stones deemed sufficient well into the mid-1960s.

Visually resembling the Fender Jaguar, the Framus Strato appeared in a number of different guises, including one model fitted with "Orgeleffekte" ("Organ Effect") circuitry, which the adverts of the day claimed could transform the guitar "into an excitingly different instrument—smooth organ tones at the touch of a fingertip!" It was, in fact, a reasonably effective volume "swell" effect.

The model shown here is an unusual, three pick-up, Strato De Luxe. Notice the positioning of the pick-ups, each one offset at an angle of its own. **TB**

Gibson
ES-335-12 1965

Type Semi-acoustic double cutaway twelve-string archtop
Body & neck Maple body, mahogany neck
Fingerboard Rosewood
Pick-ups Two humbucker pick-ups

From 1965 until 1970, Gibson produced a twelve-string version of its popular 335 semi-hollow electric archtop. The idea was to create a rival to the twelve-string Rickenbackers that were so iconic among bands like The Byrds and The Beatles at the time.

The ES-335-12 sold fairly well—just over 2,000 were sold—but never really replaced the Rickenbacker as *the* electric twelve-string. There may have been several reasons. Firstly the Gibson didn't look as cool; the headstock seemed too large, which unbalanced the guitar somewhat, and made it harder to play. Also, the Gibson was strung in a traditional style—with the higher-octave strings at the top of each pair. This meant that the higher note would sound first and strongest on a downstroke strum, creating a more biting sound. The Rickenbacker 360/12 reversed this arrangement.

Yet the Gibson could produce a warmer sound than the Rickenbacker, thanks to its humbuckers, center solid block, and choice of woods. It was a guitar that satisfied a wide range of styles. Bands as diverse as Buffalo Springfield and The Alarm and artists as different as Bruce Springsteen and David Byrne of Talking Heads used the ES-335-12. Other notable players to use the Gibson instead of the Rickenbacker include Billy Corgan of The Smashing Pumpkins, Miki Nerenyi of Lush, and Bernard Butler of Suede. **SH**

Johnny Marr used three different Gibson ES-335-12 models with The Smiths. They can be heard on tracks "Sheila Take A Bow" and "I Started Something." They can be found on *The Very Best Of The Smiths* (2001).

Gibson Firebird III "Non-Reverse" 1965

Type Solidbody electric
Body & neck Mahogany body and neck
Fingerboard Rosewood
Pick-ups Three single-coil P-90 pick-ups

The original Firebird, designed by Ray Dietrich, was a truly outstanding guitar—in the view of some people, the greatest that Gibson has ever produced. It was the first Gibson to feature a straight-through neck design, with upper and lower "wings" glued in place separately to create the body. Although this was a costly production technique, it may have enabled the Firebird to achieve its beautiful tone, and its noted ability to sustain.

Yet, in spite of the praise that was heaped upon the Firebirds by many who tried them out, they were expensive guitars, and sales during the first two years were disappointing. At the same time, Gibson had received a direct complaint from leading rival, Fender, that the Firebird's body shape had violated design patents for the Jazzmaster. A lawsuit was threatened. Unwilling to enter litigation, in 1965, Gibson took the decision to redesign the Firebird. The new look was far more conventional than the original, with the protrusions of the horns now reversed, so that it was the upper part of the body that jutted out farthest. Since the original Firebirds had a reversed look to their cutaways, the new Firebirds became known unofficially as "Non-Reverse" Firebirds.

There were more than merely cosmetic changes afoot, however. The biggest difference was the abandonment of the straight-through neck, which was replaced by Gibson's factory standard, glued-in, set necks. Although these are generally regarded as a superior construction technique to Fender's bolt-on necks, Firebird aficionados nevertheless continue to favor the original designs. **TB**

Gibson Firebird V "Non-Reverse" 1965

Type Solidbody electric
Body & neck Mahogany body and neck
Fingerboard Rosewood
Pick-ups Two mini humbucker pick-ups

The new "non-reverse" Firebirds were not only different in terms of the body shape and neck construction: there were also changes in the headstock, where the banjo-style tuners had been replaced by right-angled pegheads, so that they resembled those of a standard Fender—which was ironic, given that Fender's threat of legal action had prompted the Firebird's redesign in the first place.

As before, there were still I, III, V, and VII models available, although these now offered the player a much greater choice of sounds. Whereas the original Firebirds had been fitted with mini humbuckers, the non-reverse I and III models were fitted with two or three single-coil Gibson P-90s—these were clearly further nods toward Fender.

The Firebird V was kitted out with a pair of mini humbucking pick-ups, a Tune-o-matic bridge, and a metal vibrato cover, which was etched with the Gibson leaf design.

The new generation of Firebirds sold poorly, but remained in production until 1969. Three years later, Gibson began a relaunch of the original "reverse" Firebird shape. Unsurprisingly, given the quality of build, it's the original Firebirds that are of greatest interest to collectors.

Numerous Gibson and Epiphone Firebird reissues have since appeared, almost all of them with the reverse body shape, including, in 2008, a signature model for famed Firebird player Johnny Winter. That's not to say that there is no love for the non-reverse Firebird, which made a reappearance in 2002, courtesy of the Gibson Custom Shop. **TB**

Clarence "Gatemouth" Brown playing his Firebird V at Radio City Music Hall in New York, 2003.

Gretsch
6126 Astro Jet 1965

Type Solidbody electric
Body & neck Mahogany
Fingerboard Ebony
Pick-ups Two DeArmond Super'Tron humbuckers

It may be retrofuturistic today, but when it debuted in 1964, the Astro Jet was very much Gretsch's Guitar of the Future. Namechecking the dog in *The Jetsons*, and clearly molded to fit with that cartoon's playful space-age vision of hoverpacks, robots, aliens, and holograms, the Astro Jet was deliberately different—both from Gretsch's output at the time, and that of its rivals.

Gretsch had been dabbling with solidbodies since the 1950s, and its output largely followed Gibson's lead. 1965's Astro Jet had no direct equivalent in Gibson's lines, though it was closer in spirit to the avant-garde shapes of the Flying V, Explorer, and ill-fated Moderne of the late 1950s than Gibson's classier, more sober Les Paul and SG mainstays. With two powerful, pole-piece-less DeArmond Super'Tron humbuckers, a unique switching and control layout, and a four-and-two headstock, the Astro Jet differentiated itself sufficiently from Fender's latest Jazzmaster and Jaguar models.

The guitar was designed with input from long-time Gretsch employee and endorsee Jimmie Webster, a pioneer of the two-handed tapping playing style and the man behind 1955's White Falcon (see page 158). Webster's brief was to marry the Gretsch sound to a guitar that didn't look like a Gretsch: the large 16-in. (40.5-cm) body; lopsided, bulging outline finished in black-and-red two-tone; "melted" headstock; and hand-carved contouring took care of that. The mahogany set-neck construction was rounded off with two volumes per pick-up, a master volume, three-way tone selection, a standby toggle, and a Burns vibrato. The Astro Jet had a limited run and lasted until around 1967, meaning prices in the present are sky-high, but not astronomical. **OB**

Guyatone
Lafayette 1965

Type Twin cutaway solidbody electric
Body & neck Laminated hardwood body, maple neck
Fingerboard Rosewood
Pick-ups Three or four single-coil pick-ups

With a vaguely Fender Jaguar-like shape and a dandy metallic-finish scratchplate, the Lafayette was a mid-1960s guitar built by Guyatone in Japan. It was imported to be sold specifically in the Lafayette Electronics catalog in the United States in 1965. The catalog also used guitars built by Teisco.

It was basically a rebadged version of a Guyatone LG-140T. The Lafayette's body had very slightly different shaped horns. Versions with three or four single-coil pick-ups were produced, but all featured the distinctive chrome switchgear-splattered top and the jack socket. Strangely, the pole pieces on the bridge pick-ups were round while those on the neck pick-ups were square.

The complexity of Japanese guitars of this era is evident in the almost identical version of the LG-140T produced by Guyatone for the U.S. Bradford mail-order catalog, simply called the Bradford.

On both guitars there was a tailpiece tremolo, truss rod, plastic bridge, various pick-up selectors/preset rhythm/lead tone switches, and tone thumbwheels, plus separate volume knobs for each bank of pick-ups.

These guitars often came with a nicer-than-expected neck. Players find it chunky by modern standards, but it was very playable and was usually well finished with block positional inlays. This one seems to have been made in a less generous mood, for it only features dot inlays. Our researchers have even seen a version with a mix of dots and blocks.

The distinctive headstock was painted black and was enormous, measuring 10 in. (25 cm) from the nut to the end of the headstock. **SH**

Guyatone
LG-350 Sharp 5 1965

Type Solidbody electric
Body & neck Maple body and neck
Fingerboard Rosewood
Pick-ups Two (or three) Guyatone single-coil pick-ups

Founded in 1933 by Mitsuo Matsuki and Atsuo Kaneko, Guyatone was one of the first Japanese manufacturers to produce guitars. It was also quick off the mark to spot the electric boom in the 1950s, and became a well-known brand name exporting cheap instruments to Europe and the United States. Indeed, many a 1960s rock star cut his teeth as a teenager on one of its LG-50s (which was often sold under the Antoria brand name).

If we look at guitar production in Japan during the mid-1960s, one striking feature is the obvious influence of the Mosrite "reverse Strat" body style—this is wholly attributable to the success in Japan of U.S. surf band The Ventures—who were paid to endorse Mosrite guitars during that period. Curiously, the 1967 LG-350 Sharp 5 appears almost to mirror the famous Mosrite Ventures model (see page 308), retaining the beveled edging that comes close to a German carve, and yet there is also an undeniable Asian touch to the lines of the horns and headstock.

The guitar was built for, and named after, a popular Japanese "eleki" band of the day, The Sharp 5, and is rather more upmarket than most other Guyatones of the time. Armed with two single-coil pick-ups and an extremely sensitive vibrato mechanism, it was well suited to the instrumental guitar music of The Sharp 5 and their celebrated lead guitarist Nobuhiro Mine. **TB**

 Nobuhiro Mine was one of Japan's earliest guitar stars. His playing of his band's signature Guyatone can be heard on all of The Sharp 5's albums from the late 1960s, such as *Sharp Five Go Go* (1967).

Höfner
Ambassador 1965

Type Double cutaway semi-acoustic archtop
Body & neck Spruce body, maple back, layered neck
Fingerboard Rosewood
Pick-ups Two Höfner "Staple" humbucker pick-ups

Many European players wanted the latest Gibson semi-acoustic guitars, but simply couldn't afford the high prices of imported instruments. European guitar makers like Höfner, who had been manufacturing guitars in Bavaria since 1887, stepped into the breach with cut-price alternatives.

Höfner's Ambassador, a close relative of the Gibson Barney Kessel model, was about half the price of the Gibson version but offered many similar features. The currently contemporary shape of the twin Florentine cutaways gave maximum access to the higher frets, the dark sunburst body was thinline, there was a five-ply plastic pickguard, micromatic bridge, harp-style floating tailpiece, pinstripe binding, and headstock with inlaid vine and two Höfner pick-ups. The five-layer "Slenda-nek" with "cambered rosewood fingerboard" had an adjustable truss rod, and there were two tone controls, one master volume, and open-back nickel-plated tuners.

This standard version retailed at 80 guineas, but for an extra 6 guineas you could get the Ambassador De-Luxe. This was fitted with what Höfner's catalog referred to as "two of the world-famous American DeArmond pick-ups." Höfner's intention to compete with its revered American competitors is also underlined in its catalog by contemporary model names such as the Senator, the President, the Committee, and the Congress.

The specifications and sound were satisfactory and the guitar was sturdier than earlier Höfners. But buyers still yearned for Gibsons and fewer than 500 Ambassadors were made before production stopped in 1968. **SH/AJ**

Höfner
459/VTZ 1965

Type Hollow body electric
Body & neck Spruce and maple
Fingerboard Rosewood
Pick-ups Two 512B "Blade" humbucker pick-ups

The Höfner model 459 is the six-string version of its most famous instrument—the 500/1 "Beatle" bass, as used by Paul McCartney to this day.

"VTZ" refers to the built-in fuzz and treble boost effects—Höfner produced VTZ versions of a few of its models including the 4578 and 4571. The fuzz effect—Höfner referred to this as "dazzling built-in flip-fuzz"—sounds very similar to the Arbiter Fuzz Face pedal, which came out at around the same time. There was also an optional Bigsby-style tremolo (for an extra $40). The slim design and hollow body makes it extremely light, weighing in at 5 lb 15 oz (2.5 kg). It was manufactured between 1967 and 1970, but presumably not in large quantities as these guitars are now very rare.

According to Höfner's advertising literature: "among the first enthusiasts [for the guitar were] Bernie Mackey, original guitarist of the famous Inkspots, and Harry Chapin of The Chapins, hot new group on the record scene." **AJ**

Jolana
Alfa 1965

Type Solidbody electric
Body & neck Alder body, maple neck
Fingerboard Walnut, with pearloid dot inlays
Pick-ups Three single-coil pick-ups

Built at the Krnov factory in Czechoslovakia, the Alfa was introduced in 1965. Stylistically, this unusual model fits within the Star series of guitars that were built by Jolana from the early 1960s. Nevertheless, it was considered distinct enough to be given a separate name. Visually, it stands out because of its fragmented, three-piece pickguard, straight out of the Burns book of guitar design, and a plethora of oversized flip switches, which combine functionality and flair. Sonically, it features a trio of Jolana's Brilliant Deluxe single-coil pick-ups for that classic Jolana tone. The bottom bank of switches functions as a pick-up selector: each pick-up is controlled by its own on/off switch, allowing a variety of settings. The top knob is the master volume control; the bottom knob is a separate volume control for the middle pick-up. The top bank of switches handles the tone settings, passing the signal through high- and low-frequency cut-off filters. This schematic takes some getting used to, but allows for a variety of cool, vintage sounds. **EP**

Kalamazoo
KG2A 1965

Martin
GT-75 1965

Type Solidbody electric
Body & neck MDF (Masonite)
Fingerboard Rosewood
Pick-ups Two "Melody Maker" single-coil pick-ups

Type Hollow body electric
Body & neck Laminated maple
Fingerboard Rosewood
Pick-ups Two DeArmond DynaSonic pick-ups

Gibson's Kalamazoo, released in 1965, was the equivalent of Fender's Mustang and its family of variants—an entry-level guitar made on the cheap, to appeal to students and younger players. It wasn't outwardly branded as a Gibson; instead, the company sold it using "Kalamazoo Made in the USA" on the headstock in place of that famous logo, something it had last done in the pre-Second World War era.

By sporting a Mustang-esque outline, a bolt-on neck, single-coil pick-ups, and a six-in-a-line headstock configuration, these new student models were a pretty direct response to Fender's Mustang.

The Vibrola tremolo arm was pure Gibson, however, and the Mustang shape was superseded in 1968 by a more SG-style outline. There were four KGs, with the number designating the pick-ups, and "A" indicating vibrato. A bass model was also introduced in 1966. Bizarrely enough, Creedence Clearwater Revival's 1969 hit "Down On The Corner" references the model—then rhymes it with "kazoo." **OB**

Acoustic-guitar masters Martin couldn't ignore the electric guitar uprising forever, and in 1961, it decided to take tentative steps with its F-series archtop. This guitar borrowed its body shape from the company's archaic F-7 and F-9 archtop, and added a cutaway or two and various DeArmond pick-up configurations. These were updated in 1965 with the single-cut GT-70 and double-cut GT-75, Gretsch-like specimens with thinline hollow bodies sporting a curious "squashed space hopper."

The GT-70 and GT-75's tone was very close to that of Gretsch's classic hollow body designs, helped, of course, by the use of DynaSonic single-coils and a Bigsby option. They came in either black or burgundy finishes, and had a distinctive flared headstock. A twelve-string version was also created, with a trapeze tailpiece.

Author Michael Wright estimates 451 GT-75s were built between 1966 and 1968, making them reasonably plentiful for their relatively limited time in production. A rare electric with the timeless class of the Martin name makes the GT-75 an intriguing proposition. **OB**

Mosrite
D-100 Resonator 1965

National
Melophonic 1965

Type Hollow body electric resonator
Body & neck Basswood body; maple neck
Fingerboard Rosewood
Pick-ups Two single-coil pick-ups

Type Acoustic-electric resonator
Body & neck Fiberglass
Fingerboard Rosewood
Pick-ups One single-coil pick-up

The first resonator guitars were produced in 1929 by the Dopyera brothers' National String Instrument Corporation. Ten years later, its successor, the National Dobro Company, ceased production, as it was perceived that new electric archtops had removed the necessity for acoustic amplification. Resonator guitars, however, remained popular for their distinctive sound, and Emil Dopyera manufactured Dobros from 1959 under the brand name of "Dopyera's Original," until he was bought out by Semie Moseley in 1966. Moseley then produced a Mosrite Dobro, known as the D-100.

The body and neck—with low-profile frets, and a "zero" fret next to the nut—were based on Mosrite's Celebrity semi-acoustic, but the unique headstock was new. As well as three metal resonators, the D-100 had two single-coil pick-ups, and single tone and volume controls. Mosrite also produced a similar acoustic model, known as a "Mobro," and there was an electro-acoustic version with a single humbucker. The "Dobro" trademark was acquired by Gibson in 1993. **AJ**

Most resonator-style guitars have a pedigree of roughly the same complexity as the average stray dog, but the lineage is well documented and the family resemblance easily traced. Melophonic was a brand of resonator-style acoustic guitar made by Valco in Chicago in the 1960s; Valco was a rebranding of National-Dobro, trading since 1942; and this company was itself the result of a merger, in 1932, between the two premier resonator manufacturers. To complicate matters further, Valco made guitars and amps of many different shapes and sizes under a variety of brand names, including Supro, Airline, and National (again), and built them for other brands.

Among the guitar models was a series of Melophonic resonator-style guitars, made between the 1940s and 1960s. This spacefaring example is a long way from the Delta bluesman aesthetic with its vivid fiberglass construction and the more modern fourteenth-fret join. Valco merged with Kay in 1967, and the company went out of business in 1968. **OB**

Jose Oribe
Classical Guitar 1965

Rickenbacker
4005 Bass 1965

Type Classical guitar
Body & neck Spruce top, Brazilian rosewood back/sides
Other features French-polished top, lacquered body, Landsdorfer tuning machines, ebony fingerboard

Type Solidbody electric bass
Body & neck Maple
Fingerboard Rosewood
Pick-ups Two Rickenbacker "toaster" pick-ups

Initially a machinist, master pool player, and aspiring classical guitarist, Jose Oribe started making concert guitars of the highest quality in 1962. His combined workshop and home is in an idyllic setting in Vista, California. His machinist background served him well in applying the kind of precision and fine tolerances that goes into making guitars. Only the finest materials are used in his instruments and there is great attention paid to detail. A case in point is the care and expertise that goes into his French polish finishing process, which can take up to a year to complete. Oribe considers it an art form.

His early guitars, like this 1965 model, had a French-polished soundboard and sprayed lacquer back and sides. As the quality of lacquers improved, without a negative effect on sound quality, he began to use those for the soundboards too. Nowadays, Oribe only does French polishing to order. Another interesting feature of his guitars is their slightly taller frets that makes them, counter-intuitively, almost effortless to play. **GD**

This thinline hollow body bass model resembled Rickenbacker's 360 series of guitars, and was introduced in 1965 and discontinued in the mid-1980s. It came in standard four-string 4005 and six-string 4005-6 configurations, with a 33½-in. (85-cm) scale and twenty frets. Decidedly unstandard was a 4005L "Lightshow" version of the model, which incorporated internal colored lights that created psychedelic patterns—The Who's John Entwistle owned one, but only a few were produced, making it one of the Holy Grails in the world of the bass collector.

Entwistle also owned a 4005 in the late 1960s that he used for live and recorded work, and another famous endorsee was The Stone Roses/Primal Scream bass player Gary "Mani" Mounfield. The Pollock-style paint job on the 4005 he used for The Stone Roses' eponymous debut album has become an iconic instrument of its time. All of which has helped cement the 4005 as one of the most desirable bass models to own, particularly in rare "Mapleglo" finish. **OB**

Silvertone
1437 1965

Type Solidbody electric
Body & neck Hardwood body, maple neck
Fingerboard Rosewood
Pick-ups Four single-coil pick-ups

The Silvertone-branded electric guitars introduced in the 1960s played a major role in the pop music explosion brought on by The Beatles. Teenagers everywhere wanted to listen to music and play guitar, and the Silvertone brand was there to fill that need.

From radios to electric guitars, the Silvertone brand was a dominant force in the field of electronics. Sold by Sears from 1954 through 1969, the Silvertone brand had actually been used on instruments as early as 1915. It should be noted that Silvertone-branded instruments could have been manufactured by one of at least five different manufacturers, including New Jersey's own Danelectro, the Harmony company, Supro/Valco, Kay, and in the case of the 1437, Teisco from Japan. A large number of Silvertone instruments were imported through Chicago's WMI Corporation.

The model 1437—nicknamed "Sharkfin"—is based on the Japanese Teisco Del Rey model WG4L. It features a sharp German-carved contoured body, chrome hardware, four individual single-coil pick-ups, tremolo tailpiece, wraparound fingerboard inlay, and a unique 4 + 2 headstock tuning key layout. The shark-fin version of the body is the coolest, but there was also a variation based on a standard Stratocaster shape—this one had a simple slider for treble and bass rather than the strange tone-selector knob. **DT/AJ**

Bob Dylan can be seen playing a Silvertone 1437 in the video for his song "Most Of The Time" from the 1990 album *Oh Mercy*. It was hailed as a comeback album at the time of its release as the subject material and hazy production seemed to connect with Dylan's past.

Silvertone 1457
"Amp-in-case" 1965

Type Semi-solid electric
Body & neck Poplar frame, Masonite top/back, maple neck
Fingerboard Rosewood
Pick-ups Two Danelectro lipstick-case pick-ups

The Silvertone brand first appeared on radio sets in 1915, sold by the famous Sears Roebuck chain, and was later adopted to cover the company's own line of musical instruments and sound equipment. It last saw the light of day in 1972. Sears did not manufacture its own guitars; the Silvertone-adorned instruments were sourced from guitar makers such as Danelectro, Kay, and Harmony in the United States, and the Teisco plant in Japan. Silvertones have an important place in the history of American music, as many of the great players of the 1960s and 1970s will have cut their teeth on one of these cheap but playable instruments, often bought under duress from the Sears mail-order catalog.

Perhaps the most intriguing range of Silvertones were the "Amp-in-case" models, which first appeared in 1962 with the three-quarter-scale 1448. The electric guitar at this time was still a novelty item, and many parents buying for their teenagers didn't realize that some means of amplification was a necessity for an electric guitar. Built into the sturdy carrying case of models like the twin-pick-up 1457 was a neat little five-watt amp hooked up to an 8-in. (20-cm) loudspeaker. The guitar itself was a basic single-pick-up Danelectro, built using a cheap poplar frame covered in Masonite. The package was amazingly good value: $69.99 for the lot—less than a quarter of the price of a basic Fender. **TB**

BECK MODERN GUILT Increasingly collectible, Silvertone's highest-profile fan is Beck, who uses the single-pick-up 1448 as his main stage guitar. He can be heard playing it on the Danger Mouse-produced album *Modern Guilt* (2008).

Silvertone
1477 1965

Teisco
VN4 Baritone 1965

Type Solidbody electric
Body & neck Alder body, maple neck
Fingerboard Rosewood
Pick-ups Two DeArmond Goldtone pick-ups

Type Solidbody twin cutaway electric baritone guitar
Body & neck Laminated hardwood body, maple neck
Fingerboard Rosewood
Pick-ups Four Silvertone single-coil pick-ups

This Silvertone 1477 was sold in the United States in the famous Sears Roebuck catalogs and was aimed at young novice players unable to afford a "proper" guitar. That's not to say that these were poor instruments; they were well made, and most notably featured a pair DeArmond Goldtone pick-ups—it was quite unusual to see something of this quality on a budget instrument.

The 1477 was built for Sears by Harmony and was based on its own Bobkat H15 models that were built from 1963. The body was cut from alder, with a bolt-on maple neck and a rosewood fingerboard . . . just like a Fender, in fact. The neck was adjustable through the use of Harmony's "Torque Lok" system—a pair of truss rods accessed by removing the cover on the headstock.

With the high end of the vintage guitar market sewn up by the wealthier collector, there is a growing modern-day interest in models by Silvertone, Harmony, Kay, and other budget brands of the 1960s. **TB**

With a 27-in. (68.5-cm) scale, this solid electric was a pure piece of mid-1960s eccentricity. It could be played normally or tuned to a low B tuning (B, E, A, D, F#, D) to use as a baritone guitar.

Set in those two chrome pickguards were volume and tone rotary-wheel controls, on/off switches for each pick-up (marked as "mic" switches) plus a rhythm/solo switch for each pick-up, too.

The VN4 came with four Silvertone pick-ups; the VN2 with just two. Both versions were made in Japan by Teisco but often marketed under different brands like Ayar or Lindell. There was a string damping system at the bridge and most came with a primitive tremolo. Note the unusually modern position markers on the rosewood fingerboard.

With their raw sound, cool looks, and easy playability, cheap Teisco guitars like these were the instruments of choice for Chicago electric slide player Hound Dog Taylor, who famously was born with six fingers on his left hand. **SH**

Telestar
Sparkle 1965

Type Solid electric
Body & neck Laminated hardwood body, maple neck
Fingerboard Rosewood
Pick-ups Between two and four single-coil pick-ups

The first Telestar guitars appeared in the United States around 1965. They were budget instruments sold through a New York importer but were built at the Kawai factory in Japan.

These early Japanese imports had some of the styling features of the contemporary American Burns Bison, but at first their official and rather ridiculous name was "Professional Solid Body Speckled Electrics." Instead everyone called them "the Sparkle." By 1967, even the importers were dubbing them Sparkle.

They came in various colored sparkling finishes and configurations of pick-ups and tremolo arms. One model had four pick-ups. The pick-ups had individual on-off slider switches, a "tone modifier" toggle switch, as well as normal volume and tone controls. There was a crisp "surfer" sound from the microphone-style single-coil pick-ups that veered toward a built-in overdrive and they were usually far more playable than most Japanese guitars of the era. After decades of being unloved, they are now becoming favorites of guitar collectors. **SH**

Wandré
Davoli Selene 1965

Type Solidbody electric
Body & neck Hardwood/plastic body; aluminum neck
Fingerboard Rosewood
Pick-ups Two Davoli single-coil pick-ups

A quick glance at those Daliesque curves tell us we can only be looking at one of Antonio "Wandré" Pioli's little Italian gems. Described by some sources as the "Karak," the Selene mirrors his Rock Oval extreme cutaway model, this time lopping off a chunk from the bass side of the body. As with Pioli's other instruments, the Selene came in a bewildering variety of shades, including pink, brown, and mustard sunburst.

As with all Wandrés, once you've overcome the shock of its appearance, the most strikingly advanced aspect of its design is the aluminum neck. Pioli's first such design was in 1956, and pre-dates similar experiments by other luthiers. Pioli also pioneered the idea of a fulcrum neck, attached to the body by two bolts and a horizontally pivotal fulcrum. Final adjustments were made with a threaded truss rod. On later models, such as the Selene, he used a three-piece aluminum neck design: the headstock was bolted to the neck, which was bolted to an aluminum block that passed through the center of the body. **TB**

Ampeg
AUB-1 1966

Type Fretless bass guitar
Body & neck Maple/birch plywood body, maple neck
Fingerboard Rosewood or ebony
Pick-ups One Ampeg "Mystery" pick-up

Although a fretless bass had been used by Bill Wyman of The Rolling Stones as early as 1961, the first production fretless did not appear until five years later, courtesy of Ampeg, which now—as then—is better known for its amplifiers.

The AUB-1, as it was known, came four years before the first fretless Fender Precision and gained later publicity when Rick Danko of The Band used one on two studio albums. With their scroll headstocks, large pickguards, f-holes, bridges that extended beyond the body, and a so-called "Mystery" pick-up located beneath the bridge, the AUB models were too ungainly for mass acceptance but continue to command a small but dedicated fanbase today.

Over the years, certain defects have come to light. The body, essentially three chunks of maple glued onto a laminated hardwood back, tends to develop cracks near the tailpiece, and the lacquer finish rarely lasted more than two decades of use.

It is difficult to know how many AUB-1s were manufactured, as the serial numbers were stamped on the bridge tailpiece and lost when the strange-looking bridge unit was replaced. However, it is thought that their day was done by 1970, as was the case with so many of the 1960s' more unusual instruments. **TB**

Rick Danko played an Ampeg AUB-1 on The Band's highly acclaimed self-titled second album. Released in 1969, it is widely viewed as having contributed to the birth of country-rock.

Carvin
2-MS 1966

Type Twin-neck solidbody electric six-string and mandolin
Body & neck Maple body, bolted maple necks
Fingerboard Rosewood
Pick-ups Two AP single-coils on six-string, one on mandolin

The Carvin family had been making guitars in southern California since 1946 but usually used their own pick-ups on bodies made by Höfner. In the 1960s, they produced some innovative instruments of their own.

The MS guitars were an interesting combination of a solid six-string electric … and a mandolin. The body and neck were maple, the fretboard rosewood, and the pick-ups, of course, were Carvin's own. The Carvin catalog included hand-drawn circuit diagrams for the more technically minded customer. The MS guitars were oddly called "double-neck electric mandolin and Spanish."

"The #1-MS sold for $229.90, and the #2-MS, which was identical except for non-adjustable pick-ups, sold for $199.90."
CARVINMUSEUM.COM

It all looked slightly cranky and homemade, but the finishing details were good—the nuts were bone, the inlays were mother-of-pearl, and the hardware was all chrome. Customers could even buy a "beautiful exact color photo" of their instrument for 50 cents.

The MS-1 model was top-of-the-line, with pick-ups that featured adjustable pole pieces and on–off switches for each pick-up. The MS-2 was the same, but the pick-ups couldn't be tweaked. The twin-neck guitars weighed in at around 9 lb. (4 kg).

The U.S.-made Carvins were not expensive: the 1966 retail price of the MS-2 was $199.90 at a time when a standard Stratocaster cost around $300. Carvin also offered to fit a Bigsby vibrato system to the six-string section of your MS guitar for just $29.90. **SH**

Epiphone
Caiola Custom 1966

Type Thinline hollow semi-acoustic guitar
Body & neck Maple top, back, and sides; mahogany neck
Fingerboard Rosewood
Pick-ups Two mini humbucker pick-ups

This little-known guitar was the signature model for American jazz and country guitarist Al Caiola. It was available in a "Standard" (with P-90s) or "Custom" (humbucker) version. They both had similarities with Gibson's ES-330, with a thinline hollow body and trapeze tailpiece but, unlike the Gibson, no f-holes. The lack of sound holes reduced feedback and the mini humbuckers produced a notably warm, rich sound.

The Caiola had another very big difference from the 330—a complex mix of five two-way switches providing different tone settings by filtering at different frequencies. This "Tonexpressor" system took the place of a normal rotary tone control. It proved complicated to use, especially in live situations. And there was a volume control for each of the mini humbuckers and a pick-up selector switch (marked "rhythm" and "treble")— but you couldn't have both at the same time.

Caiola didn't seem to have much to do with the guitar but did have a very successful career in which he recorded more than fifty albums. Years later, the Caiola had a brief return to the spotlight when Tom Verlaine of Television used one, among his arsenal of unusual guitars.

The Caiola Custom is one of the rarest of the Kalamazoo factory's signature guitars. Collectors have started taking note and Caiola prices are now sometimes higher than for equivalent Gibson models. **SH**

Barry Tashian, leader of 1960s American band The Remains, used a Caiola Custom on the band's recordings and when they opened for The Beatles on their 1966 U.S. tour. He can be seen with his Caiola on the cover of *A Session With The Remains* (1996).

Fender
Coronado 1966

Type Hollow body electric
Body & neck Beechwood and maple body, maple neck
Fingerboard Rosewood
Pick-ups Two single-coil DeArmond pick-ups

Roger Rossmeisl is something of a low-key legend in the guitar world. The son of a German luthier, at the age of ten he was sent away to the prestigious Instrument Making School in Mittenwald, in the country's Alpine region. Eight years later he would emerge as one of the youngest craftsmen to graduate with a masters degree and the title "Gitarrenbaumeister" (Master Guitar Maker). Arriving in the United States in 1952, he joined Rickenbacker two years later, where over the next eight years he designed most of the company's classic models. In 1962, he joined Leo Fender who hired him to design a new assembly plant. Rossmeisl was also responsible for a number of unusual Fender guitars that appeared during that decade.

After fifteen years of producing solidbody guitars, Leo Fender had decided the time was right to offer an uncharacteristic thinline hollow body electric guitar. As the man who had designed all of Rickenbacker's classic hollow body models, Rossmeisl was the man for the job.

The back and sides of the Coronado were constructed from laminated beechwood, and featured a gently arched maple top—again, unusual for Fender. A further departure was in the use of nonstandard Fender pick-ups; the Coronado was fitted with single-coil DeArmonds.

The Coronado was produced between 1966 and 1972. The model shown features a "Wildwood" finish, a dubious-sounding process that involved injecting a chemical dye into the growing beech tree prior to harvesting. This resulted in an unusual stained grain pattern of the wood, a thin laminate of which was then used on the top of the body. **TB**

Fender
Mustang Bass 1966

Grimshaw
Bass 1966

Type Solidbody electric
Body & neck Alder body, maple neck
Fingerboard Rosewood
Pick-ups Special design split single-coil pick-up

Type Semi-acoustic bass
Body & neck Maple/spruce body, mahogany neck
Fingerboard Rosewood
Pick-ups Two single-coil pick-ups

Designed by Leo Fender prior to his leaving the company after selling it to CBS in 1965, the Mustang Bass, with its short, 30-in. (76-cm) scale and staggered split pick-up design was released the following year in Fiesta Red and Vintage White to complement its long-scaled Fender cousins. It had one pick-up, one volume/tone control, and a slab body. You don't buy a Mustang Bass for its array of features.

Its shorter scale may have produced the occasional intonation issue, but that did little to dent what became an enviable celebrity pedigree. A Mustang Bass was used by Roger Glover on Deep Purple's *Fireball* (1971); The Beach Boys' Carl Wilson played one in their "Good Vibrations" video; The Rolling Stones' Bill Wyman used them throughout the late 1960s and into the early 1970s; and Tina Weymouth used them in the early days of Talking Heads; as well as many other famous players. Continuously in production until 1981, the Mustang Bass was reissued by Fender Japan in 2002. **BS**

Like so many instrument manufacturers of the early to mid-1960s, Grimshaw was not averse to producing basses in tandem with its six-string instruments, leaning very heavily toward popular Gibson designs. The fact that these were hand-built set them above most of the budget instruments on the market at the time.

The year 1966 saw the SS Deluxe bass replaced by the SS5 model, a semi-acoustic bass resplendent with f-holes for greater resonance and bass response, a good idea considering the limited capacity of amplifiers at this time. The popularity of the guitars—which were used by the likes of Alvin Lee, The Shadows, Joe Brown, and Pete Townshend—meant that there were plenty of bassists willing to take the bass versions out for a spin. A floating bridge tailpiece, multiple controls, and pick-up selector gave the player some control over the sound, and with two pick-ups set far apart, it had some tonal variation to offer. It was later followed by the release of the Les Paul-inspired GB30 bass. **JM**

Kapa
Continental 1966

Musicka Naklada
Special 64 1966

Type Solidbody electric twelve-string
Body & neck Mahogany
Fingerboard Rosewood
Pick-ups Two Kapa humbucker pick-ups

Type Twin cutaway solid electric
Body & neck Laminated body, maple neck
Fingerboard Rosewood
Pick-ups Three single-coil pick-ups

Made in Maryland, United States, in the 1960s by Koob Veneman, a Dutch immigrant, Kapa (an acronym from his family's names) guitars came in a variety of models, mostly with a Fenderish flavor: the Wildcat, Cobra, Challenger, and this Continental were among them. Kapa made hollow bodies as well as solidbodies, and produced another electric twelve-string, the teardrop-shaped Minstrel.

    The Continental was available in six- and twelve-string versions, and debuted in 1966, being made until 1970, when Kapa closed shop and sold stock to Mosrite and Microfret. It had a slim body and slim neck, which was a trend at the time among guitar makers, and a brave move on the part of Kapa, considering the extra tension a twelve-string setup produces. Unusually for a twelve-string, the Kapa Continental was available with a vibrato-bridge system, which added $50 to the standard version's $169.50 list price. Notable players include Sonic Youth noisenik Lee Ranaldo, who used and abused one live in the late 1980s. **OB**

In the 1960s, it was fashionable to have lots of buttons, switches, and dials on your guitar's scratchplate. This Yugoslavian-made Musicka Naklada showed that players behind the Iron Curtain were also attracted to a complex array of electronics. This Special 64 offered a master tone control, three individual pick-up volume controls, and a master volume. There were also three on-off switches for each of the pick-ups.

    It was a beginner-level guitar, but, as well as all that switchgear, the pickguard was laminated wood with a metallic-gold sparkle finish. The pick-up covers were built to match that finish. There was also an interesting asymmetrical headstock, truss rod, block inlays, and an elaborate covered bridge and tailpiece tremolo system.

    Musicka Naklada operated a small factory and a handful of shops in Zagreb, now in the independent country of Croatia. They also made and sold semi-acoustic guitars and basses but seem to have gone out of business at some point in the 1970s. **SH**

Ovation
Balladeer 1966

Type Acoustic/electroacoustic guitar
Body & neck Sitka spruce top, Lyrachord back and sides, maple neck
Fingerboard Rosewood

The Ovation Balladeer was conceived by Charles Kaman, a successful aeronautical engineer and amateur guitarist. His basic idea was to use a parabolic shape, or "bowl," for the back of the guitar, thus offering greater volume and projection than a conventional dreadnought model. This was further aided by a substantially larger sound hole and an alternative system of bracing. Instead of using wood for the guitar, Kaman's company developed a powerful, strong synthetic material made from layers of bonded resin, which he named "Lyrachord."

The Ovation also had a slim neck. Kaman had wanted the guitar to feel and play more like a modern electric instrument, and many players found it easier to play than a conventional acoustic model.

Launched in 1966, the first Balladeers were entirely acoustic, until the company's trailblazing Piezo bridge transducer pick-ups were added in the middle of the 1980s. Later versions of the Balladeer were also offered with a thinner bowl, which were less prone to feedback but had a thinner tone and lower acoustic volume. **JB**

Rickenbacker
336/12 1966

Type Twin-cutaway semi-hollow electric twelve-string
Body & neck Maple body, maple and walnut neck
Fingerboard Rosewood
Pick-ups Two single-coil pick-ups

The 330 had become Rickenbacker's best-selling guitar and one of the key instruments of the jangly pop-rock sound of the 1960s. By 1966, Rickenbacker had started to experiment with offshoots of the basic semi-hollow six-string design.

The 336/12 was a twelve-string "convertible" version of the 330. It featured Rickenbacker's ingenious "comb" system to disengage six of the strings, reverting the guitar to a normal six-string. The 360 and 450 models were also given a twelve-string comb version.

This comb was designed by James Gross of Illinois. It worked when the player pulled a lever. This yanked up to six extra strings downward, pressing them firmly against the frets and hopefully enough out of the way that a strum would not catch them and make them sound. Paul Kanter from Jefferson Airplane liked the idea and started using one.

But not only did the comb system look ungainly on the guitar, it was often tricky to use. No strings could be bent, for example, in six-string mode. **SH**

Simpson
Pan-O-Sonic 1966

Standel
Custom Deluxe 1966

Type Solidbody twin-cutaway electric
Body & neck Kauri body, white birch neck
Fingerboard Rosewood
Pick-ups Three Jansen single-coil pick-ups

Type Double cutaway solidbody electric
Body & neck Mahogany body, maple neck
Fingerboard Rosewood
Pick-ups Two single-coil pick-ups

Young New Zealanders wanted electric guitars just like the rest of the world. But the only guitars available to them were overpriced imports. Auckland electrical repairman Bruce Eady saw the gap in the market and hired radio apprentice Ray Simpson from Nelson, who built his first guitar aged just seventeen. It was perhaps one of the first solid electric guitars in 1945—a lap steel instrument with a car magneto converted into a pick-up.

Eady and Simpson used kauri wood from beams from demolished houses for the guitar bodies and white birch from Simpson's old hometown for the necks. They worked on designing innovative pick-ups, researching waveforms and using the expertise of one of their designers, Paul Crowther. Crowther later left to form world-famous Kiwi band Split Enz.

This innovative guitar was a prototype, with a built-in tremolo arm and separate bridge. Although it was modeled on the Stratocaster, it featured an on–off switch for each pick-up, which gave combinations and sounds no traditional Strat had ever been able to achieve. **SH**

This eccentric electric was made by Bob Crook's Standel company in mid-1960s California. Standel was better known for making amplifiers.

The Custom Deluxe was an interesting instrument. It came as either semi-hollow or solid electric. The hollow body guitars had fiberglass bodies with stuck-on paper f-holes while the solidbody models had the pick-ups, bridge, and tremolo mounted on one wide, solid aluminum casting. Other features included Grover tuners, a neatly bound neck, and a Plexiglas scratchplate.

There were two low-output pole-less resin-filled pick-ups. Each had a volume and tone control. Through some amplifiers, the guitar sounded hopelessly weedy. Through a Standel amp, or any amp with a low-power input, it had a clear ringing tone that captured the era.

Sadly, within a year the factory closed and several smaller U.S. companies bought up the remaining parts. That's why some very similar guitars appeared for the next few years bearing other brand names like Hallmark, Gruggett, and Epcor. **SH**

Teisco
Decca DMI-203 1966

Type Solidbody electric
Body & neck Hardwood body, bolt-on neck
Fingerboard Rosewood, bound
Pick-ups Three single-coil pick-ups

The British Invasion of the mid-1960s, spearheaded by The Beatles, had a profound effect on the U.S. music industry. As myriad garage bands formed to emulate their musical heroes, the demand for electric guitars skyrocketed. To meet this demand, established guitar manufacturers increased production, new companies jumped on the bandwagon, and by 1966 the guitar boom was well on its way.

Around this time, Decca Records diversified into musical instruments, and a line of guitars and amplifiers bearing the Decca brand was produced. As was common practice, these guitars were sourced from a Japanese manufacturer, which kept prices very competitive. Then, as now, such manufacturers simply placed the necessary brand on a line of instruments already in production, and perhaps available to other distributors under different brands as well. This is why one can find the same model under several different names, and determining its actual origins is not always easy.

No such problem with this Decca, however: the "tulip" body shape, the striped, brushed aluminum pickguard, and the distinctive 4 + 2 headstock simply scream "Teisco"! The DMI (Decca Musical Industries) model 203 sports three pick-ups, a vibrato, and a rather fancy schematic with lots of knobs and switches. There was also a two-pick-up model with vibrato, the DMI-202, and a bottom-of-the-line DMI-201 (single pick-up, hardtail). All came in a snazzy shaded sunburst finish.

The heyday of Decca guitars was short-lived. In 1967, Teisco was bought by Kawai, and by 1968 the guitar boom went bust, forcing Decca out of the guitar business altogether. **EP**

Vox V251
Guitar Organ 1966

Type Solidbody electric with organ circuitry
Body & neck Maple/ash body, maple bolt-on neck
Fingerboard Rosewood
Pick-ups Two single-coil pick-ups

The Vox Guitar Organ combined solid-state circuitry from a Vox Continental organ with the body of a Vox Phantom guitar. It could be played as a conventional guitar or a guitar that sounded like an organ—or as both simultaneously. This experiment by Vox engineer Dick Denney was one of a series of innovations the company introduced in the mid-1960s.

Six organ tone generators—one for each string—were fitted inside the enlarged body of the guitar, and these were operated by contacts in the frets. Twenty-one resistors connected to the frets determined the

> *"The Vox Guitar Organ was one of the most complicated and innovative products attempted by JMI Vox in the 1960s."*
> VOXSHOWROOM.COM

pitch of the tone. To produce an organ sound, you could either hold down a fret, press one of the six "open-string" buttons, or bring a brass plectrum that was connected by a cable into contact with the body of the guitar. There were octave and effects selectors, a four-way selector for organ percussion, a flute selector, and a knob to silence the bottom two strings. The guitar's power supply also provided outputs to an amplifier.

The main drawback to the V251 was that it was heavy and awkward to play—additionally, you couldn't bend the strings when in organ mode because this would push them onto the wrong fret contacts.

Reputedly V251s were supplied to John Lennon and Brian Jones, but neither of them was impressed enough either to endorse it or to use it on records. **AJ**

Yamaha
SA15 1966

Type Hollow body electric
Body & neck Maple
Fingerboard Rosewood
Pick-ups Two mini-humbucker pick-ups

As the guitar boom of the 1960s progressed, Yamaha was keen for a piece of the archtop action, and its SA series was the result. The SA5 was first to appear, debuting in 1966, and is one of the company's earliest forays into electric guitar manufacture.

The next two years also saw the release of the thin hollow body SA15 and SA15D. Quite a departure from the SA5 and a clear nod to the Rickenbackers of Beatlemania, they featured irregular "slashing" f-holes, a Rickenbacker-esque teardrop-shaped scratchplate, and an elongated lower horn. The fretboard featured either

"The Yamaha SA15 is not a 1967 Gibson 335. But it's still a very cool guitar to have."

HARMONYCENTRAL.COM

dots or Gretsch-style semicircular bass-side "fingernail" position markers. The SA15's control layout featured separate volume and tone controls for each mini humbucker with a three-way position switch on the scratchplate. A simple though slightly obtrusive vibrato system and inlaid trapeze-type tailpiece completed the still-elegant picture. The SA15s were available in Sunburst, Black, and Maroon, and had a 24¾-in. (63-cm) scale length with a slim neck profile.

Later SA models returned to the 335 template, adding twelve-string variations and different vibrato systems. The range continues to evolve today, making Yamaha's semi-hollow body line a near-fifty-year-old success story—and one that started with the forward-looking lines and distinctly Eastern flavor of the SA15. **OB**

Yamaha SG5a "Flying Samurai" 1966

Type Solidbody electric
Body & neck Alder body, maple neck
Fingerboard Rosewood
Pick-ups Three single-coil pick-ups

Now one of the world's biggest producers of electronic musical instruments, Yamaha was founded in Japan in 1897 as a manufacturer of pianos and reed organs. It wasn't until the Second World War that the company began looking at guitar manufacture, building its first classical models in 1941. Although electric guitars were built in Japan from the late 1950s, it wasn't until 1966—with Japan's "eleki" pop boom well underway—that Yamaha introduced its first electric models.

Guitar manufacture in Japan at this time was in thrall to the American Mosrite models, played by The Ventures, the most popular and influential Western band among Japanese teenagers of the mid-1960s. So it's perhaps not surprising that the first Yamaha solidbody electric had the subtle influence of the band's Mosrite Ventures Mark I signature model, with its "reverse Strat" body shape and pronounced lower horn. However, this is in no way a mere copy; the asymmetric curves and the dropped end of the extended horn are unmistakably Eastern in character, not to mention the narrow headstock carved to simulate the handle of a traditional Japanese katana sword.

These fine guitars were produced with a variety of pick-up options and were exported in modest quantities to Europe and the United States, where they quickly picked up the tag of "Flying Samurai." **TB**

The SG5a had an abundance of single-coil twang, and it was perfect for guitar instrumentals. Japan's top guitarist Takeshi "Terry" Terauchi's Yamaha SG5a can be heard on his 1960s work with popular "eleki" combo Terry And His Blue Jeans.

Ampeg
ASB-1 Devil Bass 1967

Type Double cutaway electric bass
Body & neck Maple body, bolt-on maple neck
Fingerboard Rosewood or ebony
Pick-ups One Ampeg Epoxy-covered "mystery" pick-up

In the early 1940s, when bass player Everett Hull began experimenting with a microphone pick-up designed to fit on the end of an upright bass, the electric bass guitar revolution that accompanied the launch of the Fender Precision was still a decade away. Hull dubbed his invention the Amplified Peg—or the "Ampeg."

Unsurprisingly, Ampeg also dabbled, albeit in a small way, in the instrument market, with a range of guitars and basses. Although not hugely popular among musicians, these instruments were often distinctive—both visually and in their features.

"Very few Devil basses are in good condition today ... they're mysterious and charming, but they're also heavy and clumsy to play."

BRUCE JOHNSON, BUILDER OF MUSICAL INSTRUMENTS

Ampeg first produced electric upright basses, popular predominantly with jazz and orchestra pit musicians. This heritage was honored when the first Ampeg bass guitars appeared in 1966, the scrolled headstock design featuring classic rear-pointing tuners.

Produced briefly from the end of 1966, the ASB-1 (and the fretless AUSB-1) was designed by Ampeg employee Mike Roman, inspired by the stylings of the earlier Danelectro Longhorn. Its most unusual feature was the pair of triangular cutouts that passed through the body. With its red and black sunburst finish and sharp horns, the ASB-1 quickly acquired the tag of "Devil Bass."

Unpopular even among Ampeg employees, it's estimated that no more than 100 were built, a quarter of which were fretless. They are now highly collectible. **TB**

Aria
Diamond ADSG 1967

Type Solidbody electric twelve-string
Body & neck Hardwood laminate body, maple neck
Fingerboard Rosewood
Pick-ups Two single-coil pick-ups

From the brand's first appearance in the mid-1960s, the Aria name guaranteed a certain degree of quality at a time when Japanese guitars were better known around the world for their cheap, low-end copies of Fender and Gibson models.

Arai and Company began trading in 1954. After a failed business venture that saw founder Shiro Arai homeless, he found initial success importing and retailing European classical guitars, strings, and printed music to the emerging Japanese market. In 1960, he commissioned Guyatone to manufacture acoustic guitars for export to the United States, but the guitars failed to adjust to the dry U.S. climate and began to split.

Although Arai had imported Fender guitars to Japan from the late 1950s, his his personal interests had been in classical guitar, so it wasn't until 1963 that his first electric appeared. Built at the Matsumoko factory, these guitars were variously branded as Arai, Aria, Aria Diamond, or Arita. The Diamond line became the most highly regarded, and represents some of the best Japanese guitar manufacture of the period.

Although Aria produced high-quality guitars based on existing U.S. designs, the Aria Diamond ADSG electric twelve-string shown here is an original design—albeit a rather stylish reworking of the Fender offset body. Neck construction was impressive; the three-piece maple neck is of a standard comparable to anything being produced at the time in the United States.

From 1975, Arai positioned all of his electric models under Aria Pro II brand. Along with Yamaha and Ibanez, it formed the vanguard of Japan's challenge to the established U.S. market leaders. **TB**

Baldwin
706 1967

Type Double-cutaway hollow body semi-acoustic
Body & neck Sycamore body, mahogany neck
Fingerboard Rosewood
Pick-ups Two single-coil pick-ups

Inspired by the Gibson 335, this model came from the Baldwin guitar company in the mid-1960s. It has the same style of double cutaway thinline hollow body, two pick-ups with two controls each, and a floating tailpiece, and like the Gibson, it came in cherry or sunburst finishes.

Look closer, though, and the 706 has plenty of differentiating features. The pick-ups are Italian bar-type humbuckers with adjustable pole pieces. They create a rich, jangly sound that has been used in everything from jazz to country twang.

Stylewise, the guitar has some charming period details, like the scroll headstock, the "B" built into the tailpiece, and the name "Baldwin" stamped across the floating pickguard. Many came with Bigsby-style vibratos.

The guitar was thought of as a budget model, yet it was an international project: the body and electronics were made in Italy, the neck was made in England by the former Burns company, then everything was shipped to the United States to be assembled in Arkansas. **SH**

Coral
3S18 Electric Sitar 1967

Type Hollow body electric
Body & neck Pine frame, Masonite top/back, maple neck
Fingerboard Rosewood
Pick-ups Three single-coil lipstick pick-ups

Inspired in part by George Harrison, the psychedelic era saw a surge of interest in Indian culture: the sounds of the acoustic sitar had become a familiar component of The Beatles' recordings since *Revolver* in 1966. Session guitar player Vincent Bell increasingly found himself asked to create sitar sounds. However, the sitar was difficult to transport, tune, and play, so Bell created his own electric instrument that any guitarist would be able to play. The basic sound of the sitar was imitated by using Bell's flat bridge design, which caused the strings to create the characteristic "buzz" of the original instrument. Also fitted to the body was a set of thirteen short "sympathy" strings that would vibrate when the main strings were plucked.

Bell himself used the teardrop-shaped Coral Sitar on many hit records during the 1960s, including "Green Tambourine" by The Lemon Pipers and Freda Payne's "Band of Gold." Although Bell's Coral model was only in production for two years, electric sitars continue to be built for a niche market. **TB**

Danelectro
E2N4 Dane E 1967

Domino
California Rebel 1967

Type Solidbody electric bass
Body & neck Double cutaway poplar body, poplar neck
Fingerboard Brazilian rosewood
Pick-ups One single-coil lipstick pick-up

Type Semi-solidbody electric
Body & neck Mahogany
Fingerboard Rosewood
Pick-ups Two single-coil pick-ups

In 1967, Danelectro was a subsidiary of MCA, but still under founder Nathan Daniel's direction. Up until MCA's acquisition in 1967, with the exception of some of the Silvertone logo instruments built by Danelectro for Sears Roebuck, and the short-lived Danelectro Hawaiian lap steel that appeared in 1958, all of the company's Danelectro production guitars were built using the familiar Masonite and pine frame hollow construction. The Dane line was the first Danelectro solidbody production-line series. The standard finish was brown, with options of blue, red, and black. All instruments had "Totally Shielded" electronics. The offset body design with sculpted contours and the newly designed six-in-a-line headstock were well received. Daniel's "positive action adjustment" was also incorporated, enabling the neck angle to be adjusted, raising or lowering the playing action of the strings. Daniel failed to initiate a patent on the design and soon after, Leo Fender "borrowed" the idea and patented it himself. Nat remarked that it was so simple that he had no inclination to patent the idea. **DT**

Maurice Lipsky Music Co. was a prominent distributor and importer of electric guitars in the 1960s, and the New York–based company had been known for its Orpheum brand since the 1940s. In 1967, it began importing a range of designs and selling them under the Domino moniker. Models all took design inspiration from the usual suspects.

True to its name, the California Rebel bucked this trend and presented an original design. Its mahogany body had a sound cavity beneath the f-hole, and painted binding framed a German-carved outline. The offset trapezoid body shape has the merest glimmer of the rock body shapes of the 1980s, while the imitation-wood plastic full-body pickguard was ahead of its time. The peculiar slotted headstock must have seemed a "natural" choice for a guitar so brazenly defying categorization, adding up to a look that even today teeters precariously on the cusp of retro and modern.

The Rebel came in one, two, and three-pick-up versions, a twelve-string model, and possibly a bass. **OB**

John Entwistle
"Frankenstein" 1967

Type Solidbody bass
Body & neck Alder body, maple neck
Fingerboard Rosewood
Pick-ups One P-pick-up

From the mid-1960s for almost two decades, The Who were one of the most vital forces in rock music, shifting from arty mod band, through psychedelia and groundbreaking concept albums, and emerging in the 1970s as one of the most powerful stadium rock bands. In the band's engine room was the pounding thrash of drummer Keith Moon and the altogether more sophisticated and intricate bass work of John Entwistle.

A year after Entwistle's death in 2002, 350 of his personal items were auctioned at Sotheby's in London. Perhaps the most interesting artifact on offer was his "Frankenstein" bass, which he constructed in 1967, and which for many years he used to the exclusion of all others, using it on some of the band's benchmark works.

As the name suggests, Frankenstein is built from the parts of different instruments—five smashed Fender Precision basses and the machine heads of a Fender Jazz. But this was by no means the work of a master luthier. As Entwistle admitted: "Two hours with a Phillips screwdriver and a soldering iron and I was ranting around my hotel room screaming, 'It's alive, it's alive!'" In a 1994 interview he said, "I have about thirty-five Precisions, all with different colors and from different eras, but I always go back to Frankenstein."

At Sotheby's, Frankenstein had been expected to raise around $7,000; bidding ended at $100,000. **TB**

Entwistle's Frankenstein featured on such classic Who albums as *Quadrophenia* (1973). When Entwistle retired it from live use in the mid-1970s, he had it refinished from Sunburst to the Salmon Pink shown here.

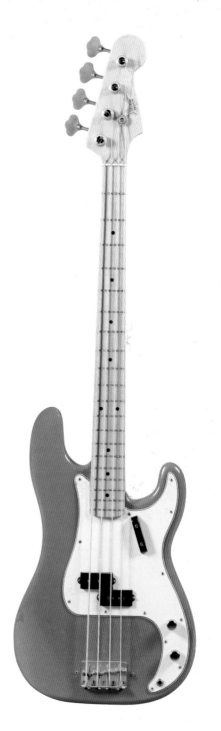

← John Entwistle with his home-built bass on the BBC's *Top Of The Pops* (1969).

Fender
Bronco 1967

Type Solidbody electric
Body & neck Alder
Fingerboard Rosewood
Pick-ups One Fender single-coil pick-up

As the CBS era began in earnest in the mid-1960s with the completion of a new factory, Fender indolently tweaked the brand's established designs and debuted Roger Rossmeisl's electric hollow bodies with bolt-on necks such as the Coronado. However, the distinct lack of headline news didn't prevent the company bringing its latest student solidbody, the Bronco, to market in 1967.

Initially sold along with a namesake amplifier (a six-watt rebadged Vibro Champ) as a package, the Dakota Red Bronco had the same body as the earlier Mustang, but updated that model's 22½-in. (57-cm) scale to 24 in.

"Bronco—a heavyweight performer at a lightweight price. You'll learn pronto on the fast-action, adjustable neck."

FENDER ADVERTISING

(61 cm) and twenty-two frets, removed the neck pick-up, and added a new "steel vibrato" bridge design. The unit had six adjustable saddles, was mounted on a spring inside a body cavity, and had a removable arm, but was unceremoniously dropped when the Bronco's tour of duty came to an end in 1981, and was never to return.

Despite their "student" status and diminutive stature, both physically and in the grand scheme of the Fender story, short-scale guitars such as the Bronco and particularly its cousin, the Mustang, have enjoyed the attention of the odd guitar hero along the way. Arctic Monkey Alex Turner has repeatedly used a later-period black Bronco, and Kurt Cobain was so enamored with his Mustangs that he enlisted Fender's help to mate one with the Jaguar, to produce the Jag-Stang. **OB**

Alex Turner of the Arctic Monkeys performs onstage with his Bronco in 2007. ➡

Fender Stratocaster "Rocky" 1967

Type Solidbody electric
Body & neck Alder body, maple neck
Fingerboard Rosewood
Pick-ups Three single-coil pick-ups

As celebrity guitars go, "Rocky" sits right near the top of the pile. A standard 1961 Fender Stratocaster would now be a desirable five-figure vintage instrument, but when it's been artfully decorated/defaced by one of the most famous rock guitarists of them all, its value becomes difficult to assess.

In the early days of The Beatles, George Harrison and John Lennon had largely been seen sporting Rickenbacker or Gretsch guitars. During the recording of *Rubber Soul* (1965), George and John sent their road manager Mal Evans on a mission—to procure for them

> "… I got some DayGlo paint, which was quite a new invention in those days … and just sat up late one night and [painted] it."
>
> GEORGE HARRISON

Fender Stratocasters. He returned with a pale blue pair and Harrison immediately began using his in the studio on tracks such as "Nowhere Man." And then one fateful evening in 1967, Harrison got to work with assorted pots of glow-in-the-dark paint and his wife Patti's nail polish to create his masterwork of psychedelic art.

Christened "Rocky"—as the name on the headstock shows—he would continue to use it with The Beatles: indeed, it can be seen in the groundbreaking live satellite broadcast of "All You Need Is Love" on June 25, 1967.

As Harrison became interested in slide guitar, in 1969 he raised Rocky's bridge and fitted it with thicker strings. He continued to use it for slide work until his death in 2001. "Rocky" remains in the possession of Harrison's family. **TB**

Gibson Flying V
"Love Drops" 1967

Type Solidbody electric
Body & neck Korina body; mahogany neck
Fingerboard Rosewood
Pick-ups Two humbucker pick-ups

Jimi Hendrix will always be associated with one guitar: the Fender Stratocaster. Indeed, it was this connection that has played such a big part in the guitar's modern-day iconic status. However, Hendrix was by no means a one-guitar man. He was known to have played Gibson Les Pauls and SGs, Fender Jazzmasters, and was even photographed playing one of Paul Barth's early Black Widows. Hendrix also owned three Gibson Flying Vs: a black 1967; a tobacco sunburst 1968; and a black left-hander built specially for him by Gibson in 1969.

Hendrix gave the 1967 Flying V his own personal touch: a fabulous, brightly colored, psychedelic paint job . . . or perhaps "nail polish job" would be more accurate. It was dubbed "Love Drops."

This Flying V saw active service in concert and on TV in Europe in 1967–1968. After Hendrix's death, the story took a peculiar turn. A new owner decided to remove Hendrix's art, and return it to its original black finish. By the time it had turned up in an English pawn shop in 1995, its pedigree would seem to have been lost. However, detective work by the latest buyer, David Brewis—who noticed traces of the original artwork under the pickguard, and that it showed signs of having been restrung for a lefty—led him to suspect its true identity. Authenticated by Gibson and Sotheby's, Brewis then had the original artwork painstakingly recreated.

In 2006, Jimi's Flying V was commemorated as the inaugural model in the Gibson Custom Shop's new "Inspired By" series. It was reissued in a limited run of 300, with the original design reconstructed by artist Bruce Kunkel. **TB**

Gretsch
6105 Rally 1967

Type Hollow body electric
Body & neck Maple body and neck
Fingerboard Rosewood
Pick-ups Two Gretsch HiLo'Tron single-coil pick-ups

One of a few Gretsch models from the mid-1960s with the same dual HiLo'Tron pick-up configuration, the Rally was another of Gretsch's attempts to be right up to date along the lines of their Monkees model that had failed to take off as hoped the previous year when it turned out that really serious musicians didn't like The Monkees (yet). According to the advertising literature: "The Gretsch Rally hollow body electric has got the 'now look and now feel' and delivers the 'now sound' with features you'd expect only from the most exclusive guitars. But its price is cool. Check out all it offers and you'll see that this is the guitar that's tops."

Visually striking, with its sporty stripes on the pickguard and truss rod cover, the Rally came in two versions: the "6104" in rally green and, even more vivid, the "6105" in two-tone copper mist and bamboo yellow. Features included one tone and two volume knobs and either a bar or a roller bridge with a Gretsch Bigsby vibrato. The two switches on the left shoulder were a standby and a treble booster, which kicked in the active electronics—that would be the "now sound" they were talking about in the brochure. It had thumbprint fingerboard inlays and a "T-zone tempered treble-end fingerboard" with dot inlays from the fifteenth fret—and a zero fret.

Another Gretsch model called the "Songbird," which was sold exclusively through music and entertainment retailer Sam Goody's stores, was identical to the Rally except that, flying in the face of normal convention, it had strange G-shaped sound holes. But there were no sporty stripes. **AJ**

Gretsch
6123 Monkees 1967

Type Twin cut-away archtop semi-acoustic
Body & neck Maple neck, hollow laminate maple body
Fingerboard Ebony
Pick-ups Two Super'Tron pick-ups

The Gretsch Monkees guitar was a fine instrument but a victim of lousy marketing. Gretsch had already tried to get official endorsement from George Harrison in the 1960s and failed. Sales were nonetheless strong, however, as Beatles fans had seen Harrison playing a Gretsch.

Instead, the company tried to cash in on the Monkees' newfound fame, producing this neat two-pick-up semi-acoustic, vaguely reminiscent of the Gibson 330 but with a Monkees-branded scratchplate and truss rod cover. It was the only official Monkees guitar and the group were huge worldwide stars at the time.

> *"The Gretsch Monkees model features a Bigsby tremolo ... original Gretsch Super'Tron pick-ups, and double thumb-print inlays exclusive to this model. Now I'm a believer!"*
> MODERN ONLINE ADVERTISING FOR USED MONKEES GUITAR

Sales, however, were underwhelming. Not only were the Monkees known for not actually playing their instruments, they appealed to young fans who were unlikely to buy guitars. Shops requested truss rod covers and scratchplates without the band's logo to help shift the stock. The model was discontinued within a year and replaced by the similar, un-Monkee-branded, Streamliner.

Yet the Monkees guitar was a high-quality archtop with two f-holes and two punchy Super'Tron pick-ups. The neck had double "thumbprint" fret markings top and bottom, and there was a Bigsby tremolo unit.

Ironically, the Monkees later evolved into a band that did write their own material and play their instruments ... including plenty of Gretsch guitars. **SH**

La Baye
2x4 1967

Type Solidbody electric
Body & neck Hardwood body, maple neck
Fingerboard Rosewood
Pick-ups Two single-coil Sensi-Tone pick-ups

This is an enigmatic guitar with a background story to match. Hailing from Green Bay, Wisconsin, guitarist and teacher Dan Helland was the man responsible for creating this minimalist masterpiece—the La Baye 2x4. The humorous name he chose was quite literal, since this guitar really is not much more than a neck bolted onto a block of two-by-four hardwood. ("La Baye" was the local name for a stretch of water on nearby Lake Michigan, and home to a community of people of French descent—it means "the bay.")

Helland had been experimenting with his idea when he came into contact with the owners of the Holman-Woodell guitar factory in Neodesha, Kansas. The company had previously secured a deal to produce "The Wild Ones: Stereo Electric Guitars" branded for Wurlitzer—a company better known for its organs and electric pianos. However, problems with flaking paint finishes led to large numbers of these guitars being returned to dealers, and the contract was quickly voided. The company plowed on, trying with limited success to sell the guitars under the Holman brand. At this point, Helland suggested producing his La Baye, fixing leftover necks and hardware to the new body. During 1967 the plant built fifty-seven guitars (including a dozen twelve-strings) and four basses and took them to the NAMM trade show. They created a stir but failed to secure any orders. Shortly afterward, Helland retired from the music business to become a photographer.

The guitar itself was playable enough. The single-coil Sensi-Tone pick-ups produced a pleasant sound. But few showed any great interest in the 2x4 as anything more than a curiosity. **TB**

Micro-Frets
Golden Melody 1967

Type Semi-solid electric
Body & neck Maple body with maple bolt-on neck
Fingerboard Rosewood
Pick-ups Two single-coil hi-fi pick-ups

The 1960s saw the emergence of a number of individualistic U.S. guitar makers, including Ralph S. Jones who produced such wonderfully eccentric instruments as the Micro-Frets Golden Melody. In the early 1960s, Jones concentrated on selling his own inventions, such as the Micro-Nut, which was an early approach to dealing with the "tempered intonation" issues that would later be famously treated by the Buzz Feiten tuning system. Jones also developed the Calibrato vibrato arm which, unlike standard vibrato units of the time, made it possible to bend chords that

> *"It can go from Country Tele twang to Hendrix in a heartbeat. Don't let the retro looks and light weight fool you into thinking it's a cheapie."*
> HARMONYCENTRAL.COM

would remain in tune as the pitch altered—and return to the correct tuning.

The first Micro-Frets guitars appeared in 1967, and, in accordance with the times, were presented in such exotic color schemes as Venus Sunset and Martian Sunrise. With its maple semi-hollow body, Golden Melody bore a passing resemblance to a Rickenbacker body shape, but its uncluttered appearance was aided by the volume and tone controls concealed beneath the floating pickguard and accessible via a pair of transistor radio-style "wheels." The Golden Melody could produce a fine selection of biting tones courtesy of the two Hi-Fi pick-ups designed by Bill Lawrence. **TB**

Micro-Frets
Orbiter 1967

Type Hollow body electric with FM transmitter
Body & neck Maple body and neck
Fingerboard Rosewood
Pick-ups Two single-coil pick-ups

Another of Micro-Frets' radical, way-before-its-time experiments was the Orbiter, a guitar with an in-built FM transmitter that could relay stereo sound to specifically tuned, nearby radio. These were the first cordless guitars—precursors to the radio-transmitter systems that have since become commonplace. The photograph shows the extended bass horn housing an antenna that was extended when in use. Separate from the guitar was an FM tuner box, which sat on top of the guitarist's amplifier and received transmissions from the guitar at a tuned frequency.

"[Ralph Jones] worked the whole factory… he was at every station at some time every day making things."

DAN "ELECTRIC BANJO MAN," MICRO-FRETS DESIGNER

Much of what we know about Micro-Frets comes from a series of sometimes contradictory postings in 2003 on the GuitarAttack online forum by two former employees, Gary Free and Dan "Electric Banjo Man," who described life at the company's small factory in Frederick, Maryland. It was an environment where Ralph Jones was clearly head honcho, and involved in every part of the design and building process; his wife, Mary, could be found winding pick-up coils and sanding between coats of paint.

Sadly, the Micro-Frets story came to a grinding halt in 1974. Following the sudden death of Ralph Jones, his wife decided to force the closure of the company. As Dan recalled: "'It's his invention,' she used to say. 'I don't want anybody to take credit for it.'" **TB**

Mosrite Strawberry Alarm Clock 1967

Type Solidbody electric
Body & neck Alder body, bolt-on maple neck
Fingerboard Rosewood
Pick-ups Two single-coil pick-ups

Semie Moseley had enjoyed success with his Mosrite brand, primarily through the upmarket signature models he had designed for The Ventures. They were, however, costly instruments, retailing at a substantially higher price than the most popular Fender models.

In 1967, Moseley hoped to reach a new market by aligning himself with the hippie movement dominating America's cultural landscape. With the aim of creating a guitar that visually mirrored the times, who better to endorse this model than America's most popular psychedelic pop band, The Strawberry Alarm Clock, then enjoying what would be a brief flurry of success.

The instrument that emerged from this curious alliance was unlike any other electric guitar around at that time. Although it shared the same hardware and construction as a standard Mosrite, the body structure featured a bizarre wooden skeleton, which stretched above and below the neck, coming together at the rear of the headstock. To give the instrument its wonderful period look, the completed guitars were shipped out to Californian artist Kenny "Von Dutch" Howard for custom paint jobs, a figure well known at the time for his flamboyant work on surfboards and automobile bodies.

The Mosrite Strawberry Alarm Clock appeared in three different guises: the green six-string, the purple bass, and the fabulous red twelve-string. **TB**

The Strawberry Alarm Clock may not have been at the cutting edge of psychedelia but their music evokes the period beautifully. Their second album, *Wake Up…It's Tomorrow* (1968) spawned the hit singles "Sit With The Guru" and "Tomorrow."

Musicraft
Messenger ME-1 1967

Type Hollow body electric
Body & neck Maple neck
Fingerboard Rosewood
Pick-ups Two DeArmond single-coil pick-ups

Glen F. Burke's Tuning Fork Guitar Company produced guitars with aluminum necks in Astoria, Oregon, between 1960 and 1965. Tuning Fork was eventually taken over by Musicraft Inc. which retained the aluminum neck concept for its Messenger models, which were manufactured in San Francisco for a very short period before the company relocated to Astoria in 1968, and then quickly disappeared. If it wasn't for Mark Farner of Grand Funk Railroad, the Messenger might have been completely forgotten.

The pictured guitar, which we believe is an ME-1 (although historian Tom Wheeler states that they made three six-string guitars: the ME-10 Morning Sunburst, the ME-11 Midnight Sunburst, and the ME-12 Rojo Red) features an aluminum neck that extends into the body—it was apparently tuned to A440 to assist resonance. The guitar also has stereo output—each pick-up could be sent to a separate amplifier—and an onboard fuzztone known as the "Tone Messer."

Mark Farner's Messenger was heavily modified— the hollow body was stuffed with foam and he taped over the "cat's-eyes" sound holes to reduce feedback. Eastwood Guitars, a modern-day manufacturer specializing in retro designs, currently makes a visual replica, but it's all wood with no fuzztone. **DB/AJ**

Classic footage of Grand Funk Railroad shows Farner's Messenger in use. "I'm Your Captain" from the band's second album *Closer To Home* (1970), will give you an idea of the Messenger's true tone.

Avalon
AV-2T 1968

Type Solidbody electric
Body & neck Laminated maple body, bolt-on neck
Fingerboard Rosewood
Pick-ups Two single-coil pick-ups

Just like the band that it is associated with, the Avalon AV-2T ("Shaggs") guitar remains something of an enigma. Originally sold for just under $50 in 1968, it currently commands prices of at least ten times that amount. While both the band and the guitar remain obscure to the mainstream, each is a well-known quantity among hip record collectors and connoisseurs of kitsch. Nobody knows much about The Shaggs beyond the basics: three teenage sisters, a domineering father, a naïve stab at pop stardom through utter disregard of all musical conventions, and an unlikely record destined for obscurity until its rediscovery by Frank Zappa. And the same holds true for the Avalon.

So where did this bizarre guitar really come from? We do know that it was made in Japan and appeared in the 1968 Harris-Teller catalog, priced at $47.50, along with claims of "professional quality and workmanship, an ultra-slim neck, and all chrome-plated parts." Whoever produced the Avalon certainly studied current trends, with the overall design being influenced by both Mosrite and Burns. Very cool for 1968.

So how does it sound? No matter what you do to an Avalon as far as setup attempts go, play it—and you will sound just like The Shaggs. Which explains why both the band and the guitar remain a rather acquired taste. **EP**

Every hipster music collection must have a copy of *Philosophy Of The World* (1969) by The Shaggs. It was one of Kurt Cobain's favorite albums. The Wiggins sisters only released this album and disbanded in 1975 after their father died.

John Bailey
JBSG2 1968

Type Custom-built solidbody electric guitar
Body & neck unknown
Fingerboard Ebony
Pick-ups Two handmade pick-ups

John Bailey was an English luthier who started out as a woodwork teacher at Hampstead Comprehensive School, and after rubbing shoulders with the folk community in London for several years, he eventually relocated to rural Dartmouth in Devon. Here he concentrated on making guitars for the new wave of 1960s folk music. He was also the author of *Making a Folk Guitar* and *Making an Appalachian Dulcimer*. Among his customers were the cream of British folk in the late 1960s, including Bert Jansch, Gordon Giltrap, Al Stewart, Richard Thompson, and John Renbourn.

"John's guitars had a very sweet tone but not a very loud voice."
GORDON GILTRAP

Bailey built this one-off guitar in Wembley, London, in 1968, before he moved to Devon. It was one of his first electric solids and was commissioned by a bluegrass band called The Echo Mountain Boys led by American Bill Clifton. The guitar has ended up in the enormous collection of Guy Mackenzie.

The uniquely shaped body wasn't just eye-catching, it was specially designed by Bailey to make fingerpicking easier on the electric guitar. There were two deep cutaways with no horns and a scalloped-out area between the pick-ups, which tends to give the presumably unintentional impression that The Echo Mountain Boys were a little rough with it on stage one night and smashed all the corners off. Bailey made the pick-ups and tailpiece himself by hand. He died in 2011. **SH**

Danelectro "Baby Sitar" 1968

Type Solidbody electric
Body & neck Poplar body and neck
Fingerboard Rosewood
Pick-ups One single-coil lipstick pick-up

The year 1968 was full of great new designs from the Danelectro company. The flagship Vincent Bell-designed Coral Electric Sitar was certainly one of them. This groundbreaking creation allowed guitarists to mimic Middle Eastern sounds without having to learn an entirely new instrument—and also enabled them to add electrification, which made it extremely useful in the studio.

Its launch was highly publicized, accompanied by a major advertising campaign, and its immediate success inspired the creation of a Danelectro-branded budget model. This new, stripped-down version, nicknamed the "Baby Sitar," lacked the thirteen sympathetic drone strings that were standard on the Coral model, and had only one pick-up with simple controls. (There had been three pick-ups on the original Coral.) Interestingly, the brass nut, a standard on the high-end Coral instruments, was retained on the "Baby," because, the makers claimed, it enhanced the distinctive tone.

A very small number of "Baby Sitars" were built, as few as 100 instruments before, in 1969, owners MCA closed down the factory in Neptune, New Jersey.

Ron Wood of The Rolling Stones has used his Danelectro "Baby Sitar" to great effect: live performances of "Paint It Black" feature the instrument prominently. Both versions of the electric sitar were used on a wide range of music styles, from pop to rock to country: classics such as "Band Of Gold" by Freda Payne, B.J. Thomas' "Hooked On A Feeling," Steve Miller's "Wild Mountain Honey," and Guns N' Roses' "Pretty Tied Up." **DT**

Fender
Montego II 1968

Type Hollow body archtop
Body & neck Spruce top, maple back and sides
Fingerboard Ebony
Pick-ups Two humbucker pick-ups

Solidbody pioneer Fender had all but steered clear of the airy world of hollow body jazz guitars, leaving that area to its main rival, Gibson. However, as the 1960s progressed and the folk revival brought a resurgence of interest in acoustic guitars, Fender employed German luthier and ex-Rickenbacker designer Roger Rossmeisl to create its acoustic range, and the Gibson-like semi-acoustic, the Coronado. Encouraged, Leo Fender channeled his passion for high-end jazz-oriented instruments into the luxurious LTD and its more affordable sibling, the Montego.

"The Montego combines both beauty and performance in a high-quality, great-sounding guitar."

1969 FENDER CATALOG

The Montego I was a single-pick-up version—with the II adding a second humbucker along with the appropriate knobs and switches. The II was aesthetically similar to guitars such as Gibson's Super 400 and the high-end jazz artistry of D'Angelico, but its Fender genes manifested themselves with an incongruous bolt-on neck, practically unheard of among guitars of this type. It was a looker though, with Rossmeisl's German carve creating an attractive outline topped off with pearl inlays and a decorated mother-of-pearl headstock. There were two humbucking pick-ups teamed with a Gibson-style three-way selector, two volumes, and two tone controls. It was discontinued in 1974, and fewer than 100 were built. In 1972, it retailed for $850 without the case. **OB/AJ**

Fender
Palomino 1968

Type Steel-string acoustic guitar
Body & neck Mahogany back and sides, spruce top, bolt-on maple neck
Fingerboard Rosewood

In the late 1960s, Fender launched a line of acoustic guitars incorporating features that had recently been developed for its electric guitars. The most popular of the line of these acoustics was the Palomino. This used a bolt-on twenty-fret maple neck from Fender's popular Stratocaster solid electric with no heel to obstruct access to the higher frets.

It had an odd feature often called "the broomstick"— an aluminum bar running inside the body from the neck to the end piece, which supposedly added structural rigidity to the body.

> *"Your Fender Palomino acoustic guitar … incorporates many new developments by Fender engineers. "*
> FENDER PALOMINO OWNER'S MANUAL

The metal bridge was an electric style too, similar to a Jazzmaster—with individual string adjustment for height and intonation. The Palomino also had in-line Kluson tuners, a three-ply screw-on gold pickguard, and a metal Fender screw plate at the back of the neck joint.

The sound was average, but the Palomino's electric guitar features made it very playable, even high up the neck. The action was low, the intonation could be spot-on, and the feel was just like a solid electric. Of course, the sound was a bit feeble compared to the best acoustic instruments, but the new generation of players didn't mind. Soon stars like Stephen Stills, Joan Baez, Eric Clapton, Waylon Jennings, Buck Owens, and Jerry Garcia played Palominos. A special black Palomino owned by Johnny Cash recently sold for $62,500 at auction. **SH**

Fender Stratocaster
240981 1968

Type Solidbody electric
Body & neck Alder body, maple neck
Fingerboard Maple
Pick-ups Three single-coil pick-ups

So, could this be the most iconic guitar in rock history? This modest Fender Stratocaster in Olympic White, serial number 240981, belonged to Jimi Hendrix, perhaps the single most important figure in the history of rock guitar. It was on this very guitar that he played his earth-shattering version of "The Star Spangled Banner"—his eloquent protest at America's continued involvement in the Vietnam War—performed at the closing of the Woodstock Festival in August 1969. There was nothing remarkable about this stock production-line guitar. Indeed, as an example of a post-CBS Fender, most aficionados would agree that any Strat made more than three years prior to this is likely to have been a superior instrument.

Hendrix was a left-handed player who played right-handed guitars, so the only alteration he had made to his Strat was removing and reversing the nut so that it could be strung in reverse.

After Hendrix's death in 1970, the guitar resided, in its case, unopened, with his band's drummer, Mitch Mitchell. In 1990, he put it up for auction at Sotheby's and saw it attract a winning bid of £198,000—a record for its time. The guitar was later acquired by Microsoft executive Paul Allen, at a cost rumored to be in the region of $1.3 million. It is now on permanent display at the Experience Music Project Museum in Seattle. **TB**

Jimi Hendrix's historic interpretation of "The Star Spangled Banner" can be heard on the album *Live At Woodstock* (1999). This rereleased two-CD version features Hendrix's entire Woodstock set.

Jimi Hendrix with his legendary Olympic White Strat. →

Fender "72" Thinline Telecaster 1968

Type Semi-solidbody electric
Body & neck Ash or mahogany body, maple neck
Fingerboard Maple
Pick-ups Two single-coil (two humbuckers on '72 Thinline)

Pick up a Telecaster from various periods of its production and you might be surprised at the dramatic difference in weight between any two models. These variations can be attributed the type of wood used in the body. During the 1960s, the light ash used on many Fender bodies became difficult to source. As a result, the more plentiful heavy ash was introduced, turning some Teles into weighty beasts that were, for some players, uncomfortable to play for long periods.

German Luthier Roger Rossmeisl, a full-time Fender employee since 1962, offered an experimental solution in 1968 by cutting a number of cavities into the body from the rear and then covering them over with a thin panel. The result was a great success; the new instrument was around 50 percent lighter than its contemporary solidbody counterpart. Later that year, Fender launched the new model as the Thinline Telecaster.

Visually the Thinline resembled a classic Tele with the obvious exception of the large f-hole cut into the upper body. Gone also was the standard chrome control panel, now replaced by a Strat-style pearloid pickguard on which the volume and tone controls and pick-up selector switch were mounted. Two versions of the Thinline were available on launch: one with an ash body; the other cut from mahogany. Both were given a "natural" finish. A sunburst option was added a year later.

In 1972, the single-coil pick-ups were replaced by Fender Wide Range humbuckers—these are shown on the model pictured here. Usually referred to as a "'72 Thinline," this model remained in original production until 1980. A number of reissues have subsequently appeared, under both the Fender and Squier brands. **TB**

Fender "George Harrison" Telecaster 1968

Type Solidbody electric (later chambered body)
Body & neck Maple/rosewood body, rosewood neck
Fingerboard Rosewood
Pick-ups Two single-coil pick-ups

In December 1968, an unknown courier began a journey from Fender HQ at Fullerton, California, and boarded a London-bound flight; in his hand, a custom-built Telecaster, a gift from Fender to be delivered in person to George Harrison of The Beatles.

Designed and built by Roger Rossmeisl and Phillip Kubicki (later the creator of the noted Factor bass), two prototypes of a stunning rosewood Telecaster were built, the better of which was sent to the Beatle. The guitar body was constructed from a thin layer of maple, with a solid rosewood back and top. There was also a rosewood neck, and a separate rosewood fingerboard. The guitar was finished in a non-standard, satin polyurethane varnish.

The rosewood Teles went on general sale in 1969, and were priced at $375 each. The production model was not identical to the prototypes: it had a one-piece neck, a gloss finish, and, to reduce weight, a chambered body. Not a great commercial success, the rosewood Telecasters were discontinued in 1972.

Harrison was evidently very happy with the guitar, though, and used it extensively during the sessions for *Let It Be* (1970), and, most famously, in the band's final live performance, on the rooftop of Apple's London HQ.

In 1969, Harrison gave the guitar to Delaney Bramlett, who sold it after Harrison's death in 2001. At auction, the Tele went for $434,750. The buyer was later revealed to be the late Beatle's widow, Olivia.

In 2012, Harrison's son, Dahni, conceived the idea of an iPad app that would enable fans to study seven of his father's guitars interactively, among them the "Rocky" Strat, and the rosewood Telecaster. **TB**

Fender "James Burton" Telecaster 1968

Fender Telecaster Bass 1968

Type Solidbody electric
Body & neck Alder body and neck
Fingerboard Maple
Pick-ups Three Fender single-coil pick-ups

Type Electric bass
Body & neck Alder body and neck
Fingerboard Maple
Pick-ups One single-coil pick-up (later a humbucker)

Louisiana-born guitar legend James Burton's long and distinguished career has seen him earn the title "Master of the Telecaster"—some honor, considering the sheer number of contenders there have been over the guitar's sixty-plus-year lifespan.

During his time with Elvis, from 1969 up until the singer's death in 1977, Burton became synonymous with the "Pink Paisley" Telecaster he was given by Fender's Vice President, Chuck Weiner. For Fender, the guitar was an out-of-character psychedelic experiment, featuring self-adhesive patterned wallpaper under clear lacquer, and came in two finishes: Blue Flower and Red Paisley.

Burton was nervous that Elvis wouldn't like it, but he needn't have worried. From its onstage unveiling onward, every "Play it, James!" the King uttered was answered by the resounding twang of the Telecaster. Burton later said, "This guitar had a sound, y'know? It was different to my original Tele, a little fatter. I had my back pick-up custom-wound by a friend of mine, Red Rhodes. Hit that switch, and the notes sound that big and round." **OB**

Fender's Telecaster Bass was a first for Fender on two very important fronts. Firstly, it was the company's first "reissue"—in the sense that it was a re-release of the first design of the all-conquering Precision Bass of 1951. Secondly, it was perhaps the first and only bass ever to use wallpaper in its construction, for the pink paisley and blue floral finishes it was briefly paraded in.

The Telecaster Bass's initial design had a two-saddle bridge, a string-through body, a Telecaster headstock, and a lone single-coil pick-up. In 1972, the design was updated with a humbucker and an extended scratchplate and was discontinued in 1979. However, both permutations of the Telecaster Bass received a new lease on life in modified form when Fender Japan released the Reissue '51 Precision Bass in 1994 and the Modern Player Telecaster Bass in 2011, and Squier created the Vintage Modified Precision Bass TB in 2007. Famous players of the Telecaster Bass include Dusty Hill of ZZ Top, Ron Wood, Paul McGuigan of Oasis, and Mike Dirnt of Green Day. **OB**

Fender Wildwood Coronado XII 1968

Type Hollow body electric
Body & neck Laminated beechwood body, maple neck
Fingerboard Rosewood
Pick-ups Two DeArmond single-coil pick-ups

Designed by ex-Rickenbacker man Roger Rossmeisl, Fender's Coronado line was marched out in 1966 to cash in on the thinline, hollow body craze instigated by British Invasion bands. In 1967, Fender added the Coronado XII, which was influenced by the jangly twelve-string of Roger McGuinn.

Hollow bodies were a natural development for Fender, but the company went a groovy step further by adding a Coronado XII Wildwood to the line— essentially an option in which the double-cutaway body's beechwood was dyed in one of six choices: green, gold and brown, gold and purple, dark blue, purple-blue, or blue-green. The dyes were injected into growing trees, resulting in some truly crazed patterns appropriate to the period.

Beyond the "hockey stick" headstock was an eminently serviceable ax. The XII featured two sizzling DeArmond pick-ups, two volume and tone controls, fingerboard inlays, a suspended tailpiece, and a Tune-o-matic-style bridge. **DP**

Hagstrom H8 1968

Type Eight-string electric bass
Body & neck Mahogany (sometimes birch) body and neck
Fingerboard Rosewood
Pick-ups Two Hagstrom bass pick-ups

Eight-string basses are commonplace these days, but in 1968, the idea of doubling each string of a standard four-string model for a more percussive tone was almost unthinkable. The treble sound produced by the secondary strings didn't have a place until the late 1960s, when bassists began to consider the benefits of a tone that could be clearly heard. Enter the Hagstrom H8.

Around 2,200 H8s were manufactured with a regular four-string design but with two extra strings above each string. These were tuned an octave higher than usual, enabling a very resonant, high-end sound.

The number of strings permitted experimentation with tunings, and Hagstrom recommended that each group of three strings be tuned to a major third, a perfect fifth, and a major seventh.

Jimi Hendrix is known to have used the sixth-ever H8, playing it on jammed tunes such as The Beatles' "Day Tripper". His bassist, Noel Redding, also used one on "Spanish Castle Magic." **JM**

Hallmark
Swept-Wing 1968

Type Semi-hollow electric
Body & neck Alder, laminated hardwood
Fingerboard Rosewood
Pick-ups Two high-output single-coil pick-ups

In the mid-1960s, guitarist-turned-luthier Joe Hall set up in Bakersfield, California, in close proximity to his former employer, Mosrite, and with the aid of colleague Bill Gruggett, set about emulating the success he'd seen first-hand while learning from Semie Moseley. A major factor in Mosrite's success had been the Ventures model, and when the band's bassist, Bob Bogle, approached Hall with a radical design idea, the spectacular Swept-Wing was the result.

Whether it was Bogle's supposed research into the tastes of guitarists of the time or merely the popularity

"I love the new Hallmark Swept Wings! ... For a combination of classic Jetsons styling, and great guitar tones, you can't beat 'em."

DEKE DICKERSON

of the *Batman* TV series that was the inspiration for its amazing outline is unclear. But the stage was set for the 1968 NAMM show in Chicago. However, the late 1960s war in Vietnam created a secondhand surplus. And the Swept-Wing was only one of many bizarrely shaped sirens attempting to seduce the six-stringers of the psychedelic era. Despite making semi-hollow, solidbody, double-neck, and bass variants, and although they were placed in the hands of players from The Doors, The Grateful Dead, and Jefferson Airplane, Hallmark declared itself bankrupt in 1968.

Perhaps fewer than 100 guitars were initially produced, but the brand and model was resurrected by Maryland maker Bob Shade in the late 1990s, and Swept-Wings are enjoying a new lease of life today. **OB**

Kawai
Concert 1968

Type Hollow body twin cutaway electric six-string
Body & neck Laminated maple body and neck
Fingerboard Rosewood
Pick-ups Two single-coil pick-ups

Japanese guitar making in the 1960s wasn't all about making cheap copies of Western models for mail-order catalogs—there were some truly innovative designs too. The Kawai Concert was a unique electric guitar with a body formed by sticking two hollow pieces together.

Kawai, already a thriving instrument maker, had purchased the Teisco guitar company in 1967. While the Teisco company continued to produce a series of big-selling instruments, Kawai seemed to take the merger as the signal to create some extraordinary guitars with a whimsical Japanese personality of their own.

As well as this thinline ax-shaped ax, there was a sixteen-string violin-bodied guitar, a banjo-shaped guitar with a tremolo arm, and a combined sitar guitar. And the "Flying Wedge" it produced at this time looked more like a shovel than a guitar.

With its awkward side cutaways, the Concert held its own among this quirky range. Its lightweight body was paired with a neck made from multiple thin laminations of maple. There were two beefy single-coil pick-ups. The guitar had a single f-hole, a tailpiece tremolo system, a Burns-style scroll headstock, and came in either Black or Sunburst.

Some of these Kawai Concert guitars were exported but may have been sold under different brands, like Winston or Splender. In fact, around this time Kawai and Teisco guitars carried more than fifty different invented brand names.

Today Kawai is still a large successful company with thousands of employees that has returned to its original core business: making pianos and keyboards. **SH**

Kawai
Teardrop 1968

Type Semi-hollow double cutaway six-string electric
Body & neck Spruce top, mahogany back/sides, maple neck
Fingerboard Rosewood
Pick-ups Two single-coil pick-ups

In 1968, Kawai produced this new guitar clearly based on the British Vox Mark VI Teardrop design. The Vox was famously used at the time by Brian Jones of The Rolling Stones.

The Kawai was, of course, cheaper, but to some players it sounded better than the Vox. The Japanese quality was clearly matching much of the European output at the time.

In Kawai's catalog of 1968 there was a bass and six-string version. Both had a semi-hollow construction and two pick-ups. But just to confuse the job of guitar historians, Kawai also launched a solidbody version of the Teardrop at the same time. This was called the PM-2V and had a similar arrangement of two single-coil pick-ups but no f-hole and a different-shaped scratchplate.

As with many Japanese guitars of this period, sometimes these instruments were labeled Kawai, sometimes Teisco, and sometimes Winston. There also seem to be some other unidentified teardrop guitars built by the Kawai empire at this time.

What is clear today, though, is that the Japanese Teardrop six-string was well appointed for the era. It featured a sprung tremolo tailpiece and a hand-rest cover on the rosewood bridge. The body, neck, and f-hole were fully bound, the hardware was all chrome (even the pick-up housings and control knobs), and there was a floating three-ply tortoiseshell pickguard. The rosewood fingerboard had chunky pearl block inlays. The neck itself was bolted to the guitar body with four screws and was adjusted via a truss rod at the playing end. **SH**

Kustom
K200C 1968

Type Semi-hollow twin cutaway electric
Body & neck Laminated maple body, bolt-on maple neck
Fingerboard Rosewood
Pick-ups Two DeArmond "anti-hum" single-coil pick-ups

The K series were thinline semi-hollow electric guitars modeled on the popular Rickenbackers that had become fashionable upon The Beatles' success. Kustom was much better known for its amplifiers, but owner Bud Ross assembled a team of designers that may have included Roy Clark (country musician) and Semie Moseley (founder of Mosrite guitars), as well as some local woodworking teachers. The guitars they eventually designed were built in Chanute, Kansas.

Features of the new instruments included two DeArmond pick-ups, which, although large, were still

"The … Kustom … was created to offer today's guitarist a quality instrument with excellent playing features and superb tonal qualities."
KUSTOM ADVERTISEMENT

single-coil. More distinctive was the unique arrangement of dot fret markers on the six-string guitars. The bodies were made of four pieces of wood glued together with a routed cavity inside and a single "cat's-eye" sound hole.

There were three main versions: with and without a factory-fitted Bigsby tremolo system, and a bass model. Over time, some guitars had more lavish trim and some models had pick-ups with adjustable pole pieces.

The K200C's maple neck was neatly bound, with a steel nut and zero fret. It was very slim and fast to play. The curved truss rod was a cleverly bolted steel plate at the end of the neck and this exerted pressure across the entire width of the guitar, providing extra neck control.

The K200C went on sale at $195 in 1968 and around 2,500 K-series guitars were sold in the next two years. **SH**

Maton
Wedgtail 1968

Type Semi-hollow twin cutaway electric
Body & neck Laminated maple body, bolt-on maple neck
Fingerboard Rosewood
Pick-ups Two DeArmond "anti-hum" single-coil pick-ups

The sense of earnestly wanting something because we know we can't have it has a name—economists call it the Scarcity Principle—and when this principle is applied to guitars, the Maton Wedgtail is one guitar that would be the cause of some considerable angst.

Maton, one of the oldest makers of electric guitars in the world, began in Australia in March 1946 when a young Melbourne-born jazz musician named Bill May and his older brother Reg unveiled their custom guitar-manufacturing and repair company—Maton Musical Instruments. Eleven years later, Elvis Presley played a

"'Gimmie Shelter' was done on a full-bodied Maton electric ... it sounded great. It made a great record."

KEITH RICHARDS

Maton "hillbilly" acoustic flat-top in the 1957 movie *Jailhouse Rock*. The Wedgtail came along in 1968, and Maton's own company history confirms about 110 were produced over five years, making it the most sought-after Maton ever made. Available colors were Flare Sunburst, Flare Red, and Natural Mahogany.

Wedgtails were always characterized by big Bigsbys, routed into the body for a lower profile that had a great look and feel to them but occasionally were thought to have pretty weak, dry pick-ups—a problem not helped by the fact that the bodies were often made with light timbers. Light timbers or not, the horns were massive, and with their eye-catching Bigsbys, the Wedgtails proved a difficult guitar to look past, even when placed alongside comparative Gibsons and Fenders. **BS**

Mosrite
Joe Maphis 1968

Type Solidbody electric
Body & neck Walnut body, maple neck
Fingerboard Rosewood
Pick-ups Two single-coil pick-ups

"Mosrite" was an amalgamation of the names Semie Moseley and Ray Boatright. Moseley was the guitar builder; Boatright, his mentor. The company was established around 1952. Moseley had worked for both Rickenbacker and Paul Bigsby's guitar-making company, learning to build quality handmade instruments.

The fledgling company gained fame by making a double-neck electric solidbody for country-picking maestro Joe Maphis. Maphis played on the local TV show *Town Hall Party* as well as cutting records featuring his supercharged flatpicking, almost always with his new trademark guitar on the cover. The dramatic double-neck instrument quickly brought both Mosrite and Maphis fame. It was thus little wonder that country bandleader Hank Thompson would soon mosey into the Mosrite workshop seeking a guitar of his own. He purchased this Joe Maphis Mark I: a single-neck version was enough for him.

The body was made from a heavy walnut slab and routed out from behind to hold the electrics. A flat back piece cleanly covered up the insides. The guitar featured a unique body shape with offset top horns and lower body. The tilted single-coil neck pick-up added to the offset effect. Moseley also made custom models for artists from Larry Collins of The Collins Kids to Nokie Edwards of The Ventures and Buck Owens. **MD**

Joe Maphis often proudly displayed his glorious Mosrite double-neck guitar on his album covers, including this aptly named country classic full of breakneck-speed instrumentals, *Fire On The Strings* (1957).

Rubio
Classical Guitar 1968

Type Classical guitar
Body & neck Spruce top, rosewood back and sides, mahogany neck, ebony fingerboard
Other features Six-fan brace design, Landstorfer tuners

From 1965 to 1968, in the period after playing guitars by Robert Bouchet and before those of Hermann Hauser, Julian Bream played guitars by David Rubio (1934–2000), instantly bringing renown and a long waiting list to this English maker who had only started making guitars a few years earlier, after having earned his living as a flamenco guitarist and ending up in New York, by way of Spain.

Having "discovered" Rubio, Bream invited him to set up his workshop at his property in Wiltshire, United Kingdom. Rubio accepted and worked there from 1967

> "In Spain I had sat shooting the breeze in the back of the guitar makers' shops … and I decided one day that I wanted to make guitars."
> DAVID RUBIO

until 1969, when he moved to Oxfordshire, vacating the workshop for another Bream protégé, José Romanillos. Rubio would go on to make about 1,000 instruments, including lutes, harpsichords, and violins.

This guitar from 1968 is from the period when Rubio was using a bracing system similar to that of Bouchet, though using six braces rather than the more usual five that Bouchet favored. It was Bream who introduced Rubio to Bouchet guitars in 1964–65, when he needed a repair to one of his and took it to Rubio in New York. Rubio guitars over the next three or four years were strongly influenced by Bouchet and it was not until 1969 that he would start evolving that general design. Bream played a 1965 Rubio on his landmark album *Twentieth-Century Guitar* (1993). **GD**

← Julian Bream playing his Rubio guitar in 1970.

Teisco Del Rey
May Queen 1968

Teisco Del Rey
Spectrum 2 1968

Type Hollow body electric
Body & neck Laminate body, maple neck
Fingerboard Rosewood
Pick-ups Two single-coil pick-ups

Type Solidbody electric
Body & neck Laminate body, maple neck
Fingerboard Rosewood
Pick-ups Two single-coil pick-ups

One of the most significant Japanese exporters, the Tokyo Electric Instrument and Sound Company (Teisco) helped fuel the electric guitar boom of the 1960s by providing cheap guitars—often blatant imitations—for novice players. The guitars were usually ordered directly, and in large quantities, by distributors: hence, identical guitars could be found in different territories under assorted names, including Jedson, Kent, Arbiter, Audition, and Top Twenty.

The 1968 May Queen was imported and branded in the United States as Teisco Del Rey. It's weird, though, since it seems to have been modeled on a British Vox Mandoguitar—an obscure, twelve-string electric mandolin with what has been described as an "artist's palette" body shape. Unlike the tiny Vox, however, the May Queen is a hollow body guitar, with a visually pleasing "cat's-eye" sound hole.

Soon after the launch, Teisco was taken over by the Kawai Corporation. By the end of the 1960s the company had ceased production altogether. **TB**

Of the many variations of twin-horn Stratocaster/Jaguar-shaped guitars produced by Teisco during the 1960s, the most sought after tend to be the more original designs produced under the Teisco Del Rey name. This one appears to be a variation of the Teisco Del Rey "Spectrum 2"—although without the split pick-ups labeled "Treble" and "Bass" that were found on most Spectrums. The issue of its identity is also slightly clouded by the fact that after Kawai took over the Teisco company in 1967, many of the model names were changed.

Between 1967 and 1970, the Spectrum line became increasingly exotic—the Spectrum 4 had four pick-ups and an inscrutable way of selecting them, and the upmarket Spectrum 5 had a long row of brightly colored pick-up selectors and a weird tremolo mechanism with no springs. The Spectrum 2, however, with its unimpressive two pick-up switches and the not-terribly-modern floral decorations on the scratchplate, has a much cheaper feel to it. **AJ**

Tokai
Hummingbird 1968

Type Solidbody electric
Body & neck Alder body, maple neck
Fingerboard Rosewood
Pick-ups Two single-coil pick-ups

Before Japanese guitar manufacturers became obsessed with copying Gibson and Fender guitars, there were some pretty wild designs unleashed. The Hummingbird was one of Tokai's first solidbody electrics. This is a good example of the way young Japanese "eleki" bands had so curiously been in thrall to the U.S. Mosrite brand—a fact entirely attributable to the popularity of The Ventures, the company's official endorsees. But although the Hummingbird has the Mosrite Mark I's extended lower horn, beautiful German carve, and dramatically offset neck pick-up, it is no crude copy of the American guitar. The horns themselves are exaggerated, and have sharper points, and the overall contour of the body has an unmistakably Japanese feel.

Aimed primarily at the home market, these guitars were not exported in huge numbers, so they are now very collectable in the West. In 2005, the U.S. Eastwood company produced a faithful reproduction of the Hummingbird in small numbers. **TB**

Welson
Jazz Vedette 1968

Type Double cutaway, solidbody electric
Body & neck Maple
Fingerboard Rosewood
Pick-ups Two humbucker pick-ups

Welson was an Italian guitar manufacturer which began producing solidbody electrics in 1962. Ironically all but ignored in Italy where Eko and Crucianelli dominated the guitar scene, Welsons were exported successfully to the United States and much of Europe.

Noted for its panache for copying others, particularly Gibson, Welson produced a design of its own in 1968—the Jazz Vedette. Inspired by Fenders and infinitely more playable than their trademark "glitter" models, the Vedette had block inlays, a thin, narrow neck, low fret profiles, and an adjustable truss rod. Available in selected colors including sunburst, they had two channels with a rhythm/solo selector, two-tone volume controls for each channel, and twin pick-ups with a three-position switch to activate them. With the distinctive crown logo on the pickguard and the Welson-engraved bridge cover, its low action and straight sound saw the Jazz Vedette soon enter the genre of "collector's item" and added to Welson's growing reputation as "Italy's answer to Gibson." **BS**

Wurlitzer
Cougar 2512 1968

Type Double cutaway solidbody electric
Body & neck Maple body and neck
Fingerboard Maple
Pick-ups Two Holman Sensi-Tone single-coil pick-ups

The thing about Wurlitzer guitars is, of course, that they were not Wurlitzers at all—they were, in fact, Holman-Woodells, made in the Neodesha, Kansas, guitar factory of Howard Holman and Victor Woodell, who simply chose the well-established Wurlitzer Music Company to be their national distributors. The first Holman-Woodell guitar—a Wurlitzer Cougar solidbody—debuted at the Neodesha Lion's Club on November 24, 1965, and was played by (and by all accounts designed by) a former wood-shop teacher, now Holman-Woodell's production supervisor, Doyle Reading.

> *"The next time you land on one of these guitars from Kansas, click your heels together and go for it."*
>
> **KEVIN MACY, THE DIFFERENT STRUMMER**

By the time the 1968 Cougar came along, however, the guitar boom in the United States was over and the company's demise was imminent. Wurlitzer had already abandoned Holman-Woodell, who had endured a takeover in 1967 and became Alray, although Holman characteristics, including its own peculiar Bigsbys (so-called Wurlitzer "Vibratron" on base plates with a "W" cutout), would persist. Necks were maple, the bodies a mix of locally sourced timbers and Canadian maple, and they had a Tunemaster adjustable bridge.

Though minus the trademark "W" in its base plate and sporting a very different, cooler-looking 3x3 headstock, the Cougar 2512 shared the same pick-ups and circuitry as other earlier "Wild One" series. **BS**

Ampeg Dan Armstrong "Plexi" 1969

Type Twin cutaway solidbody
Body & neck Plexiglas body, bolt-on maple neck
Fingerboard Rosewood
Pick-ups Modular slot-in interchangeable pick-ups

Well established for its innovative bass amplification, in 1968 Ampeg engaged the services of well-respected guitar and amplifier technician Dan Armstrong. His brief was to modernize Ampeg's less-revered instrument range. Armstrong would enjoy a long and varied career in the world of guitar technology until his death in 2004, but the innovation for which he is perhaps best remembered is the plastic "see-through" guitar body.

Armstrong chose Plexiglas for the body of his new instruments, as it had enormous on stage visual appeal, appearing as if it were carved from glass. However,

> *"I've had that guitar for a long time and it just has that real sort of twang when you pull it with your fingers. It sings a lot more than a normal guitar does."*

JUSTIN HAWKINS, THE DARKNESS

Plexiglas has a density that far exceeds any wood, and thus—in theory, at least—should enable the instrument to produce a greater level of sustain.

Available in both guitar and bass forms, Armstrong's designs were also electronically innovative. Working with pick-up legend Bill Lawrence, the pair conceived a set of modular, slot-in pick-ups, designed to be changeable within a few seconds: there were six available for the guitar, and two for the bass.

Too heavy for the liking of many, the Plexiglas models nonetheless became desirable when they were adopted for stage use by The Rolling Stones. Sadly, production was dramatically halted in 1971 following a contractual dispute between Ampeg and Armstrong. **TB**

Fender
Swinger 1969

Type Solidbody electric
Body & neck Alder
Fingerboard Rosewood
Pick-ups One single-coil pick-up

The Fender Swinger, also unofficially known as the Musiclander or Arrow, was produced in 1969 but never appeared in any of Fender's official catalogs. It was a creative solution to the problem of Fender's surplus of short-scale necks and bodies for its student guitars: the company had offered its Musicmasters, Duo-Sonic, and Mustang models with 22½-in. (57-cm) or 24-in. (61-cm) necks, and with the latter proving more popular, there were hundreds of the former left over.

Fender Product Manager for Stringed Instruments Virgilio "Babe" Simoni was the designer of the Swinger,

> *"I made [the headstock] more rounded, like an acoustic. Then somebody came along and cut the end off—made it look like a spear."*
>
> VIRGILIO SIMONI, FENDER

and, as he'd go on to do with the Maverick model using Fender XII leftovers, he proved a resourceful recycler. Both Musicmaster and Bass V model bodies were shown the band saw, and the resulting body shape had a subtle offset arc at the base and a foreshortened left horn. The larger size of Bass V bodies required more machining to cut them down to size, of course (to work out which body your Swinger was derived from, look for a rout under the pickguard, which was originally intended for the Bass V's pick-up).

For guitarists, this particular Swinger is destined to always be one of the last sets of keys in the bowl. But it did at least dress the part, coming in a range of attractive Fender colors, including Daphne and Lake Placid blues and Dakota and Candy Apple reds. **OB**

U.S. multi-instrumentalist Ben Kweller on stage with his Swinger in New York City, 2006. ➡

Gibson
Crest Gold 1969

Type Hollow body electric archtop
Body & neck Rosewood top/back/sides, mahogany neck
Fingerboard Brazilian rosewood
Pick-ups Two Johnny Smith mini-humbucker pick-ups

One of the most sought-after and distinctive thinlines Gibson produced, the Crest came in two versions, Silver and Gold, depending upon the plating that was used. Only fifty-six in total were made in 1969, and just 162 overall during its three-year production run.

The gold hardware found on the double Venetian cutaway Crest includes its two suspended Johnny Smith humbucker pick-ups, its beautiful tailpiece infilled with Brazilian rosewood and containing a pearl "Crest" nameplate, its adjustable Tune-o-matic bridge, its volume and tone knobs, its engraved truss rod cover

> *"The ornamental backstripe is a common feature of expensive flat-top guitars but is not found on any other Gibson archtop."*
>
> GEORGE GRUHN

and even the support brackets of its Brazilian rosewood pickguard. The headstock also sports a pearl-inlayed Gibson logo. The profusion of sought-after Brazilian rosewood, rather than the more typical maple common to other thinlines, gave the Crest a depth and resonance difficult to emulate even on other Gibsons. The backs of most Crests were flat, too, unlike almost all other Gibson double cutaway electrics.

Weighing in at 6 lb. 10 oz. (3 kg), the Crest was noticeably lighter than many contemporary Gibson thinlines. John Wilkinson, rhythm guitarist for Elvis' TCB band, used a Crest Gold (which he nicknamed "Mr. Murphy" after his pet dog) on the 1973 *Aloha From Hawaii* concert, and last used it in the presence of The King during a concert in Las Vegas on December 12, 1976. **BS**

Gibson
Les Paul Bass 1969

Type Solidbody electric bass
Body & neck Mahogany body and neck
Fingerboard Rosewood
Pick-ups Two low-impedance humbucker pick-ups

Guitar great Les Paul's star may have been on the wane in 1969, but his long association with Gibson was still ongoing. The inventive guitar player had approached the company in 1967 with a new revelation—the low-impedance pick-up—and two years later Gibson introduced three new Les Pauls housing them. The Personal and Professional six-strings were joined by the Les Paul Bass, the first bass to feature the guitarist's endorsement. By today's standards, it's a peculiar beast.

Physically, the new models were ½ in. (1 cm) bigger in outline, so they would be more visible on TV.

> *"This was the bass I came to England with in 1971 … Soooo heavy! I loved this bass … and played it for about five years … My best friend."*
>
> SUZI QUATRO

The extra heft was not thought to be a problem, because the three new models, with their sophisticated tone-sculpting circuitry and phase-switching capabilities, were intended more for studio use than for touring. Gibson's 1970 Les Paul catalog promised that "the frequency response, range of harmonics, and crisp, clear tones of the Les Paul Bass will exceed that of any electric bass on the market to date."

The low-impedance output required either a dedicated low-impedance amp, or an AD1 converter lead. Perhaps due to the fuss this entailed, the Les Paul Bass was replaced in 1971 by a lighter version, the Triumph, which had a high/low impedance switch, and which lasted until 1980. Gibson has returned to the concept of a low-end Les Paul several times since. **OB**

Gibson Les Paul Professional 1969

Type Solidbody electric
Body & neck Mahogany/maple body, mahogany neck
Fingerboard Rosewood
Pick-ups Two low-impedance humbucker pick-ups

The Les Paul Professional was one of a series of low-impedance guitars that Gibson introduced in 1969. The theory is that if the output from the guitar has a low impedance, it loses fewer high frequencies and is less prone to distortion and interference. Gibson provided a special lead for use with the Professional with the instruction: "You must use a Gibson low-to-high impedance transformer cord with your conventional amplifier. If you do not use the cord, your instrument will not function properly." But you don't absolutely need it in practice.

The first two guitars in this line were the Les Paul Personal and the Les Paul Professional. Neither was very successful, however, and they were both discontinued by 1972. The two models were generally similar in appearance except that the Professional had a rosewood, rather than an ebony, fingerboard, and a plain headstock. According to Gibson, "The Les Paul Professional has many of the same exciting features found on the LP Personal: low-impedance pick-ups; fast, low-action neck; and a 24¾ in. (63 cm) scale. But perhaps the feature you'll enjoy most is the modest price tag that accompanies this 'professional' guitar."

Slightly larger than a Standard Les Paul, the Professional has a distinctive panel on the body housing four knobs labeled "Bass," "Treble," "Volume," and "Decade"—the last, mysteriously named, control is an eleven-way switch for tuning treble harmonics. There is also a sliding phase control and a three-position toggle switch.

The Les Paul Recording guitar replaced these models in 1973. **AJ**

Teisco
ET-200 1969

Type Solidbody electric
Body & neck Hardwood body, maple neck
Fingerboard Rosewood
Pick-ups Four single-coil pick-ups

The Teisco company was founded in Tokyo in 1946—depending on which account you believe, the name either stands for "Tokyo Electric Instrument and Sound Company" or was coined at random by co-founder and classical guitarist Atswo Kaneko. It produced its first solidbody electric guitar, a bizarre-looking version of a Les Paul, in 1954. Teisco started exporting guitars to the United States in 1961—these were originally rebranded as Kingston Guitars, but by the mid-1960s the brand names Teisco, Teisco Del Rey, World Teisco, Kent, Kimberly, and Heit Deluxe among others were being used. In the United Kingdom they were imported as Arbiter, Top Twenty, Audition, and Kay.

These cheap instruments were sold in large quantities and, while not highly valued at the time, they are now, like most 1960s guitars, very collectible.

Their first "tulip"-shaped guitar, the E-100, was introduced in 1965—the "1" indicates that it has a single pick-up. This four pick-up guitar in the same style seems most closely related to the ET-200, which appeared shortly after Teisco was taken over by Kawai in 1967. The first version of the ET-200 had a different "satin-finished metal pickguard," but by 1969 it had a black plastic one similar in shape to the four pick-up guitar. It also had "individual, noiseless, velvet touch On/Off switches for each pick-up"—Teisco was famously generous with knobs—and a "rosewood fingerboard inlaid with eight position markers." The list price in the United States was $90 or $81 without the tremolo.

So this guitar is either a rare deluxe version of the ET-200 or a one-off custom creation; either way it's of great interest to collectors of 1960s guitars. **AJ**

Teisco
Prestige 1969

Type Solidbody electric
Body & neck Laminate body, nato neck
Fingerboard Rosewood
Pick-ups One single-coil pick-up

Taken over by Kawai in 1967, Teisco entered a golden age of bizarre psychedelic guitar design and produced some of the weirdest-looking instruments the world had ever known. This was the era of the artist's palette-shaped "May Queen," the banjo-shaped "Splender" and the tiger-striped Prestige "Tiki-Mask." The "shark-fin" Prestige is relatively conservative but, with its angular, pointed-bottomed body, is still a long way from a predictable Fender copy.

Prestige guitars are another close relative of Teisco's "Audition" and "Cameo" models. These were very basic instruments, constructed from plywood and nato wood from southeast Asia. The hardware erred on the side of rough and ready, and the pick-ups—even the "gold foil" ones that were used on other Teisco-built models and which are prized by some collectors—weren't very fussy about what they picked up. Nonetheless, their ready availability in U.S. outlets like Sears Roebuck and Woolworth's, and their striking looks, made them decent entry-level players (and, latterly, collectors' items).

This Prestige has a generic Teisco neck, with a zero fret and the end of the truss rod visible at the bottom. There are two knobs, for volume and tone, and a slider-switch to select bass or treble. There's no tremolo, but that was an optional extra. There was also a two-pick-up version. The small-scale shark-fin body design aside, this model's most distinctive feature is the reflective metal scratchplate.

With bigger fins, the guitar evolved into the more upmarket Teisco K4L (or ET-460), with four pick-ups and a less rudimentary construction. **AJ**

Zemaitis
"Ivan The Terrible" 1969

Type Twelve-string acoustic
Body & neck Rosewood back, mahogany top and neck
Fingerboard Ebony

On June 24, 2004, Eric Clapton held an auction at Christie's in New York to fund his Crossroads charity—a drug rehabilitation center on the Caribbean island of Antigua. Lot 33 was a twelve-string acoustic guitar that Clapton had commissioned from luthier Tony Zemaitis.

Zemaitis learned woodcraft during a five-year cabinet-making apprenticeship. His attentions were turned when he applied this training to a damaged guitar found in the attic of his family home. In 1955 he set up his first workshop and, by the end of the 1960s he had built up an impressive client roster, including Jimi Hendrix, George Harrison, and Eric Clapton.

The twelve-string conceived by Clapton and Zemaitis featured a highly decorated top and back; the ebony fingerboard was bound and inlaid with silver. The guitar was referred to as "Ivan The Terrible."

Clapton used the guitar with his short-lived supergroup Blind Faith, and he also lent it to friends such as Harrision and Dave Mason.

Zemaitis became celebrated for his extraordinarily decorative, metal-fronted, solidbody instruments, and by the time of his death in 2002, prices for some of his guitars had already begun to hit six figures. At Christie's, the more modestly turned out "Ivan" fetched $253,900. **TB**

George Harrison borrowed "Ivan The Terrible" during the recording of the triple album *All Things Must Pass* (1970), his first solo work after the break-up of The Beatles. The guitar features on the single "My Sweet Lord," a worldwide number one.

TREBLE

1970s

Fender "Blackie" Stratocaster 1970

Type Solidbody electric
Body & neck Alder body, maple neck
Fingerboard Maple
Pick-ups Three single-coil pick-ups

Eric Clapton has never been one to do things by half measures. After nearly a decade of fame found largely playing Gibson guitars, he made a dramatic switch. In 1970, he visited the Sho-Bud music store in Nashville, Tennessee, and came out with six 1950s Fender Stratocasters. This was at a time before the concept of a "vintage" solidbody electric really existed. They were old Strats and they were cheap—between two and three hundred dollars each. Back in the United Kingdom, he gave one each to George Harrison, Steve Winwood, and Pete Townshend. Of the remaining three—

> *"He bought a bunch of Strats in 1970 when they were going for nearly nothing. He gave a few to his buddies."*
>
> **LEE DICKSON, CLAPTON'S GUITAR TECH**

models from 1956 and 1957—he liked the black body of one; the feel of the neck of another; and the sound of the pick-ups of the third. So he ripped them apart, and built a composite model: thus was born "Blackie," perhaps the most famous celebrity guitar of them all.

Blackie featured on almost all Clapton's recordings and concerts from 1973 to 1985, after which the guitar was retired following issues with the neck. It made a memorable appearance as Clapton performed with The Band in the movie *The Last Waltz* (1978).

But Blackie's most famous appearance came at Christie's in New York in 2004, when the guitar was auctioned for Clapton's Crossroads charity and raised a startling $959,500—at the time the world's most expensive guitar. **TB**

Clapton plays the guitar that "has become a part of me" on stage in the late 1970s. ➡

Fender
Maverick 1970

Type Solidbody electric
Body & neck Alder body and neck
Fingerboard Rosewood
Pick-ups Two split single-coil pick-ups

Fender's Custom was also released under the name "Maverick," and was a curio made out of leftovers from the discontinued Fender Electric XII. The design task was overseen by Virgilio "Babe" Simoni, a longtime company employee who was product manager of stringed instruments, and like Simoni's other design, the Swinger (see page 406), it wasn't a product of Fender's R&D department.

Simoni converted the XII's "hockey stick" headstock to carry six rather than twelve tuning pegs. The offset body shape featured a "contoured waist design for

"They asked if anyone had any ideas … That's when I converted them to six-strings and carved the bodies into a different design."

VIRGILIO SIMONI

maximum playing comfort," and the twelve-string bridge assembly was replaced with a Mustang Trem unit. The guitar was finished in sunburst on the front, with an all-black back to hide the filled-in string-retainer cavity.

The Custom appeared in Fender's 1970 catalog for one year, but gathered dust in music stores for many more. It was originally priced at $289.50—more than a standard Telecaster—but the price was reduced in 1971.

You can't help but feel for the Custom. It became an icon of the malaise that Fender was suffering under the CBS era of ownership. Yet the Custom's bound 25½-in. (64.75-cm) scale neck is quality, and its split pick-ups and four-way switch offered intriguing phase-reversal effects. Surely this ugly duckling is the perfect candidate to be the next Indie Guitar Hero's ax of choice? **OB**

Giannini
Craviola 1970

Type Acoustic
Body & neck Sitka spruce top, rosewood back and sides, mahogany neck
Fingerboard Rosewood

Woodworker Tranquillo Giannini established a workshop in São Paolo, Brazil, back in 1890, to take advantage of the South American country's renowned timbers. He made guitars for his friends in his spare time, and eight decades later the guitar company that grew out of his hobby created one of the most distinctive acoustic guitars of all time—the Craviola.

Sketched out by famed Brazilian guitarist-composer Paulinho Noguiera and built by Giorgio Giannini, the Craviola's distinctive teardrop body shape produced a sound combining elements of the harpsichord and the

"It sounded … like the Harpsichord ('Cravo' in Portuguese) and … the ten-string Brazilian Viola; thus the Craviola name was born."
PAULINHO NOGUIERA

Brazilian viola caipira. The body lacked a treble bout, and had a severely cutaway bass equivalent. The D-shaped sound hole with mosaic marquetry and pointy pickguard added to the offset angularity. It originally came in three versions: the CRA6N Classic with no pickguard or fret markers, the CRA6S Steel String with diamond inlays and a tortoiseshell pickguard, and the CRA12 Twelve-String.

Once exported internationally, the Craviola's compellingly asymmetrical allure caught on: Jimmy Page owned a twelve-string version, which he used live in the early 1970s, and Puerto Rican guitarist José Feliciano, whose version of The Doors' "Light My Fire" shot him to international attention, also played a six-string version. Feliciano's first Craviola is now on display in New York City's Hard Rock Café. **OB**

Hayman
1010 White Cloud 1970

Type Solidbody electric
Body & neck Obeche body and neck
Fingerboard Maple
Pick-ups Three Superflux single-coil pick-ups

In 1969, James Ormston ("Jim") Burns, the UK guitar maker whose Fender-rivaling solidbody electrics had become synonymous with The Shadows earlier in the decade, joined the British Dallas Arbiter organization. His remit was to produce a new line of guitar designs to be marketed under the Hayman brand name, and he worked in tandem with ex-Vox guitar man Bob Pearson. The pair wasted no time, and in 1970, the first Haymans appeared.

Sporting a body shape vaguely reminiscent of a Telecaster that Burns had prototyped for his previous company, Ormston Steel Guitars, the first Haymans were the solidbody 1010 and semi-hollow body 2020. These were joined the following year by the twin-pick-up 3030 (see page 427), and the 4040 Bass. The 3030H with two Re-An humbuckers joined the line in 1973. The White Cloud also materialized in 1970, just as the Dallas Arbiter company hit stormy weather and collapsed.

The 1010 and 2020 both initially paired mahogany bodies with maple necks, but the 1010 had three Superflux single-coil pick-ups and a three-way selector switch, whereas the 2020 had two, and a semi-hollow construction. The later solidbody double-cut White Cloud looked more elegant than its forebears, but suffered from the large body-cavity rout for the three-pick-up unit it inherited from the earlier designs. Combined with a body cavity for the truss rod (adjustable from the body end) and the lack of mass from the double cutaways, this left the guitar somewhat light on wood around the neck pocket, resulting in a lack of sustain. **OB**

Landola
Double Neck 1970

Type Twelve- and six-string double-neck acoustic
Body & neck Spruce top, rosewood back and sides, mahogany neck
Fingerboard Rosewood

Multineck guitars have been made since the Renaissance but still never fail to be head-turners. This rare instrument has a mysterious history but is a well-made example of a twin-neck acoustic guitar.

It is a twelve- and six-string combo, with the twelve-string neck on top. The design includes one extended oval sound hole beneath both sets of strings and one long bridge containing both sets of string pins. Both necks have truss rods and open headstocks. Apart from that, little is known about the woods used or indeed why it was made.

The background of the guitar is lost in the mists of Scandinavian guitar making. Originally Espana guitars were a marketing invention of Swedish guitar maker Karl Hagstrom. Some were made by Bjärton in Sweden; several were produced by Crucianelli in Italy. Other companies may have been involved and distributors Buegeleisen & Jacobson exported them to North America. The best Espanas were very good but quality was uneven.

The established Finnish manufacturer Landola started producing Espana guitars in the late 1960s. The Landola logo is a crown, so this 1970 model is believed to be one of its creations rather than a Swedish-built instrument.

By the 1970s, Espana guitars were generally midpriced, competing with Yamaha and other similar brands. Typical Espanas had solid spruce tops with laminated sides and backs. They were all acoustic—either six- or twelve-string—classical or specialty guitars like this one, or short-scale, alto guitars shaped much like violins. **SH**

Ralph Smith
Eighteen-string 1970

Type Eighteen-string acoustic
Body & neck Unknown but likely to have been spruce top, rosewood back and sides, mahogany neck
Fingerboard Rosewood

After leaving the U.S. Army, Ralph Smith settled in a remote rural backwater in Kansas. He worked as a machinist in Cessna's aircraft factory and in his spare time experimented with making guitars. The most interesting one was an acoustic eighteen-string with an extreme cutaway body to allow access to the highest frets, an enormous headstock to cater for eighteen tuners, and a wide bridge hosting eighteen endpins.

People seemed to like his work, so Smith opened a professional guitar-making workshop near Wichita. Smith was a meticulous craftsman. His spotless workshop was entered through a "vacuum chamber." Often helped by members of his family, Smith went on to build around twenty of these impressive eighteen-string instruments.

The headstock was one of the biggest ever made, and Smith reduced the string tension on the neck by using extralight strings. Nevertheless, they had sturdy internal bracing. They were strung like this: E and A were both accompanied by two different octaves; D and G were both main and two-octave unisons; B and E were three unisons. This made tuning surprisingly easy. It was almost as easy to play as a conventional twelve-string, and the sound was striking. It was described by one owner as "like playing two twelve-strings at once."

Smith's deep cutaway neck joint design was innovative, too. He patented it in 1972 and later successfully sued Washburn for infringing his copyright.

Professionals appreciated Smith's innovation and quality. The first eighteen-string guitar was bought by Gordon Terry, Merle Haggard's fiddle player, and country singer Joe Maphis owned at least four Smith guitars. **SH**

Peter Cook
"Entwistle" Bass 1971

Type Solidbody bass
Body & neck Maple/ash body, maple neck
Fingerboard Rosewood
Pick-ups Two single-coil pick-ups

When it comes to the title of "God of Thunder," there's only one winner, and he went by the name of John Entwistle. It's only fitting then that this particular beast should come in the shape of a lightning bolt.

Peter Cook built a number of basses for Entwistle, but this eye-catching number was featured on the cover (drawn by Entwistle himself) of *The Who By Numbers* (1975), and was used on a number of tracks on the album. It clearly takes its initial inspiration from the Gibson Explorer and Thunderbird body shapes that Entwistle approved of so highly, but then it takes a very novel twist in terms of appearance—all under his direction, of course. Comfort doesn't appear to have been much of a concern, but, visually, it's certainly unique. It now resides as part of a memorabilia display at the Hard Rock Café in New York.

Many fans have attempted to make their own copies of this iconic design, but there is only one original. It could easily be said that this bass laid some foundations for the Buzzard design that would follow in the 1980s, with its crazy body lines and extended headstock. The fact that it is so well remembered and carries such legendary status goes some way to highlighting what an ostentatious and eccentric design it really was, but if anyone could carry it off with aplomb, it was The Ox. **JM**

Peter Cook's lightning bolt bass can be heard on The Who's eighth album, *The Who By Numbers* (1975), including John Entwistle's song "Success Story." The thunder-fingered bassist's cover cartoon of the band also shows him playing this particular instrument.

D'Aquisto
Archtop Mandolin 1971

Type Archtop acoustic guitar
Body & neck Maple body, spruce top, maple neck
Fingerboard Ebony

In more ways than one, James D'Aquisto followed in the footsteps of his mentor, the maestro of luthiers, John D'Angelico. Like his elder, D'Aquisto made more than just carved archtop guitars: he also crafted flat-top guitars, classical guitars, even solidbody electrics. But like D'Angelico, he also made mandolins, harking back to their shared Italian ancestry. D'Aquisto built just three mandolins, each of them a masterpiece.

This was the first mandolin at which D'Aquisto tried his hand. He began building it in 1971 for musician Lydia Merriman, but didn't finish it during his lifetime.

D'Aquisto roughly followed the A-Style mandolin design popularized by Lyon & Healy and Gibson, but with D'Angelico's two-point body. D'Aquisto's jewel-like mandolin boasted much of the exquisite workmanship and fine features of his most beautiful guitars.

He made the back and sides of flamed maple, topped by a carved spruce soundboard. Carved-top mandolins were an American invention, created by Orville Gibson in the 1890s by adapting violin construction techniques to the mandolin. D'Aquisto added a maple neck, capped by an ebony fretboard. The headstock followed D'Angelico's ornate Art Deco design. The whole of the instrument was highlighted by inlays and bindings made from mother-of-pearl and celluloid.

During construction, the mandolin developed a crack in the top, and D'Aquisto set it aside to be fixed and finished later. After his death in 1995, the instrument was restored to playing condition and used for several years. In 2009, it was restored by renowned luthier John Monteleone of Islip, Long Island. **MD**

Epiphone
6832 1971

Type Steel-string acoustic
Body & neck Rosewood back and sides, spruce top, maple neck
Fingerboard Rosewood

The Epiphone brand had an illustrious history; right up until the early 1950s the company was producing some of the most beautiful archtop guitars around. But company fortunes waned after the death of founder Epi Stathopoulo, and by the end of the decade a takeover by Gibson saw a slow transformation into the diffusion brand we know today. Epiphone guitars were built at the Gibson factory in Kalamazoo, Michigan, until in 1971 a cost-cutting decision was taken to move production to Japan.

Although neither Gibson nor Epiphone had been especially celebrated for their flat-top acoustic guitars, this first generation of Japanese acoustics proved popular, providing a good, playable instrument at a relatively affordable cost. The full-bodied 6832, with its rosewood sides and spruce top, was equipped with a very slim bolt-on neck and so was particularly well suited to guitarists who primarily played electric instruments. It boasted a rich, mellow tone and fine projection. The 6832 was produced until around 1981.

The model shown originally belonged to Ramases (see below). It found its way into a British second-hand shop, where it was sold cheaply because he had autographed the body in Biro. It has since featured on many recordings by the subsequent owner, including The Chrysanthemums. **TB**

Ramases was the alter ego of British prog-rock musician Martin Raphael, a one-time associate of the musicians who became 10cc. His second and final album, *Glass Top Coffin* (1975), was released on the Vertigo label. He committed suicide in 1978.

Gibson Les Paul Recording 1971

Type Solidbody electric
Body & neck Mahogany/maple body, maple neck
Fingerboard Rosewood
Pick-ups Two low-impedance humbucker pick-ups

Just as Fender had gone through "corporatization," following its sale to CBS, Gibson followed suit as it came under the wing of Norlin Industries, a business conglomerate with interests in such diverse fields as brewing, technology, and music. First on the new owners' to-do list was a new range of Les Paul models. The Standard had already enjoyed a year-long resurrection, alongside the Deluxe. A year later, the first Norlin-era Les Pauls emerged with a number of critical changes: the former one-piece mahogany body with maple top was now constructed from multiple slabs of mahogany and maple, and the neck woods had been changed from one-piece mahogany to three-piece maple. That same year saw the appearance of a new Les Paul model: the Recording.

A radical instrument by any standards, the Recording featured a complex array of knobs and switches that gave the kind of on-board control that could only otherwise be achieved by an amplifier with a wide selection of equalization parameters. The most unusual of these controls was the eleven-way "Decade" switch, which allowed for the alteration of treble harmonics. Also unorthodox were the low-impedance humbuckers, which were so sensitive that the pick-up height had to be set at the factory for optimum performance: this was no guitar for the hot-rodder. **TB**

Even in his later years, Les Paul was precisely the kind of musician to make good use of the complexities of the Recording model: indeed, he further customized his own model! It can be heard on *Chester And Lester* (1976), an album of duets recorded with Chet Atkins.

Hayman
3030 1971

Type Solidbody electric
Body & neck Obeche body and neck
Fingerboard Maple
Pick-ups Two Superflux single-coil pick-ups

Jim Burns was one of the truly great names in British musical equipment building, and the Hayman guitars he co-designed with ex-Vox man Bob Pearson between 1969 and 1971 are a part of his legacy. The 3030 was a simplified version of the pair's debut guitar, the 1010, and at £160 was comparable in price. While it shared many design and construction features with its elder brother, the 3030 had two Superflux pick-ups instead of three, though it still retained the three-way selector.

The 3030 loosely mimicked the no-frills stylings of the Telecaster and the versatile-yet-simple circuitry of

> "The 3030's body is of selected obeche, and sealed inside is an exclusive Vibrasonic chamber to give long sustain on all notes."
>
> HAYMAN ADVERTISING

the Stratocaster, and had the 25½-in. (64.75-cm) scale length familiar to Fender fans. However, it had distinctive and important design differences that harked back to earlier "Burns-family" designs: former Burns men Jack Golder (woodwork), Derek Adams (finish), and Norman Holder (truss-rod design) all worked on the model. The 3030's truss rod was adjustable at the body end, requiring an extra cavity to be hollowed out of the body in addition to the one for the pick-ups; Hayman added its own all-metal "MicroTune" string-through-body adjustable bridge design; and the large cavity inside was renamed as a "Vibrasonic" chamber to aid sustain—a major selling point for any guitar at the turn of the 1970s, and a property Hayman was keen to promote in its marketing, at any chance it had. **OB**

Herman Hauser II
Llobet 1971

Type Classical acoustic
Body & neck Spruce top, Brazilian rosewood back, sides, and bridge, mahogany neck, ebony fingerboard
Other features Torres-like bracing, Landstorfer tuners

Hermann Hauser II (1911–88) worked with his legendary father for more than twenty years before taking over the business in 1952 and making about 550 guitars. His instruments were made to essentially the same design principles and aesthetics established with Hermann Hauser I's famous guitar made for Segovia in 1937 (though he experimented with different bracing patterns), and preserved the same rich and distinctive sound. When Segovia's 1937 guitar was played out and retired in the late 1950s, he played a 1956 Hauser II for several years before switching to

> "The [Hauser] instrument has ... the very essence of classicism in guitar sound ... ideally suited for use as a concert instrument."
> JULIAN BREAM

José Ramírez III guitars in 1960. Julian Bream played a 1957 instrument by Hauser II at the end of the 1950s; it features on *The Art Of Julian Bream* (1959).

The Llobet model is a tribute to Miguel Llobet's Torres guitar of 1859, which influenced Hauser guitars for three generations. Bracing system, head, bridge, purfling, rosette, and other features all resemble the Torres style. A closely guarded Hauser secret, a feature of all its guitars, is the presence of a $\frac{1}{32}$ in. (1 mm)-thick component between the fingerboard and soundboard from the twelfth to the nineteenth fret. The Hausers have always been very evasive when asked about it, and no one has apparently gotten to the bottom of it, even when given the clue that there are four good reasons for it being there. **GD**

Jedson
"Telecaster" Bass 1971

Type Solidbody electric bass
Body & neck Plywood body, maple neck
Other features Rosewood
Pick-ups Two single-coil pick-ups

By the late 1960s, many Japanese manufacturers had begun to cut back on the large-scale production of guitars seen during the previous decade. During this time, some major companies, such as Guyatone, went out of business or were bought out. While the 1970s saw the very gradual shift toward the kind of high-quality instruments we associate with Japanese brands today, some of the large factories, such as Teisco, continued to churn out cheap models "inspired" by Gibson and Fender.

The Jedson brand name had been familiar to musicians in the United Kingdom since the 1920s, when it adorned banjos produced by John E. Dallas & Sons of London. By the late 1960s, the company had been bought out by another London music distributor, and was trading as Dallas Arbiter. In 1969, the Jedson name was resurrected for a range of electric guitars and basses imported from Teisco in Japan. These Fender and Gibson "copies" (as they were known at the time) were ubiquitous among Britain's impoverished teenagers throughout the 1970s—and later in junk shops.

Curiously, it was the Fender Telecaster shape that appeared in the widest array of variations: there were single- and twin-pick-up guitars (and one model with pick-ups that looked as if they might have come from the real thing), and short-scale basses. The bodies were made of cheap plywood, the neck of maple, and the fingerboard of beech or rosewood. The guitars generally came with horrific vibrato systems, the slightest touch of which would send the instrument out of tune. But with care in setting them up, these could be serviceable guitars for beginners. **TB**

Lviv
Electric Guitar 1971

Type Hollow body electric
Body & neck Laminated birch body, bolt-on beech neck
Fingerboard Rosewood
Pick-ups Two single-coil pick-ups

The hollow body guitars built in Ukraine (then part of the Soviet Union) by the Lviv Experimental Factory of Folk Musical Instruments are classic examples of consumer goods production under the communist system. A central planning committee decreed that a certain number of electric guitars needed to be built, and designated a factory to carry out the production. A design was drawn up, calculated to meet certain standards that had been determined by another committee. Once the design was approved, and production quotas met, that was it. The model then remained in production for many years. Thus, an antiquated hollow body design—of a kind that was on its way out in the West by 1971—continued to be made until the late 1980s. Of course, consumers would take what they could get: if you wanted a basic, hollow body electric, and couldn't get your hands on a much more expensive Orpheus or Jolana, then Lviv was the only game in town.

Built of laminated birch with a thick birch neck, the Lviv guitar has a weird feel that takes a bit of getting used to. The fretboard radius, as well as the top of this guitar, are absolutely flat. The tailpiece is stamped with a rampant lion, the heraldic device of the city of Lviv. The bridge is of a basic, floating type, and the pick-ups are screwed directly to the body, without the possibility of height adjustment. The fretboard, the body, and the curiously reversed f-holes are all bound. The glow-in-the-dark flip switches on the polymethyl methacrylate (PMMA; Plexiglas) control panel turn the pick-ups on and off—these are identical to light switches still found in some of the older buildings in modern Russia. **EP**

Orpheus
Hebros 1971

Type Hollow body bass
Body & neck Laminated body, bolt-on beech neck
Fingerboard Beech
Pick-ups Two single-coil pick-ups

Built by Orpheus in Plovdiv, Bulgaria, well into the 1980s, while the nation was still under Commuinst rule, the Hebros is a classic Eastern European short-scale—30 in. (76 cm)—hollow body bass guitar. In common with most Orpheus models, its name is historic, as befits a product made in a city with a 6,000-year history: Hebros is the ancient name of the Maritsa River in southern Bulgaria (a part of ancient Thrace), which forms part of the frontier with Greece.

The Hebros bass was available in two finishes: either the more common, two-tone, red-to-black sunburst, as shown here, or the rarer, striped, Art Deco green version. In addition to the bass, there was also a matching guitar, which was available in both the same color schemes.

The pick-ups, which were the same on both bass and guitar versions, were typical Orpheus single coils with a rather interesting construction: they were built around a trio of square magnets set on edge, with the coil loosely wrapped around them, and tied in place with string. The assembly is concealed under a chrome cover. A piece of photographic film with the Orpheus logo serves as an insert. The pick-ups are set in plastic surrounds, and held in place only by a tight fit; they are screwed directly to the top of the instrument, without the possibility of height adjustments. Each pick-up has a separate volume control; the tone control is a master that governs both pick-ups. As on all Orpheus models, the input jack accepts a DIN-5 plug, rather than a standard ¼-in. (0.6-cm) plug: these are the same as those installed on Russian-made guitars of the Soviet period. **EP**

Ovation
Breadwinner 1971

Type Solidbody electric
Body & neck Lyrachord-coated mahogany body, maple neck
Fingerboard Ebony
Pick-ups Two toroidal single-coil pick-ups

Aeronautical engineer Charles Kamen's Ovation company built its reputation on scientific innovation, creating a range of radical fiberglass-backed acoustic guitars and, later, leading the way in transducer pick-ups that revolutionized the way acoustic musicians were amplified on stage. Ovation also tried its hand at solidbody electric guitars; the results were curious but not exactly earth-shattering.

Launched in 1971, the Breadwinner was Ovation's first attempt at a non-acoustic instrument. From a visual perspective, it was certainly a bold statement, and one that has since continued to divide opinion among collectors. Neither is there clear agreement as to the story behind the guitar's curious mahogany body: an advertising blurb noted that it was all about balance; the original designer, however, claimed ignorance of such matters, and that he came up with the "ax head" shape simply because the word "ax" was then popular slang for a guitar.

Electrically, the Breadwinner was also unusual. An early example of an active guitar, the guitar featured Toroidal single-coil pick-ups; humbuckers were added later (as on the 1973 model shown). Unusually, the front and middle positions of the three-way selector switch activated just one pick-up; in the back position it switched on both pick-ups out of phase. **TB**

Colin Newman of British art-punk band Wire was a prominent user of the Breadwinner. It can be heard on the band's excellent third album, *154* (1979). The album is named for the number of live gigs the band had played up to the point of release.

Colin Newman of Wire on stage with his Breadwinner in 2011. →

Rickenbacker
331 Lightshow 1971

Type Semi-acoustic guitar with internal lightshow
Body & neck Maple body, plastic top, walnut/maple neck
Fingerboard Rosewood
Pick-ups Two Hi-gain Rickenbacker pick-ups

Rickenbacker has always been known for innovative guitars—this 331, nicknamed "The Lightshow Guitar," was one of the most original of all. It was basically a 330 model with the addition of a psychedelic sound-to-light unit that operated nine colored lamps inside the translucent plastic body cover.

Rickenbacker used car light bulbs, which lit up when different pitches of note were played. Treble sounds lit the red light, yellow was illuminated by midrange frequencies, and blue reacted to the bass notes. The lights were controlled by a sensitivity dial.

"Internally lighted by a set of frequency modulated lamps, this [guitar] will shimmer with infinite color and pattern variety. "
RICKENBACKER'S ADVERTISING

The guitar needed a second cable—a power lead that plugged in next to the jack socket for the lights. Many were later converted by owners to work on battery power. It had two of Rickenbacker's own Hi-gain pick-ups and two outputs: normal and "Rick-O-Sound" stereo.

Early models had primitive wiring that heated up quickly, sometimes making them too hot to actually play. By 1971, this was rectified with improved circuits and a heavier-duty transformer. The size of the bulbs was also reduced. There were twelve-string and bass versions of the Lightshow, but these are very rare.

Roger McGuinn of The Byrds played Lightshow guitars live and on TV during the late 1970s, and good-quality examples are today priced at over $20,000. **SH**

Zemaitis
Electric Guitar 1971

Type Solidbody electric
Body & neck Honduran mahogany body and neck
Fingerboard Ebony
Pick-ups Two humbucker pick-ups

The first year of the 1970s was a landmark one for Antanas Kazimeras "Tony" Žemaitis. He had already established a reputation as luthier-to-the-stars, thanks to associations with Eric Clapton, George Harrison, and Jimi Hendrix. Working from a house in South London, his stock-in-trade was twelve-string acoustics, then hard to find in Britain.

An inveterate experimenter, Zemaitis built numerous prototypes. One idea proved especially fruitful: to combat the problem of microphonic feedback in electric guitars, he tried positioning a thin aluminum alloy shield on the top of the body. It worked—but, to make the guitars more visually attractive, he commissioned gun engraver Danny O'Brien to create intricate etchings in the panels.

The guitars were now eye-catching works of art, and the Zemaitis order-book quickly began to bulge. Thereafter, Tony Zemaitis rarely made acoustic instruments. He continued his small-scale manufacture until his retirement in 2000, usually building between six and ten guitars a year. Since his death in 2002, some Zemaitis guitars have become extremely valuable—unsurprising as it was generally only wealthy rock stars who could afford them in the first place. But even non-celebrity examples are liable to push toward six figures. **TB**

In 1971, Ronnie Wood—then with The Faces (whose hits feature on 2012's *Stay With Me* anthology)—used a Zemaitis on British TV's *Top Of The Pops*, putting the make on the map. Wood continued to use Zemaitis guitars for the next four decades with The Rolling Stones.

Acoustic
Black Widow 1972

Type Solidbody electric
Body & neck Maple body and neck
Fingerboard Rosewood
Pick-ups Two humbucker pick-ups

The Black Widow has a strange history. Although now a largely forgotten instrument, an early incarnation was photographed in studio use by Jimi Hendrix. It was also used by Frank Zappa and Steely Dan's Skunk Baxter, and endorsed by jazz rocker Larry Coryell.

The guitar was designed in the late 1960s by early Rickenbacker pioneer Paul Barth, who first produced this long-scale instrument under his own Bartell brand name. In 1972, Barth signed to make a revamped Black Widow to be sold under the brand name of the Acoustic Control Corporation, whose reputation was founded on high-end, solid-state amplification for guitar and bass. (The late 1960s saw a shift in guitar technology, as valve amplification was superseded by cheaper, more reliable solid-state circuitry.) The Black Widow was the only guitar to bear the Acoustic name.

Production difficulties arose almost immediately, when Barth realized that facilities were insufficient to produce the numbers required by Acoustic. He struck a manufacturing deal with Matsumoku in Japan, who then produced most of the thousand Black Widows estimated to exist today.

In 1975, for reasons that are not entirely clear, production switched back briefly to the United States, where Semie Moseley's Mosrite factory produced the last 200 or so models before Acoustic pulled the plug. The small number of models produced by Bartell are the rarest and most collectible of the Acoustic Black Widows, but not necessarily superior in quality to those from Japan. Later in the 1970s, Barth would forge a similar arrangement with Hohner to produce another Black Widow variant. **TB**

Alembic
001 1972

Type Electric bass
Body & neck Zebrawood body, purpleheart/maple neck
Fingerboard Ebony
Pick-ups Two movable active pick-ups

When, in 2011, *Vintage Guitar* magazine ran a feature on the twenty-five most valuable bass guitars of all time, the list included four Alembic models. Founded in 1969, Alembic was the brainchild of electronics wizard Ron Wickersham, an ex-employee of recording specialists Ampex. Initially Wickersham was hired as a sound consultant by The Grateful Dead and Jefferson Airplane, who wanted to improve their concert sound systems to produce higher-quality live recordings.

Having forged close relationships with both bands, Alembic experimented with guitar and bass pick-ups, creating a low-impedance unit with a signal boosted by an "active" onboard preamp, thus producing a wider audio bandwidth than was possible using conventional passive high-impedance pick-ups. If not the first of their kind, these units were certainly the most advanced, and they were installed on all the Dead's instruments.

This led to the creation of the first Alembic model: an active bass for the Airplane's Jack Casady. The unorthodox "001" was built from exotic woods such as purpleheart and zebrawood. Fitted to the body were a pair of brass tubes on which the pick-ups could slide, allowing players to position them as they wished. The protrusion at the bottom of the body was reputedly to encourage players to use a guitar stand! **TB**

Jack Casady used an Alembic bass guitar on *The Phosphorescent Rat* (1974), the fourth album by Hot Tuna, an offshoot of Jefferson Airplane, which also featured Jorma Kaukonen on guitar and Sammy Piazza on drums and percussion.

Fender
Telecaster Deluxe 1972

Type Solidbody electric
Body & neck Alder body, maple neck
Fingerboard Maple
Pick-ups Two Wide Range humbucker pick-ups

By the mid-1960s, the difference between the Fender and Gibson "sounds" was well defined: guitarists knew that the single coils on a Strat didn't sound the same as the humbuckers on an ES-335. Fender guitars had nonetheless been more popular among rock and pop players, until, that is, the resurgence of the Les Paul, which, following its 1968 relaunch, was fast becoming the instrument of choice for the new breed of heavy rock bands—its appeal was largely down to the thickness in sound of the Gibson twin-coil PAFs.

Fender's response was typically pragmatic—it hired the man who invented the Gibson humbucker. Seth Lover came up with the Fender Wide Range pick-up, wound around individual Cunife magnets—a humbucker that still retained some of Fender's single-coil sound. The first guitar to be kitted out with Wide Range pairs was the new flagship Telecaster Deluxe. In addition to its powerful new electronics, the Deluxe featured an enlarged headstock and a maple fingerboard with medium-jumbo sized frets. The body also departed from standard Telecaster design, with a Strat-style "belly contour" that made it more comfortable to play.

Fender dropped the Deluxe in 1981, but revived it in 2004 with Alnico bars instead of magnets for a more conventional humbucker sound. **TB**

You can hear a Fender Telecaster Deluxe played by lead guitarist and vocalist Alex Kapranos on the early albums of Scottish band Franz Ferdinand, including their sophomore effort, *You Could Have It So Much Better* (2005).

Alex Kapranos of Franz Ferdinand with his Telecaster Deluxe. →

Gretsch 7690/1 Super Chet 1972

Type Hollow body electric
Body & neck Maple body and neck
Fingerboard Ebony
Pick-ups Two Filter'Tron pick-ups

Not to be confused with the later Gretsch Atkins Super Ax, the 7690/1 Super Chet was a more elegant affair. A product of the Baldwin era, the Super Chet was a deep-bodied hollow maple archtop redolent of jazz-era guitars and was designed by Atkins along with Gretsch's Dean Porter and Clyde Edwards.

Available in either Wine Red or Walnut, with white-bound f-holes offsetting the cream-bound 17-in. (43-cm) body, the Super was a looker: it had a beautifully ornamented fingerboard and headstock with more abalone than Liberace's bathroom mirror, and an extremely unusual control configuration on its Bakelite pickguard housing no fewer than five tone and volume buttons. It also had a superstylish ebony-insert tailpiece with yet more abalone, teamed with an adjustable Tune-o-matic bridge. A 24½-in. (62.25-cm) scale neck joining up at the eighteenth fret completed a very pretty picture. This particular Super Chet was Atkins' own, and he added the mini-toggle effects switches on the upper bout. **OB**

Hayman 4040 Bass 1972

Type Solidbody bass
Body & neck Obeche body with maple neck
Fingerboard Maple
Pick-ups Two split-coil pick-ups

When Burns and Arbiter joined forces in the early 1970s, the 4040 was the only bass that Hayman would go on to design and produce: eventually it formed the blueprint for the Shergold basses. Made in the United Kingdom, the 4040's look is very much rooted in the 1970s, complete with Plexiglas pick-up covers, string dampeners, and a tone that sits somewhere between a Fender Jazz and a Rickenbacker. Despite its period look (a precursor to the body shape used by Wal, perhaps?), it still maintains a fanbase among players, many of whom report that the guitars remain sturdy and reliable today. This is no mean feat for a 1970s-manufactured product, and probably explains why the instrument still has a high resale value.

With rock bands making the most of what the bass had to offer (Mud and The Sweet were early adopters), 4040s could regularly be seen on TV music shows of the day, reinforcing their rock credentials. Mark King of Level 42 used one to record his band's first single, "Love Meeting Love." **JM**

John Veleno
Veleno 1972

Yamaha
SG-60T 1972

Type Double cutaway electric
Body & neck Aluminum body and neck
Fingerboard Aluminum
Pick-ups Two or three humbucker/single-coil pick-ups

Type Solidbody electric
Body & neck Nato body, mahogany neck
Fingerboard Rosewood
Pick-ups Two humbucker pick-ups

American metal craftsman John Veleno's aluminum electric guitar had a unique sound, characterized by a bright, cutting top end. That's why it had such an abnormally high rate of use by top guitarists.

The list of Veleno players is extraordinary, considering he made only about 200 guitars as a part-time job. Users include Eric Clapton, Mark Bolan, Greg Allman, Lou Reed, Johnny Winter, Todd Rundgren, Dolly Parton, Jeff Lynne, and Robby Krieger.

It was certainly a distinctive instrument, with a ruby built into the headstock and pick-ups that could convert from humbucker to single coil at the flick of a switch. Yet the bolt-on aluminum neck was guaranteed never to warp or even need adjustment.

The ultralightweight guitar was machined from aircraft-quality aluminum and could be ordered with gold or chrome plating.

Only a few Velenos were produced with three pick-ups. The one shown here was made for English guitarist Peter Haycock of the Climax Blues Band. **SH**

The SG-60T was from the second generation of Yamaha electric instruments, and part of a new line introduced in 1972.

The SG-60T was a single cutaway guitar, its body built from nato and shaped vaguely like a Les Paul, albeit with much deeper carving. The neck was a mahogany bolt-on construction with a twenty-two-fret bound rosewood fingerboard. The 24¾-in. (63-cm) scale length was also of Gibson proportions, although the nut was fractionally wider, with a diameter of 1¾ in. (4.5 cm).

The SG-60T was given either a vibrant red or a sunburst finish with matching headstock, equipped with Yamaha machine heads.

Sound came from a pair of humbuckers, the neck pick-up being set at an angle following the same line as the fingerboard. The electrics featured an unusual three-stage "Tone Selector" control, along with the standard treble and bass potentiometers. The SG-60T was a well-balanced guitar with a versatile range. **JB**

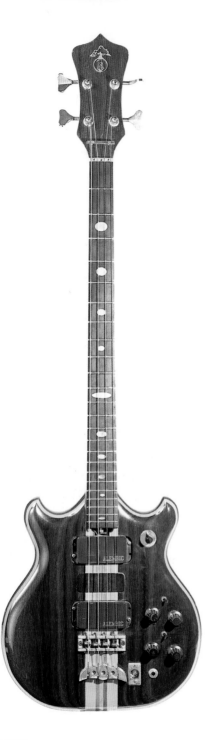

Alembic
Tenor 1973

Type Electric bass
Body & neck Mahogany/maple body, maple/walnut neck
Fingerboard Rosewood
Pick-ups Two active pick-ups

Although Alembic is known for its highly crafted, technologically innovative instruments, the company was created by a bunch of Californian techno-hippies building sound systems for psychedelic giants The Grateful Dead and Jefferson Airplane. The bass they built in 1972 as a one-off for the Airplane's Jack Casady (page 437) convinced them to try their hand at guitar making. Within two years, their workshop was producing a dozen instruments a month, made to the highest specification and with eye-watering prices to match. And although Alembic built strikingly beautiful six-string guitars, it quickly became clear that its most prized creations were its electric bass guitars.

Early takers included jazz fusion star Stanley Clarke, then playing with Chick Corea and Al Di Meola in Return To Forever. Until the emergence of Jaco Pastorius, Clarke was regarded as the first virtuoso electric bass player in jazz, and his influence crossed over into the rock world. With such a high-profile customer, Alembic saw interest in their basses soar.

Clarke's Alembic has an unusually short scale—30¾ in. (78 cm)—and has been restrung as a "tenor" bass, each string a perfect fourth above standard tuning; this was integral to his melodic style. Clarke also used "piccolo" tuning on his Alembic basses, with each string an octave higher than standard. **TB**

The title track of Stanley Clarke's *School Days* (1976) is a classic of the jazz fusion genre—as anyone who ever worked in a music store selling bass guitars in the late 1970s would probably attest, from the number of copies of the album they rang up and wrapped.

D'Aquisto
Seven-string 1973

Type Solidbody acoustic
Body & neck Maple sides, spruce top, maple neck
Fingerboard Ebony
Pick-ups Two DeArmond pick-ups

New York-based guitar maker James D'Aquisto made a series of just eight seven-string guitars during his highly acclaimed career as a custom luthier. Seven were carved top semi-acoustics; one was a solid-bodied instrument. This fine example of the arch-top New Yorker seven-string guitar used imported highly-figured maple and European spruce for the body, and maple and ebony for the neck and fingerboard.

The neck was built slightly wider to accommodate the extra string and one more tuner was added to the headstock. Otherwise, the guitar maintains many characterisitics of D'Aquisto's other New Yorker instruments, like the slightly modernistic f-holes, the adjustable ebony tailpiece, and the adjustable 'Accutone' bridge. The asymmetric headstock features the D'Aquisto scroll motif and signature.

At first glance, the tobacco sunburst model looks somewhat plain—there is, for example, no pearl inlay along the one-piece maple neck. D'Aquisto believed decorative artifice detracted from the most important feature of his guitars: the sound they made. In this case it was a beautifully detailed but warm jazz tone.

Nevertheless D'Aquisto did permit the luxury of gold-plated Schaller tuners and intricate ivory binding. The design also boasts pick-ups made by either DeArmond or Kent Armstrong. **SH**

New Jersey-born jazz guitarist Bucky Pizzarelli—the father of guitarist John and bassist Martin—had a D'Aquisto New Yorker seven-string made for him. His album *April Kisses* (1999) even bears the legend "Solo 7-string Acoustic Guitar."

Gibson Grabber
G-1 Bass 1973

Type Electric bass
Body & neck Maple body, maple neck (later alder)
Fingerboard Maple
Pick-ups One sliding pick-up

Launched alongside the Ripper, Gibson's entry-level Grabber was the starter instrument of choice for a generation of rock and metal bassists, owing to its appearance on the cover of Kiss's classic *Alive!* (1975).

Like the predominant American bass, Fender's Precision, the Grabber had a bolt-on 34½-in. (87.6-cm) neck and a V-shaped headstock along the lines of the Gibson Flying V. Its large body, made initially from maple and later from alder, made it slightly difficult to manipulate for smaller players, but there was no denying that the purchase of a Grabber gave you a lot of bass for your buck. Furthermore, owners could boast to other bassists about the Grabber's sliding pick-up, which could be moved from neck to bridge position to allow the user to access a wider range of tones. This innovation should, in theory at least, have made the Grabber one of the most user-friendly bass guitars ever designed; however, bassists didn't seem able to accommodate this paradigm change, and even Gibson switched to fixed pick-ups on a later version, the G3. Perhaps aware that the tone range was one of the Grabber's most attractive features, the designers added three pick-ups to this later model, all of them humbuckers, which could be used either as adjacent pairs or with all three in unison for a configuration labeled "a buck and a half" by owners. **JM**

The Grabber can be heard in the introduction of "Stuart And The Ave." on Green Day's *Insomniac* (1995). "I actually played a Gibson Grabber 3 with the three pickups…" recalled bassist Mike Dirnt. "I played that for about 700 shows. Then I broke the neck."

Gibson Ripper
L9-S Bass 1973

Type Electric bass
Body & neck Maple or alder body, maple neck
Fingerboard Maple
Pick-ups Two humbucker pick-ups

Back in the dark ages—say about 1972—American guitar makers noticed that so-called "heavy rock" was popular among the youth of the day. Spearheaded by stadium-filling behemoths such as Grand Funk, the new music demanded bigger, tougher guitars than those of yore, and thus the Gibson Ripper was born, alongside the Grabber model. Both were chunky basses that demanded serious upper-body strength, but even so, kids snapped them up by the thousands.

The Ripper was produced between 1973 and 1983 (1976 was its peak year). Most models were built with a maple neck/body combo that kept retail costs down, although an alder version appeared, too. In 1975, a slimmer-bodied Ripper utilized beveled edges for a more playable experience. A variety of body and pickguard finishes kept the brand interesting for the restless rock-consuming customer base.

Tonally, the Ripper had a broad range of options courtesy of a four-way pick-up selector that had also appeared on the earlier EB-3 bass. With this, users could select series, parallel, and bridge-only options—a complex system by modern standards, but not one that deterred many buyers in the 1970s. Both the Grabber and the Ripper were reissued in the 2000s for the nostalgists of the fanbase, and cheaper Epiphone versions of the originals are still around. **JM**

Mark Evans was an early bass player for Australia's premium rockers AC/DC. He played a Gibson Ripper on *T.N.T.* (1975), their second album in their native land, tracks from which were included on the band's international debut recording, *High Voltage* (1976).

Masaru Kohno
Classical 25 1973

Type Classical guitar
Body & neck Spruce top, rosewood back and sides
Fingerboard Ebony
Other features 26-in. (66-cm) strings, French polished

Masaru Kohno (1926–98) is synonymous with the highest-quality Japanese concert classical guitars. Sometime after 1948, having taken a degree in woodcraft, he took an interest in guitar making and in 1960 spent six months in Spain learning the craft from luthier Arcángel Fernández. On his return, he set up shop in Tokyo, had an initial client base among Japanese guitarists, and then became internationally renowned when, in 1967, he won a gold medal for an individual instrument in a prestigious guitar-making competition in Belgium.

> *"The older I get, the more I realize that each maker somehow builds into his instrument quite a lot of his own personality."*
>
> **JULIAN BREAM**

Kohno guitars, like this 1973 model, were built in the Spanish tradition. It is a big-sounding instrument, akin to a Fleta. (Celebrated maker Ignacio Fleta was on the panel that awarded Kohno a gold medal in 1967.) In general, Kohno's guitars, at the highest levels of evaluation, must have lacked something, because although guitarists like Julian Bream, Oscar Gighlia, Sharon Isbin, and Xuefei Yang all own or have owned Kohno guitars (mainly because they were gifts from Kohno), none of them is known to have played them very much. For many lesser mortals, however, to own a Kohno guitar is a dream come true.

Kohno's workshop is now in the capable hands of his nephew, Masaki Sakurai, a master luthier who worked alongside Kohno for over twenty years. **GD**

Arbiter
E320 1974

Type Double cutaway solid electric six-string
Body & neck Mahogany body, maple neck
Fingerboard Rosewood
Pick-ups Three Greco humbucker pick-ups

It was 1974, and the era of excellent guitar copies imported to the West from the Far East. At the same time, the real Gibson SG was everywhere: this year Black Sabbath played in front of 250,000 fans in California, AC/DC played their first gig, and Santana released their *Lotus* live album.

Those who could not afford the real Kalamazoo-made SG chose from an array of copies arriving from Japan. This Arbiter E320 was a well-made SG Custom look-alike, with three humbucker pick-ups, chunky block inlays, and a copy of a Bigsby tremolo system.

> *"Unlike the original … this Arbiter guitar is much more affordable—if just as cool! It plays and sounds extremely good."*
> MODERN-DAY ADVERTISEMENT FOR THE E320

In the tangled world of Japanese manufacturing at this time, this Arbiter was actually made by Greco. It was marketed in the United Kingdom as either a Greco or an Arbiter. The E320 had a British price tag of just £85.

The guitar's construction was Gibsonesque, with a bolt-on maple neck with truss rod, open-book-style headstock, and a mahogany body. Features included gold-plated hardware, a multi-adjustable bridge, and two separate scratch plates.

These Gibson copies were designed with the help of Japanese guitarist Shigeru Narumo. During their development, Narumo and his band were all given a real Gibson, a real Fender, and the latest Greco prototype to play while blindfolded. The story goes that they all preferred the Greco. **SH**

Bruce BecVar
Snake Guitar 1974

Type Solidbody electric
Body & neck Various exotic-timbered bodies and necks
Fingerboard Ebony
Pick-ups Two ceramic magnet pick-ups

Bruce BecVar, born in Kentucky in 1953, built his first guitar at the age of twelve. In 1973, he began hand-building a guitar that would be displayed, somewhat controversially, the following year in the André Mertens Galleries for Musical Instruments at New York City's Metropolitan Museum of Art—a remarkable feat for a largely self-taught guitar maker. The instrument, called "Guitar" by the museum (and "Snake Guitar" by Bruce) is now in the museum's permanent collection.

Combining traditional materials and designs with contemporary aesthetics, BecVar's guitar was an

> *"Composing and recording is for me a very spiritual practice … it is an exacting process of listening to the creative impulses of Spirit."*
> BRUCE BECVAR

artistic triumph. Encircling the body are two snakes, carved from bird's-eye maple. Timbers include Benin wood, flamed ebony, and Brazilian rosewood. The neck is Hawaiian koa. The guitar was left unpainted, the natural wood grains giving it extraordinary depth and contrast. On the body is an image of the Biblical David and Goliath in rosewood, bone, and abalone. Its tailpiece and bridge are handmade from solid brass, and there are patterned inlays on the fingerboard.

A successful composer of melodic ensemble music, BecVar is now considered a veteran of the acoustic guitar. In the 1970s, he set up a workshop in Sonoma in Northern California and made electric guitars for The Who, The Jackson Five, Led Zeppelin, The Peter Frampton Band, and Carlos Santana. **BS**

Burns UK
Flyte 1974

Type Solidbody electric
Body & neck Body and neck of selected hardwoods
Fingerboard Ebonized maple with aluminum dot inlays
Pick-ups Two Burns Mach One humbucker pick-ups

Having established Burns as a major British force in the early 1960s, originator Jim Burns was less involved after a sell-out to the U.S. Baldwin Piano and Organ Company. He toyed with a secondary brand, Ormston, from 1966 to 1968, and was involved in the Hayman brand from 1970. In 1973, he returned with Burns UK Ltd—he was employed by a Newcastle-based musical instrument retailer, and the range kicked off with the futuristic-looking Flyte. The high-quality wood parts were made by the Shergold company, with fittings provided by Re-An and Eddie Cross.

"The Flyte ... was originally to be named the Concorde, after the supersonic plane, because of its shape."

HENDRIXGUITARS.COM

The Flyte featured a complex Dynamic Tension bridge/tailpiece and Schaller tuners plus two Mach One humbucking pick-ups, a three-way pick-up selector, and master volume and tone. The primary finish was silver, but others—dark or light natural, white, silver, or white with red or blue shading—were offered. There was also a bass version.

Its unusual shape fitted perfectly into the glam-rock style of the United Kingdom in the early 1970s. T. Rex's Marc Bolan used one, as did Slade's Dave Hill. But ultimately, the sounds of the Flyte were more ordinary, and the powerfully named pick-ups were actually a little weak-sounding. The guitar ceased production in 1977, but its futurism lived on with the Artist, the Mirage, and the more conventional LJ 24. **DB**

Chapman
Stick 1974

Type Solid elongated fretted one-piece fingerboard
Body & neck Originally ironwood body and neck
Fingerboard A variety of woods and synthetic materials
Pick-ups Two-channel split/EMG active pick-ups

One of the most interesting attempts at a conceptual redesign of the electric guitar, the Chapman Stick superficially resembles an overlong, wide fingerboard. Yet the required playing technique is arguably closer to that demanded by a keyboard instrument. The Stick is a "tapping" instrument: sounds are made by pressing the strings down onto the frets, rather than by fretting with one hand and plucking notes with the other. In its original form, the Stick comprised ten strings; the right hand taps the top five strings, while the left hand taps the five at the bottom. This enables the player to double up combinations of bass parts, chords, and lead lines.

The Stick was developed in 1969 and launched five years later by American guitarist Emmett Chapman, who had previously created his own double-handed tapping style on a long-scale guitar. The technique of string tapping has a long history, ukulele player Roy Smeck having used this idea as early as 1932. Nor was the Stick even the first dedicated instrument of its type—Dave Bunker's "touch-guitar" had made a brief appearance more than a decade earlier. Nonetheless, the persistence of the inventor—who was still nurturing the Stick's development four decades later—has been rewarded with an ever-growing worldwide base of players. **TB**

Tony Levin has played bass with such diverse artists as Peter Gabriel, Alice Cooper, Buddy Rich, and John Lennon. His precision Stick work can be heard on King Crimson's *Discipline* (1981), interlocking to great effect with the guitars of Robert Fripp and Adrian Belew.

Tony Levin, the most prominent exponent of the Chapman Stick. →

Framus
Super Yob 1974

Type Ray-gun-shaped solidbody electric
Body & neck Alder body, bolt-on maple neck
Fingerboard Maple
Pick-ups Two humbucker pick-ups

During the first half of the 1970s, the UK pop landscape saw the curious emergence of glam rock. Not a musical movement as such, common ground among the leading lights was more about extravagant dress than sound. With brash guitars and the raucous terrace-chant choruses on hits such as "Cum On Feel The Noize," Slade were one of the least-convincing converts to glam—indeed, the term was only really applicable to the sparkly stage persona of guitarist Dave Hill.

In 1974, at the height of the band's fame, Hill commissioned British luthier John Birch to produce the "Super Yob" with its sci-fi ray-gun styling. For several years, Hill was rarely seen on stage using any other instrument. However, he found the original model overly heavy, and asked German manufacturer Framus to produce an updated version.

Birch will still build the guitar to order; the Super Yob 2 features the option of LED inlays and a laser light in the headstock! **TB**

Ibanez
2347 SG 1974

Type Solidbody electric
Body & neck Mahogany
Fingerboard Rosewood
Pick-ups One single-coil pick-up

The first electric guitars produced by Ibanez, like those of most other Japanese manufacturers during the first two decades of the rock 'n' roll era, were copies of Western designs—initially Hagstrom and EKO—and then principally Gibson and Fender by the 1970s.

The 2347 closely resembled a Gibson SG but with a scratchplate design derived from a Les Paul Junior. It was available in either of two colors: Cherry Red (like an SG), or White (like a Les Paul Junior). Its superior build quality and set-in neck made it rather more playable than most of its competitors.

Ibanez pushed its luck by taking over an American company to produce guitars in the United States, and at this point Gibson decided that it ought to put a stop to this sort of thing. In 1977, it sued the Elger Company—Ibanez's U.S. distributor at the time—for copyright infringement, focusing on the design of the guitar's headstock. This was settled out of court, and Ibanez subsequently produced its own original designs. **AJ**

Jolana
Iris 1974

Type Solidbody electric
Body & neck Alder body, bolt-on maple neck
Fingerboard Beech, with pearloid dot inlays
Pick-ups Two single-coil pickups

"We will go a different way," said Lenin in 1887, after a failed attempt to assassinate the Czar. And from then on, the Eastern Bloc way differed from the ways of the West. When the time came to design a domestic version of the Telecaster, Czech manufacturers Jolana engineered one that differed from the American classic in almost every way possible. At first glance, the Jolana Iris appears to be a copy of a Telecaster Thinline.

In fact, only in the most general and superficial sense is the Iris a Telecaster-type instrument, deceptive appearances nonwithstanding. The standard Jolana floating bridge and top-mount vibrato combo, as found on many Jolana models dating back to the early 1960s, are perhaps the most obvious deviation. This type of bridge ensures a lack of traditional Telecaster-style sustain, while the vibrato, of course, allows for an effect that Leo Fender had never envisioned on this type of instrument.

The Iris, one of Jolana's most popular models, remained in production into the late 1980s. **EP**

Musima
Elektra Deluxe V 1974

Type Solidbody electric
Body & neck Alder body, bolt-on beech neck
Fingerboard Ebony, bound, with pearloid inlays
Pick-ups Three Simeto single-coil pick-ups

Musima's long-running senior solidbody model was updated for the 1970s with redesigned Simeto pick-ups that were now height-adjustable, and a more modern Hagstrom-styled vibrato. The body was elongated slightly, losing the old blocky shape found on the early versions of the Eterna. The pickguard was now more free-flowing, while still accommodating a full array of knobs and switches. While the guitar's circuitry remained idiosyncratic and complex, gone was the famous "trick switch" that graced many earlier Musima models and provided "Shearing" and "Banjo" settings. The guitar still featured such upscale features as pearloid inlays and binding.

A simplified model called the Elektra was built alongside the Eterna. It was very similar in overall appearance, but lacked the pearloid, and featured a simpler circuit with only two pick-ups, as well as more color options. Both models were produced by the East German factory until the end of the 1970s, when they were replaced by the newly redesigned "25" series. **EP**

Rickenbacker
481 1974

Type Double cutaway solidbody electric
Body & neck Maple body and neck
Fingerboard Rosewood
Pick-ups Two humbucker pick-ups

The Rickenbacker 481 was released in 1974. Its design was based on the body and headstock shape of the maker's ever-popular 4001 bass. Rather unusually for a Rickenbacker, however, instead of the "neck-through" construction, the 481 featured a Fender-style bolt-on neck. The fingerboard was varnished rosewood with plastic triangle inlays; the headstock was fitted with Grover Rotomatic tuners.

The most unusual feature of the 481 was its use of twenty-four slanted frets, set at a slight angle and running in parallel along the fingerboard. Offered on some Rickenbackers since 1969, this was a feature intended to improve playing ergonomics, being more in keeping with the angled, natural position of the fretting fingers. Although this made for a fast neck, some found playing chords slightly cumbersome.

Also unusual for a Rickenbacker were the 481's two humbucking pick-ups, which had dedicated volume and tone controls and a three-way switching mechanism; a smaller phase-reversal switch was conveniently positioned alongside, with two volume and two tone controls.

Popular throughout the remainder of the 1970s, Rickenbacker 481s subsquently fell from favor, but interest in them revived when they were adopted by some rock guitarists of the 1990s and 2000s, including Serge Pizzorno of Kasabian and Tim Christensen, and then by various thrash bands. Today, 481s are rare and costly—as this book went to press, used prices were typically in the region of $2,000. Copies by Ibanez and Greco are slightly easier to acquire, but not a great deal less expensive. **JB**

Tonika
Urals-built Model 1974

Type Solidbody electric
Body & neck Hardwood body, bolt-on beech neck
Fingerboard Beech
Pick-ups Two single-coil pick-ups

Tonika is one of the most distinctive and historically significant Soviet guitars. The first thing one notices is the bizarre body shape. "Strange design, super heavy, hardly playable…" Russian luthier Iouri Dmitrievski told *Making Music*, "yet we teenagers were fascinated. It was a subject of our dreams! But, pretty soon, it was evident that they could hardly compete with our own home-made axes, although we could just dream about all the woods spoiled by Tonika makers. Those first Russian electrics had ebony fingerboards!

Unlike the derivative shapes of other Soviet models, the Tonika's free-flowing lines are unique, albeit influenced by German and Italian electric guitar design. Those familiar with Musima guitars of the 1960s will detect some of these influences, most notably the vibrato unit. The Italian connection is less obvious, but one can tell that Tonika's designers were familiar with Eko's triple cutaway models.

While the resultant guitar ended up relatively bulky and heavy, the body shape nevertheless proved fairly comfortable. The historical significance is also easily explained: the Tonika represents the first mass-produced solidbody electric guitar to be marketed in the USSR. The earliest examples were produced by the Lunacharsky factory in Leningrad, circa 1969. Later Tonikas were built by both the Ural and the Rostov factories, as were matching basses. Despite bearing different features, all shared the same distinctive shape. The example illustrated was built by the Ural factory in 1975, about two years before this model was discontinued, and supplanted by the equally legendary Ural (see page 506). **EP**

Travis Bean
TB1000 1974

Type Solidbody electric
Body & neck Koa body, aluminum neck
Fingerboard Brazilian rosewood
Pick-ups Two humbucker pick-ups

Travis Bean became well known in the mid-1970s for his innovative use of aluminum necks in guitar and bass design. The brand that bears his name caused a stir when it was founded in 1974 owing to what was seen as its novel use of materials, even though Antonio Pioli's Wandré guitars had used the same method well over a decade earlier.

The TB1000 was launched in two versions: the Standard "S" and the rarer Artist "A." Only 2,177 were built, making them comparative rarities. Both models were made with one-piece, solid, machined-aluminum necks, which were held onto the body by four counter-sunk bolts. The fingerboards were Brazilian rosewood inlaid with mother-of-pearl blocks. The distinctive headstocks feature a dramatic "T" cutout, the machine heads lined up along each side of the stem of the letter. The necks were set three-fifths of the way into the rear of the routed body, which gave the top a traditional appearance. The Artist had a two-piece koa body with a beautifully carved top.

Like all Travis Bean guitars, the TB1000 had a unique sound and was particularly prized for its levels of sustain. On the negative side, however, it was too heavy an instrument for some players.

Travis Beans were briefly fashionable; players at the time included Jerry Garcia, Keith Richards, Ronnie Wood, Joe Perry, and Brian Robertson of Thin Lizzy.

One of Bean's partners, Gary Kramer, went his own way in 1975, and produced a variation on the same theme with greater commercial success. After his company folded in 1979, Bean remained a small-scale guitar maker until his death in 2011. **JB**

Keith Richards wields a Travis Bean in 1979 with his band, the New Barbarians.

B.C. Rich
Mockingbird 1975

Type Solidbody electric
Body & neck Koa or mahogany body, maple neck
Fingerboard Ebony with mother-of-pearl cloud inlays
Pick-ups Two DiMarzio humbucker pick-ups

With a background making and playing flamenco and classical guitars in his family's store—Bernardo's Valencian Guitar Shop in Los Angeles—Bernardo Chavez Rico would seem an unlikely creator of some of the most striking and innovative electric guitars ever made. He chose the working name B.C. Rich and became interested in electric guitars, apparently, after repairing Bo Diddley's famous rectangular-bodied Gretsch. His first original design was the Seagull with a neck-through-body heel-less design that appeared in the early 1970s. Later designs were conceived by Neal Moser, who worked with Rico from 1974 and added his tricky electronic designs to the Seagull.

The next design, the Mockingbird—designed from a sketch by bassist Johnny "Go-Go" Kallas—was to become more famous: it surfaced in its "shorthorn" shape in, according to Kallas, 1975 (other sources say 1974). It was redesigned by Rico into the better-known—and better-balancing—"longhorn" version in 1978 and remains a striking update of the Gibson Explorer, adding more graceful curves and points.

The Mockingbird employed much of the cutting-edge design of the day, not only in the Alembic-inspired through neck but also in the active electrics, the early DiMarzio humbucker pick-ups, and the then-fashionable Leo Quan Badass wrapover bridge. **DB**

Slash is closely associated with Les Pauls, but his B.C. Rich Mockingbirds—he has a few—have seen action on stage (notably at Michael Jackson's *30th Anniversary Special* in 2001) and in the studio. Check out "The Truth" and "The Alien" from *Ain't Life Grand* (2000).

Defil
Jola 1975

Type Solidbody electric
Body & neck Beech body, bolt-on spruce neck
Fingerboard Rosewood
Pick-ups Two Muza single-coil pick-ups

Dolnoslaska Fabryka Instrumentow Lutniczych (Defil) was the main guitar maker in Poland for many years. Its mid-1960s Jola, which followed the Hagstrom-inspired Samba and Lotus models, was clearly influenced by Eastern European neighbors: Musima of East Germany and Jolana from Czechoslovakia.

The Jola was equipped with the then-new Muza pick-ups that became standard on guitars, basses, and mandolins until well into the 1980s. With an average resistance of 4.75 kOhms, these single-coils had low output by today's standards—but, back then, pick-ups were not intended to overdrive their amplifiers.

The Jola's controls by no means followed a usual scheme. There's a bass potentiometer for the neck pick-up, and a treble potentiometer for the bridge pick-up, which could be switched by two sliders that also served as pick-up selectors. The output socket is surprisingly a familiar ¼-in. (0.6-cm) jack rather than the DIN5 deployed by most Eastern Bloc instruments.

The bolt-on neck with zero fret features a skunk stripe on the back that almost reaches double thickness at the thirteenth fret or the neck heel. The three-bolt joint is covered with triangular neckplate, which only sometimes bears a serial number. All early Defils—Samba, Lotus bass, and now Jola—were red, and it's unclear if other colors were ever available.

So who played Defil instruments? Hordes of young Polish musicians who fought against the thick necks behind the Iron Curtain, as they played American and English rock. Now considered collectible, these guitars were simply the most readily available instruments in communist Poland. **IS**

Gibson
S-1 1975

Type Solidbody electric
Body & neck Alder body, maple neck
Fingerboard Rosewood
Pick-ups One to three Bill Lawrence single-coil pick-ups

The modern guitarist has little expectation of radical new designs bearing the Fender and Gibson logos. Technological innovation still exists—look at the Gibson "robot" guitars, for instance—but these instruments are, without exception, based on designs conceived fifty or more years earlier. The guitar market of the mid-1970s was a more curious place, where the big names were unafraid to try something new.

While quality control at Fender had continued to diminish during this time—a result of long-term cost-cutting by parent company CBS—the classic Strats and Teles remained the most popular solidbody electrics. Consequently, Gibson decided to try its hand at producing a Fender-style single-coil. The Les Paul–styled 1974 Marauder sold in small numbers—around 1,400 were made—but was received with sufficient enthusiasm to continue the experiment: a year later, the Marauder was superseded by a second single-coil instrument, the S-1. With the same single-cutaway Les Paul Junior-style flat body, the S-1 was, unusually for a Gibson, fitted with a bolt-on neck—in this case, with a Flying V-style headstock.

The S-1 featured elaborate wiring for a non-active guitar. Designed by top pick-up man Bill Lawrence, up to three "see-thru" single-coil pick-ups were wired to a two-way toggle switch and a four-position "chicken head" rotary switch, enabling a wide range of sounds.

Despite endorsements from stadium-fillers like Santana and The Rolling Stones, the S-1 sold modestly until it was withdrawn in 1980. It remains a cult guitar, and is still surprisingly affordable on the secondhand market. **TB**

Allan Gittler
"Fishbone" 1975

Type Electric guitar
Body & neck Stainless steel body and neck
Fingerboard None
Pick-ups Individual pick-up units for each string

Over the years there have been some pretty wild attempts at reinventing the electric guitar. Few, however, have been as radical as Allan Gittler's "Fishbone." The New York artist and inventor began by studying each element of a conventional electric guitar and questioning its role and design. What emerged was a radical rethink that he believed would have repercussions on the future of luthiery.

Gittler's lack of a traditional background in instrument design perhaps helped him in his quest. He questioned whether traditional references to acoustic guitars were relevant to modern electric instruments. This product of his labor was truly unlike anything that preceded it; constructed wholly from stainless steel, it seemed more like the skeleton of a guitar. The neck was a thin bar that ran the full length of the instrument on which thirty-two frets had been pressure-fitted. There was no fingerboard as such beneath the frets, so care was needed when pressing down on the strings to avoid wrecking the intonation. Also unusual, the guitar featured individual pick-ups for each string. We can only guess whether it had a direct influence, but elements such as the removal of any discernible headstock, with the tuners fitted behind the bridge, certainly preempted the later Steinberger models.

Gittler built only around sixty Fishbone guitars before relocating to Israel in 1982. Andy Summers of The Police was an early owner, and can be seen with one in the video for "Synchronicity II." Sadly, Fishbones are today more likely to be found in galleries such as New York's MoMA than in the hands of musicians. **TB**

Hang Dong
Electric Guitar 1975

Ibanez
Iceman 1975

Type Twin cutaway solidbody electric
Body & neck Laminated hardwood body, maple neck
Fingerboard Rosewood
Pick-ups Three single-coil pick-ups

Type Single cutaway solidbody
Body & neck Mahogany body, maple neck
Fingerboard Rosewood
Pick-ups Super 70 anti-hum, Super 2000, or V2 pick-ups

In the mid-1970s, everyone was rushing to try to make copies of the big-name American guitars. Even in Thailand there was a company churning out cheap instruments using templates based on U.S. originals.

Hang Dong might not have survived to become a household name today, but back in the 1960s and 1970s it churned out guitars like this three-pick-up solidbody electric guitar that was clearly "influenced" by the Fender Jaguar.

Hang Dong might well have been lost in the mists of time had it not been for the fact that many U.S. servicemen bought the guitars while serving in Vietnam. Some examples made it back to the United States, where they became very rare collectors' items.

The guitar had no truss rod, but four micro adjustment screws under the neckplate for altering the neck angle. There is a Fender Jaguar-style tremolo, and a bridge mute system. The neck inlays are mother-of-pearl and the pickguard is classic period pearloid plastic. **SH**

The 1970s were a landmark decade for most of the Japanese guitar makers, as companies such as Hoshino Gakki—owner of Ibanez—moved away from replicating U.S. models in favor of original designs. The Ibanez Iceman came about through a collaboration between Hoshino and the Greco guitar company. The outcome was a fabulously Asian take on the original Gibson Explorer body shape.

Known in Japan as the Mirage, the Iceman came in different varieties, whose pick-up configurations, woods, and construction methods varied with price. Production continued into 1983 when the Iceman II was issued, and the headstock design changed in favor of a six-in-a-line system of tuners.

Paul Stanley of Kiss was the first celebrity to use an Ibanez guitar, eventually launching a Washburn signature model based on the Iceman he used at the peak of his band's popularity. More recently, Daron Malakian of System Of A Down put his initials to a signature version of the Iceman: the DMM1. **TB**

Ned Callan
Cody 1975

Ovation
1281 Preacher 1975

Type Solidbody electric
Body & neck Obeche body, maple neck
Fingerboard Rosewood
Pick-ups Two Alnico single-coil pick-ups

Type Solidbody electric twelve-string
Body & neck Honduras mahogany body and neck
Fingerboard Ebony
Pick-ups Two humbucker double-coil pick-ups

Built in Britain, the Cody had been developed by luthier Peter Cook under the Pseudonym "Ned Callan." Some models were also made for the London-based Rose-Morris music store—the "Shaftesbury" name appears on the headstock of these models.

The Cody—or "Nobbly Ned," as it was sometimes known—featured an unusual offset body design made from African obeche with a sunburst finish, and with a bolt-on maple neck. The bridge was reminiscent of an original Telecaster unit, and similarly came with its own steel cover. The sound came courtesy of a pair of resin-filled Alnico pick-ups, each with its own dedicated volume and tone control.

The Cody's unusual looks polarized the opinions of players, but even its detractors admitted that its sound and "vintage" feel were surprisingly good for what was at the time a cheap instrument. It was certainly very different from the American guitars being built during that period. The Cody is now something of a collector's piece. **JB**

After the disappointing commercial performance of more adventurous designs—the Breadwinner and the Deacon—in the early 1970s, Ovation introduced the relatively conventional 1281 Preacher. It retained the two-octave neck from the earlier models, and had two small humbuckers, a three-way pick-up selector, two knobs each for tone and volume, and two jacks for mono or stereo output. The 1285 Preacher twelve-string, introduced shortly afterward, was essentially the same guitar with a twelve-string bridge and tailpiece and a wider neck.

Although it was initially perceived as an expensive Gibson SG copy, the high quality of the instrument ensured it a growing reputation. In 2004, Roger Waters donated the 1285 that he had used on his album *The Pros And Cons Of Hitch Hiking* (1984) to Eric Clapton's Christie's auction in aid of the Crossroads drug and alcohol addiction rehabilitation center on the Caribbean island of Antigua. With a guide price of $5,000, it rather surprisingly sold for $31,070. **AJ**

Ovation
Viper 1975

Type Solidbody electric
Body & neck Two-piece maple body, one-piece maple neck
Fingerboard Ebony
Pick-ups Two or three PAF humbucker pick-ups

Advertising blurb for this new line of guitars said it all: "For years, performers have been asking Ovation to make a conventional-shaped guitar." The company's first foray into the solidbody market had produced the Breadwinner. This was an excellent-sounding guitar featuring unusual innovations, but it had one obvious drawback: in spite of its cult following, the majority of musicians thought it looked dreadful! So after four years of fighting a losing battle in the marketplace, in 1975 Ovation introduced two new guitars. The Viper and the Preacher were essentially the same instrument—they broadly resembled a scaled-down version of the company's Balladeer acoustic, only with cutaways: a single for the Viper; twin for the Preacher.

With these two models, Ovation seemed to be actively pursuing Fender players. The scale length was increased from Gibson's 24¾ in. (63 cm) to Fender's 25½ in. (64.75 cm). And it switched back to single-coil pick-ups. Ovation's marketing offensive claimed that these new pick-ups had 30 percent more windings than similar (presumably Fender) single-coils, which could generate 6dB more output. They were certainly capable of producing a powerful, cutting tone.

The Viper appeared in various guises, including the three-pick-up Viper III, from 1979 to 1980. The final Viper came off the production line in 1983. **TB**

Alex Turner of the Arctic Monkeys frequently uses an Ovation Viper in concert. *Favourite Worst Nightmare* (2007) was the band's second album, released just over a year after their phenomenally successful first album, *Whatever People Say I Am, That's What I'm Not* (2006).

Rickenbacker
362/12 1975

Type Thin, semi-hollow body electric
Body & neck Maple body and neck
Fingerboard Rosewood
Pick-ups Two humbucker pick-ups per neck

During the 1960s, Rickenbacker, like many other makers, custom-built the rare double-neck guitar for special customers. But in 1975, the firm offered its first production double-necks—and it went all the way, offering a choice of three models. The first was the solidbody 4080, combining a 4001 bass with a 480 guitar. A variation was the 4080/12, which substituted a twelve-string guitar into the duo.

The 362/12 was Rickenbacker's ultimate model. It grafted two 360s—a six-string and a twelve-string—onto one expanded body. As with the regular 360, the 362/12 was a thin semi-hollow body, but a player still needed a strong back to support it. With two pick-ups per neck, the sheer number of controls was daunting; it almost required having your owner's manual handy on stage to remember what everything did. There was a volume and tone knob for each neck, two three-way pick-up selectors, and a blend knob for the stereo output—all in close proximity on the pickguard.

Perhaps the most interesting feature of the 362/12 was that the necks were not parallel to each other. The top twelve-string neck was angled slightly upward, designed to facilitate easier access to the upper frets. Rickenbacker's 362/12 boasted a ten-year production run until 1985, although few were built and they remain a highly collectible rarity.

In 1966, Rickenbacker had unveiled its Convertible guitar line, which changed from a six- to a twelve-string with the flip of the "converter comb." But the feature never caught on—and it didn't evoke the rock 'n' roll glamour of a double-neck, such as the amazing 362/12. **MD**

Alembic
Spyder 1976

Type Solidbody/chambered bass
Body & neck Maple/walnut body and through-neck
Fingerboard Ebony
Pick-ups Two humbucker pick-ups, one hum-canceling

Among John Entwistle's most famous creations, the Gibson Explorer–inspired Alembics of the mid-1970s— complete with side LEDs, sterling-silver spider inlays on the body, and no expense spared—were a mainstay of the Who star's arsenal for almost a decade.

When loud was no longer loud enough, Entwistle's Fender and Gibson basses gave way to the Alembics, which provided all the bottom-end power and top-end clarity that his style required. Ergonomically, the Spyder looks and feels a bit suspect, and the dimensions probably won't appeal to every player, but then it was built for a unique bassist using premium materials and electronics.

Previously, Alembics had purely been the domain of the hippie brigade on the West Coast and a select band of jazz and funk players. But, by the time Entwistle got his hands on his first Series 1 in 1974, the Alembic bass had been well and truly dragged kicking and screaming into the rock arena. And what a sound it had. Listen to any recordings of this period or watch the Live Aid footage to receive a kick in the pants based on what Entwistle is able to coax from this beauty: twang and boom in equal measure, a player and instrument in perfect harmony. When Entwistle's basses were auctioned, these particular Alembic models went for very tidy sums indeed. **JM**

Who Are You (1978) was cut during Entwistle's Alembic phase. "The extra treble and the facility to get up high means that I can take more solos," he said. Of Entwistle's "Trick Of The Light," Pete Townshend wrote: "[The Alembic] solo on this sounds like a musical Mack truck."

B.C. Rich
Bich 1976

Type Solidbody ten-string electric
Body & neck Maple body and neck, basswood "fins"
Fingerboard Ebony
Pick-ups Two Rockfield Mafia humbucker pick-ups

B.C. Rich is indelibly linked to the metal scene, his guitars' angular body shapes a major influence on many subsequent brands. Leaving his flamenco roots aside, acoustic guitarist Bernardo Chavez Rico's first "B.C. Rich" electric guitars were a batch of twenty instruments inspired by Gibson's Les Paul and EB-3 basses. In 1972, the Seagull took flight, showcasing the first of his visually distinctive body shapes.

The Bich of 1976 features a striking rear cutaway housing four machine heads. The reason for this is the fact that the Bich is a ten-string guitar, the top four strings doubled up in a similar fashion to a twelve-string model. These extra four strings are tuned from behind the bridge.

The most common tuning for the Bich is unison for the top two pairs with the middle two tuned an octave apart. This creates a big, powerful sound when chords are played with distortion, while the single bottom strings provide a clearer tone.

Like most B.C. Rich guitars, the Bich was principally popular among the hard rock fraternity. Dave Mustaine was a notable user, in both Metallica and Megadeth; his chosen model being a Rich Bich Perfect 10 (like Joe Perry—see below—he used only six strings). The company embraced this link, with such neat touches as coffin-shaped flight cases. **TB**

"The thing screams," Aerosmith's Joe Perry enthused. "I used the Rich Bich on 'I Wanna Know Why' (from 1977's *Draw The Line*, left)." Perry removed the extra four high strings: "[It] felt so good and sounded so good that it seemed ridiculous to have extra strings there."

B.C. Rich
Eagle 1976

Type Solidbody electric
Body & neck Maple, koa, and maple combinations
Fingerboard Rosewood
Pick-ups Two DiMarzio (PAF and Dual Sound) pick-ups

Bernie Rico's B.C. Rich Guitars started in Los Angeles in the early 1970s. The Eagle, launched in 1976, is probably the most traditionally shaped of all the B.C. Rich guitars. The Eagles built at this time were entirely handmade and are unquestionably superb.

B.C. Rich offered what was effectively one of the first custom shops—a place where musicians could specify different options for their guitars—so the Eagle came in many variations. Standard, however, was the complete neck-through-body design, with body "wings" glued on either side. As the Leo Quan

"I was playing a B.C. Rich Eagle through late-'60s Marshall heads (in Alice Cooper's band). Mine was one of the first Eagles ever made."

DICK WAGNER

"Badass" combined bridge/tailpiece was mounted on the center/neck section, sustain on the Eagle was excellent. The center/neck was constructed either of maple, with strips of koa and maple, or vice versa.

There were two models: the Standard, which featured an unbound fingerboard with diamond mother-of-pearl inlays, and the Supreme, featuring a bound fingerboard and "'cloud" inlays. The woods used on the Supremes tended to be more exotic. Two DiMarzio pick-ups were fitted to the Eagle: a PAF at the neck and a Dual Sound at the bridge, all powered by on-board active electronics. Switching options included booster volume, phase, and series/parallel switching, and a Varitone "wah" filter. Celebrity players included Aerosmith's Brad Whitford. **JB**

Burns UK
Mirage 1976

Type Solidbody electric
Body & neck Alder body, maple neck
Fingerboard Maple
Pick-ups Two Mach 1 Humbuster pick-ups

With one of the strangest-shaped bodies of any production guitar, the Mirage was a final, and ultimately ill-fated, attempt to salvage the commercial fortunes of Burns UK.

The big secret of the Mirage's design—there was no sci-fi, drugs, or enormous inspiration behind it— was simply the transposition of the body of its predecessor, the Flyte, through 180 degrees. Burns UK just attached the neck where the endpin had formerly been situated.

That was the instrument's most readily apparent selling point, but closer examination revealed that it was not the only one. Apart from the body rotation, the guitar had two Mach 1 Burns Humbuster pick-ups, a three-way selector switch, two volume and two tone controls, and a "phase switch," which put the two pick-ups out of phase to create a brighter hollow tone. It came with Schaller tuners, a three-way adjustable bridge, and a steel adjustable truss rod in the neck. The headstock was an exotic design using three-a-side offset tuners and three string-trees.

The Mirage, which Burns claimed was perfectly balanced for playing, was available in a wide range of striking color schemes, including metallic shades and colored fingerboards. The successor to the Flyte didn't last long, however. Within a year, Burns UK had folded, and the Mirage disappeared with it.

The guitar shown here was owned by Black Lace, the British band that had a series of novelty pop hits in the late 1970s and early 1980s, including "Agadoo" and "Do The Conga." It is now owned by UK guitar collector Guy Mackenzie. **SH**

Fender
Starcaster 1976

Type Twin cutaway semi-solidbody electric
Body & neck Maple with three-bolt maple neck
Fingerboard Maple
Pick-ups Two Fender Wide Range humbucker pick-ups

By the mid-1970s, the quality of Fender's guitars was in decline, but Strat and Tele designs still dominated the solidbody guitar world. The Starcaster was Fender's second attempt to challenge Gibson's ES-335 as the semi-solid electric market leader. Roger Rossmeisl's Thinline Telecaster, introduced in 1969, had found its own niche, continuing in production in relatively small numbers throughout the 1970s, but it was not the strong competitor that Fender had sought.

Designed in 1975 by Gene Fields, the Starcaster was intended as a high-end semi-acoustic instrument. Yet, unlike Gibson's "semis" that featured neck joints set in the bodies, the Starcaster retained Fender's bolt-on technique—at that time using a three-screw joint. Its pick-ups—Wide Range humbuckers, designed by Seth Lover in the 1960s—were capable of an unusually broad range of sounds. The Starcaster's most curious design feature is the headstock, with its painted lower edge; the asymmetric offset-waist body is also unusual in non-solidbody instruments.

In retrospect, Fender's treatment of the Starcaster seems half-hearted; it debuted in 1976 to little fanfare, and remained in production for only six years. Indeed, the Starcaster would be viewed as little more than a footnote in guitar history were it not for its revival in the 1990s by Radiohead's Jonny Greenwood. **TB**

Dave Keuning of The Killers uses a Starcaster in the video for "Read My Mind," from their 2006 album *Sam's Town*. "A friend in Vegas had one," he recalled. "I played it and it sounded great. I had to have it shipped in from Japan. I love it. I used it a lot on *Sam's Town*."

The Starcaster was salvaged from obscurity by Radiohead's Jonny Greenwood. ➔

Gibson Les Paul Deluxe "#5" 1976

Type Solidbody electric
Body & neck Mahogany/maple body, set mahogany neck
Fingerboard Rosewood
Pick-ups Two Gibson mini-humbucker pick-ups

Until the early 1970s, Pete Townshend was an avid fan of the Gibson SG Special—a number of which were badly damaged during the violent climaxes of The Who's concerts. When that model was discontinued, he looked elsewhere. And, as The Who's music was becoming increasingly "heavy," he needed a different tool for the job. He needed a Les Paul.

The star plumped for the rather unfashionable Les Paul Deluxe, with various modifications. From 1976, this entailed putting a powerful DiMarzio humbucker between the two Gibson Minis.

Townshend needed particular set-ups for specific numbers, often using a capo in different places on the neck so he could play powerful open-string chords in different keys. He ended up with as many as nine different Les Pauls on stage—in order that his tech knew which to give him, each had a large number stuck to its body. Shown here is #5: a customized "Wine Red" Deluxe, serial number 00129875.

Until 1979, Townshend could—in Pearl Jam singer and Who fan Eddie Vedder's words—often be seen "leaping into the rafters wielding a 1970s Gibson Les Paul, which happens to be a stunningly heavy guitar." Thereafter, however, he fell for Dave Schecter's high-performance custom shop Telecaster-style guitars.

Of the nine numbered guitars, only #8 remains in Townshend's possession—although #1, displayed at the Hard Rock Café in Dallas, Texas, does still belong to him. #4 was smashed in 1976 in Toronto and never replaced. The others are either lost or in private collections. From 1998–2007, #5 was displayed at the Rock and Roll Hall of Fame in Cleveland, Ohio. **TB**

← Townshend rocks California's Oakland Coliseum in October 1976.

Gibson
Les Paul 1976

Type Solidbody electric
Body & neck Mahogany/maple body, set maple neck
Fingerboard Ebony and rosewood
Pick-ups Two Super humbucker pick-ups

Accounts vary as to what prompted Gibson to ask its luthiers to create the ultimate limited-edition Les Paul series. Speculation ranges from a 1974 prototype commemorating the eighty years since Orville Gibson began selling instruments, to a model in honor of the U.S. Bicentennial in 1976. What is clear, however, is that they built one of the most lavishly finished guitars ever to emerge from the Kalamazoo factory.

To start, they used extraordinary quality flame maple over a mahogany body. Then they made a maple neck with a fingerboard of alternating strips of rosewood and ebony. Almost everything else was made of rosewood—including body binding, pickguard, cavity covers, pick-up surrounds, and even control knobs, which were carved by hand.

The hardware was gold-plated, the block inlays were abalone, and there was an engraved ebony-and-rosewood truss-rod cover. An abalone plate behind the headstock showed each guitar's number and date of production. The quality of wood meant the guitar sounded brighter and richer than a normal Les Paul.

Model No. 1 was given to Les Paul. He played it at the 1976 Grammys, where he won an award for *Chester And Lester* (1976), made with Chet Atkins.

With a price tag of more than four times that of a Les Paul Standard, however, the Les Pauls were more likely heading for collectors than working musicians. When the models appear at auction today, they command five-figure prices. Most are immaculate: they've hardly been played because of their value, their heritage, and their weight—some tipped the scales at 15 lbs (6.8 kg). **SH**

Godwin
Organ 1976

Type Hollow body electric
Body & neck Laminated hardwood body, maple neck
Fingerboard Rosewood
Pick-ups Two single-coil pick-ups

Godwin was not the first firm to offer a guitar organ, but by most accounts it offered the best. The question of whether the instrument was aimed at organists interested in guitars, guitarists interested in organs, or musicians of both types is beside the point. The point is that, like the guitar organs from Vox and Musiconics, the Godwin Organ never caught on.

Still, nearly everyone who has strapped on one of these behemoths marvels at the sonic similarity to a Hammond B3, particularly when the Godwin is run through a Leslie speaker. As with other organ guitars, each fret is divided into six sections. When a string is depressed, a signal is sent to a dedicated circuit inside the body's large rectangular chamber, generating the appropriate note. The volume is pedal-controlled.

Thirteen knobs serve the same function as an organ's drawbars, manipulating pitch, and, when used in combination, the tone of the note being played. As with an organ, the Godwin's knobs can be operated in real time. As if the prospect of choosing from thirteen knobs in midsong isn't daunting enough, the Godwin also features nineteen switches to help conjure other organ qualities, including percussion, sustain, and tremolo. If this all seems vaguely accordionlike, consider that Godwin was owned by the Italian firm Sisme, and that Italian electric guitars often seemed to take inspiration from accordions, albeit not quite to this degree.

If this all seems a bit much, Godwin also offered a model with only four knobs and sixteen switches. Alternatively, you could simply plug in and, thanks to two pick-ups, play it like a normal guitar. **DP**

John Birch
AJS Custom 1976

Type Solidbody electric
Body & neck Maple body and neck
Fingerboard Ebony
Pick-ups Two John Birch single-coil pick-ups

"The Bat" is a design by English luthier John Birch, also known as "the father of custom guitars in the United Kingdom." He founded his company, with John Diggins and Arthur Baker, in Birmingham in the early 1970s—just in time to cater to the tastes of some of the more flamboyant members of the Midlands musical community at the height of glam rock. Readers of the right age and nationality to have been watching *Top Of The Pops* in the 1970s are likely to remember some of the more idiosyncratic John Birch custom guitars of the period: the star-shaped model he built for Gerry Shephard of The Glitter Band, the heart (with Cupid's arrow) built for Rob Davies of Mud, and the "spade" that Roy Wood played in Wizzard.

Dave Hill of Slade owned several John Birch guitars including the J2 model and probably the most "1970s" guitar design of all time: the Superyob (although, according to Hill, it was horrible to play). He also owned the second of only four "Bat" guitars that John Birch manufactured, having been impressed when he saw the first one. Hill's "Bat" was plain white rather than cream and was unfortunately stolen before he ever gigged with it. It never resurfaced.

The earliest John Birch guitars were inspired by Gibson designs, such as the modified SG it created for Tony Iommi of Black Sabbath in 1975—it's possible to see how the inspiration for the Bat might have come from that direction. And, if nothing else, it's more tasteful than either the Hallmark "Wing-Bat" guitar or the "Bat-i-tone" baritone guitar. Such is its rarity, however, than even the John Birch company's website makes no reference to it. **AJ**

Kramer
450G 1976

Type Solidbody electric
Body & neck Walnut and maple body, aluminum neck
Fingerboard Ebonol
Pick-ups Two humbucker pick-ups

Travis Bean—with his partners Marc McElwee and Gary Kramer—pioneered the mass production of aluminum-necked guitars in 1974. Built to an extremely high specification, Travis Beans created a great deal of interest in the music world. They were built using a straight-through aluminum neck to which the bridge and pick-ups were attached— wooden "wings" were also added. But while everyone loved their sound and sustain, the aluminum was heavy and responded poorly to temperature change, which could cause tuning difficulties.

> "We loved Mercedes Benz, so we thought why not name the first guitar the 450G, after the 450 SL Mercedes."
>
> GARY KRAMER

In 1976, Gary Kramer left Travis Bean to form a new company with Dennis Berardi and luthier Phil Petillo. Still pursuing the aluminum dream, an alternative was created that would be lighter and sufficiently distinct to not infringe Bean's patent. This was achieved with a T-shaped piece of aluminum, with maple or walnut inserts secured with an epoxy resin. It was lighter yet retained the wood feel of a regular guitar neck.

The first guitars to come out of the workshop in New Jersey were the 450Gs and cheaper 350Gs. The 450 had a walnut body with a pair of maple strips down the center. It featured a pair of humbuckers with a three-way selector switch, and dedicated volume and tone controls for each one. These highly regarded early models are very collectable. **TB**

Kramer
650G 1976

Type Solidbody electric
Body & neck Maple/walnut body, aluminum neck
Fingerboard Ebonol
Pick-ups Two humbucker pick-ups

The 650 series guitars and basses were the flagship models of Kramer's "aluminum era." They had all of the characteristic features of the brand, such as the distinctive "tuning fork" headstock that housed a pair of tuners on each side. The fingerboard was also noteworthy, created from a man-made material called "Ebonol"; almost unbreakably strong, it was the same material used in the manufacture of bowling balls. The bodies differed slightly from the earlier 450, taking on a more symmetrical shape. The body was a thick slab of bird's-eye maple with walnut "wings." The body was finished with a routed edging not dissimilar to a "German carve."

There was a general perception that the aluminum Kramers were better suited to the needs of the bass player than the guitarist, which may be down to bassists being more accustomed to playing heavier instruments. Or perhaps, that as a breed, they are more willing to experiment—a glance at models produced at the top end of the bass market certainly suggests that this might well be the case. But there's no doubting that the levels of sustain and tone offered by Kramer and Travis Bean guitars was particularly well suited to bass.

In 1981, Kramer built its first models with wooden necks and the expensive aluminum models were phased out. After pioneering the Superstrat with huge success, Kramer fell foul of the economic turbulence of the early 1990s and the New Jersey firm ceased trading in 1991. The Kramer brand name eventually found itself under the wing of the mighty Gibson Corporation. Once serving the top end of the guitar market, modern-day Kramers are resolutely affordable. **TB**

A Kramer 650B bass guitar sees action with The Boomtown Rats in the late 1970s.

MusicMan
StingRay 1976

Type Solidbody electric bass
Body & neck Ash body, maple neck
Fingerboard Rosewood
Pick-ups One or two humbucker pick-ups

For those proclaiming that Fender guitars were now a shadow of what they once were, the MusicMan brand must have seemed like a godsend. Long-serving employees like Forrest White and Tom Walker found life tough under corporate ownership and, in 1971, left to form a new brand with none other than Leo Fender. With four years left on a contractual clause preventing Fender from working on rival guitars, it was not until 1975 that he was able to produce instruments with his colleagues under the MusicMan banner. Inevitably, the early MusicMan instruments drew on Fender's illustrious heritage but with interesting new twists.

Visually reminiscent of Fender's pioneering Precision bass, the StingRay—designed by Fender, Walker, and Sterling Ball—featured innovative technology. A soap-bar humbucking pick-up was set close to the bridge and controlled by an active preamp powered by a nine-volt battery; this is widely considered to have been the first production guitar to feature such active circuitry. Later innovations included an optional piezo pick-up built into the bridge.

Like other MusicMan instruments, the StingRay also featured an asymmetric tuner arrangement— here, the "3 + 1" design where the G-string tuner is fitted to the underside of the headstock. **TB**

The StingRay may be heard on recordings by bands as diverse as Queen, Rage Against The Machine, Radiohead, Journey, and the Red Hot Chili Peppers. Played by Bernard Edwards, it features prominently on *Magnifique: The Very Best Of Chic* (2011).

← Bernard Edwards of Chic—purveyor of the hottest bass lines of the disco era.

PRS
Peter Frampton 1976

Type Solidbody electric
Body & neck Mahogany body, set neck
Fingerboard Rosewood with bird-shaped inlays
Pick-ups Two P-90-style single-coil pick-ups

Born in 1956, Paul Reed Smith started playing the guitar at age fourteen. He made his first instrument—an electric bass—in high school around 1972. But there was little to indicate that he would become the most famous guitar maker of modern times.

The pictured Peter Frampton guitar was only the tenth instrument Smith had built. By 1976, he had already been repairing instruments and showing up at Washington-area venues to pitch for commissions from rock stars—Ted Nugent was an early taker. When Smith showed the guitar he had made for Nugent to former Humbie Pie man Peter Frampton—in the process of becoming a household name in the United States, thanks to *Frampton Comes Alive!* (1976)—the guitarist ordered one for himself. This all-mahogany model, based on the double-cut Gibson Les Paul Special, had a carved top featuring the bird-shaped inlays that were to become synonymous with Smith's guitars when he formed a production company in 1985.

Smith charged Frampton $500 (it would be worth considerably more if sold today!) for the handmade instrument, which still plays beautifully and typifies the all-mahogany/P-90 growl that had influenced Smith's earlier work. The guitar-maker himself later worked with a more enduring six-string supremo: Carlos Santana (see page 536). **DB**

Backstage at a Santana/Return To Forever gig in 1976, an affable roadie said he'd show the guitar to Santana. First he showed it to Return To Forever's guitarist Al Di Meola, who ordered an electric twelve-string that he'd use on the title cut of his solo album *Elegant Gypsy* (1977).

SD Curlee
Aspen AE-700 1976

Type Solidbody electric
Body & neck Mahogany body, maple neck
Fingerboard Maple
Pick-ups One DiMarzio humbucker/single-coil pick-up

Randy Curlee owned a music shop in the Midwest and wanted to market his own guitars. He joined with luthier Randy Dritz and woodworker Sonny Storbeck to start producing SD Curlee instruments in 1975. At first, the operation was homespun. The brass hardware was cast in the back of a farmer's barn; the tuners in particular proved troublesome. Many were even changed in the shops before they were sold.

Soon Curlee licensed the making of many of his instruments to Korea and Japan (the Aspen was made by Hondo). This was one of the first instances of U.S.

"Very cool in a 1970s way, it reminds me of some one-night stand between a Les Paul Jr, B.C. Rich, and a Travis Bean."
ADVERTISING FOR ASPEN

guitar manufacturers enlisting Asian factories to produce cheaper versions of their own guitars.

Japanese models, made by Matsumoku, were sold mainly in Asia, but Hondos were also sold in the United States and Britain. Some models were branded as the SD Curlee Design Series, others as SD Curlee International.

The Aspens had similar features to the U.S.-made Curlees. The thick maple neck ran three-quarters of the way through the center of the mahogany body, where it was fixed in place with a big brass plate. The six-string models were fitted with two DiMarzio high-output pick-ups that screwed directly into this neck extension. Other features included a fixed Strat-style hardtail bridge and a two-volume-one-tone control set-up. **SH**

Shergold
Marathon Bass 1976

Type Electric bass
Body & neck Obeche body, maple neck
Fingerboard Maple
Pick-ups One split humbucker pick-up

Shergold Woodcrafts was founded in 1967 in London, England, by two former employees of Jim Burns. Jack Golder and Norman Houlder set up shop primarily to produce woodwork for other guitar companies. In 1969, they began designing and providing woodwork for the new Hayman company; when that firm collapsed in 1974, they opted to continue themselves.

Much of the Shergold line is derived directly from four original Hayman designs. One interesting aspect of Shergolds is the uncommon use of obeche wood for the bodies. A mighty tree found in parts of West Africa—up to 164 feet (50 m) high and 5 feet (1.5 m) in diameter—the obeche produces a light hardwood. Its appeal as a raw material is that it can be dried quickly and is easy to work, although it isn't the strongest wood. Its relatively light weight does mean that, for some, Shergolds are problematic to balance.

The Shergold Marathon bass evolved from the Hayman 4040, and was made available in a wide variety of string configurations. In addition to fretted and fretless four-string versions, there were the more unusual—for the time—six- and eight-string versions. The electrics were also noteworthy; the single-humbucking pick-up was wired to a two-channel output socket, so the bass could be recorded in a rudimentary type of stereo. **TB**

Shergold's most celebrated user was Genesis bassist Mike Rutherford. "I tried a Shergold 12-string in a shop, and I liked it very much," he recalled in 1977. "So I said, 'Do you make basses?'" He used some of Shergold's arsenal on his solo album *Smallcreep's Day* (1980).

Shergold
Modulator 1976

Type Solidbody electric
Body & neck Obeche body, maple neck
Fingerboard Maple
Pick-ups Two humbucker pick-ups

If we were looking for a single word to describe London-based Shergold guitars it could perhaps be "quirky." The models had a certain inelegant look that some thought downright ugly. But they were affordable—nearly a third cheaper than a Fender Strat —and, during the second half of the 1970s, were a popular choice for young players graduating from Japanese Top Twenty copies. And these were good professional instruments: well-constructed, capable of a nice selection of tones, and comfortable to play.

Shergold guitars also offered a variety of unusual features, such as split pick-ups providing an optional "stereo" output between the bottom and top two strings. But the most innovative idea came in the form of the Modulator. A few years earlier, Ampeg had offered Dan Armstrong models featuring detachable pick-ups. The Shergold Modulator, however, was a guitar that featured a slot-in control panel.

Modulators—whether bass or six-string models —were routinely sold with Module 1, a basic Telecaster-style panel with master volume and tone controls and a three-way pick-up selector. Seven other modules could be bought separately. To get more tonal variety out of the Shergold humbuckers, Module 2 offered a variety of coil-tap phase switching. The quirkiest, though, was the Model 7, which gave the option of four separate outputs; one from each coil in each pick-up (this module was advertised but may not have actually gone into production).

However, noted Shergold's best-known player, Mike Rutherford of Genesis, "The best thing about them is not the modular idea but the sound." **TB**

Yamaha
SG2000 1976

Type Solidbody electric
Body & neck Maple and mahogany body, maple neck
Fingerboard Rosewood
Pick-ups Two Alnico V humbucker pick-ups

After its first Flying Samurai models appeared in the mid-1960s, Yamaha won a name for well-made electric guitars at reasonable prices. Yet in spite of the fine Yamaha and Ibanez guitars being produced in Japan, the general reputation of instruments produced in the Far East was tarnished by barely playable plywood "knock-offs" that flooded into the West to meet growing demand.

By the mid-1970s, the big American names were having problems of their own; Fender, Gibson, and Gretsch all suffered from corporate takeovers. Yamaha saw an opportunity to make a bold statement, and approached Carlos Santana to endorse a Japanese-built instrument intended to match the best of the West. That instrument was the SG2000.

OK, it wasn't a radical reinvention of the electric guitar. Indeed, its double cutaway body strongly resembled a similarly named classic Gibson. However, this was a deluxe instrument, with such features as a straight-through neck, gold-plated hardware, opulent binding, and the radical "T-Cross" neck construction.

Santana—one of the most highly regarded guitar heroes of the period—used the SG2000 extensively in the studio and on stage, proving once and for all that the construction of high-end electric guitars was not the exclusive preserve of North Americans. **TB**

Several tracks on *Moonflower* (1977)— Santana's platinum-certified, twenty-one-track double album of live and studio recordings—feature band leader Carlos Santana showcasing the full range of the Yamaha SG2000's amazing capabilities.

Carlos Santana and his SG2000, rocking London's Hammersmith Odeon in 1976. →

Epiphone
Scroll 350 1977

Gretsch
7629 Committee 1977

Type Solidbody electric
Body & neck Mahogany body, bolt-on mahogany neck
Fingerboard Rosewood, dot inlays
Pick-ups Two humbucker pick-ups

Type Solidbody electric
Body & neck Walnut body and neck
Fingerboard Rosewood
Pick-ups Two humbucker pick-ups

Epiphone originated in Turkey in the 1870s. It started making guitars in the United States in the 1920s, and by the end of the 1930s it had become a major rival to Gibson, which eventually purchased the brand in 1957. In 1969, Gibson was purchased by Norlin, and by the early 1970s Epiphones were being manufactured in Japan. By the end of that decade, however, Epiphone's star had waned.

The Scroll models were based on a Les Paul-style body, but, instead of a bass-side upper shoulder, there was a hooked, scroll-like horn. In many ways, it was typical of the rather awkward Japanese designs of the period—the controls (volume and tone) were too close to the Tune-o-matic bridge and stud tailpiece, and although the design looked to follow Gibson's set-neck principles, the SC350 was in fact a bolt-on.

Along with the SC350 was the more upmarket maple SC450, with a rosewood fingerboard and dot inlays, and the SC550 with ebony fingerboard and block inlays. **DB**

From Gretsch's Baldwin era, the Committee was made between 1977 and 1981 and is now quite rare. The sales promo literature claimed it was "designed by a committee of experts," a boast that was widely and predictably derided. In truth, the construction, sound, and aesthetics were far removed from the iconic Gretsches of old. The Committee was a rock-ready ax casting jealous glances over its contoured shoulders toward Gibson's SG. It used Gretsch's shorter-than-Gibson 24½-in. (62.25-cm) scale length, with a twenty-two-fret neck joining at the eighteenth fret. The 7629 was a low-end sibling with a close family resemblance.

Sturdy and workmanlike rather than stylish and inspirational, the Committee's main selling points were thru-body construction and a thru-body-strung "Terminator" bridge coupling that was meant to deliver unrivaled sustain at its price point. Reasonably priced in today's market due to its unfancied status, the Committee remains a fuss-free "players' guitar" that will see you through many a night on stage. **OB**

Gretsch
7625 TK-300 1977

Gretsch
7681 Super Axe 2 1977

Type Solidbody electric
Body & neck Maple body and neck
Fingerboard Rosewood
Pick-ups Two humbucker pick-ups

Type Single cutaway solidbody electric
Body & neck Maple body and neck
Fingerboard Ebony
Pick-ups Two DiMarzio humbucker pick-ups

There are many reasons why the 1970s was a terrible decade . . . and for some people, the Gretsch TK-300 might be one of them!

It was hailed as a "brand new solidbody electric guitar within everybody's price range." Described as a "workhorse guitar," the word "rock" was significantly mentioned several times throughout the advertising. It was clear that this instrument was not being pitched at Gretsch's usual market.

Priced at less than $300, the TK-300 had, to quote Gretsch, a "unique" look: a curiously angular body with an unusually large, offset headstock featuring six-in-a-line tuners. It also boasted a pair of powerful humbucker pick-ups, and what Gretsch called a "Terminator" bridge. The electrics were rudimentary, with a single volume and tone control fitted to a rather unsightly scratchplate.

Traditionalist Gretsch players saw the TK-300 as a low point in the company's history; yet fans describe it as an undervalued classic of the 1970s. **JB**

In the days before the brand vanished for several years in 1980, Gretsch went out on a Gibsonesque limb. The Super Axe was a well-appointed model sporting a punchy pair of DiMarzio humbucker pick-ups. Crucially, it also boasted a phaser module that—in the words of Gretsch's excitable marketeers—"produces the greatest sound variations you'll ever hear" and a compressor that "squeezes the tone and feeds it out for an infinite tonal response and sustain."

Gretsch hoped to appropriate a slice of the rock market (the body shape represented a nod to the Les Paul), and the brand's endorser supreme Chet Atkins declared it "the ultimate guitar for the rock musician." Sadly, most rock musicians—with a few exceptions, including Rick Springfield, who clutches one on the cover of his *We Are The '80s* album (1980), and John Entwistle (whose sunburst model was auctioned in 2003)—stuck to what they knew. Gretsch aficionados now regard the Super Axe with a sheepish affection that may be familiar to Rick Springfield fans. **BM**

Hamer
Standard Sunburst 1977

Type Solid electric double cutaway
Body & neck Mahogany body and neck, maple top
Fingerboard Rosewood
Pick-ups Two DiMarzio PAF humbucker pick-ups

After building its first guitar, the ultra-expensive hand-made Standard, Hamer produced only about 75 instruments in the following two years. The U.S. company needed a more affordable model—so the Sunburst was launched.

This was no cheap budget guitar though—the Sunburst was still a high-end instrument with a one-piece mahogany neck and a one-piece mahogany body with a curly maple top. Its attractive features included through-body stringing, a fixed bridge (sitting on a rosewood shim), Grover machine heads, and two DiMarzio humbucker pick-ups. True to its name, the double cutaway body was at first available only in a cherry-red sunburst finish.

The Sunburst soon established itself and was a great success. Within three years, 1,500 had been sold. The design of the guitar evolved, with a three-piece mahogany neck for greater stability, improved Schaller tuners and, strangely, a variety of non-sunburst finishes. So many were sold that Hamer was able to move to a bigger factory.

Sunburst sales really took off when professionals started appearing with it. Famous users included Rick Nielsen of Cheap Trick, Ian Anderson and Martin Barre of Jethro Tull, Andy Summers of The Police, and Dave Edmunds and Billy Bremner of Rockpile. **SH**

The Police's Andy Summers (bottom right) used a variety of Hamer guitars. The Standard Sunburst featured on several tracks on the album *Zenyattà Mondatta* (1980), as well as on stage during the band's Ghost in the Machine World Tour of 1981–82.

Odyssey
G100TS 1977

Type Solidbody electric
Body & neck Mahogany body, maple/mahogany neck
Fingerboard Ebony
Pick-ups Two DiMarzio humbucker pick-ups

The Odyssey brand was born when Canadian retailer Iron Music joined forces with Hungarian émigré Attila Balogh, who ran a small repair business nearby. Rarely seen outside North America, Odysseys were what we now term "boutique" guitars: made to a high specification; with high-end production techniques such as straight-though necks and brass hardware— also used in the nifty little headstock logo; and a variety of classy natural finishes. They were serious guitars with prices to match, up in Les Paul territory.

From a small industrial park in North Vancouver, Balogh and co-founder Ken Lindemere built their range of guitars and basses with a workforce numbering no more than six. The G100 series featured mahogany body halves with a carved and bound maple top. The necks were maple and mahogany veneers, topped with a 24-fret fingerboard cut from ebony with abalone dots. Most of the fittings were made at the factory, including the knobs and buttons machined from solid brass. The sound came from a pair of DiMarzio humbuckers.

Although Balogh is often credited for much of the design and craftsmanship, Lindemere maintains that Odyssey guitars were very much a collaboration: "I've seen the occasional Odyssey on the internet claiming to have been handmade by Attila. Bullshit! All the instruments were produced with several people, each doing their part in the production."

In the end, the Odyssey brand struggled to establish itself. Lindemere sold his share in 1980 and two years later—following Balogh's death—the last guitars were produced. **TB**

Roland
GS500 1977

Type Solidbody electric with external synthesizer unit
Body & neck Mahogany body, maple top, maple neck
Fingerboard Rosewood
Pick-ups One humbucker pick-up

The idea of using a guitar to control electronic keyboard sounds was not a new one; more than ten years before Roland unleashed the mighty pairing of the GS500 guitar and GR500 synthesizer, Vox had attempted to compress the gadgetry from one of its Continental organs into the body of a Phantom guitar. It worked well enough, but with one overwhelming problem: few people actually seemed to want a guitar that could sound like an organ. By 1977, the musical landscape had changed and synthesizers had evolved from complex monstrosities into compact units commonly seen in rock bands. So perhaps the time was right to revisit the idea.

Founded in 1972, Japanese electronics giant Roland established itself as a company intent on bringing innovative electronics to the masses. Five years later it produced the first guitar-synthesizer. Making no attempt to create a single instrument, the Roland system comprised two parts: the GS500 was a decent, if unremarkable, Ibanez-built guitar; the GR500 was an external synthesizer that connected to the guitar via a twenty-four-way cable, enabling the knobs on the guitar to control the synthesizer.

At the heart of the system was a divided pick-up that could accurately convert the vibration of each string individually into the control voltage data needed to drive the synthesizer.

The GR/GS500 proved far too difficult to use for any but the geekiest of guitarists, so it was not hugely popular. Nevertheless, those who embraced its complexity still rate it as one of the most versatile attempts to fuse the two instruments. **TB**

Univox
Hi Flyer 1977

Type Solidbody electric
Body & neck Poplar body, bolt-on neck
Fingerboard Maple
Pick-ups Two humbucker pick-ups

Blame The Ventures. Being instrumentalists, the U.S. band achieved the kind of international popularity that few singing groups ever attain abroad. In 1962, they became one of the first American rock 'n' roll outfits to tour Japan, where they were welcomed with an adoration that bordered on fanaticism. Being Mosrite endorsers throughout most of the 1960s, they were thus principally responsible for the Mosrite mania that influenced Japanese guitar design for many years.

Every major Japanese guitar producer, from Guyatone to Teisco, produced Mosrite copies to meet the insatiable demand of emerging Japanese "eleki" bands. Toward the end of the 1960s, Matsumoku got in on the act, too: its Hi-Flyer, made for Merson/ Unicord, was introduced in 1968.

Significantly cheaper than the guitar that inspired it, the Hi-Flyer remained in production for a decade. The styling updates that occurred over the period are divided into four phases. The Phase I Hi-Flyer had a three-tone sunburst finish, a pearloid pickguard, and a truss rod cover. Phase II added two further choices to the finish—black and white—and changed the pickguard to a plain white, three-layered version. Phase III, introduced in 1974, added "Natural" to the choice of finishes, and replaced the original single-coil pick-ups with twin humbuckers.

The illustrated example is a typical Phase IV Hi-Flyer, featuring a hardtail and a classic natural finish. A year after this model came onto the market, the parent company, Unicord, phased out the Univox brand in favor of a new line called Westbury. **EP**

Van Halen "Frankenstrat" 1977

Type Solidbody electric
Body & neck Ash body, maple neck
Fingerboard Maple
Pick-ups One Gibson PAF humbucker pick-up

The "Frankenstrat" was devised by Eddie Van Halen because he liked the shape of a Fender Stratocaster but wanted it to sound like a Gibson.

The body and neck were made by the Boogie Body company who supply parts for DIY guitar makers —the body was purportedly discounted to $50 because there was a knothole in it. The PAF humbucker was taken out of Van Halen's Gibson ES-335, "rewound to my specifications," and mounted at an angle to compensate for the smaller string spacing of the bridge, which was the Fender tremolo

> "I see so many people who have these space-age guitars… Give me one knob, that's it. It's simple and it sounds cool."
>
> EDDIE VAN HALEN

system from his 1958 Stratocaster. The electronics consisted of one pick-up, two knobs for volume and tone, and an output jack. The wiring was covered by part of an old vinyl record that had been cut to shape. Finally, it was painted black and white using masking tape to create stripes at random angles.

Van Halen continued to mess with it in ensuing years: replacing the neck several times, changing the bridge to a Floyd Rose, and adding a layer of red paint. He also added a neck pick-up and a three-way switch —neither of which actually did anything but were there just to throw imitators off the scent.

He eventually retired the original guitar in order to "show it some respect and let it survive." However, he has played replicas on tours as late as 2012. **AJ**

Aelita
Electric Guitar 1978

Type Solidbody electric
Body & neck Veneered hardwood body, beech neck
Fingerboard Beech
Pick-ups Three single-coil pick-ups

Named after the heroine of the celebrated Russian science-fiction novel, *Aelita: Queen Of Mars*, by Alexei Tolstoy (1883–1945), and the 1924 film of the same title, directed by Yakov Protazanov (1881–1945), one of the founding fathers of Soviet cinema, this guitar was introduced by the Rostov-on-Don musical instrument factory in the mid-1970s.

The name was chosen to reflect the themes of space travel and science fiction—basically everything futuristic, as a reflection of the image of the electric guitar at the time. For much the same reason, a later Rostov model was called Stella ("star"). Similar space-age nomenclature was a worldwide trend, of course, from Japanese brands such as the Astrotone and the Galaxy, to the early Jolana Star models. Even the Fender Stratocaster alluded to outer space. But in the communist Soviet Union, the electric guitar was still a vision of cutting-edge modernism for many people well into the 1970s, long after it became taken for granted as an everyday object in the West. It was, after all, only just over twenty-five years since jazz had first been allowed in the Soviet Union—under Stalin, it had been banned as a decadent, Western practice.

Today, of course, the Aelita appears rather retro-futuristic, with its sparkly pickguard, and numerous push-button controls. However, several of its visible components, which are obviously based on outmoded Japanese designs of the 1960s, make it appear simply old-fashioned. Yet for all its limitations, the Aelita retains its aura as an object of desire rather well: what fan of cheesy guitars would deny this beauty a prized spot in his or her collection? **EP**

Aria Pro II SB-1000 Bass 1978

Type Solidbody electric
Body & neck Ash body, maple/walnut neck
Fingerboard Ebony
Pick-ups One double-coil pick-up

It was a radical design that kick-started the iconic bass sound of the 1980s. The Aria Pro II SB ("Super Bass") 1000 was the first high-quality Japanese bass to arrive on the market, and it was soon adopted by leading players including Jack Bruce (ex-Cream), Cliff Burton (Metallica), and John Taylor (Duran Duran).

An important part of the new Aria's secret was the single MB-1 double-coil pick-up, which was boosted by an eighteen-volt preamp. This was Aria's "BB Noisekiller Circuit"—its first active pick-up system. The Aria also included a coil tap switch and six-position tone switch to give players unprecedented versatility.

The basics were good too: a Canadian ash body in plain sight, not hidden away beneath a paint job, and a rigid neck-through construction for sustain. The strip of lighter neck wood created a stripe right down the natural wood body, a style that became much imitated. Of course, it helped that the SB-1000 had a beautifully finished five-ply maple-and-walnut neck with a 34-in. (86.4-cm) scale and twenty-four frets.

Other details included a heavy brass bridge, a brass nut, brass covers on the access cavity on the back of the bass, and closed-back Gotoh tuners.

Others bassists soon followed—among them Sting and Trevor Horne—and the SB-1000's brighter, fuller sound became THE bass of the era. **SH**

Metallica bassist Cliff Burton played an Aria Pro II SB-1000 and is likely to have used it on their 1986 breakthrough, *Master Of Puppets*. Tragically, he was killed in a bus crash later that year—but, two decades later, Aria launched a Cliff Burton signature model SB1000.

Armstrong "Cornflake" 1978

Type Electric guitar
Body & neck Cornflakes packet body, Perspex neck
Fingerboard Rosewood
Pick-ups Two humbucker pick-ups

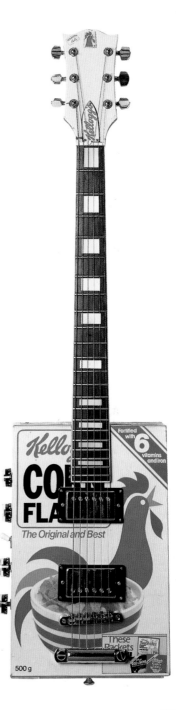

Rob Armstrong began producing beautiful acoustic guitars in the garden shed at his home in Coventry, England, in the early 1970s. He estimates that he has since produced more than 700 instruments, always by hand, and, when using wood, never with anything less than twenty-five years old. Among the leading musicians who have played his creations are George Harrison, Gordon Giltrap, Alvin Lee, and Bert Jansch.

This quirky electric proved a real wake-up call for other novelty guitar makers. Armstrong said: "It just came to me, as ideas do, who knows where they come from? I managed to get a pristine packet, and made a wooden box that fitted inside it, then I covered the outside with Perspex to protect it . . . all the attention for something that silly!"

It was sold to Fairport Convention's Simon Nicol, who used it on the BBC's *Old Grey Whistle Test*, and it continued life on the road with Nicol's son.

Armstrong's other custom creations include the Pudsey Bear acoustic guitar for the BBC's Children In Need charity, a British Legion Poppy guitar, and a steel-string acoustic made from polystyrene. Giltrap's *Echoes Of Heaven* (2011) featured Armstrong's Secret Valentine hybrid polymer guitar. Armstrong has also experimented with fiberglass, flax, linen, and other unorthodox synthetic materials.

Master Craftsmen (2002) is a fourteen-track tribute album that features contributions from Giltrap, Jansch, Dave Mattacks, Dave Pegg, Martin Allock, Phil Beer, Vikki Clayton, Kevin Dempsey, Martin Jenkins, Pete Laity, and other musicians who regard Armstrong as one of the greatest luthiers of his era. **OB**

Clearsound
Strat 1978

Eko
BA4 1978

Type Solidbody electric
Body & neck Cutaway Lucite body; bolt-on maple neck
Fingerboard Maple
Pick-ups Three single-coil pick-ups

Type Acoustic bass guitar
Body & neck Mahogany neck, back & sides;
spruce top
Fingerboard Rosewood

Fender's iconic Strat had launched in 1954, and by 1957 the company began work on a completely see-through Strat. It took four years to build this one guitar, which was then used to show trade delegates and schoolchildren the instrument's internal electrics.

Fender's rather odd promotional project sparked something in the imagination of guitar makers all over the world. Since then various see-through guitars have been made and are still being made . . . usually with dismal sales.

In 1978, Japanese manufacturer Fujigen created one of the best see-through models: the Clearsound Stratocaster, which is today a sought-after rarity.

The body of the Clearsound Strat was constructed from a type of transparent thermoplastic known by the trade name Lucite. Unlike Fender's original transparent ax, the Clearsound had a normal maple neck and headstock. It was fitted with three standard Strat-style single-coil pick-ups and controls set into a semi-transparent pickguard. **SH**

The Italian guitar manufacturer Eko had already made itself a name for building basses. Its violin-style bass guitars had been popular since the 1960s, and in the 1970s Michael Bradley of The Undertones used a semi-acoustic Eko bass on the single "Teenage Kicks."

But the acoustic BA4 series became the best-known Eko bass of all after The Cure's Phil Thornalley starting using one in the band's mid-1980s videos. The Cure would soon become fashion icons for many youngsters, so the acoustic bass suddenly achieved widespread popularity.

These Eko BA4s were certainly interesting looking instruments, with a normal acoustic dreadnought-sized guitar body, a wide Selmer gypsy-style oval sound hole and an old-fashioned floating tailpiece.

Unlike many electroacoustic basses of more recent vintage, these pioneering Ekos are renowned for their full, booming acoustic sound. Which was probably just as well, as there was no pick-up installed in them. **SH**

Gibson Kalamazoo Award 1978

Höfner Pro Sound Graphic S-5E 1978

Type Cutaway archtop
Body & neck Spruce top, maple back, walnut neck
Fingerboard Ebony
Pick-ups One BJB humbucker pick-up

Type Single cutaway solid electric
Body & neck Maple body and neck
Fingerboard Rosewood
Pick-ups Three single-coil pick-ups

The Kalamazoo Award was a labor of love for Wilbur Fuller, who worked for Gibson between 1954 and 1980. A high-end, fancily appointed, sumptuous tone machine, this 17-in. (43-cm) full-depth archtop was a first for the company in that it was hand-tuned—entirely by ear—by Fuller himself. The Award stemmed from his experience seeing the company's craftsmen tune the tops and backs of the Citation archtop (to which the Award pays homage).

Fuller went further by tuning the wood used for the internal braces. He buttoned the guitar together, and carved the braces, tuning the wood as he went.

Thanks to this care and attention to detail, the Award's sounds live up to its profile as Gibson's most exquisite archtop—its status is due to the highly figured woods, the hand-rubbed varnish finish, and the rainbow-abalone eagle-in-flight motif on the pickguard. It is also one of the company's rarest guitars: it was produced for only six years, and only eighty-five left the factory with Fuller's signature. **OB**

In 1978, Höfner introduced a solid electric that looked like a copy of a Gibson LS6. But the Pro Sound Graphic S-5E was much more than a cheap replica.

The German guitar's solid body hid state-of-the-art electronics: a five-position switch to select pick-up combinations, an active built-in preamp, a five-band graphic equalizer with slider controls, and a "sensitivity" switch to lower the output when EQ settings were boosted, to prevent overdriving the amp.

Some models had another ten-position switch for selecting different preset sounds. Others came with the Höfner version of the Bigsby palm pedal bridge.

The guitar's details were good, too: a brass bridge with individual string adjustments and Höfner-branded cover, Schaller machine heads, individual pole-piece adjustment on all the pick-ups, a neat battery compartment behind a cover on the side, and through-body stringing, or "back-side stringing" as the English manual described it. Some experts regard the S-5E as one of the best-playing Höfners ever. **SH**

Ibanez
George Benson 1978

Type Single-cutaway hollow body electric
Body & neck Spruce and maple body, maple neck
Fingerboard Ebony
Pick-ups Two humbucker pick-ups

The George Benson GB-10 jazz guitar made its debut in 1978, after a period of close collaboration between the makers, Ibanez, and the multi-Grammy Award-winning American musician whose name it bears.

The design was developed in an effort to overcome the main difficulty that Benson had encountered with the larger, standard, electric jazz guitars: namely, their feedback at high volumes. The small-bodied GB-10 solved this problem without compromising tonal quality.

> *"[Benson's] primary goals were to create a guitar that was solid as a rock, easy to play, and not unruly when volume creeps past coffee shop levels."*

PREMIER GUITAR

The single cutaway body, featuring thick, heavily braced spruce and bright-sounding maple on the back and the sides, produced a remarkably tight and responsive sound.

The bound fingerboard was cut from ebony, inlaid with decorative mother-of-pearl and abalone, and featured a combined brass/bone nut.

The GB-10 also has a pair of specially designed humbuckers, "floating" so as not to interfere with the resonance and also reducing feedback.

The tailpiece can be adjusted to allow the string pressure over the ebony bridge to be altered, allowing the player to precision-tune this fine instrument to any preferred style. In the view of many guitarists, the GB-10's only downside is its price. **JB**

George Benson on stage in New York with his signature Ibanez in 1978.

Koontz Custom Flat Top 1978

Type Flat-top acoustic
Body & neck Maple body, mahogany neck
Fingerboard Ebony
Pick-ups One single-coil pick-up

Sam Koontz was a New Jersey guitar maker who many thought was way ahead of his time. He made his first classical guitar in 1959. His work in the 1960s included a triple-neck chambered electric, with twelve-string, six-string, and bass guitar necks, a Bigsby vibrato, and handwound pick-ups. Other models had hinged f-hole covers or built-in amplifier and speakers. He even built an electric with an onboard taping facility.

After working for Standel, Harptone, and Framus guitars, Koontz set up his own workshop in which he

> *"Whenever [Koontz] built a guitar he would call me and play it on the phone ... Sam was an innovator and his guitars kept getting better."*
>
> JAZZ GUITARIST JACK CECCHINI

produced only around 200 guitars. Their craftsmanship and sound attracted top contemporary local players such as George Benson and Pat Martino.

One of Koontz's major innovations was a double treble and bass truss rod system for more precise control of neck adjustment. The Koontz guitar shown is a flat-top acoustic, whose seven-string layout must have seemed very exotic when it first appeared in 1978. It features large block inlays on the fretboard and bridge, an oval sound hole, a carefully carved headstock, and an ornate floating tailpiece.

Koontz was a perfectionist, who would travel to Germany to select the finest wood for his instruments and became very anxious about any criticism of his guitars. He committed suicide in 1981. **SH**

Martin
EM-18 1978

Type Solidbody
Body & neck Mahogany body and neck
Fingerboard Rosewood
Pick-ups Mighty Mite pick-ups

Brainchild of Dick Boak—draughtsman, woodworker, and amateur guitar builder who came to work for Martin in 1976—the EM-18 was the firm's final, and most successful, attempt to break into the Fender/ Gibson-dominated electric guitar scene, a market it had tried unsuccessfully to crack since the late 1950s. This inability to make inroads continued with the E-18 and EM-18, but just because they failed commercially is not to say that Martin and Boak did not produce a couple of very fine guitars.

> *"This guitar [is] comparable to some of the better custom-made solidbody electrics of the era like Alembic and Moonstone."*
> AL PETTEWAY

The external appearance of the EM-18s reflected the late-1970s interest in natural-looking guitars. Their bodies had nine individual laminates of mahogany, maple, and rosewood that together produced a striped effect as well as a "neck-through-body" appearance, which was deceptive because the neck was in fact a glued-on addition. EM-18s had screaming-hot Mighty Mite pick-ups and Stauffer-styled headstocks, though their smallish frets were awkward when playing the blues.

A total of 1,375 EM-18s were made, but the design began to look dated. The EM-18 and the fancier E-28, with its twenty-four frets, ebony fretboard, and sunburst finish, would be Martin's last forays into solidbody electric guitars. After all, it was by then the early 1980s: the Superstrats were coming. **BS**

Peavey
T-60 1978

Type Solidbody electric
Body & neck "Select hardwood" body, rock maple neck
Fingerboard Maple or rosewood
Pick-ups Two blade-pole humbucker pick-ups

Like many teens, Hartley Peavey fancied himself as a rock star, but came to the devastating realization that his playing couldn't cut it. But he was pretty handy at designing and building amplifiers for his bandmates. In 1965, he set up his own electronics company: designing, building, and running the business in a small room above his father's music store. Five decades on, the Peavey brand is established as one of the biggest names in global audio electronics.

The first guitar to bear his name was the 1978 T-60. Designed by Peavey and Chip Todd, it was also

> *"I'm not so great at the guitar, but I am pretty good at building things. So I decided that's what I would do."*
>
> **HARTLEY PEAVEY**

the first to be produced with CNC mechanized cutting machines. "As a gun collector," Peavey recalled, "I was amazed at how precisely gun manufacturers can mass-produce the wooden stocks that fit on the barrel of a gun. I said, 'If a machine can make stocks like that, it could make guitars.'"

The well kitted-out T-60, which emerged when quality control at Fender and Gibson was in freefall, earned healthy reviews and sales. Innovative features included a patented bi-laminated neck, designed to avoid warping, and circuitry that combined the tone control with a coil tap for the pair of humbuckers.

Peavey remains primarily an amplifier company, but the success of the T-60 kicked off an interesting secondary string to the business. **TB**

Blues player Johnny Copeland is one of a small band of notable players to embrace the T-60.

Shergold Custom Masquerader 1978

Type Solidbody electric
Body & neck Ash body, maple neck
Fingerboard Maple
Pick-ups Two Shergold humbucker pick-ups

Jack Golder had cut his teeth in the 1960s working with Jim Burns and with Hayman guitars in the early 1970s. He was evidently a single-minded man who was more interested in the sound and playability of his Shergold guitars than their appearance, which even at the time looked rather retro. There's certainly something rather quaint about a 1977 sales leaflet for the Shergold Masquerader telling us—at the height of punk—that it "embodies all the refinements suggested by top players in the beat scene."

It's likely that more Shergold Masquerader Customs were built than any other British guitar of the 1970s. First appearing at the end of 1975, early Masqueraders were fitted with Hayman necks. The first Custom models were launched in 1977. Like most other Shergold guitars, the neck of the Masquerader was extremely playable. The twin humbuckers with various switching options were capable of an array of useful tones, although not perhaps for those looking for aggressive, cutting lead sounds. It retailed at a very reasonable price of £170.28.

Particularly attractive are models with Shergold's stunning apple green sunburst finish. These are highly collectible, although finding one without cracked varnish—common to even the most well-maintained Shergolds—or with the black plastic detachable "ashtray" bridge cover intact is increasingly difficult.

Shergold was the last large-scale British guitar manufacturer. And it harks back to an era long before that of the global village, where it didn't sound weird to set up a business servicing rock 'n' roll musicians, with the aim "to prove that Britain can make it." **TB**

Thompson
Custom Bass 1978

Type Electric bass
Body & neck Customer's choice
Fingerboard Customer's choice
Pick-ups Customer's choice

New York luthier Carl Thompson (born 1939) started building his exclusive handmade basses in 1974, and since then he has completed them at the rate of around ten a year. These top-end instruments have been used by many of the world's leading pros, including Anthony Jackson and Les Claypool: the latter, a member of the band Primus, famously uses Thompson's "Rainbow" six-string bass made of contrasting strips of six different woods.

Thompson claims to be the creator of both the first six-string electric bass and the first piccolo bass (four strings an octave higher than normal). He was assisted in both enterprises by another of his customers, American bass legend and jazz composer Stanley Clarke.

Thompson's instruments are all unique, and at the time of the publication of this book the cheapest of them was on sale for $4,000. Each takes more than three years to complete in his Brooklyn workshop, and there is currently a three-year waiting list. Although Thompson is frequently asked to create a new instrument exactly the same as one of his previous works, he always refuses on the grounds that to do so would debase his currency. He has been described as "the Stradivari of the electric bass guitar."

The Thompson bass shown here is a left-handed two-pick-up model with distinctive hand-carved body styling (every one of his guitars has a different design). It was built for Colin Hodgkinson, virtuoso bassist and former frontman of the British jazz rock trio Back Door. Hodgkinson has also played with Chris Rea, Whitesnake, and Alexis Korner. **SH**

Ural
Electric Guitar 1978

Wayne
Hydra 1978

Type Solidbody electric
Body & neck Hardwood body, bolt-on beech neck
Fingerboard Beech
Pick-ups Three single-coil lipstick pick-ups

Type Solidbody electric
Body & neck Alder body and neck
Fingerboard Rosewood
Pick-ups One or two humbucker pick-ups

"No worse than a Gibson, the Ural guitar/Hit an enemy with it and knock him out/There's nothing better if you need to pound in a nail/Another hit, and it'll smash right through the wall . . . " so sang the Russian band Chaif, in praise of the most iconic electric guitar of the Soviet era. The Ural has become an urban legend. If you believe the stories, a Ural will survive a nuclear blast; touring American punk bands will gladly trade their Fenders for one because only a Ural can deliver a true punk sound; Brian Eno brought one to England to amaze his avant-garde friends; the pick-up cover design was a Zionist plot; the model was discontinued because it was deemed a weapon of mass destruction; every guitar ever built in the U.S.S.R. was called Ural. The truth can be even more bizarre: the Ural's design was derived from a 1960s Yamaha SGV and then reversed, just as Semie Moseley came up with the shape of his Mosrite guitar by tracing a Stratocaster upside down. The Ural was produced by the Sverdlovsk factory from 1976 to around 1992. **EP**

Although its name may sound like that of one of Marvel's more ordinary superheroes, the Wayne Hydra is a guitar that is anything but mundane. It was originally produced by Californian Wayne Charvel, the luthier and former Fender employee who became synonymous with the customized, hot-rodded Superstrat style of guitar. It was a Charvel custom-built instrument which, in the ridiculously skilled hands of his close friend and long-time endorsee Eddie Van Halen, took the electric guitar world by storm throughout the 1980s.

The Hydra was originally designed in around 1977 by Charvel employee Jerry Sewell. It first attracted Eddie Van Halen's attention when he saw it lying on a workbench during one of his regular trips to the Charvel factory. EVH ended up with a yellow one with resplendent gold hardware; you can still place your own custom order today, although you will, of course, then have to go and make an equally wild-looking stand for it. **OB**

Wilson
Sapphire III 1978

Zemaitis
Hollow Bass 1978

Type Solidbody electric
Body & neck Timber body and neck
Fingerboard Rosewood
Pick-ups One Magnadur-magnet dual-coil pick-up

Type Acoustic bass guitar
Body & neck Mahogany and spruce body,
mahogany neck
Fingerboard Rosewood

This guitar was a cause and an effect of the rapid development of the pop scene in postwar Britain.

Its origins may be traced to Watkins Electric Music (WEM), a London-based manufacturer of cabinets for speakers and amplifiers, which was set up in the late 1940s by the brothers Charlie, Reg, and Sid Watkins. The company became well known for its pioneering Copicat echo unit, which is still in production; it also had a sideline in affordable amplifiers.

Reg and Sid then diversified into guitars, and, to avoid a clash with Charlie's operations, started trading under their mother's maiden name of Wilson.

Many teenagers of the 1960s learned their trade on Wilson guitars. Among Wilson's bargain models, which included the Rapier 22, 33, and 44 (with two, three, and four—yes four!—pick-ups), was the more upmarket Sapphire. Looking like a cross between a Stratocaster and a Burns Bison, it came in a range that included a bass and a twelve-string as well as two- and three-pick-up variations. **OB**

Despite many a British rocker owning a Zemaitis guitar in the 1970s, this bass is today an exceptionally rare instrument. Indeed, Tony Žemaitis built only a limited number of acoustic basses before his death in 2002.

The few current owners include such luminaries as David Gilmour (who has a 1978 model) and Ronnie Wood, so it's no surprise that you'll need plenty of cash to acquire one. It is said to be a great instrument to play, and certainly looks and feels like the real deal, giving the impression that time and love went into its construction. The simple design features—the heart-shaped sound hole (a feature that Tony liked to modify and customize with each instrument), the large body to convey the lower frequencies, the hand-carved bridge, and the string retainer—combine to form an instrument of immense distinction.

Devoid of many characteristic Zemaitis hallmarks, such as metal and pearl tops, this really is a simple instrument that speaks for itself without much fanfare: it really doesn't need it. **JM**

Burns
Scorpion 1979

Type Solidbody electric
Body & neck Material unspecified, bolt-on neck
Fingerboard Bound maple with black-dot inlays
Pick-ups Two Burns humbucker pick-ups

Another year, another comeback by Jim Burns. Or so it seemed at the time. After the demise of Burns U.K. Ltd., a new company—Jim Burns Actualisers—was set up and spearheaded by two, typically left field Burns designs, the Scorpion and the Steer, that appeared in 1981 and 1982 respectively.

Even for the period, the Black Scorpion (as it was originally called) remains highly distinctive, with the horns and general outine of the Gibson SG but a substantial cut-out in the lower body that more than one commentator referred to as a "toilet seat." The twenty-two-fret Scorpion, however, was a credible sounding and playing guitar. Blondie's Chris Stein was a notable user—Burns made him a special guitar with a six-a-side headstock; the standard model had a three-a-side head, the tip echoing the "scorpion" cutout on the body. The six-saddle bridge was part of the central, chrome-plated brass plate that also held the two humbucker pick-ups, and the headstock-placed string guides used ball-bearing "pulleys" to reduce friction. The standard finish was black. It also featured a pick-up phase switch and single- or double-coil modes switched via the two-tone controls.

The Steer was in some ways more conservative with its non-cutaway, more acoustic-like outline. Made from plywood, it again featured a central metal plate that held the six bridge saddles and pick-ups. Billy Bragg used a Steer for many years. Other designs from this period included the Magpie, the more classic Burns-style Marvin Custom and Bison, and the more radical Bandit—the last Jim Burns design. Burns left the company in 1982 and died in 1988. **DB**

Doug Irwin
Tiger 1979

Type Solidbody electric
Body & neck "Hippie Sandwich" body, maple neck
Fingerboard Ebony
Pick-ups Three DiMarzio pick-ups

California-based Doug Irwin designed and built five custom guitars for Jerry Garcia of the Grateful Dead. The most famous was known as "Tiger," which became Garcia's main guitar from 1979 to 1989. According to co-designer Thomas Lieber, its working name while under construction was "The Garcia."

The body was created from layers of cocobolo, maple, vermilion, and flame maple, in what was known as a "Hippie Sandwich." (Similarly colorfully, the maple neck boasted a padauk skunk stripe.) The exotic look was completed with brass binding and inlays. The Tiger's electrics were also unique, featuring an onboard preamp and an effects loop. The latter inserted an output directly from the pick-ups—a single-coil in the neck, and Super II humbuckers on the bridge and in mid-body—into Garcia's outboard effects rack. The output was then channeled back into the guitar where the signal was governed by the guitar's volume and EQ controls. The final output went into a Fender Twin Reverb, modified so the signal from the preamp passed into a pair of McIntosh power amps.

In 1989, Garcia took another Irwin creation, "Rosebud," as his main guitar, keeping Tiger as a backup. After Garcia's death in 1995, Irwin regained Tiger—only to sell it in 2002 for $957,500: at that time the highest price ever paid for a guitar. **TB**

Tiger made its live debut on August 4, 1979, at California's Oakland Auditorium, and remained Garcia's principal on stage guitar for the next decade. Among the Dead's many live albums is 1981's *Dead Set*, taped in 1980—the electric counterpart to the acoustic *Reckoning*.

Earthwood
Acoustic Bass 1979

Type Acoustic bass
Body & neck Spruce body top, walnut back and sides, maple neck
Fingerboard Rosewood

The very first Earthwood acoustic bass was produced in 1972 as the result of a collaboration between Ernie Ball (1930–2004)—inventor of a set of light guitar strings that both Fender and Gibson refused to produce—and George Fullerton (1923–2009), a former Fender designer. Although its launch generated significant media attention, sales proved sluggish; Ball and Fullerton gradually lost enthusiasm and the guitar was discontinued in 1974. A few years later, however, Ball was persuaded by Dan Norton, one of his employees, to reintroduce it.

"If there were electric bass guitars to go with electric guitars then you ought to have acoustic basses to go with acoustic guitars."
ERNIE BALL

It came back onto the market in 1979, but this time it was no ordinary acoustic. Modeled after the guitarrón, the Mexican mariachi bass guitar, the new Earthwood had a shorter neck, greater body width, and a depth of almost 7 in. (17.5 cm), which gave it significantly greater volume than its predecessor, particularly in the lower registers.

These departures from conventional design were plain to see, and even more striking when viewed alongside comparable acoustic guitars. Yet sales remained disappointing, and production was halted after only six years. Perhaps the Ernie Ball Company was right to describe it as "an idea before its time": today, however, it is regarded as the first truly modern acoustic bass guitar. **BS**

Erlewine
Chiquita 1979

Type Solidbody electric travel guitar
Body & neck One-piece mahogany body and neck
Fingerboard Rosewood
Pick-ups One humbucker pick-up

Recent years have seen a proliferation in the manufacture of travel guitars—scaled-down models that can be stowed away on a journey. Yet this is by no means a novel idea: indeed, in the late nineteenth century, virtuoso Francisco Tárrega commissioned master luthier Vicente Arias to build for him a guitar that could be concealed beneath his cloak. Since then, there have been many variations, from experiments with body dimensions and scale lengths to folding or fully detachable necks.

In the late 1970s, luthier Mark Erlewine and Billy Gibbons of ZZ Top came up with their own idea—the Chiquita travel guitar. While many travel guitars have been either little more than toys, or barely usable junk, the Chiquita was a highly playable reduced-scale electric guitar. Ergonomic design enabled a respectable 20-in. (50.75-cm) scale length to fit into an instrument only 8 in. (20.25 cm) longer from the base of the body to the tip of the headstock. And with its mahogany body and humbucking pick-up, it was also capable of matching most serious electric guitars in tonal quality.

The Chiquita achieved iconic status when it appeared in the movie *Back To The Future* (1985): hero Marty McFly finds one in Doc Brown's garage, plays a chord on it, and gets thrown across the room!

Erlewine subsequently licensed production to International Music Corporation, which manufactured them in large numbers under the Hondo brand. Unhappy at the inconsistent quality of these instruments, when the deal ran out Erlewine again took control of production. **TB**

Gibson
Flying V2 1979

Type Solidbody electric
Body & neck Mahogany and walnut body and neck
Fingerboard Ebony
Pick-ups Two "Boomerang" humbucker pick-ups

The Flying V2 was a controversial guitar. Advertised as "a new look for a new decade," the instrument certainly had a slice of 1980s glam about it.

Gibson created a five-ply laminate sandwich of mahogany and walnut for the elaborately carved pinstripe body and neck. Then it gold-plated all the hardware, fitted the jack socket on the inside of the lower V, and added a brass nut and brass tailpiece.

The V2 was pricey—at $1,199, it was Gibson's third most expensive guitar. Sales struggled, and it was withdrawn in 1982.

> *"These are the monster cool guitars. You have a humbucking single-coil. It sounds like a Telecaster."*
>
> SCOTT GROVE, U.S. GUITARIST

The V2's biggest problem was its Boomerang pick-ups in V-shaped housings. The neck pick-up even intruded into the fretboard. Not everyone liked this.

Even more radical were the pick-ups themselves, which were not used on any other Gibson. They were a high-output hybrid of two small single-coil pick-ups placed end to end, making a new, unique variety of humbucker with a single-coil sound. However, this was not what traditional Flying V fans wanted. The Boomerangs were later replaced with Dirty Finger humbuckers but by then the V2 was doomed.

Flying Vs have plenty of celebrity users. Not the V2, though. Albert King is said to have played one but, like most V-enthusiasts, he always reverted to the mahogany/humbucker models. **SH**

Gibson
RD-Artist 1979

Type Solidbody electric
Body & neck Walnut body and mahogany neck
Fingerboard Ebony
Pick-ups Two "Boomerang" humbucker pick-ups

Roused into action by the popularity of synthesizers and competition from the likes of B.C. Rich and Alembic, whose latest models offered advanced active circuitry and switching options, Gibson enlisted synth pioneer Robert Moog to create the RD range. (RD was shorthand for Research and Development.)

There were three models—the regulation-electric Standard, the enhanced Custom (later given a Fender-ish 25½-in. [64.75-cm] scale), and the 24¾-in. (63-cm) scale Artist, with a curious new body shape that was essentially a Daliesque take on a Reverse Firebird. The

> "RDs are awesome. It's like holding a kitchen table over your chest and having it scream like a jet airplane."
>
> DAVE GROHL, FOO FIGHTERS

Artist was top dog, and the ES Series and Les Paul were also given the Artist treatment in 1979.

Perhaps because of *Star Wars* (1977), the company proceeded to gleefully pack R2D2-esque amounts of circuitry into the RD's body cavities. As well as the four control knobs and three-way selector, a second three-way switch brought the battery-powered active electronics into play, offering neutral, bright, and a third setting to provide "expansion" on the neck pick-up and compression on the bridge.

Despite Led Zeppelin's Jimmy Page using one on "Misty Mountain Hop" at Knebworth in 1979, the active-circuit sounds of the RDs were not to the taste of most contemporary players, and by 1982 they had disappeared from Gibson's catalog. **OB**

Gretsch
BST 1000 Beast 1979

Type Solidbody electric
Body & neck Mahogany
Fingerboard Rosewood
Pick-ups Two special design humbucker pick-ups

For those accustomed to the beauty of Gretsch's White Falcon semi-solidbody, the BST line must have been a shock. The Beast range came in single-cut bolt-on twenty-four-fret neck 1000 and 1500, double-cut twenty-two-fret 2000, and thru-neck twenty-four-fret 5000 permutations, with various pick-up and switching options and a range of fancy body appointments. The 1000, 1500, and 2000 had string-through body bridges; only the 2000 had a 25½-in. (64.75-cm) scale; only the 5000 had Gretsch's patent Geared Truss Rod and coil-tapped pick-ups.

"…All the sound you can ask for. New pick-ups, new electronics, new designs make it all happen…Are you ready for the Beast?"
1979 GRETSCH CATALOG

Gretsch had been bought by Ohio's Baldwin company in 1967, and the BST marked the final new model of the Baldwin era, which had been characterized by uninspiring forays into the solidbody realm and a succession of retro Chet Atkins models. Given this ill-starred provenance, the BST range might have been expected to crawl into the back of pawnshops and there gather dust for evermore.

Over time, however, the Beasts earned a cult following as fierce blues-rock and rock workhorses, with the higher-numbered models' high-output stock DiMarzio Super Distortion pick-ups making them ideal valve-amp drivers. This is reflected in today's prices, which are highly respectable for guitars so unfancied throughout their two years in production. **TB**

Guild
S70D 1979

Type Double offset cutaway solidbody electric
Body & neck Mahogany
Fingerboard Rosewood
Pick-ups Three DiMarzio SDS-1 single-coil pick-ups

The Guild Guitar Company was founded in 1952 by Alfred Dronge, a guitarist and the owner of a music store in Manhattan, New York, and George Mann, a former Epiphone executive. At the start, Guild specialized in acoustic instruments for folk singers, but in the 1960s the company responded to the emergence of rock by moving assertively into the electric market.

Not all of its creations were unqualified successes. The Guild S70D ("D" for DiMarzio pick-ups) had a particular problem when it came to aesthetics—most people simply did not like the look of it. "Fantastic but ugly" was the prevailing sentiment. Some owners complained of questionable paintwork, though few questioned the guitar's dependability, longevity, and the fact that it was good for almost any sound.

The S70D used three high-output DiMarzio pick-ups (they do the job but can be augmented with a virtual vintage on the bridge) over a seriously large scratchplate, and a Strat-styled, five-position lever with phase reversal switch. Only about 250 were ever made, which today makes them a little hard to come by—particularly in the United States—although they are more readily obtainable in Europe.

The S series—designed to mimic bell-bottoms and replace Guild's SG series—was an unlikely offering from a guitar maker noted mainly for its acoustics. Nevertheless, it has since carved out a respectable niche in the vintage 1970s genre.

Although Guild was taken over in 1995, its name survives as a brand of the current owners, the Fender Musical Instruments Corporation. **BS**

Hamer
12-string Bass 1979

Type Solidbody electric twelve-string bass
Body & neck Maple body and neck
Fingerboard Rosewood
Pick-ups Two EMG humbucker pick-ups

In the late 1970s, U.S. company Hamer Guitars created "the world's first twelve-string bass" with four groups of three strings: each low-octave standard bass string is augmented with two thinner strings tuned an octave up.

It started life in 1977 as a custom order for Cheap Trick's Tom Petersson. Designer Jol Dantzig recalls: "We were going to make him an eight-string bass and he said, 'Why don't you make a twelve-string bass?' We thought there would be too much tension on the neck and it would be difficult to control. I think I may have come up with the compromise, saying, 'Why don't we just triple the D and G strings and we can get away with that tension as a halfway measure?' Tom agreed and we built a ten-string for him."

The ten-string worked well, and the twelve-string bass quickly followed: it was intended to be stereo but Petersson suggested it should be quadraphonic, each string group having its own pick-up. These are the so-called Hamer "Quad" twelve-string basses that are credited as the first of their kind, although very few were made. The simplified design of the electronics evolved into the B12S, which, like many of Hamer's instruments, used the Gibson double cutaway Special outline along with the split-V headstock. It remained in standard production until 2001. **DB**

The original Hamer twelve-string, made for Tom Petersson, debuted on the title track of *Heaven Tonight* (1978). Its distinctive sound then featured on 1978's live *Cheap Trick At Budokan*. "I really haven't had one since that has worked as well," Petersson said in 1997.

Ibanez
Roadster 1979

Type Twin cutaway solidbody electric
Body & neck Mahogany or ash body, maple neck
Fingerboard Maple
Pick-ups Three Super 6 single-coil pick-ups

"It's about time someone improved on the old designs," trumpeted the Ibanez Roadster catalog of 1979. Many buyers felt it was time for a new type of guitar to cater for the new techniques of electric playing. These guitars were more likely to come from the more innovative Japanese manufacturers.

So this was the cue for the birth of one of the first Superstrat guitar series. The Ibanez Roadster replaced the straightforward Strat copies and led to the Blazer and the Roadstar guitars, heralding a new wave of faster, heavier, Stratocaster-style instruments.

> "The Roadster series features ... combine to make it the most advanced high-performance guitar of its type."
>
> 1979 IBANEZ CATALOG

The Roadster launched with a Strat-style body and a bolt-on maple neck, but added several features: the Accu-Cast bridge/tailpiece had a string-through design and sustain block, with two-way adjustment for each string. The double-wound Super 6 pick-ups, claimed to be the hottest ever, were kept quiet with interior shielding for the wiring. There was a Strat-style five-way selector switch and a brass nut for sustain.

The base model was the RS100; the flagship was the RS300, with an ash body, natural finishes, and coil-tap switch to the basic specification.

Some of the "new features" were more marketing-speak than innovation: the "Quadra-lock" neck system was merely stuck to the body with four screws; the "Sure Grip" knobs were just plastic rotary controls. **SH**

Musima
Deluxe 25 1979

Type Solidbody electric
Body & neck Alder body, bolt-on beech neck
Fingerboard Rosewood, bound, with pearloid inlays
Pick-ups Three Simeto single-coil pick-ups

These guitars were produced in Markneukirchen, East Germany, by Musima, which, for much of the nation's communist period (1949–90), was one of the world's largest musical instrument factories. The 25 series electrics quickly became the essential tools of Eastern European rock 'n' rollers, who had little or no access to guitars produced in the capitalist West.

Although the etymology of the name of this instrument remains partly shrouded in Marxist mystery, it is believed that the number refers to the twenty-fifth anniversary of the Musima brand, which was established in 1953. Therefore, the 25 series is thought to have been introduced in 1978 or 1979, although not even that is certain.

The Eterna Deluxe 25 was the top-of-the-line model and featured the same circuitry as the Eterna Deluxe II that it replaced. The main differences between the old model and the new were the body shape, which now resembled that of a Fender Jaguar rather than an overweight Hagstrom, and a change of color: the later instrument came in a three-way sunburst finish, whereas previously purchasers could have any color they liked as long as it was black.

The bridge of the Musima Deluxe 25 was newly designed to feature chromed plastic saddles; three Simeto single-coil pick-ups, in their final, black plastic-covered version, completed the ensemble. Early models were good, but as mass production revved up over the following years, overall quality fell off somewhat. Nevertheless, these Musimas were still solid and durable. Surviving examples have become something of a collector's item. **EP**

Ovation
Adamas 1979

Type Electroacoustic guitar
Body & neck Lyrachord body; maple neck
Fingerboard Rosewood
Pick-ups One piezo bridge transducer pick-up

Ovation had already caused one guitar revolution by replacing the instrument's traditional wooden back and sides with a fiberglass "bowl" molded from Lyrachord, a synthetic fiber developed by Charles Kaman's aeronautical company. The models that followed, such as the flagship Adamas, were excellent lightweight instruments, and the molded back was so strong that it required no bracing, thus reducing interference with the sound.

In the 1970s, Kaman introduced another hugely significant innovation—a pick-up that, when amplified, still managed to sound like an acoustic guitar. This was a piezo transducer built into the bridge saddle and housed beneath the soundboard that connected to a built-in preamp, thus creating a new type of guitar—the electroacoustic.

Kaman's Ovation Adamas was unlike any acoustic guitar that had gone before it. While previous Ovations had topped the Lyrachord "bowl" with sitka spruce—a wood commonly used on guitar soundboards—the Adamas had a thinner surface with carbon-based composites laminating a thin layer of birch. Instead of a single hole, the sound was dissipated using twenty-two small sound holes in the upper chamber of the body, facilitating greater acoustic volume and a reduction in feedback. **TB**

Junior (2010) is the fifth album by American guitarist Kaki King, one of most highly regarded young steel-string acoustic players to emerge in the twenty-first century. She has been honored with her own signature Adamas model.

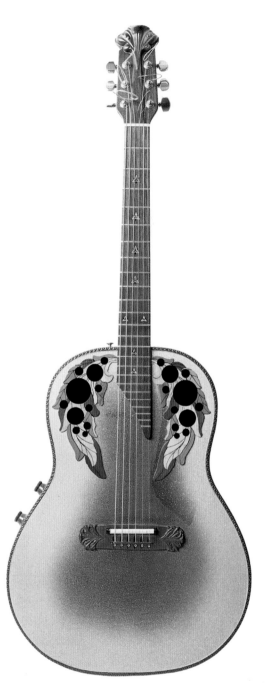

Pedulla
Pentabuzz 1979

Type Electric bass
Body & neck Maple body and neck
Fingerboard Ebony
Pick-ups According to requirements

Michael V. Pedulla has long enjoyed a reputation among electric jazz players as a luthier of some of the finest boutique bass guitars in the United States. Curiously, however, for a luthier so strongly associated with the electric bass, Pedulla's first personal creations were banjos and acoustic guitars.

Pedulla set up his first workshop in 1975 in Rockland, Massachusetts. His early bass instruments attracted attention and resulted in him taking on customization and repairs for Mark Egan (Pat Metheny Group) and Tim Landers (Al Di Meola), two stars of the fusion scene in the late 1970s. The work he did for them influenced the design of his signature model, the MVP, and its fretless counterpart, the Buzz.

Gradually expanding his business throughout the 1990s, Pedulla, like many successful artisans, became frustrated at having to devote increase amounts of his time to management and administration. Taking the dramatic step of downsizing his business, thereafter he would work on every Pedulla instrument throughout its construction.

In spite of the number of high-end endorsees, these players get no freebies. As Pedulla says: "All those in our artist program purchase their Pedulla basses. They play them because they want to."

The Buzz range is visually exotic, sporting a striking flame maple body. The heavily varnished fingerboard protects the ebony from the wear and tear of roundwound strings. For bass players looking beyond four strings, the Buzz range also includes Pentabuzz (five-string), Hexabuzz (six-string), and Octabuzz (eight-string) models. **TB**

← Mark Egan was one of Pedulla's earliest customers—he is well known for his work with the Pat Metheny Group.

Rick Turner
Model 1 1979

Type Solidbody electric
Body & neck Mahogany body, graphite/maple neck
Fingerboard Rosewood
Pick-ups One Rotatron pick-up (piezo optional)

The Rick Turner Model 1 was first built in 1979 for Lindsey Buckingham, then enjoying worldwide success with Fleetwood Mac. At first glance, it appears to be a hollow-body/electroacoustic guitar, its smallness reminiscent of acoustic instruments built in the early-nineteenth century Viennese tradition. It is, in fact, a solidbody guitar cut from mahogany.

Its most striking feature is Turner's Rotatron pick-up. Cradled in what appears to be the guitar's sound hole, the unit can be rotated to fine-tune the tonal balance across the strings. An optional bridge-built piezo can provide a more acoustic type of sound. Instead of a conventional pick-up selector switch, the Model 1 uses what Turner described as "blending electronics" and likened to "a zoom lens on a camera."

Around 600 Model 1s have been built since production began in the early 1980s. But Turner—who had spent most of the 1970s as a key figure at Alembic—seems content: "We currently make about five a month ... pretty steady."

Fledgling luthiers would do well to download free from the Internet Barry Price's *Making The Turner Guitar: An Architect's Illustrated View Of The Guitarmaking Process*. This fascinating and beautifully illustrated pamphlet details visually every part of the Model 1 construction process. **TB**

"I asked him if he could design me something that had a fatter sound—something between a Les Paul and a Stratocaster—but that had the percussive elements that would respond well to my style," said Lindsey Buckingham, who first used his Model 1 on *Tusk* (1979).

Schecter
"Telecaster" 1979

Type Solidbody electric
Body & neck Mahogany body, maple neck
Fingerboard Maple
Pick-ups Two Schecter coil-tapped humbucker pick-ups

Having run a repair shop in Van Nuys, California, since 1976, David Schecter announced a range of his own models in 1979. Based on the two main Fender designs, they were expensive and sold in fewer than twenty of the United States's most exclusive stores.

Schecter swam into the mainstream in late 1979 when The Who were in New York for shows at Madison Square Garden. Guitar tech Alan Rogan discovered a Schecter "Telecaster" at Manny's Music on West 48th Street. Pete Townshend took to the guitar immediately and phased out the numbered Les

> "These Schecter guitars are superbly made and easy to play and they sound glorious. They are capable of anything."
>
> PETE TOWNSHEND

Paul Deluxes he used on stage. Townshend would use Schecter Teles throughout the 1980s, although later models were built for him in Britain by Roger Giffen, using Schecter parts. "They have humbucking pick-ups as opposed to single-coil pick-ups…" Rogan told *Guitar World*. "And instead of having the three-way Fender-type switch, they have a Gibson-type toggle switch so you can flick it much easier when you're playing—up and down as opposed to left and right. That's about as customized as it gets."

Visually stunning, and kitted out with the highest-quality components, the Schecter Tele was one of the first successful "boutique" guitars. "Don't be fooled by imitations of old guitars," Townshend enthused in a 1982 ad. "These Schecters are unique!" **TB**

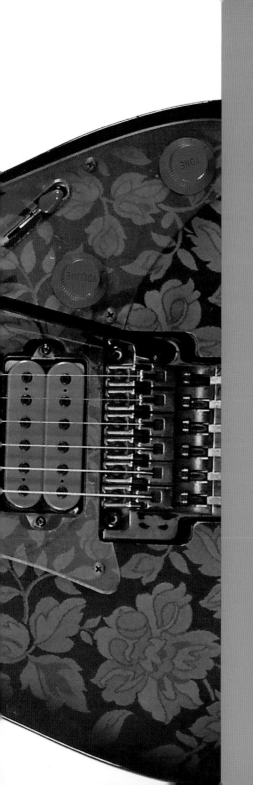

1980s

Bontempi
Memo 1980

Type Electric toy guitar
Body & neck Yellow plastic body; brown plastic neck
Fingerboard Brown plastic with note buttons
Pick-ups No pick-ups

The early 1980s was a great time to be a kid. Santa delivered sackfuls of Transformers, Cabbage Patch dolls, and Rubik's Cubes on both sides of the Atlantic. The luckiest children got one of these extraordinary state-of-the-art electronic guitars.

The Memo—marketed by Bontempi but made by Comus in Italy—was a plastic electric guitar powered by four C batteries in a special compartment in the back of the body. The specification included a built-in amplifier and speaker in the center of the body.

The brown neck featured a complex array of labeled note buttons, including flats and sharps and octave shifters. The synthetic buzzing sound that they produced was very similar to that emitted by the great musical toy of the 1970s—the Stylophone. Players could press a button marked "Glide" for a very basic slide effect between the notes.

The Bontempi could produce little tunes itself when set to "Auto" mode, and a "Tempo" switch altered their timing. It also featured a primitive recording system to play back, stop, or clear a sequence of notes previously pressed.

Bontempi have been selling toy instruments for more than fifty years. They are best known for their small electronic keyboards of the 1970s and 1980s that produced distinctive thin sounds by blowing air over reeds for each note. Still in business, Bontempi currently offer a range of miniature wooden guitars and plastic electric guitars, all of which come with pre-recorded tunes that can be simply played at the touch of button—a feature that might be as valuable to accomplished guitarists as to beginners. **SH**

Dean
Golden E'lite 1980

Type Solidbody electric
Body & neck Mahogany body and neck
Fingerboard Ebony
Pick-ups Two DiMarzio humbucker pick-ups

The three guitars in Dean Zelinsky's Dean brand, which first surfaced in 1977, are instantly recognizable by their oversized, inverted V-shaped headstocks: the shape of the V is based on that of the Gibson Flying V; the Z is derived from the Gibson Explorer; the ML combines the top half of the Explorer with the bottom half of the Flying V. Zelinsky used the same "cut-and-paste" style for his E'lite and Cadillac designs of the late 1970s, which fused the rounded lower bouts of the Gibson Les Paul with the top half of the Explorer.

The new design was certainly more conservative than the first trio of Deans, and the E'lite originally came with dual DiMarzio zebra-coiled humbuckers, and body and neck made of solid Honduras mahogany. Like many makers at the time, Zelinsky was refining a basic Gibson blueprint for the modern player, especially in terms of the neck shape and heel design, and also in the provision of easy access to the top, twenty-second fret. While many makers were experimenting with complex control circuits and active electronics, the E'lite's electronics were passive, in classic Gibson style, with a volume and tone control for each pick-up, while, like the Explorer—and the Dean Z and ML—the three-way pick-up selector toggle switch was placed on the elongated treble horn.

Dean's January 1980 catalog showed a trio of models with the same outline shape: the bound rosewood fingerboard E'lite, the Golden E'lite (with gold hardware and ebony fingerboard), and the Cadillac, which upgraded the Golden E'lite spec through the addition of a third humbucker, and mother-of-pearl block position inlays. **DB**

Defil
Aster Rock 1980

Type Solidbody electric
Body & neck Maple/mahogany/beech body and neck
Fingerboard Rosewood
Pick-ups Two Muza humbucker pick-ups

Many guitars look like other brands, either by accident or design. This is a notable exception: anything more than the most cursory glance at the Aster Rock will reveal clearly that it was built and assembled at the Lubin plant of Defil, the most productive Polish manufacturer of the Communist era. The telltale signs are the hardware and the electronics.

The Aster Rock was part of a series that also included the cheaper Aster Lux, as well as a bass guitar, and a Les Paul-style guitar—neither had a model name; they were both known simply as Asters.

The Aster Rock looks like the neck is a straight-through construction, but, in fact, it's a bolt-on. Both body and neck are cut from several pieces of maple, mahogany, and beech.

The Rock came in many variations, including a batch with a two-piece body and a translucent green finish. Similarly, there are several different control panel layouts: one is a three-knob configuration, with two different arrangements; another is a four-knob set-up.

In spite of all the variations on offer, the Rock consistently featured high-output Muza humbucking pick-ups—the guitar was clearly aimed at heavy metal players. During the 1980s, Defil also produced the Kosmos, whose source of inspiration was unusual: it was based on the Gibson Moderne.

The Aster brand would turn out to be one of Defil's final attempts to maintain its niche in a rapidly changing musical world. By the end of the 1980s, the fall of Communism had given Polish rockers access to Western electric guitars; within a few years Defil would produce only acoustic instruments. **IS**

Eastwood Blue Moon Special 1980

Type One-off solidbody electric
Body & neck Beech
Fingerboard Beech
Pick-ups One single-coil pick-up

Retro British eight-man pop band Showaddywaddy commissioned this one-off guitar to mark the launch of a single at the height of their success in 1980. The song, an updated version of "Blue Moon," the 1934 classic by Richard Rodgers and Lorenz Hart, hit the charts quicker than expected, so guitar-maker Brian Eastwood had to complete the instrument in a sleepless non-stop seventy-two hours.

The paint was still drying when lead guitarist Russ Field strapped on the Blue Moon Special and strode on stage for a live television appearance on British TV's *Top Of The Pops*. Yet the cartoon-like guitar actually worked well. Its star-shaped headstock has no tuners because they are hidden under the "clouds" at one end of the guitar. There are six holes where the mirror-faced star joins the neck: these act as a through-body tailpiece, as in a headless guitar.

Lightning bolts across the clouds emanate from the volume and tone controls for a purpose-built, powerful pick-up concealed in the body, from which dangled two detachable "legs" clad in denim and wearing blue suede shoes.

Like the single that inspired it, the eye-catching Blue Moon Special was a big success, and it was used extensively in Showaddywaddy's live act.

More recently, Eastwood's Blue Moon was featured in BBC TV's *History Of The Guitar* (2008). The forgotten original was rediscovered by collector Guy MacKenzie, who lent it to Showaddywaddy (now minus Russ Field, who left in 1985) to use for a live performance, thirty years after they first commissioned it. **SH**

Hondo
M-16 1980

Type Solidbody electric
Body & neck Plywood body, maple neck
Fingerboard Rosewood
Pick-ups Two humbucker pick-ups

Hondo was formed in 1969 when Jerry Freed and Tommy Moore of the International Music Corporation of Fort Worth, Texas, formed a partnership with Samick, a company based in South Korea. Initially they produced cheap and not terribly good acoustic guitars but by the time the company relocated to Japan in the mid-1970s it had moved on to better-quality copies of American electric designs. In 1976 it produced a fairly successful banjo.

The M-16 appeared two years prior to the frenzy surrounding *First Blood* (1982), the original Rambo movie. It was supplied with a faux sheepskin-lined case and a strap that looked like an ammunition belt with bullets: presumably Colt the gunmaker had a relaxed attitude to copyright infringement. A particularly nice touch was the "trigger" that doubled as the pick-up selector.

The Hondo name was mothballed in the mid-1980s when Freed and Moore moved on to the Charvel/Jackson company. **AJ**

Ibanez
Musician Bass 1980

Type Solidbody bass
Body & neck Mahogany/ash body, maple/walnut neck
Fingerboard Ebony/rosewood
Pick-ups Two single coil pick-ups

Introduced when Aria and Ibanez were leading the way with cheap copies of Fenders and Gibsons that were as good as, if not better than, the originals, the Musician bass was an all-new design that remained in the Ibanez catalog until the introduction in 1987 of the company's SR Soundgear range. Available in two versions—the MC-800, with a single pick-up, and the MC-900, featuring a pair of humbucking pick-ups and a three-band EQ—the bass came in either a natural or a dark-stain finish. Fretless and left-handed models were later added, but the basic design never changed. Sting and John Entwistle were early users of the Musician and gave it the swagger it required for success. The fretless model became an icon for fans of The Police and Adam Clayton of U2. Over its eight-year life, the Musician was used by bands of every genre, such was its adaptability and versatility, and even now it retains cult status among players—so much so that it still holds its value secondhand and even saw a Thirtieth Anniversary issue by Ibanez in 2009. **JM**

Martin
EB-28 1980

Mates Custom-built
Parlor Guitar 1980

Type Solidbody electric bass
Body & neck Mahogany body and neck
Fingerboard Ebony
Pick-ups Two DiMarzio pick-ups

Type Flat-top, parlor-style acoustic
Body & neck Spruce body top, solid rosewood back and sides, ebony fingerboard with floral patterns
Other key features Floral patterns on head

Martin had dipped its toes into the electric market on several occasions: pick-ups attached to standard designs like the D-28 in 1959; the F-50 hollow body series in 1962; and the similar GT-70/75 models in 1966. Sales were limited to around 500 of each model.

In 1979, with a decline in the sales of acoustics, Martin took the solidbody route, launching a pair of six-strings (E-18, EM-18) and a solidbody electric bass, the EB-18. The following year, they were superseded by a costlier second generation: the E-28 and EB-28.

These were beautifully made, high-performance instruments featuring modern technology. The EB-28 boasted a mahogany neck-through-body design with an ebony fingerboard, and a pair of DiMarzio pick-ups connected to nifty active tone circuitry. It was capable of a wide range of sounds, the active controls helping the bass achieve a tight and powerful bottom end.

Sadly, the EB-28 suffered because of the identity of the brand: the rockers at whom it was aimed simply didn't see Martin as an electric guitar company. **TB**

For decades, London luthier Tom Mates has been an indispensable custom maker, technician, and repairman to numerous great guitarists, including Eric Clapton, Ralph McTell, Fairport Convention's Dave Pegg, and Gordon Giltrap. A custom-made Mates guitar is a favorite among McTell's twenty guitars. Giltrap speaks of Mates as "my guitar man."

Mates has made many dreadnought and parlor-style flat-top guitars based on classic Gibson and Martin models. He reportedly copied McTell's Gibson J-45 for him when the original became too fragile to tour with. He made this 1980 flat-top parlor-style guitar for Dave Pegg about the time the bassist joined Jethro Tull after (temporarily) leaving Fairport Convention, with whom he had played for ten years.

The guitar is something of a hybrid: its head, neck, and bridge are typical of the Martin dreadnought range; its body resembles that of a vintage Martin parlor guitar; and the floral patterns suggest 1930s "decalomania" as much as "flower power." **GD**

Mighty Mite
Mercury 1980

Type Solidbody electric
Body & neck Ash body, maple neck
Fingerboard Rosewood
Pick-ups One triple-coil pick-up

The Mighty Mite name first appeared in the mid-1970s. This American company was an important player at the start of the hot-rodding vogue, initially producing high-quality Fender-style guitar parts that were, at the time, generally considered to be superior to the originals. The idea was an appealing one for anyone who liked the idea of a custom-built guitar but lacked the necessary carpentry skills to produce an original creation. Every part of the guitar's anatomy was made available in an ever-growing variety of options—from the body and neck to the pick-ups and circuitry. All that was needed was a screwdriver and soldering iron and a few hours of free time. That said, as late-1970s advertising from Mighty Mite's UK distributor Rosetti illustrates, some of Britain's top independent luthiers of the time—including Peter Cook, Pete Back, and Ashley Pangborn—were using Mighty Mite parts on their own custom guitars.

Eventually Mighty Mite began to deviate from the Fender classics, creating their own unique designs—like this eccentrically shaped Mercury body. An interesting feature of this particular example is the curious "triple-coil" pick-up with three individual coil switches.

Mighty Mite did not offer completed instruments, but the choice of a complete kit or a carte blanche selection from an ever-growing list of optional parts. The quality of any Mighty Mite guitar was, therefore, down to the assembler. There were many satisfied customers at the time, among them no less than a young Eddie Van Halen.

Mighty Mite foundered in the mid-1980s, before reappearing a decade later on, supplying parts sourced mostly in the Far East. **TB**

Mosrite
Custom 1980

Type Solidbody electric
Body & neck Laminated walnut body, maple neck
Fingerboard Rosewood
Pick-ups Four single coil pick-ups

This magnificent guitar now forms part of the collection of the Smithsonian National Museum of American History in Washington D.C., in which are preserved "three million artifacts, from the original 'Star-Spangled Banner' and U.S. President Abraham Lincoln's top hat to Dizzy Gillespie's angled trumpet and Dorothy's ruby slippers from *The Wizard Of Oz.*" The collection also contains more than 5,000 musical instruments, including such interesting electric guitars as Prince's "Yellow Cloud" and Eddie Van Halen's "Frankenstein Replica."

The Mosrite Custom was handmade in 1980 by company founder Semie Moseley (1935–92), in gratitude to a backer who had rescued him from disaster: the firm had precarious finances throughout its existence, and while its trade sales were seldom healthy, it survived mainly on the income generated by the production of custom guitars such as this.

In style, the instrument is somewhat reminiscent of a couple of custom models that Moseley made in the 1960s for the self-styled "King of the Strings," American country guitarist Joe Maphis—particularly the baroque curl of the horn on the single cutaway, which puts one in mind of what an eighteenth-century Les Paul might have looked like.

The extraordinarily beautiful body is made from laminated walnut and maple, and the bronze hardware has been painstakingly cast by hand. The frets of the Mosrite Custom have an interesting and unusual design that reduces vibration by connecting to an interior bar that runs through the length of the guitar's neck. **AJ**

Ovation
UKII 1980

Type Solidbody electric
Body & neck Foam body, aluminum/mahogany neck
Fingerboard Ebony
Pick-ups Two humbucker pick-ups

At first glance, the UKII may look like a conventional wooden solidbody guitar with a mahogany top, but it is actually built using an aluminum frame, which gives anchor points for the bridge and the neck, beneath cast Urelite foam—a material more often associated with the construction of helicopters, the industry in which Charles Kaman made his name before founding Ovation in 1965. (UK stands for Ultra Kaman.) The use of Urelite evolved out of the Applause range of acoustic guitars—the ones with the rounded backs—and another antecedent is the 1970s Ovation Viper range, which used the same body shape.

According to Ovation, the humbucker pick-ups on this guitar were the highest output and quietest on market at the time. Although there was some criticism that the Urelite foam had a habit of soaking up high frequencies, it was possible to use them in single-coil mode if you didn't think they sounded bright enough.

Considering the quality of its components— gold-plated hardware throughout, mono or stereo jack outputs, Schaller sealed tuners, brass Schaller bridge, and brass nut—the original price of £431.25 seems more than reasonable, but back then it wasn't cheap enough to seduce prospective purchasers away from more conventional choices such as the Gibson Les Paul. The UKII was discontinued in 1983. **AJ**

Several members of Genesis have used a few Ovation guitars in their time, and even the lesser-known UKII was played by Steve Hackett on *Highly Strung* (1982), his sixth solo album, which effectively showcases the instrument's impressive capabilities.

PRS
Electric Guitar 1980

Type Solidbody electric
Body & neck Mahogany with flame maple cap, set neck
Fingerboard Rosewood with bird-shaped inlays
Pick-ups Two humbucker pick-ups

In 1976, Paul Reed Smith showed the tenth guitar he had built—the Peter Frampton guitar—to Carlos Santana. Although Smith later recalled Santana saying that the instrument "had a lot of love in it," the guitarist did not order one immediately because he was tied to an endorsement deal with another manufacturer.

In early 1980, Smith completed his first guitar with a carved maple top, which—along with the bird inlays first seen on that Frampton guitar—would become synonymous with PRS production guitars from 1985.

The figured "curly" maple actually came from the drawer fronts of a friend's dresser. The first maple-topped Paul Reed Smith guitar was originally made for a local musician but Smith bought the guitar back and sold it for $2,000 to Heart's Howard Lesse, who dubbed it the "Golden Eagle." It became Lesse's first-choice instrument for nearly two decades. Lesse swiftly ordered another, this time with a single humbucker pick-up.

It was a picture of that guitar that Smith showed to Santana later in 1980, and after a series of false starts Smith finally hooked his hero. The Santana guitar features two pick-ups made by Seymour Duncan and a modified Stars Guitars brass bridge, a roller nut, and locking tuners: the genesis of Smith's vibrato system that would grace his production guitars. **DB**

Zebop! (1981) was the first Santana album on which the band's eponymous founder used a Paul Reed Smith guitar. Carlos Santana has remained a devotee ever since, and his multi-million-selling *Supernatural* (1999) became a showcase for the PRS sound.

Robert Ruck
Classical Guitar 1980

Type Classical guitar
Body & neck Cedar body top, with rosewood back and sides, ebony fingerboard on neck
Other key features Fan bracing, rosewood bridge

Testimony to the quality of Robert Ruck's guitars is in the fact that one of his earliest models, built in 1972, is used by the eminent classical guitarist Manuel Barrueco in concert and for all of his recordings. It is a similar association between guitarist, luthier, and specific instrument as we saw with Andrés Segovia and his 1937 Hauser, or with Julian Bream and his 1973 Romanillos. It was Barrueco's rising fame that brought Ruck renown and an order book that had players waiting many years: his client list now reads like a who's who of leading classical players.

Ruck is an innovator and experimenter in guitar construction who is driven by design targets that include power, a big dynamic range, a wide spectrum of tone color, evenness across registers, and ease of playing. His early guitars were cedar topped and made in the José Ramírez III style of the instrument shown here, but his influences also include Hermann Hauser and Masaru Kohno. After 1990 he moved away from the classic Torres seven-fan braces system, making guitars with either six, seven, or nine fan braces, all with diagonal treble cut-off bars—his nine-brace system becoming his standard design. In recent years Ruck has also made guitars with composite tops and acoustic ports with two small holes on the sides near the heel of the neck. **GD**

Cuban classical guitar virtuoso Manuel Barrueco travels into crossover territory on *Sometime Ago* (1994), a delightful album of transcriptions of music by Chick Corea, Keith Jarrett, Paul Simon, and Lou Harrison—all played on his trusty 1972 Robert Ruck guitar.

← Manuel Barrueco is the most prominent player to use a Ruck.

Steinberger
L2 1980

Type Solidbody electric bass
Body & neck Steinberger Blend graphite/carbon fiber mix
Fingerboard Steinberger Blend
Pick-ups Two low-impedance EMG pick-ups

Since the birth of the solidbody electric guitar, New Yorker Ned Steinberger is one of an elite set of luthiers who can lay claim to having produced a design that was both revolutionary and commercially successful.

The first Steinbergers were the L-series guitars and basses. Launched in 1980, they were unorthodox in both their looks and construction. Sometimes likened to a broomstick or cricket bat, the L2 bass is perhaps the best-remembered model—a fabulous period piece that enjoyed enormous success in the first half of the 1980s before falling out of fashion.

"Sting turned me on to the Steinberger. The first time I ever saw one was when I went to see The Police ... They're real good basses."

JACO PASTORIUS

Most visually arresting is the headstock—or the lack of one. Specially created, double-ball-ended strings are threaded from behind the nut, and tuned from behind the bridge. To further alienate more conservative musicians, no woods were used in the L2's construction. The neck was made entirely of the Steinberger Blend, a proprietary mix of graphite and carbon fiber. The result was denser than the hardest wood, but extremely lightweight.

L-series basses came with one or two pick-ups: high-impedance DiMarzio or low-impedance EMGs—the L2 had two of the latter. And, in 1990, the series won Ned Steinberger the coveted "Design Of The Decade" award from the Industrial Designers Society of America. **TB**

Sting (with fellow Police-man Andy Summers) plays a Steinberger in 1982. ➔

Wal
Pro Fretless 1980

Type Solidbody bass
Body & neck Ash body, exotic wooden neck
Fingerboard Ebony
Pick-ups One or two humbucker pick-ups

The Wal name is synonymous with high-quality basses with a uniquely identifiable tone. The legend created by Ian Waller and Pete "The Fish" Stevens in 1973 and 1974 continues to this day under the keen eye of Paul Herman, following Stevens' death in 2011.

The Pro Series went into production in 1978 and continued into the early 1980s, when the Custom range was introduced. The four models—Pro I, Pro II, Pro IE, Pro IIE—each had one or two pick-ups and passive or active electronics, although only around 700 instruments were ever produced. As with all Wal basses, function and flexibility were priorities, so these basses featured extensive tone shaping on the active models, and a "pick attack" switch (courtesy of push/pull controls) to give a high-end boost to emulate the use of a pick. A balanced XLR output for studio use, which later became a standard feature on Wal basses, could be specified as a custom option.

Fretless Wals were revered, with bassists such as Mick Karn (Japan) and Percy Jones (Brand X) making a bold case for the singing, almost vocal nature of the bass. Although it was regarded as a "production" bass, its numbers were restricted by the high standards the builders set for themselves and the fact that only the tuners were off-the-shelf components: everything else was designed in-house. **JM**

In 1981, Mick Karn switched from Travis Bean to Wal basses. His fretless Wal features on that year's *Tin Drum*, Japan's final studio album. The instrument can also be heard played by John Illsley on Dire Straits' *Alchemy* (1984) and by Colin Edwin on early Porcupine Tree albums.

Alvarez
5058 Artist 1981

Type Dreadnought acoustic
Body & neck Spruce top, rosewood back and neck
Fingerboard Rosewood
Features Rosewood headstock, chrome tuners

Alvarez, a brand established in 1965 by St. Louis Music of Missouri, worked in partnership with established Japanese classical guitar maker Kazuo Yairi from the late 1960s to manufacture a range of steel-string acoustic guitars that came to be played by famous names such as Johnny Cash; Crosby, Stills, and Nash; Jerry Garcia; and Ani DiFranco. The guitars were made in Kani, a small community high in the mountains of Honshu, Japan. Yairi chose the finest craftsmen and housed apprentices in dormitories, with mandatory communal morning exercises before work. Mrs. Yairi

"I've been playing Alvarez guitars ... my whole career, and they've served me really well. The company has been a great friend."

ANI DIFRANCO

cooked for everyone. Many Alvarez guitars are made in China nowadays, but St. Louis Music has retained an Alvarez-Yairi line for its top line of acoustic guitars, still handcrafted in Japan.

The unique nine-string configuration of this 1981 model is considered ideal for slide playing, open chords, and open-string phrasings. It provides clear and well-defined basses with brightly resonant trebles, and is sometimes known as the Harry Chapin model for the singer-songwriter who would remove the bottom three octave strings of a twelve-string guitar to achieve the same result.

The Alvarez 5058 Artist is the only known production model of a nine-string guitar. But, for all its qualities, it was never popular. **GD**

B.C. Rich
Warlock 1981

Type Solidbody electric
Body & neck Mahogany, bass, or maple body; maple neck
Fingerboard Ebony
Pick-ups Two DiMarzio humbucker pick-ups

By 1979, B.C. Rich had been making guitars for a decade, and although the California-based brand had started with acoustic instruments, electric solidbodies soon became its primary focus. Four main designs had already emerged—the Seagull, the Mockingbird, the Eagle, and the Bich—but the Warlock, which crashed onto the scene in 1981, took B.C. Rich further into the heavy metal scene with which it would become primarily associated.

Although clearly inspired by the lower cut-out of the B.C. Rich Bich, the Warlock featured much more angular lower bouts, and equally angular and pointed offset horns that were dramatically different from the Seagull, the Eagle, and even the Mockingbird.

Originally, the Warlock, in spite of its shape, was similarly constructed, with a through neck flanked by exotic wood wings, dual DiMarzio humbucker pick-ups, a Leo Quan Badass bridge, and some complex switching. As the guitar and subsequent bass were adopted by the metal fraternity—early users included Mötley Crüe's Mick Mars and Nikki Sixx, Lita Ford, and Paul Stanley—numerous versions appeared with Kahler and Floyd Rose vibratos, and later with bolt-on necks. Today, B.C. Rich offers nearly twenty variants, including Lita Ford, Terrence Hobbs, Joey Jordison, and Kerry King signatures.

The Warlock opened the floodgates for new B.C. Rich designs that continued to reflect the heavy metal genre: among the subsequent newcomers were the Widow, designed by Blackie Lawless, and the Stealth by Rick Derringer (a noted Mockingbird user), which followed in 1983. There were many more to come. **DB**

Lita Ford in 2012, the year B.C. Rich launched her signature Warlock. ➡

Burns Actualizer Ltd Bison 1981

Type Twin cutaway solid electric
Body & neck Body unknown, maple neck
Fingerboard Maple
Pick-ups Two Burns humbucker pick-ups

The final incarnation of Jim Burns' guitar-making company was Burns Actualizer Ltd, which was established in 1979 and lasted for four years. The Burns Steer (used by Billy Bragg) and Scorpion (used by Blondie's Chris Stein) were notable guitars of this era, but here we feature a rare reissue of one of the most eccentric Burns body styles of the 1960s, the Bison.

The Cambridgeshire workshop created this remake of the distinctive design with inward curling body horns. It now featured two Burns humbucker pick-ups. They were selected and combined via a five-way selector switch. The tailpiece featured a Fender-like vibrato, and the headstock featured three-on-a-side tuners, mirroring its contemporary, the Scorpion, rather than the original Bison.

The new Bison sold for around £370 and was probably the best Burns guitar of the Actualizer era, but the mix of modern humbuckers and 1960s styling didn't sell well. So the 1980s Bison remains one of the rarest Burns guitars. **SH**

Daniel Friedrich Classical Guitar 1981

Type Classical guitar
Body & neck Cedar top and neck, Indian rosewood back
Fingerboard Ebony
Other key features Rosewood bridge, French polished

Born in Paris, France, in 1932, Daniel Friedrich was a cabinetmaker before he began making classical guitars as a sideline in 1955. Five years and fifteen guitars later, he showed one of his creations to master luthier Robert Bouchet, who encouraged him to become a full-time luthier. Friedrich went on to make exceptional concert instruments that have been played by many of the greatest classical guitarists.

By 1981, Friedrich had stopped using spruce for soundboards, and his subsequent guitars are all the more prized for their power, balance, and sound quality. Friedrich fine-tunes each guitar to each buyer's sound preferences and playing style, his own being (as he describes it) "a sound that is full-bodied, full of charm and depth, more like a piano than a harpsichord." These variations are achieved by the woods chosen and the use of three different bracing systems: a classic seven-fan brace system; a complex asymmetrical system used for his standard guitars; and soundboards that are flexible lengthwise. **GD**

Fender
Bullet 1981

Type Single cutaway electric
Body & neck Plywood body, maple neck
Fingerboard Rosewood
Pick-ups Two single-coil pick-ups

Created by Fender R&D engineer John Page to replace the aging Mustang and Musicmaster student guitars, the Bullet's design was derived from that of the Telecaster (most notably in the shape of the headstock), but built with components of lesser quality. It came in two versions, a standard and a deluxe, most of which went on to become some fortunate teenager's very first electric.

This was Fender's response to the influx of cheap, Korean-made, entry-level "Strat" copies. However, at the time, Fender was owned by CBS, and subject to budget cuts that were not conducive to quality craftsmanship. Available in red or cream, the Bullet's treble-rich sounds were reminiscent of a Telecaster, and the instrument was nicely playable thanks to its slim, smooth neck. Versatility came through a three-way pick-up selector switch. The standard version had a one-piece aluminum pickguard and bridge. The deluxe had a plastic pickguard and a heavier body that produced wonderfully warm tones. **BS**

Gibson
Flying V Heritage 1981

Type Solidbody electric
Body & neck Korina body and neck
Fingerboard Rosewood
Pick-ups Two humbucker pick-ups

The Heritage was Gibson's first (fairly) authentic revival of the 1958 Flying V. The original, along with the Explorer and mythical Moderne, had been designed to propel Gibson into the space age, but was so ahead of its time that it failed to take off. Reputedly only 120 were made—each is now worth up to $250,000.

There had been other reissues such as the 1971 "Medallion," created to commemorate 1972's Olympic Games, and 1979's V2. But the Heritage was the first to revert to the Korina wood used for the 1958 model. Korina, also known as limba, is a strong but light relative of mahogany, also found in table tennis paddles.

The Heritage isn't an exact replica of the original: the body dimensions vary slightly; it has a three-piece neck instead of a one-piece; and the two wings of the body have the wood grain running parallel to the neck instead of diverging from the middle.

The limited edition FF-82—the Heritage with minor differences—was created for a 1982 trade fair. The Heritage itself was discontinued in 1984. **AJ**

Gibson
Victory MVX 1981

Type Cutaway electric
Body & neck Maple body and neck
Fingerboard Ebony
Pick-ups Two humbucker pick-ups and one Super Stack

Created when financial challenges forced Gibson to discontinue underperforming models, the Victory series MV2 and MVX (multi-voice) were made to challenge the popularity of Fender's Telecasters and Stratocasters. They were a departure from the accepted Gibson shape—no more roundness around the handle—and came with a double notch and fixed body microphones with new pick-ups, and circuitry able to produce single-coil sounds. Rather than mimicking Fenders, the MVX was an original attempt to produce a Stratocaster-like guitar that would not be written off as a mere Fender copy.

Available in candy apple red, antique cherry sunburst, and twilight blue, the MVX still had plenty of traditional Gibson features, such as a glued-in maple neck and humbucker-induced fat, Gibson-like tones. The solid construction produced some brilliant sustains and a wide tonal palette—but also meant that these guitars were seriously heavy.

It is hard to understand why they didn't enjoy more commercial success, although the early 1980s was an era of falling guitar sales. Alternatively, perhaps Gibson customers just wanted traditional Gibson styling instead of Fender-esque double-cut bodies and offset horns. Both the MV2 and MVX were discontinued in 1984 after only a short run. **BS**

Ray Davies of The Kinks played a blue MVX on *State Of Confusion* (1983) and live on stage during the tour to promote the album. One of the tracks, "Come Dancing," gave the band their biggest U.S. hit single since "Tired Of Waiting For You" in 1965.

Ray Davies of The Kinks performing with his MVX . ➡

Jackson
Randy Rhoads 1981

Type Solidbody electric
Body & neck Maple body and straight-through neck
Fingerboard Ebony
Pick-ups Two Seymour Duncan humbucker pick-ups

Randy Rhoads is as pivotal a figure in the story of Jackson guitars as Eddie Van Halen is in that of Charvel. In 1981, Rhoads, the highly rated young shredder on Ozzy Osbourne's *Blizzard Of Ozz* (1980), asked Charvel's Grover Jackson to build him a high-spec Flying V-style instrument. Rhoads later commissioned a second instrument, a Flying V with heavily asymmetric wings shaped like a shark's fin: he named it "The Concorde," and it quickly became his main guitar. Jackson then decided to launch the guitar as a production model, but felt that the unusual body shape didn't sit comfortably among the Charvel Superstrats. Tragically, on March 19, 1982, before the guitar went into production, Rhoads was killed in an air crash. Jackson named the guitar in his honor.

A high-performance rock guitar, the first Jackson Randy Rhoads models featured a maple body and through neck, with high-output Seymour Duncan humbucking pick-ups. The hardware was state-of-the-art, featuring a Floyd Rose locking tremolo system (before it had become de rigueur on metal guitars), and flattened frets to aid the high-speed player.

Randy Rhoads became a posthumous legend, hailed by later speed merchants like Zakk Wylde as a major influence. And his legacy lives on as his guitar remains popular in the metal world. **TB**

Randy Rhoads uses his beloved "Concorde" throughout Ozzy Osbourne's *Diary Of A Madman* (1981). This was the last album on which Rhoads played: just under a year after its completion he died in a plane crash in Leesburg, Florida.

The late and much-lamented Randy Rhoads. ➡

Kay
K45 Travel Guitar 1981

Type Solid electric travel guitar
Body & neck Mahogany body, maple laminate neck
Fingerboard Ebony (with brass inlays)
Pick-ups Two DiMarzio humbucker pick-ups

This was no flimsy fold-up for tourists: Kay's electric travel guitar was a well-made, full-scale instrument.

Okay, the body was almost a stick, and the compact headstock featured special mini three-a-side Grover tuners. But the K45 was neatly designed, with a laminated neck running right through the body, two quality humbucking pick-ups, each with coil tap switches, through-body stringing and a brass nut, a fixed bridge, and fret position inlay markers.

Built in South Korea, it came with a strap that was integral to the design, along with a brown, fitted leatherette case. Cleverly, the strap also served as a handle when the guitar was in its case.

It sounded good, and it was cheap: in spite of its high specification and build quality, when it first appeared, it sold for only £109 in the United Kingdom.

With its gunstock-shaped body, the Kay was known either as "the rifle guitar" or, in the United States, where it was marketed as the "Austin Hatchet," as "the hatchet guitar." **SH**

Kay
LP Synth 1981

Type Single cutaway solid electric
Body & neck Mahogany laminate body, neck unknown
Fingerboard Rosewood
Pick-ups Two humbucker pick-ups

This Korean Les Paul copy wasn't a real synthesizer—it just had a panel of effects built into the guitar.

These were "fuzz," "echo," "wah," "tremolo," and "whirlwind" (the last was like a phaser). They were battery-powered, with an overall speed control that applied to whichever effects were selected. The Kay also featured a volume and tone control, a phase switch, and a headphone output jack (as well as the normal amp socket). However, there was no way of selecting between the two humbucker pick-ups.

The Kay LP Synth was otherwise loosely based on the Les Paul Recording, with Gibson details such as twin humbucker pick-ups, carved top, and pearl block neck inlays. The sunburst body, neck, and headstock all have a neat, three-ply binding. The neck, however, is bolt-on. There is a cover for the battery compartment in the back, which is made of plywood.

Although this instrument was made for Kay, that name does not appear on it, which may lead to identification problems today. **TB**

Ken Smith
BT Custom V 1981

Type Solid electric bass
Body & neck Wide choice of wood for "wings" and "core", five-piece maple neck with graphite strips
Fingerboard Ebony

After a distinguished career playing professional bass, backing a host of top singers including Shirley Bassey and Johnny Mathis, self-taught American luthier Ken Smith turned to making innovative basses in his Brooklyn apartment.

His output of world-class instruments includes the world's first wide-spaced, proper six-string.

Produced in 1981, the Custom V is a five-string instrument, with a low B below the normal E. It also features BT (bass/treble) active tone controls. Today, Smith makes four-, five-, six-, and seven-string basses. His customers have included legendary players such as Stanley Clarke, Bill Dickens, Jon Patitucci, and Anthony Jackson.

Smith's highly-rated basses are still hand-built, but the workshop has now been moved from New York City to Pennsylvania. The woods are all selected by Smith himself—in fact, he keeps an exotic wood lumberyard on site, with more than twenty different aged tonewoods readily to hand. **SH**

Robin
RDN 1981

Type Twin-neck solid electric, standard and octave
Body & neck Ash body, maple neck
Fingerboard Maple
Pick-ups Four single-coil pick-ups

Robin Guitars was formed by David Wintz in Texas in the 1970s. Among its more eccentric creations was this double-neck guitar featuring a standard six-string and a neck with six strings an octave higher—the effect of which has been likened to that of a guitar with a capo at the twelfth fret. The Robins were available in sunburst or metallic red.

The Robin Double Neck, or RDN guitar, as it became known, had parts made for Robin by ESP in Japan but disappeared from the catalog in 1985 due to lack of sales. The single-neck Octave guitar was more successful, and enjoyed a long production run. Robin Guitars stopped making instruments in 2010.

Only about twenty-five RDN guitars were made before production ceased. They later became famous when, in 1987, the MTV cable channel showed a sensational video of Stevie Ray Vaughan and his brother Jimmie playing a blues instrumental on the same RDN at the same time at a live gig in New Orleans, Louisiana. **SH**

Veillette-Citron
Shark Baritone 1981

Type Solidbody baritone
Body & neck Maple body, koa neck
Fingerboard Rosewood
Pick-ups Veillette-Citron single-coil pick-ups

Architect-turned-luthier Joe Veillette partnered with his friend Harvey Citron to form Veillette-Citron in 1975. During their seven-year run from a workshop in Brooklyn, they created some original high-end guitars and basses that were played by members of Blondie, the B-52s, ABBA, Van Halen, and Devo, among others.

The Shark Baritone (a lower-tuned guitar, in this case to A) was requested by Lovin' Spoonful founder John Sebastian, and led to VC creating the first production baritone guitar. "I had been playing a six-string bass for a few years, so I knew what was wrong with it as a baritone," Sebastian told *Fretboard Journal*. "The strings were too close together."

The menacing body shape was reminiscent of the Guild Thunderbird favored by the Spoonful, and featured a twenty-two-fret thru-neck with 24¾-in. (63-cm) scale, twin custom-designed single-coil pick-ups, a tremolo unit, and a brass nut.

VC made only around 500 guitars in total, and no more than fifteen of these Sharks. **OB**

Washburn
Stage A10 1981

Type Double cutaway solid electric
Body & neck Ash body, maple neck
Fingerboard Rosewood
Pickups Two Washburn humbucker pick-ups

Washburn's Japanese-made Stage series were striking solid electrics designed for heavy metal guitar buyers.

The maple neck was thin, and speed merchants were helped on their way by a polished rosewood fingerboard. The exciting "sawn-off Explorer" body shape was outlined with edge binding around the flat top and along the sides of the fretboard. The back of the body was carved with a big indent to fit against the player's body.

The two Washburn "Power Sustain" humbucker pick-ups were helped in the quest for everlasting notes by through-body stringing and Washburn's own "Harmonic Lock" bridge, with brass saddle rollers and individual adjustments.

The Matsumoko-made instruments had varying specs, but even the base model, the Stage A10, had pearl dot inlays, bone nut, wooden back covers for body cavities, six-on-a-side Washburn tuners, and an adjustable, three-ply neck. Top of the extensive line was the Washburn A20. **SH**

Washburn
Stage A15 1981

Type Solidbody electric
Body & neck Ash body and neck
Fingerboard Rosewood
Pick-ups Three Washburn single-coil pick-ups

Washburn's first "A"-designated guitars were lavishly appointed acoustics from the 1920s. By the time this photogenic rocker appeared on the U.S. market in 1980, under the Washburn trademark revived in Japan in 1964, tastes had most definitely changed. Sharing some of the DNA of Gibson's Explorer in terms of headstock and angles, the Japanese-made Stage series included the stripped-down A-5 with Tele-esque controls, the A-10, the A-15, and the neck-through-body A-20. There was also a bizarre twelve-string version of the A-10 that housed six of the tuning pegs in the base of the guitar body.

The A-15 had three single-coil pick-ups, two volume controls, one tone control, and a five-way pick-up selector. It also had single-edge binding, and a Washburn "Harmonic Lock" bridge system. Those with "V" suffixes had vibrato units.

The line went on until 1985, when it was replaced by the HM Tour Series. However, it was revived in 1996 by the addition of the A-30 Artist Series. **OB**

Westone
Thunder III 1981

Type Solid double cutaway electric
Body & neck Ash/maple/walnut body, maple/walnut neck
Fingerboard Ebony
Pick-ups Two F530 humbucker pick-ups

Westone Thunder guitars were the first solid electric guitars produced at the Matsumoko factory that had previously turned out instruments for Ibanez, Yamaha, Aria, Vox, and Washburn.

The Thunder was the former sewing-machine manufacturer's attempt to create a world-famous brand. The range was wide, and covered most 1980s fashions, with six-strings and basses, bolt-on necks and through necks, passive and active electronics.

At first sight, it seemed like just another Japanese guitar. Its body shape was uninspiring, its name a bit corny. But that was before it got played.

The Thunder was great value. Around sixty per cent of its construction—including fretting, painting, and assembling—was by hand. The top-of-the-line Thunder III had a five-piece through-neck design, active electronics, with two humbucker pick-ups with phase and coil-tap switching, and brass hardware.

In 1988, production was moved to Korea. Quality declined, and the brand vanished around 1991. **SH**

Yamaha
SC400 1981

Type Solidbody electric
Body & neck Alder/ash body, maple/mahogany neck
Fingerboard Rosewood
Pick-ups Three Yamaha single-coil pick-ups

The SC400 was the more affordable sibling of the fancier SC600, and had a set neck rather than the 600's through-body design. It also lacked the bright tone option that the 600's coil tap provided. On the plus side, it had gotten away lightly on the finish front, and lacked the now-dated go-faster stripe design that blighted the 600's body. Both guitars came in either Persimmon Red or Oil Stain.

Aside from these differences, the 400 and the 600 shared the same vaguely Yamaha SGV-like styling and

> "The Yamaha SC guitars give a new dimension to one of the electric guitar's most popular formats."
> PRESERVATIONSOUND.COM

construction, with a twenty-two-fret, 25½-in. (64.75-cm) scale, a slimline, beaky headstock, a peculiar, reversed, offset-cutaway body, and an overwound trio of single coils. As a bonus, Yamaha also fitted a "High-Performance" through-strung bridge, with a shallower angle at the saddles and a larger baseplate contact area to transmit vibration from the light guitar body—at least, that was the theory.

The SC400s were designed to give lower-range Strats of the era a run for their money. That they failed to do so is plainly evidenced by the fact that production ended in 1983, only a year after they were initially launched. Today, they are fairly rare, but if you can find one, it might well be a worthwhile purchase, especially for beginners, to whom it will offer more character than the venerable Pacifica. **OB**

Gibson
Chet Atkins CEC 1982

Type Single cutaway electroacoustic nylon string
Body & neck Mahogany body and neck
Fingerboard Ebony
Pick-ups Six piezo transducer pick-ups

The Chet Atkins CEC was developed by Gibson in 1982 in collaboration with the legendary American country picker who lent it his name. It was a hybrid of different types of guitar: a classical, nylon-stringed instrument with a single cutaway and a pick-up system that could easily be amplified. The model letters "CEC" denote "Classical Electric Conventional." "Conventional" refers to the neck width: the original CEC model had a standard classical-width fingerboard. Gibson later introduced a second model, the CE, which had a narrower neck, similar to that of an electric guitar.

The guitar has a mahogany body with chambers hollowed out for weight reduction, and a cedar or spruce top. The one-piece neck joins the body at the twelfth fret.

The active pick-up system is especially powerful, built beneath the bridge, with an onboard preamp and a single volume and tone control. The sound balance is controlled by the fine adjustment of the six individual piezo pick-ups under each string. This system allows the guitarist to play at relatively high volumes without feedback.

In 1987, Gibson introduced a variation on the Chet Atkins, the steel-string "SST" model, which was also briefly available as a twelve-string. The series was discontinued in 2006. **JB**

Throughout most of the 1980s, Mark Knopfler used a Gibson Chet Atkins CEC when playing live with Dire Straits. "It's a beautifully made thing," he said. The guitar can be heard on cuts like "Private Investigations" and "Romeo And Juliet" from *Alchemy: Dire Straits Live* (1984).

Gibson
Corvus III 1982

Type Solidbody electric
Body & neck Select American hardwood body, maple neck
Fingerboard Rosewood
Pick-ups Three single-coil pick-ups

The early 1980s was a curious time for the guitar world. Newer U.S. manufacturers such as B.C. Rich, Kramer, and Jackson began selling large numbers of unusually shaped instruments, often geared to metal musicians. For the first time, the giants—Fender and Gibson—found themselves in the unusual position of looking elsewhere for inspiration. So while Jackson and Kramer were producing pointy Superstrats and B.C. were conjuring creations that looked like spiders and bats, Gibson came up with . . . a bottle opener!

The Corvus was heralded in Gibson's 1982 American Series catalog as "an instrument with a look as daring as it sounds." It certainly was unlike any previous Gibson, but it did hark back to Ovation's Breadwinner: a fine guitar that had first appeared in the early 1970s, but that few players embraced.

In spite of the looks that are—let's be honest—a bit silly, the Corvus was an extremely capable rock guitar. And Gibson clearly had high hopes, producing no fewer than three different models, with pick-up configurations to suit all tastes. The Corvus I and II were both armed with single or double high-output Alnico 5 humbuckers. The Corvus III saw Gibson once again in Fender territory, with a selection of three single-coil pick-ups. And, like the mid-1970s S-1, the Corvus was constructed with a bolt-on maple neck.

However, this creation was poorly received and remained in production for just two years. Now something of a cult guitar, it made a surprising reappearance in the popular *Guitar Hero* video games—and it probably represents Gibson's last stab at producing a strikingly "original" instrument. **TB**

Gibson
Moderne 1982

Type Solidbody electric
Body & neck Korina body and neck
Fingerboard Rosewood
Pick-ups Two PAF humbucker pick-ups

It was 1957. Gibson, stunned by the success of the modern Tele and Strat shapes appearing from Fender, responded by designing the "Futura" trio of exotically shaped guitars. The Flying V and the Explorer made it to production. The Moderne didn't.

It's uncertain if there was even a prototype. Perhaps Modernes were just too futuristic and ended on a Kalamazoo bonfire. Whatever, this strange narrow-bodied guitar became a holy grail for collectors—the rarest Gibson ever.

"A musical chimera, shrouded in the silvered mists of myth and legend … the enigmatic 'guitar that never was.'"

GIBSON USA

In 1975, Ibanez made a few Moderne copies, named Futuras, which have since also become rare. Seven years later, Gibson finally built official Modernes —but only 143 of them. Today, the few that ever surface command thousands of dollars at auction.

The Moderne featured one of Gibson's strangest headstocks, requiring four additional string guides. The uniquely-shaped body was made of rare African korina. The pick-ups were late-1950s style, the hardware was gold, and there were two volume controls and a tone control. The sound was smoother and jazzier than that of its Futura siblings.

In 2001 Epiphone made a few Korean Modernes, which again became rare. Finally, in 2012, Gibson launched the Moderne as a normal production model with a conventional mahogany body and neck. **SH**

Santa Cruz
Tony Rice 1982

Type Flat-top acoustic
Body & neck Indian rosewood body, mahogany neck
Fingerboard Ebony

Its values informed by 1960s Californian hippie ideals —"sharing, teaching, and challenging"—Richard Hoover's Santa Cruz Guitar Company can now be counted among the most highly regarded in the world of the flat-top steel-string acoustic guitar.

In the early 1970s, Hoover ran a small-scale repair and manufacturing workshop. There, he encountered a new generation of young guitar builders like Jean Larrivée and Bob Taylor, who shared techniques and tools—a vital collaborative process in a pre-Internet age in which reference books were hard to come by.

His Santa Cruz Guitar Company, founded in 1976 (when Hoover was approached by investors offering finance in exchange for lessons in luthiery), became the brand of choice for an emerging new generation of progressive steel-string players, such as Dale Miller, Will Ackerman, and, most significantly, Tony Rice. In the early 1980s, Hoover collaborated with Rice to produce a signature dreadnought based on the guitarist's own modified 1935 Martin D-28. This Santa Cruz model was designed to provide an enhanced treble and midrange for Rice's rapid, single-note playing style.

Unsurprisingly, Santa Cruz guitars—in common with Martins—don't come cheap, but the roster of artists using their instruments reads like a "who's who" of American country and folk music. **TB**

The Pizza Tapes is a collaboration between Santa Cruz figurehead Tony Rice, mandolin player David Grisman, and Jerry Garcia of The Grateful Dead. A home studio recording from 1993, it was belatedly released in 2000, five years after Garcia's death.

Tokai
Talbo A80D 1982

Type Hollow metal electric
Body & neck Aluminum body, maple neck
Fingerboard Rosewood
Pick-ups Two Blazing Fire single-coil/humbucker pick-ups

Innovative band Devo needed a stage guitar that reflected their eccentric futuristic uniqueness: the Tokai Talbo fit the bill perfectly.

Tokai was trying to branch out from making respected copies of American instruments. The Talbo was certainly a great leap into the unknown for them.

The unusual body was made of aluminum, partly because of fears about the sustainability of using wood for guitar bodies, and partly because it gave a cool, bright sound. The metal inspired the name, which is derived from Tokai ALuminum BOdy. Tokai was so proud of its creation that the headstock bore the slogan: "The new legend of the guitar history."

The skewed teardrop body was chunky but had a big hollow for wiring and to reduce the weight. On close inspection, the internal wiring was visible through the plastic scratchplate. The guitars came with various combinations of humbucking or single-coil Blazing Fire pick-ups.

One oddity was a truss-rod in the maple bolt-on neck—this was adjusted with an Allen key from the side of the neck near the heel.

The Talbo was not a big seller overseas, but thanks to its popularity in Japan it stayed in production for decades. Later, Tokai offered a maple hollow-bodied version, and, in 2000, a Talbo with a built-in amp. **SH**

"I use these live and in the studio," enthused Tim Farriss of INXS. "I absolutely love them. The tone and sustain achieved with the aluminum design is beautiful." At the 1986 MTV Awards, he played it on "What You Need," from their breakthrough album *Listen Like Thieves* (1985).

Tokai
TST50 1982

Type Solidbody electric
Body & neck Alder body, maple neck
Fingerboard Rosewood or maple
Pick-ups Three single-coil pick-ups

The Tokai TST50 was one of a generation of Japanese instruments that had a wide-reaching impact on the future of the global guitar market. It first appeared in 1982, when the trajectories of the American and Japanese industries finally intersected.

Tokai Gakki was founded in 1947 in Hamamatsu, Japan. Like every other Japanese manufacturer in the 1960s, Tokai mixed cheap imitations with its own original designs. During the 1970s, Tokai's business was concentrated on making copies of Fender Strats and Teles, and Gibson Les Pauls and SGs: by the end of the decade, partly because of what many saw as a decline in quality at Fender and Gibson, the gap between American and Japanese standards had narrowed quite dramatically.

Appearing in the early 1980s, Tokai's TST range was widely praised in guitar magazines. The TST50 was an absolutely blatant rip-off of a Fender Stratocaster, even down to the logo on the headstock, where Tokai's stylized "T" bore more than a passing resemblance to Fender's "F"! But the quality of the guitar was beyond dispute, leading some reviewers to question why one would choose a genuine Fender when you could have something that looked identical and played just as sweetly for around half the price.

Fender came up with a creative solution that avoided the need for legal redress: they reasoned that, if they were to produce a range of cheaper Japanese Fenders, then surely nobody would want to buy the copies. Thus was born Fender Japan, whose Fender Squier guitars were built in the same factories that had previously been making the copies. **TB**

Westone
Padauk II 1982

Type Solidbody electric double cutaway
Body & neck Ash body with padauk top, maple neck
Fingerboard Maple
Pick-ups Two F540 humbucker pick-ups

Time moves on, fashions change, and what once looked cool can later look downright ugly. In modern surveys, the Padauk is regularly cited as one of the ugliest guitars of recent times—but, in the early 1980s, this was a striking instrument.

At the time, adding a layer of padauk (an exotic, dark-grained South American wood) to a contoured, flat-topped ash body with stumpy little horns and offset cutaways seemed a great idea. It gave the original single-pick-up Padauk an exclusive edge.

Its electrics were state-of-the-art for 1981—the single-magnet humbucker pick-up was wired through volume, tone, coil tap, and active boost switches. It was well built and assembled at Japan's Matsumoko factory and, with a starting price of around $300, it seemed great value compared to established brands.

However, Westone was always tinkering with its model lineup. A year after the Padauk I's debut, Westone upgraded it with the addition of a heavy-duty brass bridge with through-body stringing and a padauk skunk stripe along the back of the neck. The Padauk II arrived in 1982 with two humbucker pick-ups and opulent detailing that included solid maple necks, brass nuts, and knurled brass knobs. Within a year, however, all the Padauks had disappeared from the Westone lineup forever. **SH**

Dave Brock, known as "The Captain" of enduring underground rock band Hawkwind, played a Padauk throughout the 1980s, including on the album *Church Of Hawkwind* (1982). Brock had his Padauk's top covered with a hand-painted "warrior" design.

Zon Legacy
Elite 4 1982

Type Electric bass
Body & neck Mahogany body, carbon fiber neck
Fingerboard Phenowood
Pick-ups Two Bartolini soapbar pick-ups

While makers and buyers of six-string electric guitars conspire to recreate a 1950s golden age, it's been left to the four-string brigade to push the envelope with new materials and construction techniques. Joe Zon epitomizes this type of modern-day bass luthier.

Establishing himself in New York in the 1980s, he combined playing with a reputation for high-quality repairs, before producing his own fine instruments.

Zon bass guitars are noted both for their sound and the neck design, which makes extensive use of "composite" materials. Besides enhancing clarity in the lower bass register, these—according to Zon—provide greater consistency from one bass to another. The necks are built from carbon fiber originally developed for the aerospace industry. This carbon fiber, he says, is then "rayon-extruded under extreme heat and pressure, a process that changes its molecular structure on a sub-atomic level." This process maximizes the ratio of strength to weight, making the necks strong, stable, and enviably light. In another departure, each neck is topped with a "phenowood" fingerboard. This process, developed in the 1950s, injects a piece of wood—generally birch or maple—with a carbon resin, heated to an extremely high temperature, then compressed.

The bodies of Zon basses are built from a variety of woods—swamp ash, mahogany, maple, alder—and topped with master-grade bookmatched tops. Taking a slab of figured hardwood, slicing it down the center, and opening it like a book produces the beautiful effect of a symmetrical grain running along the center of the body. **TB**

Contreras
Carlevaro 1983

Type Classical acoustic
Body & neck Spruce/rosewood body, mahogany neck
Fingerboard Ebony
Other key features Side slits instead of sound hole

The Carlevaro model was a fruitful collaboration between the Spanish luthier Manuel Contreras and Abel Carlevaro, the Uruguayan classical guitarist, composer, teacher, and creator of the influential Carlevaro Technique. Carlevaro was looking for improved sound production from the guitar, in particular from the basses, and came up with an idea for a design that Contreras would refine and execute at his Madrid workshop in 1983. The idea was to increase volume and improve tone by having a top with a bigger surface area. Other innovations include an internal set of back and sides to reduce the damping effect of the player's body, and, instead of a conventional sound hole, slits along the edge of the top and between the sets of sides. The design features make for a heavier instrument, but volume and tone are measurably enhanced.

Born in Madrid in 1928, Manuel Contreras was a cabinet maker until the late 1950s, when José Ramírez III invited him to join his guitar atelier. There he remained until 1962, when he set up on his own. In 1974, Contreras sealed his reputation as an innovator with the "Double Top" model. He continued to develop designs until his untimely death in 1994. Now run by his son, the Contreras workshop continues to make superb instruments. **GD**

Carlevaro Plays Carlevaro (1985) features the composer and guitar maker playing eleven of his own pieces on his own instrument. The collection includes "Preludios Americanos," five colorful pieces full of the captivating melodies, harmonies, and rhythms of Latin America.

D'Aquisto
Flat Top 1983

Type Cutaway auditorium flat-top acoustic
Body & neck Spruce/maple body, mahogany neck
Fingerboard Ebony
Other features Oval sound hole, ebony bridge

Apparently master archtop jazz guitar maker Jimmy D'Aquisto started making flat-top guitars by chance after he received a wrong delivery of flat-top woods from a supplier. He is known to have made only sixteen flat-top instruments between 1973 and 1984, including dreadnought and auditorium models with and without cutaways, like this 1983 example. They share other features, such as the bracing system, oval sound hole, and asymmetrical bridge design, all of which contribute to superior tonal balance, great sound projection, and robust-sounding bass. Like much of the rest of D'Aquisto's exceptional output, they are masterpieces of design and style, somewhat minimalist, and devoid of ornamentation.

This model of guitar has been seen strung with both nylon and steel. In nylon, it is ideal for playing smooth jazz, classical crossover styles, and Latin-inflected jazz music. In steel, classic Django Reinhardt or more recent versions of the French manouche style of gypsy jazz could suit it perfectly. **GB**

Defil
Kosmos 1983

Type Solidbody electric
Body & neck Laminated body, bolt-on beech neck
Fingerboard Beech
Pick-ups Two single-coil pick-ups

While Polish-built Defil electric guitars were mostly original creations, some were inspired by established Western models. The Defil Lotos was reminiscent of a Hagstrom, and the Defil Aster took after the Gibson Les Paul. But, in the early 1980s, somebody at Defil must have come across photos of a 1950s Gibson prototype that never went into production—and that is how the world ended up with an Eastern European version of the famous Moderne.

In the early 1980s, as unusually shaped guitars became all the rage, Gibson thought about reissuing the Moderne. Defil saw this as an opportunity to "catch up with and overtake" the West. The resultant guitar, of course, owes nothing to Gibson beyond its shape. With its bulky bolt-on neck, anemic single-coils and 1960s-era hardware, it doesn't play, sound, or intonate anything like a Gibson. However, the visual impact was just right for the times and the Kosmos remained a popular choice with Polish heavy metallists and punks well into the 1990s. **EP**

Elektra
Lady 1983

Type Solidbody electric
Body & neck Solid maple body, maple neck
Fingerboard Rosewood
Pick-ups Two humbucker pick-ups

The early years of the 1980s, just before the coming of the Superstrats, was the era when the images of guitarists were often built around the sort of instrument that they played. It was the era of Van Halen, of New Age heavy metal, and of an all-too short-lived craze for the pointed guitar. And few examples exemplified this brief flirtation with outrageous geometry better than the Elektra Lady.

The Elektra was manufactured by the Japanese company Matsumoku in 1983, in the midst of a takeover by its U.S. distributor, St. Louis Music (SLM). What made this guitar, and the various other pointy creations of Matsumoku/SLM, so special were their unique pick-ups—twin humbuckers, set on either side of a reverse-wound single coil (the product of guitar designer Tom Presley), with three pull-up pots allowing for eleven different pick-up combinations, one of the most varied tonal setups ever devised for an electric guitar. And they are rare too, with fewer than 200 having been produced. **BS**

Franklin
OM 1983

Type Orchestra model steel-string acoustic
Body & neck Spruce/koa body, mahogany neck
Fingerboard Ebony
Other features Fourteen-fret neck, ebony bridge

The inspiration for this guitar, by Missouri luthier Nick Kukich, was the original C.F. Martin & Co. Orchestral Model (OM) from the late 1920s, which was famed for its superior sound and distinctive styling. Since forming the Franklin Guitar Company in 1974, Kukich has made more than 600 guitars, almost exclusively OM and Jumbo models. The latter's inspiration were vintage Larson Brothers' Prairie State guitars from about the same period as the Martin OM, and they were marketed at one time as the Franklin Prairie State.

Through experimentation, Kukich modified the OM's internal construction to improve projection and clarity, incorporating hand-carved interlocking braces that reportedly improve the top's vibration.

Stefan Grossman played a Prairie State Jumbo in the early 1980s, and soon converted his collaborator, John Renbourn, to Kukich's guitars: the latter's preferred model was an OM. Kukich is still making guitars, which cost around twice as much as modern C.F. Martin & Co. equivalents. **GD**

Gibson Les Paul
Spotlight Special 1983

Type Solidbody electric
Body & neck Mahogany/maple body, mahogany neck
Fingerboard Rosewood
Pick-ups Two humbucker pick-ups

The rumor is that Gibson found some leftover pieces of maple dating back to the 1950s in a corner of the Kalamazoo factory. The pieces of curly and quilted maple were beautiful but had been discarded because they were not big enough to cover the front of a Les Paul. So this design was created, using a contrasting strip of walnut down the center.

The Spotlight was a limited edition of 211 that were assembled in Nashville and badged "Custom Shop" on the rear of the headstock. Experts believe

"The strip of walnut is an interesting idea— and this is what it sounds like (*bursts into heavy riff and solo*)—wooooo, yes!"

PHIL X (BON JOVI, ALICE COOPER)

that many of the parts were leftovers, which would explain the variable quality of the material used.

There were two finishes available: ASB (antique sunburst) and ANT (antique natural). The ANT guitars get more attention from collectors today because of their unusual contrasting dark binding and walnut strip against the light maple body. It's not a familiar Les Paul look.

The best Spotlight Specials are great. The body is lightweight and its look and finish are unique; the maple tops are beautiful and the sound is awesome: a classic 1950s Les Paul fullness with bite and warmth.

A Spotlight Special Custom Shop Reissue was made in small numbers in 2008. These weren't such a success though—they used a wider walnut strip and less dramatically figured maple. **SH**

Paul Fischer
Classical Guitar 1983

Type Classical guitar
Body & neck Rosewood sides and back with spruce soundboard, Brazilian mahogany neck
Fingerboard Ceylon ebony

With a career that began in 1956 under master harpsichord maker Robert Goble, Paul Fischer is today a renowned classical guitar luthier, with clients in twenty-five countries. Working out of a workshop in Britain's scenic Cotswolds, Fischer is renowned for both elegant craftsmanship and innovation.

He estimates that he crafted 150 examples of the design seen here, beginning in 1977. With a stunning hand-carved rosette of natural and dyed woods complementing the spruce soundboard, it features a

> *"I believe some of the skepticism toward alternative woods was born out of the natural conservatism of classical musicians."*
>
> PAUL FISCHER

Brazilian rosewood body and headstock facing, and a mahogany neck. "I held a presentation in London where these instruments were played and the audience was asked to judge the results…" he said. "No one could pick out the Brazilian instrument from the others. However, the general response of the audience was skepticism, partly because they assumed wrongly that I was trying to catch them out… That was not the purpose at all. It was a serious endeavor to deal with a looming problem." (By 1992, use of the wood had been banned.)

Shortly after completing this instrument in 1983, Fischer switched from traditional fan-bracing to a low-mass/high-strength grid-like "taut" bracing of his own design. "To be rigid about tradition," he told *American Lutherie* in 1998, "is to stagnate." **DP**

Peavey
Razer 1983

Type Solidbody electric
Body & neck Alder body, maple neck
Fingerboard Maple
Pick-ups Two Super Ferrite twin-blade humbuckers

Although better known for its amplification, Peavey made a mark in the guitar world with the T-60 guitar and the T-40: the first production guitars made using precision numerical carving machines. In 1983, Peavey entered the exotic metal market with a pair of non-traditional body shapes. The Mystic was a very metal, B.C. Rich-style design; the Razer, on the other hand, seemingly had no precedent.

For starters, the body styling borders on the brutal. Its most striking visual aspect is the "unwaisted" hard edge of the body's bass side—a straight line that passes from the tip of the horn to the pointed lower bout. It's rare to note, but there really is no other guitar that looks like this. And, as far as the majority of guitarists are concerned, that would probably be viewed as a good thing.

Looks aside, there were unusual construction ideas going on. Most notable was Peavey's patented bilaminated maple neck, in which strips of laminate were run in opposite directions to increase stability.

There was also a curious tone circuit that integrated a coil tap switching mechanism with the tone pot. By turning the control in one direction, the very hot twin-blade Super Ferrite humbucker switched to a single-coil pick-up.

The Razers were not produced in large quantities, and nor were they endorsed by any notable players. Strangely, however, for such an individualistic guitar the Razer seems to have completely avoided the radar of the collecting fraternity. They rarely come up for sale and, when they do, they often go for surprisingly small amounts. **TB**

Rockinger
Lady 1983

Type Solidbody electric
Body & neck Maple body and neck
Fingerboard Maple or rosewood
Pick-ups Two single-coil Rickenbacker-style pick-ups

The German designer Dieter Gölsdorf established Rockinger Guitars in Hannover, Germany, in 1978, and found almost immediate success selling electric guitar kits and spare parts. His growing company then rapidly established an international reputation as a good source of supplies for amateur luthiers or players wanting to hot-rod their guitars.

Two years later, a demonstration of the new Rockinger Tru-Tone tremolo—one of the first locking/fine-tuning systems to be produced—was licensed by Kramer guitars in the United States. At around the same time, emergent rock legend Eddie Van Halen was searching desperately for a tremolo that stayed in tune. When introduced to the Tru-Tone he was so impressed that he agreed to become an endorsee, reportedly remarking that he would make Kramer "the number one guitar company in the world." Indeed, the Rockinger system was introduced by Kramer as "The Edward Van Halen Tremolo."

The fame, success, and profits that followed were significant, but they did not last for long. By 1983, the Rockinger/Eddie Van Halen tremolo had been largely superseded by the Floyd Rose system. Thereafter, Rockinger maintained a somewhat low-key guitar manufacturing operation, introducing models such as the offset-waisted Lady.

In the mid-1990s, Gölsdorf turned his attentions to a new brand, launching the first Duesenberg models, and thereby gaining the approval of players such as Ron Wood, Elvis Costello, and Mike Campbell of Tom Petty & The Heartbreakers, who later had his own signature model. **TB**

Bond
Electraglide 1984

Type Solidbody electric
Body & neck One-piece carbon fiber body and neck
Fingerboard Anodized aluminum stepped fingerboard
Pick-ups Three humbucker pick-ups

With synthesizers and electronic music all the rage, during the early 1980s, the electric guitar began to seem rather passé. This period saw several attempts to redefine the instrument, one of the more exotic examples of which was the Bond Electraglide.

Alan Bond conceived an instrument built from a single piece of carbon fiber, with integrated digital electronics. Visually, the twin-cutaway Electraglide was styled on a Gibson Melody Maker, and featured three humbucking pick-ups selectable with the use of five push-button switches. The volume and tone controls were entirely digital: incremental rocker switches, connected to an internal motherboard, passed on data to the volume, bass, and treble controls; the player was able to view settings via a three-color digital readout. Unfortunately, the state of digital technology at that time required this system to be fed by a bulky external power supply.

The most radical aspect of the Electraglide's design, however, was the fingerboard. Dispensing with traditional frets, the black, anodized aluminum fingerboard was shaped in steps, the peak of each positioned where each fret would have been located.

The Bond Electraglide received a lukewarm reception and remained in production until 1986. Between 1,000 and 1,400 were produced. **TB**

The Edge played an Electraglide on U2's *The Joshua Tree* (1987), including the solo for "One Tree Hill." "The strings started to vibrate on the fretboard…" he recalled. "The guitar having no true frets, it created a different kind of effect. It was an attempt to sound obnoxious."

Mick Jones used the Electraglide during his time fronting Big Audio Dynamite.

G&L
Cavalier 1984

Type Solidbody electric
Body & neck Single cutaway korina body, set korina neck
Fingerboard Rosewood
Pick-ups Two PAF humbucker pick-ups

G&L—set up by Fender lynchpins George Fullerton and Leo Fender in 1980—succeeded Music Man as the outlet for Leo's restless creativity: he remained there until his death in 1991.

The Cavalier resembled both the Strat and the Mustang, albeit with period-correct rock trimmings, and had the former's 25½-in. (64.75-cm) scale length. Its most distinctive features were Leo's patented offset Magnetic Field Design H62R pick-ups. Brighter than ordinary humbuckers, hand-wired with adjustable pole pieces, and with a slanted configuration, they

> *"Leo died in '91 and he worked right up until literally the day before he died."*
>
> STEVE GROM, G&L PRESIDENT

produced an idiosyncratic tone that makes the Cavalier ideal for recordings that need an unusual second guitar to double guitar parts. It had master volume, treble and bass controls, and a three-way pick-up selector. (The example shown here also has a Dual Fulcrum bridge.)

Around 800 were produced between 1983 and 1986. G&L—endeavoring to reconcile 1980s tastes and Fender's heritage—produced a series of models that remain underrated. The Comanche, with its split Magnetic Field Design Z-Coil dual-coil pick-ups, is a versatile tone machine; the ASAT is a renowned Telecaster alternative; the Interceptor, with its X-shaped body and option of offset MFD humbuckers similar to those in the Cavalier, is a true original. **OB**

Jackson
Soloist 1984

Type Solidbody electric
Body & neck Alder body with maple top, maple neck
Fingerboard Ebony
Pick-ups Various single-coil and humbucker options

In the 1970s, rock guitarists began souping up basic Strats with the latest innovations, like humbuckers, active pick-ups, and locking vibrato systems that enabled "dive-bomb" pitch bends to be made.

The first great Superstrat was Grover Jackson's Soloist. Although only launched on the market in 1984, prototypes combining Stratocaster-type bodies with Gibson Explorer-inspired headstocks had existed in Jackson's Charvel workshop since the late 1970s. At this time, Jackson was essentially a custom guitar maker, so the Soloist was made available with a wide

> *"I don't think they [Fender] ever made it right—I think they got lucky."*
> GROVER JACKSON
> (on when Fender last made a truly great guitar)

array of user options: Floyd Rose or Kahler tremolos, or a string-through-body fixed bridge. Seymour Duncan pick-ups were standard, although any type desired by customers was possible. Finishes were near unlimited.

The 1980s are sometimes seen as a dark time for guitar design: a period when pointy Superstrats ruled the roost. Yet the original, custom-built Soloist was a finely crafted, high-performance guitar. Jackson took a Fender-style body, gave it a Gibson-esque neck, added the premium neck-through construction not offered by the Big Two, and topped it off with versatile electrics and hardware. The Soloist exerted a powerful influence, effectively kicking off the Superstrat phenomenon—and for a decade, Fender, Gibson, Ibanez, and ESP followed. **TB**

Jaydee
Mark King Bass 1984

Type Solidbody bass
Body & neck Five-piece laminated body and neck
Fingerboard Ebony
Pick-ups SN 2000 active pick-ups

The brainchild of English luthier John Diggins, Jaydee produces some of the best hand-built guitars and basses to be found outside the United States.

Mark King bought his first Jaydee "Supernatural" Series-1 Bass in 1980, and used it with Level 42, the decade's best-known British jazz-funk band. The instrument played a major role in the development of his trademark "thumb-slapping" sound.

The Jaydee bass has a five-piece laminated neck-through-body design with an ebony fingerboard, features that produce a strong and stable neck joint and improve sustain. Brazilian mahogany was most commonly used for the body's wings. Jaydee basses are also highly regarded for the quality of their active onboard electronics.

These basses were usually finished naturally, to highlight the patina of the woods. Their hardware was eye-catching brass, and the covers of the SN 2000 pick-ups were set in a polished hardwood casing.

King and Diggins then collaborated on a signature model: the "Mark King Classic." A later variant in white with ornate fingerboard inlays became known as the Starchild bass, after a Level 42 song. Mark King basses were also offered with mother-of-pearl "Saturn/Crescent" fingerboard inlays as alternatives to the dot inlays of earlier Classics. **JB**

Mark King's handiwork can be admired on *The Very Best Of Level 42* (1998). Of luthier John Diggins, he said in 2000: "I last saw John in 1994, and he seemed to be doing just fine. He is a lovely guy, and made a special bass for my birthday that year!"

Kinkade
Dave Gregory 1984

Type Solidbody electric
Body & neck Mahogany/maple body, mahogany neck
Fingerboard Ebony fingerboard
Pick-ups Two Schaller humbucker pick-ups

Most players welcome an opportunity to have a guitar specially made for them—and, in the summer of 1984, I was lucky enough to meet the men who would not only indulge my slightly naïve requirements, but also build me a first-rate, top-quality instrument at a reasonable cost.

The Kinkade brothers, Simon and Jonathan, had restored an old Gibson for me and made such a fine job of it that I asked them to build from scratch something that I would design. I wanted it to sound like a 1958 Les Paul Standard, but to look unusual; the guitars seen in ZZ Top's then-current promotional videos had left a deep impression on me!

To assist sustain, the center body section and neck were cut from a single length of mahogany 3¾-in. (9.5-cm) wide, with glued mahogany "wings" forming the body shape. The top is carved from two pieces of book-matched flame maple, and finished in the Royal Tan sunburst copied from my Epiphone Riviera. All hardware is gold-plated, and sourced from Schaller in Germany. The upper edge of the headstock is formed to resemble a traditional f-hole. The beautiful, bound-ebony fingerboard, with its individually-cut pearl "eyebrow" inlays, is a work of art.

The finished guitar is perhaps too big. Acoustically it's quiet, and to get any real tone was a challenge. In 1991, Jonny suggested a hotter pick-up, and installed a Schaller "Two-In-One" at the bridge, with a "Golden 50 Super" at the neck. It was impossible to fit the gold cover to the back pick-up due to feedback issues, but my guitar now delivers the vintage Les Paul tone more accurately than any real Gibson. **DG**

Manzer
Pikasso 1984

Maya
8029 1984

Type One-off forty-two-string multineck acoustic electric
Body & neck Rosewood body, mahogany necks
Fingerboard Ebony
Pick-ups One piezo pick-up

Type Solidbody electric travel guitar
Body & neck Body unknown, maple neck
Fingerboard Maple
Pick-ups One humbucker pick-up

The American jazz-rock guitarist Pat Metheny commissioned acclaimed Canadian luthier Linda Manzer to produce a guitar with "as many strings as possible." The multi-necked guitar she devised was named for Picasso's distorted Cubist guitar images.

It included piezo pick-ups linked to Metheny's computer system to trigger sampled sounds. The guitar can be heard on many of Metheny's recordings.

Manzer made a second Pikasso in 1995 for wealthy American collector Scott Chinery. This instrument was similar to the original, but entirely acoustic. Chinery's collection was thought to be the world's largest, with at least 1,400 instruments, many of them very rare. He later lent his Pikasso II to the Boston Museum Of Fine Arts.

Both Pikassos had four necks, two sound holes, and forty-two strings. The body of each is tapered, so that the side closer to the player is thinner than the side resting on the player's knee. This makes it more comfortable and easier to see all the strings. **SH**

One of the first solidbody electric travel guitars came from the mysterious Japanese Maya brand. It was small—measuring just under 34 in. (86 cm) from headstock to endpiece—but contained its own built-in amp and speaker.

The guitar's speaker was mounted in the center of the body under the strings, which left room for just one pick-up: a humbucker next to the bridge.

Although Maya guitars were built in Japan, their exact provenance is harder to pin down precisely. The brand was made by various manufacturers, only one of which was the Maya Guitar Company. To add to the confusion, some were badged Maya, others El Maya. The instruments were distributed by a Japanese exporter called Rokkoman in the United States and by Stentor in the United Kingdom.

Although very few top players ever used the Maya travel guitar, a black ST type was found in the collection of rock guitarist Gary Moore (formerly of Thin Lizzy) after his death in 2011. **SH**

Modulus Graphite Quantum Bass 1984

PRS Electric Guitar 1984

Type Electric bass
Body & neck Alder body (maple top), carbon fiber neck
Fingerboard Ebony (chechen also used)
Pick-ups Three active EMG pick-ups

Type Solidbody electric
Body & neck Mahogany body, set neck
Fingerboard Rosewood with bird-shaped inlays
Pick-ups Two humbucker pick-ups

Building a guitar isn't rocket science . . . unless you are Geoff Gould. He, in fact, *was* a rocket scientist, and part of the team behind the *Voyager I* space probe. Frustrated by instruments built from mere wood, he saw man-made materials as the solution to such issues as acoustic dead spots and warping of the neck.

He found a sympathetic ear in Rick Turner, one of the founding figures of Alembic. In 1976, Turner used his luthiery skills to realize Gould's idea of creating a bass with a carbon fiber neck. Their first designs came to the attention of The Grateful Dead's Phil Lesh, who would become a key figure in Gould's success.

In 1979, Gould set up a workshop in San Francisco to develop his ideas. Among the finest instruments to appear under his Modulus brand was the startling Quantum, which boasted a body of exotic tonewoods, a hand-laid carbon fiber neck, an ebony fingerboard, and high-fidelity EMG active soapbar pick-ups.

Gould sold his interest in the company in 1995, but the brand remains a force for innovation. **TB**

In 1982, Paul Reed Smith designed the "Sorcerer's Apprentice," a guitar with a Gibson-derived body shape but featuring what is now known as the PRS headstock. He approached Yamaha, but no deal was made, so he had to go it alone. But he still needed an original body shape: "I knew that, if I didn't draw a line down the middle and combine the best features of the Fender and Gibson designs, I was dead."

In 1984, Smith perfected the classic PRS body shape: elegant, referenced from the past, but no copy. The design used a unique vibrato with locking tuners and a friction-reducing nut; the scale length of 25 in. (63.5 cm) sat between Fender's 25½ in. (64.75 cm) and Gibson's nominal 24¾ in. (63 cm); the two PRS pick-ups offered five humbucking and single-coil tones via a rotary switch.

This was a classy hybrid, but you still couldn't buy one. Smith built some prototypes, one of which is shown here. U.S. retailers saw their merit, and, by October 1985, Smith had built his hundredth PRS. **DB**

Roland
G-707 1984

Type Solidbody with graphite stabilizing bar
Body & neck Alder body, set maple neck
Fingerboard Rosewood
Pick-ups Two humbucker pick-ups

Until the relatively recent development of guitars fully kitted out with onboard processing capabilities, Japanese technology giant the Roland Corporation was the only company in the world to persist seriously with the idea of merging the seemingly incompatible and constantly divergent worlds of the guitarist and the synthesist.

The features that had won the earlier Roland GS-500 a lasting place in the hearts of a small coterie of fans were precisely the causes of its commercial failure: the instrument was much too complex for the "ordinary" player to master.

Roland attempted to simplify matters by taking advantage of recent developments in synthesizers: the 1980s saw a great increase in the use of stored preset sounds, as a result of which musicians were no longer required to create what they required from scratch. Thus was born the G-707, a stomp-box unit housing banks of preset sounds that could be recalled from a footswitch.

The guitar itself had a highly distinctive look that many potential customers viewed with ill-disguised derision. However, its most striking idiosyncrasy—the graphite bar that joined the body to the headstock—was no mere embellishment to give the instrument a futuristic appearance. On the contrary, it was, in fact, an essential, practical feature: converting a vibrating string into consistent control data had long been a problem with the more volatile construction of a regular guitar. Thus, the G-707 was a technological breakthrough; sadly for Roland, however, it was no more successful than its ill-fated predecessor. **TB**

← Billy Idol's sideman Steve Stevens made extensive use of the G-707 in the mid-1980s.

Squier
Stratocaster 1984

Type Solidbody electric
Body & neck Alder body, maple neck
Fingerboard Rosewood or maple
Pick-ups Three single-coil pick-ups

Until the middle of the 1970s, the big American guitar manufacturers largely ignored the cheap plywood imitations that flooded the budget end of the market. After all, poverty notwithstanding, no serious player would choose a Top Twenty "Strat" produced at the Teisco factory in Japan over the real thing. It could even be argued that the sheer ubiquity of the imitations played a part in building up the Fender Strats/Teles and Gibson Les Pauls/SGs to their iconic status.

There was a problem, however. By the late 1970s, the quality of post-corporate Fender and Gibson guitars was on a clear downward trajectory . . . just as Japanese copies began to show a big improvement. Gear reviewers suddenly began rating "Strat-a-likes" from the Tokai or Greco factories as approaching the quality of the originals. In 1982, Fender came up with an imaginative response: it launched a Japanese manufacturing wing, collaborating with some of the builders and distributors of its imitators. Now, officially sanctioned guitars could be built under the Fender Squier brand name, removing a chunk of the competition at a stroke.

The first models were a great revelation. In 1984, the Squier Stratocaster retailed at $369, only $40 more than a U.S.-built model. Many players felt they were just as good. The multi-tiered ethos behind the Squier brand soon become central to Fender's business: Fender's premium guitars are now built in the United States and Japan, and cheaper models in Mexico; the high-end Squiers come from Japan, while the budget models are produced in factories in Korea, China, India, and Indonesia. **TB**

Stonehenge
Model II 1984

Type Semi-hollow body electric
Body & neck Metal/inlaid wood body, mahogany neck
Fingerboard Rosewood
Pick-ups Three DiMarzio pick-ups

Stonehenge tubular metal-bodied guitars were made entirely by hand in the early 1980s by luthier Alfredo Bugari in Castelfidardo, Italy. These strikingly beautiful, triangular-bodied instruments have minimal timber infills, and more than half of what would ordinarily be the body is simply empty space. Such a lack of substance must have a detrimental effect on the instrument's sustain, but who cares about sustain when you're playing one of the coolest guitars on the planet?

The body of the Stonehenge II was almost completely empty, apart from, across its center, a monolithic block of metal reminiscent of a prehistoric stone on the monument in Wiltshire, England, for which it is named.

The circular design of the tubular frame echoed Bugari's theories about the tonal qualities of Stonehenge itself. Although no one knows the original purpose of the stone circle, studies of its acoustics have revealed some of its singular qualities—the echoes, resonances, and whispering-gallery effects that it creates are almost unparalleled in any building constructed before the modern age. This may come as a surprise to those who assume that Neolithic people were primitive, and concerned only with survival. But there is strong evidence that they were at least as aware as we are of the way that space reacts to acoustic activity.

For all their palpable merits, none of the three guitars that Bugari produced with this design ever made any real impression on the market: it quickly became apparent that musicians did not subscribe to his sound theories. **BS**

Vigier Nautilus Arpege 1984

Type Solidbody bass
Body & neck Maple/alder body, maple neck
Fingerboard Phenowood
Pick-ups Two single-coil pick-ups

In the wake of French manufacturer Patrice Vigier's developments in graphite neck production and phenolic resin fingerboards, the Nautilus Arpege was the first bass instrument to feature a processor-based ROM electronics system that allowed players to avail themselves of nineteen EQ and tonal presents for instant call-up.

With an extensive array of controls (twelve, to be precise), there was plenty of technology for the player to get used to, although whether a bass player really needs so many different sounds is a contentious issue. In fact, the vast available choice may go some way to explaining why this system never really took off from a commercial viewpoint. Then again, the Nautilus was developed in the 1980s, when more was good and even more was better still, and this was a time when developments in the bass world were unfolding on a weekly basis.

With very few extant examples, and not much information available, it is hard to know quite how good an instrument this actually was, but considering the esteem in which most Vigier instruments are held, it is quite likely that the Nautilus-equipped basses will have been imbued with the same level of quality, playability, and craftsmanship that was afforded to all other Vigier instruments.

Neck stability will certainly have been a prime consideration, because Vigier were not only producing graphite-necked instruments around this time; they were also pioneering the use of graphite inserts to improve neck rigidity and to prevent necks from warping and twisting. **JM**

Vox
White Shadow 1984

Type Solidbody electric
Body & neck Nato body and neck
Fingerboard Maple
Pick-ups Two humbucker or three single-coil pick-ups

During its unfashionable years in the 1970s, Vox ceased producing guitars altogether. After the last of the Phantom series, and a couple of other models, including the frighteningly ugly Marauder, in 1969, it didn't produce another guitar until 1982, when it introduced the Custom and Standard ranges. These were superseded in 1984 by the White Shadow.

Moving away from the Stratocaster-like design of the Standard, the White Shadow had a mid-1960s flavor to it, and was reminiscent of the earlier Vox Bulldogs and Invaders—although with an incongruous, 1980s-style headstock instead of the 1960s Vox shape that the Standard had retained. It still had a Strat-like pick-up configuration, with three DiMarzio FS-1 single coils and a five-way selector switch. (FS-1s are claimed to be 25 percent more powerful than standard single coils.) There was a single volume knob, and a tone control for each of the neck and middle pick-ups—the bridge pick-up bypassed the tone circuit. White Shadows came in red, blue, black, and white, and they were supplied with a sympathetically designed 1960s-style case.

Ironically, potential buyers found Vox's retro-design just a bit too far ahead of its time. Sales were disappointing, and the White Shadow remained in production for only a year. **AJ**

The Vox White Shadow is the main instrument of Andy Export of UK punk band Unlucky Fried Kitten. He can be heard playing it on such albums as *Napoleonic Enid Blyton* (2008) and *Unlucky Fried Kitten Present Loserville.com* (2010).

Dupont
MD50 1985

Type Steel-string acoustic
Body & neck Rosewood and spruce body, walnut neck
Fingerboard Ebony

With the revival of interest in Django Reinhardt and Gypsy jazz in the 1980s, a new jazz guitar was needed to replace the aging, fragile Selmers that Django originally played and could now be afforded only by wealthy collectors. Enter Maurice Dupont, who set up an atelier in France's Cognac region in 1981, and began constructing Gypsy guitars in 1985.

As the new generation of Gypsy jazz players unreeled an ever faster, more virtuosic, and athletic style, Dupont's guitars were up to the task. Copying the construction of the Selmer—and later, the Busato—Dupont used a blend of traditional and modern techniques to construct strong instruments. He wisely incorporated truss rods into the necks, experimented with different woods, and produced his own updated tuners. Like the so-called "Superstrats" then popular in hard rock and heavy metal, Dupont's new Gypsy guitars were truly Super Selmers.

The MD50, Dupont's main model, is lightweight yet rock solid, built for life on the road. Like all Duponts, its voice improved the more it was played.

Dupont still restores old Gypsy guitars, and builds Selmer- and Busato-style guitars, as well as classical, flamenco, archtop, and Hawaiian instruments. He also offers reproductions of Django's favored Stimer add-on pick-ups and Stimer amplifiers. **MD**

Romane is one of Dupont's greatest endorsers, playing the top-of-the-line Vieille Reserve guitar, an exacting Selmer replica with a vintage vibe and relic-like finish. The instrument is showcased on *Roots & Groove: Live At The Sunset* (2011).

Fender
Katana 1985

Type Solidbody electric
Body & neck Basswood body, set maple neck
Fingerboard Rosewood
Pick-ups Two humbucker pick-ups

By the start of the 1980s, Fender was in decline: cost-cutting by the parent company, CBS, had seen a gradual yet palpable drop in quality. This was combined with a crisis of identity, as newer brands such as Kramer and Jackson, with their unorthodox angular designs, found favor with rock players. As a consequence, Fender found itself under pressure from sales agents to come up with something contemporary that might re-establish the brand.

There was little appetite within Fender to produce a guitar like this. Marketing director Dan Smith disliked the new trend for "pointy" guitars: "These things are revolting . . . but to pacify the dealers we needed something. So I sat down with the art program on the Macintosh and screwed around."

Thus was born the Katana, which was named after the Japanese Samurai broadsword that it mainly resembled (but with more than a passing nod to the Jackson Randy Rhoads), and then rather half-heartedly offered to Fender dealerships across the world.

The Katana's looks divided opinion, but there was no doubt about it as a rock guitar, kitted out with Superstrat accoutrements, such as locking tremolo and humbucker pick-ups. Indeed, constructed with a set neck by Fender Japan, it was arguably better than almost anything then coming out of Fender U.S.

But sales were poor, and within a year the Katana had disappeared from Fender's list. By then, an employee buy-out had seen the formation of the Fender Musical Instrument Corporation, and the brand began a gradual recovery. The Katana later found a place on Fender's budget Squier roster. **TB**

Fender
Performer 1985

Type Solidbody electric
Body & neck Alder body, bolt-on maple neck
Fingerboard Rosewood
Pick-ups Two covered humbucker pick-ups

Seeking a solution to the firm's long-term decline, William Schultz, the president of parent company CBS's Musical Instruments Division, began in 1985 to lay the ground for the employee buy-out that would see the formation of the Fender Musical Instruments Corporation. This transition period saw Fender's final attempt to produce "original" instruments, before the company decided to trade wholly on the brand's illustrious history.

After the controversial Katana, Fender hedged its bets on a second Japanese-built model. Whereas the Katana was almost guaranteed to alienate Fender devotees, the Performer resembled a hybrid of a Strat and one of B.C. Rich's more conservative angular body designs. The Performer had, in fact, originally been conceived in the early 1980s, designer John Page working to a brief to produce a deluxe edition of the Jazz bass, but it would hit the shops with a new identity in both six-string and bass guises.

The Performer was a high-end rock instrument on a par with any Superstrat, kitted out with a two-octave fingerboard, locking nut, and floating tremolo system. The humbucking pick-ups, wired with a coil-tap switch, enabled the guitar to produce a wide range of sounds, from fat, Les Paul-type tones to the crisp, sharp, single-coil sound of the Stratocaster. **TB**

BLOC PARTY.

The Performer was in production for only a year, which may explain why there are so few recorded examples of its use. However, Bloc Party frontman Kele Okereke used one on their debut *Silent Alarm* (2005), and plays it in the "Helicopter" and "Little Thoughts" videos.

Gibson
Alpha Q-300 1985

Type Solidbody electric
Body & neck Mahogany body, maple through-neck
Fingerboard Ebony
Pick-ups Three single-coil pick-ups

Traditionally minded devotees of Gibson's gifts to the guitar world, such as the Les Paul and the SG, were set for a culture shock in the 1980s. The company feared that such classic instruments, even though they still generated a hefty chunk of income, were starting to appear outdated and out of step in the eyes of the next generation of potential customers. After all, the Les Paul Goldtop had been around since 1952; the SG since 1961. By contrast, the Jackson Soloist seemed to be ushering in a new era—that of the so-called Superstrat. With this in mind, Gibson set the past aside, and tried to win a coiffeured lock or two of the lucrative hair-metal market. One of the results, along with the US-1, the M-111 Standard, and the eccentrically styled Corvus, was the Q-3000, which was also known as the Q-300.

The Q-3000, which became known for a neck that was fast and fluid, was part of a range that also included the Q-1000 (with a single humbucker), and the Q-2000, which was configured with one single-coil pick-up plus a humbucker. Only a few hundred of the Q-3000s, with its Strat-like shaping, emerged onto the market. Like many of Gibson's models around this period, it didn't last long after launching. There was also the ultra-rare Q-4000, made in very restricted numbers and shouting from the rooftops in pink or red. If you have an Alpha Q-3000 in spanking condition—and if you actually wish to part with it, which you probably won't—recent estimates suggest that you could pick up something around the $700 mark, and double that amount if it's a Custom Shop edition. **CB**

Gibson
Spirit II XPL 1985

Type Solidbody double cutaway
Body & neck Mahogany/maple body, mahogany neck
Fingerboard Rosewood
Pick-ups Two Gibson "Tim Shaw" humbucker pick-ups

Now a rarity, the Spirit was produced between 1982 and 1986. First launched as an Epiphone, it was later remarketed under the Gibson banner. It was based on a double-cutaway Les Paul Junior, but kitted out with humbuckers instead of the single-coil P-90, and neck joints taken further into the body to create a stronger heel. The Spirit's bodies were mainly mahogany flat-tops, some with figured maple, but most in sunburst or plain colors. The pick-ups were "Tim Shaw Humbuckers," which are now highly prized.

The basic Spirit I had a single-pick-up with volume and tone controls, and a "wrap-around" combination bridge/tailpiece. Later models had a separate tailpiece, a Tune-o-matic bridge, and a pickguard similar to that of the Junior. The Spirit I was discontinued in 1984.

The Spirit II had two pick-ups, and humbuckers with exposed coils, but no pickguard. The pick-ups were selected using the three-way switching found on most Les Pauls. It had a volume control for each pick-up, and a single master tone control.

Produced from 1985, the top-of-the-line XPL had an Explorer-style headstock, with six-in-a-line machine heads rather than the three on each side of the I and II models. It came with a Kahler Vibrola and locking nut, and a single humbucker in the bridge position, with an optional second in the neck. **JB**

During the mid-1980s, Chris Hayes from Huey Lewis And The News could be seen playing a Spirit XPL in concert. The band's *Sports* (1983) was one of the period's biggest-selling albums. Hayes left the News in 2000, but returned briefly for the band's *Plan B* (2001).

Ibanez
Axstar 1985

Type Solidbody electric
Body & neck Basswood body, bolt-on maple neck
Fingerboard Rosewood
Pick-ups Two humbucker pick-ups (on the Ax30/Ax40)

"X" marked the spot for a slew of guitar manufacturers in the middle of the 1980s, but none of the x-shaped guitars that hit the market during that period could lay much of a claim to originality. As far back as 1958, Gibson was fashioning the Explorer and the Moderne, for example. The design lived on through the Gibson Firebird of 1963. Then there was Ibanez's own Destroyer in the mid-1970s. All the same, the first generations of the light-bodied Ibanez Axstar made striking visual impressions in 1985, with competition coming from the similarly styled B.C. Rich Stealth and the Carvin-220.

The Axstar series was designed to revive Ibanez's share of the market. Initially, there were three to choose from, each individual selection depending on pick-up preferences: the Ax30 came with two humbuckers, the Ax35 weighed in with two singles and a humbucker, while the Ax38 reversed that. A second wave of guitars—the Ax40/45/48—included fine tuners at the back of the bridge.

The Axstar range extended to the bass, with a Steinberger-like model. Where that headless bass had led, in 1986 its six-string sibling followed. There were significant changes to the design of both ends of this guitar: the Ax70 and Ax75 sacrificed the x-shape for a curved rear; alder replaced basswood for the body, with ebony on the fingerboard in place of rosewood.

However, this was not the end of the x-shaped guitar. The Jackson Warrior appeared as the 1980s crossed over into the 1990s, then made a comeback in the early 2000s. Ibanez itself returned to essentially the same shape for the Xiphos series in 2007. **CB**

Ibanez
XV500 1985

Type Twin cutaway solid electric six-string
Body & neck Basswood body, maple neck
Fingerboard Rosewood
Pick-ups Two V5 blade-pole humbucker pick-ups

The mid-1980s was an era of bands with lots of hair and pointy guitars . . . and none was more pointy than this Ibanez XV500. It was so pointy, in fact, that players had to take care that no one was impaled on it during live shows. Yet the distinctive-looking, lightweight, Z-shaped Ibanez was all the rage throughout its short period of production.

Adverts at the time called these guitars "the shape of the future." Around half of them were made in a purply pink called "violet halfburst," and half of them in a two-tone blue called "blue burst."

This Japanese-built guitar was obviously aimed at metal musicians, with a slim, bolt-on neck and enormous cutaways giving speedy fingers plenty of assistance. Other features included Ibanez's Pro Rock'r version of a locking, top-mounted, Kahler tremolo bridge, a slippery graphite nut, and Ibanez's own sealed "Smooth Tuner II" black machine heads on the pointy headstock. Everything else was minimalist—just a single volume control and pick-up selector. **SH**

Karnak
Isis 1985

Type Solidbody electric
Body & neck Mahogany or ash body and neck
Fingerboard Rosewood or maple
Pick-ups One "Hot Stuff" humbucker pick-up

This Glasgow-based firm, established by Maurice Bellando and James Cannell (a.k.a. Jimmy Egypt), created a range of Egyptian-themed guitars and basses between 1985 and 1987. There were three lines, Karnak, Luxor, and Pharoah, each adding more luxurious woods and different electronic configurations, and each with two models: the Isis and its reverse-bodied counterpart, the Osiris. There were also two basses: the Nefertiti and the fretless Nofretiti.

The basic colors were Anubis Black, Cleopatra White, Nubian Blue, Rosetta Red, and Aurora Tobacco, although some custom-colored examples were also made, and the Pharoahs were honored with offerings of figured tops of various woods and pyramid inlays on their ebony fingerboards. Twin-pick-up models had a separate tone control for each pick-up, a three-way toggle, and a coil-split.

The Karnak range had Schaller pick-ups, whereas the Luxors and Pharoahs boasted custom pick-ups and passive and active electronics, respectively. **OB**

Kramer
Ferrington 1985

Type Acoustic/electroacoustic
Body & neck Maple body and neck
Fingerboard Rosewood
Pick-ups Piezo transducer pick-ups

In the mid-1980s, if you were walking your retriever on the beach in the blazing sunshine, you'd be sure to wear a black, full-linen, jacket-and-trouser combo, and take along a hybrid acoustic-electric with a very easily scuffable black finish. This was the Bob Perine-esque vision for a Kramer/Ferrington marketing campaign featuring Edward Van Halen's latest endorsement—the Kramer/Ferrington acoustic.

Sporting a slim, asymmetrical body and a bolt-on neck, it was the guitar reborn in strummer-friendly form, with a banana-shaped (and, later, a pointy) headstock, diamond inlays, and—on the acoustic-electric model—a built-in bridge transducer. The designer, Nashville luthier Danny Ferrington, was already making similar hybrids, so Kramer offered the classic Fender-shaped KFS-1 and KFT-1 in black, white, red, and cherry sunburst. Many lines followed, updating the look, and adding an Explorer shape, two basses, and a twelve-string, before Kramer launched a Signature Series, which survived into the 1990s. **OB**

Pangborn
Mini Guitar 1985

Type One-off, three-quarter-size solid electric
Body & neck Mahogany body, maple neck
Fingerboard Rosewood
Pick-ups One single-coil and one humbucker pick-up

Ashley Pangborn was a young English guitar maker who worked from a small workshop in South London. At first, he made classical guitars, but he became more successful when he switched to making basses. He counted Level 42's Mark King and The Who's John Entwistle among his customers.

Pangborn also made six-string electrics. Several of these were "mini" guitars, commissioned by private clients who wanted small instruments for travel, convenience, or practice. This one-off custom model was built for Phil Manzanera, Roxy Music's guitarist. It's a three-quarter-size copy of a Gibson Explorer.

Manzanera has long been associated with Gibson Explorers and Firebirds—he eventually made a solo instrumental album entitled *Firebird VII* (2008). But little is known about why Manzanera wanted the mini Explorer, or what became of the instrument.

Pangborn later abandoned his business and went to work for Gibson's Custom Shop in Germany, but still built occasional one-off guitars privately. **SH**

PRS
Custom 1985

Type Solidbody electric
Body & neck Mahogany with maple top, set neck
Fingerboard Rosewood with bird-shaped inlays
Pick-ups Two humbucker pick-ups

A decade after he'd hand-built his first guitar, Paul Reed Smith formed his own company, PRS. PRS products all bear the Paul Reed Smith signature logo on the headstock.

When it began trading, PRS offered three guitars: the maple-topped Custom, the custom-painted Metal, and the PRS, an all-mahogany instrument that by 1987 would be called the Standard.

The Custom soon established itself as the most popular member of the trio, and it has remained in production ever since. It was never cheap, originally retailing for $1,550 (an early example is worth way more today). Its maple top was a major draw, recalling the classic Les Paul of the late 1950s, but in a more modern setting, with figuring that became more and more exotic as time went on. With vibrant, translucent color finishes, it was as if the Les Paul had been pulled kicking and screaming into the modern world.

The early Custom, with its twenty-four-fret fingerboard, felt almost skeletal, like a supermodel, compared to the bulk of the Les Paul. Soundwise, the Custom, with its humbucker/single-coil pick-ups switching from a five-way rotary switch, referenced both Gibson and Fender without, perhaps, nailing either. In fact, it would take many years before Smith was happy with the sound of his creation. **DB**

"The first time I played a PRS…" remembered Mikael Åkerfeldt of Opeth, "I was like, 'Wow, I can actually hear every single string ring in this chord, yet it sounds like a full chord." He uses a variety of PRS Custom models on the Swedish metal band's *Watershed* (2008).

← Opeth's Mikael Åkerfeldt on stage in 2008.

Jose Romanillos
La Buho 1985

Steinberger
GM4T 1985

Type Classical guitar
Body & neck Spruce/rosewood body, cedar neck
Fingerboard Ebony
Other key features Torres-based fan bracing system

Type Double cutaway solidbody electric
Body & neck Maple body, graphite/carbon fiber neck
Fingerboard Phenolic
Pick-ups Two Hotrails, one custom humbucker pick-up

A self-taught luthier, José Luis Romanillos Vega (b. 1932) trained as a cabinetmaker in his native Spain before emigrating to England, where he started making guitars, initially for his own use. In 1969, he showed one of his instruments to Julian Bream, who invited him to set up a workshop on his property. It was there in 1973 that Romanillos created his first masterpiece, a guitar that Bream played for well over a decade, and which became almost as famous as Segovia's Hermann Hauser guitar of 1937.

In fact, Romanillos based a lot of its design on Hauser guitars. He has always sought a characteristic Spanish sound, and this end is achieved by observing design principles established by Torres a hundred years earlier, and later refined by Hauser.

Romanillos is fond of giving his guitars Spanish names. This one from 1985 is called "La Buho" (the owl). With its beautiful lines, trademark rosette, striking head pattern, and perfect finish it is a tour de force, the quintessential Romanillos. **GD**

American luthier Ned Steinberger had great success with his revolutionary L-series instruments, especially the L2 bass guitar.

These models polarized opinion. No one doubted that they were excellent, but many people disliked their looks. As the decade proceeded, Steinberger looked to integrate the innovations of his earlier models into a more conventional-looking guitar.

The 1985 GM4T was a good compromise. It still featured Steinberger's proprietary graphite and carbon fiber neck—lightweight but denser than the heaviest wood—and no headstock, the double-ball-ended strings threaded behind the nut, and tuned from behind the bridge. The neck was, however, bolted to a double cutaway maple body, giving the appearance of a relatively normal guitar.

The GM4T also featured Steinberger's latest innovation—the Trans-Trem, a vibrato unit that detuned strings in tensioned parallel, enabling entire chords to be "bent" but remain in perfect tune. **TB**

Takamine
F-150 1985

Westone
Rail 1985

Type American parlor guitar (replica)
Body & neck Spruce/rosewood body, rosewood neck
Fingerboard Ebony
Other key features Antique finish

Type Headless four-string electric bass
Body & neck Maple body and neck
Fingerboard Rosewood
Pick-ups One Magnaflux RB pick-up

Takamine—named after Mount Takamine in Gifu, central Japan, at the foot of which it has its factory—was founded in 1959 and, in the space of about twenty years, went from being a small workshop to a major manufacturer of a wide range of acoustic and acoustic-electric guitars, from student to professional standards of quality. The company is proud of its innovation capabilities, and, in particular, of its integral Palathetic pick-up system.

In 1984, Takamine, by then an established brand, marketed this limited edition of 150 hand-made parlor guitar replicas to coincide with 150 years since the founding of C.F. Bruno, one of the largest guitar wholesalers of the second half of the nineteenth and early twentieth centuries. All came with certificates of authenticity: in other words, they were authentic replicas. Owners appear to have been delighted with the vintage appearance and distinctively vintage sound of their instruments, though for a little bit more money they could have had the real thing. **GD**

One of the most eye-catching bass designs ever created, the Westone Rail was little more than a neck with a pick-up at the end, a "headless" guitar. Strings were attached to the top of the neck via a bar clamp, and a truss rod ran through the neck. The instrument also had a unique, sliding pick-up assembly, set within the body's mid-section, that also housed a volume control and an output socket, and which slid along the instrument's two uncoated steel rails, making it possible to achieve tonal variations without any electronic gimmickry by sliding the assembly up and down the rails. Its original U.S. list price was $499.50; in the United Kingdom it went on sale for £240.

A common complaint about the Rail is that, owing to the absence of a weighty body, it provides little resistance to hand movements, and moves about easily when the strings are played hard. The Rail takes standard strings, thanks to a clamp at the top of the neck, and was available in three colors: black, red, and white (white models had black rails). **BS**

Ashbory
Bass 1986

Type Solidbody bass guitar
Body & neck First poplar, then agathis, body and neck
Fingerboard Plastic
Pick-ups One piezo transducer pick-up, fitted to bridge

Designed by folk musician and pick-up designer Alun Ashworth-Jones and luthier Nigel Thornbory, this one-piece reproduces the deep, resonant tone of a plucked double bass—a remarkable feat given that, with a scale length of 18 in. (45.75 cm), it is almost half the size of a standard bass guitar. Yet, in spite of its toy-like appearance, the Ashbory is a credible instrument, its tiny, plastic, fretless fingerboard requiring considerable skill to intonate with accuracy.

Its unique tone is derived from special silicone rubber strings, which stretch across an acoustic piezo-

> "Al discovered that a rubber band stretched over one of his guitar transducers produced an impressive bass note when plucked."
>
> NIGEL THORNBORY

transducer pick-up fitted to the bridge. The instrument's short scale length meant a reduced level of tension in the neck, so, unlike other bass guitars, the Ashbory requires no truss rod, making it—like the bridge—non-adjustable. The instrument is most effectively played with the fingers, rather than with a pick, and because of the natural grip of the rubber, dusting the strings with chalk or talcum powder is necessary for any nimble fingerboard movement.

The Ashbory was produced by Guild Guitars until 1988, using a one-piece poplar body and neck. An attempt to launch a Mark II model stalled in 1990. By then established as a cult instrument, the Ashbory was reintroduced in 1999 under Fender's DeArmond brand, this time using cheaper agathis wood. **TB**

Barker
Archtop 1986

Type Acoustic electric archtop
Body & neck Spruce/maple body, maple neck
Fingerboard Ebony with mother-of-pearl markers
Pick-ups One adjustable floating pick-up

It is not often that an individual guitar is credited with turning a musician's life around, but an early William G. ("Bill") Barker archtop from 1964 did just that for Martin Taylor. Having hit a very low point in his career in the 1980s, the British jazz guitarist began the process of selling all his instruments, seemingly intent on giving up on music. The Barker was to be the last to go, but, playing it for what he thought was the final time, he was suddenly inspired to come back from the brink. Taylor later set up a new group, which he named Spirit of Django in honor of Django Reinhardt, whose work with the Quintette du Hot Club de France he particularly admired. After Taylor was reborn in this way, he reportedly vowed never to part with the guitar that had saved him.

This rare archtop from 1986 is one of only a few made with seven strings among Barker's total known output of around 120 guitars, which were produced between the 1960s and the 1980s, the earlier ones in Toledo, Ohio, and the later ones in Bartonville, Illinois.

Barker was part of an elite—one commentator has observed that, during this period, the number of archtop guitar makers could be counted on the fingers of one hand. Rarity alone would have ensured that Barker guitars became highly collectible, but their desirability—and, hence, the prices that they now fetch—have been greatly increased by their immaculate craftsmanship and playability.

After Bill Barker died in 1991 at the age of 63, the business was taken over by Bill Cook, one of his former apprentices, who continues to make top-grade archtops using the same traditional methods. **GD**

Charvel
Model 4 1986

Type Solidbody electric
Body & neck Basswood body, maple neck
Fingerboard Rosewood
Pick-ups Two Jackson J200s and one J50BC pick-up

Charvels played a central role in making "Superstrats" fashionable in the 1980s. They exerted a massive influence on the competition through their combination of single-coil and humbucking pick-ups, and their use of sharply pointed, drooping headstocks.

In 1978, Wayne Charvel sold his share of the business to Grover Jackson, under whose aegis the brand moved from hot-rodding Fenders to producing Charvel guitars and, later, Jacksons.

A list of early Charvel users is a who's who of rock—Eddie Van Halen, Richie Sambora, Warren DeMartini, and Eddie Ojeda. Californian Charvels were hand-built and expensive.

In 1986, Jackson transferred production of some of the most popular configurations to Japan. The Model 4 was one of five Charvels. It featured all the Superstrat accoutremonts—a fast fingerboard, a powered preamp, and a locking tremolo system. Japanese Charvels from this period are regarded as some of the best imported production-line instruments. **TB**

Gittler
Gittler II 1986

Type Skeletal electric
Body & neck Plastic and stainless steel
Fingerboard None as such
Pick-ups Six Gittler pick-ups

Allan Gittler, who died in 2003 at the age of seventy-three, was a virtuoso jazz guitarist and boffin. His experiments in pushing the boundaries of minimalist electric guitar design led to the production of the Gittler guitar—of which sixty examples were produced in New York in the late 1970s. Devoid of a conventional wooden body and made of stainless steel, the instrument looked like the internal workings of a cyber eel from the future—it's sometimes referred to as the "fishbone guitar."

Just as the guitar was gaining popularity in the United States, Gittler changed his name to Avraham Bar Rashi and immigrated to Israel. Here he licensed production of the Gittler guitar to a company called Astron Engineer Enterprises Ltd, based in Kiryat Bialik. It produced the Gittler II model, which faithfully followed the original design but added a molded plastic body and neck to make it easier to handle. Gittler later disowned this version of the guitar because he didn't think the workmanship was up to scratch. **AJ**

Gordon-Smith
Gypsy 60 SS 1986

Knight
Mandola 1986

Type Semi-solid single cutaway
Body & neck Mahogany body and neck
Fingerboard Rosewood
Pick-ups Gordon-Smith humbucker pick-ups

Type Solidbody electric
Body & neck Sycamore/ Sitka spruce body, laminate neck
Fingerboard Maple
Pick-ups One Fishman M-100 piezo pick-up

With the demise of Shergold in the early 1980s, high-volume guitar manufacture in Great Britain looked set to disappear altogether. However, with more than three decades in business, having built and sold more the 10,000 instruments, Gordon-Smith is now the country's only large-scale guitar builder.

Gordon Whitham and John Smith established their firm in 1979 in Partington, near Manchester, with the aim of producing affordable, high-quality, hand-made instruments for working musicians. Their most popular models are based on classic Gibsons, such as the Gypsy series, inspired by the Les Paul Junior. The company also designs its own humbucking pick-ups, and claims to be one of the first to offer a coil-tap switch.

The Gypsy range comprises both solid and semi-solid models, with either single or double cutaways. For comfort and playability, the neck is set into the body at an angle of around eighty degrees. The semi-solid Gypsy 60 (shown here) is visually distinctive due to the unusually large f-holes. **TB**

Knight has been hand making jazz guitars in England since the 1940s—usually by request only. It also specializes in repair work, its website bearing testimonials from Jimmy Page and Pete Townshend, the latter of whom says: "I smash them into a thousand pieces—Knight Guitars put them back together again."

The Mandola isn't actually a guitar, of course—it's the big brother of a mandolin, with eight strings in four pairs, tuned a fifth lower than a mandolin (C-G-D-A). They're commonly used in folk music, especially in Italy, and British folk-punk poet Attila the Stockbroker regularly uses one.

It features a Fishman M-100 piezo pick-up, which is embedded in the bridge, and mother-of-pearl block inlays on the fretboard. It's constructed from high-grade sycamore and Sitka spruce.

"Unplugged or plugged in," say Knight of its instrument, "this will make the hair stand up on the back of your neck." **AJ**

MusicMan
Silhouette 1986

Type Double-cutaway solidbody
Body & neck Poplar, alder, or ash body; maple neck
Fingerboard Maple or rosewood
Pick-ups Three single-coil/humbucker pick-ups

Throughout the early part of the 1980s, MusicMan was almost constantly beset with problems, most of which were caused by the unusual structure of the business network of which it formed a part. The firm originally marketed and sold guitars and basses supplied by CLF (a company whose name was derived from the initials of its owner, Clarence Leo Fender). When a rift emerged between the two businesses in 1979, CLF withdrew from the arrangement; Fender launched a new company to take over MusicMan's former role: this was G&L Musical Instruments (G for George Fullerton; L for Leo Fender; the third co-founder was marketing executive Dale Hyatt).

Left to its own devices, MusicMan struggled on until 1984, when it came under the ownership of Ernie Ball, the guitar string manufacturing company. The MusicMan brand then enjoyed an unexpected resurrection, profitably producing a range of guitars and basses that combined Fender-style bodies with the characteristic asymmetric tuner arrangements of its existing guitars.

In its new form, MusicMan's first significant success was the Silhouette. Launched in 1986, this "Superstrat" featured a 25½-in. (64.75-cm) Fender-style fingerboard extended to twenty-four frets. The meat of the instrument was in the combination of DiMarzio single coils and hand-wound humbucker pick-ups.

MusicMan would continue to be a significant name in the upmarket guitar world, thanks in no small part to successful tie-ins with the likes of Eddie Van Halen and John Petrucci, a founding member of the progressive metal band Dream Theater. **TB**

Stepp
DG1 1986

Type Guitar synthesizer
Body & neck Polycarbonate body and neck
Fingerboard Polycarbonate
Pick-ups In-built synthesizer sounds

A guitar so 1980s that it should have come with its own silly haircut, the Stepp DG1 looked like an unholy hybrid of a digital watch and a Rush fan's imagination, and was impossible to service unless you had a degree in computing. To inventor Stephen Randall, however, it was nothing less than "the logical step in the evolution of the guitar."

In *The Complete Simmons Drum Book* (1987), author Bob Henrit recalls Randall visiting the Simmons company—best known for its electronic drums—"with a sketch of a guitar on the back of a cigarette packet." Simmons agreed to build prototypes, but "ran into so many problems" that they eventually opted to pass on the idea. Randall then took his designs to a consultant in Cambridge, England, and together they brought the Stepp to life.

A distant descendant of Vox's pioneering V251 guitar organ, the DG1 had built-in sounds, mimicking everything from flutes to organs. Whooshy effects were available, too—essential in the unlikely event of your repertoire including Pink Floyd's "On The Run." A later model, the DGX, was a MIDI [Musical Instrument Digital Interface] guitar controller, putting it in the same lineage as the equally 1980s SynthAxe.

For all its flaws, the DG1 was a plucky attempt to think outside the box. "It's not a bastardization of an acoustic instrument," observed Henrit, "and they haven't simply mounted a pick-up and endeavored to pluck control signals from the strings. They've taken a sideways look at the whole concept . . . If you're going to do something different, then you might just as well go the whole hog." **BM**

SynthAxe
SynthAxe 1986

Type MIDI controller
Body & neck Metal chassis with glass fiber covering, metal neck
Fingerboard Glass fiber

Not a guitar as such, the SynthAxe is nonetheless a historically significant slice of technology. Some people back in the 1980s really did think that this synthesizer hybrid was going to be the future of the world's most popular musical instrument.

The instrument was the brainchild of Bill Aitken, who had cut his teeth as a composer/experimenter at the BBC's Radiophonic Workshop sound effects unit. Launched in 1986, the SynthAxe was one of the first dedicated MIDI controllers: it made no sounds of its own, but triggered suitably equipped synthesizers, drum machines, and digital samplers.

The first guitar synthesizers faced a tricky problem: accurately converting the vibrations of a guitar string to digital data without it being corrupted by standard techniques such as bending and vibrato. The SynthAxe's nifty solution was to create two independent sets of strings: a short group on the body was picked to trigger notes, while the set on the neck was fretted to determine the pitch of the note. The pitch data, however, was generated electronically, the frets themselves forming part of the circuit when the string was pressed down.

Although the SynthAxe worked brilliantly, it proved a completely alien playing experience for most guitarists, not least in that all of the frets were spaced equally. "I used to do clinics for SynthAxe and audience members would ask if I could make it sound like a Strat," recalled Allan Holdsworth. "It was pretty funny. They would want to play blues licks on it." A bold failure, very few were built—the $10,000 price tag inevitably limiting its consumer base. **TB**

Casio
MG-500/510 1987

Type Solidbody electric/MIDI guitar
Body & neck Basswood body, maple neck
Fingerboard Rosewood
Pick-ups Two single-coil, humbucker, hexaphonic pick-ups

If one company typified the way the music world seemed to be rolling in the early 1980s, that company was Casio. In an era when the guitar was beginning to look prehistoric, when bands appeared on stage in big shoulder pads, funny haircuts, and wearing their keyboards, Casio was one of a number of—mainly Japanese—companies that saw the only future for the guitar was in combination with the synthesizer.

Founded in Tokyo in 1946, Casio's success was based almost entirely on having developed the world's first all-electric compact calculator in 1957. Two decades later, Casio had developed the era-defining Mini calculator and the Casiotron multifunction watch. It wasn't until 1980 that Casio decided to muscle in on the musical instrument market, with the VL-Tone compact synthesizer/ sequencer/rhythm machine.

In 1987, Casio moved into guitars, with a pair of modestly playable three-pick-up models. Both included a hexaphonic pick-up, which was fitted to the bridge, and capable of creating MIDI (Musical Instrument Digital Interface) data. Vibrations from each of the strings were converted by the guitar's internal circuitry into MIDI "pitch," "gate," and "bend" data, which could then be passed down a cable and connected to external MIDI sound sources, such as synthesizers and drum machines, or used for sending "recording" data MIDI sequencers.

Although kitted out identically, the two guitars were differently styled: the MG-510 had a Strat-shaped body; the MG-500, shown here, had a futuristic design in keeping with the spirit of the age. **TB**

Ibanez
Jem 1987

Type Twin-cutaway solidbody
Body & neck Basswood or alder body, maple neck
Fingerboard Rosewood, maple, or ebony
Pick-ups Two humbuckers and one single-coil pick-up

By the time Ibanez collaborated with Steve Vai to produce the monumental Jem series of Superstrats, it was already among the leading guitar manufacturers, with one of the largest ranges of production instruments—a far cry from the early days of producing Fender, Gibson, and Burns knock-offs.

In 1986, Frank Zappa protégé Vai designed his own instrument for Ibanez. "When I started playing in David Lee Roth's band," he told *American Songwriter*, "all the major manufacturers were very interested in having me play their guitars. I sent out the design to a lot of the companies and they sent me back their standard guitars with a couple of little tweaks, except Ibanez. They gave me back the exact guitar I wanted and it hasn't changed since." The Jem is well suited to the high-speed playing for which Vai is renowned, and its unusual combination of DiMarzio pick-ups—wired so that different positions of the five-way selector engage different humbucker coils—provides every possible sound a rock guitarist could require.

The Jem's garish looks, clashing colors, and floral patterns divided opinion. Another unusual design feature was the "monkey grip" handle, carved into the top of the body. Visuals aside, this is a serious player's guitar, from the dive-bomb Floyd Rose vibrato to the scalloped frets at the top of the scale. **TB**

The Jem and its seven-string counterpart, the Universe, were debuted on Steve Vai's award-winning instrumental album *Passion And Warfare* (1989), which he described as "Jimi Hendrix meets Jesus Christ at a party that Ben Hur threw for Mel Blanc."

Steve Vai, the shredders' shredder. ➡

Ibanez
RG550 1987

Type Solidbody electric
Body & neck Basswood body, maple neck
Fingerboard Maple and rosewood
Pick-ups Two humbuckers and one single-coil pick-up

Ibanez brought out the RG550 in 1987 as a more affordable version of its Jem 777—the first of the series of guitars, developed with Steve Vai, that became the quintessential heavy metal instruments of the era. While using arguably inferior proprietary pick-ups rather than DiMarzios, and leaving out some of the cosmetic features of the original, such as the cut-out "monkey grip," the RG550s retained the Jem body shape (like a Stratocaster with thinner, sharper-looking horns), and the maple neck. Also in place was the "Edge" tremolo, a standard feature on many Ibanez models, which was recessed into the body to allow for a lower action than a standard Floyd Rose system, and had locking studs, which made it so stable that you could shred all day without the strings going out of tune.

For players who absolutely had to play as many notes as possible in any one bar, the RG550 offered advantages over the Strat that it superficially resembles: an ultra-fast, thin neck with wide frets, satin finish, and a tremolo that allowed the use of strings so thin that they were almost invisible. The unfinished fingerboard, although prone to accumulate dirt, is said to reduce drag during fast playing.

The original RG550 was discontinued in 1994 but reintroduced three years later, and again in 2007 for its twentieth anniversary.

According to legend, the RG550 was designed by Rocky George, lead guitarist with the band Suicidal Tendencies, and the "R" and the "G" are his initials. In truth, the initials stand for "Roadstar Guitar" (the RG550 was part of Ibanez's Roadstar Deluxe series). **AJ**

James Tyler
Studio Elite 1987

Type Twin cutaway solidbody electric
Body & neck Alder body, maple neck
Fingerboard Maple or Indian rosewood
Pick-ups Two single-coil pick-ups and one humbucker

Based in California since 1972, James Tyler began his working life repairing and servicing guitars for the cream of LA's studio session scene—outstanding players such as Dann Huff, Steve Lukather, and Mike Landau. Tyler's reputation for fine workmanship quickly spread, and he soon found himself building his own range of boutique guitars.

The Strat-inspired Studio Elite emerged in 1987 and, as its name suggests, came about very much as a result of the company he was keeping. One's eyes are first drawn to the unusual headstock: this may well have been conceived to circumvent Fender's own design patent, which had polarized guitarists for more than three decades. The lower bout of the body also deviates from the Strat, its deep cutaway allowing for easy access to the upper frets. Particular attention is given to the finish of the necks, the much-desired Fender "59" contour aiming to give a vintage "feel."

The Studio Elite's electrics were designed for maximum versatility: a pair of original Tyler single coils and a humbucker in the bridge position, a mid-boost preamp, and a switch to preset the volume for soloing.

Early Tyler guitars are much sought after by players and collectors alike—and, in 2011, the U.S. magazine *Guitar Player* listed the Studio Elite among its fifty greatest guitars of all time. **JB**

In 1986, Steve Lukather commissioned James Tyler to produce a customized Studio Elite with a Floyd Rose vibrato system. Lukather called the guitar "Puffy" and used it throughout the sessions for Toto's *The Seventh One* (1988).

Martin
B-65 Bass 1987

Type Acoustic bass
Body & neck Spruce/maple body, mahogany neck
Fingerboard Ebony
Pick-ups Optional Fishman bridge transducer

When C.F. Martin launched its first electric bass, the EB-18, in 1979, it was greeted with little enthusiasm. So it was perhaps a surprise when, eight years later, the B-65 appeared; designed by Dick Boak, it was Martin's first acoustic bass guitar.

The body of the B-65 was essentially that of a regular Martin jumbo: 16 in. (40.5 cm) wide, 4⅞ in. (12.4 cm) deep, and constructed using solid, flamed maple back and sides, spruce top, and tortoiseshell binding. The neck was mahogany, with twenty-three frets set into a 34-in. (86.4-cm) scale-length ebony fingerboard. It was also offered as a fretless model.

Unlike Martin's six-string guitars, the B-65 featured only side dot markers. The headstock was a typical Martin shape, but fitted with Schaller bass machine heads. A further option was a Fishman bridge transducer with an onboard preamp. This model was designated the B-65-E.

Learning a lesson from the poor sales of the EB-18, Martin looked toward their classic designs with the B-65: visually it was very much in keeping with the styling of their jumbo acoustic, even down to the scratchplate. Although smaller that most other acoustic bass guitars, the B-65 had a fine tone and dynamic range and projected a surprisingly high volume given the size of its body.

Martin later produced a B-65 in a cutaway version, which provided much more comfortable access to the higher frets.

The B-65 remained in production until 1994. A variation of the B-65 design—the B-28KV signature "Klaus Voorman" model—appeared in 2008. **JB**

Ovation
Thunderbolt 1987

Type Shallow cutaway acoustic electric
Body & neck Spruce/plastic body, mahogany/maple neck
Fingerboard Ebony
Pick-ups One piezo pick-up

Some acoustic players were bored with the same old traditional look of their instruments. In the late 1980s, Ovation offered them striking styling previously found only on electric guitars.

The Thunderbolt's shallow synthetic back had been used on several previous Ovations, but the spruce top—with angular sound holes shaped like thunderbolts either side of the upper bout—was new. The walnut bridge was shaped like a thunderbolt, too. And there were no simple wood finishes here—the top was painted red, white, or black.

"Thunderbolt—the amazing new roundback from Ovation that's taking guitarists by storm."

OVATION ADVERT, 1988

The headstock was another change from Ovation's normal design, with six-on-a-side black Schaller tuners looking more like those of an electric guitar. The ebony fretboard had small black dots on the neck binding, rather than the normal position inlays.

Some of the best bits were hidden. The truss rod adjustment was accessible through a door in the back of the instrument, and there was a piezo pick-up under the bridge saddle with its own OP-24 active preamp. Ovation's longitudinal bracing, with the grain of the spruce, gave the wood more chance to vibrate.

The sound, though bright, was more limited than that of a full-bodied wooden guitar. Best in electric mode, the Thunderbolt became popular for live work —Janick Gers of Iron Maiden used one on stage. **SH**

Pensa
MK1 1987

Type Solidbody double cutaway electric six-string
Body & neck Mahogany/maple body, mahogany neck
Fingerboard Rosewood
Pick-ups One EMG humbucker and two single-coil pick-ups

Mark Knopfler met guitar makers Rudy Pensa and John Suhr at the height of Dire Straits' fame in 1980. Together they drank coffee and planned a new instrument on a café napkin. This guitar has since become known as the MK1—a highly sought-after, custom-made instrument used not only by Knopfler, but by many other top players, too.

The shape is roughly along the lines of the Stratocaster, although it's all made of mahogany. The fretboard is rosewood, and the body is topped by a decorative slice of maple.

Knopfler's first MK1 was designated serial number 001. It had an EMG humbucker pick-up in the bridge position, with two SA single-coils in the middle and neck positions. The electronics featured a "presence boost" acting on the mid range, which was activated by pulling up the tone control. Other features included a Floyd Rose locking tremolo, Sperzel locking tuners, black headstock, and gold hardware.

Suhr later left to work with Fender in 1990 and the guitars became known simply as Pensa. The MK1 is still made—a new one will cost you more than $7,000. Knopfler has since switched to other Pensa MK evolutionary models, including the MK2, and the MK80. Other Pensa players include Peter Frampton, Lou Reed, and Eric Clapton. **SH**

The Pensa MK1 was used by Mark Knopfler on *Neck And Neck* (1990), his celebrated collaboration with legendary country picker Chet Atkins. "Poor Boy Blues," a single from the album, won a Grammy Award in 1991.

PRS
Signature 1987

Type Solidbody electric
Body & neck Mahogany/maple body, set neck
Fingerboard Rosewood with bird-shaped inlays
Pick-ups Two humbucker pick-ups

The original PRS Custom was so expensive that one might have thought that the next step for its creator, Paul Reed Smith, would have been to produce a more affordable instrument. But PRS, in only its second year of production, introduced a guitar that was nearly $1,000 more expensive. Smith later recalled: "I showed a guitar to William Compton, a psychologist and teacher, and he said 'You don't charge enough.' My mind just reeled. So we thought: let's take absolutely the best maple tops, put them on the guitars, and I'll sign them. And it worked."

While only 1,000 Signature guitars were made, it was the first "ultimate" PRS guitar. More followed—often small runs featuring the finest available woods, and often with highly decorative inlays.

Aside from the exclusive wood choice and that hand-signed headstock, the Signature was identical to the Custom, including a "sweet switch"—a passive tone filter that attenuated the high-end—instead of a conventional tone control.

Ultimately, it proved difficult to make, as Smith wasn't always available to sign the headstock of the guitars, leading to hold-ups in the spray department. "They had me sign model decals, and they put those under the finish a couple of times. They even threatened to sign 'em themselves. So that was the end of that!" The price of the Signature gave fuel to detractors who claimed that PRS made guitars only for "lawyers, doctors, and dentists."

Smith revived the "signature" concept in 2011. A year later, PRS's first official multi-artist endorsement became the 408 standard production model. **DB**

Bourgeois
Martin Simpson 1988

Type Acoustic guitar
Body & neck Mahogany/spruce or rosewood/spruce body, maple neck
Fingerboard Ebony

English folk virtuoso Martin Simpson collaborated with New England luthier Dana Bourgeois to design and construct this high-end, special edition, acoustic guitar in 1988.

The dreadnought-sized acoustic was specially tailored to fingerstyle or flatpicking players, with a wide neck—1¾ in. (4.5 cm) at the nut—providing room for fancier fingerwork.

The sloped cutaway gave the player access up to the fifteenth fret, but the design of the guitar's internal bracing helped retain power and projection

"A great twelve-fret jumbo guitar for fingerstyle or flatpicking. Martin and Dana created something unique with this model."
AL PETTEWAY

in the sound. The result was one of the best-sounding fingerpicking acoustic guitars available.

Buyers could choose either the warmth of mahogany or the clarity of rosewood on the back and sides of the guitar: both versions had resonant tops of solid spruce. The decorations were discreet—there was no need for ostentation—with subtle abalone rosette, gold Schaller tuners with ebony buttons, and a simple ebony bridge.

The Martin Simpson was never intended for plectrum strumming, so there was no scratchplate fitted. However, the acclaimed K&K Pure Western transducer pick-up could be specified.

Bourgeois has built guitars for many other leading musicians, including Ry Cooder and James Taylor. **SH**

D'Aquisto
Avant Garde 1988

Type Steel-string acoustic
Body & neck Spruce and maple body, maple neck
Fingerboard Ebony

Many people now regard Jimmy D'Aquisto as the greatest twentieth-century luthier. Since all his instruments were personally hand-crafted to such a high standard, his output during a thirty-year career was not huge—even at his peak, during the 1980s, he was building no more than fifteen guitars a year. This limited supply made D'Aquisto guitars mind-bogglingly expensive, and, at the time of his death in April 1995, his order books had a ten-year waiting list.

Although D'Aquisto was an avid experimenter, most of his guitars were largely traditional in appearance, heavily influenced by his mentor John D'Angelico. Not so the model shown here. One of D'Aquisto's most unusual designs, the Avant Garde is a strikingly uncluttered vision, which features two oval sound holes, a raised ebony pickguard, and a pair of unusual headstock cutouts—it really does look as if it ought to be on permanent display at the Met in New York. D'Aquisto built only custom-order guitars, with specifications tailored to suit the needs of the purchaser, although he would refuse requests that he felt lacked merit. The wealthy Californian vintage guitar dealer who, in 1988, commissioned the prototype of the Avant Garde evidently contributed construction ideas as well as the model's name.

After D'Aquisto's death, prices for his guitars quickly rocketed. Shortly afterward, the dealer sold his Avant Garde for approaching $150,000—although at current market values that seems like a snip. Indeed, if a non-celebrity guitar ever manages to surpass the million-dollar mark, it is very likely to be one built by James L. D'Aquisto. **TB**

Fender Stratocaster
Eric Clapton 1988

Type Solidbody electric
Body & neck Alder body, maple neck
Fingerboard Maple
Pick-ups Three Gold Lace Sensor single-coil pick-ups

The antecedent of Fender's first signature guitar was "Blackie"—a guitar that Eric Clapton assembled from parts of three different mid-1950s Strats and which had been his favorite since Derek And The Dominos.

Fender used the body of an Elite Stratocaster with a neck based on that of a Martin acoustic—Clapton's preference—but with an even softer "V." The Elite's pick-ups were replaced with Gold Lace Sensors, which have metal barriers surrounding the single-coils that reduce electro-magnetic interference, and a mid-boost circuit that makes them sound more like humbuckers. Clapton was evidently trying to recreate the tone he had developed during the Cream era when he was mainly playing Les Pauls and SGs.

The 1988 model was essentially a recreation of a 1957 Strat: twenty-two vintage-style frets, Gotoh/Kluson tuners, TBX tone controls (that allow frequencies to be boosted or cut), and an active 25dB boost circuit. The vintage synchronized tremolo bridge was blocked with a piece of wood to disable the mechanism—Clapton liked the bridge but tended not to use the tremolo. The Lace Sensors were replaced by Fender Vintage Noiseless pick-ups in 2001. There have been many custom variations over the years including a short run with a rosewood fretboard and one finished in gold leaf, with gold-plated hardware. **AJ**

Clapton used a prototype for his signature Fender on *August* (1986). A reconstructed version—with the neck put on a black body—was his main stage guitar from 1990 to 1993, and hence features on *24 Nights* (1991), taped at London's Royal Albert Hall in 1990 and 1991.

Fodera
Anthony Jackson 1988

Type Electric six-string bass
Body & neck Alder/maple body, maple neck
Fingerboard Brazilian rosewood
Pick-ups One humbucker pick-up

A Grammy-nominated New York bass player with over 3,000 sessions and 500 albums to his name, Anthony Jackson is also a pioneer of the six-string bass guitar, using models built two decades before they gained common currency. Frustrated by the limitations of four strings, Jackson argued: "As the lowest-pitched member of the guitar family, the instrument should have had six strings from the beginning. The only reason it had four was because Leo Fender was thinking in application terms of an upright bass."

In 1975, luthier Carl Thompson built a six-string "contrabass" for Jackson, adding a low "B" and a high "C" to the standard four strings. By 1981, Jackson was using custom-built six-string basses exclusively. In 1988, he asked luthier Vinnie Fodera to create a new instrument. The result was his signature model, a monster with a 30-in. (76-cm) scale and a twenty-eight-fret fingerboard, but with surprisingly basic electrics—just a single, humbucking pick-up wired directly to the output socket, with not a tone or volume control in sight.

The brand was established in 1983 by Fodera and bassist Joey Lauricella, who aimed to produce high-end, handmade instruments that were also visually distinctive. Intended for professionals, Fodera basses have been adopted by the likes of Victor Wooten. **TB**

Anthony Jackson's bass work has graced many genre-defining albums, including *The Nightfly* (1982), the widely acclaimed solo debut from Steely Dan's Donald Fagen, which featured all-original material plus a version of "Ruby Baby" by Leiber and Stoller.

Gibson
US-1 1988

Type Solidbody electric
Body & neck Balsa/maple body, maple neck
Fingerboard Ebony
Pick-ups One PAF humbucker and two ML-180 pick-ups

The US-1 was possibly one of the oddest instruments that Gibson ever made. First produced in 1988, it was evidently an attempt to create a "pointy headstock" guitar in the style of the many "Superstrat" guitars that had flooded the market during the earlier part of the decade.

The US-1 had a short lifespan, but it made its mark with Gibson aficionados. The body shape was closer to a Jackson Soloist than a regular Stratocaster, but it was very light because it was made largely from balsa wood. (Gibson kept his choice of material quiet during the development stage, throughout which it was codenamed "Chromyte.") The rims, back, and top were made from maple. So, too, was the neck, which had a bound, twenty-two-fret, ebony fingerboard with attractive "Double Triangle" pearl inlays. The US-1 also had an atypical scale length—25½ in. (64.75 cm), as usually found on a Fender, rather than Gibson's regular 24¾ in. (63 cm). The US-1 was available with a Tune-o-matic bridge and stop tailpiece, a Kahler Vibrola, or a Floyd Rose unit.

The headstock was widely regarded as a rip-off, but Gibson could reasonably have argued that they'd merely produced a pointed version of their own Explorer headstock from the late 1950s—which had itself been copied by Jackson, Kramer, ESP, and other makers of contemporary rock guitars.

The pick-ups certainly gave more than a passing nod to the Superstrat: they were a combination of single-coils and humbuckers: a PAF at the bridge, and two ML-180s in the center and neck positions. All in all, the US-1 was indubitably a cool guitar. **JB**

Gilbert
Classical Guitar 1988

Type Classical guitar
Body & neck Spruce/rosewood body, rosewood neck
Other key features Fan bracing similar to Hernandez y Aguado guitars, distinctive rosette design, French polish

A tool engineer for almost two decades, John Gilbert (1922–2012) started making guitars in his spare time in 1965. In 1974, he decided to make it his career. Two years later, David Russell was introduced to Gilbert's guitars, became a convert, played several for many years, and introduced other concert guitarists to (in his own words) "the bright, strong sound of his guitars." Soon, everyone wanted one, and eventually there was a twenty-year waiting list. Guitarists Raphaella Smits, Benjamin Verdery, and David Tannenbaum, to name but a few, played Gilbert guitars; Russell himself had three, including an eight-string model.

Constantly experimenting to improve all aspects of the instrument, Gilbert introduced "T"-shaped braces that are lighter and stronger than traditional ones, did away with saddles, and devised an electronic tool to find and remove wolf notes. Such exceptional details make this 1988 example a superb concert instrument. Having made around 120 guitars, Gilbert handed over production to his son, William, in 1991. Thereafter he focused on developing his own superior brand of tuning machines.

John Gilbert believed that guitar making was a mixture of about ninety percent science with ten percent art. "The art comes in how you use the science," he once said. **GD**

Grammy-winner David Russell's *The Music Of Barrios* (1995) features a guitar made by John Gilbert. The album comprises a series of twenty-one romantic pieces by the prolific Paraguayan guitarist-composer Agustín Barrios (1885–1944).

Gretsch Traveling Wilburys 1988

Type Single cutaway solidbody
Body & neck Maple body and neck
Fingerboard Ebony
Pick-ups One single-coil pick-up (on original TW100)

In the 1980s, Gretsch was in the doldrums. Stray Cat Brian Setzer kept the flame burning, but the revival began only when Fred Gretsch—great-great-grandson of the founder—repurchased the brand from the Baldwin Music Company in 1985. "There was another boost when George Harrison collaborated with Gretsch designers to produce the unique Traveling Wilburys collector guitar," Fred recalled. "By 1989, Gretsch guitar production had begun in earnest."

This was not the first time that Harrison had influenced the history of the company. His use of a Gretsch Chet Atkins Country Gentleman guitar in The Beatles had, Gretsch noted, "ignited a frenzy for that model among aspiring guitarists." (Moreover, a Gretsch Duo Jet graces the cover of Harrison's 1987 album *Cloud Nine*.)

Signature models were created for Harrison, Bob Dylan, Tom Petty, Roy Orbison, and Jeff Lynne—although the signatures in question, reproduced on the back of the body, were those of their Wilbury pseudonyms, Nelson, Lucky, Charlie T., Lefty, and Otis. The white bodies had Wilbury-themed graphics silk-screened on the front. "They bore no resemblance to any other past or current Gretsch," observed gretschpages.com. "Truth be told, they were sort of a Danelectro/Tele hybrid." Although the group's debut was cut before the guitars were ready, Harrison plays one in the "Handle With Care" video.

Over the next three years, there followed six further models, with varying graphics and features, including a humbucker, dual single-coils, and, on the TW600, a Floyd Rose tremolo system. **BM**

Hermann Hauser III
Classical Guitar 1988

Type Classical
Body & neck Cedar/rosewood body, mahogany neck
Fingerboard Ebony
Other key features Torres-like bracing system

Following in the footsteps of his grandfather, father, and elder brother, three of the greatest luthiers of the twentieth century, Hermann Hauser III (b. 1958) learned the craft of instrument-making at the Staatliche Geigenbauschule in Mittenwald, Germany. Asked by *Guitars International* if it was easier to receive the baton from such distinguished forebears, he sounded unsure: "I think maybe a person who starts fresh has it much easier, because he can do what he likes. I have always had the tradition in my head. So maybe in some things I'm not so free."

"Only build few instruments, so that you can vouch for each single instrument, and only work for few, but content, artists."
HERMANN HAUSER I

Hermann Hauser III started constructing guitars with his own labels in 1977, independent of his father, with whom he shared a workshop in Reisbach.

Hauser currently manufactures a maximum of seventeen guitars per annum, with each instrument carefully and painstakingly calibrated to the purchaser's exact requirements. His work retains all the style and aesthetic of Hermann Hauser I, creator in 1937 of Segovia's best-known instrument, but features new improvements, including Reischl tuners, occasionally a four-piece back consisting of two outer pieces of Brazilian rosewood and two maple pieces in the center, the occasional use of cedar for the top (as in this 1988 example), and lacquering on all but the soundboards, which are French-polished. **GD**

Jackson Instant Sex Custom 1988

Type Solidbody electric
Body & neck Maple and poplar body, maple neck
Fingerboard Ebony
Pick-ups One humbucker pick-up

In the Jackson Custom Shop in Ontario, California, the philosophy is simple: no guitar design is too far-out or too crazy to try. Their craftsmen may seem demented, but what else would you expect from the guys who gave the world the Concorde? With the Instant Sex Custom, they went one better—hardly a surprise, perhaps, for a guitar maker that began as a custom shop. Hardly a surprise, either, for a team of luthiers with over 170 years of combined experience, and who pride themselves on the manufacture of unique, occasionally outlandish, one-off instruments.

"A small Southern California guitar repair shop became the epicenter of a new level of shred-approved excellence."

JACKSON GUITARS ADVERTISING

Jackson's popularity took off in the mid-1980s, and in 1988 the craftsmen, led by the company's creator Grover Jackson, came up with the Instant Sex Custom, an instrument that was typical of the high-quality, high-performance metal "shred machines" that they were becoming increasingly proficient at producing, and which—along with the Soloist, King V, Double Rhoads, and the X-shaped Warrior—have become icons of the brand.

The motifs that adorn the face of the Instant Sex Custom were typical of the hard rock era. And of course there were all the usual characteristic Jackson trademarks, such as the pointed headstock. Jackson still produces cutting-edge guitars for thrash metal, speed metal, death metal, rap metal, and grunge. **BS**

Marlin Masterclass Sidewinder 1988

Type Hollow body electric
Body & neck Plywood body, maple neck
Fingerboard Rosewood
Pick-ups Two single-coil humbucker pick-ups

Marlin was the brand name of a Korean-made range imported into Britain in the late 1980s by British Music Strings. This Wales-based company made a name for itself with imports, but by designing and building very decent guitars, including the Sidewinder.

Maligned by some, the imported Marlins were, in fact, highly creditable budget guitars. The Masterclass MMC-11 was well rated on launch, but it was the Sidewinder that perhaps best typifies the Marlin legacy. Extremely weighty (owing to a multi-ply body through which it acquired a reputation for being near-indestructible), with an ugly bridge, and a little too angular on its edges, the Sidewinder was a standard Strat-style copy, with a humbucker pick-up at the bridge, and a three-spring tremolo.

For a time, the Sidewinder dogged the sales of Squier Strats in Britain, and even spawned a bass counterpart. According to an entertaining defence of the guitar by Bob Leggitt on the Planet Botch website, it was, at one point, the United Kingdom's best-selling guitar. "The Sidewinder came in a choice of seven finishes," Leggitt adds, "including Black, Pearl White, Charcoal Fire, Candy Apple Red, Midnight Blue, Flamingo Pink, and Purple Haze. The inclusion of some rather attractive metallic finishes was another surprise on such a cheap guitar, and the actual standard of assembly was usually impressive for the price."

Occasional debates about Marlin's merits on forums are notable both for the Flat Earth Society-esque fervor of those who remember the brand with affection, and for the inevitable comic consequences of Marlin being mixed up with Martin. **BS**

McGlincy
Custom Acoustic 1988

Onyx
1030 1988

Type Hollow body electric
Body & neck Spruce/rosewood body, mahogany neck
Fingerboard Ebony
Other key features Purfling, transparent pickguard

Type Twin cutaway solid electric
Body & neck Laminate body, unknown neck
Fingerboard Rosewood
Pick-ups Two humbucker pick-ups

There are thought to be nine of these custom-made guitars, made by L. Edward ("Ed") McGlincy of Bayville, New Jersey. All are slightly different, and seemingly inspired by the Martin 000 and OM Auditorium, their ornamentation suggesting vintage instruments from fifty or sixty years earlier.

Apparently Bob Dylan was among the first to own a McGlincy Custom Acoustic. He showed it to Gordon Lightfoot, who then ordered one for himself. Lightfoot's guitar, very similar to this 1988 example, but with simpler bridge and rosette designs, can be seen on the cover of his *Dream Street Rose* (1980).

Lightfoot showed the guitar to Terry Clements, the lead guitarist in his band, and he ordered one, too. A McGlincy would be a fixture in Lightfoot's band thereafter. Johnny Cash was another famous owner. With such eminent musicians owning and playing his clearly desirable guitars, it is unfortunate, that due to ill health and early retirement, Ed McGlincy did not leave behind a greater legacy. **GD**

These guitars were built in Korea and China but marketed in Australia under the Onyx name. Most Onyx instruments were entry-level copies, but the 1030 was more interesting. Its body seemed inspired by a U.S.-made Mosrite of the 1960s, but the hardware was more in tune with the 1980s: the uncovered humbucker pick-ups featured tone and volume controls, plus two micro switches to turn each pick-up on and off.

Distinctive features included a shapely, curved scratchplate, and a neck pick-up at a heavy slant to the strings. The black-and-gray sunburst effect was repeated on the three-on-a-side Gibson-style headstock, which also featured a black truss rod cover. However, the non-locking tremolo bridge/tailpiece unit caused tuning problems, as did the unbranded machine heads. Many owners replaced both sets of hardware.

While the original instruments have faded from guitar history books, Onyx Guitars has recently resurfaced as an imported brand in Australia. **SH**

Overwater
C Bass 1988

PRS
Classic Electric 1988

Type Solidbody electric bass
Body & neck Maple top, ash body, maple neck
Fingerboard Ebony fingerboard with twenty-four frets
Pick-ups Two Overwater custom humbucker pick-ups

Type Solidbody electric
Body & neck Alder body, maple neck
Fingerboard Maple with dot inlays
Pick-ups Two humbucker pick-ups

The pioneering, low-range C Bass is part of an elite stable of electric basses from Chris May of Overwater Basses in Carlisle, England. At 36 in. (91.4 cm), it was for some years the longest-scale bass guitar around, until surpassed by Knuckle Guitar Works' Quake bass. It is a striking instrument, with sinuous lines, stretched-out look, and beguiling geometry that recalls images by Salvador Dalí. It is tuned C-F-B♭-E♭, four semitones below standard four-string bass tuning. It predates Overwater's earliest five-string basses, and basses that were extended to eight-string configurations.

The first C Bass—a variant of Overwater's Original Series from 1979—was built for bassist Andrew Bodnar when he played in the Thompson Twins' live band in the early 1980s. Overwater customers have included John Entwistle, David Gilmour, and Martin Kemp. It has manufactured around 3,400 instruments since inception. More recently, Overwater designed a series of mid-price basses that are manufactured and distributed by Tanglewood Guitars. **GD**

The original Classic Electric was PRS' first bolt-on instrument, the first PRS with a maple fingerboard, the first with an alder body, and the first to feature the bold capital-letter PRS logo.

If the body, neck, and fingerboard recalled the Fender—although the guitar still featured the 25-in. (63.5-cm) scale length, twenty-four frets, and body shape of the Custom—the effect was short-lived, with maple tops soon added. "Classic Electric" was later abbreviated to "CE."

The guitars were then simplified, with just a three-way mini toggle pick-up selector (with an enlarged chromed switch tip) that voiced either humbucker or inside coils together, unusually, in series. Although this was changed to the standard five-way rotary pick-up selector, it gave the original Classic Electrics a voice more like that of a hot Fender.

Classic Electric/CE guitars remained in production for two decades, and laid the foundation for future bolt-ons: the EG series, and Swamp Ash Special. **DB**

Washburn
EC36 1988

Type Solidbody electric
Body & neck Maple body and neck
Fingerboard Ebony
Pick-ups One Washburn humbucker pick-up

Even Malcolm Young, co-founder of AC/DC, who allegedly referred to the upper reaches of his guitar's neck as "the dusty end of the fingerboard," might have to admit that Stephen Davies' extended cutaway designs were nothing to, well, sneeze at.

A luthier and guitarist who eventually grew frustrated by the limitations of four octaves, Davies created designs that evolved into a line of electrics introduced by Washburn in 1988 as the Stephen's Extended Cutaway series. The most notable of the lot was the thirty-six-fret EC36, of which 500 were made.

"The guitarist is now free to write and play guitar music that previously existed only in theory."

WASHBURN GUITARS ADVERT, LATE 1980s

The EC36 had a deep, sweeping, lower cutaway that provided access to five full octaves of shred. Davies's through-neck construction, which Washburn literature described as "extensively carved," eliminated the neck-joint heel to allow maximum reach. The EC36's short scale length made for some crowded fretwire, however, which Washburn "compensated" '(i.e., narrowed) beyond the twenty-fourth fret.

Arriving at the zenith of the Superstrat era, the EC36 came standard with a Floyd Rose tremolo for dive-bomb runs, and "crackle" finishes in a variety of colors. The fingerboard left room for a single proprietary "hum-canceling" pick-up. The model shown here features an Ibanez-style "monkey grip," which could be ordered as an option. **DP**

Yamaha
G10 1988

Type Solidbody MIDI controller
Body & neck Plastic body and neck
Fingerboard Plastic
Pick-ups Three sensors: pitch, bend, and velocity

The marriage of the guitar and digital technology seemed to open up endless possibilities in the 1980s. It was a time when MIDI (Musical Instrument Digital Interface) was all the rage. The SynthAx arrived in 1984. Four years later, Yamaha unleashed the G10, cheaper (though still pricey by the standards of the day), and much less cumbersome.

Strictly speaking, the G10 was a MIDI controller rather than a MIDI guitar. It made no sounds of its own, but could draw on the aural options available on a compatible synth. However, efforts were made to make guitarists feel as much at home as possible while still pushing the boundaries. Players reaching for the whammy bar encountered the controller arm, which offered a wide palette of options, including altering the pitch and the volume levels. The headless style brought to mind the Steinberger basses from earlier the same decade. Yet none of this was enough to attract buyers in sufficient numbers.

There was the transition—which some didn't make—to a situation where the G10 worked best with unwound strings, all of the same weight. As the guitar was set up to sense where a string was hit, it was not even necessary to conform to any conventional tuning. Where the G10 did score highly was in speed of response for the sound, processing the information very quickly, even with pull-offs and hammer-ons.

Press releases trumpeted the G10 with the line: "Now guitarists can control the world." The fact that the model was discontinued within a year rather suggests that they preferred a different route to global domination. **CB**

Zemaitis
Solid Bass 1988

Type Solid electric four-string bass
Body & neck Mahogany body and neck
Fingerboard Rosewood
Pick-ups One Seymour Duncan pick-up

Boutique guitar maker Tony Žemaitis had already been using metal scratchplates for years when he came to build this striking four-string bass guitar.

Some of these metal tops completely covered the face of the guitar, and allowed Zemaitis' Danny O'Brien a chance to engrave elaborate decorations. Players found that the metal added a unique flavor to the sound. Yet the original idea was simply to provide a shield for the guitar's electrics to reduce hum. In fact, Zemaitis's first metal-topped guitar was made in the late 1960s for Tony McPhee of The Groundhogs.

The decorated metal became one of Zemaitis' best known styles, used by artists including Ronnie Wood and Marc Bolan. O'Brien, formerly a shotgun engraver, has now became well known for the distinctive decorative work. Today, his name normally appears on the decorated metal tops between the bridge and tailpiece, like an artist's signature.

Zemaitis started making metal-topped basses in the 1980s, too. Now the company has a range of nine metal-fronted bass guitars. Like the early model shown here, these feature a hand-crafted Zemaitis-designed solid aluminum bridge with large thumb wheels for adjusting the string height.

On this particular Zemaitis bass, the engraving is less intricate than the style would later become. Nevertheless, this is clearly a top-end guitar. The single Seymour Duncan pick-up has an ebony cover, and there are engraved metal plates for the headstock logo and truss-rod cover. Even the tailpiece is decorated. The company name is engraved prominently in the middle of the scratchplate. **SH**

Fender Twin-Neck
Custom 1989

Type Solidbody electric
Body & neck Ash body, maple neck
Fingerboard Rosewood
Pick-ups Three single-coil (one on Esquire) pick-ups

This formidable twin-neck was one of the first guitars produced by the Fender Custom shop—a division of Fender Musical Instruments that was established in 1987 in an attempt to revive the craftsmanship and attention to detail that the company was known for back in its golden age, before the CBS takeover. It was built by master luthier Michael Stevens, one of the co-founders of the Custom Shop—he had made a Fender-style twin-neck for Christopher Cross a few years earlier, but this was the first ever double-neck guitar that was an actual Fender. According to Stevens: "They had a double-neck 'plank' bass for testing strings in R&D, but it was not a product for sale, nor very pretty." In view of the fact that Gibson had produced double-neck models as far back as 1958, and that Gretsch had been doing the same since 1961, this is perhaps surprising. With a retail price of $3,688, the Twin-Neck Custom also had the distinction of being Fender's most expensive guitar to date.

Avoiding the usual approach of combining two different types of guitar—guitar and bass or one six- and one twelve-string instrument—the upper half of this guitar is based on a Stratocaster, and the lower half on a Fender Esquire. The body contours on each side are appropriate to each of these guitars, with rounded edges on the top, and square, Telecaster-style, edges on the bottom. The tone knob can be pushed or pulled to switch necks, and the Stratocaster half of the instrument has a "Synchronized Tremolo" combined bridge/tailpiece with the tremolo arm on the wrong side, in order to keep it out of the way of the Esquire part. **AJ**

G&L
Commanche 1989

Type Solidbody electric
Body & neck Alder body, maple neck
Fingerboard Rosewood
Pick-ups Three Z-coil pick-ups

In 1979, after business disagreements with Forrest White and Tom Walker—former colleagues and fellow co-founders in 1971 of MusicMan—Leo Fender extricated himself from the company and teamed up with George Fullerton—with whom he had designed the epoch-defining Telecaster—to establish an entirely new enterprise, G&L Guitars. (The letters were a combination of their first initials.)

Unsurprisingly, G&L guitars traded heavily on the two men's illustrious heritage. Nevertheless, although they leaned heavily on the Fender classic body shapes, there was one overwhelmingly significant new development—G&L moved away from single coils, and installed humbucking pick-ups on its guitars. The aim was to produce updated interpretations of the kinds of instrument on which the Fender company had built a reputation that had sadly declined after the sell-off to CBS in 1965.

Making its entry toward the end of the Superstrat era, the highly regarded Commanche was a slim, spiky take on the classic Strat body—in this case somewhat elongated—with three split Magnetic Field Design Z-coil humbuckers. An immediate commercial success, the Commanche has remained in production ever since, although the period-style sharpness of the body has gradually evolved into more conventional, Strat-like contours.

Leo Fender died in 1991; George Fullerton in 2009. Some feared that G&L might lose its identity, but it has since faithfully maintained the founders' production values, and the guitars produced by the company today are fully in keeping with its original vision. **TB**

Godin
LR Baggs 1989

Type Electroacoustic guitar
Body & neck Mahogany body, rock maple neck
Fingerboard Rosewood
Pick-ups One LR Baggs pick-up

Robert Godin is a guitar maker from Quebec, and this model helped establish his company as one of the most innovative makers of acoustic instruments.

Glance at the Godin LR Baggs "acousticaster"— "LR Baggs" refers to its pick-up and electronics—and you could be forgiven for thinking you are looking at a Fender Telecaster (not least because the neck is bolted to the body, Fender-style). But closer examination reveals that, although the body shapes are similar, this is in fact an acoustic guitar.

The body is cut from mahogany, with two interior sound chambers, and capped by a solid spruce top finished in gloss black with cream binding. The guitar was also available in natural, white, cherry sunburst, and turquoise. The ebony bridge appears to be of traditional design, with a single saddle and bridge pins, but there are eighteen metal "tines" that are tuned. These vibrate sympathetically and help give the "acousticaster" its unique sound. The rock maple neck has a scale length of 25 ½ in. (64.75 cm) and is topped with a twenty-two-fret rosewood fingerboard with small dot inlays.

The headstock is equipped with Schaller machine heads and two string trees. The LR Baggs preamp controls—a gain and three unobtrusive EQ sliders— are mounted on the top of the body.

Lightweight and very comfortable to play, this proved popular with electric players who wanted an acoustic guitar with a familiar feel. "Adaptable and unusual . . . a rare combination," enthused *Guitarist* at the time. And it sounded great, both acoustically and amplified. Every guitarist should have one. **JB**

Heartfield
Talon 1989

Type Solidbody electric Superstrat
Body & neck Basswood body, maple neck
Fingerboard Rosewood
Pick-ups Two single-coil pick-ups, one humbucker

Fender started making Heartfield guitars in the late 1980s in the acclaimed Fujigen Gakki factory in Japan, which had been making high-end Ibanez guitars. The factory produced four types of six-string electrics and two basses in the four years before the yen/dollar exchange rate made the arrangement unsustainable.

The Elan was the top of the line: a Superstrat aimed at the new breed of metal players, with the two Fender single-coil pick-ups supplemented by a Heartfield humbucker. After that, Fujigen continued making Elan guitars under its own name, mainly for the Japanese market.

At the time the Elan was considered a cutting-edge instrument. With its Floyd Rose tremolo system, pointy headstock, deep cutaways, and slim horns, it was a very radical guitar for Fender. The guitars were labeled in various ways: "Heartfield," "Heartfield by Fender," or just plain "Fender."

Today, Heartfield instruments are highly sought after and command top resale prices. **SH**

Ibanez
Maxxas MX3 1989

Type Semi-hollow electric
Body & neck Mahogany body, maple neck
Fingerboard Rosewood
Pick-ups Two DiMarzio humbucker pick-ups

In 1989, Ibanez was worried that its new experimental lightweight guitar, designed to avoid the pointy headstocks common to the Jacksons and Kramers of the time, would not be a commercial success. So, instead of putting the Ibanez name on the headstocks, it chose to label them "Maxxas: A Division of Ibanez." That way, if they happened to fail, they would not tarnish the good name of Ibanez. Hoshino Gakki, the company president, wasn't overly fond of these models, either, and worried that they would not fit into the Ibanez range.

The first Maxxas guitars were released in 1987, but it was the MX3 in 1989 that would be most faithful to the original concept of its designer, Ibanez's own Rich Lasner. It had a carved, semi-acoustic sound chamber, which was made from a single block of Honduras mahogany, split into top and back, and then carved both inside and out to create its resonant tones. It also had an HQ tremolo. Colors included Fountain Blue and Cranberry Red. **BS**

Kramer Floyd Rose Sustainer 1989

Type Double cutaway solidbody
Body & neck Alder body, maple neck
Fingerboard Rosewood
Pick-ups One humbucker and one single-coil pick-up

Gary Kramer had made a big splash in the 1970s guitar world with his use of aluminum necks. But neither he nor his erstwhile partner, Travis Bean, could create sustainable businesses. By 1981, Kramer had left the company he founded, and the radical designs had been replaced by instruments geared toward the rock and metal markets.

The success of the transition was due in no small measure to the patronage of the guitar hero of the era, Eddie Van Halen, who, for the entire decade, played an assortment of personally modified Kramer guitars.

Kramer was the first major company to see the potential of the Floyd Rose locking tremolo system, which by the mid-1980s was fitted to all its guitars.

The 1989 Sustainer is also notable for another Floyd Rose innovation; a neck pick-up capable of emitting an electromagnetic signal strong enough to make the strings vibrate and sustain indefinitely. Sadly, shortly after the introduction of this device, the debt-ridden Kramer company went out of business. **TB**

Kubicki Factor 4 Bass 1989

Type Four-string electric bass
Body & neck Maple body and neck
Fingerboard Ebony
Pick-ups Two Kubicki humbucker pick-ups

When Philip Kubicki was a teenager, he would visit his grandparents' house and play with an old guitar that his grandfather kept locked away in a closet. "I think all of us instrument makers have had that kind of fascination—some little spark, back at the very beginning," he later recalled.

In 1964, Kubicki was hired by Fender to work in its R&D division, which he left in 1973 to create his own company. He began by making acoustics—including a dulcimer for Joni Mitchell, and George Harrison's legendary Telecaster—but it would be his line of bass guitars, culminating in the first Factor bass in 1985, and popularized by Duran Duran's John Taylor, that would bring Kubicki national acclaim.

Instead of threaded claws, which are prone to wear, the strings wrap around drums on the Factor 4's bridge. Innovative in sound and appearance, the guitars' contoured bodies were "headless," with tuner and bridge built into the body, which consisted of thirty-four pieces of laminated maple. **BS**

Spector
NS-6A 1989

Type Solidbody electric
Body & neck Maple body and neck
Fingerboard Rosewood
Pick-ups One single-coil and one humbucker pick-up

Founded by New York luthier Stuart Spector, Spector originally serviced the high-end bass market, but turned its attention to souped-up rock guitars.

There were two models: the NS-6 ($2,000), which replaced the standard Strat tremolo system with a Floyd Rose; and the Korean-built NS-6A ($900), with a Floyd copy. Both boasted neck-through designs, making them more secure and stable, and offering more sustain, than a regular Strat. The NS-6's gold-plated hardware was a late-1980s fashion statement; the NS-6A had more hardcore black hardware.

The NS-6 had two EMG active pick-ups—one single-coil, and one humbucker. The Korean version's three pick-ups were Spector-branded passive units—one humbucker and two single-coils.

The NS models were named for Ned Steinberger, a furniture maker who helped Spector with the design (and who went on to create his own range of electric guitars and basses). Sadly, they were abandoned in the wake of Spector's takeover by Kramer. **SH**

Starforce
8007 1989

Type Solidbody electric
Body & neck Wood/laminate body, maple neck
Fingerboard Maple, rosewood, or ebonol
Pick-ups One humbucker and one single-coil pick-up

The Starforce "Superstrats" emerged from Korea around 1988, and were imported to the United States in a wide variety of versions and confusing model names. Many were branded "Starforce USA," for sale to Latin American countries. Few seem to have made it to Europe. The U.S. importer was based in Miami, so today most used versions seem to turn up in Florida.

This is an 8007 with a slightly more original body shape than most, and distinctive star-inlay fret position markers. It has the classic Superstrat arrangement of humbucker and two single-coil high-output "SkorCherz" pick-ups. For low-priced copies, they had good specifications: the bolt-on, solid maple neck has a steel truss rod, six-on-a-side Gotoh-style tuners, and a locking nut. There was also a Floyd Rose or Wilkinson tremolo bridge, depending on the model, and matte black hardware.

Like many Asian copies of the era, they enjoyed a brief shelf life; by 1990, the importers had moved on to work with another manufacturer. **SH**

Sunn
Mustang 1989

Type Solidbody double cutaway electric
Body & neck Black limba (korina) body, maple neck
Fingerboard Rosewood
Pick-ups Three single-coils (or two plus humbucker)

In the late 1980s, facing a wave of cheaper copies from Asia, Fender licensed the building of its Precision Bass and Stratocaster guitars to Sunn in India. In many countries, these were sold as Squier guitars. In the United Kingdom, they were imported as Sunn Mustangs.

Since then, the Stratocaster copies' reputation has grown. Some guitarists swear that these Mustangs are better than U.S.-made models. They were certainly built carefully, mostly by hand, using good-quality, unbranded Fender parts. The slim, maple necks are especially well thought-of. Sunn used korina, which is more highly rated today, for the bodies, and local rosewood for the fretboards.

Yet Mustangs cost only £98 in the United Kingdom. They were initially available in red, white, or black, all with white scratchplates. According to a 1988 advert: "The new Sunn Mustang brings you quality not seen before on a budget-priced instrument." The guitars, it claimed, "are capable of producing sounds to complement many different musical styles." **SH**

Synsonics
Terminator 1989

Type Solidbody electric with built-in amp and speaker
Body & neck Particleboard body, rubberwood neck
Fingerboard Rubber
Pick-ups Two single-coil pick-ups

This was an innovative instrument that offered truly portable electric guitar playing. The three-quarter sized, Strat-style body contained its own battery-powered amplifier and speaker.

The Terminator was built cheaply in Korea: the body was particleboard, and the neck and fretboard were a single piece of rubber wood, stained black to match the rest of the guitar. The minimal plant costs were reflected in the retail price: the Terminator cost only around $40 in the United States.

Synsonics could be played through an external amplifier, or switched to their on-board amps, when the pick-ups became active. Each pick-up had a volume control, and there was an overall tone control. There were even plug-ins for headphones, enabling the instruments to be played silently.

Perhaps surprisingly, this meager features list also included a Bigsby-style tremolo bridge. But, according to one reviewer, this had the effect of "knocking you into a tuning known only to dolphins." **SH**

Tune
TWB6 1989

Type Solidbody electric bass
Body & neck Alder body, bolt-on maple neck
Fingerboard Mix of exotic woods on body, maple top/neck
Pick-ups Two slim active-bar pick-ups

Tune Guitar Technology started making original modern bass guitars in Osaka, Japan, in 1983—its stated aim to manufacture and distribute "virtually everything that a bassist needs to perform." To this end, they launched wave upon wave of guitars: the brilliantly monikered Bass Maniac series in 1984, the TWB series in 1985, the "hot-slapping" SWB series in 1986, the Casiopea TWX series (named in honor of the jazz fusion band whose bassist Yoshihiro Naruse was a Tune aficionado) in 1987, and the Supernova ZI series and Modern Acoustic Bass in 1989. Notable players included Bachman Turner Overdrive's Fred Turner.

The TWB6—an advanced, six-string bass—was released in 1989 and was regarded as the company's flagship instrument. It boasted all the features of an expensive high-end professional guitar, other than the price, which was less than that of the average American equivalent. It was also an original design, not a copy of anything else, so seemed great value.

The TWB6's technical specs gave weight to such good first impressions: it had polished brass hardware (including the nut, and Gotoh machine heads), a four-piece bolt-on, hard maple neck, a mix of exotic woods for the body, which is hand-oiled, an ebony fingerboard with simple dot position markers, and two active Tune pick-ups.

The tone variety is wide, thanks to controls for volume, pan between pick-ups, bass, middle, treble, and a filter/trim control. On the downside, though, the guitar has a finger-stretching neck—the six-string configuration means that the neck is 3½-in. (9-cm) wide at the twenty-fourth fret. **SH**

Valley Arts
Custom Pro 1989

Type Solidbody electric
Body & neck Ash or alder body, maple neck
Fingerboard Maple
Pick-ups Three EMG humbucker pick-ups (plus other options)

The 1980s: a time when all the top metal guitarists decided that not only could you not play fast enough on the old Fender guitars, but the horns weren't pointy enough. And they didn't have enough frets. Enter that six-string savior, the "Superstrat," courtesy of pioneers Jackson, Charvel, and Valley Arts.

Mike McGuire and Al Carness had founded the company in the San Fernando Valley in the mid-1970s. Two decades later, an attempt to expand faltered: they partially sold out to the Korean company Samick and were eventually taken over by Gibson.

The pre-Samick guitars are the company's most highly regarded and sought after by collectors, and the Custom Pro was the flagship model. It had a wide variety of custom options: you could choose between EMG, OBL, Tom Anderson, Seymour Duncan, Ultra Sonic, DiMarzio, and Alembic humbuckers, and a wide range of colors and finishes were available (although most existing examples seem to sport an aggressively orange fireburst appearance).

The hardware, including the ubiquitous Floyd Rose tremolo, came in a choice of chrome, gold, or black. Another option, for an extra $250, was Valley Arts' own "Interlock Neck System," which used slide-in elements between the body and neck and was claimed to yield enhanced sustain and resonance. **AJ**

Steve Lukather, a Valley Arts fan, played one on his band Toto's 1978 debut. By the mid-1980s, he had his own signature model and, although he parted ways with the company when Samick came along, he used a Custom Pro on Toto's *Kingdom Of Desire* (1992).

Wal
MIDI Bass 1989

Type Solidbody bass guitar
Body & neck Hardwood/timber body and neck
Fingerboard Rosewood
Pick-ups One or two humbucker pick-ups

The MB4/MB5 Wal four- and five-string MIDI (Musical Instrument Digital Interface) basses were designed at a time when MIDI systems for guitars were improving greatly, although there always seemed to be a delay in the tracking, with the bass sound lagging behind the strings being played.

In an attempt to remedy this problem, the guys at Wal, along with an Australian designer named Steve Chick, developed a system whereby sensors were built into the frets to determine the pitch of each note, while the pick-up dealt with attack, dynamics, and pitch-bending information. The bass could function in two ways: either as a normal bass, or by hooking up to a supplied MIDI controller and a collection of pedals via a fifteen-pin cable that was attached to the rear of the bass.

By these means it became possible to make your electric bass sound like a sixty-piece orchestra . . . at least, sort of. A double-necked version of the guitar was also produced. Although players such as Mark King and Pino Palladino took the instrument on board, the system was eventually sold on to Peavey for its MIDI Bass project at the start of the 1990s, bringing to an end its association with Wal. The bass itself feels like a regular Wal instrument, but how the systems are faring these days is hard to say. **JM**

Level 42's bassist Mark King shows the Wal Midi Bass's capabilities during a demanding work-out on "Lasso The Moon," a track from *Guaranteed* (1990). This was the band's first album on the RCA label after the previous year's split from Polydor.

Yamaha
Pacifica Series 1989

Type Double cutaway electric
Body & neck Alder body, maple neck
Fingerboard Maple
Pick-ups Two single-coil pick-ups and one humbucker

Designed by Rich Lasner (ex-Ibanez), the Pacifica was one of the best-value electric guitars of the 1990s. Early models may have lacked the extra tones that distinguished a great guitar from a good one (the tuning was a touch unstable, especially when using the tremolo), but for beginners who found it hard to justify spending money on a Fender, the Pacifica—particularly the Series 112 shown here—was too good to ignore. It came with a heap of color options (including a stunning Ice Blue Metallic), and was equally at home playing blues/jazz, rock, or metal.

"This classy looking double-cutaway guitar ... delivers a punch that can't be touched in its price class."

ULTIMATE-GUITAR.COM

And it produced a sound that truly defied its price tag. It also came with contoured, comfy bodies, five-way switching of its H-S-S pick-ups, and vintage-style vibratos. Unlike other beginners' guitars, such as the Squiers, the Pacifica's single-coil pick-ups generated clear, deep tones without any annoying fizz, and the bridge-positioned humbucker was seriously raunchy. The bridge and headstock were solid, and the word "tank" was used more than once to describe the reliability of its hardware and its "untarnishable" finish.

Most models have double cutaways with horns for great fret access, and the solid body was a relief at a time when many entry-level guitars were laminated hardwood. The Pacifica 112 proved you don't have to spend a lot to get a great-sounding guitar. **BS**

Yamaha
TRB6P 1989

Type Solidbody electric bass
Body & neck Maple/rose body, maple/mahogany neck
Fingerboard Ebony
Pick-ups Two single-coil and piezo pick-ups

Jazz and session bassist Anthony Jackson is usually credited with inventing the six-string bass as we know it—he asked luthier Carl Thompson to build him the first one in 1975. Jackson contended that six was the logical number of strings for a bass guitar—they only had four because Leo Fender couldn't get the idea of a bass fiddle out of his head when he was designing the Precision in 1951.

Fender and Danelectro had, admittedly, made six-string basses. These, however, were tuned an octave below standard guitar tuning, while Jackson's was tuned to B-E-A-D-G-C—the low B leading him to call it a "contrabass." Demand for such instruments evidently suffered in the early 1960s because record players couldn't reproduce the necessary low frequencies. That, and jazz funk hadn't been invented yet.

Bassists who prefer more than four strings speak well of Yamaha's TRB6P contrabass, owing to the quality of its construction and competitive price. It has a neck-through design, three-band active electronics and, in addition to the standard single-coil pick-ups, a piezo element for each string that picks up the resonance of the maple.

It has now been superseded by the TRB6PII, available in ovangkol and bubinga as well as maple, and humbuckers instead of the single-coils. **AJ**

Brooklyn-born jazz bassist John Patitucci endorses Yamaha and has two six-string signature models: the TRB-JP and TRB-JP2. His playing can be enjoyed on work by acts ranging from B.B. King to Bon Jovi, and solo albums such as *Sketchbook* (1990).

Yellow Cloud
Electric Guitar 1989

Type Solidbody electric
Body & neck Maple body and neck
Fingerboard Maple
Pick-ups One humbucker and one single coil pick-up

This is the guitar that the artist previously known as Prince Rogers Nelson suggestively attempts to wrap around the waist of Diamond (Lori Elle) in the video for "Gett Off," the lead single from the New Power Generation's *Diamonds And Pearls* album (1991). Keen-eyed fans who could drag their gaze away from his Purpleness for just a moment might have spotted the rising star's bassist sporting a four-stringed precursor of this instrument as far back as the promo for 1979's "Why You Wanna Treat Me So Bad?"

The story picks up again in the 1980s, when David Rusan and Barry Haugen of Knut-Koupee Enterprises Inc., in Minneapolis, were commissioned by Prince for a custom-build with a similar upper horned piece, its phallic significance all too obvious for the oversexed star. The extension proved to be a relatively fragile part of the guitar, especially given Prince's notorious treat-'em-mean attitude to his equipment, but it does lend the instrument an utterly distinctive air.

In various iterations, the guitar resurfaced in white, black, peach, and blue (that final one during the U.S. number one "Batdance" era), all with sexuality symbols in the fingerboards.

Prince donated a Yellow Cloud to the Smithsonian National Museum of American History in Washington D.C. For lesser mortals who wanted to get hold of one of these guitars, in 1989 Schecter was awarded a license to produce them in limited numbers, although these versions had bolt-on necks, and different pick-up arrangements. When Prince entered his own symbol phase soon afterward, the artist and his guitars were about to get even weirder. **CB**

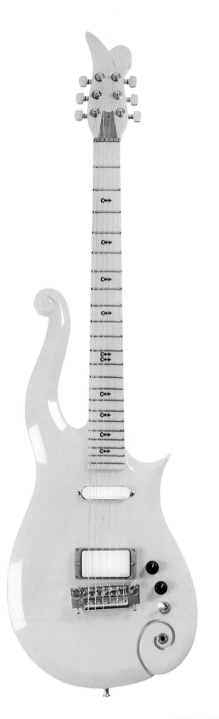

Ernie Ball
Music Man EVH 1990

Type Solidbody electric
Body & neck Basswood/maple body, maple neck
Fingerboard Maple
Pick-ups Two DiMarzio EVH Custom pick-ups

The Ernie Ball Music Man Eddie Van Halen model (EVH) was designed for the virtuoso shredder in 1990. Intended as a limited run of 1,000 guitars, demand was so great that production was increased to around 5,500.

The EVH was a radical departure from Van Halen's mainstay "5150": gone were the red, black, and white stripes, the Explorer–style headstock, and the weird electrics. One of Van Halen's stipulations was that he could go into any store, anywhere in the world that stocked his guitar, pick it up and play it, and they would all be of equal quality.

The body of the EVH is made of basswood with a beautifully bound quilted maple top. The one-piece, twenty-two-fret neck is made from bird's-eye maple, and has a matching fingerboard. The neck was copied from Eddie's original "5150" using digital mapping, so as to give it an identical feel to his old instrument. The headstock featured Schaller tuners in a four-plus-two configuration, and the guitarist's signature.

Like many rock guitars of the time, the EVH was equipped with a Floyd Rose-licensed vibrato unit with a locking nut, enabling dive-bomb pitch bends without putting the instrument out of tune.

The electrics were fairly straightforward, with two DiMarzio EVH Custom pick-ups and a single volume control with a Strat-style knob and a three-way selector switch.

The EVH is widely regarded as an outstanding modern rock guitar by players and collectors alike, and is certain to be highly sought after in the future. Definitely one to watch. **JB**

Fender
Jazz Plus V 1990

Type Five-string electric bass
Body & neck Pao ferro or alder body, maple neck
Fingerboard Rosewood
Pick-ups Two Lace Sensor pick-ups

Fender introduced its four-string Jazz Bass Plus in 1989 and, a year later, brought out its first modern five-string, the Jazz Plus V. In an age when basses were becoming more affordable and plentiful, something special was required to make one stand out from the crowd . . . and the Jazzes were certainly eye-catching.

The first thing you notice is the absence of both a pickguard (nothing to "ugly up" the body) and the usual chrome control cavity cover. The Plus V featured a larger body, a twenty-two-fret neck, and a very beefy-looking Gotoh, vintage-style top-loading Schaller "Elite" fine-tuner bridge, a wonderfully deluxe piece that added to the instrument's long sustain. But it was the five-string's Lace Sensor active pick-ups, and its Philip Kubicki-designed nine-volt preamp, that really made the difference.

Although four- and five-string Jazz Pluses are regarded as the forerunners of Fender's 1995 American Deluxe, there have been concerns that they never really captured the essential bass sound. But the Jazz brand's active tonal controls—a notched switch with three positions (active, mute, and passive)—provided a range of tonal options, from bright to flat.

According to guitarist Scott Grove, the four- and five-string Fender Jazz basses are "as good as a Fender ever got." Standard colors included black and sunburst, but there were also questionable pastels, and reverse fade finishes. In production for only four years, the Jazz Plus V is now a highly sought-after instrument. And why wouldn't it be, when it featured Kubicki-engineered electronics? (Premium models had the even rarer eighteen-volt Kubicki circuitry.) **BS**

Ibanez
Universe 1990

Type Twin-cutaway, seven-string solidbody
Body & neck Basswood body, bolt-on maple neck
Fingerboard Rosewood
Pick-ups Two humbuckers and one single-coil pick-up

Having laid down a marker for innovation in 1987 with the Jem, Ibanez now produced the first seven-string electric guitar to go into large-scale production.

Guitars with more than six strings were not new. In Russia, for example, the seven-string acoustic guitar was the norm during the nineteenth century. The Universe was not even the first seven-string electric guitar: in 1938, Epiphone built a seven-string archtop for American jazz musician George Van Eps.

Although Fender produced a prototype seven-string Stratocaster in 1987, it never went into production. Unlike the Van Eps model, which added a low "B," the additional string was a high "A," extending the upper range of the guitar.

Steve Vai, flushed with the success of his Jem, encouraged Ibanez to produce a seven-string version. After experimenting with high and low strings, Vai went for a low B, giving the twenty-four-fret fingerboard an extraordinary note range of four octaves and five half-steps. He first played the Universe live with Whitesnake, and later used it on his award-winning solo album, *Passion And Warfare* (1990).

The Universe started a trend in the modern electric guitar: every manufacturer of instruments for the rock and metal markets now produces at least one seven- and/or eight-string model. **TB**

James "Munky" Shaffer used an Ibanez Universe on Korn's self-titled debut album (1994). "It just plays *sweet*," he enthused. The Californian nu-metal five-piece band helped to establish trends for seven-string guitars and for the down-tuning of instruments.

James "Munky" Shaffer of Korn performing with his Universe in 2004. →

Jackson
Warrior Pro 1990

Type Solidbody electric
Body & neck Maple straight-through neck, poplar wings
Fingerboard Ebony
Pick-ups Three J-200R humbucker pick-ups

The Warrior was quite a radical design for Jackson. Custom models aside, it had specialized in fairly conventional instruments, such as the Soloist "Superstrat'" and the Flying V-inspired Randy Rhoads. The Warrior prompted contrasting opinions but— although initially only in production for two years—has become one of Jackson's most popular designs.

The original Warrior, made in the U.S., featured a neck of quarter-sawn maple, while the bound ebony fingerboard had Jackson's characteristic "Sharkfin" pearl inlays. But most striking was the body shape— look closely to see how it resembles four Jackson headstocks positioned at different angles. A second unusual feature was the extended fingerboard, set at an angle along with the pick-ups, which all added to the overall quirkiness. The guitar was not in fact designed by Grover Jackson, who withdrew from the company that year, but head of R&D Mikey Wright.

The hardware was given a black finish and included a Jackson Floyd Rose-licensed vibrato and three J-200R "Rail" humbuckers. The control layout was appealingly simple, consisting of a single volume and tone control and a pick-up selector switch.

The Warrior was not only a success story for Jackson, but also spawned a whole bunch of similar designs from other guitar manufacturers. **JB**

Limp Bizkit's idiosyncratic guitarist Wes Borland wields a Warrior in the video for the title track of their 2011 comeback album *Gold Cobra*. Jackson gave Borland three—"probably the nicest guitars I've ever owned"— for the accompanying tour.

Jerry Jones
Master Sitar 1990

Type Solidbody electric
Body & neck Masonite/poplar body, maple neck
Fingerboard Rosewood
Pick-ups Three balanced lipstick pick-ups

Until 2011, when Jerry Jones retired and closed his factory, his firm manufactured electric guitars in Nashville, Tennessee. It specialized in recreating Danelectro designs from the 1950s and 1960s, together with a few more exotic variations, such as a six-string version of the Longhorn Bass, and the Guitarlin (half guitar, half mandolin).

The Master Sitar was the middle instrument in a family of three: the others were the "Supreme" and the "Baby." It was a re-creation of the Coral Sitar designed by Vincent Bell for Danelectro in 1967, and used to psychedelic effect on such hit singles as "Green Tambourine" by The Lemon Pipers, and "Do It Again" by Steely Dan.

The sitar-like whirring effect is achieved on the guitar by making the strings vibrate against what Jones calls a "buzz bridge"—a raised, height-adjustable piece of rosewood, about 1½ in. (3.8 cm) long. There are thirteen sympathetic strings to the left of the six main ones—these are all .010 in. (0.2 cm) gauge, and can be tuned to a chord or scale according to personal preference. There's a clear Perspex guard that prevents the player from hitting these by accident. Each of the three pick-ups has dedicated volume and tone controls. Overall, the construction is somewhat better than the Danelectro original. **AJ**

Dave Gregory played a Jerry Jones Master Sitar when The Dukes Of Stratosphear (a pseudonym of British rock band XTC) briefly reunited to record the track "Open A Can (Of Human Beans)" for the compilation album *The Wish List* (2003).

Norman
B50 1990

Type Acoustic flat-top
Body & neck Solid spruce top, maple back and sides,
Honduras mahogany neck
Fingerboard Ebony

Norman guitars—now known as "Canada's guitars"—
began production in the early 1970s. Its first
instrument was the B20, with three-layered laminates
of cherry wood that gave deep, rich tones. In 1990
came the B50, one of Norman's "Studio Series," with an
ebony fingerboard and bridge, pressure-tested solid
spruce top, three-way laminated maple back and
sides, a high-gloss custom polished finish, and
optional Fishman Presys electronics. Later models
came with maple-leaf inlays around the sound holes.

The origin of the Norman brand is complex. There
were several guitar-making concerns in La Petrie,
Quebec, including Godin, Kamouraska, and Seagull.
The town was also home to a luthier who learned his
craft moving from one of these companies to the
next—Normand Boucher (the "d" was later dropped).

Boucher then set up a guitar-making business of
his own, but after suffering various financial setbacks,
and a factory fire, he sold a controlling interest to the
Godin company, which retained the Norman name.

At the end of the manufacturing process, every
Norman guitar spends several days receiving a
custom polished finish which, unlike a typical
polyester finish that can imperceptibly dampen the
acoustic properties of even the finest guitars, creates
maximum vibration and a superb sound. The way a
Norman guitar's neck is attached to the body
maximizes neck pitch, because the neck is joined
"wood-to-wood" to the body without any adhesives
or finishes that might impede the transference of
vibration. A Norman guitar represents the very best of
the luthier's art. **BS**

Ovation Collector's Edition 1990

Type Six-string acoustic-electric flat-top
Body & neck Maple/fiberglass body, maple neck
Fingerboard Ebony
Pick-ups One piezo electric pick-up

Spotting an Ovation acoustic guitar from a distance has never been difficult. The company's signature bowl-shaped, semi-parabolic body—developed by its own aerospace engineers in 1965 to enhance its instruments' projection—did away with the sharp perpendicular edges common to traditional flatbacks that so bedeviled the rib cages of many a guitarist, and gave responsiveness and efficiency in sound generation a whole new meaning.

The Collector's Series made its first appearance in 1982 as the R&D department's latest effort to find the next commercial model. The prototype's body shape preserved the traditional Ovation curves, and was constructed from maple and Lyrachord. The latter—a composite of fiberglass and bonding resin tweaked at the molecular level to increase its resonance—had a perfectly smooth interior that reflected sound more efficiently than traditional timbers, which are absorbent and porous. The fact that it was mold-cast gave it an inherent strength that obviated the need for internal bracing.

Engineers at the Ovation factory in Hartford, Connecticut, called these guitars "roundbacks," and the name stuck. The 1990 Ovation Collector's Edition came with a walnut bridge, custom five-piece epaulet rosettes, and gold Schaller tuners. However, it was its stunning, highly figured top, made from bird's-eye maple—a quirk of nature caused by unfavorable growing conditions—with matching overlays on the headstock, that really set this instrument apart, and made it one of the most beautiful and distinctive stars in the guitar universe. **BS**

Alvarez
Dana AE650 1991

Type Six-string acoustic-electric flat-top
Body & neck Maple/fiberglass body, maple neck
Fingerboard Ebony
Pick-ups One piezo electric pick-up

Beyond the striking visuals of Dana Sutcliffe's Scoop design, there's a practical benefit—improving sustain and resonance. But it all came about by accident.

By 1988, Sutcliffe was producing his own line of guitars for Westone, a division of SLM (St. Louis Music). While working on a Westone body, one of Sutcliffe's employees hit a knot in the wood near the cutaway, and accidentally cut a gash into the body. Another employee decided to finish assembling it. Sutcliffe played this oddity, and discovered that the resonance he was looking for happened only when the "scoop" appeared at the twenty-fourth fret. This helped eliminate the phase cancellation that is caused when two different and incompatible vibration frequencies collide in the bridge area. The scoop itself enhances natural harmonic resonance.

With the prototype completed (this first model had a reversed headstock) in 1989, Sutcliffe was approached by SLM to market the guitar under the Alvarez brand.

By 1992, the Scoop was available in four Korean-made guises, including this AE650, all featuring pick-ups that ran in series with Dana's active Harmonic Enhancer electronics. Production ceased in 1995, after disagreements between Sutcliffe and SLM, but their work together produced a truly unique guitar. **RL**

A number of Scoop guitars were customized for various artists, including one for Eddie Van Halen, and three for former Runaways guitarist Lita Ford, who endorsed the model before she recorded *Black* (1995), her sixth solo album.

Banzer
Classical Guitar 1991

Type Cutaway electro-classical
Body & neck Classical body and neck
Fingerboard Ebony
Pick-ups Humbucker pick-up

Don Banzer was a guitar maker in Ashtabula, Ohio. He was never prolific—before his death in 1995 from lung cancer, at the age of 50, he produced only around 200 instruments. Most of these were classical, but he also turned his hand to six- and twelve-string steel-string guitars. Neither was he ranked among the leading luthiers of his era: many players found his build quality uneven, and some critics questioned his undoubtedly quirky craftsmanship, which eschewed truss rods, and never really got to grips with the practicalities of dovetail joints.

Nevertheless, Banzer acquired and retained a loyal coterie of admirers, one of the most distinguished of whom was Jorge Morel (b. 1931). The virtuoso Argentine-American guitarist-composer is renowned for his encouragement of emerging musical talent of all kinds, but he does not give his endorsements frivolously or in return for sponsorship payments. Praise from him is therefore praise indeed, and goes a long way toward outweighing those who disparaged Banzer's creations.

Morel owned and played a Banzer guitar in concert, using it on a world tour in 1980 to play his own compositions and arrangements of a wide range of works by classical composers such as Heitor Villa-Lobos, and popular musicians such as John Lennon and Paul McCartney. Morel liked his Banzer so much, he ordered a second one.

The guitar shown here is a typical Banzer classical design, custom-built with cutaway and pick-up system. The headstock and bridge designs are also similar to those of other Banzers. **GD**

Brune
25th Anniversary 1991

Type Classical guitar
Body & neck Spruce body and neck
Fingerboard Rosewood
Other features Carved ebony headstock

Just twenty-five models were produced to celebrate Richard E. Brune's quarter-century in the classical and flamenco guitar-building business. For a one-man operation crafting world-class instruments, that represents a significant run.

Brune's original 1966 workshop was at his home in Dayton, Ohio, to which he would return between stints playing flamenco guitar in professional troupes around the United States and Mexico. In 1973, he decided that his future lay in construction rather than performance, and he thereafter dedicated himself full-time to lutherie. His clients have included Andrés Segovia and Julian Bream; there is typically a five- to six-year waiting list for a Brune original.

Brune is now based in Evanston, Illinois. Attached to his workshop are a showroom, which contains some of his own creations and a collection of rare classical and flamenco guitars by other hands, and an extensive reference library that can be used by visitors. Also on-site are the Brune archives, comprising thousands of photographs of fine instruments, along with original manuscripts of correspondence from various makers, and hundreds of measured drawings.

This Anniversary model features a special-edition rosette, and an internal label with the model number to mark it visually. Even more distinctive is the carved ebony headstock in a shield with a garland pattern. Unsurprisingly, this model is highly sought after, and examples rarely surface on the collectors' market. However, in 2010, one Anniversary model (SN: 24/25) did appear for sale from an American collection: it was priced at $20,000. **RL**

← Flamenco star Pepe Romero is one of many noted players to use an Richard E. Brune guitar.

Charvel
Surfcaster 1991

Type Semi-hollow electric
Body & neck Mahogany body, maple neck
Fingerboard Rosewood
Pick-ups Two single-coil lipstick pick-ups

Grover Jackson may have been the father of the Superstrat, running two of the genre's preeminent brands, but he was no great businessman: "I didn't understand money. I was just thinking about the product." After accepting investment from music giant IMC, Jackson found himself unsuited to corporate life and, in 1989, sold his interests in Charvel and Jackson.

The aftermath saw the birth of the most unlikely guitar to bear the Charvel name. Among the most attractive designs of the past twenty-five years, the Surfcaster paved the way for boutique hollow-body electrics, servicing demand for a contemporary high-performance-fused-with-classic-retro-American guitar. This was not a guitar for the usual Charvel/Jackson pointy-headstock metal crowd.

The semi-hollow body (originally mahogany and later basswood) combined a Fender Jaguar-style outline with Rickenbacker stylings, including the cat's-eye f-hole and a "reverse-Gumby" headstock. The sound came from a pair of newly designed single-coil Danelectro-type "lipstick case" pick-ups, which certainly delivered plenty of classic "twang."

First built in Japan, the Surfcaster underwent minor alterations each year until 1997, when production shifted to India and the brand from Charvel to Jackson, which saw a marked deterioration in quality. Production ended when Jackson/Charvel came under the wing of Fender. The design later re-emerged with the Charvel Desolation Skatecaster solidbody range.

The Surfcaster was never a commercial success. But after *Guitar Player* listed it as a "Pawn Shop Prize" in 2003, early models have become collectible. **TB**

My Bloody Valentine's Bilinda Butcher rocking out with her Surfcaster. ➡

Eggle
Berlin 2 1991

Type Solidbody electric
Body & neck Maple/mahogany body, mahogany neck
Fingerboard Ebony
Pick-ups Two humbucker pick-ups

The reunified German capital was much in the news in 1991, so British guitar maker Patrick Eggle's first model was named the Berlin. Acclaimed as "the British PRS," it evolved into a range, with the Berlin Standard, higher spec Berlin Plus, and even higher spec Berlin Pro. The last—the most popular—is still made.

The Berlin was quite small, with an asymmetric headstock bearing Eggle's signature. He added further Berlin variants, such as the DLX, Stage, Anniversary, and EVO. The company also developed other ranges, including the New York and Los Angeles.

Book-matched flame, quilted, or bird's-eye maple tops lay on a well-sculpted, Brazilian mahogany body, with an ebony fingerboard on a one-piece, set mahogany neck. Premium features included Sperzel locking tuners, a Wilkinson locking tremolo, and twin Kent Armstrong humbuckers with coil tap switching.

Unusually, there was no standard tone control—instead, players created different sounds using the pick-up and coil-tapping selections. **SH**

Fender
Prodigy 1991

Type Solidbody electric
Body & neck Poplar body and neck
Fingerboard Rosewood
Pick-ups One humbucker and two single-coil pick-ups

Just in time for the grunge era, Fender released this beefy, angular competitor to the "Superstrats" from companies such as Jackson, Charvel, Yamaha, and Ibanez. It had an offset waist, with pointier horns and a smaller headstock than a standard Strat, and the humbucker plus two single coils confirmed what Fender traditionalists had feared—that this was the Devil's own take on a Strat.

One universally unpopular design decision made with the Prodigy was to retain only a single volume and a single tone control, and to place the jack socket where the second tone knob would have been on a Strat. This led many Prodigy owners to scurry off and invest in a right-angled jack, and left others paranoid about the risk of snapping off the bottom corner of their pickguard.

The Prodigy, which in spite of its "Made In USA" tag, was part-built in Mexico, was introduced in 1991 and discontinued in 1993. It is now a curious and rare, if still not particularly fashionable, find. **OB**

Fender Stratocaster Jeff Beck 1991

Fender TLAC-950 HMT Acoustic Electric 1991

Type Solidbody electric
Body & neck Alder body, maple neck
Fingerboard Rosewood
Pick-ups One "dually" and two single-coil pick-ups

Type Acoustic electric
Body & neck Mahogany/spruce body, maple neck
Fingerboard Rosewood
Pick-ups One piezo and one single-coil pick-up

The 1986 prototype of this instrument was finished in bright yellow—Jeff Beck told Fender that he wanted his signature guitar the same color as an automobile featured in the film *American Graffiti*.

The production model—which replaced that finish with Surf Green, Midnight Purple, and Vintage White options—was based on the Stratocaster Plus, but with several differences. On early models, the necks were the biggest Fender had ever used on a Stratocaster; U-shaped and 1-in. (2.5-cm) thick without a taper, they resembled the early Les Paul "baseball bat" style. This feature was later discontinued.

The Beck model had a Wilkinson roller nut and Sperzel locking machine heads, staggered in height to reduce friction or the need for string trees. There was also a two-point Fender Vibrola which was capable of staying in tune, even with extreme usage.

The electrics were radical, with the pick-ups, including, at the bridge, a "dually"—two Lace pick-ups side by side, with a coil-tap switch. **JB**

This rare Japanese model should not be confused with the HMT (Heavy Metal Telecaster), produced in the same year. The TLAC-950 is a far subtler-looking guitar that offers its own distinctive sonic charms.

Essentially, it's a hybrid electric and acoustic guitar. Designed to be played with acoustic strings, the TLAC is equipped with an acoustic-style bridge that has a piezo pick-up, and active (battery-powered) circuitry. The Lace Sensor, Strat-style pick-up brings the electric tones to the table with a blend control that allows players to balance between piezo and single-coil sounds.

The TLAC-950 became the 100 model in 1992. The new name didn't reflect any change in the guitar's features, though—the only difference was an increase in the Japanese RRP from 950,000 to 1,000,000 yen. The models remained a discontinued oddity on the secondhand market until 2010, when Fender released the Mexican Acoustasonic Tele, which carried some of the TLAC's versatile qualities into a new era. **RL**

Fender **Stratocaster Richie Sambora** 1991

Type Solidbody electric
Body & neck Alder body, maple neck
Fingerboard Maple
Pick-ups One humbucker and two single-coil pick-ups

In the wake of Bon Jovi's success, Kramer scrambled to manufacture a signature model for guitarist Richie Sambora in 1986, the year everything went *Slippery*. It had a sticker of a star on the body. It had a pointed head. It was so mid-1980s metal-lite, it might even have had mascara brushes for frets.

When *New Jersey* (1988) confirmed Bon Jovi as one of Earth's biggest bands, Sambora kicked Kramer to the curb and hooked up with Fender. Fender rewarded him with a signature Stratocaster model that, in keeping with Bon Jovi's straddling of the rock/pop divide, featured a DiMarzio PAF humbucker, Texas Special single-coils in the middle and neck positions, and that hard-rock staple, the Floyd Rose tremolo system. Variants emerged from the U.S. (Cherry Sunburst and Olympic White), Japan (Snow White), and Mexico (with a rosewood fretboard and Duo-Sonic pick-ups replacing the Texas Special single coils). With beaten-up grunge chic yet to fully hit, it had Kramer-evoking stars on the fretboard and Sambora's signature on the headstock.

Sambora later hooked up with Gibson, ESP, and even—for those moments when Bon Jovi would have us believe they're a country band—Martin. But it is for his Strat association that even those who wouldn't be caught dead whistling his band's tunes give him grudging respect. **BM**

With Bon Jovi on a strained hiatus, Sambora's solo debut *Stranger In This Town* (1991) earned Top Forty placings on both sides of the Atlantic. Among its impressive guests was fellow Stratomaster Eric Clapton, who solos, appropriately enough, on "Mr Bluesman."

Gibson
MIII Standard 1991

Type Solidbody electric
Body & neck Solid poplar body, maple neck
Fingerboard Maple
Pick-ups Two humbuckers and one single-coil pick-up

By the start of the 1990s, most major guitar companies were launching models to chase the glam and metal markets, while established classics had begun to fall out of favor in the decade before. Fender and Gibson were later to the mosh pit than most, perhaps aware of how far outside their proven traditions Floyd Rose tremolos and pointy headstocks lay. In addition to Fender Japan's very un-Tele-esque Heavy Metal Telecaster, 1991 saw the launch of a guitar that many would struggle to name as a Gibson at first glance.

The MIII's tone and volume knobs evoked the Les Paul, but its body shape, Schaller-made Floyd Rose, and almost tiger-stripe effect on the oddly shaped pickguard were bold steps for Gibson. Also courageous was the pick-up switching system—a combination of a five-way blade selector and two-way toggle meant nine different sounds were possible, with a standby mode for killswitching effects.

Soon the tide of taste turned against the MIII. Shred and hair metal looked passé next to the Seattle grunge scene, which championed classic models, such as the Les Paul and the Jaguar. The MIII was discontinued in 1994, but its shape lived on until 2010 in Epiphone's EM models. In the meantime, this unique Gibson's tonal versatility earned it an enthusiastic cult following. **RL**

Like the MIII, Memphis band Roxy Blue were also created in the dying days of the glam metal boom. Their guitarist, Sid Fletcher, used an MIII Deluxe in the video for the distinctly Van Halen-flavored "Rob The Cradle," from the band's only album, *Want Some?* (1992).

PRS
Artist I 1991

Type Solidbody electric
Body & neck Mahogany with maple top, set neck
Fingerboard Rosewood with bird-shaped inlays
Pick-ups Two humbucker pick-ups

Between 1985 and 1990, PRS established itself as a company that was going places. But Paul Reed Smith wasn't happy. Endorsements and use by high-profile players were crucial to any guitar company, and although numerous players loved the look, feel, and build of the instruments, many were looking for a bigger, more traditional sound, with more low-end.

In a move that it would often repeat, PRS released an "ultimate," high-end, limited production guitar to try something new. That was the thinking behind the Artist I. As Smith said: "The old PRSs didn't sound bad, but they had a thinner tone. The whole idea was that I wanted a better acoustic sound."

Smith was one of the first modern luthiers to openly discuss the acoustic resonance of an electric guitar as being fundamental to its tone—something that was virtually forgotten in the gain-laden, shred days of the 1980s. "We experimented with all kinds of things. We found out that making the necks a little bigger, the bodies a little bigger, and the necks a little shorter got closer to where we wanted to be."

PRS said they chose Smith's "favorite stains, violin glues, abalone inlays, vintage tones," for the Artist I, which they called "Our very best." It might have remained part of the "ultimate" tradition, but instead it paved the way for a new PRS guitar for the 1990s. **DB**

Finnish power-rock guitarist Matias Kupiainen joined Stratovarius in 2008, replacing Timo Tolkki, who had left to develop *Saana: Warrior Of Light Part 1*, a rock opera. Kupiainen plays a PRS Artist model on *Polaris* (2009), the band's first album with the new lineup.

PRS
EG II 1991

Type Solidbody electric
Body & neck Maple body and neck
Fingerboard Rosewood with dot inlays
Pick-ups Different options available

In 1990, PRS unveiled the first EG guitar, with a new, more Fender-like shape, but without the famous carved top and bolt-on neck. The first PRS with twenty-two frets, it aimed to provide a truly affordable instrument after the commercial failure of the Classic Electric/CE. Among its Fenderisms were scratchplate-loaded pick-ups—either three single-coils (EG 3), or a humbucker and two single coils (EG 4). The market, especially in Europe, was enthusiastic, but Paul Reed Smith, who apparently had less to do with the design than he would have liked, was unhappy.

A second attempt surfaced in 1991 with a more PRS-like outline, again with a flat top (and maple-top options), and a bolt-on neck. This time, three different scratchplate-mounted pick-up configurations were offered: three Lindy Fralin Zero Noise "domino," hum-canceling, single coils; one PRS HFS humbucker, with two Fralin Zero noise single coils; or two PRS HFS humbuckers with a regular Fralin single-coil pick-up.

The EG II Series lasted until 1995, and again proved popular with the market, but not with Smith. Like the original Classic Electric, they offered more Fender-like percussion tonality. The series also provided the first left-hand PRS models, and were the first PRS guitar bodies to be cut outside the factory on computer-assisted (CNC) machinery. They remain affordable, and are popular with collectors.

The slab body, bolt-on guitar returned to the PRS line in 2010, with the introduction of the NF3 and DC3 bolt-ons with, respectively, Korina and alder bodies. Both used proprietary PRS pick-up designs, which were very popular with players. **DB**

Rickenbacker
Tom Petty 660/12 1991

Type Solidbody electric
Body & neck Maple body and neck
Fingerboard Rosewood
Pick-ups Two single-coil pick-ups

The Rickenbacker 600 series goes all the way back to a 1958 design by Roger Rossmeisl. The template for the 660/12TP (Tom Petty signature model) was a 1963 prototype twelve-string version of its 625. On the cover of *Damn The Torpedoes* (1979), Petty wears a Rickenbacker 625. This instrument, which belonged to Heartbreakers' guitarist Mike Campbell, is used in the opening of "Here Comes My Girl." ("I love Rickenbacker guitars as works of art," Petty himself enthused, "and for the sound they make.")

Twelve years and four best-selling albums later, Petty—then between *Full Moon Fever* (1989) and *Into The Great Wide Open* (1991), and moonlighting with the Traveling Wilburys—was apparently keen to widen the neck, which was duly altered from 1⅝ in. (4 cm) to 1¾ in. (4.4 cm) at the nut. The bridge was an adjustable, twelve-saddle design, previously used on the 1988 Roger McGuinn signature model.

The Tom Petty guitar also features two of Rickenbacker's own Vintage single-coil "Toaster Top" pick-ups. The 1950s-style, gold-colored pickguard has a silk-screen impression of Petty's autograph on it. Each guitar was handmade in the United States from solid, "charactered," Eastern Rock Maple.

Rickenbacker Tom Pettys were produced in a limited edition of 1,000—813 of them with a red, "Fireglo" finish, and the remaining 187 in black "Jetglo." The manufacturers previewed the new instrument at NAMM (National Association of Music Merchants) show in 1988, and formally introduced it to their line in 1991. The original list price was $1,279. Buyers agreed it was worth every cent. **AJ**

← Mike Campbell, Tom Petty's long-standing sideman, performs on an original 660/12 in 1981.

Robin
Machete Custom 1991

Type Solidbody electric
Body & neck Maple body and neck
Fingerboard Ebony
Pick-ups Two humbucking pick-ups

Of all the Texan company's eye-catching designs, the Machete is probably Robin's greatest head-turner. If the asymmetrical single cutaway body and split, V-shaped headstock aren't enough, Robin's patented three-layer figured maple body, with its bold "steps," up the ante further. Introduced in 1989, the neck-through Machete Custom was the result of a sudden burst of inspiration for its designer.

"I saw a guitar that another company was making," Robin's David Wintz told *Vintage Guitar* in 2003. "It looked nothing like [the] Machete, but it inspired me . . . I went home and came up with the Machete in about thirty minutes."

Although Wintz's original Machetes featured mahogany necks, these were switched to maple on this model. The designer explained the terraced cuts in the Machete's body that have remained a trademark feature: "The view from the rear end of it is unique; it has three 'stairstep' drops of a quarter-inch each, and that look is fully patented. Something like a Firebird has one drop of maybe a sixteenth of an inch, but the Machete really has a great aesthetic."

Not everyone agreed, but the Machete deserves respect for being a bold U.S. design in a guitar industry that often toes a conservative line with body shapes. It's still a key part of Robin's model line. **RL**

The most notable Machete player is Jay Yuenger of industrial metallers White Zombie. His Robins—tuned in D♯, and loaded with Duncan Custom TB humbuckers—were used heavily on the band's standout final studio album, *Astro-Creep: 2000* (1995).

Tom Anderson
Drop T 1991

Type Single cutaway solidbody
Body & neck Wide range of woods for body, maple neck
Fingerboard Maple, rosewood or pau ferro
Pick-ups Array of humbucker and single-coil pick-ups

Tom Anderson has been active on the U.S. guitar scene since 1977, when he took a full-time job at Schecter Guitar Research in Van Nuys, California. David Schecter had set up shop a year earlier to exploit the growing market in hot-rodding production guitars—these were often the popular Fender models that by this time were perceived as having taken a severe fall in quality. Initially, there was a strong demand for replacement parts, but within two years Schecter was offering fully-assembled high-end guitars based on classic Fender designs. As Schecter's business thrived,

"We are ... dedicated to creating the world's finest feeling, playing, and sounding electric guitars—Period!"

TOM ANDERSON

parts were increasingly sourced from Japan, and when the company was sold in 1984, Anderson, with Schecter's encouragement, set up on his own, initially providing his former employer with Stratocaster pick-ups that were built in his own kitchen!

Tom Anderson Guitarworks used pioneering construction techniques: in 1988, they were the first guitar company to use CNC (computer numerical control) to maintain consistency in the manufacturing process; they were also early adopters of the Buzz Feiten tuning system.

The Drop T model shown here is a flame-maple-topped, Telecaster-style instrument. The sounds come from an array of Anderson H-Series pick-ups, wired with every switching option imaginable. **TB**

Paulino Bernabé
Bernabé 1992

Type Classical
Body & neck Spruce body and neck
Fingerboard Ebony
Other key features Rounded bridge and headstock

Paulino Bernabé (1932–2007) learned to make guitars in the workshop of José Ramírez III in Madrid, Spain, where he spent years researching, experimenting, and attempting to make guitars that would satisfy the exacting requirements of Andrés Segovia.

Opening his own workshop in 1969, Bernabé immediately marked himself out as an innovator. From the early 1970s, in a quest to improve the sound quality and volume projected from his guitars, he experimented with different bracing systems, going from five braces to seven, and later developing a

> *"What I believe is missing from foreign guitars is what we call the 'duende,' that soul ... that we always had in Spain."*
>
> PAULINO BERNABÉ

complicated arrangement with four braces radiating from the sound hole, along with three fan braces of varying profiles, coupled with an innovative back design. Another thing that sets Bernabé apart is his selection of rare and exotic woods, many of which he sourced from antique furniture purchased in Madrid's flea market, the Rastro.

This 1992 Bernabé guitar incorporates its creator's innovations to striking effect. Another original instrument he made was a 1972 ten-string guitar for Narciso Yepes, which for decades remained that guitarist's trademark. In the late 1970s, Bernabé's son, also called Paulino, started his own apprenticeship. Father and son worked side by side for almost forty years until Paulino senior's death in 2007. **GD**

Fender Stratocaster
Alex Gregory 1992

Type Solidbody electric seven-string
Body & neck Maple body and neck
Fingerboard Maple
Pick-ups Three Seymour Duncan single-coil pick-ups

Classically trained British musician Alex Gregory decided that the only way he could play his virtuoso rock versions of violin melodies was with a seven-string guitar. The instrument would have a top A string above the normal E string, allowing him to play four full octaves.

He designed the instrument, patented the idea, and approached Fender and Gibson. Both were interested, but Gregory took Fender's offer.

Fender built three prototypes to Gregory's specifications, but modeled them on the normal Stratocaster format. The third was the most successful, and became Gregory's choice for his recording career. It is generally thought of as the first solidbody seven-string guitar. Fender's project never reached normal production, however, for financial reasons.

At first, the guitar was beset with difficulties with the high A string, which had to be specially made by D'Addario. Breakages were common.

Gregory went on to build seven-string guitars with Hamer, Ibanez, and Schecter. Produced in limited numbers, all are collectors' items. Gregory's design, however, was the blueprint for most seven-string electric guitars since, although they have generally used an additional B string below the bottom E, instead of the troublesome higher A string. **SH**

Maestro Alex Gregory's prototype seven-string Fender was used extensively on *Paganini's Last Stand* (1992), his classical rock set that became a cult hit. "I would rather use my seven-string Stratocaster with high A than a five-string mandolin with a low C," he explained.

Fender Stratocaster
Stevie Ray Vaughan 1992

Type Solidbody electric
Body & neck Alder body, maple neck
Fingerboard Pao ferro
Pick-ups Three single-coil pick-ups

An immensely nimble soloist who fused the influence of the great Chicago bluesmen with Jimi Hendrix, Stevie Ray Vaughan (1954–90) spent the early years of his professional career being described as a "guitarist's guitarist"—a double-edged compliment for any musician. He reached an international audience in 1983 as David Bowie's sideman on the hugely successful *Let's Dance* album, and the following tour. He also fronted Double Trouble, a highly acclaimed blues band, but generally worked in areas in which he was never likely to achieve massive commercial success. Vaughan was at the peak of his powers as a player when he was killed in a helicopter crash in Chicago, Illinois.

Throughout his career, Vaughan was an exclusive Stratocaster player who heavily customized his own guitars. His main instrument was a battered hybrid that had been given to him, and which was built from a pair of 1962/1963 Strats. He called it "Number One" (and sometimes even his "First Wife"). The most unusual modification Vaughan made to his guitar was the fitting of a left-handed vibrato, so that he could use it in the same way as his idol, Hendrix, who had played a right-handed guitar left-handed.

Early in 1990, Vaughan and Fender had begun discussing the idea of a signature model. Following the guitarist's sudden tragic death in August of that year, Fender chose to commemorate him with a replica of "Number One." The finished instrument was supplied complete with Vaughan's distinctive "SRV" logo, fake-shabby paintwork, and—most authentically —a left-handed trem. **TB**

Gibson
Starburst 1992

Type Electroacoustic single cutaway
Body & neck Maple body and neck
Fingerboard Rosewood
Pick-ups One Fishman transducer pick-up

The Gibson Starburst was made for only one year, so is highly prized by collectors. It was an electroacoustic with a single sharp Florentine cutaway, all solid wood and distinctive star-shaped pearl neck inlays. There are star motifs on the headstock and bridge, too.

The Starburst was made in Bozeman, Montana, and had a distinctive acoustic sound with a bit more sparkle and less bottom end than a traditional Gibson, thanks to the unusual all-maple construction.

Features included Grover deluxe gold-plated machine heads, rosewood bridge, ebony string pins, and an under-the-saddle pick-up. Mounted on the upper bout are electric-guitar-style volume, treble, and bass control knobs. The endpin serves as a jack socket. The back of the maple neck featured distinctive rosewood "stripes."

There was a standard model with star decorations, and an "Elite" version, which added binding to the design, an ebony fingerboard, and a quilted maple top. Starbursts were made in a range of colors, including bright green, pink, and orange.

Buyers loved the amplification, but there were problems: the preamp required a battery, which was secured inside the body with Velcro straps. Those wanting the trademark Gibson sound were disappointed by the bright maple tone. **SH**

Jorma Kaukonen, formerly of Jefferson Airplane and Hot Tuna, has used Starbursts since they were released. He mentions the guitar in the sleeve notes of *The Land Of Heroes* (1995), and is pictured playing one on the cover of *Too Many Years* (1998).

Martin
Backpacker 1992

Type Straight acoustic
Body & neck Solid spruce body,
hardwood neck
Fingerboard Rosewood

With a body that is little more than an extension of its rather chunky neck, the Backpacker was, as its name suggests, designed with the budget traveler in mind. Slim enough to fit into an aircraft's overhead baggage locker, or to be slipped into a rucksack, the Backpacker is just 35 in. (89 cm) in length, weighs less than 2.5 lbs (1.1 kg), and is supplied in its own black, padded nylon gig bag.

The instrument is never going to sound like a Martin D-28, although, considering its size, it does sound surprisingly rich and tonal. This is partly due to the size of the neck, which is around 50 percent thicker than almost any other guitar, and partly to the lack of a truss rod. The nut is cut back, and too far off the fretboard, and the frets can sometimes stick out beyond the neck, which means getting out a metal file if you want to keep the skin on your fingers. The strap button is located in the middle of the neck—at the tenth fret—which means that, when you want to play high notes, you have to move your thumb over the strap to get to them. The neck is a little heavy, but that isn't a real problem because, after all, you're holding on to it, anyway. And its short length makes it perfect for rhythm work, although it does lack bass.

Still, who's going to notice a lack of bass when sitting on a beach, or watching a sunset? **BS**

Backpackers have been used by stars ranging from Ani Difranco to Jon Anderson. Multi-instrumentalist John Jennings uses one on *A Place In The World* (1996) by singer Mary Chapin Carpenter, a set that features "Keeping The Faith," and the hit "Let Me Into Your Heart."

Ovation
Standard Elite 1992

Type Electroacoustic guitar
Body & neck Lyrachord body, mahogany/maple neck
Fingerboard Rosewood
Pick-ups One piezo pick-up

The Ovation Standard Elite is a single-cutaway, electroacoustic guitar, similar in appearance to the flagship Adamas models, but much more affordable.

It quickly became popular with musicians because of its stunning good looks and its ease of amplification in concert environments, in which acoustic players often struggle.

It featured Adamas-style "epaulet" sound holes cut from exotic hardwoods, and inlaid into the solid grade AA sitka spruce top. In place of the usual sound hole in the center of the body, the Standard Elite has eleven epaulets above the fingerboard and four below. The bound top has scalloped bracing and a rosewood bridge, which houses the piezo pick-up. An onboard OP-24 preamp controls EQ.

The deep-bowl body is made from Lyrachord, which was specially designed by aerospace engineers at Ovation's parent company. It is a composite, fiberglass material that is extremely durable yet lightweight, perfectly smooth inside, and does not require any bracing or support. It enables the instrument to produce greater volume.

The neck is constructed from two-piece mahogany, with a central "sandwich strip" of maple/mahogany/maple to provide extra strength and prevent twisting. It has a rosewood fingerboard, with pearl dot and diamond inlays, which extends into the body, allowing full access to the twenty-two frets. The headstock is fitted with the same machine heads that are used on most other Ovation models.

The Elite is available in a variety of natural finishes or exotic black. **JB**

PRS
First Dragon 1992

Type Solidbody electric
Body & neck Mahogany with maple top, set neck
Fingerboard Rosewood with dragon inlay
Pick-ups Two humbucker pick-ups

If it was the PRS Artist I that started the redesign of the original PRS recipe, it was the PRS Dragon that kicked it into the stratosphere. As before, PRS used a high-end, limited edition model to experiment with new design features, although, for many, the innovations were completely overshadowed by the inlaid dragon that draped itself along the entire fingerboard. The First Dragon was a fifty-piece-only edition, with a list price of $8,000!

While it was the sinuous dragon inlay—drawn by Jude Van Dyke, and realized by Larry Sifel's Pearlworks company—that attracted nearly all the publicity at the time of the launch, the guitar itself was worthy of attention because it differed so remarkably from previous high-line PRS instruments. It used a shorter, twenty-two-fret neck (it was the first set-neck PRS to do so), with a longer heel and the "wide-fat" profile (the biggest neck offered by PRS).

The First Dragon also introduced the "hardtail" Stoptail wrapover bridge—previously all PRS guitars, apart from a few limited editions and custom builds, had featured Smith's vibrato. Also new were the Dragon Treble and Bass humbucker pick-ups.

"The Dragon I was all about bigger necks, twenty-two frets, and the Brazilian rosewood fretboard," said Paul Reed Smith in retrospect. It was highly successful, too, and inspired the Dragon II in 1993 and the Dragon III in 1994—both of which were, according to Smith, "identical, just different fingerboard inlays."

The Dragon I was an instrument of change: in one way or another, it influenced the structure and/or the appearance of every subsequent PRS guitar. **DB**

Greg Smallman
Aboriginal 1992

Type Classical guitar
Body & neck Cedar/rosewood body and neck
Fingerboard Ebony
Other key features Lattice bracing system

It's still too early to tell, but Australian luthier Greg Smallman may one day be regarded as the twentieth century's equivalent to Antonio Torres. Like Torres, Smallman revolutionized classical guitar design, primarily through a groundbreaking new lattice bracing system that has been much imitated since its creation in 1980; and as with Torres, it was a famous guitarist who championed his instruments and brought him fame and glory. In Torres' case, it was Francisco Tárrega; in Smallman's, it was John Williams.

Smallman started making guitars in the style of Fleta in 1972—this is particularly interesting, because Fleta was also an innovator in bracing systems. Having listened to Williams' views on the Fletas he had been playing for two decades, Smallman began reinventing the guitar's internal architecture to improve sustain, resonance, and projection, and to provide a consistent sound quality across the full dynamic range. Williams has been playing Smallmans since 1981, inspiring a generation of guitarists and luthiers.

This 1992 guitar has the best of Smallman's new design features, refined since their conception more than a decade earlier. Smallman went on to produce instruments with a truss rod, an adjustable neck, and a floating armrest to avoid the damping effect of the player's right arm. **GD**

The Black Decameron (1997) brings together three major classical guitar forces: John Williams playing works by neo-Romantic guitarist-composer Leo Brouwer (including the Afro-Cuban-inflected Concerto de Toronto) on a guitar by Greg Smallman.

Somogyi
OM 1992

Bozo
Requinto 1993

Type Handmade, single cutaway, dreadnought acoustic
Body & neck A choice of fine woods for body and neck
Fingerboard Ebony
Other key features Built with local weather in mind

Type Acoustic
Body & neck Spruce/laminated body, maple neck
Fingerboard Rosewood

Ervin Somogyi made his first guitar from a cigar box when he was a Cub Scout, and progressed from there. He has progressed a long way.

Born in Hungary in 1944, Somogyi later immigrated to the United States, and is now based in California. His handmade, custom-designed instruments are highly sought after, and command high prices (at least $30,000). There is a waiting list of more than a year.

Somogyi's attention to detail is extraordinary. Buyers have to send a tracing of their left hand, and details of the seasonal humidity in the area they live in, even before discussing the types of woods to be used, and the effect they will have on the guitar's tone.

He writes about, and lectures in the principles of, guitar making, and has taught many of America's up-and-coming luthiers. The standard of his woodworking is so high that Somogyi is also considered an accomplished artist, and sells pieces of wooden art based on the mosaic patterns from guitar rosettes and sound holes. **SH**

The Serbian luthier Bozo Podunavac was born in Belgrade (then Yugoslavia, now Serbia), immigrated to the United States in 1959, and settled in Chicago, Illinois, where he found work in the repair shop of a musical instrument dealer. In 1964, Bozo opened his own shop, "Wooden Magic," where he specialized in creating highly decorative guitars. Six years later, he relocated his business to California, settling first in Escondido, and then San Diego.

Bozo adopted "old-school" craftsmanship— adding one-off rosettes, herringbone and abalone inlays, and his own signature flowerpot design to hand-selected European woods—and sold his creations to musicians such as Leo Kottke and Cat Stevens. The Requinto (a nineteenth-century Spanish word for clarinet) was a small-bodied guitar with a higher-than-usual pitch, which made it popular for use as lead guitar in mariachi bands. But Bozos are not for everyone. Heavily built, they are most assuredly, in the words of Jim Earp, a "man's guitar." **BS**

Fender Harley Stratocaster 1993

Fender "Mini-Stratocaster" 1993

Type Twin cutaway solidbody electric
Body & neck Hollow aluminum body, maple neck
Fingerboard Ebony
Pick-ups Three gold-plated single-coil pick-ups

Type Solidbody electric
Body & neck Basswood body, maple neck
Fingerboard Rosewood or maple
Pick-ups Two or three single-coil pick-ups

Only 109 of these Custom Shop Stratocasters were made to celebrate the ninetieth anniversary of Harley-Davidson motorbikes. The guitar was built by two of Fender's top luthiers, Scott Buehl and Jason Davis.

It was certainly one of the most distinctive special editions, with a chromed, hollow aluminum body decorated with hand engravings, gold hardware, chrome scratchplate, and stainless steel inlaid fret markers. The headstock was black, with a prominent Harley-Davidson logo. Even the gig bag was special—a black-leather, embossed carrier, complete with a leather-jacket style fringe.

Look hard and you'll see there was also some wood involved on the neck and fingerboard.

Although one Harley Strat was played by wild country star Travis Tritt in concert, most of the examples seem to have been bought by collectors, locked away in vaults to appear only occasionally, and then sold on for enormous sums to other collectors. Recent examples have hit the $20,000 mark. **SH**

Three novelty instruments arrived from Fender Japan in the early 1990s in the form of scaled-down versions of the Stratocaster, Telecaster, and Precision Bass guitars. It is possible that they were intended for children—but, no matter what the target market may have been, these instruments missed it by a wide margin because they were too difficult to play and keep in tune.

The Stratocaster model MST-32 featured a scale length of 18¾ in. (47.6 cm), a twenty-one-fret neck with no truss rod, and two or three pick-ups. It had a full-sized headstock, jack cup, and bridge assembly, complete with vibrato system. It was initially offered in a choice of either sunburst with a rosewood fingerboard, or black with a maple fingerboard. It remained in production for about three years, eventually being replaced in 1999 by Squier's Mini series, in which the scale length was extended to 20¾ in. (52.7 cm), the center pick-up was restored, and the tremolo system removed. **DG**

Gibson Nighthawk Special 1993

Type Single-cutaway electric
Body & neck Mahogany body and neck
Fingerboard Rosewood
Pick-ups Two humbuckers and one single-coil pick-up

The Nighthawk series was an attempt to modernize the Gibson image, to produce a "guitar for all seasons" capable of playing a new range of sounds. The Nighthawks had cutting-edge electronics, including a coil tap switch that doubled as a tone control which, when moved up or down, converted the humbuckers to single-coil pick-ups, giving guitarists a whole new array of potential tones. The slanted bridge humbucker and mini humbucker at the neck were aimed at lovers of blues and classic rock.

There were three variations: the Custom, the Standard, and the Special. The Special was the budget version, costing $200 less than the Standard, and lacking some of the latter's cosmetic features. Only its body was bound, for example, as opposed to the bound body, neck, and headstock of the Custom, and it had dot inlays instead of the patterned inlays found on the Standard. And it lacked the holly crests that adorned the headstocks of both other models.

Resembling a squashed Les Paul, the Nighthawk was structurally a Gibson but had decidedly Fenderish features, such as the slanted bridge humbucker, which had sharper tones and less gain than standard Gibson humbuckers, a Fender-style string-through bridge, and a longer scale neck length of 25½ in. (64.75 cm), which meant increased string tensions that gave it something of a Fender sound. The series never gained a huge following, however—in spite of being lighter, less expensive, and more versatile than their Les Paul "cousins," and maintaining a sustain remarkably well considering its small stature. All three Nighthawk models were discontinued in 1998. **BS**

Gretsch Nashville Setzer 1993

Type Hollow body electric
Body & neck Maple body and neck
Fingerboard Ebonized rosewood
Pick-ups Two Gretsch Filter'Tron humbucker pick-ups

Some signature models seem destined to be. After Stray Cat Brian Setzer spearheaded the rockabilly revival in the 1980s, and thus renewed interest in Gretsch guitars, it was only fitting that the company should find a way of returning the favor.

Setzer's signature guitar is based on the Gretsch 6120, popularized in the 1950s by Eddie Cochran, Chet Atkins, and Duane Eddy. But two decades later, sales had declined, and by the time Setzer needed a replacement for his trusted original, they were no longer in production. "Vintage Gretsch guitars need

> *"I bought my first Gretsch 6120 when I was a kid. When I plugged it into my Bassman amp, I went, 'There it is!'"*

BRIAN SETZER

to be maintained and refurbished," Setzer explained to *Guitar Aficionado* magazine in 2011. "You can't play a stock Gretsch from 1959. It probably won't play in tune, and the fretboard will probably be warped and pitted. You can get it refurbished to make it playable, but that takes away some of its value."

Gretsch's Japanese-made version of Brian's old 6120 was the solution: a balance of old and new. While Setzer encouraged Gretsch to look back to its roots—avoiding the thicker maple tops that they'd subsequently adopted—the signature model also discards the zero fret of the old 6120s. The dice controls are another Setzer touch, and the results are a guitar that helped re-establish Gretsch's reputation and popularity with new players. **RL**

Thomas Humphrey
Millennium 1993

Type Classical acoustic
Body & neck Spruce/rosewood body and neck
Fingerboard Ebony
Other key features Sloping top from tail to fingerboard

Born in 1948, by the 1970s Thomas Humphrey was building guitars in the style of Hermann Hauser out of his New York apartment. His instruments were played by some of America's leading concert artists. Then, in 1985, he dreamed of a radical new design, inspired by that of the harp, for a guitar with the soundboard sloping down from the lower bout to the fingerboard, which would now be raised—strange to look at in profile, but easier to play than conventional guitars beyond the twelfth fret. The new guitar design was named Millennium, and guitarists David Starobin, Eliot

"The tradition of the guitar is its evolution. The fact that it does change ... is because of the players, who say, 'Give us more.'"

THOMAS HUMPHREY

Fisk, and Sharon Isbin, among others, started favoring them for their superior tone and projection, as well as for their playability. The early Millennium guitars had fan bracing, but, in the 1990s, Humphrey began experimenting with a lattice bracing system.

This 1993 Millennium guitar was built during that transitional period. Humphrey also made several quirky and unique guitars, one with f-holes and a strange retro head, and others with surreal paintings by Tamara Codor on their backs. The Millennium design was licensed to C.F. Martin for a special line of guitars, one of which was custom-made for Sting.

Humphrey was much loved by guitarists, who congregated in his workshop and home until his untimely death in 2008. **GD**

MusicMan
Albert Lee 1993

Type Solidbody electric
Body & neck Ash body and neck
Fingerboard Maple
Pick-ups Two Seymour Duncan single-coil pick-ups

Herefordshire's (in the United Kingdom) finest country guitar picker also happens to be one of the best guitarists on the planet, whatever the genre, and celebrated his fiftieth year as a pro player in 2010. Though once synonymous with vintage Telecasters, his trusted weapon of choice since its 1993 debut has been the MusicMan Albert Lee signature model. This quirky, angular slice of retro-futuristic Americana grew out of Lee's friendship with company owner Ernie Ball and his son Sterling, and the guitarist's love for and use of the Silhouette, a more conventional and classic

"It's quite different from a Tele, more like a Strat, with three single-coils and a five-way switch … I just fell in love with that guitar."

ALBERT LEE

MusicMan model. Lee's guitar was a prototype that was given to him to try out on the road.

Its scale length is the same as the Strat's, though the compact body makes it seem shorter. This, along with the four-and-two headstock that's now standard on MusicMan electrics, makes for a guitar which, Lee swears, sustains more than a Strat. As you'd expect on a country player, the bridge pick-up has a metal plate underneath it, and is hotter than a Strat equivalent.

The MusicMan Albert Lee model has been modified at various times to accommodate P-90s, a vibrato, and a B Bender. The latest HH incarnation features two DiMarzio-designed humbuckers, versatile switching, and a choice of stoptail or vibrato tailpiece. It is played live by Joe Bonamassa. **OB**

Parker
Fly Artist 1993

Type Solidbody electric
Body & neck Tonewoods/carbon fiber body and neck
Fingerboard Carbon fiber
Pick-ups Two humbuckers and one piezo pick-up

Once every decade or so, a new instrument appears that shakes the foundations of the guitar industry. It is usually radical in design, becomes briefly fashionable, is expensive, and then gradually begins to influence the way others think about guitar design. The original Parker Fly solidbody electric was a leading example of this type of instrument: there are very few subsequent guitars that owe nothing to its innovations.

The Fly was developed in 1993 by Ken Parker. His aim was to create an instrument that was lower in mass than—but just as strong as—a conventional solidbody electric. The original, acclaimed design consisted of a wooden frame, its exoskeleton made of a powerful carbon fiber/epoxy composite, and a neck ("Better than any neck I've played," enthused Adrian Belew) topped with a similar composite fingerboard.

The Fly's radical, active, on-board electronics were critical to the guitar's sound. Great tonal variety was made possible by the combination of a pair of switchable humbuckers with Larry Fishman's piezo bridge saddle pick-up—the latter could also be used on its own to create a highly effective, amplified acoustic guitar sound.

Parker Guitars was sold to U.S. Music Corporation in 2003, after which the Fly was given a cost-cutting revamp. None of the changes was an improvement. Although later guitars in the line are good, they nevertheless represent a dilution of the original strength: if you are looking to recapture the "Wow!" factor experienced by the first people who picked up the Parker Fly, there really is no alternative to seeking out one of the earliest models. **TB**

← Well known for his work with King Crimson, Adrian Belew was an early adopter of the Fly.

PRS
Custom 22 1993

Smith BT Custom
Bass V 1993

Type Solidbody electric
Body & neck Mahogany/maple body and neck
Fingerboard Rosewood
Pick-ups Two humbucker pick-ups

Type Electric bass guitar
Body & neck Various woods, including acacia and maple
Fingerboard Ebony
Pick-ups Two humbucker pick-ups

While the PRS Dragon I guitar was aimed at collectors, the rest of us could reap the benefits with this production model, the Custom 22. It didn't use the heavily inlaid Brazilian rosewood fingerboard of the opulent Dragon, but constructionally it featured the same wide-fat, twenty-two-fret neck, with its longer heel. It also boasted the Dragon humbucker pick-ups, and was offered with either the new stoptail wrapover bridge or the standard PRS vibrato.

Comparisons with the twenty-four-fret Custom (which, confusingly, wouldn't become the Custom 24 until 1998) were illustrative of the change. Here was a guitar that felt and sounded beefier; less skeletal. The stoptail bridge added focused character, while the humbuckers provided vintage tonality, but still with plenty of power.

Although at the time not everyone liked the change, early Customs have since become prized collectors' pieces. The PRS Custom remains, to this day, PRS's best-selling instrument. **DB**

Ken Smith has been making beautiful, hand-crafted instruments since 1979, and has served such leading musicians as Stanley Clarke and Marcus Miller.

The BT Custom V five-string was introduced in 1993. A wonderful, handmade instrument, it incorporated many of Smith's characteristic features, including exotic woods, such as acacia koa for the body's wings, mahogany for the center block, and a laminated three-piece "aged" hard rock-maple for the neck, which also contained graphite for stability, and had ebony strips.

The scale length is 34 in. (86.3 cm), and the BT has a full two-octave range, the body cutaways allowing easy access to the upper registers. The hardware is also noteworthy: the Smith bridge is fully adjustable, and, like the tuners, gold-plated. The pick-ups are Smith's own humbucking soapbars, connected to a two-band active preamp and volume control.

Ken Smith basses use so many different woods that you are unlikely to find two that are identical. **JB**

Warwick
Thumb Fretless 1993

Type Solidbody bass
Body & neck Bubinga body, wenge neck
Fingerboard Tigerstripe ebony
Pick-ups Two active MEC pick-ups

Warwick—founded by Hans-Peter Wilfer in Markneukirchen, East Germany, in 1982—originally specialized in premium instruments made from exotic tonewoods. At a time when graphite was the fashionable material for bass guitar construction, Warwick's motto was "The Sound of Wood."

These days, it is possible to find more affordable Warwick designs made in China or Korea out of more conventional wood—their Rockbass and Pro & Artist subsidiaries produce the "Vampyre," the "Alien," and the BO (bolt-on neck) version of the Thumb bass. Warwick also owns the Framus trademark. Its guitars have been endorsed by, among others, Jack Bruce, Bootsy Collins, and John Entwistle, who have all had their own Warwick signature models.

The Thumb bass shown here belonged to Bruce. The pick-ups are balanced with a blend control, and there are dual stacked treble and bass knobs. Further sounds can be created by pulling out the volume knob to defeat the active electronics. **AJ**

Brian Moore
MC/1 1994

Type Hollow body electric
Body & neck Composite/maple body and neck
Fingerboard Ebony
Pick-ups Customized

Aiming to create "the perfect balance between wood and composites for a completely new instrument," former Gibson employee and musician Patrick Cummings, businessman Kevin Kalagher, and Brian Moore of Steinberger joined forces in 1992 to found a high-end guitar design company (now named iGuitar). Its first product was the MC/1.

The guitar combined sustain with strength, through Moore's blend of synthetic materials and traditional wood. Unlike carbon-fiber composites, Brian's blend was designed to resonate like aged woods, aided by the MC/1's neck-thru construction.

The first 200 MC/1s—custom-made to order at the company's original shop in Brewster, New York—used hollow body construction, with the pick-ups mounted directly on the maple top. Later models were semi-hollow guitars with center blocks for routing the pick-ups.

The instrument shown here features two single-coil pick-ups and one humbucker. **RL**

Buscarino Virtuoso 1994

Fender Egyptian Telecaster 1994

Type Hollow body archtop with single Venetian cutaway
Body & neck Maple/spruce body, maple neck
Fingerboard Ebony
Pick-ups One floating or fitted humbucker pick-up

Type Solidbody electric
Body & neck Ash with Corian veneer body, maple neck
Fingerboard Corian veneer
Pick-ups Two single-coil pick-ups

A one-man company, John Buscarino boasts impressive credentials, having been apprenticed to both classical guitar builder Augustino LoPrinzi and highly-regarded archtop producer Robert Benedetto. Buscarino's guitars are prized, not only for their acoustic properties and playability, but also for their beauty. In 1996, Buscarino was one of twenty-two leading luthiers commissioned by collector Scott Chinery to produce a themed series of blue guitars.

Buscarino builds acoustic and solidbody guitars, but it is archtop models on which his reputation rests. At the top of this range is the Virtuoso. A magnificent example of the luthier's art, its back and sides are carved from quarter-sawn flame maple, its top from aged and seasoned sitka spruce; burl is used on the headstock, and the tailpiece is carved from ebony. The guitar may be amplified using a "floating" humbucker, designed by Kent Armstrong to eliminate unwanted feedback. Such exclusivity does not come cheap—Virtuosos currently start at $25,000. **TB**

Since 1987, the Fender Custom Shop has provided discerning players and collectors with the resources to commission ground-up one-offs. Custom Shop output has comprised everything from painstakingly detailed "relics" to eye-popping art guitars. There is no doubt where on that spectrum this Egyptian Telecaster lies.

Former Custom Shop master builder Fred Stuart recalls that they would routinely build art guitars for what he calls "dog-and-pony shows." He explains that his own fascination with "primitive art" was the inspiration for a Telecaster festooned with Egyptian motifs. (Similar Aztec, Mayan, and Celtic guitars followed.) Stuart laminated the ash body and maple neck with a veneer of Corian, a synthetic stone, which was then carved by his colleague, George Amicay. Stuart remembers that the electronics were "off-the-shelf," but also notes that, as outlandish as the Custom Shop "art guitar" may have appeared, above all it was important to "make sure it worked as a guitar." **DP**

Fender Urge Stuart Hamm 1994

Type Solidbody electric bass
Body & neck Alder body, bolt-on maple neck
Fingerboard Rosewood
Pick-ups Two "J" pick-ups, one "P" pick-up

Stuart Hamm spent his adolescence in thrall to The Partridge Family. "I was a big Danny Bonaduce fan," he said of the popsters' bassist, "because I was a pudgy red-haired geek, as he was."

Practicing the root notes on "I Think I Love You" paid off: Hamm went on to play with legends from Joe Satriani to Robert Fripp (both of whom grace his 2010 album *Just Outside Of Normal*). However, Hamm's most impressive achievement was in becoming the first bassist to create a signature Fender (an honor shared on the six-string side with one E. Clapton).

"The first Urge was a 32-in. [81.3-cm] scale bass," he recalled. "We had the active electronics . . . We worked real hard to make it sound great for a short-scale bass, but some people said, 'A short-scale bass? That doesn't sound manly—I can't play that.' Plus, I looked really big wearing a small bass." The next stage was Urge II, which came out in 1999. Boasting a pau ferro fingerboard—and, later, a Hipshot Drop D-tuner—it remained in Fender's catalog until 2010. **BM**

Ibanez PGM500 1994

Type Solidbody electric
Body & neck Basswood body; maple neck
Fingerboard Rosewood
Pick-ups Two humbuckers, one single-coil pick-up

Debuting in 1990, the PG series was a collaboration between Ibanez and Paul Gilbert, guitarist with U.S. rock band Mr. Big, who were at that time hugely popular in Japan. Emerging at the end of the "Superstrat" boom, the PGM500 is unusual for its lack of a Floyd Rose-style locking vibrato system—indeed, at this time, it was the only Ibanez guitar to feature a fixed bridge.

Gilbert chose to use a "non-trem" model because in the early stages of his career he couldn't afford the luxury of a guitar tech, and, laborious as they can be to maintain, he "didn't want to spent hours in his hotel room every night restringing four or five guitars." Bowing to inevitable demand, later versions would be kitted out with a trem.

Visually, the guitar is notable for its faux f-holes, which are simply stenciled onto the body—a characteristic of the PG range. Also unique among Ibanez models was the reverse headstock design that saw the tuners aligned along the bottom edge. **TB**

Ibanez
Talman TC530 1994

Type Semi-solid electric
Body & neck Resoncast body, maple bolt-on neck
Fingerboard Rosewood
Pick-ups Three single-coil Korean Sky lipstick pick-ups

The three original models in the Japanese-made Talman line debuted in 1994. Their offset double-cutaway body shape was partly inspired by Fender's iconic trio of Telecaster, Jaguar, and Jazzmaster. With their vibrato and Korean Sky lipstick single-coil pick-ups—styled after the original hot Danelectros—the TC530s were also ideal for the Ventures-style surf rock that Fender's latter two models handled so well.

The initial Talman runs were constructed from a body material unusual in guitar manufacturing—Resoncast—MDF that was only used in production for

"Talman guitars might have been created by the imaginative designers of the 1950s and '60s, if they had today's technology…"
1994 IBANEZ SALES CATALOG

a few years before being replaced with wood for later Talman models. The TC530 appeared with two sibling Talmans: the TV650 and TV750 models came with a combination of single-coil lipstick pick-ups and Sky mini humbuckers. The two "TV" models were similar but for the 650's top bound in pearloid celluloid. The TC530 itself was replaced after a year with the TC630.

Punk rockers The Offspring were one of the world's biggest bands in the Talman's maiden year. Their guitarist, Kevin "Noodles" Wasserman, was so enamored of its shape that he asked Ibanez to base his 1994 duct tape-bound NDM1 signature model on it. Another noted user was Rage Against The Machine's Tom Morello, whose Talman was given a custom finish featuring the national flag of Kenya. **RL**

PRS
McCarty 1994

Type Solidbody electric
Body & neck Mahogany/maple top, set neck
Fingerboard Rosewood
Pick-ups Two humbucker pick-ups

David Grissom had been an early adopter of PRS in the late 1980s. After gigging and recording with the guitars for a number of years, he put in a custom order. "My complaint had always been that they [PRS guitars] were all midrange. Up to that point, it had suited me really well, because I was looking for this supercharged Telecaster sound. I think some of the thoughts I was having, Paul [Reed Smith] was having at the same time: he wanted the guitars to appeal to a broader range of players that might be looking for more lows and a little bit more vintage tone."

"The McCarty is a wonderful instrument but the DGT is just a product of a lot of miles down the road, a lot of gigs, a lot of records."
DAVID GRISSOM

Grissom "wasn't ready" for a signature guitar at that time (his David Grissom Tremolo would launch in 2007), so his custom order became the McCarty model—named after Ted McCarty, president of Gibson guitars during its golden period (1950–65), who'd consulted for PRS. The name certainly tied in with the vintage ethos of the McCarty, which used the same outline as the Custom, but had a body that was 1/8 in. (0.3 cm) thicker, twenty-two frets, and new-design McCarty humbucker pick-ups with, for the first time on a PRS, covers, and a three-way toggle pick-up selector switch with a pull-push coil-split on the tone control.

The McCarty took PRS onto a more vintage-aimed route, and laid the foundation for the Singlecut. **DB**

Tobias
Standard V 1994

Type Solidbody electric bass
Body & neck Ash/maple/bubinga body and neck
Fingerboard Rosewood
Pick-ups Two Bartolini humbucker pick-ups

Before he became involved with Gibson, Michael Tobias spent thirteen independent years building a reputation among players for both his custom basses and his repair work. A guitarist himself, he began making them too, but soon found his basses were appreciated more.

The Tobias brand is unusual in that serial numbers didn't begin at 01; instead, the first Tobias Guitars instrument denotes the year of its creation—0178 (January 1978). Until 1992, Tobias basses were built by Michael's core team in Los Angeles, California, but demand increased beyond his ten-man team's capacity to cope with it. The decision was therefore taken to use an outside vendor to build for the company. However, an attempt to outsource to Japan for the first Standard model basses was not economically viable, because of the unfavorable dollar/yen exchange rate. Only 400 Standard models were made in the Nagoya factory before December 1992, when Tobias production moved to Gibson's home city of Nashville, Tennessee. But the original team declined to move with it. By the end of the year, its founder had left the company (he went on to found Michael Tobias Design basses), and Gibson had taken over production.

Today, the pre-Nashville Standards are the most desirable. The four-, five-, and six-string models were discontinued in 1996, but the Standard has made a comeback of sorts. The Tobias Standard IV is available through Epiphone, with its shape intact, but with the high-end spec reduced to match an entry-level price. Only the Tobias Deluxe-V offers five-string thrills. **RL**

Zon
Hyperbass 1994

Type Solidbody bass guitar
Body & neck Mahogany/maple body, composite neck
Fingerboard Composite
Pick-ups One humbucker pick-up

Two octaves of bass notes not enough for you? Then you probably need a Zon Hyperbass, with its slick, playable, three-octave neck, made of graphite composite, and extended more than halfway into the actual body of the bass. Don't worry, the dusty end of the fretboard is made accessible by a deep cutaway, but be warned that you might fall off your stool if you're playing that high.

Although the Hyperbass comes with only a single humbucker pick-up, it's an active unit, powered by Zon's own magical circuit, and fully able to deliver a wide tone range. Developed in consultation with

> *"The bass plays great! To borrow from Jeff Berlin: 'It's like playing in melted butter on a Teflon surface in zero G.'"*
>
> MARK BEEM, TALKBASS.COM

Windham Hill/New Age bassist Michael Manring—a one-time student of the great Jaco Pastorius—this curious, but frankly extremely desirable, instrument is popular among soloists and jazz ensembles alike, particularly in the anything-goes world of modern jazz fusion. No expense has been spared on the components, as your bank manager will not fail to notice if you buy one—a fully specified Hyperbass will set you back in excess of $10,000.

Zon book-match a curly maple top to the poplar core in order to make the Hyperbass sound full and look lovely. If you choose a fretless model, like the one shown here, you'll be able to do your best Jaco Pastorius impression all the way up that neck. **JM**

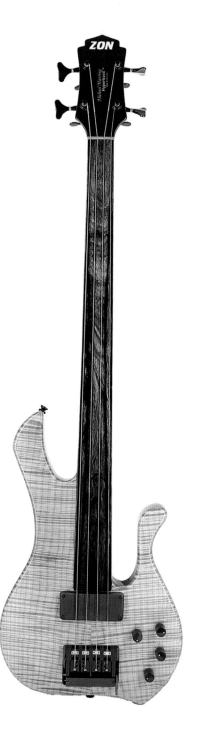

Breedlove
SC20 1995

Type Steel-string acoustic
Body & neck Spruce/walnut body, mahogany neck
Fingerboard Ebony
Other key features Gold Grover tuners, ebony bridge

Larry Breedlove and Steve Henderson met while working at Taylor Guitars in Anaheim, California, and later decided to set up their own company, making innovative top-end instruments in a rural location.

They established Breedlove Guitars in Bend, Oregon, in 1990. Years of experimenting led them to some distinctive ways of building acoustic guitars.

The SC20 was their most popular early design. It featured a pinless bridge, a narrow, tapered headstock to ensure the straightest string path between nut slots and tuning pegs, and an inventive new system of bracing to improve tone, volume, and strength.

The SC20 was a concert-style guitar, with a deep body for enhanced tone and projection. The finish was understated, but of the highest quality—with gold Grover tuners, a one-piece wooden rosette decorating the round sound hole, and ebony fingerboard and bridge. The walnut back and sides of the instrument shown here give it a warm and balanced sound ideal for more technical playing. **SH**

Campellone
Special 1995

Type Acoustic archtop cutaway
Body & neck Spruce/maple body, maple neck
Fingerboard Ebony
Other key features Ebony bridge

Considered one of today's finest archtop guitar makers, Mark Campellone of Grenville, Rhode Island, had considered an art career before pursuing an interest in guitar playing by attending Berklee College of Music, and then becoming a professional musician. He began repairing and building guitars in the 1970s, patiently learning the craft before building his first archtop in 1988. By 1990, he had become a full-time luthier. His archtop guitars are masterpieces of design, harking back in their styling to a bygone Big Band era. Campellone's guitars are not just beautiful *objets d'art*, but instruments that rival the best of Gibson archtops from the 1950s.

The Cameo is now Campellone's top-of-the-line guitar, but the Special (like the 1995 custom model shown here) is next in line, followed in descending order by the Deluxe, Standard, and EP models. There is no expense spared in the quality of materials, and all models, with or without optional pick-up, come in a range of colorful and dazzling finishes. **GD**

Fender D'Aquisto Custom Ultra 1995

Type Archtop acoustic
Body & neck Spruce/maple body and neck
Fingerboard Maple
Other key features Adjustable, carved ebony bridge

In 1984, luthier James D'Aquisto teamed with Fender to produce the D'Aquisto Standard and Elite models. Featuring laminated bodies, these Japanese-built guitars were intended to fill a gap in the market for modestly priced jazz boxes. Ten years later, D'Aquisto and Fender hooked up again, but this time the results—the D'Aquisto Deluxe and Ultra—were a far cry from archtops for econo-minded jazz cats.

As apprentice and successor to famed master luthier John D'Angelico, Brooklyn-born D'Aquisto was a thoroughbred of the guitar world, and his 1994 offerings via the Fender Custom Shop reflect that. The Ultra, retailing for $15,000, featured a carved spruce top with "highly figured" maple sides and back. The three-piece, 12-in. (30.5-cm) radius neck was likewise carved from figured maple, and featured a 25⅛-in. (63.8-cm) ebony fingerboard with twenty-two frets and rectangular shell inlays.

By the time of his death in 1995, James D'Aquisto had logged 371 guitars in his ledger. **DP**

Fodera Victor Wooten Monarch 1995

Type Electric bass
Body & neck Alder/ebony body, maple neck
Fingerboard Ebony
Pick-ups One P-style and one J-style pick-up

If ever there was a bass-playing match made in heaven, it would surely be this one: a signature model produced by the elite, Brooklyn-based Fodera company—a brand geared to the requirements (and the pockets) of the professional market—for Victor L. Wooten, one of the most influential bass guitarists of his generation.

An established Fodera player, Wooten approached Vinny Fodera in 1995 with the idea of having a yin-yang symbol inlaid on his Monarch bass; Fodera went further, covering the entire front of the body with the design, and making it available in Standard and Deluxe models.

The Victor Wooten Yin-Yang Deluxe takes twice as long to build as a regular Fodera bass. Consequently, it is available only as a special, Custom Shop order, and even then only in small quantities—a maximum of six are built per year. Then again, the number of bass players with $14,000 burning a hole in their pockets must be quite small. **TB**

Gibson **Les Paul 60 Corvette** 1995

Type Mahogany/maple body, maple neck
Body & neck Rosewood
Fingerboard Richlite
Pick-ups Two humbucker pick-ups

During the 1990s, both Fender and Gibson began marketing promotions with leading brand names from other industries: the Fender Custom Shop hooked up with motorcycle manufacturers Harley-Davidson; Gibson's Custom Shop forged a link with automobile giants Chevrolet, particularly with the Corvette model. The synergy was that of firms that were young and hip during the 1950s, the first decade of rock 'n' roll.

Commercial "tie-ins" are sometimes tawdry, exploitative affairs, aimed purely at maximum cash extraction, but the Gibson Corvette is a very classy piece of kit. What we have here is one of a limited edition of 200 Les Paul Standards, styled after a 1960 Chevy Corvette automobile. For starters, the guitar was available in a variety of authentic General Motors color finishes. And then there were the Corvette touches: the smooth curves of the chrome-edged white panel that envelops the bridge and pick-ups, and imitates the contours of the panels on either side of the original cars. Conventional fingerboard inlays are here replaced with the Corvette's famous logo script in mother-of-pearl between the second and thirteenth frets; the classic Chevrolet crossed flags symbol is inlaid on the headstock. Engraved legends on the two pick-up covers—"283" and "Fuel Injection"—relate to the small-block V8 engine of the original car.

In 2003, Gibson reprised the link with a limited edition of fifty guitars celebrating the Corvette's half century, this time based around a Les Paul Junior "twin-cut" design. **TB**

Heritage
H150 CM 1995

Type Single cutaway solidbody electric
Body & neck Mahogany/maple body, mahogany neck
Fingerboard Rosewood
Pick-ups Two Seymour Duncan '59 humbucker pick-ups

Heritage Guitars set up in old Gibson workshops in Michigan, using old Gibson machinery operated by former Gibson employees—so it's no surprise that the Heritage Les Paul-style models are so good.

The H150 is obviously a classic Les Paul in all but name. Only the headstock logo tells you otherwise. The Heritage has the mahogany body and neck, twin humbucker pick-ups, and single cutaway design that are so familiar. However, close examination reveals that the Heritage's headstock is a slightly different shape, and has an increased angle to the neck, for improved tuning stability.

Heritage fans love the H150's craftsmanship and attention to detail. The specification is impressive: the CM (custom maple) has a solid, carved, curly maple top on its one-piece mahogany body, and a cream, bound-rosewood fretboard on the one-piece mahogany neck. The pick-ups are Duncans, not Gibsons; there are mother-of-pearl trapezeoid inlays on the fretboard, and all the hardware is chrome-plated. The Heritage bodies are usually heavier, and the necks slimmer, although there is more variation in their hands-on build than in Gibson's more mechanized production.

H150 players include Testament's Alex Skolnick, for whom Heritage produced a signature model. **SH**

Gary Moore was one of the biggest Heritage endorsees. He played an H150 CM in many live shows, videos, broadcasts, and recordings, including the album *After The War* (1989). In 1991, Heritage produced a Gary Moore signature model.

Krawczak Twin Soundboard 1995

Martin 000-42 ECM 1995

Type Acoustic with second soundboard
Body & neck Spruce and maple body, maple neck
Fingerboard Ebony

Type Steel-string acoustic guitar
Body & neck Rosewood and spruce body, hardwood neck
Fingerboard Ebony

Polish immigrant Kaz Krawczak settled in Rhode Island, and began building eccentric acoustic and electric guitars, including this extraordinary handmade "twin soundboard" instrument.

Krawczak experimented with designs to reduce stress on the soundboard while amplifying the vibrations. To this end, he patented an innovative "acoustic arm" device. This is an extension of the neck, running inside the soundbox, and emerging through the soundboard as a tailpiece. The strings, in effect, join the bottom of the neck, not the top of the soundbox. Guitar collector Scott Chinery bought one of these handmade instruments in 1995.

Using this arrangement with a second floating soundboard creates extra vibrations, and relieves the original soundboard of all tension from the strings. Bracing can be much lighter, which improves tone and volume. Krawczak also devised a unique acoustic guitar bridge that includes height adjustment, but no major manufacturers have so far taken up his idea. **SH**

Although widely revered as one of the the greatest blues-based rock guitarists of them all, Eric Clapton is no mean acoustic picker, either. This was amply demonstrated in 1992, when he took part in MTV's acclaimed "Unplugged" series—performing acoustic versions of some of his rock classics, such as the evergreen "Layla."

For the show, Clapton used his two favorite Martin guitars: a 1939 000-42, and a customized 1966 000-28. Such was the interest aroused by the broadcast—including a Grammy-winning album that would shift more than ten million units—that Martin approached Clapton with a view to launching a signature model.

Launched in 1995, the limited-edition Martin 000-42 ECM was a blinged-up replica of Clapton's own model that would set the buyer back more than $5,000. It was, of course, a magnificent instrument, the "000" body size prized for both its tonal balance and its clarity in the treble register, making it the perfect guitar for fingerpicking styles. **TB**

Monteleone
Radio Flyer 1995

Type Archtop
Body & neck Spruce and maple body and neck
Fingerboard Ebony

Long Island-based John Monteleone is a crafter of exquisite mandolins and archtops, and is considered one of the finest luthiers at work today. His Radio Flyer was designed as a tribute to the power of radio, and to acknowledge the medium's far-reaching effect on the guitar. "My imagination was nurtured by radio and most of the great guitar recordings I ever heard were brought to me via radio," Monteleone has explained. "I would eventually turn this influence into an inspiration for the Radio Flyer."

Monteleone describes the Radio Flyer's sound as accelerated and immediate in response, with a wide dynamic response, power, and sustain, and likens it to a magic-carpet ride for the player. The "Dolphin" sound holes in place of f-holes add a futuristic air to the proceedings, balanced by the obvious quality of the tonewoods, and the stylish air of refinement of its tailpiece, guard, and headstock. And luminaries such as Mark Knopfler and Kevin Bacon play them, so they're definitely good enough for most of us. **OB**

Peavey
Cropper Classic 1995

Type Solidbody
Body & neck Maple/mahogany body and neck
Fingerboard Rosewood
Pick-ups One neck and one bridge humbucker pick-up

Steve Cropper (a.k.a. "The Colonel") has one of the most impressive guitar résumés imaginable: indeed, *Mojo* magazine put him second in its poll of all-time greats. His classic recordings with Stax, Booker T & The MGs, and on countless sessions and collaborations are filled to the brim with sinuous, deft licks, mostly conjured out of a '59 Esquire or a '63 Telecaster, using a tricky pick-and-fingers technique.

When Peavey showed Cropper the prototype of a new guitar, he liked it. "With all due respect to Fender, it just ate all my Telecasters. The pick-ups were hotter, and the sound was thicker," he told Brian D. Holland. A tour with Dave Edmunds followed, and he played it for well over a decade. Peavey's Cropper Classic had an intriguing quad-blade humbucker in the bridge, and a proprietary Maxcess neck joint system that provided better access to the dusty end.

Cropper himself was impressed by this, as well: "A guy named Jim DeLuca made that guitar . . . I played it for a long time," he said. **OB**

Ribbecke
Blue Mingione 1995

Type Archtop acoustic
Body & neck Spruce/maple body and neck
Fingerboard Ebony
Pick-ups None

Tom Ribbecke began building guitars in 1974, and currently has a workshop near Santa Rosa, California. He grew up in Brooklyn, and built his first guitar while in college, going on to play for years in San Francisco before moving to Healdsburg, California. Nowadays, Ribbecke Guitars employs nine craftsmen and creates custom-order, high-end archtop guitars, including the ingenious Halfling design, for an exclusive clientele.

In the mid-1990s, Ribbecke was one of twenty-two luthiers chosen to contribute to Scott Chinery's "Blue Collection," a celebration of the archtop guitar,

"[Chinery] told us it had to be … of certain dimensions, and it had to be blue. Other than that, we were given free rein."

TOM RIBBECKE

which was exhibited in the Smithsonian Institution in Washington D.C., and then at the Museum of Musical Instruments in Boston, Massachusetts.

Ribbecke's Blue Mingione was named after jazz player Andy Mingione. Its A-shaped sound holes, wooden pickguard and tailpiece, and body shape are characteristic of Jimmy D'Aquisto, the Sorcerer's Apprentice of the archtop world, and Ribbecke's main guitar-crafting inspiration. One idiosyncrasy of the Blue Mingione is the inclusion of an ebony sound port on the side of the guitar's upper bout, which enables the player to insert a "sound horn" to act as a kind of "monitor" for the left ear. Like the rest of the blue guitars in the Chinery Collection, its value is estimated at around $30,000. **OB**

Teuffel
Birdfish 1995

Type Solidbody electric
Body & neck Mahogany/maple body, maple neck
Fingerboard Ebony
Pick-ups Two single-coil and three humbucker pick-ups

Although he may once have seemed something of a rebel, the electric guitar player of the twenty-first century can sometimes cut a somewhat conservative figure. Especially when most youngsters seem to be happily wielding designs conceived more than fifty years earlier. And more often than not, attempts to rethink the fundamentals of the instrument are met with caution or a haughty sneer.

One of the most radical reinventions of the electric guitar appeared in 1995, when a young Bavarian luthier named Ulrich Teuffel came up with the Birdfish. A former student of industrial design, Teuffel's starting point was brutally fundamental, questioning the function of every part of the electric guitar. The instrument that resulted was constructed as a frame of "modules."

The core of the body consists of two aluminum pieces, described by Tueffel as the "bird" and the "fish." The two sections are joined by a pair of strong wooden "tonebars." The neck is fixed to the upper element (the bird), while the lower element (the fish) houses the electronics.

This modular approach extends to the body and hardware. The Birdfish comes with two single-coil and three humbucking pick-ups, any of which can be fitted into the three available slots. Furthermore, the wooden tonebars can be exchanged—two pairs are provided, one in maple, the other in alder—to modify the guitar's tonal characteristics.

It may seem surprising that an instrument of such beauty and versatility is not more widely embraced, until you see the $15,000 price tag! **TB**

Vanden
Archtop Guitar 1995

Type Cutaway archtop acoustic-electric
Body & neck Spruce/maple body, maple neck
Fingerboard Ebony
Pick-ups One custom humbucker pick-up

Mike Vanden is a maker of high-end archtop guitars, mandolins, and world-class pick-up systems, who runs his own workshop in Scotland. He has a felicitous association with jazz guitarist Martin Taylor, who collaborated with him on designing the Martin Taylor Artistry model archtop.

They both wanted an integrated design, with a dual pick-up system, and a 15-in. (38-cm) body that would be equally suitable for fingerstyle or for using with a pick.

Taylor describes the result in glowing terms: "What I like most about it is that it is a small-bodied jazz guitar that's comfortable to play. It has a great, woody sound, but also has a lot of bass, and nice high frequencies. Also, we designed it so that it has more sustain than most jazz archtops."

The creation of this instrument inspired Vanden to experiment with other pick-up systems. His earlier efforts, aimed at flat-top guitars, had been licensed to Fishman, and became their Rare Earth line.

For archtops, Vanden preferred two pick-up sources, but the problem lay in making them user-friendly, without leads everywhere. In the Mimesis Jazz Blend, Vanden came up with an easy, "plug-and-play" system: a suspended humbucker pick-up, Fishman piezo bridge elements, preamps, and controls, all of which are fitted to the pickguard.

The Vanden archtop featured here is similar to the Cadenza model, but with a Venetian cutaway. The luthier himself generally favors a less pronounced, almost Maccaferri, shape, but in this case he acceded to Taylor's wishes. **GD**

B.C. Rich
EMI-1 Exclusive 1996

Type Solidbody electric
Body & neck Mahogany/maple body, maple neck
Fingerboard Ebony
Pick-ups Two humbucker pick-ups

Guitar maker extraordinaire Ed Roman, never a man short of an opinion or ten, united in the mid-1990s with Bernardo Chavez Rico of B.C. Rich to produce a guitar that both men hoped would undercut and outperform the popular PRS range.

The EM-1 Exclusive was, indeed, a thing of beauty, but Roman and Rico diverged on the intention to market it under the B.C. Rich name. Since that company was closely associated with metalheads, Roman was convinced that the target market would immediately be alienated, and look elsewhere for their

> "B.C. Rich was a quality guitar, but the average PRS lover would never even consider a guitar with a metal heritage."
>
> ED ROMAN

next purchase. People who choose their purchases exclusively on the basis of the name of the manufacturer, rather than appreciating the attributes of each individual model, were a big bugbear for Roman. In the streams of invective for which he was famous, he often inveighed against what he called "misdirected, ignorant brand loyalty."

In this case, his fears were not unfounded. When the Exclusive—whose sober, effortlessly classy styling set it apart from other guitars in the B.C. Rich range—failed to find buyers in significant numbers, Roman took over the marketing himself, and relaunched it as the intriguingly titled "Mystery Guitar."

The Mystery is over, but the Exclusive remains available as a B.C. Rich custom build. **CB**

Benedetto La Cremona Azzura 1996

Type Acoustic archtop cutaway
Body & neck Spruce/maple body, maple neck
Fingerboard Ebony
Other key features Blue sunburst nitrocellulose finish

One of the twenty-two guitars custom-built for Scott Chinery's "Blue Guitar" project, Robert Benedetto's "La Cremona Azzurra" (The Blue Cremona) is remarkable, not only for its unique styling, but also for the quality of its tone and projection. It was one of the loudest of the twenty-two, a distinction it achieved through the position of the foliated sound holes, and the additional openings cut into its side. Professionals such as veteran jazz guitarist Bucky Pizzarelli speak of Benedetto guitars as being among the very best; other notable players include Chuck Wayne, Martin

> *"My orders have been from mainstream jazz players, so I've been able to ... continue my pursuit of the ultimate jazz guitar."*
>
> ROBERTO BENETTO

Taylor, Andy Summers, and Kenny Burrell. His work has also been admired by the great luthiers John D'Angelico and Jimmy D'Aquisto.

Instruments in this league don't come cheap: Benedetto guitars start at $4,000; the classic Cremona model with standard f-holes costs $30,000; $40,000 buys you the Sinfonietta model.

Robert Benedetto (b. 1946) is part of a small elite of contemporary U.S. luthiers making archtop jazz guitars. Benedetto has personally made about 500 since his first in 1968. In the late 1990s, he licensed Fender to produce his guitars. In 2006, he joined forces with guitarist-businessman Howard Paul to found Benedetto Guitars, Inc., and took manufacture in-house again. **GD**

Carrington
Classical Guitar 1996

Type Classical acoustic electric
Body & neck Spruce/rosewood body, rosewood neck
Fingerboard Ebony
Pick-ups One internal B-band pick-up

Immediately recognizable by their unique, "Gothic" headstocks, and the dotted inlays around the sound hole, Chris Carrington's guitars stand out from the crowd, both visually and acoustically. They are big-sounding instruments, even without the aid of their internal electronics. Enthusiasts extol their traditional, warm, Spanish sound, with singing trebles, and good sustain, and they can hardly believe how accessible their prices are. Guitarists who have owned and played Carrington guitars include Andy Summers, Fred Hand, and Benjamin Verdery.

"Because I play … I know exactly what needs to go into the instrument from a player's point of view."

CHRIS CARRINGTON

Based in Texas, Carrington is not only a maker but also a professional musician of high standing. He majored in classical guitar, and earned a Masters of Music degree in classical guitar performance. With more than 500 international concerts to his credit, the high point of his career to date has been recording and touring with Al Di Meola during the 1990s in the acoustic ensemble World Sinfonia.

Carrington embarked on his parallel career as a luthier by making himself guitars that he could amplify on stage when playing large venues, and which satisfied his own exacting standards—this is a very direct, experience-based process of learning the craft of guitar making from a luthier who is, extraordinarily, also a world-class guitarist. **GD**

Carvin
H2 1996

Type Semi-hollow electric
Body & neck Alder body with alder or maple neck
Fingerboard Ebony
Pick-ups Two H22 pick-ups

For more than six decades, the Carvin Corporation has plowed its own furrow in the world of American guitar manufacture. Founded in 1946 by Lowell Kiesel, who initially produced pick-ups and lap steel guitars, the brand first appeared in 1949, selling guitars and basses built from bodies and necks imported from Höfner in Europe. In the 1970s, Carvin found its niche: designing and building its own instruments and selling them via mail order from the company's headquarters in San Diego, California.

As Carvins are built to order, they are effectively custom instruments—but, with no distributors or retailers cutting into the profits—they can be sold at very reasonable prices. And if you want to save a bit more cash, Carvin offer high-quality DIY kits— quaintly offered as a "perfect father–son project." But with instruments endorsed by such names as Frank Zappa, Steve Vai, and Allan Holdsworth, it's clear that Carvin can make pretty serious guitars.

British-born jazz-fusion guitarist Allan Holdsworth would certainly seem to be a good name to have on board if you're trying to appeal to the speed merchants—since, in his hands, guitar playing just doesn't get any faster! Holdsworth first came into contact with Carvin when he moved to California in the 1980s. The most unusual aspect of his two signature models—the single-pick-up H1 and the twin-pick-up H2—was their semi-hollow body construction, which featured two "i-beam" braces into which the neck was set. The top of the body was glued into place without coming into contact with the two beams. **TB**

Fender
Jag-Stang 1996

Type Solidbody electric
Body & neck Basswood body, maple bolt-on neck
Fingerboard Rosewood
Pick-ups Single-coil pick-up (neck), humbucker (bridge)

In 1993, Kurt Cobain approached Fender with a design combining elements of the Mustang and the Jaguar. Cutting up two Polaroids and sticking them to a piece of paper, Cobain added annotations like "Mustang pick-ups and electronics," "very thin neck," and "left-handed" to convey his hybrid dream guitar.

Two prototypes, in the classic Fender colors of Fiesta Red and Sonic Blue, were made under the direction of Custom Shop master builder Larry L. Brooks and delivered to Cobain early the following year. Rumored to be dissatisfied with how the design had worked out, Cobain played the blue prototype only a handful of times on Nirvana's 1994 European tour. After his death on April 5, his widow, Courtney Love, gave the guitar to R.E.M.'s Peter Buck.

The design went into production in 1996 and, although popular as a tribute to Cobain, divides opinion among players. The short 24-in. (61-cm) scale suits smaller hands but can be awkward for those with larger ones. Reliable tuning is impaired by the Mustang-style floating bridge that makes vibrato risky and sustain impossible. Many owners replace the shop pick-ups with beefier options to drive fuzz or distortion, as per Cobain's preference. However, it retains a loyal following for its quirkiness, neat form, and features like three-way switches (on-off-reverse phase) on both pick-ups. **JMB**

Set-up for right-handed use, Cobain's blue Jag-Stang is played by Peter Buck in the video for "What's The Frequency, Kenneth?," from R.E.M.'s *Monster* (1995). Mike Mills also used it in concert when the band played the same album's Cobain requiem, "Let Me In."

Gibson Les Paul Premium Plus 1996

Gibson Les Paul Ultima 1996

Type Solidbody electric
Body & neck Mahogany/maple body, maple neck
Fingerboard Rosewood
Pick-ups One 496R and one 500T humbucker pick-up

Type Solidbody electric
Body & neck Mahogany/maple body, mahogany neck
Fingerboard Ebony
Pick-ups Two '57 PAF humbucker pick-ups

How do you tweak an established classic? This is a difficult question, because what one player welcomes as an improvement, another may regard as sacrilege. For many, Gibson peaked in 1959 and 1960 with its Les Paul. Decades later, guitarists were looking for some of that vintage magic to be repeated.

The Les Paul Classic was introduced in 1990, and then produced for four years before being reissued between 1999 and 2001. It was made for a specific market—players who wanted a slimmer, 1960 neck profile, and higher output with hotter, ceramic magnet pick-ups. The 1993 Plus and Premium Plus variations gave the Classic the figured tops previously found on Gibson's Les Paul Reissue model. The Plus featured AA-grade flame maple; the Classic Premium Plus shown here had the more highly figured AAA grade. With the possibility of overlap between the grades, the models are differentiated by handwritten initials under the rhythm pick-up. On this guitar, they are "LPPP" (Les Paul Premium Plus). **RL**

The Ultima was one of Gibson's fanciest-ever guitars. It was the Nashville Custom Shop's attempt to create the ultimate Les Paul.

Its most striking feature was the lavishly decorated fretboard: the ebony was inlaid in abalone and mother-of-pearl. Buyers could choose one of three designs—flame, tree of life, or harp—all of which dominated the whole fretboard.

Other top-of-the-line ingredients included a high-grade quilt or flame maple top, elaborately inlaid headstock and binding, gold hardware, pearl tuning buttons on Grover tuners, and an elaborate trapeze-style tailpiece.

It was great to play too: chambers in the body made it one of the lightest Les Pauls—less than 8 lbs (3.6 kg)—but improved sustain from the vintage style humbucker pick-ups. The Ultima's refined sound can make a standard Les Paul seem muddy. It was beautiful, too. One reviewer warned buyers: "Be careful—it will make you look ugly." **SH**

Grimes
Jazz Laureate 1996

Hollenbeck
Ebony 'n' Blue 1996

Type Archtop (optional single cutaway)
Body & neck Maple/spruce body, spruce neck
Fingerboard Ebony
Pick-ups Optional

Type Hollow body jazz
Body & neck Bird's-eye maple body and neck
Fingerboard Ebony
Pick-ups None

Steve Grimes is guitar maker to some of the world's top players. His customers include Hank Marvin, Willie Nelson, Walter Becker, and Steve Miller. Jazz player George Benson has four Grimes guitars, including two of these Jazz Laureate archtops.

Grimes' workshop, up Mount Haleakala on the Hawaiian island of Maui, produces only around twenty guitars a year, each costing about $16,000. There is usually an eighteen-month waiting list.

The Jazz Laureate is available in cutaway or non-cutaway shapes, and various sizes. The key to Grimes' success is his choice of timber. He selects from hundreds of samples of master-grade wood. Backs and sides are cut from the same piece of German curly maple, so that they match visually and tonally. Grimes personally chooses and tests this wood for lightness, stiffness, sustain, and purity of tone.

Decorations are exquisite. They include inlaid diamond, and alternating strips of paua shell, abalone from New Zealand, and mother-of-pearl. **SH**

Bill Hollenbeck's Ebony 'n' Blue was one of twenty-one guitars commissioned by archtop aficionado Scott Chinery for his "Blue Guitar" collection. The project—which also featured Linda Manzer's Blue Absynthe (see page 709), Tom Ribbecke's The Blue Mingione, and Bob Benedetto's La Cremona Azzurra—was triggered by a blue sunburst D'Aquisto Centura Deluxe that Chinery commissioned luthier Jimmy D'Aquisto to build in 1993. The guitar, completed a couple of years later, was one of the last that D'Aquisto built before his death in 1995. As a tribute, Chinery commissioned twenty-one top luthiers to build a classic 18-in. (45.75-cm) wide format archtop jazz guitar, the main stipulation being that each should be finished in the same Ultra Blue Penetrating Stain #M520 hue as the D'Aquisto model.

For Ebony 'n' Blue, Hollenbeck (who passed away in 2008) used beautifully figured bird's-eye maple for the body and neck, and luxuriously dark ebony for the bridge, scratchplate, and fingerboard. The guitar was framed with lustrous gold hardware. **EM**

Ibanez
Pat Metheny 1996

Type Hollowbody electric
Body & neck Maple body, mahogany neck
Fingerboard Ebony
Pick-ups One IBZ Super 58H humbucker pick-up

The PM-100NT was a collaboration between Ibanez and jazz fusion guitarist Pat Metheny. It is essentially a modern take on the Gibson ES-175, but sounds brighter, and is less susceptible to feedback.

The slim-line, 16-in. (40.5-cm), body has a maple back and sides, and a carved maple top. The shape is unusual, with a large, Florentine cutaway on the lower bout, and a smaller offset cutaway on the other side of the neck: these features facilitate access to the uppermost frets, and contribute greatly to the elegant appearance of the instrument.

The neck is cut from a single piece of mahogany, with a twenty-two-fret, bound-ebony fingerboard inlaid with mother-of-pearl blocks with diagonal abalone centers. The headstock features an attractive pearl "lightning-strike" inlay.

The neck joins the body at the seventeenth fret rather than at the more traditional fourteenth.

The high-quality hardware is gold-plated, and features either a fully adjustable, Ibanez Full-Tune II bridge or a Gotoh 103-B bridge, mounted on an ebony base. There is also a new tailpiece, designated the PM-100 by Ibanez.

This instrument's sound comes from a single humbucker. Ibanez also produced the more elaborate PM-120, which had an additional pick-up. **JB**

PAT METHENY
TRIO →LIVE

Pat Metheny used the twin pick-up version of his signature Ibanez on much of *Trio: Live* (2000). This album—which features Larry Grenadier on bass and Bill Stewart on drums—was recorded live during a tour of the United States, Europe, and Japan.

Manzer
Blue Absynthe 1996

Type Single cutaway archtop acoustic-electric
Body & neck Maple/spruce body, spruce neck
Fingerboard Ebony
Pick-ups Kent Armstrong pick-ups

There are normal, top-quality guitars, but above all of them is a class most of us never get to play: "museum-class" instruments. Toronto-based guitar maker Linda Manzer's Absynthe archtops belong in this category: they cost more than $20,000, and are so exquisitely crafted that they are bought only by top-level professionals or very wealthy collectors.

Each of her guitars takes around 200 hours to build, using the highest grade, aged, and matched woods. These include curly maple for the backs and sides, spruce for the hand-carved tops, and ebony for the

"Linda Manzer is one of my all-time favorite luthiers. Her work is so original and so perfect… This guitar is a phenomenon."
SCOTT CHINERY

fingerboards, bridges, tailpiece, and floating pickguards. All the binding is solid wood. Decorative features include gold-plated height adjustment for the tailpiece, and engraved mother-of-pearl orchid headstock inlays.

On the upper bout there is an innovative sliding panel: its two thin veneers of ebony and curly maple run on a mahogany track. This is an adjustable sound port, which allows the player to hear sound that normally projects forward. Body depth is 3 in. (7.6 cm) at the side, and 5 in. (12.7 cm) in the middle.

Scott Chinery ordered one for his "Blue Guitar" collection and Manzer spent five months building it. The model was later exhibited at the National Museum of American History in Washington, D.C. **SH**

Megas
Athena Custom 1996

Nickerson
Equinox Jumbo 1996

Type Hollow body archtop
Body & neck Spruce/maple body, maple neck
Fingerboard Ebony
Pick-ups One floating full humbucker pick-up

Type Acoustic archtop
Body & neck Spruce and maple body, maple neck
Fingerboard Ebony

Oregon-based Ted Megas is famous for the detailing and craftsmanship he brings to every instrument he fashions, but this hollow body archtop represents the pinnacle of his art. The Athena is in the classic style, with split block mother-of-pearl inlays on the fingerboard, a hand-carved, aged spruce top, and flamed maple back with matching sides, all in a luminescent, dark sunburst finish. Its large f-holes are reminiscent of contemporary Gypsy-style jazz guitars, and all the trimmings are what you'd expect from a Megas guitar, from the multi-lined plastic bindings throughout, to the graphite-reinforced truss rod, gold Schaller tuning machines, solid ebony pickguard, and hand-knurled brass height adjusters on the bridge.

Optional extras include a seventh string, a master fiddleback, a built-in pick-up, a back-through neck-heel construction, and a bound pickguard. The blond or golden amber finishes are nice additions to the twenty-four carat gold-plated hardware, and the high-gloss, nitrocellulose-lacquered finish. **TB**

Born on Cape Cod, Brad Nickerson made his first handmade guitar in 1982, and continues to build them today in a world where so-called handmade guitars can at times involve CNC machines and various other technical assists. He built his first Equinox Jumbo in 1996, the same year he began to teach archtop guitar building at the Leeds Guitarmakers' School in Northampton, Massachusetts.

The sweeping, elliptical shape of the Equinox sound holes was carefully designed to enhance its acoustic response, and its modified bracing provided some additional strength. But it was the beautiful blue of the Equinox and the distinctive scrimshaw blue macaw on its headstock that made it so distinctive. The guitar took Nickerson in excess of eight months to construct, six times the amount of time that this skilled craftsman generally requires. Sean McGowan, Professor of Music at the University of Colorado, has called Nickerson a luthier who works at the highest possible level of creativity. **BS**

PRS
Private Stock #13 1996

Type Hollow body electric
Body & neck Red maple body, set neck
Fingerboard Rosewood
Pick-ups Two humbucker pick-ups

By the mid-1990s, PRS was well into its production stride, but founder Paul Reed Smith's nostalgia for pre-corporate days inspired his Guitars of the Month program—twelve one-off instruments. He followed this with his Private Stock program—an initiative to build one-off custom instruments for anyone with the money who wanted to prototype new concepts. The Private Stock #13 is one of the fruits of this endeavor. It's a fully hand-carved, hollow body, archtop guitar.

Since then, many new PRS designs have started in Private Stock, most recently the 2011 Signature, which showcases a culmination of years of artist input, and boasts PRS's first-ever multi-endorsement guitar. In 2012, it became the PRS 408 Maple Top.

Not all Private Stock owners take their instruments on the road, but Scottish steel-string player Tony McManus is an exception. "It has been all over the United States, all over Canada," he says of his own signature model. "It's been to Australia, and to Japan twice. It just comes out of its case and plays." **DB**

Rozas
Classical Guitar 1996

Type Classical guitar
Body & neck Spruce/rosewood body, mahogany neck
Fingerboard Ebony
Pick-ups Two single-coil pick-ups

Ignacio Rozas made his first "1a" Especial Guitar #230 in 1996. This quintessential concert instrument was characterized by an ebony crown carved onto the headstock, just one of many decorative flourishes that also included hand-crafted, gold tuning mechanisms, over-fifty-year-old timbers that are given a French polish finish, and Rozas' own signature just inside the sound hole.

Rozas studied with the best. Born in Guadalajara, Spain, in 1943, he began his working life as a cabinetmaker before becoming an apprentice guitar maker under José Ramírez from 1959 to 1969. In 1970, he began making classical and flamenco guitars under the guidance of Spanish luthier Manuel Contreras, the creator of the Double Top, before setting up his own shop in 1987—Ignacio M. Rozas Classical Guitars. Rozas continued to make guitars until 2001, when he took a year's absence, before resuming in 2002. He retired in February 2008, and since then his guitars have become increasingly sought after. **BS**

Scharpach
Blue Vienna 1996

Takamine
GB7C 1996

Type Acoustic archtop
Body & neck Cello wood body, maple neck
Fingerboard Solid ebony
Other features Buffalo horn and titanium tuning pegs

Type Electroacoustic steel-string
Body & neck Rosewood/cedar body, mahogany neck
Fingerboard Rosewood
Pick-ups One palathetic piezo pick-up

Austrian Theo Scharpach began making classical guitars in 1975. He set up a workshop in the Netherlands, where business remained steady until the mid-1990s, when he became the sole European luthier to be invited to build a guitar for Scott Chinery's "Blue Guitar" collection. Scharpach's contribution—Blue Vienna, a homage to guitar-making legend James D'Aquisto's Centura Deluxe—gained him superstar status.

Like all the guitars commissioned for this project, the Blue Vienna was painted in the same color as D'Aquisto had used. The detail is correspondingly gorgeous: the bridge wood is 100 years old, the tuning pegs are a fusion of buffalo horn and titanium, an Art Deco motif of sea shells adorns the pickguard, the gold-plated tailpiece is cut from a solid block of brass, and its precut top is hewn from 250-year-old cello wood.

Theo Scharpach has never accepted another order to reproduce the Blue Vienna. **BS**

The workshop from which the Takamine brand evolved opened in 1962 in Nakatsugawa, Japan. It soon profited from the Western folk boom that hit Japan toward the end of the 1960s, but it was not until master luthier Mass Hirade joined the company in 1968 that it began to establish a reputation for quality and design. When Hirade took over as president in 1975, Takamine gained an international profile.

The GB7C—built for country star Garth Brooks—is a dreadnought-style acoustic with a single cutaway giving access to the twenty-first fret, which covers only the top two strings. This is more cosmetic than functional; Brooks wanted the traditionally circular sound hole to complement the contours of the body, hence the cut twenty-first fret reflects the cutaway. The CT4B II preamp, built into the top of the body, houses a three-band graphic equalizer, volume control slider, and a built-in chromatic tuner.

Brooks was reportedly given sixty of the guitars, many of which he in turn gave to fans at concerts. **TB**

Triggs
New Yorker 1996

Walker
Empress 1996

Type Solidbody electric archtop
Body & neck Spruce/maple body, maple neck
Fingerboard Ebony
Pick-ups One Johnny Smith pick-up

Type Acoustic archtop
Body & neck Spruce and maple body, maple neck
Fingerboard Ebony

Prior to joining Gibson's Custom Shop in 1986, where he contributed to the famous Super 400s and L-5 archtops, luthier Jim Triggs made mandolins—almost 150 of them. Having helped Gibson get "back on track" producing quality instruments, he left the firm in 1992, determined to use his accumulated skills to develop his own line of guitars.

The New Yorker—completely handmade, of course, by Jim and his son, Ryan—was created in the style of the great D'Angelico guitars of the 1950s, and rivals them for craftsmanship and sound quality. It has a very New York-looking, stepped tailpiece, and a Big Apple, stepped-skyscraper inlay on the headpiece, as well as a bound, firestripe pickguard, and a bound ebony fretboard.

Jim and Ryan have also built custom, solidbody guitars for Aerosmith, The Cars, Steve Miller, and country artist Alan Jackson. Triggs Senior still builds mandolins, too, in the Gibson F style, and every year organizes a bluegrass festival in Kansas City. **BS**

Paul Heumiller, the American guitarist and founder of Dream Guitars, Inc., in North Carolina, has described Kim Walker as "one of the best builders I've ever had the pleasure to play," a luthier who "reproduces the vintage look, feel, and, most importantly, the tone of the best vintage Martins."

Kim builds only twenty guitars a year, and for his "Blue Guitar" collection had but a single aim: to create the very best 18-in. (45.75-cm) acoustic archtop that he could. By all accounts, he succeeded. In the book *Blue Guitar*, co-author Ken Vose described the sound of the Blue Empress as "very lutey—medieval—an original, strong sound," and concluded that it was one of the most delicately-made guitars he'd ever seen.

After working for guitar maker George Gruhn in the 1980s, and later at Guild, Kim Walker entered a league of his own. His craftsmanship, according to the great archtop maker Bob Benedetto, became "set apart from anyone else's work that I had ever seen, mine included." **BS**

Washburn
Bettencourt N8 1996

Type Double-neck electric
Body & neck Swamp ash body, maple necks
Fingerboard Ebony
Pick-ups Three humbuckers and one L500 pick-up

The Washburn Bettencourt N8 was one of a series of signature models for Nuno Bettencourt, guitarist with the band Extreme. This is a "12/6" double-neck, designed primarily for stage use so that Bettencourt could emulate the sounds of his regular Washburn N4, and do the odd bit of twelve-string work. The N8 is so named as it is an "N4 times two."

Both bolt-on, one-piece maple necks are identical, featuring twenty-two-fret ebony fingerboards with dot inlays. Both also feature the same "reverse Stratocaster" headstocks used on other Washburn Bettencourt models, and, indeed, many guitars built during this period. Each headstock had six-in-a-line tuners; the "octave" strings on the twelve-string were adjusted using a set of tuners behind the bridge—the ball-ends were secured at the nut.

The large body was cut from two-piece swamp ash, given a satin coat. Fittingly for such an attractive guitar, it was available only in a "natural" finish.

The cutaways are notable for the neck joints, known as "Stephens Extended Cutaways," which allow easy access to the upper frets on both necks, and reduce the overall weight. The upper neck was held in place by six bolts; the lower neck by four bolts.

Two different pick-ups were chosen for the N8: the six-string neck was fitted with a Bill Lawrence L500 at the bridge, and a Seymour Duncan 59 humbucker in the neck position; the twelve-string had a pair of 59s. The electrics were simple: both necks shared a single volume control, a two-way neck-selector switch, and a three-way pick-up selector switch. **JB**

Nuno Bettencourt playing his single-neck signature N4—half an N8. →

Zeidler Jazz Deluxe Special 1996

Type Hollow body archtop
Body & neck Curly maple body and neck
Fingerboard Ebony
Pick-ups None

Over the course of a twenty-seven-year career, John Zeidler, who died in 2002 at the age of forty-four, crafted just about every type of stringed instrument, from mandolins to pedal steels to double-necked solid-body electric guitars. However, his favorite instrument was the archtop hollow body.

Zeidler's reputation as a craftsman was such that he became one of twenty-two luthiers commissioned to contribute an instrument to Scott Chinery's "Blue Guitar" collection. The guitar he submitted was a suitably blue-hued example of his Jazz Deluxe Special, which featured an amber finish. Based around an 18-in. (45.75-cm) archtop hollow body, with curly maple back and sides, and a hand-split select Adirondack spruce top, the guitar took around eight weeks to complete.

Zeidler paid remarkable attention to every detail. He hand-tooled the guitar's English-scroll design tailpiece, which was then rhodium-plated and engraved. The two-piece, laminated maple neck was topped with an ebony fingerboard and twenty-two frets, and crowned with machine heads equipped with buttons that were hand-turned from celluloid tortoiseshell material.

Following Zeidler's death, fourteen of the best luthiers in America collaborated on the construction of a one-off tribute guitar. Many of the luthiers involved in the Zeidler Project had also contributed archtops to Scott Chinery's "Blue Guitar" collection. The completed tribute guitar, built using Zeidler's favored woods and techniques, was later sold to benefit his family. **EM**

Fano Satellite DG Custom 1997

Type Solidbody electric
Body & neck Solid mahogany body, set mahogany neck
Fingerboard Rosewood
Pick-ups Two custom-wound pick-ups

Early in 1996, XTC's Andy Partridge was contacted by a fan from Bloomfield, New Jersey, requesting permission to build him a guitar. Intrigued, Andy specified a list of requirements, faxed some drawings, and, later that summer, took delivery of the "Partridge," an electric guitar based loosely on the shape of an Encore student model he'd taken to. The build quality and attention to detail were exceptional, and Andy was very impressed.

The fan in question was twenty-five-year-old Dennis Fano, anxious to get a foot on the ladder and make a career for himself as a luthier. He already had a line of solidbodies, the Satellites, which he was happy to tailor to the needs of his clients while retaining the basic body shape and structure. He then contacted me [Dave Gregory of XTC, the writer], asking if I'd like a Satellite, and, if so, what would I wish to put in it?

I'd always wanted a solidbody Gretsch, but found "that great Gretsch sound" strangely elusive on the few expensive models I'd tried. The closest I had to the sound came from a Gibson SG Junior; I suggested a Filter'Tron pick-up on a mahogany platform, with a simple wrap-over bridge. Dennis obliged, and placed a second pick-up near the neck with just a switch and a volume control in the circuit. It worked brilliantly.

The fingerboard features the same hand-cut pearl eyebrow inlays I'd requested for my earlier Kinkade Custom (see page 577).

Today Dennis Fano has a successful guitar-making business, his highly desirable Alt de Facto retro-look electrics contrasting strikingly with his modern-as-tomorrow "AlumAcrylic" Sphear series. **DG**

Fender
ST-Champ 10 1997

Type Short-scale travel guitar
Body & neck Basswood body, bolt-on maple neck
Fingerboard Maple or rosewood
Pick-ups Single humbucker pick-up

Like the chassis of a Model T Ford, the utilitarian bolt-together nature of the Fender Stratocaster has allowed myriad variations on a theme to be spawned over the years.

Produced for the home market, the Japanese-built ST-Champ 10 was Leo Fender's most iconic design rebooted as a scaled-down travel guitar. Built around a classic double-cutaway basswood body, mated to a chunky 21-in. (53.25-cm) scale bolt-on maple neck, the guitar housed a 10-watt Champ amplifier circuit and speaker, an old-school "Synchronized vibrato," and a single humbucking pick-up. The instrument's blade switch had three settings: off; onboard speaker with clean tone; and onboard speaker with distortion. A jack socket allowed the ST-Champ 10 to be connected to an external amplifier and the specification list featured master volume and master tone controls and a red status LED to show when the onboard amp was activated.

The ST-Champ 10 was available in three-tone sunburst (with a rosewood fingerboard) and black (with a maple fingerboard) finishes. The JM-Champ, a Jazzmaster-shaped variant, was also available. Fender was by no means a pioneer when it came to producing an instrument with an in-built battery-powered amplifier, and while its appeal as a bedroom practice guitar or an instrument to have in your backpack during your travels is clear, the toy-like nature of the Champ may be a little off-putting for some—a reason, perhaps, that they were never given a worldwide launch. As such, few of these guitars have found their way outside of Asia, giving them a certain collectible cachet in the West. **EM/TB**

Fender
Cyclone 1997

Type Solidbody electric
Body & neck Poplar body, maple neck
Fingerboard Rosewood
Pick-ups One bridge-mounted atomic humbucker pick-up

The 1997 Cyclone was similar to the Mustang, Fender's student guitar, first released in 1964, and eventually made famous by Kurt Cobain. It had a nicely contoured poplar body, and a one-piece maple neck, but the fact that it was made in Mexico—albeit at Fender's state-of-the-art facility at Ensenada in Baja California—meant it came with a multi-laminate body and paper-thin laminate top over a less-than-attractive solid wood core, a common cost-cutting trick. However, the pick-up from its bridge-mounted atomic humbucker lived up to expectations, and its nicely shielded electronics virtually eliminated hum. Yet it still managed to look a lot like a Duo-Sonic, in spite of its Strat-style tremolo, its bridge humbucker, and 24¾-in. (63-cm) scale length, vintage machine heads, and cool colors, such as "candy apple," which gave it a great retro look and made it just plain fun to play.

Although it was a Fender, the Cyclone always struggled for acceptance. Its body was ¼ in. (0.6 cm) thicker than the Mustang's, which led to concerns about its weight. It was never used by well-known players, apart from the Japanese guitarist Char, and John Paul Pitts of the American indie rock band Surfer Blood. But that was not the point of the Cyclone, which was always a "student's guitar," and never meant to rival, say, a PRS.

A 1998 Fender ad claimed that the Cyclone was "stirring up the dust with a radical new design," but it never really did. Fender discontinued the Cyclone and its variants, the Cyclone II and the Cyclone HH, in 2007. They are now considered a short-term experiment—a design for a budget-conscious market. **BS**

Fender Jazz Marcus Miller 1997

Type Electric bass
Body & neck Ash body, maple neck
Fingerboard Maple
Pick-ups Two single-coil pick-ups

New Yorker Marcus Miller is a classically trained clarinettist, jazz composer, and multi-instrumentalist. He is perhaps best known for his bass guitar work with such giants of jazz as Miles Davis and Herbie Hancock.

Miller's main instrument throughout much of his professional life has been a Fender Jazz bass—particularly, models built in 1977. However, his instruments were not standard production-line models: wanting greater control over the range of sounds he could produce in the studio, Miller took his Jazz to Roger Sadowsky—a noted guitar builder in his own right—who carried out significant modifications. The installation of a Bartolini active preamp enabled Miller to achieve what he describes as "scooped mids," which are central to his sound. Sadowsky also replaced the stock Fender bridge with the heavier Leo Quan Badass II model.

In 1997, Fender announced the production of the Marcus Miller signature bass, which incorporated all the original modifications. It has remained in production ever since, and become one of the most popular models in Fender's Artist series.

In many ways, this is an unsurprising success, since the instrument combines the tradition of one of the most famous bass guitars ever made with active on-board circuitry—a feature popular with many professional bass players over the past three decades. Indeed, many would regard active electrics as better suited to bass instruments than to their six-string counterparts, and this is especially true on the five-string version of this instrument, with a tighter sound on the low B. **TB**

Marcus Miller with his own heavily modified Fender Jazz. →

Fender Stratocaster Catalina Island 1997

Type Solidbody electric
Body & neck Ash body, maple neck
Fingerboard Rosewood
Pick-ups Three Danelectro-style lipstick pick-ups

The relationship between John Page, manager of the Fender Custom Shop in Corona, Riverside County, California, and Pamelina Hovnatanian ("Pamelina H"), an airbrushing artist originally from Carmel, was a fruitful one that started out on a very informal footing. As Page remembers it: "I'd give her some bodies and [say] 'Do what you do,' and she'd take off and create these ultra-cool pieces."

At first, Pamelina was given carte blanche. "I believe the very first guitar I painted," she recalls, "was a woman's ass clad in shiny leather hotpants!" While retaining her ability to shoot off at imaginative tangents when the opportunity arose, she also demonstrated a strict rigor that enabled her to fulfill the most demandingly exact briefs to the satisfaction of those who'd commissioned her: such talent and discipline rarely combine in a single being, and they have since brought her considerable success. By the end of 2012, Pamelina had painted more than 2,000 guitars for Fender, Ibanez, Washburn, Roscoe, and other guitar manufacturers, in addition to her work for private individuals.

Among Pamelina's most desirable pieces was the one she designed for the 1999 Catalina Island Blues Festival, then in its third year. She created her original topless mermaid design, which was subsequently relief-carved by George Amicay, and had a wood veneer applied to the artwork. Lastly, the bodies were returned to Hovnatanian for a final painting.

The Island is a particularly unusual Stratocaster in that it is equipped with three gold-plated, Danelectro-style, lipstick pick-ups. **TB**

Fender Squier
Vista Venus 1997

Type Solidbody six- and twelve-string electric
Body & neck Basswood body, maple neck
Fingerboard Rosewood
Pick-ups Various (see below)

Following the suicide in 1994 of her husband, Nirvana frontman Kurt Cobain, and her critically acclaimed performance alongside Woody Harrelson in the Miloš Forman movie *The People vs. Larry Flynt* (1996), Courtney Love's profile, and that of her band, Hole, were at an all-time high when Fender offered her the opportunity to design a signature guitar. She accepted without hesitation.

Crafted in Japan, and with shapes influenced by those of Mercury, Stratocaster, and Rickenbacker solidbody guitars, the Vista Venus Series was launched in 1997 in six- and twelve-string formats. At the time, the only other female musician to have her own signature series of guitars was Bonnie Raitt.

Both models featured a basswood body, a bolt-on 25½-in. (64.75-cm) maple neck, a bound rosewood fingerboard studded with twenty-two frets, and a choice of Black and Sea Foam Green finishes, with body-matching painted headstocks.

The six-string model (original retail price: $699.99) came loaded with a bridge humbucker, a neck position single-coil pick-up, and a classic Strat headstock. The twelve-string variant (first offered for one cent less than $1,000) featured a pair of Seymour Duncan split single-coil pick-ups, and a 1960s paddle-style headstock.

In spite of heavy promotion by both the artist and the manufacturer, the Vista Venus line wasn't the sales success that Fender had hoped for, and both models were dropped from the brand's catalog in 1998. Their stock has since risen, however, and they have become sought-after cult classics. **EM**

Froggy Bottom
D Standard 1997

Gibson
Les Paul DC Pro 1997

Type Acoustic dreadnought
Body & neck Spruce and mahogany body, maple neck
Fingerboard Ebony

Type Solidbody electric
Body & neck Mahogany/maple body, mahogany neck
Fingerboard Rosewood
Pick-ups Two Burstbuster humbucker pick-ups

Michael Millard made his first guitar in 1970 in his apartment on the Lower East Side of Manhattan, New York City. He put a bend in its side by placing the wood against a heat pipe that ran up through his kitchen floor—an inauspicious beginning for a man who would soon be acclaimed as one of America's finest luthiers. At the time, Millard was working for Gurian Guitars, but in 1974 he struck out on his own. He built one guitar at a time, slowly, working by himself, and orders came in by word of mouth as his reputation grew.

The Froggy Ds, like all Froggy Bottom guitars, are unique creations, with custom models designed specifically to cater for the clients who originally ordered them. Even standard models are individually crafted. Thin, highly arched, back braces are a trademark of Froggy Bottom guitars, as are the woods they are made from, which are all sourced in the forests of Vermont and New Hampshire by the very person who makes them. **BS**

Les Paul double cutaways (DCs) may have a less distinctive shape than classic Gibsons, but there are compensations, most notably their reduced body weight, which means more high-fret access. They were a good idea, but they were not a new one: Duane Allman had often used a double-cut Les Paul back in the 1970s.

The Pro was Gibson's response to the success in the 1990s of PRS double cutaway guitars. It also mimicked PRS's single volume and tone controls. The Pro's feature list included Burstbuster humbucker pick-ups, a stopbar tailpiece, chrome hardware, and green tuner keys.

Japan's top rock guitarist, Tak Matsumoto of B'z, often uses a DC, and has a Gibson signature DC model of his own.

The DC Pro has a slightly lighter and cleaner sound than the thicker, heavier Les Paul Standard, although the hotter Burstbuster pick-ups supply a good dose of sustain when required. **SH**

Gretsch G6120-6/12 Nashville 1997

Type Hollow body electric
Body & neck Laminated maple body, maple necks
Fingerboard Ebony
Pick-ups Four Filter'Tron humbucker pick-ups

Although the iconic Gretsch 6120 Chet Atkins model—famously beloved by Eddie Cochran, Duane Eddy, and, more recently, Stray Cat Brian Setzer—has been tweaked many times since its launch in 1954, it received its most radical makeover in 1997.

Built in Japan, the aptly designated 6120-6/12 model featured a heavily modified, laminated-maple, hollow body that played host to both a six- and a twelve-string neck. The six-string side of the body had a Bigsby True Vibrato; the twelve-string part featured a classic G cut-out tailpiece. While its ergonomically compromised body shape makes it arguably not as pretty as its standard six-string ancestor, it has all the eye candy that gave the 6120 its enormous stage presence. The gold hardware and the orange stain finish are both present and correct.

The guitar is a tonal monster, too, thanks to a quartet of Filter'Tron humbuckers. Incidentally, Gretsch also launched a double-neck version of its 6128-T Duo Jet model in the same year. **EM**

Klein/Taylor Acoustic Bass 1997

Type Acoustic bass
Body & neck Buyer's choice of woods
Fingerboard Buyer's choice of woods
Other features Asymmetric "flying buttress" bracing

California's Sonoma Valley is best known for fine wine, but it also produces great musical instruments, thanks mainly to Steve Klein, whose works include a nineteen-string electric harp, and an electric sitar (for Steve Miller).

In 1991, Klein teamed with Taylor Guitars on the AB acoustic bass series, with features later incorporated into his own acoustic bass. The aim was to increase the efficiency with which string energy creates sound. Placing the wood-bound sound hole on the treble side of the upper bout utilizes an area of the soundboard that typically does little to transmit vibration, and frees a large portion of the soundboard for an unusual, asymmetric, "flying buttress" bracing pattern that produces better sound. For player comfort, the large body is narrower at the upper bout.

Another feature of the Klein design is the bridge, which creates greater tonal separation for the strings. Being a custom-built instrument, it is offered in a variety of wood choices. **DP**

Schecter
Hellcat 1997

Type Solidbody electric
Body & neck Basswood body, maple neck
Fingerboard Rosewood
Pick-ups Three mini-humbucker pick-ups

The Hellcat was the product of a meeting of minds. Schecter President Michael Ciravolo was determined to distance his company from its Fender-referencing models of the early 1980s. Schecter had built its reputation in the hands of guitarists such as Pete Townshend of The Who, and Mark Knopfler of Dire Straits, but Ciravolo decided that the brand needed to develop its own identity. At the same time, a group of Texan businessmen who had invested in the Schecter company were keen to capitalize on the firm's reputation for quality.

"We could see a need for affordable guitars designed for a younger audience, and we developed the Hellcat."

MICHAEL CIRAVOLO

Although the Hellcat was hailed at the time of its release as one of Schecter's first original designs, its offset body borrows from the blueprints of Fender's Jaguar and Jazzmaster, while its headstock references the design of the Japanese pawnshop-prize Teisco Del Rey guitars of the mid-1960s.

Nevertheless, the project was not merely an exercise in reinterpretation. With the Hellcat, Schecter cleverly spliced the eye candy of classic surf-era instruments with the playability and firepower of modern rock guitars, something that Fender would also attempt with its Toronado model.

In 1998, Schecter added the Hellcat model to its enormously successful, Ciravolo-designed, Korean-made, Diamond Series. **EM**

Warr
Phallanx 1997

Type Twelve- or fourteen-string touch guitar
Body & neck Ash body, various necks
Fingerboard Wenge
Pick-ups One Bartolini pick-up

For many, the vogue for two-handed finger tapping seemed to come from out of the blue with Eddie Van Halen's blistering guest spot on Michael Jackson's "Beat It" (1982). In fact, the technique—producing a note by "hammering" on the fingerboard with both hands—dated back to the 1940s. Early experimenter Jimmie Webster even wrote a "Touch System" playing guide in 1952. And, in the 1970s, Emmett Chapman specially designed his Stick guitar for just this technique. Ever since then, a small number of builders have supported a group of players whose numbers are, slowly but surely, increasing year on year.

The original tapping instrument, the Chapman Stick, was launched in 1974. When Mark Warr started up as a competitor in 1991 a good deal of bad blood was spilled, especially in 1996, when Chapman filed a lawsuit against him. Both sides went public on the Internet to make their cases. How did it play out? Inconclusively: at the time of publication of this book, both brands remained in business.

Even if they are both tapping guitars, there's quite a difference between the two instruments. The Stick is essentially a long neck with pick-ups, whereas the Warr Phalanx takes on a more conventional appearance, with an identifiable body and neck—albeit a very wide one. Stringing conventions are also different, with the Warr's bass and treble sections reversed—thus the left hand would typically play the bass lines, and the right hand the chords and melodies—which many find more intuitive. Finally, Bartolini pick-ups are used to give the Warr its powerful sound. **TB**

Antigua Casa Nuñez 1998

Type Classical guitar
Body & neck Spruce top, hardwood back and sides
Fingerboard Ebony
Other features Carved headstock, rosewood bridge

Argentina had seen a major surge in interest in the guitar at the beginning of the twentieth century. There were reportedly over 5,000 guitarists in Buenos Aires alone in the 1920s, many of them women. The guitar has become as much a part of the national psyche in Argentina as it is in Spain. Among the nation's most distinguished modern exponents are guitarist-composer-poet Atahualpa Yupanqui, guitarist-composers such as Eduardo Falú, Jorge Morel, Juan Falú, and Maximo Diego Pujol, and virtuoso guitarists such as Victor Villadangos.

"My first real guitar … I couldn't get my hands off it … It was an Antigua Casa Nuñez Diego Gracia, made in 1928."

JORGE MOREL

The history of the Antigua Casa Nuñez goes back to 1870 when Francisco Nuñez (1841–1919) founded a guitar-making, retailing, and publishing business in Buenos Aires. The tone of some of his higher-quality guitars was said to rival Torres. In 1925, Francisco Diego, Dionisio Gracia, and other investors bought the business, and over the following decades expanded the manufacturing side from a production rate of 100 guitars per month in 1950 to 2,000 a month by 1970.

This concert guitar from 1998 traces its design and aesthetics to the kind of guitars that Enrique Garcia and Francisco Simplicio were exporting from Spain about seventy years earlier, even down to a similarly carved headstock—a feature that has always been very popular in Argentina. **GD**

Aria
NXG-01 1998

Type Hollow body electric
Body & neck Spruce/mahogany body, mahogany neck
Fingerboard Rosewood
Pick-ups Piezo and internal mic pick-ups

The traditional shape of the classical guitar had remained substantially unchanged little for hundreds of years. The Japanese company Aria was one of several guitar manufacturers who decided in the 1990s to ignore purists, and create nylon-strung guitars for the modern electric age.

Aria had originally been Arai and Company, a musical equipment retailer founded in 1953 by Shiro Arai. In 1960, he started specializing in guitars. Four years later, he licensed Matsumoku to build acoustic guitars for his firm, which he renamed so that Westerners would find it easier to say and remember. (In the same way, Kiichiro Toyoda had changed the name of his automobile company to the more Anglophone-friendly "Toyota.")

With its slim, hollow body, and offset sound hole, the NXG-01 was a revolution for classical, jazz, and Latin players. Suddenly, they could reap some of the benefits of the progress that had been made in solidbody electric guitars.

The body was shaped more like a Telecaster than a classical guitar, and it had a thinner, faster, bolt-on neck, which extended to a full two-octave range, and was made more accessible by the single cutaway. The nut measured 1⅘ in. (4.5 cm)—at the time, the standard, classic nut was 2 in. (5.2 cm).

The electric sound produced by the NXG-01 was innovative and versatile, thanks in large measure to Aria's PCM-1 Hybrid System—a combination of a bridge piezo and an internal condensor mic that could be blended by the player, as well as using the active bass and treble controls. **SH**

Conklin
GT-4 1998

Type Solidbody electric bass
Body & neck Ash/maple body, wenge/purpleheart neck
Fingerboard Purpleheart
Pick-ups One, two, or three P- or J-style pick-ups

When top American jazz funk bassist Bill Dickens used a Conklin GT-4 on his instructional DVD, the music world began to notice these little-known instruments.

Bill Conklin is based in Springfield, Missouri, where he designs high-quality electric guitars and basses. The "Groove Tools" basses have been his most successful range. They are made in Korea by Westheimer to Conklin's detailed specifications.

There's a GT-5 five-string, a GT-7 seven string, and a special Bill Dickens version, but the GT-4 is the standard model featured here.

"The neck is made to precision and it's very comfortable on the hands. The playability is outstanding and the sound is incredible."
KELLY CONLON, SESSION BASSIST

It comes with a 34-in. (86.3-cm), twenty-four-fret neck, and its wine red or natural finish shows off the figured-maple top. The sculpted body and neck heel make it a comfortable, well-balanced bass to play, and the deep cutaway allows access to the highest frets. Other notable features include the five-piece wenge and purpleheart laminate neck, locking jack socket, off-set neck position markers, and pick-ups made in California by Pat and Bill Bartolini.

The active electronics include a Mighty Mite preamp with controls for volume, blend, bass, mid, and treble, and a "Slap" switch to cut the midrange for percussive styles of playing. This can be customized by fine-tuning two hidden pots controlling the relative gain and output of the slap sound. **SH**

ESP
LTD M-250 1998

Type Solidbody electric
Body & neck Basswood and maple
Fingerboard Rosewood
Pick-ups Two regular and one single-coil-size humbucker

Introduced in 1995, ESP's Korean and Indonesian-made LTD line made the parent company's Japanese-made guitar and bass designs accessible to less well-heeled customers for the first time. Based on ESP's immensely popular M-II "Superstrat" design, the LTD M-250 can also trace its lineage back through to the late 1980s' MM-250 and MM-290 model ESPs (also based on the M-II format) used by Kirk Hammett of Metallica.

Hammett's long-term loyalty to ESP—he's still one of their highest-profile endorsees, alongside bandmate James Hetfield—would be rewarded with his custom KH signature models featuring through-neck body construction, active EMG humbuckers, and his now-iconic skull and crossbones fingerboard inlays. Aside from his Les Paul Junior-shaped guitars, over the past twenty years most of Kirk's signature range has been based on the design of the M-II.

ESP has been accused by some of plagiarizing the design of the Jackson Soloist, one of the most popular rock-guitar brands of the 1980s. There is a strong resemblance but, to be fair, both Jackson and ESP took their cue from the Fender Stratocaster—Superstrat isn't just a clever term. The kids didn't let the debate stop them from lapping up the charms of the LTD M-250. They were sold on what was essentially a budget Kirk Hammett-style electric with great playability, a locking Floyd Rose vibrato, and plenty of rock-star curb appeal in features such as the reverse pointed headstock. ESP would eventually release an official Chinese-made LTD KH-202 Kirk Hammett signature in 2004. The latest descendants of the LTD M-250—the M-50, M-100, and the M-330R—can be found in the 2013 ESP catalog. **EM**

Fender Stratocaster
Relic 60 1998

Type Solidbody electric
Body & neck Alder body, maple neck
Fingerboard Rosewood
Pick-ups Three Fender Custom '60s single-coil pick-ups

The concept of the "relic" is one of the most divisive in the world of guitar. The idea of buying a brand-new instrument with the distressed signs of decades of roadwear manufactured onto it is a bizarre preference for some; and yet, for other players, old-looking guitars are simply cooler.

Fender began to acknowledge the concept of vintage character in 1995 with its Custom Shop-produced Relic models. It's often wrongly reported that Rolling Stone and early Custom Shop customer Keith Richards was the inspiration for the cosmetically

"Jay and I reasoned that if people bought distressed leather jackets, jeans, and reproduction antiques, why not guitars?"
VINCE CUNETTO

aged Relic, asking for his guitars to be "bashed-up" before he'd play them. But the true story stemmed from Stones producer Don Was. The Custom Shop master builder Jay Black attended a Rolling Stones recording session in Los Angeles in 1994. Was wanted Black to beat up the new Sadowsky bass that he was due to play with Bonnie Raitt at a Grammy Awards ceremony—he felt it looked too squeaky clean.

This 1998 Relic is especially desirable for collectors, as it was made during the Vince Cunetto era. Cunetto's reputation for distressing guitar parts was a significant factor in the Relic idea getting the official green light, and it was decided to outsource the Fender-made components that needed to be distressed to Cunetto Creative Resources Inc. **RL**

Fender Telecaster
"Go Cat Go" 1998

Type One-off solid single cutaway electric
Body & neck Unknown
Fingerboard Unknown
Pick-ups Two single-coil pick-ups

American rock 'n' roll star Carl Perkins seldom kept an instrument for long. He was sometimes known as "the rockabilly king who played a thousand guitars."

Finally, just before he died in 1998, Fender made a special one-off guitar that seems to have satisfied him. The headstock was normal, but that was about the only thing that was. The guitar had a unique, sparkly blue finish, with a matching blue scratchplate, in honor of Carl's biggest hit, "Blue Suede Shoes." It also had a Bigsby tremolo system that Carl particularly liked for its rockabilly twang.

"Carl changed guitars several times looking for a sound and a look … The Tele gave him part of what he wanted."

JERRY ELSTON, CARL'S RHYTHM GUITARIST

Even more distinctively, the guitar had Perkins' "Go Cat, Go!" inlaid down the fretboard in mother-of-pearl. The line had become Carl's catchphrase, and was the title of his 1996 autobiography. It's a lyric from "Blue Suede Shoes," which was written as "Go man go" by Sam Phillips, owner of Sun Studios in Memphis, Tennessee, but changed by Perkins because he wanted it to sound more in tune with the new rock 'n' roll vibe.

The "Go Cat Go" Telecaster suited Carl's playing style. His finger-picking mix of bluegrass, country, and rockabilly meant that his right hand was always busy in the center of the guitar body. He often found guitars had a pick-up right where he wanted to place his fingers. This Telecaster, however, had a nice clear space for his picking action. **SH**

Fender
Toronado 1998

Type Solidbody electric
Body & neck Alder body, maple neck
Fingerboard Rosewood
Pick-ups Two humbucker pick-ups

First rolling out of the Fender factory in Ensenada, Mexico, in 1998, the Toronado model was the firm's first successful attempt to update its iconic Jaguar and Jazzmaster models for a new generation. The familiar, offset body style was stripped of its single-coil pick-ups, and the love-it-or-leave-it, surf-friendly, vibrato unit, to be substituted with twin covered Atomic humbuckers, and a six-saddle hardtail bridge with through-body stringing. Interestingly, Fender chose a classic Gibson 24¾-in. (63-cm) scale length for the Toronado. This, coupled with the twin humbuckers and two-volume and two-tone control layout, made the guitar a serious competitor to the Gibson and lower-priced Epiphone SG models.

The original spec Toronado ran from 1998 to 2003 before being reissued in 2004 with open-coil humbucking pick-ups, and a new range of colors. In 2002, the short-lived, higher-spec American Deluxe and American Special Toronados were launched in twin humbucker and P-90 single-coil formats. Other variants followed, notably the Korean-made Toronado GT HH in 2005, with its mahogany body, Seymour Duncan humbuckers, and hot-rod body stripe.

Sadly, the Toronado line was dead by 2007, but many still remember the model, thanks to John Frusciante, who brandished one in the Red Hot Chili Peppers' video for the 2003 single, "Can't Stop."

"The director asked me to play that, just because of the color," Frusciante revealed to *Guitarist* magazine in 2007. "I don't play guitars unless they're from the 1960s or earlier, so I wouldn't play one, but it looked all right to me. I thought the shape was pretty cool." **TB**

Gibson
SG2 Tony Iommi 1998

Type Solidbody electric
Body & neck Mahogany body and neck
Fingerboard Rosewood
Pick-ups Two humbucker pick-ups

Tony Iommi's iconic association with the Gibson SG dates back to the recording of the first Black Sabbath album in November 1969—when, during a session, the bridge pick-up on his white Fender Stratocaster cut out. "We only had two days in the studio to finish the entire record," Iommi explained to *Hit Parader* in July 1993. "So, there was no time to waste. At that moment I switched over to the SG, and I never played the Stratocaster again." That first SG, a 1965 Special, with P-90 pick-ups, was soon replaced by a black "SG," custom-built by British luthier, John Birch. The Birch guitar was itself substituted with "No. 1," "The Old Boy," a Jaydee Custom SG built by John Diggins.

When the Gibson Custom Shop began assembling the black-and-cherry-red prototypes for the Tony Iommi Signature model in 1997, it used the features found on The Old Boy as a starting point. Therefore, unlike a regular SG, which has twenty-two frets, the prototypes had a full, two-octave fingerboard with Iommi's favored cross inlays. Both guitars featured the classic SG four-control layout— albeit with the bridge pick-up tone knob disconnected—and locking Sperzel machine heads kept Iommi's unique lineup of light-gauge strings (.009, .009, .012, .022, .028 and .038) in C♯ tuning.

The prototypes—and the subsequent Gibson and Epiphone G-400 production models—featured a pair of Tony Iommi Signature humbuckers. The first-ever Gibson artist signature pick-ups, these powerful units were tonal replicas of Tony's favorite humbuckers, handmade by John Diggins for the Jaydee No.1 guitar. **EM**

Ibanez
Artstar 1998

Type Solidbody electric
Body & neck Maple body and neck
Fingerboard Rosewood
Pick-ups Two humbucker pick-ups

Originally launched in 1988, the Ibanez Artstar Series is basically the Japanese brand's answer to the Gibson ES-335 semi-acoustic. Interest exploded in Ibanez in the late 1980s, thanks to a series of high-profile endorsements by instrumental guitar heroes, such as Steve Vai and Joe Satriani. The fact that those artists are still signed to Ibanez is testament to just how fruitful that association is. It made the company one of the best-known producers of rock guitars. That said, a longer-standing working relationship with jazz guitarist, and onetime Miles Davis frontman, George Benson, helped establish Ibanez as a purveyor of fine semi-acoustic and hollow body guitars.

The Artstar Series (model designation "AS") took elements of the ES-335—laminated maple with solid center block, 24¾-in. (62.9-cm) scale length, and a twin humbucker layout—and refined the playing experience for a modern rock and shredder demographic with large frets and a slim C-profile neck. The Artstar Series made the concept of a thin-bodied, semi-acoustic guitar enticing to young musicians. There was even a locking vibrato-equipped model available for a short period in the late 1980s.

Probably the highest-profile Artstar Series owner is Tom Morello of Rage Against The Machine, Audioslave, and The Nightwatchman. His custom-built Artstar, most often used live for the Rage track "Guerrilla Radio," was based on a vintage Vox Ultrasonic (basically a 335 derivative, albeit with a six-on-a-side machine head arrangement). Morello's Artstar came loaded with on-board effects—wah, echo, distortion, and treble and bass boost. **EM**

Klein Electric Harp Guitar 1998

Type Solidbody electric harp guitar
Body & neck Swamp ash body, rosewood neck
Fingerboard Rosewood
Pick-ups One Joe Barden humbucker pick-up

There is some controversy over the exact definition of a harp guitar. The accepted meaning of the term has changed a lot over the last 200 years, but it usually refers to any kind of guitar that has at least one extra string, which is plucked, but not fretted.

This Klein electric harp guitar has an additional neck in the form of three graphite poles, which support five sub-bass strings. The traditional, acoustic version usually has a huge, surrealistic, banana-shaped extrusion, with its own sound hole coming out of the top of the main body, and supporting a row of "harp" strings above the six usual strings.

The body of this instrument is based on the radical design developed by Steve Klein with Carl Margolis, Ronnie Montrose, and Ned Steinberger. Opinions about it varied: Lou Reed said it was the most comfortable guitar that he had ever played, but it was christened "Lumpy" by David Lindley.

The Steinberger influence is evident in the disturbing absence of a conventional headstock, and also in the presence of the "Trans Trem" vibrato. This system maintains the tuning of the strings in relation to each other, and enables the tuning of the whole guitar to be changed by locking the bridge into one of several different positions—a particularly useful feature if you happen to know only three chords. **AJ**

Michael Hedges (1953–97) played a significant part in bringing harp guitars to public attention during the late 1980s. He uses a Klein harp guitar on *Taproot* (1990), which was Grammy-nominated in the Best New Age album category.

Terry McInturff TCM
Glory Custom 1998

Type Semi-hollow body electric
Body & neck Mahogany/maple body, mahogany neck
Fingerboard Rosewood
Pick-ups Two Zodiac humbucker pick-ups

Terry McInturff began making top-quality instruments in 1978 in his workshop in Siler City, North Carolina. He is a passionate fan of Honduras mahogany, which he calls "the most stable wood known to mankind." His range includes a double-cutaway Terrycaster, and a twin-humbucker Taurus. One of his guitars—the TCM Glory Custom—was auctioned as part of the "Crossroads" sale of Eric Clapton's guitars in 2004. The pre-sale estimate was $4,000 but the instrument sold for $12,548.

The Glory Custom is still available today (at a price of around $4,000). It is a twin-cutaway instrument

> *"These pieces of wood are not pulled off the top of a stack. They are sorted and chosen so they vibrate as a team in the way that I want."*
>
> **TERRY MCINTURFF**

with a small hollow chamber within the carved body, a set mortise-and-tenon neck joint, and a built-in "shock protect" circuit to safeguard against dangerous electrical problems.

The finely finished boutique instrument has gold hardware, a self-lubricating nut, and Paua shell neck inlays. The pick-ups are all custom-made (often by DiMarzio) and the electrics can be customized to any configuration. The Clapton guitar had two humbuckers and a single-coil pick-up.

In addition to Clapton, other famous customers have included Jimmy Page, Brad Whitford (Aerosmith), Brad Delson (Linkin Park), Marshall Crenshaw, David Hidalgo (Los Lobos), Chuck Garvey (moe.), Danny Flowers, and Jeff Beck. **SH**

Mobius
Megatar 1998

Type Double-handed tapping instrument
Body & neck Maple/alder/mahogany/sapele/wenge
Fingerboard Assorted: maple, rosewood, wenge
Pick-ups Two active split pick-ups and one piezo pick-ups

The three big names in the two-handed tapping world are Chapman—the first company to go into production with a dedicated tapping instrument—Warr, and Mobius. All three take slightly different approaches to the job in hand. But which one is the best? Chapman is by far the longest established, and the best known, but, as far as quality is concerned, there is no clear winner: each has a dedicated following of players who would use nothing else.

The Mobius Megatar is a twelve-string, two-handed, tapping instrument. The player holds the guitar in a broadly upright position, and plays the six treble strings with the left hand from beneath the neck; sound is achieved by pressing the strings down against the frets. The right hand plays the six bass strings from above the neck in the same way. This makes it possible to play bass lines simultaneously with chords or melodies. If it sounds difficult ... well, that's because, for most guitarists, it is: the necessary ability to make the hands finger different parts is likely to come more naturally to those schooled in the piano, and, in practice, it appears that the likeliest players to make the crossover successfully are bassists.

The model shown here is the leviathan of the Mobius range, the Hammer of Thor. It features a split Bartolini pick-up, with separate outputs and the capability of controlling external MIDI (Musical Instrument Digital Interface) devices.

The most visually striking aspect of this instrument is the ergonomically designed arrangement of fanned frets, which enables more accurate intonation, as well as deeper bass tones. **TB**

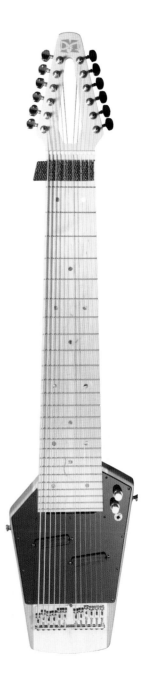

PRS McCarty
Hollowbody 1998

Type Hollow body electric
Body & neck Mahogany with spruce top, set neck
Fingerboard Rosewood with moon-shaped inlays
Pick-ups Two humbucker pick-ups

The McCarty name was used to introduce a new direction for PRS. Joe Knaggs—a gifted jazz guitarist, who had worked for PRS since its early days—instigated a design that recalled the hollow body archtops of the jazz era. It started as part of the Guitars of the Month program between 1994 and 1996. Knaggs also hand-built two further hollow-bodied guitars with f-holes for the Private Stock program in late 1996 and early 1997.

Two production models appeared in 1998: the deep-bodied Archtop, and the shallower Hollowbody.

"This instrument is not only one of the best sounding, but one of the best playing guitars I've ever picked up."

PAUL JACKSON, JR., JAZZ GUITARIST

Both used the outline of the PRS Custom solidbody, but they were almost completely hollow, apart from a wooden pillar that connected the top to the back underneath the stoptail bridge—the tops and backs were carved inside and out by a complex CNC program.

Available in various specifications, including spruce or maple tops, and mahogany or maple backs, the Hollowbody also led to the creation of the PRS Piezo system, designed in collaboration with LR Baggs, which gave the Hollowbody and Archtop guitars a dual electric and acoustic-like tonality when amplified.

Perhaps not surprisingly, the thinner-bodied Hollowbody has remained in production, while the Archtop had faded from view by 2004. In 2008, the Singlecut Hollowbody was added to the lineup. **DB**

Vaccaro
X-ray 1998

Type Solidbody electric
Body & neck Alder body, aluminum neck
Fingerboard Ebonol
Pick-ups One single-coil and one humbucker pick-up

The Travis Bean and Kramer brands had both previously explored the idea of an aluminum guitar neck and its advantages in maintaining sustain. The latter's 1976 patented design was discontinued in 1981, due to the high cost of manufacture. Henry Vaccaro Sr., had been a senior executive at Kramer during the 1980s, helping it to become one of the largest U.S. guitar manufacturers. But after a decade of producing Superstrats, in the early 1990s the Kramer company went out of business.

In 1995, Vaccaro and his son, Henry Jr., obtained the ownership of Kramer's aluminum neck patents,

> *"I realized the potential of the old Kramer neck design—the tremendous sustain and attack generated by the aluminum…"*
> HENRY VACCARO

and initially attempted to revive the brand. This idea was thwarted when in 1997 Gibson acquired the rights to use the name. Undeterred, a year later, a new Vaccaro line appeared under the stewardship of one of Kramer's founding luthiers, Phil Petillo.

The interesting Vaccaro X-Ray made its debut in 1998, and featured an alternative take on the original T-bar neck design, which was heavy, cold to touch, and sometimes too responsive to temperature changes. The alternative "V-neck" design featured an aluminum core that was surrounded by wood. What's more, it was only 2 oz. (57 g) heavier than a conventional wooden neck and able to house a truss rod enabling fine adjustments not possible with the previous aluminum designs. Vaccaro sadly went out of business in 2002. **RL/TB**

Aria
M-650T 1999

Type Solidbody electric
Body & neck Agatis/maple/rosewood body, maple neck
Fingerboard Rosewood
Pick-ups Two humbucker pick-ups

In 1999, *Total Guitar* magazine judged Aria's M-650 guitar "the coolest of the year." The retro/futuristic instrument looked "suitably classy," they raved. The object of their acclaim was a quirky, but high-quality, solidbody electric with undoubted stage presence.

It was the unique shape and finish that caught the attention of guitarists like The Cure's Perry Bamonte, and French star Tommy Laurent.

The lightly sequined body finish (available in orange, blue, or red), and white, pearloid scatchplate gave the M-650 a kitsch charm. If you specified the Bigsby tremolo of the 650T version, it conjured up the style of thirty years previously—but in a highly usable modern form.

The M-650's details were excellent, too: triple rosewood binding, a twenty-four-fret fingerboard with block inlays, and a nicely carved maple top. Beneath the glitz, however, most of the Aria's features were pretty straight-ahead, and reliable: a bolt-on neck, two humbuckers, and simple, chrome hardware. **SH**

Collings
Lyle Lovett 1999

Type Flat-top acoustic
Body & neck Spruce and rosewood body, maple neck
Fingerboard Ebony

Based in Austin, Texas, Collings Guitars was founded in 1973 by medical school dropout Bill Collings. The Collings name took off in 1987, when vintage-guitar expert George Gruhn ordered twenty-five flat-top acoustics for sale at his outlet in Nashville, Tennessee. After this, Collings began to receive attention from other U.S. retailers and the guitar media.

Progressing from flat-tops through archtops and mandolins, at the NAMM show in 2006 Collings decided to expand into the electric guitar market, with a new line of Gibson-inspired instruments.

CJ ("Collings Jumbo") guitars are based on the relatively obscure Gibson Advanced Jumbo, a flat-top, round-shouldered dreadnought that was produced briefly in 1936. In 1999, Collings produced a signature CJ model for American country singer and actor Lyle Lovett, who had been a long-term player of Collings guitars. The CJ design makes for a higher-than-average-volume instrument but retains the sweet treble tone of more "delicate" models. **TB**

Danelectro
Hodad 1999

DeArmond
M-75Ty 1999

Type Semi-solidbody electric
Body & neck Laminate/Masonite body, maple neck
Fingerboard Rosewood
Pick-ups Four lipstick-tube single-coil pick-ups

Type Solidbody electric
Body & neck Agathis/maple body and set maple neck
Fingerboard Palisander
Pick-ups Two DeArmond 2K single-coil pick-ups

By the late 1990s, interest in original Danelectro guitars had grown sufficiently to justify reviving the name after thirty years, and, along with it, the models that had first made its reputation. These included the U1, the U2, and the Shorthorn, but Danelectro's comeback also brought this new design to the table.

Its offset, double-cutaway body was reminiscent of the Mosrite guitars favored by instrumental, surf-guitar phenomenon The Ventures. That may account for the model name—"Hodad" was a 1950s term for someone who pretends to be able to surf. The pick-ups were two sets of twin single-coils, offering out-of-phase and coil-tap options via push-pull controls on the tone pots, and making for an impressive total of twelve different tonal variations. With the added option of a Bigsby-style vibrato tailpiece, as in the example shown, the control over a highly versatile guitar is heightened still.

The Hodad has the vibe of a long-lost favorite, and it was no surprise when it was reissued in 2012. **RL**

Even though the DeArmond guitar line was made by Guild, and under Fender ownership in the mid-1990s, its Korean reissues of some of the former's designs were always marketed as DeArmonds. They were not available in the United States. The guitars featured the DeArmond pick-ups of their namesake, the company originally founded by Harry DeArmond, which produced classic archtop pick-ups, such as the classic 1000 Rhythm Chief. DeArmond also made the single-coils for the guitar of which this is a reissue: a 1952 Guild known as the Aristocrat, later dubbed the Bluesbird by blues musicians drawn to its charms.

The DeArmond Korean reissue adds a "T"—the Bigsby Tremolo—but differs from the originals, which were hollow bodied, unlike the rival Les Paul that was also released in 1952. Although the model was officially renamed the Bluesbird in the late 1960s, by 1973 it had switched completely to solidbody. Both guises shared the M-75 model number, just like this guitar that continued the legacy. **RL**

Fender Monterey
Pop Stratocaster 1999

Type Solidbody electric
Body & neck Ash body, maple neck
Fingerboard Rosewood
Pick-ups Three single-coil pick-ups

Pamelina Hovnatanian, known professionally as "Pamelina H," is a guitar artist who has worked on many splendid exhibits for the Fender Custom Shop. In 1997, she was given the task of producing a design for a Fender Stratocaster that celebrated the thirtieth anniversary of Jimi Hendrix's appearance at the Monterey Pop Festival. On June 18, 1967, Hendrix had given a typically electrifying performance that climaxed, during his anarchic cover of The Troggs' "Wild Thing," with the ritual sacrifice of his hand-painted Fiesta Red Strat. Famously captured on film, Hendrix first squirted lighter fluid over the body, before setting it alight, and then smashing it into pieces.

> *"The only reference I had to go by was a video of the concert. I was given a VHS that I looked at frame by frame."*
>
> PAMELINA H, GUITAR ARTIST

Hovnatanian—who had attended the show as a child with her mother—was given a brief to produce a hand-painted artwork that "evoked, rather than reproduced" the guitarist's original handiwork. Her design refined Hendrix's psychedelic floral swirls, and incorporated quirky original features, such as the backstage pass graphic above the bridge. In fact, a matching, laminated, backstage pass was included with each of the limited run of 210 guitars. Hendrix's original guitar had been a 1965 model, built during Fender's CBS takeover, and features an authentic reproduction of a period headstock, including the "transition" logo. **TB**

Fender Pastorius Tribute Jazz 1999

Type Semi-hollow body electric
Body & neck Maple body, set neck
Fingerboard Rosewood
Pick-ups Two single-coil pick-ups

Jaco Pastorius arrived on the U.S. jazz scene as a fully formed talent of extraordinary proportions, and was immediately invited to join Weather Report at jazz-fusion's top table.

Single-handedly responsible for inspiring a generation to take up the fretless bass guitar, Pastorius's own instrument was a battered, 1962 Fender Jazz he'd bought at a pawn shop in 1970, and then customized, ripping out the frets, and coating the fingerboard with heavy marine resin.

Based on a relatively slim body of work, Pastorius is now viewed emphatically as one the greatest-ever exponents of the electric bass. Almost all his work was performed with his so-called "Bass of Doom." The Pastorius reign, however, would be sadly brief: plagued by the effects of bipolar disorder and drug abuse, he died in 1987, at the age of 35.

In 1999, Fender produced the Pastorius Tribute, faithfully replicating the Bass of Doom, right down to the fret slotting on the fingerboard and distressed bodywork where the paintwork on the original would have slowly been worn away by the player's sleeve.

The original Bass of Doom—stolen from a park bench in Greenwich Village, shortly before Pastorius died—reappeared two decades later, and is now owned by Metallica's Robert Trujillo. **TB**

With his debut solo album, *Jaco Pastorius* (1976), the Pennsylvania-born musician upped the ante for every wannabe jazz bass guitarist. He continues to be an important influence in this field. Check out the opening track, Miles Davis' "Donna Lee."

Gibson Zakk Wylde
Les Paul Bullseye 1999

Type Solidbody electric
Body & neck Maple/mahogany body, maple neck
Fingerboard Ebony
Pick-ups One EMG-81 and one EMG-85 pick-up

Alternatively known as "The Grail," Zakk Wylde's trademark, bull's-eye-painted, Gibson Les Paul was lost from a truck traveling between Ozzy Osbourne gigs in Texas. After putting out a reward notice, Wylde was contacted by a fan who had bought the guitar from a pawn shop in Dallas, and then noticed that the initials "ZW" had been carved into the backs of the pick-ups. The fan arranged the return of the instrument, receiving two other Les Pauls as a reward for his honesty.

The replica version of Wylde's original Les Paul was built by Gibson, under close guidance from the guitarist himself, and features a carved-maple top with a solid mahogany back, and multiple black-and-white banding around both front and rear. It has a three-piece maple neck, with no finish, pearl block inlays, and Gibson's classic, rounded profile.

The original instrument had an ebony fingerboard, but this has been replaced on the Gibson replica with Richlite, a branded, synthetic material made from recycled paper and phenolic resin. Often used in kitchen work surfaces, Richlite does not absorb moisture, and ensures a lightning-fast action well suited to Wylde's playing style.

The Les Paul is also fitted with a Nashville Tune-o-matic bridge, and a stopbar tailpiece. There are two pick-ups. In the neck position is an EMG-85, which gives a warm, natural tone, and a beefy low end, without being muddy. In the bridge position is an EMG-81, which works excellently with high-volume, overdriven amplifiers, thus producing exciting amounts of attack and sustain. **PP**

Zakk Wylde wields his signature Les Paul. ➔

Lindert
John Henry 1999

MotorAve
LeMans 1999

Type Semi-hollow body electric
Body & neck MDF body, maple neck
Fingerboard Rosewood
Pick-ups Two hand-wound Alnico humbucker pick-ups

Type Solidbody electric
Body & neck Mahogany or cedar body, mahogany neck
Fingerboard Rosewood
Pick-ups One P-90 or humbucker pick-up

When Charles Lindert quit apple-picking to try to make it as an instrument maker, he learned from the best: Freddie Tavares, designer of the Fender Stratocaster.

The John Henry was the tenth in Lindert's locomotive-theed series; the range's individuality had been established through the radio-grille-type arrangements on the body and the distinctive headstock. The latter came about when Lindert was sketching out designs. "I just had my hand resting on the paper with my thumb kind of sticking up and I looked down and I saw it and I said: 'That's it,'" he recalled. The John Henry aimed to epitomize the "steel driving man"—the ultimate blue-collar icon of U.S. folk legend—after whom it was named. The radial arrangement of the John Henry's pickguard and cloth grilles referenced the resonator guitars of the 1920s.

It remained in production until Lindert was wound up in 2002, when, by his own account, "The whole thing turned into greed and envy and jealousy and hatred and spite." **CB**

Luthier Mark Fuqua worked with established American guitar makers like Terry McInturff and James Trussart before setting up on his own in California. He is currently based in North Carolina.

One of Fuqua's first commercially available instruments was this single-pick-up solid electric. Costing more than $3,000, the LeMans has all the attributes of a top boutique guitar: a finely finished hand-carved body in a choice of woods, a quartersawn and carved mahogany neck, and a choice of top-quality P-90 or humbucker pick-up.

Unusually, there's no tone control: the electronics include switches to provide varying degrees of treble cut instead. Other interesting features include Kluson tuners, aluminum fret-marker inlays, CTS volume control, TonePros bridge ... and a lifetime guarantee.

LeMans players include hard rocker Dimitri Coats from The Burning Brides and Off! and Tom Rothrock, the producer, composer, and musician who wrote the theme tune for the *Sopranos* TV series. **SH**

Parker
MIDIFly 1999

Tacoma
EA-14 1999

Type Solidbody electric
Body & neck Mahogany body and neck
Fingerboard Carbon-fiberglass composite
Pick-ups Three DiMarzio pick-ups and one Fishman piezo

Type Electroacoustic guitar
Body & neck Ash body, mahogany neck
Fingerboard Rosewood
Pick-ups LR Baggs Miratone pick-up

To most people, "digital music revolution" evokes thoughts of online retailing. But Parker Guitars were pioneering the form when iTunes was still a twinkle in Steve Jobs' eye.

Introduced in 1999, the Parker MIDIFly adapted Parker's acclaimed Fly to incorporate features that allowed the instrument, when used with a synth or PC, to emulate keys, woodwinds, brass, and percussion, not to mention oodles of classic guitar tones, all while presenting an intuitive user interface. Familiar tone and volume knobs, and a selector switch controlled the magnetic and piezo pick-ups, while MIDI (Musical Instrument Digital Interface) controls were limited to a volume knob, and mode and octave switches. A stereo jack (MIDI On) was positioned alongside five-pin MIDI Out and MIDI In jacks that dispensed with typical thirteen-pin MIDI connectors, while a cast-aluminum bridge housed a Virtual DSP MidiAx, and a piezo pick-up for onboard guitar-to-MIDI conversion, obviating the need for an outboard conversion device. **DP**

Olympia is the import division of the Tacoma guitar company—their guitars were originally manufactured in Tacoma, Washington, but since 2004 they have been owned by Fender.

The EA-14 lacks the "paisley sound hole" that characterizes much of the Tacoma range, but still uses a modified version of the cross-shaped "voiced bracing support" that goes with it. (The theory is that, if you move the sound hole to the left shoulder of the guitar, and have it shaped like an apostrophe, the top will be stronger, and need less bracing, thereby improving its resonance.) Another feature on this guitar is the asymmetrical bridge, which is designed to improve the response of each string.

The electronics consist of the Miratone pick-up system, which is made for Tacoma guitars by LR Baggs. In addition to volume and tone controls, the Miratone has a notch filter, which can be used to home in on troublesome, feedback-causing frequencies, and deal with them humanely. **AJ**

Washburn
PS1800 1999

Washburn
The Dime Culprit 1999

Type Solidbody electric
Body & neck Mahogany body, set mahogany neck
Fingerboard Rosewood
Pick-ups Two humbucker pick-ups

Type Solidbody electric
Body & neck Basswood body, set maple neck
Fingerboard Rosewood
Pick-ups Two humbucker pick-ups

Like so many other businesses, the original Washburn guitar company perished in the 1929 Wall Street Crash.

The re-formed company—established in 1974—has often specialized in high-quality, celebrity-tied instruments: their longest-standing signature artist is Paul Stanley of Kiss. The PS1800 model was "inspired and designed by Stanley . . . no other guitar can sustain the playing power of this legendary rocker."

Owing more than a little in body shape to the Ibanez Iceman—which is unsurprising, since it was Stanley's guitar of choice throughout the band's glory years—the PS1800 is a workhorse rock instrument that has appeared in an assortment of shiny finishes, such as the later "cracked mirror" design.

Die-hard Kiss fans can now buy a luxury package that involves meeting Stanley before a Kiss concert to be presented with a signed PS1800 . . . and then see it smashed on stage during the band's encore. At the end of the show, you get to collect and take away all of the remaining pieces! **TB**

The Dime Culprit by Washburn was one of the guitars designed for Darrell Lance Abbott—a.k.a. "Dimebag Darrell" or "Diamond Darrell"—the guitarist with Pantera and Damageplan. Darrell had been with Dean Guitars for years before signing with Washburn in 1994.

The Culprit guitar featured a mirror scratchplate, two hot, ceramic, humbucker pick-ups with chrome covers, a three-way selector switch, and two volume controls, but no tone controls. The 333 model had a Floyd Rose locking tremolo, with the 332 model having a stoptail bridge fitted. Another version of the same guitar had a mahogany body and neck, with a clear finish and a black scratchplate. Both guitars were fitted with mini Grover machine heads. The neck was 25½-in. (64.75-cm) scale, and had twenty-two frets.

On December 8, 2004, Darrell was shot dead by a member of the audience while performing live on stage with Damageplan in Columbus, Ohio. The shooter, Nathan Gale, killed three other people before being shot dead himself. **PP**

Yamaha
AES500 1999

Yamaha
Pacifica 311 1999

Type Solidbody electric
Body & neck Nato body, maple neck
Fingerboard Rosewood
Pick-ups Two Yamaha humbucker pick-ups

Type Solidbody electric
Body & neck Alder/ash body, maple neck
Fingerboard Maple
Pick-ups Two single-coil pick-ups and one humbucker

The history of Yamaha's AE series goes all the way back to the Japanese company's earliest forays into the American market in 1966, and its very first archtop, the AE11. The design of Yamaha's first series of electrics was influenced by established American designs: the AE11's dual humbuckers, rosewood bridge, and trapeze tailpiece positioned the instrument somewhere between Gibson's Byrdland and ES-125 models.

The AE12, which followed the AE11 five years later, debuted the more rounded, cutaway shape on which the Taiwanese-made solidbody AES500 later drew when it was launched in 1998.

The 500 model was the only guitar in the AES line to have a body made of nato—a hardwood that was more affordable than the mahogany used on later models, such as the AES800. For all its retro stylings, the coil tap (controlled with the tone knob) on the pick-ups brings some added versatility to a guitar that originally retailed for a relatively affordable $599. The AES500 was discontinued in 2000. **RL**

The 311 Pacifica "Telecasters" were manufactured in the wake of the acclaimed Japanese Mike Stern Signature series of the late 1990s. They came with alder/ash bodies, and a lovely string-through body design, although their neck and bridge pick-ups were considered inadequate, and were often replaced with DiMarzios. Factory-set intonations, too, were often in need of adjustment. But the 311s were capable of producing sustained, long notes—something not always associated with Telecasters—and they had a lovely responsiveness, even when unplugged.

Despite producing an impressive array of sounds, however, the 311 could never be mistaken for a metal guitar. Still, it remains one of the best-ever guitars in terms of responding to modifications, such as the addition of a coiltap to split the pick-ups, a tweak that will produce tones and resonances never heard on the factory floor. So release yourself from "badge snobbery," play it at gigs without backup, and be proud of your Telecaster. **BS**

2000s

Crafter
CTS 155C 2000

Type Electroacoustic guitar
Body & neck Spruce body, mahogany neck
Fingerboard Rosewood
Pick-ups One LR Baggs Element pick-up with LR-F Plus

The CTS 155C is from Crafter, a big South Korean manufacturer of affordable acoustic and electroacoustic guitars, some of which can be had for less than $200, and only few of which break the $1,000 barrier. Guitars in the Crafter Pro Series have better woods, and components, and cost a little more, but they are still mass-produced instruments, and serious players should not have excessively high expectations of them.

The CTS 155C is marketed as both a classical and a thin-body acoustic. With its classical guitar head and neck, black body, and a rosette reminiscent of a series

"One of the really cool things about Crafter is that they are very much a family-owned and oriented company."

DAMON JOHNSON OF THIN LIZZY AND BROTHER CANE

of black parlor guitars made by Stella in the 1930s, it is something of a hybrid, seemingly made with mix-and-match components.

Founded in 1972, Crafter originally made classical guitars branded "Sungeum" for the domestic market. They diversified into acoustic and electroacoustic guitars in the early 1980s. This CTS 155C was made in 2000, the year Crafter opened a huge factory with a workforce of 140 which, in 2001, churned out 60,000 guitars. With offices in South Korea and the United States, its instruments are now sold in forty countries.

Several artists have been recruited to be pictured playing, and, by association, endorsing, Crafter guitars, but whether they played them for pleasure as well as profit only they would know. **GD**

Gibson Les Paul Standard Raw Power 2000

Type Solidbody electric
Body & neck Mahogany and maple body, mahogany neck
Fingerboard Rosewood
Pick-ups Two Seymour Duncan 59s pick-ups

The Raw Power was a variation on Gibson's flagship Les Paul Standard series that appeared briefly in their catalog starting in 2000. The idea was to produce a stripped-down, no-frills version of the Standard that still retained its sound and playability and was also considerably more affordable—less than half the price of most Les Paul models. Visually the guitar had an unrefined appearance, with a thin satin matt lacquer finish in place of the standard nitrocellulose that revealed all the detail in the grain in the carved maple top—supposedly, the lack of a traditional finish allowed

> *"Gibson USA's Les Paul Standard Raw Power is a total natural—the Les Paul in its most basic form, yet built like none other before it."*
>
> THE GIBSON CORPORATION

the wood to breathe and you got to hear more of its natural tone. Some players also find that the lack of a glossy finish makes the guitar feel less sticky and is therefore faster to play.

The pick-ups were either two passive Seymour Duncan 59s or the classic heavy metal combination of Zakk Wylde signature EMG humbuckers—an 81 at the bridge and an 85 at the neck. The 24¾-in. (63-cm) scale neck had a rosewood fingerboard with trapezoid inlays and there was a Tune-o-matic bridge, a stopbar tailpiece and Grover Rotomatic tuners.

The Standard Raw Power was superseded in 2001 by the all-maple Studio Raw Power, which also came in a wider range of colors, and a line of Raw Power guitars including an SG version was launched in 2009. **AJ**

Lâg Tramontane T200 D12 2000

McIlroy A Series 2000

Type Twelve-string acoustic
Body & neck Mahogany and cedar body, mahogany neck
Fingerboard Rosewood

Type Mid-size jumbo acoustic
Body & neck Materials vary from model to model
Fingerboard Ebony

French company Lâg Guitars celebrated its thirtieth birthday in 2011 by winning the National Association of Music Merchants (NAMM) Best In Show for the second successive year, and the Tramontane range was awarded Best Product in its category. Lâg later opened a factory in China to satisfy increasing demand.

The Tramontane twelve-string T200 D12 and T200 D12CE have mahogany backs and sides, and cedar tops with bindings in rosewood and maple. The neck is mahogany, with a French satin finish, and has an Indonesian rosewood fingerboard with twenty silver-nickel, medium-type frets. Around the sound hole is an Occitania cross decoration made from rosewood and maple. The bridge is also made from Indonesian rosewood, with a black resin compensated saddle. The headstock is solid Indonesian rosewood, with a linseed-oil finish, the Lâg logo, and a maple inlay. It is fitted with lubricated, high-precision, satin-black machine heads, with satin-black tulip buttons. The CE version has a Nanoflex piezo pick-up under the bridge saddle. **PP**

The son of a pianist mother and a carpenter father, luthier Dermot McIlroy (b. 1963) built his guitar factory in Antrim, Northern Ireland, in 2000 after ten years as an employee at the nearby Lowden Guitar Company. All his guitars are made to order, and if you want to own one you generally have to wait several months for it—it's a point of pride to McIlroy that no guitar has ever left his workshop without having been sold first.

The A Series mid-size jumbo is the most popular McIlroy design. There are three basic forms—the "AJ" is a jumbo; the "AS" is a small jumbo; the "AD" is a round-shoulder dreadnought—and there are also various possible A Series model numbers that correspond to the wood used in the body—thus, for example, the A30 has a Sitka spruce top with rosewood back and sides. All McIlroy guitars have paua abalone rosettes, their nut and saddle material is bone, and they incorporate Gotoh machine heads. The model shown here is a McIlroy A80 made from Brazilian rosewood. **AJ**

Modulus
Vertex Bass 2000

Ovation Adamas
Melissa Etheridge 2000

Type Solidbody bass guitar
Body & neck Alder body, carbon fiber neck
Fingerboard Composite
Pick-ups One humbucker pick-up

Type Twelve-string acoustic
Body & neck Composite/carbon fiber body and neck
Fingerboard Ebony
Pick-ups One Ovation high-output pick-up

Although the hot pick-ups and wide tonal range of Modulus guitars have attracted slap bass players, such as Flea, it would be inaccurate to label the Californian company's instruments as merely funk basses. Other musicians such as Alex Webster of death metallers Cannibal Corpse have also used Modulus gear on an ongoing basis, because the instruments are solid, travel well through all climates, and are immensely playable—all of which attributes are at least partly due to their carbon fiber necks and composite fingerboards. A well set-up Modulus Vertex plays like butter, to the immense satisfaction of its numerous devotees, although some members of the bass guitar community will never accept its neck because it is not made of wood. While there is much to be said for a decent tonewood, graphite neck technology has been a proven success since the 1980s, and the quality and playability of instruments such as the Vertex make it difficult for anyone other than the most hardened purist to argue against them. **JM**

Acoustic-rock singer-songwriter Melissa Etheridge collaborated with Adamas at the Ovation workshop in New Hartford, Connecticut, to design the Melissa Etheridge Signature twelve-string. The guitar features a unidirectional, carbon fiber soundboard, with Adamas fan bracing, and a mid-depth, cutaway, composite body. Other features include a five-piece neck, with ebony fretboard and bridge, bass-side soundports with exotic hardwood epaulets, and a custom "ME" maple symbol at the twelfth fret.

The instrument is also fitted with Ovation's original high-output pick-up, and its OP-Pro preamp gives the option of dual XLR and ¼ in. (0.6 cm) output jacks that connect to virtually any recording console, stage amp, or sound system. Ovation claims that the unidirectional carbon fiber top provides strength, with very little mass, for the truest enhancement of a string's vibration. The neck has a hand-rubbed, urethane oil finish, with gold-plated machine heads. Every signature series guitar has a label signed by the artist herself. **PP**

Taylor
Kenny Loggins 2000

Type Acoustic jumbo
Body & neck Koa body, mahogany neck
Fingerboard Ebony
Pick-ups One Fishman pick-up and preamp system

As an artist now most commonly associated with synth-driven, soft-rock hits from movies such as *Top Gun*, *Footloose*, and *Over The Top*, Kenny Loggins may seem a surprising choice by Taylor for a signature acoustic. But his "I'm Alright," from *Caddyshack* (1980), was an acoustic-based strummer that harked back to the 1970s, when his work with Jim Messina had often showcased his folky playing.

"Writing and playing with acoustic guitar shifts my writing, and takes me into different places, rather than writing with keyboard players or on an electric guitar," Loggins explained in a 2009 interview.

His link with Taylor guitars had already been solidified before the manufacturer made this signature run of 100 instruments. In his introduction to a Loggins live performance in celebration of Taylor's thirtieth anniversary in 2004, founder Bob Taylor revealed: "Every time people ask, 'Who's someone famous who plays one of your guitars? Who's a great player who plays your guitars?', the first person that comes out of our mouths is almost always Kenny Loggins." High praise indeed. And, in a further tribute, Taylor added special nods to Kenny's love of Hawaii, with not just the premium koa top, but also the unusual maple hibiscus blossom inlays in the fretboard—both plants are native to the Pacific islands. **RL**

The Kenny Loggins Signature Model (KLSM) was used in the reunion gigs after Loggins and Messina got back together in 2005 following a twenty-nine year separation. Some of the best live performances are captured on *Sittin' In Again At The Santa Barbara Bowl* (2005).

Teuffel
Tesla Classic 2000

Type Solidbody electric
Body & neck Maple/alder body, maple neck
Fingerboard Maple
Pick-ups One "hot" humbucker and one split-coil pick-up

Remember that first cheap Japanese "Strat" your Dad bought you in that junk shop when you were fourteen? And how the pick-ups used to hum like crazy . . . and every time your hand went anywhere near the selector switch the sound cut out . . . and when you moved too close to your amp you were deafened by a high-pitched squeal? Ulrich Teuffel does. And what's more, he misses it. On the Tesla Classic, the creator of the Bird Fish—the world's weirdest/coolest guitar—gives us the option of reliving those moments.

> *"With the Tesla I have designed a guitar that, along with modern guitar sounds, also has these primitive sounds at its disposal."*
> ULRICH TEUFFEL

The Tesla is another of Teuffel's characteristic fantasy guitars that doesn't really resemble any other. It does have a certain essence of Steinberger about it, but it really is out there on its own. The three buttons below the pick-ups are of particular interest. When pressed, the first activates a 60 Hz hum; the second interrupts the signal; the third activates a small microphone beneath the neck pick-up, which causes it to feed back. Most guitarists see no value in such features, but once you know that two early takers were Henry Kaiser and David Torn, they do start to make sense.

Whether you view Teuffel as a genius or a crackpot—or both—he certainly challenges the orthodoxy of contemporary guitar manufacture. **TB**

Washburn Dimebag Darrell Stealth ST-3 2000

Type Solidbody electric
Body & neck Mahogany body and neck
Fingerboard Ebony
Pick-ups Two humbucker pick-ups

The Washburn brand name has been through two very distinct eras. The original company was founded in the late nineteenth century, producing very fine acoustic instruments for four decades before falling foul of the Great Depression. The "new" Washburn emerged in the 1970s, and quickly gained a reputation for its solidbody electric guitars, which were particularly popular with metal players.

In 2000, Washburn teamed up with "Dimebag" Darrell Abbott, who was at the time one of the metal scene's most significant shredders, and well known for his work with Pantera. The Washburn Stealth was based on the Dean ML that Dimebag had pioneered in the 1990s. The ML's body shape loosely resembled a Gibson Flying V grafted onto the upper half of a Gibson Explorer; the Washburn Stealth exaggerated this shape to its limit, creating surely the pointiest of pointy guitars!

Launched in 2000, the Stealth came in two versions, the upmarket U.S.-built ST-3, which was constructed with a set neck, and the budget Korean-built ST-2 with a bolt-on neck.

The ST-3 shown here has a mahogany body and neck with a luxurious ebony fingerboard; the sound comes from a pair of Bill Lawrence/Seymour Duncan humbuckers, with dedicated volume controls and a master tone pot.

The Dimebag story ended in tragedy in 2004 in Columbus, Ohio. While on stage with his new band, Damageplan, a paranoid schizophrenic ran riot with a semi-automatic handgun, killing Dimebag and three others before being shot dead himself. **TB**

The late Dimebag Darrell, one of the great shredders of the 1990s. ➡

Blackmachine
B2 2001

Type Solidbody electric
Body & neck Ash/ebony body, rosewood neck
Fingerboard Ebony or rosewood
Pick-ups Two humbucker pick-ups

With demand constantly increasing for guitars built by Doug Campbell, the waiting list for one of the British designer's most popular models continues to grow. But good things eventually come to those who wait, and the Blackmachine's enigmatic reputation among admirers in the technical metal scene is built on the firmest of foundations. London-based Campbell works alone, often putting in long hours to fulfill orders with a very keen player's eye for tonal detail. And the lucky players who have had B2s built for them since the launch of the model in 2001 tend to rate their purchases very highly indeed.

"That's a magical guitar," proud B2 owner Misha "Bulb" Mansoor of Periphery told *Total Guitar* magazine in 2012. "As mystical as people say they are, there really is something special about that guitar. They're so musical—there are a lot of guitars that come close, but that guitar is personally very special to me. That is something I will have forever." Periphery is a U.S. progressive metal band that is widely regarded as the leading popularizer of djent, a style of playing that emphasizes pick attack and the staccato. The term was coined by Fredrik Thordendal of Meshuggah to describe the mode of guitar playing with which he has become most closely associated.

The B2 has been likened to the B6, but with added beef, a sweeter midrange, and none of its stablemate's propensity for harshness. The fretboard contributes to a very punchy attack, and the BKP pick-ups facilitate easy switches between aggressive modern rock and warm, jazzy tones; the latter are further enhanced by the Schaller Hannes bridge. **RL**

Daisy Rock
Heartbreaker 2001

Type Electric bass
Body & neck Basswood body, maple neck
Fingerboard Rosewood
Pick-ups One split "P-style" pick-up

As far back as the early 1960s, Gretsch released the Princess, a guitar that didn't make too many inroads into a new hoped-for girl market. But two generations later, the idea's time had come. In 2000, Tish Ciravolo embarked on a one-woman crusade to take the electric guitar and bass to young twenty-first-century women. Ciravolo, who cites her initial inspiration as Suzi Quatro's character Leather Tuscadero on the TV show *Happy Days*—then taking time out from her own music career to raise a family—founded Daisy Rock Girl Guitars as a subdivision of Schecter Guitar Research (her husband is company founder Michael Schecter). Watching the enthusiasm drain from girls for whom standard guitars were too cumbersome inspired Ciravolo to produce models whose USP was a tailoring for the female user, with lighter weight and slimmer necks an obvious target area.

The most visually arresting guitar from the Daisy Rock line emerged from the stable early—2001's Heartbreaker, available as either a six-sting or bass. Weight was down and usability was up, with personality to burn. Courtney Love gave the range her seal of approval. A section of the market largely uncatered for was opened up, but its appeal stretched beyond that. "Along comes something brand new and shocking in its appeal," said Paul McManus, chief executive of the Music Industries Association, of Daisy Rock in 2005.

Over time, Daisy Rock has evolved from producing cute shapes, like the Lady Bug, Butterfly, Daisy, and Star models, to more conventional single- and double-cuts, along with Flying V designs. Meanwhile, Ciravolo has continued her mission publishing the *Girl's Guitar Method* series for Alfred Publishing. **CB/TB**

Dean
Tonic S 2001

Fender D'Aquisto
Classic Rocker 2001

Type Solidbody electric
Body & neck Mahogany body, maple neck
Fingerboard Rosewood
Pick-ups Two Dean Silver Rail and Mini Silver Rail pick-ups

Type Hollow body electric
Body & neck Maple body, set neck
Fingerboard Rosewood
Pick-ups Two custom DeArmond single-coil pick-ups

Although Dean guitars are traditionally associated with aggressive "metal" imagery, this is not the case with the Tonic S, a comparative demure wallflower from 2001. This South Korean-made guitar is made of a lightweight solid mahogany and is milled to create a two-tier effect. It comes well equipped, with two American Dean "Silver Rail" humbucker pick-ups (one of them a Mini), Grover tuners, and a Tune-o-matic-style bridge. Plugged into the right amp, the five-position pick-up selector switch can offer a range of sounds from those of a Tele and a Strat to that of a Les Paul, with an output level that enables clean, rich tones to grinding crunch and more.

Despite these undoubted merits and retailing at around $300 it was not a big hit, and within two years of its short run it could be found for not much more than a third of that price. Its unappealing looks didn't help. In copper/black, it was not too unpleasant, but pretty much everyone agreed the creme/red color option shown here was awful. **GD**

Jimmy D'Aquisto was considered by many the world's greatest archtop guitar maker from the late 1960s until his death in 1995. In 1984, Fender commissioned him to produce the D'Aquisto Elite, a hollow body archtop with a laminated maple body, spruce top, and traditional headstock. This was followed by a Standard model, and finally by the top-of-the-line Ultras, hand-built (only thirty were ever made), with optional floating pick-ups, solid-maple bodies, and spruce tops. It was in honor of this series of classic, highly sought-after instruments that Fender introduced its D'Aquisto Classic Rocker in 2001.

Made by Samick in Korea by craftsmen trained by U.S. master luthier Bill Comins, the 2001 Rockers are, of course, not meant to compare to the originals, and the addition of the D'Aquisto name might seem to some just a blatant example of "branding." Nevertheless with their checkerboard, multi-bound tops, inlaid fingerboards, and set three-piece figured maple necks, they come close enough for most. **BS**

Fender Squier Double Fat Telecaster Deluxe 2001

Fylde Single Malt 2001

Type Solidbody electric
Body & neck Mahogany body and neck
Fingerboard Rosewood
Pick-ups Two humbucker pick-ups

Type Dreadnought acoustic
Body & neck Pine/oak body, pine neck
Fingerboard Oak
Other key features Woods from whisky distilleries

Although Fender had been producing its budget "Lead" series guitars in the United States since the late 1970s, until the introduction of the first Japanese-manufactured Squier guitars, there had never been inexpensive versions of the classic Telecasters and Stratocasters. Fender had owned the Squier name since 1965, but it was not until 1982 that it decided to revive it for its first Far Eastern-manufactured guitars—partly in response to Japanese companies that were playing fast and loose with its designs. The first Squier Telecaster was introduced in 1982, and there have since been around twenty permutations.

The Double Fat Telecaster Deluxe was made between 2001 and 2003, by which time production had moved to the enormous Cor-Tek factory in Korea. The design featured a carved top, which immediately set it apart from a standard Tele, and it had a pair of humbuckers instead of the usual single-coil pick-ups—hence the "double fat" moniker. Many players felt that it sounded and handled like a Les Paul. **AJ**

Makers of custom guitars, mandolins, bouzoukis, and citterns, Fylde Guitars has its workshops in Penrith, in the Lake District of northern England. Its founder, Roger Bucknall, took a degree in engineering before a hobby of making guitars became a passion that drove him to found his own company in 1973. Bucknall's past and present clients include some of the greatest acoustic guitarists of the last fifty years.

Fylde Guitars' quirky combination of unique, and not always widely available, materials can limit the size of its guitars, but such restrictions did not apply in the case of this jumbo-sized, pinched-waist dreadnought.

Now it is offered as a smaller, almost vintage, Martin-styled, parlor-sized instrument known as the Ariel Single Malt—part of an eclectic range of guitars that take their names from characters in Shakespeare plays (in this case, *The Tempest*). The pattern on the soundboard pine of the Single Malt model comes from forty years' immersion in hot alcohol; that on the oak comes from scorching and seasoning. **GD**

PRS
Santana SE 2001

Type Solidbody electric
Body & neck Mahogany body, set neck
Fingerboard Rosewood
Pick-ups Two humbucker pick-ups

It took many failed attempts, and the greater part of twenty-five years, but finally PRS came up with an affordable guitar that outsold all its direct rivals—the SE (Student Edition), designed in the United States, but manufactured in one of South Korea's top guitar-making facilities.

PRS introduced the range with the plain-looking Santana SE in 2001. Its flat-topped shape was close to the original PRS outline, and featured dual, covered humbucker pick-ups, a Korean version of the stoptail, and, of course, the 25-in. (63.5-cm) scale length,

"Paul makes guitars with great consistency … from his most expensive custom models to the lowest-priced SE model."

CARLOS SANTANA

together with the three-on-a-side PRS headstock. Anecdotally, Paul Reed Smith himself was concerned that these SE guitars would undercut his own U.S.-built starter models. Consequently, no PRS logo appeared on the first version.

The same guitar was spruced up a year later, and featured the PRS block logo on the truss rod cover as well as a pickguard, vibrato option, and dual, uncovered, Korean-made SE humbucker pick-ups. An SE version of the Tremonti Model followed in 2003, and, as the decade progressed, maple tops and bird inlays were added to the burgeoning range that today includes numerous signature models, including Good Charlotte's Billy Martin, and ex-Whitesnake member Bernie Marsden's models. **DB**

PRS
Tremonti 2001

Type Solidbody electric
Body & neck Mahogany with maple top, set neck
Fingerboard Rosewood
Pick-ups Two humbucker pick-ups

There was little doubt that this solidbody was inspired by Gibson's classic Les Paul. Initially, PRS even used an advert promoting the guitar with a picture of ex-Gibson President Ted McCarty, and a strapline reading: "Ted McCarty introduced the single cutaway guitar in 1952. We learned a lot from Ted while we were working on ours."

It quickly prompted only the second-ever PRS signature instrument—the Tremonti Model, produced in honor of Creed's guitarist, Mark Tremonti. It was identical to the standard model, except for a twelve-fret inlay and different pick-ups.

The Singlecut gave PRS a new shape, and a new signature artist, but it landed them in court. Gibson started legal proceedings immediately after the guitar was launched and, in 2004, PRS was prevented from manufacturing the instrument. After appeal, the court decision was reversed, and the "notorious" Singlecut started shipping again in early 2006.

According to Paul Reed Smith, there were "about thirty differences" between a PRS Singlecut and a Les Paul, including the 25-in. (63.5-cm) scale length and the one-piece stoptail bridge. "The body outline is different in six places," he added. "It's not a Les Paul—it's one of our guitars. Anyone who thinks they're buying a Les Paul . . . well, they're not." **DB**

Mark Tremonti's signature PRS sound features extensively on Creed's third album, *Weathered* (2001). He also plays the instrument, in company with fellow PRS endorser Myles Kennedy, on Alter Bridge's double CD/DVD release *Live From Amsterdam* (2010).

Rainsong
Black Ice 2001

Warmoth
Gecko Bass 2001

Type Steel-string acoustic
Body & neck Graphite body and neck
Fingerboard Graphite
Pick-ups Fishman Prefix Plus-T

Type Solidbody bass guitar
Body & neck Customer defined
Fingerboard Customer defined
Pick-ups Customer defined

The Black Ice was the world's first all-graphite guitar. Even the fretboard and bridge were graphite (although the frets and tuners are still nickel).

Why graphite? (It's not the stuff from lead pencils, but carbon fiber.) Rainsong says that this material is lightweight, impervious to changes in humidity and temperature, that it won't warp or crack and, unlike wood, supplies uniform strength and stiffness. There's no bracing needed under the soundboard, resulting in greater volume, and a cleaner tone. Some models feature a truss rod, not to rectify twisting, but to allow players to customize the neck angle.

The range includes dreadnought, jumbo, and electroacoustic, single cutaway models with Fishman electronics. They are all high-end guitars with prices over $2,000, and feature individual sound hole decorations, making each guitar unique.

Rainsong claims that the guitars have such stable tuning that they are shipped from the factory in concert pitch and arrive still in tune. **SH**

Warmoth is perhaps the best-known supplier of high-end guitar parts. Customers are given an almost endless list of components, from which the practically minded guitarist can build an extremely high-quality instrument at a relatively low cost, and without having to master the traditional skills of the luthier.

Although the bulk of Warmoth's business is in the reproduction of classic Fender and Gibson designs, the fabulous Gecko bass is a wholly original creation. Available with five or six strings, its twin cutaway has an attractive, overextended bass horn. The fingerboard features a neatly inlaid lizard image—it may not be quite up to the level of a PRS Dragon, but it's classy and distinctive nonetheless.

Since the choice of woods and number of pick-up configurations is almost endless, there is no Gecko "sound" as such, so—and this is part of its appeal—it can be whatever you want it to be. And for anyone confident with a screwdriver and soldering iron, this must surely be an extremely attractive prospect. **TB**

Warr
Trey Gunn 2001

Art & Lutherie
AA85 2002

Type Double-handed tapping instrument
Body & neck Mahogany/maple/walnut body and neck
Fingerboard Wenge
Pick-ups Two Warr custom pick-ups

Type Dreadnought acoustic
Body & neck Cedar/wild cherry body, maple neck
Fingerboard Rosewood
Pick-ups Green antique burst finish, Godin transducer

Both leading manufacturers of double-handed tapping instruments have their own star players: the Chapman Stick has Tony Levin, and Warr has Trey Gunn. While Mark Warr, founder of Warr Guitars, may find it irksome always to be bracketed with the older, more established, Chapman, such comparisons are difficult to avoid when you consider that both Levin and Gunn fulfilled the same bass-end role in British prog rock legends King Crimson.

Gunn and Warr collaborated closely on the design of this signature model, and paid particular attention to the weight/tone formula. According to Gunn: "One of the main things we've been trying to do . . . is to bring the weight down. However, when you lower the weight, you lose the mass of the body, which changes the tone. The current instrument I'm playing is the best possible compromise."

Unsurprisingly, these beautiful instruments don't come cheap. The top-of-the-line model will leave you with only a handful of change from $5,000. **TB**

No one seems to have anything bad to say about Art & Lutherie guitars, which are good-quality, affordable instruments with the bonus that they are made by a company with a sustainability ethos: ninety-five per cent of the wood it uses comes from previously fallen trees in Canadian forests.

The AA85, in an eye-catching green antique burst finish, is from a line of acoustic guitars that includes classic parlor (the Amis), OM (the Folks), and six- and twelve-string dreadnought models, with or without cutaways. Players lavish particular praise on the dreadnoughts' earthy, rich, and woody "old-time" sound, and their easy playability.

Art & Lutherie—a brand of Godin Guitars—is based in Princeville, Quebec. It was started in the 1980s by Robert Godin, who still designs most of its wide range of traditionally styled electric, archtop, acoustic, and classical models. These are spread over several brands, and manufactured in six locations—five in Quebec, and one in New Hampshire. **GD**

Ayers
ACSM-E 2002

Type Acoustic guitar
Body & neck Mahogany/spruce body, mahogany neck
Fingerboard Rosewood
Pick-ups One Fishman Prefix pick-up

Growing up in the 1960s and 1970s, Huang Chengfa always wanted a guitar like one of those played by the Western groups he idolized, particularly The Beatles and The Eagles, but, like most of his Vietnamese compatriots at that time, he soon found that such instruments were either unobtainable or unaffordable, mainly because of the Vietnam War that devastated the country until 1975.

By the late 1980s, peace was restored, and Huang had started producing budget guitars. The success of this early foray into the market inspired him, in 1996, to found a company, which he named Ayers in honor of the advice and technical assistance he had received from Australian luthier Gerard Gilet—Ayers Rock (Uluru) is Australia's most famous natural wonder.

Ayers began mass production in 1999, and later shared its factory in Bien Hoa, near Ho Chi Minh City, with the now defunct Baden Guitars. Perhaps surprisingly for a Vietnamese company, Ayers has always made all its guitars by hand, rather than on CNC (Computer Numerical Control) machinery.

Today, Ayers uses a numerical system to classify its models, but the ACSM was named for its most important characteristics: "A" for auditorium shape; "C" for cutaway; "S" for spruce top; "M" for mahogany; and "E" to signify an electro model. **RL**

Currently, Ayers' highest-profile endorsee is Kansas fingerstyle guitarist Andy McKee, a YouTube sensation with 45 million hits and counting for his technically astounding composition "Drifting." On CD, McKee's strongest album to date is *Joyland* (2010).

Gibson Les Paul Duane Allman 2002

Type Solidbody electric
Body & neck Mahogany/maple body, mahogany neck
Fingerboard Rosewood
Pick-ups Two Gibson humbucker pick-ups

Some of rock 'n' roll's greatest guitarists are also those whose lives were taken far too soon by tragedy. Southern rock and slide guitar icon Howard Duane Allman lost his life in a motorcycle crash in 1971 at only twenty-four years of age, but the legacy of his music remains timeless. And just over thirty years after his death, Gibson decided to honor one of its greatest players by dedicating this guitar to his memory.

Allman owned three key Les Pauls during his career: a 1957 Goldtop, a 1958 cherry sunburst model, and the 1959 tobacco sunburst (a.k.a. the Darkburst) guitar he acquired just a few months before he died. It's the Darkburst on which this ultra-limited edition model is closely based.

Gibson went to remarkable lengths to replicate Allman's guitar: the stunning, "gullwing," flame maple top was so difficult to source that it took the company two years to complete the production run.

To justify the list price of nearly $14,000, Gibson went further still. The original had "Duane" spelled out in fretwire on the back—an addition that had been made several years after Allman's death by the guitarist's loyal friend and road manager, Twiggs Lyndon. Gibson also included this unusual feature on their first run of fifty-five replica models, which were aged by the Custom Shop's Tom Murphy. **RL**

The Les Paul that Gibson chose to replicate was not the guitar that Duane played on the Allman Brothers' classic live album *At Fillmore East* (1971)—he used the 1958 Les Paul. However, the Darkburst does feature on his final album with the band, *Eat A Peach* (1972).

Gretsch 6144 Spectra Sonic Baritone 2002

Type Solidbody electric baritone
Body & neck Alder/spruce body, maple neck
Fingerboard African padauk
Pick-ups Two custom TV Jones humbucker pick-ups

Most modern Gretschs seem to be close copies of guitars built in the 1950s and 1960s. Among significant exceptions are the Spectra Sonic C Melody Lead, Baritone, and Bass models, offered from 2002 to 2005. These three distinctly different Gretsch guitars were designed by Gretsch fanatic, Tom "TV" Jones—known for his own outstanding Gretsch-style pick-ups—in conjunction with Gretsch and Brian Setzer's guitar tech, Rich Modica.

Early models were made in the United States by Hamer Guitars, but the majority were built in Japan, like the standard, modern-day Gretsch instruments.

The Spectra Sonic is easily identified by its archtop-sized 15¼ in. (38.7 cm)-wide body, although it has a flat, laminated spruce top, and the alder body is chambered, though of standard solidbody depth at 1.875 in. (4.75 cm). The neck is a three-piece laminate (maple on the Baritone, mahogany on the Lead), and the fingerboard, unusually, is African padauk. A Bigsby vibrato was standard on both the Lead and the Baritone. All three Spectra Sonics featured an outsized pickguard—white on the black body finish.

The C Melody Baritone was tuned, low to high, C, F, B♭, E♭, G, C. It featured a longer, 29¼-in. (74.3-cm) scale length to support this lower tuning, and a Bigsby B-11 vibrato. The Lead had a 24¾-in. (62.8-cm) scale, and sported a Bigsby B-12. All three models used TV Jones pick-ups, controlled by master volume and tone, and a shoulder-mounted three-way toggle switch.

After Gretsch stopped production of these instruments, TV Jones continued to build Spectra Sonic Lead and Baritone guitars. **DB**

Ibanez
JS2000 2002

Type Solidbody electric
Body & neck Basswood body, maple neck
Fingerboard Rosewood
Pick-ups Two DiMarzio humbucker pick-ups

Setting aside for the moment all issues of quality, one of the reasons that Ibanez enjoys such a reputation in the modern guitar world is that the Japanese giant was able to secure the services as endorsees of two of the biggest names in late-twentieth-century guitar pyrotechnics. By the end of the 1980s, both Steve Vai and Joe Satriani had their own highly regarded ranges of signature Superstrats: Vai's Jem and seven-string Universe, and Satriani's "JS" range.

Although Joe Satriani emerged on the rock scene after Steve Vai, Satriani had previously been the young

> *"It took quite a long time … I took the guitars on tour, bring 'em back and say, this is a problem, that is a problem …"*
>
> **JOE SATRIANI**

Vai's tutor. Indeed, before he made it as a player in his own right, Satriani could count among his students Kirk Hammett of Metallica, David Bryson of Counting Crows, Larry LaLonde of Primus, and Charlie Hunter.

The first JS guitars appeared in 1988, and were essentially a continuation of the earlier Radius line, with Satriani-approved DiMarzio pick-ups installed. The JS-2000 shown here was the fifth in the series of hard-tailed JS models, and another fine example of an Ibanez Japanese-built Superstrat. The body was cut from basswood, a lightweight wood that divides opinion in some guitar circles for its tone and lack of durability. The sound comes courtesy of a pair of DiMarzios—a PAF for the neck, and a FRED for the bridge. The JS2000 was discontinued after 2004. **TB**

Yamaha
SLG 2002

Type Silent guitar
Body & neck Composite maple body, mahogany neck
Fingerboard Rosewood
Pick-ups Two pick-ups

Something of a modern-day cult instrument, the Yamaha Silent Guitar is an acoustically "silent" steel- and nylon-string guitar that players can hook up to a pair of headphones and practice without annoying family and neighbors. It achieves its silence by dispensing with the part of the acoustic guitar that projects volume—the body. But to give the guitarist the experience of playing a "real" guitar, the neck is fixed to a sleek, lightweight, composite frame contoured like a conventional guitar; thus the invisible body can still be held just like any other acoustic guitar. It also acts as a very effective travel guitar, since when you've finished playing the whole thing dismantles and fits into a compact gig bag.

These instruments look cool and produce a surprisingly rich tone through the use of custom-designed pick-up systems by LR Baggs and B-Band and smooth-sounding, built-in Yamaha digital reverbs. The SLG1000 models (suffixed with "S" for steel string and "N" for nylon) are also very comfortable to play, with a low action and wide bridge spacing.

Other onboard features include an auxiliary input that lets you plug in an external CD or MP3 player to allow you to jam in private. The EQ is basic but efficient, and the effects are usable, especially the two reverbs and the echo.

Curiously, because the SLGs looked so cool and, having no soundboard, didn't feed back when amplified, they started to turn up on stage. They have become popular with such notables as Brian May, Lee Ritenour, and the Mexican duo Rodrigo y Gabriela. **TB**

Epiphone
Airscreamer 2003

Type Solidbody electric
Body & neck Mahogany body, maple neck
Fingerboard Rosewood
Pick-ups Two EMG humbucker pick-ups

The Airscreamer is a signature model Epiphone for The Trailer Park Troubadours. The brainchild of country/rockabilly guitarist and singer Antsy McClain, The Troubadours' live show revolves around a fictional trailer park called Pine View Heights inspired by McClain's real-life upbringing when his father was a truck driver and his mother was an Avon lady. The Troubadours' songs include "Living in Aluminum" and "Aunt Beula's Roadkill Overcoat."

The design of this guitar is officially licensed from the Airstream company, which has been making an

> *"The perfect convergence of a guitar, a band, and a vehicle … A home on wheels has never sounded so good."*

JIM "EPI" ROSENBERG, PRESIDENT OF EPIPHONE

instantly recognizable brand of shiny aluminum recreational vehicles since the 1930s. Its first models were created by William Hawley Bowlus, who is best known as the Superintendent of Construction on Charles Lindbergh's aircraft, the *Spirit of St. Louis*. The Airscreamer guitar is based on the compact 1961 Airstream Bambi 422, which became a design classic. There's one in the permanent collection of the Museum of Modern Art in New York.

The "aluminum color" finish on the mahogany body doesn't quite capture the bullet-like metallic look of the Bambi, although the hardware is all chrome-plated. The controls are minimal—there's just a volume knob, which is the hubcap, and this doubles as a push/pull control for pick-up selection. **AJ**

Martin
LX1E 2003

Type Three-quarter-scale steel-string acoustic
Body & neck Mahogany body, maple neck
Fingerboard Rosewood
Pick-ups Fishman Isys T pick-up system

Affectionately known as the "Little Martin," the LX1 is the smallest conventional guitar in Martin's modern range. A three-quarter-size travel guitar with a rosewood fingerboard, it shares many construction features, such as the bracing, with its full-size siblings. However, with the exception of the solid spruce top, the mahogany HPL (High Pressure Laminate) used for the body and side of the guitar—in effect, a three-ply laminate of wood veneers—would certainly not grace one of the company's $3,000 instruments.

Anyone expecting the rich sonority of an OOO-28 will be disappointed, but you do get an even tone, with a surprisingly robust bass, and a projection volume that might not be expected on a guitar of this size. Above all, the LX1 is fun to play—which is important for a guitar aimed at student players.

For an extra $50 you can get the LX1E—an LX1 with a useful, inbuilt, Fishman Isys T pick-up system.

The Little Martin is probably the most popular upmarket, three-quarter-scale, steel-string guitar; most buyers' shortlists feature this and the Baby Taylor, though, in truth, there is probably little to choose between the two.

Although the instrument was never intended for professional, gigging musicians, Ed Sheeran performs on stage accompanied only by his trusty LX1E. **TB**

The debut album of English singer–songwriter Ed Sheeran, + (2011), has garnered huge critical acclaim, earning him a Brit Award and multi-platinum sales. In 2013 he received a Grammy nomination for his song "The A Team."

Ed Sheeran with his three-quarter-size Martin. →

Rayco Weissenborn-style 2003

Type Lap steel guitar
Body & neck Koa body and neck
Fingerboard Rosewood
Other key features X-braced, Waverly tuners; steel saddle

Deep in the Canadian wilderness, the small town of Smithers in northern British Columbia—where luthiers Mark Thibeault and Jason Friesen of Rayco Resophonic have been making guitars since 2002—seems a far cry from the swaying palms of the Pacific, yet Hawaiian guitars have a history in northwestern North America that dates back to their first appearance at the Lewis and Clark Exposition in Portland, Oregon, in 1905.

Rayco's first Hawaiian guitar was made for Scott Atchinson, who played in the Smithers bluegrass group Hungry Hill, which was fronted by Jenny Lester, and in which Thibeault himself played Resophonic guitars.

Weissenborn-style Hawaiian guitars are as wonderful as the 1920s' originals. Already very light in construction, a bigger sound was achieved by thinning down the bridge and fingerboard to make the top more responsive, along with a lighter satin finish to make them even more resonant. To hear their rich, woody, earthy sound, full of sustaining resonance, can be a mesmerizing experience. **GD**

Santa Cruz PJ Parlor Size 2003

Type Parlor-style acoustic
Body & neck Spruce/rosewood body, mahogany neck
Fingerboard Ebony
Other key features Lower bout 12⅓ in. (31.4 cm)

This instrument, from Richard Hoover's Santa Cruz Guitar Company, closely follows the style and tradition of the great luthiers of the late nineteenth and early twentieth centuries, and is constructed with comparably meticulous care.

Santa Cruz offers a range of dreadnoughts, OM, and OOO models that hark back to that period. Some of its small-bodied guitars, including this PJ parlor-style, look back even further, to the guitars that C.F. Martin made in the 1850s. Contemporary design techniques, and optimized bracing and top construction make for a strong, well-balanced sound with the projection that twenty-first century players require. Of course, the original Martins, strung as they were with gut strings, were in a totally different sound world. The short, 24-in. (61-cm) scale, and V-neck make this instrument much easier to play. To achieve consistent and superior tonal properties, Santa Cruz employs dovetail-jointed necks, and the techniques of violin luthiers to hand-voice and tune its instruments. **GD**

Squier Showmaster HSS Jason Ellis 2003

Status Buzzard Bass 2003

Type Solidbody electric
Body & neck Alder body, maple neck
Fingerboard Rosewood
Pick-ups One humbucker and one single-coil pick-up

Type Graphite bass
Body & neck Graphite body and neck
Fingerboard Phenolic
Pick-ups Two Status Hyperactive pick-ups

Introduced in 1998, the Showmaster was one of Squier's own "Superstrats." It featured a carved top with no scratchplate, twenty-four frets, and various permutations of bridge and pick-ups—"HSS" denotes a combination of a humbucker bridge pick-up (in the case of this signature model, a "Duncan Designed Detonator"), and a single-coil at the neck. The Chinese-made Squier Showmaster retailed for $499.

This Jason Ellis model also has a deeply recessed Floyd Rose double-locking tremolo. Jason Ellis, originally from Melbourne, Australia, is a radio host and former professional skateboarder—the symbol on his signature guitar is that of the Red Dragon skateboard team. Ellis has also appeared in several films, raced trucks, and written the best-selling autobiography, *I'm Awesome: One Man's Triumphant Quest To Become The Sweetest Dude Ever* (2012). He was also the singer with the comedy metal band, Taintstick, until 2012, when he announced the formation of a new band, called Death! Death! Die! **AJ**

Although it may look like the signature bass of a heavy metaller, the bold Buzzard shape was actually designed by John Entwistle, bassist of The Who. The model would pass through the workshops of three separate brands during the latter stage of his career.

The original Buzzard was designed by Warwick in 1985, with prototypes and early models made in wood. But Entwistle was keen to use a different material, and approached Modulus, a U.S. company specializing in basses with necks made of carbon fiber, which, unlike wood, was not prone to excess bowing.

Modulus made two graphite Buzzards for Entwistle, then six graphite necks to be used on his Warwick-made basses. But in 1996, the Buzzard design took flight again, this time to English maker Status.

This Buzzard was a full, one-piece graphite affair, with a basketweave design. According to Status founder, Rob Green, it took three attempts to get the mold right. The side LED lights on the twenty-six-fret neck of this version complete a striking package. **RL**

Taylor
RNSM 2003

Type Steel-string guitar
Body & neck Indian maple back and sides, Sitka spruce top, hard rock maple neck
Fingerboard Ebony

Founded in 1974 by luthier Bob Taylor, and based in El Cajon, California, Taylor guitars became firmly established over the following twenty years among the most prestigious, large-scale producers of steel-string acoustic guitars. The company grew steadily over the period, eventually running two production plants, and employing more than 500 staff.

Although even the most modest Taylor guitars could hardly be described as cheap, the brand is often seen as a more affordable alternative to a Martin, which is widely perceived as the benchmark for a flat-top acoustic guitar.

Like most major guitar companies, Taylor made judicious use of celebrity endorsement as a marketing tool. The Taylor RNSM was a signature model created for Rick Nielsen of Cheap Trick, whose hits include "I Want You To Want Me" (1977), and whose penchant was for the most absurd five-necked guitars.

However, there is nothing ridiculous about this model. With a single cutaway, it was available for a limited run, both in the exotic, rich green finish shown here, and in black, and with a beautifully inlaid "breakaway chequerboard" fingerboard.

The top of the guitar is made from solid Sitka spruce, and the back and sides are carved from big-leaf maple. The neck is hard rock maple. The tuners are gold Grovers. There are twenty frets, and scalloped X-bracing on the top. Among other notable features is the Taylor Expression System, which has been acclaimed for its unparalleled reliability, and its capacity to provide the most natural amplified sound possible. **TB**

← Rick Nielsen performing with his Taylor RNSM in 2004.

Taylor Sambora Double-Neck 2003

Type Acoustic six- and twelve-string
Body & neck Koa body and neck
Fingerboard Rosewood
Pick-ups Two piezo pick-ups

Double-neck guitars are often listed as one of rock 'n' roll's vices, but, unlike some of the medium's other excesses, they are, at least, rooted in the practical needs of bringing studio sounds to the live stage—often for one key song. For Jimmy Page, that song was "Stairway To Heaven"; for Don Felder, it is "Hotel California"; for Richie Sambora, it is "Wanted Dead Or Alive."

The Bon Jovi guitarist originally used a custom-made Ovation to deliver his favorite song from *Slippery When Wet* (1986). As the piece required a switch between six- and twelve-string acoustics before

> *"All of a sudden, the wind and the low keyboard comes in and you feel like you're in a Western town somewhere."*
>
> RICHIE SAMBORA, 1986

moving on to an electric six-string, Ovation built Sambora a custom double-neck for the first half of the song. The guitarist then convinced them to produce a triple-neck version, so that he did not have to switch to a separate electric for the latter part of the song. However, this was a step too far.

After the RSSM—the limited-edition, Sambora signature, six-string, koa model—Taylor built a custom double-neck version for live performances of "Wanted," with, unusually, the six-string rather than the twelve-string on the top. It remains one of only two double-necks Taylor ever made: the two are interchangeable; one stays at company HQ, while the other goes on the road with Richie; when the latter needs resetting, he swaps it for the other one. **RL**

Richie Sambora with his unusual double-neck Taylor acoustic. ➔

Teuffel
Niwa 2003

Type Solidbody electric
Body & neck Alder body and neck
Fingerboard Rosewood
Pick-ups One single-coil and two split-single-coil pick-ups

American red alder, claims luthier Ulrich Teuffel, is a great tonewood that was responsible for Jimi Hendrix's sound. So that is what the whole Niwa guitar—body and neck—is made of.

There's even an alder "control box" mounted on the top of the guitar, with a resonant, spherical cover. The volume, tone, and five-way rotary selector are all disks of rosewood.

It's this sort of innovation and downright eccentricity that sets Teuffel's guitars apart. The use of alder in the neck flies in the face of conventional wisdom that the wood is not stiff enough for the purpose. But Teuffel surmounted this obstacle by reinforcing the basic material with maple inserts, and adding a double-action truss rod made of hardened stainless steel. He then secured it to a matching, rounded pocket in the body with three hand-polished, precision steel screws.

Throughout this unique guitar, the level of detail is staggering: note, in particular, the two-tone side-position fret markers—black for light conditions, phosphorescent green for playing in the dark—and the nut, which includes rubber-damped rollers to prevent snagging strings.

In such a context, you might expect the pick-ups to be special, too, and you would be right to do so. Not only are they covered in rosewood, but those on the neck and the middle units are split-coil, with half the pick-up aimed at the bass strings, and the other half directed at the treble. Both halves are separately wound. The bridge pick-up is hotter, with its own custom winding pattern. **SH**

Cole Clark
Violap 2004

Type Hollow body acoustic or semiacoustic lap steel
Body & neck Bunya wood body and neck
Fingerboard Rosewood
Pick-ups One Cole Clark Horseshoe replica single-coil pick-up

A former employee of the Maton Musical Instruments Company, Cole Clark has been making guitars in Australia since the late 1990s. He specializes in the use of indigenous wood such as bunya pine, which is a stronger alternative to spruce.

Like a lot of modern lap steel guitars, the Violap is inspired by instruments produced by Hermann Weissenborn in Los Angeles in the 1920s and 1930s, which, with their cello-shaped bodies and hollow necks, are now the stuff of lap steel legend.

The two main varieties of Violap are acoustic (VL) and semiacoustic (VL2P). The former have arched tops that float above the support timber running from the neck to the bottom on the acoustic model; the latter have fixed tops. The electric version has various possible pick-up combinations including a single-coil Cole Clark horseshoe, twin humbuckers, and a dual-output preamp.

Cole Clark is particularly proud of the use of bunya in the instrument, pointing out that locally sourced materials are environmentally friendly and also that, while spruce takes several hundred years to reach a useful size for soundboard construction, bunya only takes about seventy. But if you really hate bunya, the body of the guitar can be made out of blackwood, Queensland maple, or silver quandong. **AJ**

Lap steel and dobro player Jerry Douglas uses a Cole Clark Violap on *Secret, Profane & Sugarcane* (2009), the celebrated album in which Elvis Costello crosses over from the punk/new wave in which he made his name into bluegrass and country music.

Fender "Crash-3" Stratocaster 2004

Type Solidbody electric
Body & neck Alder body, maple top
Fingerboard Rosewood
Pick-ups Three single-coil pick-ups

"Crash" is John Matos, a graffiti artist who began his career painting on subway trains in New York at the age of thirteen. In 1997, he met Eric Clapton, who was in New York filming street murals for a video, and wanted someone to show him the underground sights of the city. Clapton suggested that Crash should create some artwork using a Fender guitar.

Crash received his first Eric Clapton Signature Stratocaster in 1996. He later said: "Man, when I got it, it was so beautiful, I almost felt too intimidated to paint on it. But I did."

"The rips in the top of the body were to sort of replicate the aerodynamic designs on some of the … cars that Eric loves."

JOHN "CRASH" MATOS

The guitarist used the instrument on his 2001 tour, while the artist went on to create a total of five "Crashocasters." The most famous of these is "Crash-3," which Clapton used as his main stage instrument in 2004. This was later auctioned by Christie's in aid of Clapton's Crossroads drug and alcohol rehabilitation center in Antigua, and was sold for $321,100.

Of Crash-3, Crash has said: "I wanted to create a design that would be challenging—so that it could stand out alone in a corner or look really cool if someone was rocking it."

Fender subsequently commissioned another fifty graffiti-designed guitars for a limited edition "Crashocaster" line, and Crash also designed a line of Fender Telecasters with matching amplifiers. **AJ**

Fender "Skele Tele" Telecaster 2004

Type Solidbody electric
Body & neck Ash body, maple neck
Fingerboard Rosewood
Pick-ups Two single-coil pick-ups

There have always been those in search of a uniquely decorated guitar: the psychedelic era saw some famed personalized attempts by the likes of George Harrison, Jimi Hendrix, and Eric Clapton. One of the first major manufacturers to see the commercial value in this approach was Fender, who have combined high-end guitars built at their Custom Shop in California with the decorative skills of a number of fine artists, often skilled in the ways of the airbrush.

Taking this approach to the absolute limit, the Fender Custom "Skele Tele" Telecaster is a celebration of *Dia De Los Muertos*—"The Day Of The Dead"—a national holiday that takes place in Mexico on the first two days of November, where friends and family gather to remember those who have passed on. This Telecaster, which took six months to produce, has been "masterbuilt" by top Fender man Chris Fleming, and the ornate decoration designed by artist Kit Carson. All over the body you can see examples of hand-made sterling-silver skull overlays, many given semiprecious-stone eyeballs. Similarly, the fingerboard is adorned with beautifully ornate inlays and eighteen-karat-gold, set-ruby side-dot markers. The "ashtray" cover, usually discarded by Telecaster owners, has been hand engraved, and there's even a red die in place of the usual pick-up selector switch. Other craftsmen have also been involved in the process—the paint job provided by Dan Lawrence, and the fabulous anodized etched pickguard by Ron Thorn. Turn the guitar over and the treats continue, with more skeletons, suitably somber graphics that declare "Tone To The Bone!" and a skull etched neatly onto the neck plate. **TB**

Gibson
Johnny A 2004

Type Hollow body electric
Body & neck Mahogany/maple body, mahogany neck
Fingerboard Ebony
Pick-ups Two Gibson 1957 classic humbucker pick-ups

When it comes to jaw-droppingly beautiful instruments, few can match Gibson's 2004 Johnny A. What hits you first is its gorgeous, golden honey-hued Sunset Glow finish, then, around it, the Art Deco flourishes, from the design of the pickguard to the mother-of-pearl inlays along the neck and headstock. Tone slots are bowed, the binding is a creamy-pale yellow, and the fret markers are faux tortoiseshell. Most striking of all is the retro-looking Bigsby which, once seen, should banish any thoughts of saving money by going for a stopbar tailpiece.

"With the Johnny A model, I … have the optimal guitar for my approach, so it's a perfect blend of style and instrument."
JOHNNY A

The guitarist for whom the instrument was named, Johnny A, fell in love with Gibsons as a teenager, playing Les Pauls, ES-295s, and Firebirds. In 2003, he noticed in the Gibson Custom shop in Nashville, Tennessee, a hollowed prototype hanging on the wall. The guitar wasn't slated for production, but Johnny A saw something in it that others had missed, and persuaded Gibson to reconsider. Thus he entered an exclusive fraternity—the Gibson Signature Club—alongside Les Paul, B.B. King, Chet Atkins, and Joe Perry.

The Johnny A—an archtop, with back and sides carved from a single piece of mahogany, a figured maple top, and a 25½-in. (64.75-cm) scale—was designed and sized to fit all the requirements of its signature owner. **BS**

Johnny Antonopoulos, known as "Johnny A," playing his signature guitar. ➔

Gibson
Les Paul Voodoo 2004

Type Solidbody electric
Body & neck Ash body, mahogany neck
Fingerboard Ebony
Pick-ups Two "Black Magic" humbucker pick-ups

A black, swamp ash body with red grains, an ebony fingerboard with a red skull inlaid at the fifth fret, and even the Gibson logo in red ... the Voodoo was clearly no ordinary Les Paul.

With this guitar, Gibson was trying to recapture the heavy metal guitar market. The lighter body, with more porous wood, and the "Black Magic" pick-ups (with red and black coils), produced a more raw sound, with piercing highs, and a twangier, clean bass.

Every detail on the Voodoo got the full juju treatment: black hardware, red numbers on the controls, and a red snakeskin case. Apart from the disconcerting red skull, there were no fret markings along the fingerboard.

However, the Voodoo did not cast as strong a spell as Gibson had hoped: the new breed of shredders regarded the traditional mahogany neck as fat, rather than fast, and the weight, while ten percent less than that of a standard Les Paul, was still considered excessive. **SH**

Gretsch 6128T
Duo Jet 2004

Type Solidbody electric
Body & neck Mahogany body and neck
Fingerboard Ebony
Pick-ups Two humbucker or single-coil pick-ups

Gretsch has been making the 6128 Duo Jet for around sixty years, and it remains one of its most sought-after guitars. Today, it comes in a variety of configurations—the current Gretsch catalog lists twenty-three different models.

The standard 6128T comes with two Filter'Tron humbucker pick-ups, and a Bigsby vibrato, but there are also single-coil and hardtail models. There are even double cutaway versions.

In 2011, Gretsch added a George Harrison tribute Duo Jet to the lineup—a limited edition replica of the all-black 1957 guitar that the Beatle called his "first real decent guitar."

Gretsch later passed through changes of ownership that caused design and build-quality issues. After the company was rescued in 2003 by Fender, Duo Jet production was switched to Japan. Thereafter, designs included one-piece necks, lighter bodies, and optional sparkle finishes. Most owners believe quality improved. Some say that it has never been better. **SH**

Ovation
CSE225 2004

PRS
513 2004

Type Double-neck electroacoustic
Body & neck Maple/Lyrachord body, nato neck
Fingerboard Rosewood
Pick-ups Two Ovation Slimline pick-ups

Type Solidbody electric
Body & neck Mahogany/maple body, rosewood neck
Fingerboard Rosewood
Pick-ups Five single-coil pick-ups

In the 1970s, the double-neck guitar was linked in the popular imagination with loud, smoke-filled, hockey arenas. But that lingering image obscures the fact that the flashy 6/12 configuration was a pragmatic solution to the problem of performing nuanced arrangements in a stadium setting.

Renowned for their advanced acoustics, Ovation has produced several double-necks, including this CSE225. Featuring a super-shallow version of the iconic Lyrachord bowl back, and a figured maple top in Transparent Blue or Ruby Red Burst, the CSE225 was an acoustic double-neck. (There was also a CSD225, with a cheaper, laminated top.) Among other highlights of the CSE225 were the acclaimed Ovation electronics—a Slimline pick-up and an onboard OP-24+ preamp—and three-way toggling to access either neck or both necks at once. Slim nato necks with aluminum channel cores were capped with bound-rosewood fingerboards, while the cutaways allowed access to the upper reaches of both 25-in. (63.5-cm) scales. **DP**

One of PRS's missions, from its first Custom in 1985 to the present day, has been to create the ultimate union of the Gibson humbucker and the Fender single-coil on a single guitar. On the eve of its twentieth anniversary, PRS unveiled the 513, which, through five single-coil pick-ups—arranged in dual-coil humbucking pairs at neck and bridge, and a lone single-coil in the middle position—offered thirteen distinct tones via a five-way lever pick-up selector, and another three-position lever selector offering "single-coil," "clear humbucking," and "heavy humbucking" modes.

Among the other ways in which the 513 was a variation on the usual PRS theme were a subtly different neck joint to enhance low-end, and a slightly angled "truly compensated" nut to improve intonation.

The original 513 featured a solid Brazilian rosewood neck and fingerboard (a mahogany neck version was added in 2007). This guitar, along with the 2004 Modern Eagle, represented the ultimate in PRS production-line quality. **DB**

Jackson
Kelly 2005

Type Solidbody electric
Body & neck Alder body, maple neck
Fingerboard Rosewood
Pick-ups Two Jackson CVR2 humbucker pick-ups

The guitars of Grover Jackson and Wayne Charvel have a special place in the history of rock and, particularly, of heavy metal. Jackson started designing and making guitars bearing the Charvel name in 1978—hot-rodded instruments for the flamboyant Southern Californian rock bands that sought to emulate Van Halen. After Randy Rhoads joined Ozzy Osbourne's band in 1979, Jackson set about designing increasingly extravagant guitars, which were built to a high quality and suited the virtuosic styles of metal. These instruments, from the Rhoads co-designed Concorde onward, carried Jackson's name.

The Kelly was the fruit of a collaboration with Bradford Kelly of Australian band Heaven, who were getting international recognition for combining AC/DC raunch with Judas Priest speed. The body and string-through design are inspired by the Gibson Explorer, but the Kelly is thinner, and made of lighter wood. The neck is bolted on high up, thus allowing easy access to the top frets. The Kelly has a full, two-octave fretboard suited to high-register screaming metal solos, and two powerful humbuckers. The simple electronics (volume and tone controls, and a three-way blade pick-up selector) cover sounds from heavy to face-melt. If ever there was a guitar built for metal, this is it. **JMB**

The reputation and popularity of the Jackson Kelly were greatly increased by Megadeth guitarist Marty Friedman, who had his own signature model, "The KE1," at the time of the release of the band's fourth studio album, *Rust In Peace* (1990).

Kremona
Orpheus Valley 2005

Type Acoustic classical/flamenco
Body & neck Spruce and silver oak body, cedar neck
Fingerboard Rosewood (Rosa Dive RD model)
Pick-ups One Fishman Classic 3 or Prefix Pro Blend pick-up

Since 1924, Kremona has been making stringed instruments in the Valley of Orpheus, which, they like to point out, "nestles between the vast Balkan and the Rodopi mountains of Bulgaria and is the mythological home to the Thracian father of songs, great poet (and dog trainer) of antiquity." The company was founded by Dimitar Georgiev, who had made his name designing machine guns, but, after seeing them used in the First World War, decided that he would rather build mandolins instead. These days Kremona employs 120 people and makes violin-family instruments as well as guitars.

The Orpheus Valley Guitar series features three variant forms. The Basic series are student models—these are available in a range of reduced scales suitable for small fingers. The Performer series are intended to be used at live concerts with electric bands—they have cutaways, and either a Fishman Classic 3 or a Prefix Pro Blend pick-up system; the Fiesta Cutaway F65CW-7S is a seven-string version. The Artist series is the premium range of classical and flamenco guitars—handmade by their most experienced luthiers out of a range of exotic tonewoods. The "Sofia," for instance, has a red cedar solid top, sapele back and sides, a mahogany neck, and a rosewood fingerboard. The machine heads are gold-plated with amber buttons. **AJ**

Roberto Corrias plays a Sofia model Orpheus Valley Guitar on his album *La Calle del Pintau* (2010). Born in Sardinia, Italy, Corrias is currently based in Sacramento, California; he teaches locally and performs with other distinguished musicians worldwide.

Lado
505-QS Bass 2005

Type Solidbody five-string bass guitar
Body & neck Maple/exotic woods body and neck
Fingerboard Ebony
Pick-ups Two EMG P Bass pick-ups

In 1987, Yugoslavian expatriate Joseph Kovacic entered the *Guinness Book Of World Records* for building the largest playable electric guitar: a veritable behemoth, measuring 14 ft. 3 in. (4.3 m) in length, and weighing 309 lb. (140 kg). Kovacic's real legacy, however, will be the electric and acoustic guitars and basses he has crafted under the Lado name at his shop in Ontario, Canada.

Among Kovacic's superbly crafted instruments is this 505-QS bass guitar. It is a five-string, built to order in a choice of ten exotic body woods, including ziricote, lacewood, bubinga, afromosia (a teak substitute), and curled walnut. The highly figured woods are beautifully accentuated by any of eight, stunning, transparent colors offered by Kovacic. The body, contoured on the backside, comprises two layers to produce a sort of "low-fat" version of Alembic's famous "hippie sandwich" construction.

The Lado 505-QS is outfitted with two soapbar EMG P Bass pick-ups, and two tone and two volume pots. A 34-in. (86.4-cm), "Fender scale," five-ply through-neck is capped with an ebony fingerboard, which features understated dot markers, and is topped with a 3 + 2 headstock.

It is the headstock that is always the most easily recognizable distinguishing feature of any Lado guitar. The front of it always bears the company name, along with the maker's personal emblem, an image of a falcon. The reverse side bears a unique serial number with the model name, together with the letters "CDN" or "CND," to indicate that the instrument is constructed in Canada. **DP**

Luna
Andromeda 2005

Type Solidbody electric
Body & neck Basswood body, maple neck
Fingerboard Rosewood
Pick-ups Two humbucker pick-ups

You'll notice someone playing an Andromeda guitar. They come with either a large phoenix or dragon design inlaid in abalone across a black gloss body or a guitar body painted purple or turquoise. This eye-catching styling comes courtesy of Yvonne de Villiers, a stained-glass artist turned guitar designer.

Yvonne grew up watching her mother, a pro bassist, struggle to handle guitars that were too big and heavy for her. They looked all wrong on a small figure. So she designed a range of instruments that are lightweight, sculpted for comfort, and styled with striking looks.

Florida-based Luna now sell basses, acoustics, ukeleles, mandolins, and banjos—but here we're looking solely at the solidbody electric Andromeda line.

The bass version shown here features a slim neck profile (described as "petite" by Luna), and deep double cutaways. One of the guitar's big selling points is that highly shaped body, which is carefully designed for comfortable playing. It's made of basswood for lightness, with a string-through system to help sustain. The Andromeda range is highly decorated too, with details including a crescent moon on the headstock, and inlaid fret markers following the phases of the moon—with a full moon at the twelfth fret.

These features have achieved exactly what they were intended to do—establish the Luna as one of the top choices of female guitarists. The company's artist roster includes India Arie, Vixen, and jazz player Jenni Alpert. And, indeed, the Luna has exceeded the maker's original expectations by becoming a favorite of many male players, too. **SH**

Ovation
NSB778 Elite T 2005

Type Electroacoustic bass
Body & neck Lyrachord/spruce body, neck unspecified
Fingerboard Ebony with pearl inlays
Pick-ups High-output bass with one preamp pick-up

Nikki Sixx, one of the founders of Mötley Crüe, isn't known for playing electroacoustic bass, but he approached Ovation to build him such an instrument for the band's 2005 Red White and Crüe tour, in which he was reunited with the other original Crüe members, Mick Mars, Tommy Lee, and Vince Neil.

The original NSB778 Elite T bass was a limited edition from the factory in New Hartford, Connecticut, where USA Ovation and Adamas instruments had been made since 1967. The single cutaway design featured a synthetic Lyrachord mid-depth bowl back and solid spruce top—with bass-side sound holes—hidden under a red flame or gray flame finish. The full 34-in. (86.4-cm) scale bass came with an ebony bridge and fingerboard, the latter inlaid with Iron Cross markers.

Ovation basses have always been rare birds. The first Ovation-branded bass, the Typhoon, appeared in the short-lived Electric Storm line (made between 1967 and 1969), a now very rare series of models, built in the style of the semi-solid Gibson ES-335, and intended to give Ovation some market presence until the new-fangled bowl-back electroacoustic guitars took off.

Once market leaders, Ovation and Adamas—owned, since 2008, by Fender Musical Instruments Corporation (FMIC)—have now been overtaken by the likes of Takamine, Taylor, and Martin. **DB**

Sixx used his Ovation bass on "Life Is Beautiful," the debut single by his band Sixx:A.M. The track also featured on the *The Heroin Diaries Soundtrack* (2007), a companion album to his autobiography, which told the harrowing story of his long-standing drug addictions.

Parker Maxxfly
DF842 2005

Type Solidbody electric
Body & neck Alder body, basswood/carbon-glass neck
Fingerboard Carbon-glass-epoxy composite
Pick-ups Two humbucker pick-ups

Luthier Ken Parker is most famous for developing the Parker Fly guitar with Larry Fishman during the 1990s. In many respects, the Maxxfly series tames the design wildness of the Fly. The very angular body of the Fly is smoothed off, especially the parts that might dig in to the guitarist's lower ribs. For those who might find the Fly a little too 1990s in its aesthetic, the Maxxfly is a typical twenty-first century design—innovative, but with some concessions to more traditional "S" shape, and the use of familiar, high-quality tonewoods.

The Maxxfly's neck humbucker is positioned to allow a twenty-four fret neck, which sports a characteristic Parker thin, rectangular headstock, and locking tuners. In addition to the pair of humbuckers, the Maxxfly has piezo string saddles, and an onboard preamp to capture the acoustic sound of the guitar. The guitar's electronics are designed for flexibility.

The various combinations of the magnetic humbuckers and piezo pick-ups can be selected with a three-position switch, together with three knobs (for magnetic volume, magnetic tone, and piezo volume). The magnetic tone control is push/pull, so that the player can switch out one of the coils in each of the humbuckers to create a single coil guitar. Finally, the output socket is a "smart" switching jack that can send out split stereo or summed mono.

Unsurprisingly, the Maxxfly appeals to virtuosic guitarists with eclectic styles: players who may need to switch from acoustic guitar simulations to mellow jazz tones to outright distortion in consecutive bars. Adrian Belew, Vernon Reid, and Larry Coryell are among the notable players of this instrument. **JMB**

Ritter
Raptor 2005

Squier Black and
Chrome 2005

Type Solidbody electric bass
Body & neck Mahogany body, maple neck
Fingerboard Maple
Pick-ups Two lightwave laserbucker pick-ups

Type Solidbody electric
Body & neck Agathis body, maple neck
Fingerboard Rosewood
Pick-ups Three single-coil pick-ups

Since the 1990s, master luthier Jens Ritter has produced between eighty and ninety instruments a year at his atelier—a seventeenth-century winery in Deidesheim, in the southern Rhineland of Germany. A byword for quality, Ritter has been described as "the German Stradivarius."

Ritter's unique guitar designs have attracted many famous customers, including Prince, George Benson, Grateful Dead's Phil Lesh, and musicians playing for Madonna, Christina Aguilera, and many others. The Metropolitan Museum of Art in New York City acquired one of his instruments to start itscollection of electric bass guitars.

The Raptor model shown here is supplied in four- or six-string versions, with Ritter BT tuners custom-made by Gotoh, a bolt-on, three-piece neck with a 36-in. (91.4-cm) scale, a hard maple fretboard, which can be fretted or unfretted, and a mahogany body. The pick-ups are lightwave laserbuckers in neck and bridge positions. **PP**

The list price of Squier's 2005 special edition Black and Chrome Stratocaster was $379.99, but you could pick one up online for $150 less. These guitars were mass-produced in South Korea, clearly without the attention to detail you might expect from the Fender Custom Shop in California. And yet, if you took the trouble to try out a few different ones, you might still have ended up with a quality guitar—certainly, one that sounded similar to the American version—even if the hardware was less refined and the wood less exotic.

The body of the Black and Chrome is made of Agathis—a straight-grained wood with a good strength-to-weight ratio—which resonates well, and is cheap to produce.

The guitar features a large, painted headstock, knurled chrome knobs, black plastic pick-up covers and switch tip, and a shiny chrome scratchplate, which is useful for catching spotlights. The standard Black and Chrome had three single-coil pick-ups, but there was also a "fat" version with a humbucker at the bridge. **AJ**

Suhr
Modern 2005

Type Solidbody electric
Body & neck Mahogany body and neck
Fingerboard Pau ferro
Pick-ups Two humbuckers and one single-coil pick-up

After looking at all the most popular twenty-four-fret, bolt-on neck guitars on the market, John Suhr wanted to offer something a little different, but still familiar, to those who have played this style of guitar for any length of time.

The Modern is a twenty-four-fret, bolt-on neck, solidbody guitar that comes in several colors and configurations. The addition of two frets altered the geometry of the body and the layout of the requisite cavities for the pick-ups. The result is a slightly asymmetrical body shape that gives good access to the high end of the neck, making it possible to hit a high E. The Modern is fitted with Sperzel locking machine heads, a Tusq nut, and jumbo ss frets.

In the neck position is a JST SSV humbucker, in the middle a JST FL single-coil, and at the bridge a JST SSV+ humbucker. There is single volume and tone control, with a five-way switch. The Bridge has 510 two-post solid saddles and steel block. Hardware is chrome-finished, with a side-position jack socket. **PP**

Taylor
T3/B 2005

Type Semi-hollow body
Body & neck Sapele and maple body, sapele neck
Fingerboard Ebony
Pick-ups Two Taylor HD humbucker pick-ups

The successor to Taylor's T5 and the Solidbody, the T3 comes in two varieties, which are almost identical, apart from the fact that the T3/B has a Bigsby vibrato tailpiece with a metal roller-style bridge that lets you bend the strings a long way without putting them out of tune. Running along the center of the semi-hollow body is a solid block of wood on which the figured maple top rests. The neck joint is unique to Taylor guitars—it works like a jigsaw puzzle piece that can't move when in place, allowing it to be securely attached with only a single bolt.

The humbuckers can be made to work like two pairs of single-coil pick-ups—this is operated by pulling up the volume knob—and the tone control has a mid-boost circuit that kicks in after the first two-thirds of its rotation, giving it a midrange peak that sounds a little like a wah-wah pedal that isn't quite open all the way. At the time of writing, the list price for a T3/B was $3,198, but it was available more cheaply through online retailers. **AJ**

Washburn Bootsy Collins Space Bass 2005

Type Solidbody bass guitar
Body & neck Mahogany and maple body, maple neck
Fingerboard Maple
Pick-ups Four humbucker pick-ups

Bootsy Collins was the bassist for James Brown and then Parliament-Funkadelic. This signature Washburn bass is consonant with his extravagant image and playing style, but would probably look incongruous on any other player.

Only 100 Space Basses were made, making them instant collectables: most of them are now no doubt safely stored away, rather than earning their keep on the live circuit. It's the crazy, star-shaped body that immediately identifies the Space Bass, of course, although it shouldn't be assumed that the instrument

"The deep thing is, every crazy thing I pulled I got away with because I could hold my own with my ax."

BOOTSY COLLINS

is merely a novelty: each of the four humbuckers has its own output, for a range of effects options. Its tone range is correspondingly wide and sensitive—an important feature, given that Bootsy's style ranges from subtle pizzicato to a full-blown string pop, delivered by pinching a string between thumb and forefinger before raising and dropping it. The bass is adorned with a rhinestone-encrusted, mirrored pickguard, star-shaped pearl inlays along the two-octave fingerboard, gold tuners and bridge, star-shaped controls, and a hard case in purest white, with yet more gold hardware and a cranberry-colored, crushed velvet interior. There's even a certificate of authenticity signed by the man himself. Few guitars so strikingly reflect their owners' personalities. **JM**

Byers
Classical 2006

Type Classical guitar
Body & neck Cedar/rosewood body, mahogany neck
Fingerboard Ebony
Other key features Lattice bracing, rosewood bridge

Gregory Byers found his true vocation after trying out architecture, pottery, ecology, and evolutionary biology. In 1981, he attended a guitar-making course by José Romanillos, and was later influenced by John Gilbert, before establishing himself as a luthier in 1984. On a continuous quest to improve the classical guitar's traditional capabilities, Byers produces only twelve guitars a year. Having started building classic fan-braced instruments, his guitars now feature an elevated fingerboard, a unique system of fine tuning the nut and bridge to improve intonation, and, crucially, his own lattice bracing system that preserves the tonal nuances of classic fan-bracing, while delivering better clarity, projection, sustain, consistency across strings and registers, and more robust-sounding basses. This bracing system features in this cedar top guitar from 2007.

Prominent among the guitarists who have played Byers instruments are David Russell, Ricardo Cobo, and David Tanenbaum. Byers would send Tanenbaum all his new guitars for comments and criticism. Tanenbaum's view is that "There's a real refinement to Byers' instruments, a wonderful, fine craftsmanship, and a beautiful sense of legato. They are incredibly musical instruments and they're very, very even across the range." **GD**

Grammy Award-winning soloist David Russell plays a guitar by Gregory Byers on this 2008 selection of compositions by the Spaniard Federico Moreno Torroba (1891–1982), one of the first and most prolific composers to write music for Andrés Segovia.

← David Tanenbaum is perhaps the most prominent admirer of Gregory Byers.

Campbell American
Transitone 2006

Type Solidbody electric
Body & neck Linden body, maple or mahogany neck
Fingerboard Ebony, rosewood, or maple
Pick-ups Three DiMarzio standard pick-ups

Founded in Blackstone Valley, Massachusetts, in 2002, Campbell American has since become one of the more established names in the "boutique" guitar world. The company's mission statement, according to founder Dean Campbell, is to "build guitars here in America using old New England craftsmanship."

Campbell American concentrates on a relatively small range of designs; its most popular model is the wonderfully retro Transitone shown here. This curiously shaped instrument owes little visually to the American classics on which most custom guitars are

"The Nelsonic Transitone is an extremely versatile guitar with a wide tonal palette. I'm thrilled to bits with it!"

BILL NELSON

based, excepting perhaps a very slight nod to the Gibson Firebird.

The advantages of a custom guitar from a high-end producer such as Campbell American are the quality of the build, and the fact that it can be tailored to the specific requirements of the player. As such, the Transitone can be ordered with more options than the "name" brands could ever hope to offer: the default body material is linden, but other tonewoods are available; the neck can be rock maple or mahogany; the fingerboard ebony, rosewood, or maple; and the pick-ups by DiMarzio, Seymour Duncan, Lollar, or TV Jones, to name but some of the choices on offer.

The model shown here is the Nelsonic Transitone, a signature guitar built for British guitarist Bill Nelson. **TB**

Gibson
Les Paul BFG 2006

Type Chambered electric six-string
Body & neck Mahogany/maple body, mahogany neck
Fingerboard Rosewood
Pick-ups One humbucker and one single-coil pick-up

It was touted as "the most powerful Les Paul ever made," so the BFG had a lot to live up to. It was presented as a stripped-down rock ax, with the familiar body shape and the 1950s' rounded mahogany neck just about the only standard things on board.

The electrics are definitely non-standard issue. The high-powered, Zebra Burstbucker 3 humbucker in the bridge, and the single-coil P-90 in the neck are controlled by three knobs—two for volume, and one for tone. The traditional pick-up selector toggle has been rewired as a kill switch—pick-up selection is

> *"Blasted back to the bare essentials, the BFG guitar is the Les Paul for guitarists who want a loud, raw, and wild sound."*
>
> 2007 GIBSON ADVERTISING

controlled by a mini-toggle at the volume knobs. Thus the BFG ends up with a distinctive sound that is quite different from all other Les Pauls.

How stripped down is the BFG? Well, in some ways it has really been left raw, but in others it is a little contrived. For example, there's no truss rod cover, and the maple top is left unsanded. The control knobs are wood, the toggles have no washers or caps, and the hardware is either distressed or gunmetal, including the Grover tuners. The rosewood fingerboard has no inlays—there are side-position marking dots only. All the finishes are trans, showing the grain of the wood clearly, and the back plate is see-through. The pick-ups have no surrounds—they are simply screwed to the body of the instrument. **SH**

Gibson
SG Goddess 2006

Gibson X-Plorer New
Century Black 2006

Type Solidbody electric
Body & neck Mahogany body and neck
Fingerboard Madagascar heather ebony
Pick-ups Two clear-covered humbucker pick-ups

Type Solidbody electric
Body & neck Mahogany body and neck
Fingerboard Ebony
Pick-ups Two ceramic magnet humbucker pick-ups

When Gibson unveiled the Goddess series, it claimed to be "focusing on the female performer," and "delivering high-end quality and tone in a slim, weight relieved [sic] design." Thin it undoubtedly was, but the new instrument's most practical concessions to the supposedly weaker sex were perhaps the accommodating 24¾-in. (62.9-cm) scale neck and the 1.625-in. (4.1-cm) nut.

Made in Nashville, Tennessee, the SG Goddess was offered in a choice of five colors: Iced Burst, Violet Burst, Rose Burst, Sky Burst, and Ebony, all finished with matching headstock logos. There was a twenty-two-fret ebony neck, with trapezoid mother-of-pearl inlays, as well as chrome-plated auto-trim tuners, wrap-around bridge, and top-hat volume and tone knobs.

Like her Les Paul sister, the SG Goddess featured a single set of pots to manipulate two humbuckers: Gibson's hot 498T Alnico at the neck, and a 490R Alnico at the bridge, both with clear covers and complementary-colored copper windings. **DP**

Gibson's New Century line was not for shy, retiring types. They were all fitted with a full-body mirror pickguard, mirror dot fretboard inlays, and even mirror inlays on top of the truss rod cover and control knobs.

Of course, the X-Plorer New Century was an updated version of the Explorer that had always looked futuristic. Gibson painted it black, screwed on a couple of high-output, ceramic magnet humbuckers, and created a hardcore guitar designed to wow twenty-first century live audiences.

It was all done in the best possible taste: the mirror guard was neatly set flush with the body thanks to a 1/10 in. (3 mm) indent in the wood. The hard ebony board on a slim taper neck joined the body at the nineteenth fret—perfect for speed merchants.

The Explorer's original light limba wood was replaced with good old Gibson mahogany. It's heavier, but the classic mahogany warmth, combined with the extra abrasive edge of the ceramic pick-ups, make a killer, modern-rock tone. **SH**

Ibanez MTM100 Mick Thomson 2006

Jackson Dave Ellefson 2006

Type Solidbody electric
Body & neck Mahogany body, maple/walnut neck
Fingerboard Rosewood
Pick-ups Two humbucker pick-ups

Type Solidbody bass guitar
Body & neck Alder body, maple neck
Fingerboard Ebony
Pick-ups Two humbucker pick-ups

From the 1980s, the Ibanez brand had been trying to move away from aping other guitar manufacturers. And it was generally agreed that they succeeded. Their jazz models were approved by such stars as Pat Metheny and George Benson; their iconic rock guitars were the Iceman used by Kiss's Paul Stanley, and models produced for Joe Satriani and Steve Vai. Then, in 2006, Slipknot's Mick Thomson put his name to this formidable monster.

The guitar bore many of Thomson's calling cards: a reversed headstock, and, on the rosewood fingerboard, the trademark "SEVEN," which signified his moniker, "#7," when playing with the crushing Iowan metal masters. Set to a lower-than-normal tuning, the MTM100 doesn't feature a surfeit of knobs, just a volume control and a three-way pick-up switch. As Thomson himself said: "For playing metal, how often do you touch a tone control?" As to be expected with a neck-through design, "You hit a note and it just holds ... The sustain is pretty amazing." **CB**

In the 1980s and early 1990s, two heavy metal bass players above all others demonstrated unprecedented levels of picking-hand precision: David Ellefson of Megadeth, and Jason Newsted of Metallica. While the latter suffered the ignominy of being mixed out of his band's albums in his early years as a member, Ellefson's precise lines were always at the forefront of Megadeth's sound, leading a generation of headbangers to marvel at his picking speed and accuracy.

A quarter of a century after Ellefson co-founded 'Deth, he was rewarded with a splendid signature instrument by Fender subsidiary, Jackson, the company whose pointy-headed instruments he had helped to popularize in the 1980s.

The Ellefson bass is a replica of the Jackson Concert instrument that he used on *Rust In Peace* (1990), and which produces the same "hot" tone as its predecessors, allowing it to cut through the thickest of guitar riffs, whether as a four-string or a five-string. Watch out for that headstock now: it's sharp. **JM**

Lakland Duck Dunn
Signature Model 2006

Type Solidbody electric bass
Body & neck Alder body, maple neck
Fingerboard Maple and rosewood
Pick-ups One Fralin split-coil humbucker pick-up

The late Donald "Duck" Dunn started playing with a Kay, then graduated to his heart's desire at the time—the Fender Precision. By the late 1990s, this legend of the low-end—whose work you may have heard with Booker T and the MGs as well as on "In The Midnight Hour," "Knock On Wood," "(Sittin' On) The Dock Of The Bay," and in countless other Stax hits—was looking for something with greater ease of playing. Conversations with Bob Glaub—who has played with everyone from Springsteen to Springfield—led to substantive talks with Dan Lakin of Lakland Basses.

"The neck is fast and smooth and the bass is lightweight, but a hummer. It sounds great: quality and craftsmanship impeccable."

DUCK DUNN

The result was a new model with a thinner neck that gave the instrument a jazz feel. Dunn felt that, in terms of weight and balance, it was almost like playing a lead. He pronounced himself "extremely happy." "The bass just feels tougher," he commented.

Although the standard production body was made of alder, ash was an optional alternative, and this was Dunn's preference. U.S.-built examples had maple and rosewood necks, while Korean products were empty-shell Skylines with rosewood-only necks that had electronics added back in Lakland's Chicago factory. The latter came only in Dunn's signature candy apple red, although a wider range of colors was available on American versions. The model now trades as the 44-64 Custom. **CB**

PRS Private Stock
Gary Grainger 2006

Type Solidbody electric bass
Body & neck Mahogany body, flame maple top, maple neck
Fingerboard Rosewood
Pick-ups Two PRS/GG pick-ups

Although Paul Reed Smith has built bass guitars since the earliest days of his first workshop in West Street, Annapolis, as a brand, PRS could hardly be described as a market leader. Smith's first production basses appeared in 1986, the Bass-4 and five-string Bass-5 were solid, if unremarkable, instruments. They were also the most expensive instruments in the PRS catalog at that time. Mediocre sales combined with the early-1990s recession led Smith to abandon his bass range in 1992. Built in small quantities, some of these original models are now collectible. PRS would resume the manufacture of bass

> "These basses give me everything I need for recording and playing live ... They are works of art and great tools for working bassists."
>
> GARY GRAINGER

guitars in the twenty-first century with the Electric Bass line, but the most interesting instruments have been produced as part of the exclusive Private Stock line.

Gary Grainger may not be a household name, but is a big noise on the jazz-funk/fusion scene, having played with the likes of John Scofield, George Duke, Frank Gambale, and Earth, Wind, and Fire. In 2003, Grainger teamed up with PRS to produce his own Private Stock model. This is a characteristically beautiful instrument both to look at and to play, although perhaps the most interesting feature is the active pick-up configuration consisting of four single-coils combined into two "separated" hum-canceling pick-ups. In 2013, this Private Stock bass evolved into the PRS Grainger line of production bass guitars. **TB**

← Gary Grainger, bassist and bass designer.

Dean Dave Mustaine VMNT 2007

Type Double-neck electric
Body & neck Mahogany body and neck
Fingerboard Ebony
Pick-ups Three Mustaine Duncan Live Wire pick-ups

After speed metal merchant Dave Mustaine was kicked out of Metallica, he went on to form the influential Megadeth. It was not only Metallica with whom Mustaine had difficulties; there had been problems with previous suppliers of his guitars. But he and Dean were a match made in heaven. As he later recalled: "When I went to Dean, I found out that the guitars were very responsive. And one of the most important things was the attention to detail. Also the relationship with me as an artist. Because the previous companies I was with, the guitars were good, but the relationship was sour. And I found that being with Dean was really good for me, because they took care of me as an artist, they took care of the guitars. They also knew what the public liked."

In effect a double-necked Flying V, this Dean VMNT was built as a one-off for Mustaine before being offered as a production model in 2007. Following tradition, it combines a twelve-string upper neck and a six-string lower neck. It is built from mahogany, with set necks and twenty-four-fret ebony fingerboards; the "shark tooth" inlays are mother-of-pearl. The finish on the model shown here is described as "Blood Lust."

Double-neck guitars can be difficult to balance; to prevent the instrument becoming neck-heavy, both headstocks are the same size, and six of the twelve Grover tuners are fitted behind the tailpiece. Both necks have Tune-o-matic bridges with "V" tailpieces.

The Mustaine Duncan Live Wire pick-ups have master tone and dedicated volume controls. **JB**

Dave Mustaine—two Flying Vs are better than one. ➡

Evaline
JX 2007

Type Solidbody electric
Body & neck Swamp ash body, maple neck
Fingerboard Ebony
Pick-ups One EMG 81 humbucker pick-up

Launched in 2005, Evaline guitars are hand-made in Michigan by master luthier Gary Kozlowski. Kozlowski has been involved in the Detroit music scene for many years, managing bands, running the No Deal Records label, and making guitars for bands such as Panic Trigger and MindCandy.

The Evaline JX model was created for Jeremy Ferguson—better known as Jinxx, rhythm guitarist and violin player with numerous bands, the best-known being Hollywood glam-metal merchants Black Veil Brides. The JX was based broadly on the Wall Dogg, which was the first Evaline single cutaway. It features a swamp ash body, a maple neck, and ebony fingerboard. The headstock features six-in-a-line tuners and a unique "hooked" design common to all of their guitars. The two heavily angled humbuckers are primed to give a powerful rock sound. Appealingly for some players, electrics are kept to a bare minimum, with just a master volume control and selector switch.

In 2013, after Jinxx had ended an endorsement contract with B.C. Rich, he returned to Evaline, who presented him with a custom version of his signature guitar. The Ouija JX is similar to the original excepting some spectacular body graphics based on a classic Ouija board. Jinxx's guitar may not be able to contact the dead, but it certainly gets through to the living. **AJ**

Jinxx plays his Evaline JX on Black Veil Brides' *Wretched and Divine: The Story of the Wild Ones* (2013). This was their third studio album and their first to hit the Top Ten of the *Billboard* 200 chart on its release. It features the single "In the End."

EVH
Frankenstein 2007

Type Solidbody electric
Body & neck Ash body, maple neck
Fingerboard Maple
Pick-ups Two Seymour Duncan Custom humbucker pick-ups

Eddie Van Halen's "Frankenstrat"—the name is a portmanteau of "Frankenstein," as in Mary Shelley's fictional monster, and "Stratocaster," as in epochal electric ax—was his homemade, hybrid guitar that attempted to mix a Gibson sound with a Fender body. As a tribute to EVH, in 2007, the Fender Custom Shop painstakingly produced 300 replicas of this instrument, and quickly sold them all in spite of their astonishing $25,000 price tag.

The replica was very accurate: of course, the body had the same red, black, and white striped paint job as the original. Also featured were reproduction details, including a 1971 25¢ coin, screwed just behind the bridge to keep it in tune, and burn marks on the headstock where Eddie would keep lighted cigarettes jammed under the strings during a song.

The guitar has a bridge humbucker pick-up that was a secret EVH creation, designed by Seymour Duncan, and a neck single-coil pick-up that was not even wired in, just as it had not been wired in on the real Frankenstrat. The three-way pick-up selector switch does nothing, just like in the original. And the one control knob—the volume—is authentically covered with a plastic knob bearing the legend: "Tone."

During his 2012 tour, Eddie Van Halen played what looked like a variant form of the Frankenstrat, with a black-and-white capped bridge pick-up, a maple neck, and a black headstock. However, it remained unknown whether this was the original instrument, a replica of the prototype, one of this limited edition, or a completely new, custom-made instrument that just happened to resemble the old one. **SH**

Gibson
ES-339 2007

Type Semi-hollow body electric
Body & neck Maple/poplar body, maple neck
Fingerboard Rosewood
Pick-ups Two Gibson 1957 Classic humbucker pick-ups

Chuck Berry is synonymous with Gibson's ES-335, but the semi-hollow body guitar has made a mark, not just on rock 'n' roll, but on almost all musical genres since its introduction in 1958. In 2007, as part of the build-up to its fiftieth anniversary celebrations, the Gibson Custom Shop unveiled an evolution of the classic: the ES-339.

Comparable in size to a Les Paul, the ES-339 is designed to be less unwieldy than most semi-hollow body guitars. Gibson's Memphis Tone Circuit preserves high frequencies, allowing the guitar to retain its larger forebear's full tonal spectrum at any volume. Two Gibson humbuckers with individual tone and volume controls and three-way switching—just like on the ES-335—offer versatility, while the maple/poplar/maple laminate body is coated only lightly to enhance the tone. The guitar is complemented by nickel hardware, and Kluson tuners with keystone buttons.

Gibson notably moved the ES-339's jack to the outer rim, and offered the guitar with either a rounded, 1959-style neck or a slimmer 30/60, with 0.3 in. (85 mm) added front to back.

While some old-stagers maintained that the old ES-335 was unsurpassable, and wondered why Gibson had tried to improve on perfection, most critics were unstinting in their praise for the ES-339. Musicradar. com led the cheering in a long review that concluded:

"We strongly suggest you track down one of these guitars—you'd better get in the queue behind us though—before, in terms of price, someone at Gibson realizes they've made a terrible mistake. It really is that good." **DP**

Gibson **Robot Les Paul Studio** 2007

Type Auto-tuning solidbody electric
Body & neck Mahogany body and neck
Fingerboard Rosewood
Pick-ups Two humbucker pick-ups

When it comes down to technology, what features do most guitarists really want on their instruments? MIDI connections? In-built synthesizer sounds and effects? Pick-ups that provide never-ending sustain? Programmable touchscreens? Espresso maker? These all seem to be niche concerns, when—let's be honest—most players make limited use of their volume controls, and wouldn't even notice if the tone knobs vanished altogether. But how about a piece of technology that took care of an area that concerned all guitarists, irrespective of the style of music or the ability of the player? Tuning.

German guitarist and inventor Chris Adams spent a decade developing what would become the Powertune system, which in 2007 Gibson bought in for its first range of "Robot" guitars. Powertune is a device built into the guitar that checks and maintains the intonation of each string. The system is located on the underside of the stop bar and it checks the pitch of the note; if it is found to be out of tune, a message is sent to the automated machine heads, which retune by themselves. (Take a look online, there are plenty of videos showing the system in action—it is seriously impressive.)

The first limited run of the Robot Guitar featured a Les Paul with the Powertune system installed. It was advertised widely as a world's first, even if the similar Transperformance self-tuning system predated it by a decade; however that system also required extensive butchery to an existing guitar, at a cost of around $3,000 ... which was about the same price as the Gibson model complete. **TB**

PRS David Grissom DGT 2007

Type Solidbody electric
Body & neck Mahogany/maple body, maple neck
Fingerboard Rosewood
Pick-ups Two humbucker pick-ups

David Grissom's custom order led to the PRS McCarty Model. His next major contribution was his first actual signature guitar: the David Grissom Tremolo (DGT). Building on the McCarty, the DGT added a second volume control, a new neck shape—"We compared my 1993 McCarty and my 1987 Standard, and shot for something in between those as they are both my favorite 'feeling' guitars," said Grissom—and, most importantly, new-design pick-ups.

Initially, the DGT was offered in a nitrocellulose top-coat finish. This delayed the release of the guitar—it was announced in the summer of 2007, but not officially released until the following January.

Around four years before the launch, "Paul and I started to discuss different possibilities," relates Grissom. "I sort of felt that there were several things we could do with the [McCarty] guitar to make it better. Some of the things I was already doing on my own McCartys: different fretwire, pick-ups, changing the tuners. At the same time I had a lot of people, studio players, coming up to me that would play my main McCarty and say, 'If I could get one like this, I'd buy one.' See, you can't get a McCarty with tremolo, and I never stopped tinkering with my tone."

The DGT Standard is still in production with, since 2012, an all-mahogany option. **DB**

David Grissom has recorded and toured with a host of artists, including Buddy Guy, Chris Isaak, Sarah Hickman, and Bob Dylan. His albums *Loud Music* (2008) and *Way Down Deep* (2011) are essential listening for lovers of PRS-fueled sound.

Ruokangas
Mojo Grande 2007

Type Semi-hollow body electric
Body & neck Cedar/birch body, maple neck
Fingerboard Rosewood
Pick-ups One humbucker and two single-coil pick-ups

After training under the guidance of some of Finland's most respected luthiers, Juha Ruokangas founded his own company, Ruokangas Guitars, in 1995. Initially working alone, he now employs a small team that produces about 120 unique guitars a year.

His guitars are all designed in an old-school fashion—he still uses a 1960s drawing board and builds prototypes. It's an unusual way of working these days, but it's one that he describes as relaxing. His main focus when designing the Mojo Grande was "to create as responsive an electric guitar as humanly

> "Ruokangas sets the bar as a standard by which all the boutique guitar companies should be measured."

JAY JAY FRENCH, TWISTED SISTER

possible." He goes on to say that "The guitar is featherlight, and the tone open. It's so versatile, it works for country, rock, and blues, and you can dial in even really cool, mellower jazz tones."

The guitar features a single cutaway semi-hollow body with a thin veneer of walnut separating a Spanish cedar back and a carved top of Arctic birch. It also features a gloss finish and stylish holes carved above the bridge. In the pick-up area, Haussel provides the S/H combo, which is controlled through master volume, master tone, and three-position blade switch. The bolt-on neck is made of rock maple. A rosewood fingerboard comes with twenty-one silver/nickel frets, dot position inlays, 12 in. (30.5 cm) radius, and a nut made of moose shinbone. **RP**

Squier
Hello Kitty 2007

Type Solidbody electric
Body & neck Agathis body, maple neck
Fingerboard Maple
Pick-ups One humbucker pick-up

In 2007, BBC News reported that police officers who arrived late for work in Bangkok, Thailand, were forced to wear pink Hello Kitty armbands on their uniforms. No doubt certain heshers and thrashers would impose similar penance—or worse—on any bro who would dare to rock the Squier Hello Kitty Strat.

But, clearly, Fender did not intend this guitar for the bros. Available in pink (natch) or black with matching dot inlays, the guitar was a play to the swelling ranks of rockin' tween and teen girls (remember, emo was then at the height of its influence). In fact, Squier offered an acoustic and a bass as well. The Strat had a string-through body, a twenty-one fret neck, and a pickguard in the shape of its namesake Japanese character's head, but otherwise the instrument was a rather plain affair, with a lonely humbucker pick-up, a single knob (for volume), and an agathis body. Even so, licensing fees pushed the Hello Kitty's retail price up to $350. It was discontinued at the end of 2009. **DP**

Taylor
Classic 2007

Type Solidbody electric
Body & neck Swamp ash body, maple neck
Fingerboard Indian rosewood
Pick-ups Two humbucker pick-ups

The Taylor Classic was the last in an evolutionary acoustic-to-electric line of guitars that began in 2005. It was a highly configurable instrument, with a wide range of options, and was available in either a double-cutaway form or the original, pointy, Florentine-style, single cutaway shape of the 2009 example shown here.

The depth of this guitar ranges between approximately 1⁴/₅ in. (4.6 cm) in the center, and 1¹/₅ in. (3.0 cm) on the bass side of the rim. It also tapers from 1¾ (4.5 cm) at the bass strap button to 1⅖ in. (3.5 cm) at the neck joint. In spite of its thinness, players found it felt solid in the hands.

Innovative features of the Classic included an easily removable and adjustable neck, which was tight-fitting and stable, and incorporated the single-bolt T-lock joint design first seen on the T5; a stylish and acoustically resonant aluminum bridge; a "Fendery" range of tone colors from the Taylor pick-up system, and a reassuring, fused string ground to prevent players getting electric shocks. **GD**

Almansa Gran Professional 2008

Blindworm Cragg 2008

Type Classical guitar
Body & neck Spruce, cedar, and peroba body; cedar neck
Fingerboard Ebony

Type Semi-hollow body electric
Body & neck Poplar body, maple/birch neck
Fingerboard Maple
Pick-ups Seymour Duncan Seth Lover pick-ups

Guitarras Almansa have been making classical and flamenco guitars in Muro del Alcoy, Alicante, Spain, since 1989. Taking its initial influence from the Madrid school, its luthiers have imported skills and techniques acquired from time spent in the workshops of other makers, including Manuel Rodriguez, as well as absorbing local influences. In addition to guitars, they build bandurrias (an instrument similar to a cittern or a mandolin that is used primarily in Spanish folk music), lutes, flamenco guitars, and modern electric instruments.

Almansa produces three grades of classical guitar that it refers to as "Student," "Conservatory," and "Concert." This Gran Professional Exótico is its top-of-the-line, flagship instrument. Few compromises are made in its construction: the back and sides are carved from solid red Brazilian peroba, with its red heartwood very prettily streaked with purple and brown, and it is kitted out with luxury gold-plated machine heads. **AJ**

Colorado-based luthier Andrew Scott has a reputation for designing and making eccentric but functional instruments in his "Garden of the Gods Garage." Each one of the high-end guitars is custom-built, can be viewed only by appointment, and takes three months to construct. As well as the intricate nature of the designs, the guitars often feature inlaid mineral, dinosaur bones, and exotic woods. Scott's clientele has included Lee Renaldo of Sonic Youth. "We cater for the eccentric one percent of players and collectors," he claims, and when you look at a guitar like the Cragg you can see why. This heavily sculpted instrument, which resembles something between a dragon and a sea serpent, comprises a figured poplar body, and a firm but light seven-piece roasted maple and roasted birch neck. Its screaming head is complete with antler horns, osage orange knothole eyes, and a jade tongue. And, interestingly, the fretboard is made from 100-year-old maple wood salvaged from a table belonging to Scott's grandfather. **RP**

Brook Guitars
Parlor Guitar 2008

Dean
Amott Tyrant 2008

Type Parlor acoustic guitar
Body & neck Indian rosewood back and sides, European spruce top, mahogany neck
Fingerboard Ebony

Type Solidbody electric
Body & neck Mahogany body and neck
Fingerboard Ebony
Pick-ups Two DMT humbucker pick-ups

Set in the wilds of Devon, southwest England, Brook Guitars is now firmly established among the leading makers of acoustic guitars in the United Kingdom. Twenty years ago, however, the two founders, Andy Petherick and Simon Smidmore, were engaged in very different activities, respectively as car mechanic and builder. Fate played an interesting hand putting them together with Andy Manson, one of Britain's leading luthiers. After years of working alone, Manson had been given the opportunity to expand into a new business, so he trained Petherick and Smidmore, who worked for him for the next three years. When Manson decided to return to working alone, his students took over, founding Brook Guitars in 1995.

The model shown here is a parlor guitar based on a template provided by Jethro Tull's Ian Anderson (drawn from an 1860s French guitar the singer has hanging on his wall). It was custom-built for comedy writer Tom Cutler, the shape of the bridge exaggerated to reflect his handlebar moustache. **TB**

Tampa, Florida-based Dean Guitars has had a long association with the heavier side of rock, as exhibited by a roster that includes players like Dave Mustaine, Dimebag Darrell, and Uli Jon Roth. In 2009, the firm added another metal heavyweight to the lineup, rolling out the Tyrant, the signature model of Arch Enemy's Michael Amott.

Everything about this American-built metal monster is top-end: the Grover tuners, the pearl valknut inlays (a nod to Amott's Swedish heritage) in the ebony fingerboard, the machined aluminum pickguard, and the Tune-o-matic bridge. The Tyrant also features Dean Magnetic Technologies humbuckers, including the eponymous Tyrant in the bridge.

A classic V-shape with metal flare, the mahogany body is a string-through design because Amott took a shine to the sustain exhibited by Dean's Michael Schenker model. Originally available in Classic White, Classic Black, and (of course) Blood Red, the Tyrant was subsequently offered in several variants. **DP**

Duesenberg
Mike Campbell 2008

Type Hollow body electric
Body & neck Maple/spruce body, maple neck
Fingerboard Rosewood
Pick-ups One single-coil and one humbucker pick-up

The Duesenberg Guitar Company was founded in Hanover, Germany, by luthier Dieter Gölsdorf, whose love of Art Deco and American jazz guitar shine through in these glorious designs. They combine a retro look with modern features, and have been welcomed by many great guitarists, such as Joe Walsh, Billy Gibbons, Dean Parks, and Mike Campbell of Tom Petty and The Heartbreakers.

The Mike Campbell Duesenberg is a hollow body guitar reminiscent in outline of a Les Paul, with maple back and sides, and a spruce top with f-holes and cream binding. The set-neck is D-shaped one-piece maple, with a bound Indian rosewood fingerboard, dot inlays, and Duesenberg's own "Art-Diego" tuners.

The guitar is finished in a striking blue sparkle, with two white stripes down the center of the body. It comes with either a fixed bridge and tailpiece or a Vibrola. Two different pick-ups are used: a single-coil Domino P-90 in the neck, and a Grand Vintage humbucker in the bridge position. **JB**

Fender **Time Machine**
59 Precision Bass 2008

Type Solidbody electric bass
Body & neck Alder or ash body, maple neck
Fingerboard Rosewood
Pick-ups One custom vintage 1959 split single-coil pick-up

Introduced in 1951, Leo Fender's Precision Bass introduced a practical, tuneful, and mass-produced alternative to the percussive double bass. The "P Bass" underwent many updates in the following decades, as it became one of the most beloved electric basses of all time. Little wonder the Fender Custom Shop included the 1959 model in its Time Machine Series.

The Time Machine Series seeks to re-create vintage Fender models to the exact specifications of yesteryear. The 1959 P Bass was notable—and thus worthy of the series—because it was the year Fender switched from an all-maple neck to a rosewood fingerboard, which remained standard until 1966. The 1959 Time Machine P Bass, produced through 2008, was offered in three-color sunburst alder and white blonde ash bodies with an anodized pickguard. A 34-in. (86.4-cm) scale C-shaped neck with clay dot markers was dressed with twenty frets, while a Fender split single-coil pick-up with staggered pole pieces delivered that classic bottom end into the mix. **DP**

Fernandes Vertigo Elite Sustainer 2008

Type Solidbody electric
Body & neck Mahogany body, maple neck
Fingerboard Ebony
Pick-ups One sustainer and one humbucker pick-up

The Vertigo is an original Fernandes design—the extended bottom-left-hand side of the body is reminiscent of a Gibson Explorer. Mass produced to a high standard in the Far East, Vertigo guitars currently cost around $1,000 each. The Elite version is made of solid mahogany, and has an ebony fretboard with trapezoid abalone inlays, together with an FRT-11 Floyd Rose locking tremolo.

In addition to the usual controls, there are on/off and mode switches for the "sustainer." The sustainer system consists of a special neck pick-up and a

> "No one else was playing Explorers at that point—quite soon it became the thing we were famous for."
>
> THE EDGE

circuitboard powered by a nine-volt battery, which generates a magnetic field that causes the strings to vibrate as if they were feeding back next to a loud amplifier. The sustain will keep on going for as long as the player holds down the string. The E-bow works in a similar way—but with this system you get to keep one hand free to hold a plectrum.

Among other distinctive features of the Vertigo Elite Sustainer is a knob to control the intensity of the feedback, and you can also select between natural mode, harmonic mode (which adds a fifth harmonic), and mixed mode, which produces a sustained harmony. Also available as part of a kit is a Fernandes sustainer, which can be added to the stringed instrument of your choice. **AJ**

Gibson
Dark Fire 2008

Type Solidbody computer-equipped electric
Body & neck Mahogany/maple body, mahogany neck
Fingerboard Rosewood
Pick-ups Burstbucker 3, P-90, and piezo pick-ups

Among the big players in the world of music technology, only Roland in Japan—with MIDI systems that evolved from its original late-1970s guitar synthesizers—had shown any long-term commitment to the idea of a guitar beyond six strings and a couple of magnetic pick-ups. So it was something of surprise when in 2007 Gibson announced its first range of self-tuning "GOR" Robot guitars equipped with the Powertune system. The purists scoffed, but for once it looked as if this might be a genuine milestone on the timeline of the guitar. The initial run of Les Paul Robots was well received and extended to include SG, Flying V, and Explorer variants.

A second generation emerged a year later, featuring an updated version of the impressive self-tuning system and extended with onboard technology to alter the its tonal capabilities. The Dark Fire is a pretty cool "analog" guitar its own right, kitted out with Burstbucker 3 and P-90 pick-ups, and with a piezo bridge for acoustic-type tones, but it comes into its own when you connect it up to a computer to build your own presets using the Chameleon Tone software. Here can you not only alter tunings but configurations of the three pick-ups, along with finely drawn parametric EQ curves that can be applied to the onboard circuitry. So when your presets are stored you could, for example, change from a DADGAD tuning playing only the piezo pick-up, to Open G tuning and a tone that combines all three pick-ups… all in a few seconds and at the push of one button. Little wonder that Gibson have called it "the most versatile tone monster ever made." **TB**

Godin
Montreal 2008

Ibanez
Artcore Custom 2008

Type Semi-hollow body electric
Body & neck Mahogany body and neck
Fingerboard Rosewood
Pick-ups Two humbucker pick-ups

Type Hollow body electric jazzbox
Body & neck Maple body, maple/walnut neck
Fingerboard Rosewood
Pick-ups Two humbucker pick-ups

The Godin Montreal blends a combination of traditional magnetic pick-ups for electric sound, and saddle transducers in the bridge for acoustic sound.

The body has two hollow chambers; it is carved from a solid block of mahogany, and then capped with a carved mahogany top, with two f-holes, and finished with a cream binding. The neck is also mahogany, and has a 24¾-in. (62.9-cm) scale and twenty-two frets. The hardware is in black and gold. There are two Godin humbuckers, in the bridge and neck positions, and the bridge is loaded with LR Baggs transducer saddles. There is also a powered preamp EQ, and a five-way pick-up selector switch, giving five different tones. By adding to that the acoustic sounds from the bridge transducers, this guitar has a wide range of sounds, making it extremely versatile. There are two outputs, which can be blended in the guitar by using a single patch cord, or the outputs can be sent to two amp channels, or a mixer, to combine the sounds from bridge transducers and pick-ups. **PP**

Ibanez guitars are most commonly associated with virtuoso rockers, such as Steve Vai and Joe Satriani, and the newer breed of down-tuning metal players with their seven- and eight-string instruments. But Ibanez also has a strong jazz heritage, attracting greats such as George Benson, Pat Metheny, and John Scofield.

Archtop jazz guitars can be costly to produce, but Ibanez's Artcore range, made in China, exhibits the brand's exacting attention to detail at an affordable price. This deep, hollow body AF125 Artcore Custom, introduced in 2008, was originally listed for $1,133 yet boasts an impressive specification. The body is quilted, maple-faced laminate, the neck a five-piece maple/walnut laminate; the bound rosewood fingerboard has extremely tidy fretting, and a sumptuous shell inlay. It features wooden control knobs and tailpiece, while the gold-plated Tune-o-matic-style ART1 bridge sits on a classic-style wooden foot. Pick-ups are Ibanez's Super 58 Custom humbuckers. Guitars like these have proved that the jazz archtop is still alive and kicking! **DB**

Ibanez
Herman Li 2008

Type Solidbody electric
Body & neck Mahogany/maple body, maple neck
Fingerboard Rosewood
Pick-ups Two humbuckers and one single-coil pick-up

Herman Li is a founding member of British power metal band Dragonforce. A longtime Ibanez user, his 2008 signature EGEN18 guitar (and the more affordable EGEN8) is based on the Ibanez S series models, which he'd previously used and retired from stage performance at the end of the tour to promote the album *Inhuman Rampage* (2006).

Finished in "transparent violet flat," the twenty-four-fret EGEN18 features a bolt-on maple neck, and a flame-maple-topped mahogany body. Distinctive features include a "Kung-Fu grip" on the upper horn, and a scalloped lower horn for increased upper fret access. Three DiMarzio HLM pick-ups are wired to a five-way pick-up selector, while further sounds come from a coil-split switch on the volume control. Ibanez's Edge Zero vibrato completes the specification.

The company was evidently happy with the result: according to its advertising, "It took three years, but we did get it more than right . . . these models are perfect for ultimate shredding." **DB**

Ibanez
Noodles 2008

Type Solidbody electric
Body & neck Solid basswood body, maple neck
Fingerboard Rosewood
Pick-ups Two humbuckers and one single-coil pick-up

The Ibanez Noodles (NDM1 and NDM2)—two of the guitars in the Talman series of aggressive, punk era-inspired, electric and acoustic guitars—are the signature instruments of Kevin Wasserman, lead guitarist of the U.S. band The Offspring, who is best known by his stage name, Noodles.

"They have a cool, old-school vibe to them," Wasserman told guitarcenter.com, "but they also play easily and . . . are almost completely stock, with the exception of the DiMarzio Tone Zone pick-ups that I use on almost everything."

Both Noodles guitars are recreations of Talmans that Wasserman had been playing since 1994. The NDM1 he covered in, of all things, duct tape—a finish that Ibanez decided to call "taped stain gray" (TSG)—while the NDM2 has The Offspring's "Flaming Death or Glory!" motto and mirrored skull emblem emblazoned on the pickguard. Thus, each has its own distinctive look, but in neither case can observers ever mistake them for anything other than a Noodles. **BS**

Manson
MB-1 2008

Type Solidbody electric
Body & neck Alder body, maple neck
Fingerboard Rosewood
Pick-ups One MBK-2 and one P-90 pick-up

The Manson MB-1 was designed in collaboration with, and built for, Matt Bellamy of Muse. British luthier Hugh Manson had been building instruments for the guitarist since 1997, and the MB-1 was specifically made for live use. Only around seventy-five hand-built MB-1s have been produced, and, for those interested, the waiting list a long one.

The design is unique, and incorporates features found on some of Bellamy's other stage guitars. The body is cut from alder, and is available in a matt black or a red glitter finish, with headstocks to match. The bolt-on bird's-eye maple neck has a mild "V" shape, and is topped with a compound radius rosewood fingerboard. There are no inlays on top of the fingerboard; the only markings are side dots.

The bridge is a fixed unit, with the strings secured through the body, in Telecaster style. Hardware is a chrome finish, including Gotoh 512 tuners. The MB-1 is kitted out with Manson's own custom MBK-2 bridge pick-up, and a P-90 in the neck position.

However, there are many innovative options available for the MB-1, including an X-Y MIDI screen controller, allowing the player to control a Korg Kaoss Pad, DigiTech Whammy Pedal, or other MIDI device. It can also be fitted with a Fernandes FSK-101 pick-up, which makes possible an infinite sustain effect by electromagnetically vibrating the strings.

That, at the time of writing, this should be one of the most innovative guitars in production, is no surprise, in view of Manson's history: he was teching for the likes of Led Zeppelin in the 1970s, so he knows what it means to push the boundaries. **JB**

Matt Bellamy of Muse is big on guitar tech. →

Peerless
Monarch 2008

Type Archtop guitar
Body & neck Spruce/maple body, maple neck
Fingerboard Rosewood
Pick-ups One floating mini-humbucker pick-up

The solid top is pressed, rather than hand-carved; the Grover tuners are criticized by some for lacking the ability to maintain the tuning; and there's the problem of the absence of a tone control. But these are the worst things that can be said about the Peerless Monarch. When unplugged, it has a great jazzy sound, whose amplified tone and performance seriously rival those of guitars costing three or four times as much, and it comes across powerfully when amplified. Its mini floating pick-up produces between 80 and 90 percent of the output of a full Epiphone 1957

> *"If you are thinking of moving up to a good acoustic guitar . . . but do not have a spare thousand or two, try out this guitar."*
> MUSIC MAKE MAGAZINE

humbucker, and the instrument has a great sustain. It also has a refreshingly fast neck that can play like greased lightning, and overall is reminiscent of that classic, timeless Jimmy D'Aquisto jazz guitar shape.

The Peerless brand—first established in Korea in the 1970s—soon acquired a reputation for craftsmanship that it has maintained ever since. The Monarch—often referred to as the "working man's archtop"—maintains this tradition. A small soundpost beneath the bridge minimizes feedback issues, while the body—17 in. (43 cm) wide and 3 in. (7.5 cm) deep—produces beautifully rounded tones that enable it to play anything from the gypsyish sounds of Django Reinhardt through to the dark, brooding melodies of Jim Hall. **BS**

PRS
Sunburst 245 2008

Type Solidbody electric
Body & neck Mahogany/maple body, maple neck
Fingerboard Rosewood
Pick-ups Two humbucker pick-ups

Once the Singlecut guitar had been successfully reintroduced into the PRS line, the company decided in 2007 to split production into two distinct models: the 25-in. (63.5-cm) scale PRS 250, and the more vintage, shorter-scaled, 24½-in. (62.2-cm) PRS 245, with 245 humbucker pick-ups.

They hoped thereby to make inroads into two different markets. The 250 was aimed principally at modern rock players, while the Singlecut (SC) 245 targeted guitarists who wanted more of an old-school, Les Paul vibe. The apotheosis of the latter was

"It has to be said that if you're in the market for a singlecut electric, the 245 is gunning for your wallet."

MUSICRADAR.COM

achieved a year later, in the form of the limited-run, "Sunburst" series, a line that included the 245—the first Singlecut to feature Paul Reed Smith's new 1957/2008 (usually shortened to 57/08) humbucking pick-ups.

Smith revealed that PRS was exclusively using the same type of coil wire, made on the same machine, as that used by Gibson to wind its classic PAF humbuckers. "But it ain't just the wire," he explained, "it's the magnets too."

Limited to just 150 pieces, the nitrocellulose-finished Sunburst 245 was perhaps the ultimate vintage-style PRS Singlecut, and formed the foundation for two subsequent PRS guitars, the 2010 SC58, and the "Stripped" 58. **DB**

Samick **Greg Bennett** Cobra 2008

Type Solidbody electric
Body & neck Mahogany body, maple neck
Fingerboard Rosewood
Pick-ups One or two Duncan humbucker pick-ups

Samick is one of the world's biggest instrument manufacturers. Most of its guitars are produced in a giant factory in Indonesia. Many are made for Epiphone, and other, separate companies; some are sold under Samick's own brand names, one of which is that of Greg Bennett.

Bennett is a luthier based in Nashville, Tennessee. His Samick guitars are moderately priced, but all use distinctive tonewoods and top-grade components, such as Fishman or Seymour Duncan-designed pick-ups, Grover tuners, and Wilkinson bridges.

"… enough low-mids to fill any arena. Power trios will lose their minds … if you tear it up on stage; your shoulder will thank you."

GREG BENNETT ADVERTISING

The Cobra is a radically-shaped, solidbody electric guitar with either one or two Duncan-designed humbucker pick-ups. The thin, flat, mahogany body and slim, glued, maple neck mean it is a lightweight instrument. Add in the deep double cutaways, and striking body shape, and you have a guitar that is very practical for live use.

Some Cobras have been made in Korea, some in Indonesia. Whatever, these guitars are clearly aimed at modern metal players. The Grover tuners are black, the rest of the hardware is chrome. Some Cobras come with a metallic finish on the body. The asymmetrical body shape is matched by an offset and angled-back, three-on-a-side headstock. One reviewer described the Cobra as looking like "an SG designed by Klingons." **SH**

Squier Classic Vibe Stratocaster '50s 2008

Type Solidbody electric
Body & neck Alder body, maple neck
Fingerboard Maple
Pick-ups Three Alnico single-coil pick-ups

In 1982, the very first Squiers, by Fender guitars, came out of Asia. They were aimed at players who wanted budget guitars with top-of-the-range sounds—and sales figures soon demonstrated that the makers had scored a direct hit on the target market. Their reputation has since endured—Squiers remain highly rated by guitar enthusiasts worldwide. Today, early examples are extremely collectable, and fetch high prices at auction.

The Vibe Series was never intended to be an exact re-creation of a vintage model, but was rather meant to impart the general feel of a classic Fender design.

"We must now suggest that the Classic Vibe range has become the initial port of call if you're after your first Strat."

MUSICRADAR.COM

The Vibe Stratocaster is good-looking, and user-friendly. It has an alder body, which is finished in polyester, and a one-piece maple, modern C-shaped neck, with a 9½-in. (24-cm) maple fingerboard. The scale length is 25½ in. (64.75 cm), with twenty-one medium jumbo frets and ten dot position markers, and measures 1⅔ in. (4.1 cm) at the nut. The machine heads are chrome vintage style, as is the six-saddle tremolo bridge.

The unique features of the guitar include a two-color sunburst over alder; a vintage-tint gloss maple neck; "aged" plastic parts, including a single-ply white pickguard, and a custom Stratocaster pick-up set with magnets made of Alnico (an alloy of iron with aluminum, nickel, and cobalt). **PP**

TV Jones Spectra Sonic Supreme 2008

Type Semi-hollow body electric
Body & neck Maple/alder body, maple neck
Fingerboard Ebony
Pick-ups Two TV Classic pick-ups

The Spectra Sonic Supreme was the first guitar made by Thomas V. Jones' company in Washington State. It is a modification of an earlier design, produced by Gretsch in 2002, which had been developed as a signature model for Brian Setzer by Jones and Rich Modica. At the end of his contract with Gretsch, Jones decided to introduce the "Supreme" under his own brand name.

Jones had built his reputation at the World of Strings, a guitar repair workshop in Long Beach, California, at which one of the regulars was Setzer, whose main instrument at the time was a Gretsch 6120. Jones created a remodeled version of this 1959 guitar that was adopted by Setzer and, in 1998, by Gretsch for their Hot Rod line. The TV Jones range of pick-ups remains the company's main speciality.

The Spectra Sonic Supreme's upmarket features include Sperzel non-locking tuners, and a nut made of Delrin, a slippery thermoplastic that stops the strings getting stuck when you use the Bigsby B-11 vibrato. **AJ**

Vintage SpongeBob SquarePants 2008

Type Solidbody electric
Body & neck Maple body and neck
Fingerboard Maple
Pick-ups One humbucker pick-up

Vintage is a budget guitar maker owned by John Hornby Skewes (JHS), a company based in Leeds, England, which also owns Encore, Danelectro, and Italia.

The flagship SpongeBob SquarePants model comes as part of a package that comprises a SpongeBob-covered 10-watt amp, a carry bag, a strap, a guitar lead, a plectrum, a spare set of strings, and a tuition DVD—all packed inside a special SpongeBob display pack. There are two finishes available: either yellow or black. The recommended retail price of all this is £199, although it can be obtained for even less.

There are two variant forms of the basic item: a seven-eighths-size version, and a three-quarter-size version with a built-in speaker powered by a nine-volt battery. Optional accessories include a clip-on chromatic tuner, spare leads, and reusable overlays so that you can change the design of the guitar body.

SpongeBob SquarePants is a U.S. animated cartoon character who looks like a kitchen sponge, and lives in an undersea pineapple. **AJ**

Vox
Virage DC 2008

Warwick
Corvette 2008

Type Semi-hollow body electric
Body & neck Ash/mahogany body, mahogany neck
Fingerboard Rosewood
Pick-ups Custom triple-coil system pick-ups

Type Solidbody electric bass
Body & neck Bubinga body, ovangkol neck
Fingerboard Wenge
Pick-ups Two MEC Jazz pick-ups

Vox, the company famous for its amplifiers, also made innovative, but commercially unsuccessful, electric guitars and basses from the early 1960s and had been in a long and steady decline when Korg, the Japanese electronics company, bought it in 1992. Although its new owner reissued the classic Phantom and Teardrop guitars in 1998, it had been decades since Vox had made a newly designed guitar—and then came the Virage. Targeting high-end buyers, the Virage is loaded with innovative features, but the makers, clearly not wanting to repeat past mistakes, played safe with the styling, which is reminiscent of the Epiphone Casino, and the Gibson ES-330.

Among the unique elements of the Virage are the tone bars, carved out of the back and top, which serve to separate treble, middle, and bass tonal ranges. Its low-mass, aluminum bridge improves the transfer of string vibrations, and it produces versatile tones thanks to an exclusive pick-up system that works like a single coil, a P90, and a humbucker all in one. **GD**

Warwick Guitars is based in Markneukirchen, Germany, where it makes custom-shop and signature guitars. Warwick's Artist series guitars are made in Korea and the Rockbass series in China. The signature series—ranging from Adam Clayton and U2, through to Bootsy Collins and Jack Bruce—cover a wide range of styles and sounds. The Warwick Corvette is a five-string bass with a two- or three-piece bubinga body, ovangkol neck, and a wenge fretboard. The machine heads are Warwick's own, and the neck has a 34-in. (86.4-cm) scale, and twenty-four jumbo extra-hardened frets. The tailpiece and bridge are fully adjustable for height, string spacing, and intonation. The truss rod is accessed through a small lid system at the headstock, which Warwick named "Just a Nut 111." The battery and electrics are accessed through easy-to-open compartments on the back of the guitar. The two MEC Jazz pick-ups can be active or passive. This model was made at Warwick's German factory until 2009, but from 2010 it was built in Korea. **PP**

Caparison
Angelus 2009

Type Solidbody electric
Body & neck Various woods
Fingerboard Ebony or maple
Pick-ups Single coil + humbucker/two humbucker pick-ups

Caparison's Angelus series is produced in Nagoya, Japan. All Angelus guitars have the same, heavily carved, body shape that is almost Superstrat in style, but they vary greatly in construction and electronics.

The flagship Angelus is the signature guitar developed for Japanese metal star Captain Ace Shimizu. The Angelus ACE model added a flush-mounted tremolo unit, coil tap switches for each pick-up, and custom inlaid symbols as fret position markers.

There's also an Angelus Custom Line, which features two EMG pick-ups, a humbucker at the bridge, and a single coil at the neck. Unlike the others, it has a maple fingerboard, and a mahogany neck and body. In contrast, the Angelus M3B has a body made of a mahogany-and-maple sandwich.

In addition to these configurations, customers can specify various tone control combinations at the time of ordering. They can also choose the pots and capacitors used inside, and various combinations of pick-up selecting and coil splitting. **SH**

Collings
360 2009

Type Solidbody electric
Body & neck Mahogany/maple body, mahogany neck
Fingerboard Rosewood
Pick-ups Two Lollar mini-humbucker pick-ups

Founded in 1973, Collings Guitars of Austin, Texas, had long been famous for flat-top acoustics. In a move that surprised some observers, in 2006 Bill Collings diversified his activities into Gibson-inspired solidbody electric instruments.

The body of the 360 could be described as an offset Les Paul, with the treble cutaway drawn back to give better access to the upper frets than on a Gibson. If that visual quirk is to your liking, then you'll certainly appreciate the body, which is cut from Honduran mahogany, and optionally topped by carved quilted maple with a gentle sunburst effect around the edges: all in all, a visually stunning instrument.

However, if this comes across as just another "boutique" take on a 1950s classic, then you may be surprised by the types of sound the 360 is capable of creating. A pair of Lollar mini-humbucker pick-ups produces a variety of tones, ranging from a classic Les Paul from the neck pick-up to an almost Fenderesque clarity and bite coming from the bridge. **TB**

Duesenberg
49er 2009

Type Solidbody electric
Body & neck Mahogany/maple body, mahogany neck
Fingerboard Rosewood
Pick-ups One Domino P-90 and one humbucker pick-up

It might have looked like a Les Paul, with its mahogany set neck, mahogany body with a carved arched maple top, and the single-cutaway shape, but Duesenberg's 49er was a whole new take on this classic guitar shape.

The string-through-body system was designed to add sustain, helped by the weighty slab of mahogany; In fact, many 49ers are even heavier than Les Pauls. The 49er has a Duesenberg Domino P-90 single coil at the neck and a Grand Vintage humbucker at the bridge. These give a range from warm traditional Les Paul sounds right through to a twangier Telecaster tone. The middle position of the three-way selector switch combines the P-90 with just the inner coil of the humbucker, creating a quacky twin single-coil sound that is more like a Strat.

Other features include Duesenberg's "Z" tuners, a multi-adjustable bridge, an Art Deco "D" logo on the upper bout, and a raised metal finger rest along the edge of the scratchplate nearest the strings. The 49er is available in special editions: the classic goldtop or the bold outlaw with faux black leather grain. **SH**

Epiphone Camo
Zakk Wylde 2009

Type Solidbody electric
Body & neck Mahogany body, maple neck
Fingerboard Rosewood
Pick-ups Two Zakk Wylde EMG-81 pick-ups

Zakk Wylde, guitarist with Ozzy Osbourne and Black Label Society, reputedly intended the custom paint job on his Les Paul to be a black-and-white spiral that he'd seen in the Alfred Hitchcock movie *Vertigo*—but when it came back from the shop looking more like a bull's-eye he decided it was fine anyway: the most important thing was that it should not look anything like Randy Rhoads' white Gibson. The Zakk Wylde range of signature Epiphones not only includes a version of his Gibson Les Paul but also this version, the Camo, with a camouflage pattern beneath the circles.

The Korean-made Epiphone's main compromise with the (more expensive) Gibson version is probably that the two pick-ups are passive EMG-HZs, rather than the active humbuckers that many regard as essential if you really want to sound like Zakk Wylde. Otherwise, it has the same gold hardware throughout, a volume and tone control for each pick-up, a standard Tune-o-matic bridge, a stop tailpiece, and sealed Grove tuners. **AJ**

Epiphone G-310
Emily the Strange 2009

Type Solidbody electric
Body & neck Basswood body, mahogany neck
Fingerboard Rosewood
Pick-ups Two 750T and 650R humbucker pick-ups

Emily the Strange is a cult, counterculture cartoon figure that began life in the early 1990s as a decoration on a range of Californian skateboards. A moody, black-haired young girl with "dark" proclivities, Emily started getting noticed when she began appearing on stickers on clothing by Cosmic Debris, a skate and surfwear label. Her popularity spread on the Internet, eventually spawning comics, books, and assorted merchandising bearing her catchphrases: "Get Lost!" and "Wish You Weren't Here."

Hooking up with Epiphone may not have seemed the most obvious of partnerships, but in an era when every kid's middle-aged dad seems to play guitar in a rock band, the ebony finish with those bold/crude red-and-black graphics are sure to be pleasingly distasteful to the eyes of most adult players.

The G-310 is a basic Epiphone SG model produced between 1989 and 2011. Curiously, the 2009 "Emily The Strange" variant was designed to appeal primarily to teenage girls, so it came as something as a surprise when it began turning up in the hands of young men playing in goth and emo bands. There is nothing inherently "special" about the G-310, but it does reflect why Epiphone represents such an important part of Gibson's business: this is a more-than-decent-quality guitar, with an SG body shape that nods to Gibson's illustrious past, but which is presented at a very affordable price.

Although not aimed at professional players, when it first appeared, Epiphone's "Emily" was photographed in the hands of singer and guitarist Machy, of Mexican all-girl pop group La Conquista. **TB**

ESP
Iron Cross 2009

Type Solidbody electric
Body & neck Mahogany/maple body, mahogany neck
Fingerboard Ebony
Pick-ups Two EMG 81/EMG 60 active pick-ups

The Electronic Sound Products (ESP) store was established in Tokyo, Japan, in 1975, and earned its early reputation providing superior-quality custom replacement parts for production instruments—often Fender and Gibson. Launching in the United States eight years later, ESP quickly made a name among the high-speed thrash metal shredders who, throughout the 1980s, were driving the hot-rodded "Superstrat" vogue. By the time the scene's leading band, Metallica, had broken through into the mainstream, lead vocalist and guitarist James Hetfield was already established as ESP's principal cheerleader. Together, he and ESP would go on to produce several signature models, based broadly on classic Gibson body shapes.

The Iron Cross was a limited-edition version of ESP's Les Paul-inspired Eclipse; it was based on the model Hetfield had used on Metallica's *Death Magnetic* tour. It featured a mahogany body with a maple cap, set mahogany neck, Gibson-style 24¾-in. (62.9-cm) scale length, and high-output, active EMG pick-ups. The paintwork and hardware were purposely distressed and worn to match Hetfield's own model. And, of course, the instrument was decorated with the characteristic gold racing stripe and metal iron cross of the original. A lot of bang, but a lot of bucks, too: the ESP cost only slightly less than $10,000. **TB**

The original guitar on which the Iron Cross was modeled can be heard on *Death Magnetic* (2008). This was Metallica's ninth studio album, their fifth consecutive release to debut at Number One in the U.S. charts, and their first to feature Trujillo on bass.

Fender Make'N Music
MVP Stratocaster 2009

Type Solidbody electric
Body & neck Ash body, quarter-sawn maple neck
Fingerboard Maple
Pick-ups Three Custom Shop Fat '50s pick-ups

Fender's Custom Shop in Corona, California, is where the company's custom-ordered guitars are built. The shop also produces a number of exclusive "Dealer Select" models—bespoke Fenders for exclusive sale by a specific retailer. Between 2009 and 2011, the Fender Custom Shop produced a limited range of heavily distressed instruments for Chicago's Make'N Music, noted as one of America's earliest boutique guitar outlets—running since 1973. The range of Stratocasters and Telecasters on offer were authentic-looking replicas of specific models from the 1950s to the early 1970s, but they were given what Fender call the "Heavy Relic" treatment—although they were brand new guitars, they were made to look as if they'd had a half century or more of very heavy use. And since each guitar was hand-built, the distressing on each one was unique.

The model shown here is the Fender Make'N Music MVP (Master Vintage Player) 1950s Stratocaster, which recreates the physical appearance of an original 1956 Strat. This is not entirely an exercise in replicating an instrument from a bygone era; model by model these guitars have a variety of new features. Hidden discreetly in the center of the volume control knob is the S-1 switch, which, when activated, combines the sound of the bridge and neck pick-ups—an effect not possible on an unmodified production Strat. There are other clear design departures in the neck department, including a modern-style flat fingerboard to facilitate faster soloing.

The sound comes courtesy of three Custom Shop Fat '50s single-coil pick-ups, which are designed to deliver a 1950s Strat sound but with boosted bass and a less harsh mid-range. **TB**

Gander
Aquarius 2009

Type Solidbody electric
Body & neck Maple/ebony/bloodwood body and neck
Fingerboard Ebony and maple
Pick-ups Two Seymour Duncan humbucker pick-ups

Canadian guitar maker Ray Gander has created some of the most eye-catching and innovative modern electric guitars, all named after signs of the Zodiac.

The Aquarius was one of his earliest, and today costs more than $5,500. It features an amazing array of woods and craftsmanship. The combination of maple and ebony in the neck, for example, forms a wave shape rolling down the fretboard, with abalone block position markers set in the ebony section.

Gander specializes in exotic wood custom instruments, and has patented a construction process

> "…for those who want to wield something that walks the line between art piece and musical instrument."
>
> GUITAR PLAYER MAGAZINE

that uses a strong carbon-fiber beam through the neck and body of the guitar. Gander claims that this improves sustain, durability, and stability, especially at the traditional weak point—where the neck joins the headstock and the body.

The controls are on a panel in the bottom side of the guitar, out of the way of the picking action. The body has two large holes, and even the headstock has a carved hole.

The hardware is gold-plated, and of the highest quality: Seymour Duncan humbuckers, Grover tuners, a Schaller roller bridge, and Gander's own patented springless tremolo system, which works by compressing a rubber block. Further details may be customized to individual taste. **SH**

Gibson
Dusk Tiger 2009

Type Solidbody electric
Body & neck Marblewood/ebony body, mahogany neck
Fingerboard Ebony
Pick-ups Two Burstbucker 3 and P-90H pick-ups

The Dusk Tiger is the fourth in a series of guitars produced by Gibson that incorporated computer software to do clever things with the tuning and output. The company's HD.6X-Pro Digital Guitar had introduced the capability to output the signal from each of the six strings individually, and its Robot Guitar could send these outputs to auto-tuning software controlling motorized machine heads that could then tune the guitar automatically. The Dark Fire used an improved version of the same system.

The Dusk Tiger appeared in a limited edition of 1,000 guitars costing $4,128 each. It initially attracted criticism for its appearance, which was thought to undermine the supposed sophistication of its insides—Gibson said it was the "world's most advanced guitar"—and one reviewer referred to its "Ron Burgundy-esque name and aesthetic."

Gibson contended that the Dusk Tiger was more intuitive to use that its predecessors, and was therefore more at home in a live environment. The advanced features of the guitar are accessed from the Master Control Knob (MCK II). This has a built-in color LED display, which, when pulled, sends the guitar into tuning mode. Once it has been tuned, the player can select from presets that use onboard effects and pick-up configurations to approximate the sound of classic Gibson and Fender guitars of the past. In addition to the standard pick-ups, there's a piezo that can work with the onboard EQ to produce an imitation of an acoustic guitar. Software for the guitar, including the Chameleon Editor and Guitar Rig 4 Pro, can be downloaded from Gibson's website. **AJ**

Gibson
Eye 2009

Type Solidbody electric
Body & neck Mahogany
Fingerboard Ebony
Pick-ups Two single-coil Alnico V pick-ups

Perhaps because of the enduring popularity of its "heritage" instruments, the Gibson brand has seen few truly original designs launched over the past two decades—very little, in fact, since the Nighthawk series debuted in 1993. One oddity to emerge briefly in 2009, in a limited run of 350 guitars, was the Gibson Eye.

With its pointed twin cutaways, the Eye is superficially an SG variant but with some noteworthy differences: structurally it's similar to a regular SG, with a slim mahogany body with a set mahogany neck; visually, the most obvious deviation is the protruding bass horn, which gives it a slight Fender aesthetic. The ebony fingerboard differs in that it runs a full two octaves, the twenty-four medium-gauge frets a relative rarity on Gibson. Also unusual are the fingerboard inlays—or the complete lack of them.

Overall, the Eye cuts a somewhat brash appearance by Gibson's standards, which tend toward the classic or conservative, depending on your perspective. It is available in one color: the red shown here. Contrasting nicely is the pointed white three-ply pickguard into which the controls and pick-ups—themselves finished is a rather splendid red "Hammerite"—are housed.

The electrics are unusually simple, with single master volume and tone controls and a three-way pick-up selector switch. A 490R humbucker sits at the neck, with a 498T at the bridge. The latter uses Alnico V magnets and is "hot wound," giving it a punchier sound in the mid-range and high frequencies. This same combination is used on new SGs; indeed, for all its visual differences, at a blind listening few would be able to tell the difference between an Eye and a modern-day SG Standard. **TB**

Gibson
SG Zoot Suit 2009

Type Solidbody electric
Body & neck Birch laminate
Fingerboard Ebony
Pick-ups 496 and 500 humbucker pick-ups

Pass the smelling salts—Gibson go plywood! OK, it's not quite the way it sounds, but the SG Zoot Suit does represent something of a departure for the brand in both build and appearance.

Emerging in 2009, the fabulously psychedelic Zoot Suit may look like a slightly reserved paint job thrown together in San Francisco in 1967, but is in fact "natural" when you understand the way in which this visual effect has been created. Instead of the usual slab of mahogany used on SGs since they first appeared in 1961, the body of the Zoot Suit is constructed from birch laminate pieces; each one is under ¹⁄₁₆ in. (2 mm) thick and dyed a different color. All of the different pieces are then bonded with a proprietary glue and then compressed into a "solid" block of wood. When the curves on the body edging are carved, the different colors of the dyes become visible. It's a very pleasing visual effect. For protection, the body is sealed with two coats of satin nitrocellulose lacquer. The same principle is also used on the neck. Of course, by varying the combinations of colored laminate, different effects are possible: the Zoot Suit is available in five different finishes: black and red, black and natural, black and orange, red and blue, and rainbow, which is the one show here.

One interesting by-product of using birch rather than mahogany is that, at around 5¾ lb. (2.6 kg), the Zoot Suit is slightly heavier than a regular SG, which actually creates a slightly better-balanced instrument—the SG might be one the most famous models in guitar history, but the lower mass of the thin mahogany body can make it overly neck-heavy for some players. **TB**

Giffin
T2 Black Limba 2009

Type Semi-hollow body electric
Body & neck Black limba body, black limba/maple neck
Fingerboard Rosewood
Pick-ups Two Amalfitano single-coil P-90 pick-ups

Peripatetic guitar maker Roger Giffin's illustrious career began in the late 1960s in his native London. At his workshop alongside the River Thames he would build instruments used by the likes of Pete Townshend of The Who, Pink Floyd's David Gilmour, and Andy Summers of The Police. His life took a different tack: in the late 1970 he built the prototype of the Steinberger M-Series (the GM1TA), and as a result was poached by Gibson to run their Custom Shop in Los Angeles. Making a permanent move to the United States, he remained with Gibson until 1997, when he once again branched out on his own.

> *"My hands-on approach to guitar building still gives me the greatest satisfaction, and it allows me to produce unique ... instruments."*
> ROGER GIFFIN

Based in Portland, Oregon, since 2004, Giffin now produces a small boutique range of hollow and solidbody electric guitars selling from anything between $2,500 and $5,000. All of the Giffin guitars use the same twin cutaway body shape found on the flagship "Standard" models. The T2 range is less expensive, since the bodies are cut from a single slab of wood without the separate carved tops found on Giffin's luxury instruments. And yet, for those who favor a natural finish, the model shown here with its body carved from increasingly rare black limba is surely about as attractive as a guitar of its type can be. Of course, since these instruments are built to order, the options of wood, pick-up configuration, and finish are all but limitless. **TB**

Gilberto Grácio
Guitolão 2009

Guerilla
TR6 Tank Rust 2009

Type Twelve-string acoustic
Body & neck Spruce and pao santo body,
mahogany neck
Fingerboard Ebony

Type Solidbody electric
Body & neck Basswood body, maple neck
Fingerboard Ebony
Pick-ups Two EMG pick-ups

Many of the guitars featured in this book are broadly conventional; others are variations on a theme; a few are eccentric. None, however, is quite as innovative as this: the Guitolão is an entirely new instrument.

Gilberto Grácio is well known in Portugal as a guitar maker, the latest of a long line of acclaimed luthiers. In his Lisbon workshop, he has built guitars for many famous clients, including Led Zeppelin's Jimmy Page and Steve Howe of Yes.

The Guitolão is more influenced by the traditional music of Grácio's native land than by Western rock. The new shape and larger size of the beautifully made instrument give it a range of tones uniquely suited to, and previously unheard, in Portuguese folk music.

The lower four sets of strings are tuned in pairs together, the higher two sets are tuned an octave apart. Concerts showcasing this new sound have mostly featured the fingerstyle playing of Antonio Eustaquio, who owns one of the only two Guitolãos that Grácio has built. **SH**

Guerrilla Guitars are custom-built in Canada by the owner, "Kosta," and a pair of part-time workers. The company makes no bones about the fact that its instruments are built with metal players solely in mind. Currently under production are six-, seven-, and eight-string guitars, all of which can be configured to suit any player's personal needs—including woods, hardware, pick-ups, and paint jobs.

The necks and bodies are all hand-made at the company's small workshop, except for the pockets and tremolo cavities, which are bored by a CNC machine for accuracy. Every guitar has a paint design sprayed personally by Kosta, giving each individual instrument a one-off finish.

The Guerrilla TR6 Tank Rust has a basswood body, and a three-piece Canadian maple through-neck with a one-inch (2.5-cm) quartersawn center. All the hardware is painted black, and includes a Floyd Rose tremolo, distressed Sperzel USA machine heads, and the fabulous paint finish for which it is named. **PP**

Indie IPR-MG Myles Goodwyn 2009

Italia Rimini 2009

Type Hollow body electric
Body & neck Mahogany body, maple neck
Fingerboard Ebony
Pick-ups Two GR8 Alnico humbucker pick-ups

Type Six-string semi-acoustic
Body & neck Agathis body, maple neck
Fingerboard Rosewood
Pick-ups Two Wilkinson mini-humbucker pick-ups

The Indie guitar company was founded in England in 2001; seven years later, it expanded into Canada. The company's mid-price guitars are manufactured in its own factory in Korea. The philosophy behind the "Indie" name dictates that they sell only through independent retailers, thereby offering small shops the opportunity to stock different guitars from those on sale in the big chain stores. The savings that Indie makes by minimizing advertising—most of its promotion is by word of mouth or on YouTube—enables it to offer attractive discounts to stockists.

The IPR-MG is a signature model for Myles Goodwyn, guitarist with the Canadian rock band April Wine since 1975. It's an original design, although slightly in Gibson territory—the way the body tapers towards the horns make it look a little like an ES-335 that has started to melt. The body is solid mahogany, there are two Alnico (aluminum, nickel, and cobalt alloy) humbucker pick-ups, and one knob each for tone and volume. **AJ**

With a street price of less than £400, it's no surprise that an instrument that looks as good as the Italia Rimini was selected as one of influential website MusicRadar's twenty best budget guitars in the world.

It's a classic f-hole, semi-solid, retro-looking guitar that comes in six- and twelve-string versions. The most distinctive feature is the unique, split headstock. The tuners are arranged in normal three-a-side fashion, but the treble strings get an open slot, while the bass strings get the conventional vertical mounting.

Apart from that, it's mainly standard equipment: a set maple neck, bound rosewood fretboard with pearloid block inlays and twenty-two medium jumbo frets, and Italia's own die-cast tuners. The bridge is Tune-o-matic style; there's a master tone control, a volume control for each pick-up, and a toggle switch—all of which are mounted on a strange little oval control panel. And the Rimini comes in a range of finishes, emphasizing its retro styling with colors that include light blue and honeyburst. **SH**

Letts
Fretless Bass 2009

Type Custom bass guitar
Body & neck Various
Fingerboard Various
Pick-ups Various handmade Letts pick-ups

Bass guitar maker extraordinaire Jon Letts has a workshop in Leicester, England, where he creates unique custom instruments with no automated machinery, using only traditional hand skills, and some of the finest natural materials. The results are among the most distinctive modern bass guitars on the market.

Every wooden part is hand-carved, and shaped from scratch. Even the pick-ups are hand-wound, and these are given hand-made wooden covers, so that they match the guitar body. The control knobs are made from matching wood.

The range of Letts basses is extensive—from standard, four-string instruments to exotic monsters with thirteen strings. To specify their perfect custom guitar, buyers have to make daunting choices from many tonewoods, neck-joint constructions (maple or mahogany, with contrasting stripes, usually wenge or ovangkol), and fretboards.

For a basic starting price of (at the time of writing) only £700, Letts offers customers the following entry-level options: a single or double cutaway body shape; a single humbucker pick-up with ramp (split, hum-cancelling single coils) or a traditional humbucker without ramp; a passive EQ with CTS or Bourne "no load" potentiometers; rosewood or maple fretboard; and side dots in black or white.

Letts uses ebony on his fretless instruments, which are then either given wooden veneer marking lines or left blank. Other details usually include Hipshot tuners and bridges, although hand-made wooden bridges are also an option. **SH**

Pedulla
Nuance 2009

Type Solidbody bass guitar
Body & neck Maple/assorted wood body, maple neck
Fingerboard Ebony
Pick-ups Two Bartolini humbucker pick-ups

Michael Pedulla's Nuances are high quality, and very expensive. There are five different versions: a six-string, with a choice of ¹¹⁄₁₆-in. (17.5-mm) or ¾-in. (19-mm) string spacing, which retails at $4,895; a five-string, also with a choice of string spacing, for $4,395; and a four-string option that costs $4,395. For an extra $495, you can have your name written on the headstock.

The woods used on the Nuances are remarkable. The neck and body are soft maple, and the top is a choice of maple burl, arbutis burl, redheart quilted maple, redwood burl, or spalted chestnut.

"The inspiration was two fold; my love of all the various woods I was not using, and to complement the existing line."
MICHAEL PEDULLA

(A burl is a part of a tree in which the grain has grown in a random manner, creating unpredictable patterns that can look lovely when they've been cut and highly polished. Spalting is the discoloration, caused by fungi, which gives the affected wood surprisingly attractive rustic patterns of pigmentation, white rot, and zone lines.)

Consequently the finish on each Nuance guitar is unique. It is Mike Pedulla's view that the top wood of the guitar generally affects its tone, and that chestnut, in particular, supports tight low-mids and a crisp, focused high end.

The electronics for this guitar are all custom-made by Bartolini in California; the stainless steel strings supplied with the bass are in-house creations. **AJ**

PRS
Al Di Meola Prism 2009

Type Solidbody electric
Body & neck Mahogany/maple body, mahogany neck
Fingerboard Rosewood
Pick-ups Two humbucker pick-ups

World-renowned fusion guitarist Al Di Meola has always been held in high esteem for his acoustic and electric performances and for his recordings—not only his solo work, but also his collaborations with such notable names as John McLaughlin and Paco de Lucia, and with Chick Corea and Stanley Clarke in the band Return To Forever.

Di Meola had been using PRS Guitars for many years prior to his first signature model. The PRS Al Di Meola Prism (or "Rainbow" as it is sometimes called) was prototyped in 2008 and went into production a year later. It turned out to be arguably the most visually striking guitar ever produced and is much loved by players and collectors alike.

In essence, the Prism resembles a top-of-the-range Custom 24, but both Di Meola and Paul Reed Smith wanted a "tie-dyed" finish that would stand out.

The one-piece mahogany body was topped with book-matched, highly-flamed maple; the one-piece set mahogany neck is significantly different from other PRS styles, and was built to the guitarist's specification. The 25-in. (63.5-cm) scale-length neck features a twenty-two-fret Mexican rosewood fingerboard with abalone bird inlays. It is extremely comfortable to play.

The Prism has locking tuners, a PRS vibrola, and a graphite nut. The pick-ups are the PRS 1957/2008 humbuckers—modeled closely on the original Gibson PAF, they give the guitar a vintage sound. The controls are minimal, comprising a single volume and tone control, and three-way toggle selector switch. It is, simply, one of the best guitars PRS ever made. **JB**

PRS
Angelus Cutaway 2009

Type Acoustic guitar
Body & neck Rosewood/spruce body, rosewood neck
Fingerboard Rosewood
Pick-ups Optional pick-ups

PRS had toyed with producing acoustic guitars in the early 1990s, but it wasn't until late 2008 that two models were unveiled: the start of an upmarket range. Paul Reed Smith worked with luthier Steve Fischer to create the 15½-in. (39.3-cm) wide Angelus Cutaway, and the 16-in. (40.5-cm) wide Tonare Grand. The guitars use the old Santana-style headstock, with a hybrid Torres-inspired fan, conventional X-bracing, and, initially, a non-adjustable, graphite-reinforced neck with proprietary-design Robson tuners. The Angelus Cutaway is, perhaps, the definitive design, known for its balanced voice and strong projection.

Seasoned acoustic performers Martin Simpson and Tony McManus became signature artists with their own models (in 2011), while country artists like Ricky Skaggs and Colby Kirby (another signature artist) did much to popularize the new instruments. A Korean-made SE Angelus was offered in 2011, as were proprietary PRS pick-up systems. PRS's Private Stock program offers custom versions; the Collection series models represent the top tier in terms of price and specification.

"The Angelus is balanced beautifully across the registers. It has a powerful bass, a really strong mid feel and a singing treble," says Simpson. "The combination of wide fingerboard and wide spacing at the saddle makes it a fingerstyle guitar par excellence." **DB**

Veteran English folk guitarist Martin Simpson plays the PRS Angelus acoustic on *Purpose + Grace* (2011), which reviewer Colin Irwin described as "an album of great love and joy, [which] confirms that Simpson remains at the top of his game."

Squier Classic Vibe Duo-Sonic 2009

Type Solidbody electric
Body & neck Basswood body, maple neck
Fingerboard Maple
Pick-ups Two single-coil pick-ups

The Duo-Sonic has had a checkered career in Fender's hands, having been launched and dropped three times since 1956.

The original Duo-Sonic was a beginner's electric guitar with a short-scale neck, a simple, undecorated color scheme, and basic electronics and hardware. The guitar was revised several times before production ceased in 1969.

It was re-released in the 1990s as a reasonably-priced, Mexican-built Fender with a short-scale neck. Then production was shifted to China, and the guitar

> *"This Duo-Sonic really does a very good job of nailing the original design ... it has vintage vibe in spades."*

MUSIC RADAR REVIEW

was re-labeled as a Squier Affinity, but it was dropped again two years later.

Then, in 2009, the Duo-Sonic was released for a third time, again as one of Fender's budget Squier Classic Vibe guitars—it was now banking on its retro appeal. But to no avail: it was discontinued in 2012.

The 2009 Duo-Sonic was closely modeled on the original. It had the same maple fretboard that was later changed to rosewood, the gold pickguard, and the utility "desert sand" color scheme. What it did not replicate, though, was the ultra-short neck. The original was 22½ in. (57 cm) long—on the 2009 Squier it is 24 in. (61 cm), only 1½ in. (1.3 cm) shorter than a standard Fender neck. The Squier also featured a more modern C-shaped neck profile, and chunkier frets. **SH**

Republic
Highway 61 2009

Type Resonator
Body & neck Brass or steel body,
mahogany neck
Fingerboard Rosewood

Resonator guitars have held a niche appeal since they first appeared at the end of the 1920s: country, blues, slide, and lap players have all embraced the instrument's unique "metallic" tone. Of course, most of the original prewar National and Dobro designs are now highly collectible, and their modern counterparts are too costly for the casual player. Step forward, Frank Helsley, a Texan on a mission: "I decided I would like to make resonator guitars that were more affordable than what was being offered." Thus Republic Guitars was born.

"I bought my first resonator guitar in 1968 ... I loved to ... tinker with them and try different things to make them sound better."

FRANK HELSLEY, OWNER, REPUBLIC GUITARS

Helsley fell in love with the resonator as a teenager, when he heard Johnny Winter playing acoustic blues. In 2007, Helsley teamed up with a small workshop in China to develop a broad range of classic single-cone and tri-cone models, to which they added their own features, such as body cutaways and options of classic nickel or "distressed" metal finishes.

In 2009, Republic came up with the Highway 61, a three-quarter-scale "travel" resonator with a single cutaway. In spite of its reduced size, it can produce a surprisingly big sound, with an attractively rich tone perfectly suited to open-string slide playing.

Retailing at just under $700, these couldn't really be described as cheap guitars, but there really are few decent alternatives to be found at this price. **TB**

Schecter Robert Smith Ultra Cure 2009

Type Solidbody electric
Body & neck Mahogany body, maple neck
Fingerboard Rosewood
Pick-ups Two Seymour Duncan humbucker pick-ups

Why do people buy signature guitars? If it's in the hope that some nimble-fingered magic might rub off on them, then why would a guitar manufacturer choose someone not overly rated as a guitarist to endorse their instruments? In more than thirty years of downbeat tunesmithery and smeared lipstick, Robert Smith of The Cure has never let rip with a blistering high-tempo solo. So what was Schecter Guitar Research thinking? To be fair, a close listen to The Cure actually reveals Smith as a rather interesting and underrated guitarist—but there's no denying that what he does is very understated.

So what about the guitar? The Ultra Cure is a pretty curious retro design, especially the rather inelegant bulbous body that just looks . . . well, a bit wrong, really. In fact, Smith took an original Schecter Ultra body shape and made it larger. This really is a big body—and yet, at the same time, it is not overpoweringly heavy. In spite of an appearance that has polarized opinion, the Ultra Cure is a very playable guitar capable of a very useful range of tones. The electrics go for an American classic vibe, the Seymour Duncan 1959 humbuckers modeled on Seth Lover's original Gibson PAFs. There's a classic combination of woods—a mahogany body with set maple neck—and the headstock has a reverse MusicMan type of layout, with the tuners for E and A strings on the top, and the four higher strings positioned along the bottom. The two-octave rosewood fingerboard is decorated with some rather cute "Stars and Moons" inlays. And it is available in just one color—"Goth Black," of course. **TB**

The Cure's Robert Smith with his unmistakable Schecter. ➡

2010s

B.C. Rich ASM Zoltán Báthory 2010

Type Solidbody electric
Body & neck Maple/nato body, maple neck
Fingerboard Maple or ebony
Pick-ups Two Duncan Design Rockfield Mafia pick-ups

Hungarian-born Zoltán Báthory combines twin careers as a martial artist and the guitarist in his own aptly named metal band, Five Finger Death Punch. Hugely popular in the United States, Báthory is evidently also pretty well rated in the guitar fraternity, judging by his "Best Shredder" status at the 2010 Metal Hammer Golden Gods Awards. Little surprise, then, that B.C. Rich, longstanding purveyors of rock guitars, should honor him with the ASM Zoltán Báthory signature.

Instead of coming up with one the brand's characteristic pointy bodies—"I wasn't really into the

> *"A bigger headstock is basically going to give a guitar more sustain… actually the headstock is the loudest part of the guitar."*
> ZOLTÁN BÁTHORY

crazy shapes"—Báthory elected to take an existing model and tweak it to his own tastes. So a classic PX3 Superstrat was used as a template with a few significant mods: "We enlarged the headstock a little bit and it's a different shape," declared Báthory: this was in pursuit of greater sustain. The guitar has a "neck-through" construction, with maple neck and nato wings and a quilted maple top; depending on which of the three models you go for, the twenty-four-fret fingerboard is cut from maple or ebony. Báthory's own personalization comes in the form of the fingerboard's sole inlay—a lion rampant on the third fret. The hardware is similarly high-grade: a pair of Duncan Design Rockfield Mafia humbuckers and an original Floyd Rose system. **TB**

Zoltán Báthory of Five Finger Death Punch with arguably the soberest-looking B.C. Rich.

Brazen
Caleb Quaye 2010

Bunker
Touch Guitar 2010

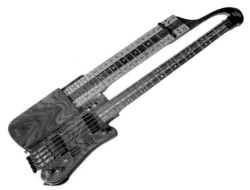

Type Solidbody electric
Body & neck Mahogany/maple body, rosewood neck
Fingerboard Rosewood
Pick-ups One humbucker and two single-coil pick-ups

Type Double-neck bass and six-string electric
Body & neck Walnut body, maple neck
Fingerboard Ebony, maple, and rosewood
Pick-ups Hex-humbucker/quad-humbucker pick-ups

English guitarist Caleb Quaye played for Elton John's band for ten years, and worked on sessions with Paul McCartney, Mick Jagger, and Pete Townshend. He later moved to California, and became a Christian evangelist.

His signature guitar was made by California-based, high-end luthiers Brazen. Unusually, it has a Brazilian Patagonian rosewood set neck matched to its rosewood fingerboard. This rare construction gives the Brazen a noticeably warm sound, an effect enhanced by the solid mahogany body.

The electronics comprise two Seymour Duncan Cool Rail single-coil pick-ups in the bridge and middle positions, and a Seymour Duncan Jazz humbucker in the neck position. A five-way Strat-style pick-up selector and a mini switch that splits the coil on the neck pick-up add to the versatility.

The instrument is based on Brazen's Fantasy series of guitars, which normally feature two humbuckers. Although the guitar is not overly personalized, Caleb's signature is a position marker at the twelfth fret. **SH**

The Bunker Touch was an eccentric twin-neck guitar originally developed by innovative American guitarist Dave Bunker in 1955. It was designed from scratch as an instrument for a two-necked tapping technique. It even had an elbow rest to hold the right arm in the correct position. More than forty years later, Bunker's strangely shaped guitar was made available commercially, with a four-string bass neck, and a choice of a six- or seven-string second neck above.

Bunker developed special "hexophonic" pick-ups for each string on his guitar: he claimed that these were ideally suited for his hammer-on style of playing. The Touch also featured his patented "electro-mute" system, which eliminated all unwanted noise by canceling all the output from each string until it was plucked. Bunker devised an individual bridge assembly system for each string, too. He even published *The Dave Bunker Guitar Method* book, to help buyers to learn to play the six-string and bass guitar at the same time. **SH**

Citron
AEG 2010

Type Hollow body electroacoustic
Body & neck Mahogany/spruce body, mahogany neck
Fingerboard Rosewood or ebony
Pick-ups One single-coil and one piezo pick-up

Citron's AEG series is an unusual combination. It has the skinny, pointed headstock, and fast, narrow neck of an electric guitar, and the hollow body, oval sound hole, and bridge of an acoustic guitar.

This lightweight instrument is purpose-built as a high-end electroacoustic, so comes with a Citron single-coil, custom-wound, magnetic pick-up mounted in the sound hole, and an EMG piezo transducer pick-up under the acoustic-style bridge.

The blending of the clean piezo under-saddle and the warm single-coil is the key to the success of the AEG. It is one of the best guitars at allowing players to get close to a genuine acoustic sound. Using the single coil alone gives a good electric sound, like a semiacoustic guitar.

Other sophisticated features of the Citron's 18-volt active EQ system include a mono/stereo switch, one control to boost or cut the midrange tones, another to cut or boost treble and bass frequencies, and a knob to blend the two pick-ups. **SH**

Collings
MF5 Mandolin 2010

Type Semiacoustic archtop mandolin
Body & neck Spruce and maple body, maple neck
Fingerboard Ebony

Collings is best known for its acoustic guitars, but it makes high-end mandolins, too. These are hand-built in its workshop in Austin, Texas. In the United States, the company has become the leading name in bluegrass mandolins.

To cash in on a resurgence in rootsy mandolin playing all over the world, Collings launched the MF5 in 2010. This is a professional-quality f-hole instrument built with seasoned woods.

The carved Adirondack spruce top, and figured maple back and sides, combine with a special form of parallel internal "tone" bracing to create a sweet playing sound.

The details show that this is a premium instrument: ebony fingerboard, bone nut, adjustable and floating ebony bridge, and an endpiece in either nickel or gold. Buyers can even choose the finish on the tuners: nickel or gold, with black or pearl buttons.

MF5 players include Sarah Jarosz, Don Stiernberg, and Marcus Mumford of Mumford and Sons. **SH**

Daemoness
Cimmerian 7 2010

Type Solidbody electric seven-string
Body & neck Swamp ash/maple body, maple neck
Fingerboard Ziricote
Pick-ups Two humbucker pick-ups

Dylan Humphries is a luthier working in Bristol, England, where he shares a workshop with his mentor, Tom Waghorn of Waghorn Guitars. Humphries is dedicated to the creation of the ultimate, no-compromise metal guitar—he speaks of metal as an ethos which deserves a quality guitar of its own. Each of his instruments is meticulously handcrafted and decorated, and has a unique identity and a name—his Cimmerian series of seven-string guitars includes the "Misha Mansoor," the "Sephiro," the "Philippians," and the "Jesus of Nazareth." His designs are often inspired by Nordic mythology and

> *"Big companies can never produce instruments that define the music because they are too closely linked with big business."*
> DYLAN HUMPHRIES

medieval art and literature. Humphries says: "I am fascinated by medieval art because it was during this time that it first entered [into Western thought] the possibility that the world could end. I detect in this a correspondence with the ideas that have inspired metal into being."

The "Crypt" Cimmerian 7 is the most Gothic of his instruments, with its dye-on-wood skull, *trompe l'oeil* flies, and maggots. The flies are created with inlaid abalone and real flies' wings, and the maggots are made of inlaid mother-of-pearl. The fretboard is made of ziricote, which has a unique spiderweb-like grain, and the subtle inlaid dot fret guides glow in the dark. Aftermath pick-ups are built by Bareknuckle for the "fast-tracking of high-speed staccato riffs." **AJ**

Eastwood
Wandré DLX 2010

Type Solidbody electric
Body & neck Mahogany body, maple neck
Fingerboard Rosewood
Pick-ups Three mini-humbucker pick-ups

The Eastwood Wandré DLX is a tribute to the Italian Wandrés, which were unusually shaped, and among the first to incorporate aluminum necks. The Wandré DLX has a more conventional bolt-on neck made of maple, but it is by no means a standard guitar.

Eastwood guitars are wonderfully eccentric, modern retro instruments, and the Wandré DLX is no different. Its looks are very 1960s, with huge horns on the upper body like an early Burns.

There are three mini-humbuckers, with a bright, clean Stratocaster sound. Each of the pick-ups has an

> *"It looks like a cartoon guitar. It's a sexy-looking thing. The pick-ups sound nice, and I really like the front pick-up."*
>
> WENDELL FERGUSON, AMERICAN COUNTRY MUSICIAN

on-off switch (shaped like a teardrop), and the various combinations give a wide variety of attractive retro- and Fender-style sounds. There are also tone and volume controls, and an optional Bigsby tremolo system instead of the standard hardtail.

There are unusual details, too: the five-ply-bound mahogany body includes hollow chambers for extra resonance and to lighten the weight; the rosewood fingerboard has inlaid star-shaped position markers; the six-a-side headstock is very distinctively shaped. The DLX comes in black, sunburst, or dark green.

The original Wandré guitars are highly sought-after by collectors with prices reaching into five figures. The Eastwood Wandré DLX was given a more reasonable RRP of less than $1,000. **SH**

Epiphone
Dave Navarro 2010

ESP M1
George Lynch 2010

Type Electroacoustic
Body & neck Mahogany/spruce body, mahogany neck
Fingerboard Ebony
Pick-ups One Shadow Nanoflex pick-up

Type Solidbody electric
Body & neck Maple body and neck
Fingerboard Maple
Pick-ups One Screamin' Demon humbucker pick-up

Dave Navarro's work with Jane's Addiction and Red Hot Chili Peppers made him one of alternative rock's first guitar heroes. He played with everyone from Nine Inch Nails to Alanis Morissette. That versatility is captured in his Epiphone signature instrument.

The Epi Dave Navarro is a solid-wood electroacoustic that has striking looks, and is equally at home on stage or played acoustically.

The all-black guitar features a solid Sitka spruce top, hand-scalloped bracing, and a solid-mahogany back. The mahogany neck is hand-fitted to the single cutaway body using a dovetail neck joint and hide glue. Acoustically, this all makes for a rich dreadnought sound. When it's plugged in, Epiphone's eSonic preamp, and the NanoFlex under-saddle pick-up, give impressive amplified tones. There's a built-in tuner and EQ system, plus distinctive decoration, including a nine-ply binding, a scratchplate line drawing, and inlaid star position markers. As a final touch, the mysterious word "Jane" is engraved on the truss rod cover. **SH**

ESP guitars are endorsed by literally hundreds of guitarists, including many of the leading exponents of thrash, not to mention several other species of metal. One of these is influential guitar hero George Lynch, who first became famous in the 1980s through his work with heavy metal band Dokken. He has at least nine signature-model ESP guitars—he is probably most closely associated with the Japanese-style, camouflage-patterned "Kamikaze" model. He also endorses some high-nickel content Dean Markley strings and the Seymour Duncan Screamin' Demon pick-up, which is used on the tiger-striped ESP M1 George Lynch model.

Underneath the eye-catching stripes, the M1 George Lynch is a heavy, utilitarian, metal workhorse. It has just one bridge-mounted humbucker pick-up, a standard black Floyd Rose tremolo bridge (all the hardware is black—it goes nicely with the yellow), and there's only one knob—a volume control—on the entire guitar. **AJ**

First Act
Red Arrow 2010

Fox Amazona
Classico Deluxe 2010

Type Solidbody electric
Body & neck Poplar body, maple neck
Fingerboard Rosewood
Pick-ups One humbucker pick-up

Type Steel-string acoustic
Body & neck Cedar/imbuia body, cedar neck
Fingerboard Braúna
Pick-ups One piezo transducer pick-up

First Act is an American company that makes a range of inexpensive instruments, including drums and keyboards, which are aimed at children and young teenagers who are learning an instrument for the first time. They also make Disney and Sesame Street branded instruments—including ukuleles and tambourines—for smaller children, as well as the Adam Levine designer series. (Levine is a coach on the American talent show *The Voice*.)

The Red Arrow is a short-scale Flying V-shape solidbody electric guitar with a single humbucker pick-up, and a single knob for volume control. It comes as part of a package that also contains some plectrums, a lead guitar cable, and a First Act MA2039 practice amp—all of which is available online for around $120. First Act claim that it's suitable for ages of fourteen and over; there are also resources on its website that answer such questions as: "I've just taken my new guitar out of the box for the first time, and the strings seem loose: do I need to tune them?" **AJ**

Fox Guitars are hand-made in Brazil using locally sourced exotic woods. Models are made in limited quantities, and each guitar is unique and individual. There is no mistaking a Fox guitar.

The Amazona is a simple but eye-catching instrument which, although solidbodied and shaped like a Les Paul, is actually a surprisingly lightweight acoustic guitar. The body is carved from solid Brazilian cedar, with chambers cut in to reduce the overall weight. The body is topped with highly figured bookmatched imbuia, a local variant of walnut. The natural variations in both the cedar and the imbuia ensure that no two Amazonas look identical. The neck is also cut from Brazilian cedar with a fingerboard and bridge made from braúna, another distinctive and highly unusual Brazilian timber.

The Amazona has a fine piezo transducer pick-up, which is mounted beneath the bridge and controlled by a Shadow T-Pro preamp, which features both comprehensive EQ and a tuner. **JB**

Giannini
GCRA 2010

Type Solidbody six-string craviola electric
Body & neck Mahogany body, maple top
Fingerboard Rosewood
Pick-ups Two humbucker pick-ups

This uniquely shaped guitar was invented by Brazilian composer Paulinho Nogueira, and produced by long-established stringed-instrument maker, Giannini.

Guitars of this type are known as craviolas. They can be six- or twelve-stringed; both have more harpsichordy sounds than normal guitars. They are used mainly like classical guitars, with the player seated, and the instrument positioned neatly on his or her thigh. But then, in 2010, Giannini attempted to broaden the appeal by launching an electric craviola, which, though designed in Brazil, used mainly Korean hardware, and was assembled in China.

It has a mahogany body with an arched maple top, and a thin, fast, mahogany set neck. Electronics consist of two original Wilkinson humbucker pick-ups, with two volume controls, two tone controls, a three-way pick-up selector, and two mini-switches for coil-tapping the pick-ups. Other details include a Tune-o-matic bridge, pearl block inlays, and white multi-ply binding around the body and the headstock. **SH**

Givson
GS 1000 2010

Type Solidbody six-string electric
Body & neck Teak body and neck
Fingerboard Rosewood
Pick-ups Two humbuckers and one single-coil pick-up

Most mentions of these guitars start with the words "it's not a Gibson," just to make sure you didn't think it was a printing error. One look at the GS 1000, however, and you'd be unlikely to confuse it with something built in Kalamazoo.

Givsons, in fact, come from India, and have an intriguing character all of their own. They originated when Western guitars were hard to find in the Indian subcontinent, and local manufacturers tried to satisfy demand by building their own.

The GS 1000 has a wacky retro shape, with three pick-ups, and flashy graphics. It's clearly not a Gibson rival, but its basic specification does include a brass bridge, two volume controls, and two tone controls. The pick-up selector allows various pick-up combinations, including series and parallel.

The use of toon (a variety of teak, a very heavy wood) is the same as in many Indian sitars. This is not ideal for a guitar: players have found that it makes the instrument very heavy to play standing up. **SH**

GMP
Cheetah 2010

Godin
MultiOud 2010

Type Boutique solidbody electric
Body & neck Alder/mahogany body, maple/mahogany neck
Fingerboard Rosewood or ebony
Pick-ups Two Seymour Duncan or Rocket humbuckers

Type Eleven-string electroacoustic
Body & neck Mahogany/spruce body, mahogany neck
Fingerboard Ebony
Pick-ups One Fishman under-saddle pick-up

Genuine Musical Products (GMP) builds its guitars in San Dimas, California. Its Cheetah has an asymmetrical body with an animal-skin graphic finish. Like many of the high-end boutique guitars produced in the United States, its precise specification is dependent on the customer's preferences.

The basic model is the Cheetah, with an alder body, maple neck, and rosewood fingerboard (starting at around $1,850). Prices rise as you ascend through the models: the Cheetah Special has a mahogany body, a bound-maple or mahogany neck, and a rosewood or ebony fingerboard; the Cheetah Standard has a carved alder body, maple neck, and bound-rosewood fingerboard; and the Cheetah Deluxe has a mahogany back and carved figured maple top, with a bound mahogany neck and ebony fingerboard (around $2,850).

Buyers can also choose between various forms of body chambering, tremolo systems, and finishes. The two pick-ups are from Seymour Duncan or Rocket. **SH**

This instrument is the latest incarnation of the oud, a pear-shaped instrument, similar to a lute, that originated in Western Asia no later than the fourth century BCE.

Godin's MultiOud modernizes the ancient. It has eleven strings, a side-mounted Aura Pro preamp, a chromatic tuner, and custom-voiced electronics, along with specially designed, precise machine heads that make it easy to tune.

The MultiOud is completely electric, and can play as loud as an electric guitar. It has a cutaway for ease of access, as well as a unique design in which the bridge sits over an ebony saddle, which aids sensors placed under the bridge.

Purists might say that the oud has always been the perfect instrument, and that it requires no modifications. However, that would be to overlook the difficulties of tuning, particularly in low humidity, and of incorporating it into a live band. The MultiOud solves both these problems. **BS**

Hagstrom
Beluga II Bass 2010

Type Solidbody electric bass
Body & neck Ash body, maple neck
Fingerboard Resinator
Pick-ups Two humbucker pick-ups

Swedish instrument maker Hagstrom ceased trading in 1983, but was revived in 2004. It has since reissued updated versions of its most famous designs, and some new ones, including the Beluga Tonemaster series bass guitars, the shape of which hints slightly at Hagstrom's Goya/Standard range from the 1960s, but perhaps bears an even closer resemblance to an Ovation Magnum.

The Beluga has an onboard eighteen-volt active preamp, with a switch on the back for selecting active or passive operation, plus a six-way pick-up selector, and a three-band, active EQ. Hagstrom's original "H-Expander" truss rod allows the bass guitar strings to be mounted on a comfortably thin neck without it breaking in half.

The "F" version has a cavity, with an f-hole above it in one half of the body, and the Beluga III is a slightly cut-down version. It may or may not be a coincidence that the Beluga II shares its name with a sailing ship owned by Greenpeace. **AJ**

Halo
GVK 2010

Type Solidbody electric
Body & neck Swamp ash or basswood/maple
Fingerboard Rosewood
Pick-ups Two Halo-Bucker pick-ups

US-based guitar builders Halo have specialized in custom made-to-order, extended range guitars since 2005—they claim that their custom shop can build a guitar for you faster and for less money than any of their American competitors.

Halo claim that "We hear a lot of people say extended range instruments are useless and a waste of money. We feel differently. There is no such thing as a one-size-fits-all instrument." The GVK guitar is available as a six- or eight-string guitar or a four- or five-string bass. It is available in a combination of neck and body woods and features two Halo-Bucker pick-ups.

"GVK" stands for Grey Van Kuilenburg—the man who hand-carved the body of the guitar in an exaggerated style that wouldn't look out of place in the Bat Cave. Kuilenburg is a horror-film-influenced artist from Alabama who also writes music and poetry and works as a tattoo artist in Hollywood. You could make an appointment with him to have your torso altered to match your guitar. **AJ**

Hoyer
ERN Prestige 2010

Hufschmid
H7 2010

Type Solidbody electric
Body & neck Mahogany/maple body and neck
Fingerboard Ebony
Pick-ups Splittable humbucker pick-ups

Type Seven-string solidbody electric
Body & neck Salvaged wood/mahogany body and neck
Fingerboard Pau ferro or West African ebony
Pick-ups Two custom humbucker pick-ups

Hoyer dates back to 1874, when Franz Hoyer opened a small luthier shop in Germany. Hoyer produced a number of respectable guitars until 1987. The brand eventually landed with a UK concern in 2009, which relaunched with a line of electrics and basses.

One of the former, the ERN Prestige is a carved-top, mahogany solidbody outfitted with Hoyer hardware and electrics. While outward appearances, apart from the double cutaway, suggest a Les Paul, closer inspection reveals a five-ply through-neck, a string-through body, one tone and one volume pot, and two splittable, proprietary humbuckers, all weighing in at just over 7 lb. (3.2 kg), making the ERN a featherweight compared to Gibson's flagship model.

The ERN Prestige's book-matched maple top is available in honey and red bursts (the back can be finished in natural or dark red), while the bird theme is expressed in a headstock logo and cloud fingerboard markers, all inlaid. Pearl-button tuners stretch the strings over Hoyer's "Tune-O-Bridge." **DP**

Patrick Hufschmid makes between eleven and fifteen guitars a year in the basement workshop of his home in Switzerland. His specialties are long-scale seven- and eight-string guitars, which take their cue from a historical tradition going back to Renaissance and Baroque lutes.

The seven-string guitar has been around in the jazz world for some time, but Hufschmid realized that many rock and metal players tune lower, and consequently miss the register of the high E string. His seven-string guitars are tuned A-E-A-D-G-B-E.

Like all Hufschmid guitars, the H7 is made using premium, eco-friendly timbers, and high-quality hardware, which includes custom-wound pick-ups, handmade by Kent Armstrong, with volume and tone controls, three-way toggle, and optional, bright red killswitch. The configuration makes for a highly versatile instrument that can handle anything from the warmest, cleanest of jazz tones to the most extreme death metal. **GD**

Italia
Modena 2010

Type Solidbody electric
Body & neck Agathis tonewood body, maple neck
Fingerboard Rosewood
Pick-ups Three WMH mini-humbucker pick-ups

Italia Guitars was founded in 2000. Its retro-styled products were designed in England by luthier Trevor Wilkinson, and manufactured in South Korea.

The Modena is based on the Crucianelli Tonemaster, which dates from 1962, and owes its appearance partly to the accordions for which Crucianelli was better known—although the headstock is perhaps more reminiscent of a Galanti, another Italian accordion/guitar company of the same period. According to Italia: "With acres of pearloid and sparkle, the Modena is a blast from the past and a definitive example of glitzy retro-chic." In fact, the entire body of the guitar has a heat-shrunk pearloid covering, which does indeed make it look rather like a giant Christmas decoration.

The first version of the Modena came with a chunkier neck, which, though faithful to the original Tonemaster, was not to everyone's taste. Italia have since modified it with something more modern. The body of the guitar still feels a little hefty—it weighs nearly 9 lb. (4 kg).

The three mini-humbucker pick-ups are selected by a five-way switch, and there are single master volume and tone controls, plus a second volume knob for the neck pick-up only—this allows it to be added to any pick-up selection, and thus provides quite a lot of tone variation. The tremolo is the Trevor Wilkinson-designed "Wigsby" which, while using the same principle, doesn't resemble a Bigsby as closely as you might imagine.

At various times, a baritone version of the Modena and a Modena sitar have also been available. **AJ**

Jay Turser
JT-LTCRUSDLX 2010

Type Semi-solidbody electric
Body & neck Semi-solid body, set maple neck
Fingerboard Rosewood
Pick-ups Two single-coil Alnico pick-ups

Imitation is the sincerest form of flattery. If Roger Rossmeisl, who designed the original Telecaster Thinline for Fender in the late 1960s, were still alive, he would surely be extremely flattered by the number of makers who copied his original design. At a time when Japanese products did not have the quality or prestige of equivalent U.S. products, Japanese-owned Ibanez USA had a cheap copy of the Telecaster Thinline in its first catalog issued in 1971, along with many other clones of popular Gibson, Fender, and Rickenbacker guitars.

> *"[In the 1950s], it was all about originality and collective research. There is an awful lot of imitation going on now."*
> STEVE LACY, JAZZ SAXOPHONIST

Today, China is where Japan was back then, and U.S. Music Corp's Jay Turser brand, which manufactures this clone of the Telecaster Thinline in that country, is one of the last in a long line of brands manufacturing guitars that look and sound not unlike the real thing, at a fraction of the price. Fender is also selling at these price points with its Squier brand.

The JT-LTCRUSDLX has been positively reviewed by buyers for the quality of its sound, playability, and finish. It certainly represents a lot of guitar for $300. That said, if a buyer wants a similar package, but is particularly brand sensitive, another $100 buys Fender Squier's Classic Vibe Telecaster Thinline, which not only has the Fender name on its headstock, but may also legitimately be called a Telecaster. **GD**

Larrivée
RS-4 2010

Type Solidbody electric
Body & neck Mahogany/maple body, mahogany neck
Fingerboard Rosewood
Pick-ups Two single-coil "toaster" pick-ups

It is a big event when a major manufacturer renowned for steel-string flat-top acoustic guitars launches a solidbody electric model. You wait for ages and then two come along together. In 2007, Californian manufacturer Taylor Guitars launched its Classic model. Canadian manufacturer Larrivée, having opened a factory in California some six years earlier, countered with the RS-4 on Taylor's home turf. It was not Larrivée's first foray into the solidbody electric market, though: the company had made them in the 1980s during a downturn in acoustic guitar sales. Both Taylor and

"We endeavored to make this instrument reach its potential through excellence in craftsmanship and superior hardware."
LARRIVÉE

Larrivée already had comparable product lines, and their pricing was similar. In launching their new electric models, they also had pretty much the same strategy of concentrating their efforts on a single model that is conservative in styling but right up-to-date in its hardware. Clearly they watch each other very closely.

Four years in the making, the RS-4 features a carved maple top on a mahogany body with a softened cutaway and two body cut-outs for playing comfort, which also reduce weight to a light 7 lb. (3.75 kg). The neck features a "spoke nut, truss rod" which enables adjustments with the strings at tension. The hardware set-up includes master tone and volume controls, a three-way selector, a pair of humbuckers, and a vintage-style tone circuit. **GD**

Line 6 James Tyler Variax JTV-89US 2010

Type Electric with built-in modeling/tuning effects
Body & neck Mahogany body, maple neck
Fingerboard Rosewood
Pick-ups One piezo plus two humbucker pick-ups

California-based Line 6 was a leading pioneer in modeling technology, with effects such as the famous Pod units. Its Variax series, however, was less successful.

These instruments offered amazing technology—including the capability of changing the guitar's tuning, and duplicating the sounds of all major guitars—but they were held back by uneven build quality, and by their looks and feel.

The James Tyler Variax (JTV) range remedied these shortcomings. They are produced in association with Tyler, a top American guitar maker.

> *"It's awesome ... If you're looking for a shred guitar that pretty much does it all, then this is the one."*
>
> ROB "CHAPPERS" CHAPMAN, SESSION MUSICIAN

The JTV-89US is a high-tech version of a shred guitar—other JTVs aim to create twenty-first-century versions of a Strat (JTV-69) or a Les Paul (JTV-59)

The onboard Line 6 technology means there are twenty-eight guitar sounds—from a Les Paul to a twelve-string acoustic—and eleven different tunings.

With its reverse headstock, black nickel hardware, and sleek horns, the 89 is clearly aimed at metal players. The thin, flat neck, with shallow "C" profile and the deep scoop in the body for high fret access mean there's nothing to slow down the fastest fingerwork. Although the camcorder-like rechargeable lithium battery inside the body gives just twelve hours' playing time, the JTV does, however, function as a straight electric guitar without a battery. **SH**

Lowden Richard Thompson 2010

Type Acoustic flat-top
Body & neck Cedar/ziricote body, maple/rosewood/walnut neck
Fingerboard Ebony

Born in Belfast, Northern Ireland, in 1951, George Lowden made his first credible attempt at building a guitar at the age of eighteen, but it would be another four years before he tackled in earnest the challenge of becoming a true luthier. "I learned everything the hard way," he said. "I had no one to teach me how to avoid the obvious pitfalls. I tried new shapes, bracing designs, and many other ideas, and gradually emerged from the 'hard school' of self-taught guitar making." He certainly did. In the late 1970s, Lowden developed a new neck block extension under the fingerboard as well as his

> "As a luthier, I find that designing a few 'special' guitars does stretch my creative abilities, and I enjoy that challenge."
> GEORGE LOWDEN

own distinctive A-frame bracing system, and when he was done, the Lowden guitar was born.

Launched in 2007, the Richard Thompson signature model is named after the British songwriter and guitarist who had been playing Lowden guitars for many years. Crafted in the family workshop in Downpatrick, County Down, Ireland, the instrument is, in Thompson's view, "loud, punchy, and sweet at the same time," and offers an "even balance between bass and treble."

Its attractions include ebony gold Gotoh tuning machines, Tasmanian blackwood binding, and a headstock of laminated rosewood. The timber combination—an AAAA cedar top and ziricote back and sides—is renowned for its clarity. **BS**

Brian Moore
iGuitar 2010

Type Solidbody electric
Body & neck Mahogany/maple body, maple neck
Fingerboard Rosewood
Pick-ups Two humbuckers and one single-coil piezo pick-up

The iGuitar is an innovative instrument that gives players various output options. There are three normal magnetic pick-ups—two humbuckers, and a single-coil operating through a five-way selector switch—that can be combined in the usual variety of ways.

In addition, the iGuitar has a sophisticated bridge piezo, with individual string sensors. The piezo output can be played alone for an acoustic guitar sound, or blended with the magnetic pick-ups for a mix of both.

Wiring the piezo through a thirteen-pin connector allows players to use a guitar MIDI-synthesizer or to link directly to a computer system to record or trigger any sounds. All three outputs can work at the same time.

Onboard electronics include an octave-shifting switch, which is especially useful when the midi output is triggering keyboard sounds. The humbuckers have a coil-splitting switch, so the range of tones from the standard magnetic pick-ups is huge.

The low-tech body is so highly contoured that there's no need for pickguards. Other innovations include a jack socket hidden in the back of the guitar for secure connection, and a headstock featuring four tuners on one side, two on the other.

The iGuitar is also available in a single cutaway shape with two humbuckers and no single coil, and in a semi-hollow version. **SH**

Guitarist Roger Adler used his Brian Moore iGuitar to create the sounds of every orchestral instrument on *The Garage* (2005), and played the iGuitar live in the same year at U.S. President George W. Bush's second inaugural ball in Washington, D.C.

MusicMan
John Petrucci 2010

Type Solidbody electric
Body & neck Alder/maple body, mahogany neck
Fingerboard Ebony
Pick-ups Two HH pick-ups and one DiMarzio pick-up

MusicMan has produced several signature models for John Petrucci of Dream Theater. Voted the seventeenth-greatest guitarist of all time by readers of *Guitar World* in 2012, Petrucci is known for his high-speed, alternate picking, metal shredding technique, and his use of seven-string guitars (such as the MusicMan JP7), which allow him to play extended runs while soloing. The JPX model was introduced in 2010 to celebrate ten years of collaboration between company and player.

This version has a thin upper horn, and a large, alder body with a series of chambers for extra acoustic

"The idea was to get a smooth feel, and I'm all about making the guitar as easy to play as possible."

JOHN PETRUCCI

resonance—this, combined with a piezo pick-up concealed in the tremolo mechanism, enables the creation of acoustic guitar-like sounds, saving the player the trouble of switching guitars during a performance. There are dual output jacks that offer the option of the signal from the piezo on its own or a stereo output. A five-way selector gives access to individual pick-up coils.

Petrucci was interested in experimenting with a flatter fretboard. He says: "We started with 20 in. (50.8 cm) to see what would happen . . . I was trying to get it so the neck was really not getting in your way . . . The rear contour also changed, so it's more symmetrical. It's a taste thing, and it's certainly not traditional, but it's really cool." **AJ**

John Petrucci performing with his signature MusicMan in 2009. ➡

MusicMan
Reflex Bass 2010

Type Solidbody electric bass
Body & neck Ash/maple/mahogany body, maple neck
Fingerboard Maple or rosewood
Pick-ups Two optional single-coil or humbucker pick-ups

Formed by ex-Fender execs Forrest White and Tom Walker (with Leo Fender as a silent partner, his no-compete with CBS still in effect), MusicMan was a pioneer in active electronics in guitars. In 1976, the StingRay 1 and StingRay became the first production guitar and bass, respectively, to offer the option of frequency boosting, thanks to onboard preamps.

Fast forward to 2010, and the MusicMan Reflex five-string bass seems the logical destination of the journey begun by the StingRay. Although the Reflex forgoes the StingRay's iconic oval pickguard and boomerang control plate, it does retain the unique MusicMan headstock shape and tuner arrangement (in this case 4 + 1 rather than 3 + 1).

MusicMan ups the ante with a four-band, active preamp (treble, high-mid, low-mid, and bass), and a passive preamp, both of which, when combined with any of the Reflex's three pick-up options, result in a wide range of tonal options. A push-button switch flips the Reflex between passive and active. While traditional volume and tone pots are used in passive mode, in active mode, two nested knobs tweak the four EQ bands. Push-buttons switch each of the pick-ups on or off in the three-pick-up version. The single- and double-humbucker Reflexes have a push-button for series and parallel switching, the latter also featuring an on/off button for each pick-up.

Available in black, white, three-tone sunburst, and gold, the Reflex also features an attractive binding, and the StingRay's beveled bass-side lower bout and barrel saddles. Notably, the Reflex line also features six-string guitars and a four-string bass. **DP**

Novax
Charlie Hunter 2010

Type Solidbody electric
Body & neck Ash, mahogany, or walnut body and neck
Fingerboard Ebony
Pick-ups Two Bartolini pick-ups

Judging by the output of the industry big guns, you could be forgiven for thinking that the vast majority of guitarists have little interest in anything other than a handful of designs created more than half a century ago. If this is indeed true, then at the other end of the scale we find a tiny number of explorers and innovators like Ralph Novak.

Novax guitars are fascinating. Their USP is clear at a single glance—the frets are "fanned," rather than running parallel to one another. What's actually happening here is that every string has a unique scale length. The explanation is best left to Novax: "Imagine six one-string guitars, each with a scale length optimized for the pitch and tone of that string. If a chord was formed by striking all of the one-string guitars at once, how might that sound compared to one six-string guitar?" It's all interesting stuff.

The highest-profile Novax user is American jazz guitarist Charlie Hunter. Making his name in the 1990s with The Disposable Heroes Of Hiphoprisy, Hunter is a player whose music seems to require two brains to play. Hunter collaborated with Ralph Novak, to produce the Charlie Hunter eight-string. It's rather like a three-string bass combined with a five-string guitar: both the pick-ups and tuners are split accordingly. This configuration is geared toward the way in which Hunter plays, with his thumb picking the bass strings and his finger the treble strings.

Sadly for most of us, these incredibly beautiful instruments don't come cheap: at well over $3,000 for a basic model, customers need deep pockets as well as exploratory minds. **TB**

Ovation DJ Ashba Demented 2010

Type Hollow body electroacoustic
Body & neck Spruce body, nato neck
Fingerboard Rosewood
Pick-ups One black Ovation slimline pick-up

Ovation's "Demented Collection" consists of four acoustic electrics made in 2010 and inspired by Guns N' Roses guitarist DJ Ashba, whose graphic designs the company decided to reproduce as a limited series.

Every audible and visual aspect of these guitars was a collaborative effort between Ashba and Ovation's R&D division. The designs were the Chrome Bone, a section of chrome-plated spinal column that Ashba himself has as a tattoo on his back; the Bone Yard, showing an olive-shaped devil dancing on a bed of skulls; the Bone Daddy, with its stitched-up heart and barbed wire encircling a red rose and skull; and an animated depiction of Ashba himself, floating before a full moon wearing his trademark stitched top hat and with a hole through his chest.

The unique Ovation slimline pick-up has an individual sensor for each string which, combined with its mid-depth roundback body, produces a guitar with a lovely tone and a compensatingly uncompromising attitude. **BS**

PRS 25th Anniversary Swamp Ash 2010

Type Semi-solidbody electric
Body & neck Swamp ash body, bolt-on maple neck
Fingerboard Maple
Pick-ups Three mini-humbucker pick-ups

PRS's twenty-fifth anniversary in 2010 signaled a huge shake-up in its electric range and, of course, a slew of new Anniversary models.

The Swamp Ash Special (SAS) was originally introduced in 1996, and by 2010 was the only bolt-on-neck guitar in the PRS range. As its name suggests, the SAS uses a lightweight, swamp ash body with a maple neck and fingerboard—a very Fender-like blend. The Anniversary version sports three new-design Narrowfield (NF) humbuckers in place of the old hum/single/hum configuration. These were controlled by a Strat-like, five-way lever pick-up selector switch.

The NF pick-ups, like those on the PRS513, are unconventionally-sized, and, like single-coil pick-ups, are able to sense any small "aperture" in the vibration of the strings: thus, they combine the character of the single coil with the fullness and warmth of the humbucker. A highly successful guitar, the PRS Anniversary Edition remains in the PRS line as the Swamp Ash Special Narrowfield. **DB**

RGB
Model B 2010

Schecter
V-1 2010

Type Solidbody electric
Body & neck Customer's choice
Fingerboard Customer's choice
Pick-ups Two Stewart McDonald Golden Age humbuckers

Type Solidbody electric
Body & neck Mahogany/ebony body, mahogany neck
Fingerboard Ebony
Pick-ups One Seymour Duncan Blackout active pick-up

Founded by original Material guitarist Cliff Cultreri, Destroy All Guitars is one of the most fascinating retail outlets for those in search of instruments that traverse function and art. Among DAG's list of clients is luthier Ryan Gray Boutté who, since 2000, has been producing hand-made electric guitars under the RGB name. Boutté produces only two different models, the twin cut Model A and the Model B (shown here).

As with many small-scale custom luthiers, much of RGB's appeal lies in the fact that every instrument is unique, and may be tailored to the desires of the player. This particular model is cut from dark meranti, a very unusual tonewood that hails from the Phillippines, with a rosewood fingerboard and flame maple and waterfall bubinga neck. It also has a free-turning glass marble fitted into the body behind the tailpiece, visible from both sides. Boutté will similarly build pieces of glass, metal, or bone into the guitar if required. Cultreri hails RGB's "exceptional build quality and playability" and a "unique and magnificent art aesthetic." **TB**

Schecter's "V-1" designation is used to describe a series of guitars broadly based around the classic Gibson Flying V. These have appeared in a number of guises since the end of the first decade of the twenty-first century, taking names such as the Hellraiser, Blackjack, and Demon. These guitars tend to share a number of characteristics, such as a mahogany body a three-piece neck, and powerful EMG or Seymour Duncan active humbuckers.

The V-1 "Jaw" shown here was built for death metal guitarist Mike Derks and incorporates an unusual variation on the Flying V design in the form of beetlelike mandibles at the head and two teethlike extrusions inside the V, making it look like the jaws of a shark. If you think that this all seems a little aggressive, then consider that Derks, whose alter ego is "Balsac the Jaws of Death" in the American heavy metal band Gwar, probably wouldn't feel as comfortable playing say, "Hail, Genocide" from their album *Bloody Pit Of Horror* (2010) on a guitar shaped like a hamster. **AJ**

Starr Labs
Ztar 2010

Type MIDI/computer controller
Body & neck Composite body and neck
Fingerboard 144 pressure-sensitive switches
Pick-ups One InBeam non-audio pick-up

In spite of retaining to the present day a niche group of dedicated followers, the guitar synthesizer must go down on the guitar's evolutionary timeline as a failed late-1970s experiment. The emergence of MIDI (Musical Instrument Digital Interface) in the decade that followed saw the introduction of guitars capable of converting picked strings into data that could control external synths, and finally the birth of guitar-shaped controllers that had no sound of their own.

Like the late-1980s Synthax, the Starr Labs Ztar completely separates the actions of the left hand and the right hand. A set of six "strings" appears on the body of the instrument; these act as triggers and can be picked in the usual way, the movement captured by the optical InBeam. The conventional fingerboard, however, is replaced by a series of six pressure-sensitive switches on each fret.

Starr Labs is a manufacturer of electronic musical instruments that was founded in 1986 in San Diego, California, by musician and inventor Harvey Starr. **TB**

Traben
Greg Weeks 2010

Type Solidbody electric bass
Body & neck Basswood body and neck
Fingerboard Rosewood
Pick-ups Two Rockfield humbucker pick-ups

The music of deathgrind band Red Chord is not for the fainthearted. Its bassist Greg Weeks needs a powerful instrument to be heard above the brutality of Guy Kozowyk's vocals, and Mike "Gunface" McKenzie's guitar. The Traben Chaos bass, customized to Weeks' specification to become the Greg Weeks Signature model, is that instrument.

The main contributor to the power, volume, and tone of Traben basses is the unique bridge, which increases mass and bridge-to-body contact. Its external parts are cast from steel, and the internal component is constructed from aluminum: the two sections combine to enhance the low end.

Traben basses normally have five-way switches, but for this signature model Weeks opted for a three-way switch, with a toggle for coil tapping, and a three-band EQ with a volume knob. He explained his choice simply: "I just wanted people to have as many options as I could to get any tone for any form of music that they're playing." **GD**

Cort Matthias Jabs Garage 2 2011

Decibel Javelin 7 2011

Type Solidbody electric
Body & neck Swamp ash body, maple neck
Fingerboard Maple
Pick-ups Two "Scorpu" humbucker pick-ups

Type Seven-string solidbody electric
Body & neck Walnut body, rosewood neck
Fingerboard Rosewood
Pick-ups Two Custom Nordstrand humbucker pick-ups

Matthias Jabs, who has played guitar for The Scorpions since he replaced Michael Schenker in 1978, is perhaps most frequently associated with the Gibson Explorer or his signature Dommenget Mastercaster. Nevertheless, in 2010 he collaborated with gigantic South Korean guitar manufacturer Cort to develop a signature line of guitars called the Garage 1 and the Garage 2.

Jabs' premise was to create an instrument that was easy to use and less fussy than the Mastercaster. The Cort Garages both use "Scorpu" pick-ups that were designed by Jabs himself—the Garage 1 has just one of them—and there's a coil-tap that gives the humbuckers a single-coil option operated by a push/pull knob with a plastic grip that is designed to make it foolproof, no matter how quickly you need to get to it. The only unusual control is the "full force" switch which bypasses the volume and tone controls. As a bonus, on request, you can have Matthias Jabs' autograph on the headstock. **AJ**

When Darren Wilson completed the Javelin Prototype 1 in 2010, news of this momentous event was quick to reach Misha Mansoor, founder and lead guitarist of progressive metal band Periphery. Mansoor sent Wilson a message asking if he could try it the next time he was in Toronto, Canada, and of course Wilson agreed. At Mansoor's request, some heavier strings were installed, it was tuned to drop-A flat, and the neck was adjusted to get the action as low as possible. Mansoor loved it so much that he played it for the first two songs at his Toronto concert, and purchased it in July 2011. This was an epoch-making event: it was the first Javelin ever offered for sale.

Wilson, a graphic designer-cum-luthier, uses only the very finest woods in his hand-built masterpieces: among the materials employed in the bodies are swamp ash, white limba, and roasted curly maple, while ziricote is used for the fingerboards. The current wait for a Decibel guitar is two years, give or take. Customers are more than happy to wait. **BS**

Fender Kurt Cobain Jaguar 2011

Type Solidbody electric
Body & neck Alder body, maple neck
Fingerboard Rosewood
Pick-ups One DiMarzio and one PAF humbucker pick-up

To mark the twentieth anniversary of Nirvana's album *Nevermind* (1991), Fender launched this special-edition "artist signature" Jaguar. It was modeled on a customized 1965 guitar used by Kurt Cobain, the band's frontman, whose style and sound helped to launch grunge music worldwide.

Fender was careful to replicate the distressed finish of the original—and the changes that Cobain had made to it. The carefully recreated details include the Strat headstock shape with 1950s style "spaghetti" Fender logo, Gotoh tuners, four-ply scratchplate, a

> *"Meticulously modeled on the battered and highly unusual 1965 Jaguar that Cobain wielded… when Nirvana ruled rock …"*
>
> 2011 FENDER ADVERT

floating, lockable tremolo system, white neck binding, and a synthetic bone nut.

The replica also includes the two-position slide switch, for changing between preset "lead" and "rhythm" circuits, that was in place on the original when Cobain acquired it.

The body finish was an aged sunburst, and all the hardware was aged and heavily road-worn to recreate the multiple knocks the original received during Nirvana's lively and chaotic life on stage.

The Jaguar was accompanied by an authentic black vinyl hard-shell case and an exclusive Kurt Cobain book, which included interviews with Nirvana's guitar technician Earnie Bailey. It was made in Mexico and cost $1,850. **SH**

← Kurt Cobain plays the very Jaguar that the 2011 Signature model aims to replicate.

Fender Stratocaster Pro Closet Classic Pine 2011

Type Solidbody electric
Body & neck Pine body, maple neck
Fingerboard Maple or rosewood
Pick-ups Three "Master Design" single-coil pick-ups

Pine? To many traditional guitar fans it seemed an unlikely choice of material for a new Stratocaster. But pine is a perfect tonewood—after all, spruce is a type of pine, and that's the commonest wood used for building acoustic stringed instruments.

Fender launched this rare solidbody electric in 2011. It was a high-end Strat with a high price tag to match, so Custom Shop workers used all their skills to create something special. The body was finished in a special lacquer, and the neck was slightly tinted to give the whole instrument a retro feel. The sales blurb

> *"A truly remarkable guitar, with a body fashioned from hundred-year-old pine and a distinctive closet classic lacquer finish."*
>
> **FENDER ADVERT**

described it as "the look of a long-lost but newly rediscovered instrument."

The quartersawn maple neck had a large "C" profile, vintage-style truss rod adjustment at the headstock, and fingerboards with jumbo frets. Other classic touches included a single-ply scratchplate, and the standard Stratocaster five-way pick-up selector. But there were modern touches too: like the Fender Master Design pick-ups and the Gotoh locking tuners. The guitar was available only in white, black, or copper.

Players found that the lightweight, resonant body, and the stainless steel saddles and block created a very bright-sounding guitar, while the pick-ups added warmth. For all its merits, the Closet Classic Pine was withdrawn after only one year in production. **SH**

Gibson Les Paul Studio Baritone 2011

Type Solidbody electric baritone
Body & neck Mahogany/maple body, mahogany neck
Fingerboard Rosewood
Pick-ups Two Gibson humbucker pick-ups

Gibson built six-string basses decades ago, and a few years ago the company tried a brief run of a Les Paul baritone guitar. It was well received by critics, but took time to gain general acceptance. However, after it went out of production, demand grew until the pewter-finished instruments were worth more than twice the original price. So it tried again in 2012 with this limited-edition Les Paul Studio Baritone.

The new bari Les Paul had the same 28-in. (71-cm) scale as its predecessor. That's 3½ in. (8.9 cm) longer than on a standard Les Paul—two extra frets' worth of

"If you're looking for tones that are even more burly and muscular than a standard Les Paul, this unique instrument can definitely deliver."
JORDAN WAGNER FOR PREMIER GUITAR MAGAZINE

neck. This keeps the string tension tight if players opt for lower tunings, such as C (C-F-B♭-E♭-G-C), B (B-E-A-D-F#-B), and A (A-E-A-D-F#-B). The sound is still tight in a way you couldn't get if you tuned a standard guitar down that low.

Apart from that, this is classic Les Paul: a one-piece mahogany neck with a rounded, 1959 shape, and a mahogany body with maple top. The body is actually a two-piece affair, with internal tone chambers that reduce the weight and increase the resonance.

For the electrics, Gibson used a pair of uncovered ceramic-magnet humbuckers—a 496R in the neck position, and a 500T at the bridge pick-up. These hotter units are able to handle more low frequencies than the pick-ups on other Les Pauls. **SH**

Gibson Midtown Custom 2011

Type Semi-hollow body electric
Body & neck Maple/mahogany body, mahogany neck
Fingerboard Richlite
Pick-ups Two Burstbucker pick-ups

The Midtown Custom is a scaled-down descendant of Gibson's ES-335, the world's first thinline, archtop, semi-acoustic guitar. Although the latest version bears a resemblance to its legendary forebear, its dimensions have been scaled down—the widest part of the Midtown Custom's body is 1½ in. (38 mm) narrower than that of the ES-335, so it's quite a bit easier to get your arm around.

Whereas the ES-335 was constructed with a laminate top and bottom, connected with a central block, the Midtown Custom is a solid piece of mahogany, with chambers carved into it, and a maple top with f-holes, a combination that gives the guitar some of the quality of a solidbody.

Other twenty-first-century features include the fingerboard, which may look like ebony but is in fact made of Richlite—a mixture of recycled paper and phenolic resin that supposedly works the same as the real thing but lasts longer. Gibson publicity claims that it offers "the constructional and resonant properties of fine hardwood, but with improved durability, for a superb feel."

The inlays may superficially resemble pearl block markers, but they are acrylic. The Midtown Custom also features Burstbucker pick-ups: these latest versions of Gibson's original PAFs provide players with plenty of scope to contrast openness and dynamism.

The slim-taper neck has Gibson's standard 1⁷⁄₁₀-in. (4.3-cm) nut width, and the joint at the nineteenth fret makes access to the upper reaches easier than on a Les Paul. All in all, this is a supremely versatile guitar that can handle anything from classic rock to funk. **AJ**

GMW Guitarworks
Empire Custom 2011

Type Custom electric
Body & neck Various available
Fingerboard Various available
Pick-ups Various available

California-based luthier Lee Garver's GMW company specializes in creating distinctive custom guitars for clients all over the world. It builds electric guitars using a wide variety of woods, and numerous different shapes of bodies and construction styles, and it gives buyers a choice of any pick-up produced by EMG, DiMarzio, or Seymour Duncan. GMW is also known for its unique graphic design finishes, which are normally painted by Lee himself. The range of detailed options for buyers is immense, right down to a choice of fretwire and the color of the side dots on the neck.

Prospective buyers can simply run through an extensive online menu of options to create their ideal custom-made guitar. Also notable are the amazing graphic paint jobs that GMW offer, which in the past have included an image of ancient Egyptian Pharaoh Tutankhamen, realistic snakeskin finishes, and a hand-painted scene from the Quentin Tarantino film *Inglourious Basterds* (2009). Impressive decorative extras have included pearl "bullet-hole" inlays as neck markers, rose and vine abalone decorations on a guitar body, and flames painted across a headstock.

Prices start at $1,200 for the base one-pick-up model, and the line ascends right up to special models such as the GMW Firefox. This two-pick-up, through-neck, solid mahogany electric guitar, based on a Gibson Firebird shape, was built to specifications supplied by Michael Sweet, lead guitarist of Californian glam metal band Stryper. The model shown here is an Empire LTS Standard. With its tri-leaf inlays, bone nut, Sperzel Trim Lock locking tuners, and 6150 Dunlop frets, it is the most popular member of the Empire family. **SH**

Ibanez
FRM100 Fireman 2011

Type Solidbody electric
Body & neck Mahogany body, mahogany/maple neck
Fingerboard Rosewood
Pick-ups Three single-coil pick-ups

Well established for his complex noodling in the bands Racer X and Mr. Big, Paul Gilbert deservedly finds himself in *Guitar World* magazine's list of the fastest guitarists of all time.

Gilbert has long been an endorsee of Ibanez. His PGM (Paul Gilbert Model) line had Ibanez RG-style bodies with pairs of Gretsch-style, painted f-holes that created the impression of a hollow body instrument. In 2009, Gilbert came up with his own design for a reversed classic Ibanez Iceman body shape: with its bright red finish, Gilbert naturally called it the Fireman!

Originally a high-end custom instrument, in 2011 Ibanez launched a more affordable, Chinese-built version, the FRM100. Unlike other Ibanez shred guitars, the neck profile is chunky and wide: 0.86 in. (22 mm) at the first fret; 0.9 in. (24 mm) at the twelfth.

The sound emanates from of a trio of hum-canceling Alnico DiMarzio single coils: Gilbert's signature Injector models in the bridge and neck positions, and an Area '67 in the middle. These nicely combine the beefy sound of a humbucker with the clarity and bite of a single coil. They are offset, and housed in a tortoiseshell pickguard. Control comes via a five-way pick-up selector switch with master volume and tone pots—the volume, unusually, in the farthest corner of the lower bouts. **TB**

Paul Gilbert can be seen wielding his Fireman on the cover of *Fuzz Universe* (2011). Most of the thirteen tracks on this acclaimed album are original compositions, but there are also pieces by Johnny Cash, Todd Rundgren, and J.S. Bach.

Paul Gilbert—one of the speediest of the speed merchants. →

Mayones
Regius 6 Mosaic 2011

Type Six- or seven-string solidbody electric
Body & neck Ash/mahogany/maple body, or ash top; maple/mahogany/wenge/amazaque neck
Fingerboard Ebony

Mayones guitars and basses have been hand-made in Gdansk, Poland, since 1982. They are custom-finished to the customer's specification, and have been purchased by, among others, Led Zeppelin's John Paul Jones, and Wes Borland of Limp Bizkit.

The Regius series have a sturdy neck-through construction, a sleek Superstrat shape, and a couple of high-powered humbuckers. There is a six-string version, the Regius 6, plus a Regius 7, and Regius 8. The Regius Thirtieth Anniversary is a twin-neck with a twelve-string and a six-string. Within these categories is a variety of finishing touches: the Regius Gothic with hard ash top, ebony fingerboard, and optional Iron Cross-inlaid fret position markers; the Regius Pro with a Schaller Floyd Rose PRO tremolo unit; the Regius KLR 6 with a Kahler tremolo bridge.

The standard Regius model comes with either a mahogany or a swamp ash body, and a choice of pick-ups. Other options include a normal or long-scale baritone neck, and black or chrome hardware. **SH**

Michael Kelly
Patriot Evan 9 2011

Type Solidbody electric
Body & neck Mahogany/maple body, mahogany neck
Fingerboard Rosewood
Pick-ups Two MK PAF humbucker pick-ups

Evan Rodaniche, a.k.a. Evan 9, formerly guitarist with American alternative metal band Powerman 5000, played a Gibson Les Paul until it "snapped in half" before a live show. A guitarist in a support band lent him a Michael Kelly Patriot guitar to do the gig. Evan liked it so much that he bought two of them.

Later, Evan 9 customized his Patriots with a unique spray paint job. He became such an outspoken fan of Patriot guitars that Michael Kelly set about building him a signature instrument.

Every Evan 9 Patriot is hand spray-painted in the workshop and no two are the same. The guitar itself has a lot of similarities with the Les Paul. The fingerboard is rosewood with abalone block inlays, the tuners are by Grover, and there's a Tune-o-matic bridge and tailpiece. In standard Les Paul style, there are two volume and two tone controls.

But the pick-ups are Michael Kelly's own PAF-Plus humbuckers, with coil tapping, and all the hardware has a distinctive antique-bronze finish. **SH**

Sadowsky
Walter Becker 2011

Type Solidbody electric
Body & neck Swamp ash/maple body, maple neck
Fingerboard Rosewood
Pick-ups Three Lollar P90 pick-ups

Roger Sadowsky produces an unusually wide range of solidbody and archtop electric guitars and basses at his workshop in Long Island City, New York.

Based on Sadowsky's NYC range, the Walter Becker Model was built as a signature instrument for the celebrated Steely Dan guitarist. Immediately striking is the sumptuous finish—a flamed, spalted maple top fitted to a chambered swamp ash body; a rosewood fingerboard with pearl dot inlays, and black Sperzel and Gotoh hardware complete the guitar's opulent look. A highly versatile instrument, the Walter Becker Model is by any other name a Superstrat, albeit one kitted out with three single-coil Lollar P90s (with "F-spaced" pole pieces on the middle and bridge pick-ups). A push-pull tone control combines with the five-way selector switch to provide an extraordinary variety of tonal combinations.

Like most boutique guitar brands, the customer pays a premium for such a beautiful hand-built instrument—in this case, the price is nearly $5,000. **TB**

Viktorian
Ruth 2011

Type Hollow body electric
Body & neck One-piece composite
Fingerboard One-piece composite
Pick-ups Two Viktorian custom humbucker pick-ups

Viktorian guitars were born out of a research project at Florida State University's Applied Mathematics Department and luthier Boaz Elkayam's concept of minimizing the use of tooling in guitar construction. Elkayam, a classical guitarist from a family of violin makers, had developed methods of making small, portable guitars out of limited materials, and he subsequently applied the revolutionary acoustical theories developed at Florida State to their design.

The construction of the Ruth initially involves making a model out of foam and wood, which is then used to produce a mold for the carbon fiber body of the guitar to be poured into. The resulting hollow body includes the neck and headstock as a single component. It's strong and light—4.4 lb. (2 kg)—and there's nothing inside the body to disrupt acoustic resonance, but, because it's sealed, it sounds like a solidbody guitar. It has a classic Tune-o-matic-style bridge, a couple of Viktorian's in-house humbuckers, and volume and tone knobs for each pick-up. **AJ**

Waterstone 12-string Bass 2011

Amfisound Atrain 2012

Type Hollow body electric bass
Body & neck Mahogany body, maple neck
Fingerboard Rosewood
Pick-ups Two humbucker pick-ups

Type Solidbody electric
Body & neck Alder body, maple neck
Fingerboard Rosewood
Pick-ups Two Lundgren humbucker pick-ups

Tom Petersson of Cheap Trick is probably the world's best-known twelve-string bass player, although former Metallica bassist Jason Newsted and King's X frontman Doug Pinnick have also made the unusual instrument their own at times. Petersson's current signature guitar, the hollow body Waterstone which bears his initials, is a custom instrument with the very high specifications that are essential to enable it to achieve the requisite intonation. Waterstone luthier Bob Singer makes the TP-12 in Korea, keeping costs to a manageable level, and is reported to arrange personally for Petersson's signature to appear on each model. Playing this beast requires serious accuracy, as well as finger strength, because of the enormous effort required to fret three strings at a time and then pluck them with fingers or pick them with equal force. Get it right, though, and the TP-12 produces a ringing, plangent tone with more volume than standard bass guitars, due to its body cavity and the huge string mass over the pick-ups. **JM**

This handmade instrument comes from the workshops of Amfisound in northern Finland, and is marketed in their "Extreme" line of instruments—an apt term for something that looks more like a medieval weapon than a traditional guitar.

It is the work of two Finnish luthiers who met on a college guitar-making course and ended up establishing Amfisound in the small port of Haukipudas, just below the Arctic Circle.

The Atrain's specification is high, with sanded, satin-finish, three-piece, quarter sawn maple neck, and specially-made "non-slip" control knobs. The price tag of over 3,000 euros on the top model, the T6 Master, reflects this level of quality.

The Atrain has a sturdy and resonant neck-through construction and Lundgren pick-ups from Sweden set in carefully worked rings to match the body decoration. The level of detail is impressive, with shielded control and pick-up cavities, a jack socket lock, strap locks, and a graphite bridge saddle. **SH**

Aristides Instruments
OIO 2012

Type Solidbody electric
Body & neck Arium body and neck
Fingerboard Ebony
Pick-ups Two single-coil pick-ups and one humbucker

Aristides guitars are made from a specially formulated synthetic wood substitute called arium. This sturdy, resonant, composite material allows the guitar to be molded in one piece.

This innovative instrument was designed by a Dutch design agency, then tested by guitarists including Adrian Vandenberg, formerly of Whitesnake. Now these high-quality guitars and basses are hand-built in Haarlem in the Netherlands.

The OIO—those are letters not digits—comes in a standard form with two single-coil pick-ups and a humbucker, or as a Custom model, which features two EMG active humbuckers.

The standard OIO is finished in metallic colors like red or gold, but the Custom is available only in white. The unusual scoops and cutaways on the top of the guitar's body make the Aristides look unique.

Other features are a five-way pick-up selector, locking tuners, Gotoh tremolo, Aristides leather strap, and a scannable security microchip in the body. **SH**

Babicz
Spider 2012

Type Electroacoustic
Body & neck Spruce/mahogany body and neck
Fingerboard Rosewood
Pick-ups One LR Baggs Element under-saddle pick-up

Company founder Jeff Babicz began building acoustic guitars in the late 1970s, and went on to work with the legendary Ned Steinberger in the 1980s and early 1990s. However, it was arguably only after he took a Babicz prototype—featuring a continually adjustable neck and torque-reducing split bridge—to the Healdsburg Acoustic Guitar Festival in 2003 that his guitar designs started gathering the acclaim his innovations warranted.

The Identity Series Dreadnought and Jumbo models followed, and these led in turn to what the company has termed its "paradigm breakthrough"—the Spider, which would win a prestigious *Guitar World* magazine Gold Award.

The Spider has a thin body, a fast neck, and strings that form a web as they fan out at the top of the guitar. Attracted by its appearance, numerous star players were smitten by its resonance and projection. Among its army of celebrity fans are Todd Rundgren and Chrissie Hynde. **CR**

B.C. Rich Kerry King Jr V-Tribe 2012

Type Solidbody electric
Body & neck Maple body and neck
Fingerboard Ebony
Pick-ups Two MG Kerry King signature pick-ups

The more affordable of the B.C. Rich Kerry King 25th Anniversary guitars—the other being the similarly V-shaped USA Handcrafted 25th Anniversary Kerry King V-Tribe—this is one of many current B.C. Rich Kerry King models, which also include the Beast V, Warlock, and Wartribe shapes, all with graphic finishes and either B.C. Rich or EMG active pick-ups.

Kerry King formed Slayer in the early 1980s. *Show No Mercy* (1983) put the band on the metal map. Fourteen albums and numerous collaborations later, they are established metal royalty.

> *"I like pointy guitars that look like weapons. My first was a 1977 red B.C. Rich Mockingbird."*
>
> KERRY KING

The Jr V reflects B.C. Rich's transformation from small, hand-crafted beginnings, which attracted such classic rock players as Joe Perry and Slash, into a metal-brand company. The Jr V's EMG Kerry King pick-up set features an EMG81 active humbucker at the bridge, with an EMG85 in neck position. "When he [King] needs something extra to cut through the mix," says EMG, "he flips the switch on his PA2 Preamp Booster for an additional 20dB of gain." As a consequence, the guitar features master volume and tone controls, a three-way toggle pick-up selector, and a toggle selector for the PA2 booster. More signature action comes in the form of the Kerry King Signature Kahler Tremolo.

The Gibson Flying V on which the Jr V is based was not popular in 1958: how times have changed. **DB**

Kerry King of Slayer performing with his B.C. Rich in 2012.

B.C. Rich
Widow 4 Bass 2012

Type Solidbody electric four-string bass guitar
Body & neck Mahogany body and neck
Fingerboard Ebony
Pick-ups Two active EQ black P-style pick-ups

The makers promote this uncompromising bass guitar with an equally uncompromising slogan: "The WMD Widow is designed to do some serious damage!" And it's hard to dismiss this claim as advertisers' hyperbole: even for B.C. Rich, it's a radical creation.

The Widow 4 is a twenty-four-fret, four-string version of the WMD. It has an all-mahogany, neck-through-body construction, body wings, and dual active EQ P-style pick-ups. To the onyx finish are added red pinstripes, to resemble the markings on the back of the lethal black widow spider.

"Few guitars can match what BC Rich's Widow offers in its price range … Rest assured, it will serve you well."

CHORDER.COM

Among numerous other facets, the Widow boasts die-cast B.C. Rich tuners, a wrap-around bridge, chrome hardware, a three-way pick-up selector, and tone and volume controls.

Over and above all these undoubted virtues, the Widow's principal attraction is its price: this whole package, which is ready to play straight out of the box, is listed at a highly competitive $699, and may be obtainable even more cheaply through certain online outlets. Unlike the U.S.-built originals, it is constructed in South Korea.

The Widow is thought by some to have evolved from an original design drawn in the 1980s by Blackie Lawless of WASP—this might explain the retro charm of the modern instrument. **DB**

Buscarino
Mira 2012

Type Solidbody electric
Body & neck Ebony/maple body, maple neck
Fingerboard Rosewood or maple
Pick-ups Two humbuckers and one single-coil pick-up

Luthier John Buscarino studied under Augustine LoPrinzi and Robert Benedetto, and has been building guitars in Franklin, North Carolina, since the 1980s. In that it's a solidbody guitar shaped like a Stratocaster, the Mira represents a partial return to his rock 'n' roll roots after several years of building classical instruments and semi-acoustic archtops for jazz musicians like Corey Christiansen and George Benson.

As you would expect from an instrument costing $3,800, the Mira has many luxurious features, including a patented DeadBolt neck joint which, although bolted

> *"Although ... designed with the jazz player in mind ... jazz, country, rock, or blues— you name it, this guitar can handle it."*
>
> JOHN BUSCARINO

on, has a curved heel that gives the feel and the sustain of a through-neck. The unconventional pick-up configuration, which sandwiches a single coil between two humbuckers, features Buscarino Signature pick-ups, which are custom made by Kent Armstrong. These have "series and parallel" wiring and a push/pull knob in conjunction with a five-position selector, which, according to Buscarino, makes it "virtually impossible not to find the perfect tone for whatever style of music you are playing."

The most striking visual aspect of the instrument is the wood—especially the optional quilted maple top, which resembles an unusually restrained tartan—and the bird's-eye maple, with mysterious little dots, used for the neck and as an option for the fingerboard. **AJ**

Campbell American
Space Biscuit 2012

Type Solidbody electric
Body & neck Linden (basswood) body, maple neck
Fingerboard Rosewood
Pick-ups Two Custom DiMarzio humbuckers (different

Since 2002, Campbell American has been producing hand-built guitars in the New England town of Westwood. Run by cofounder, luthier Dean Campbell, until 2012 his small operation had been building twenty to thirty new guitars each month until he took the decision to cut back production, enabling him to focus more on his art and less on the business.

That Campbell American should produce such an unorthodox-looking guitar as the beautifully named Space Biscuit should come as no surprise to anyone who has seen the company's earlier fabulously retro

"We wanted to make something that looks like it would have been in a window in 1970."

DEAN CAMPBELL

Transitone. The Space Biscuit however has a look that is paradoxically futuristic and retro at the same time. Whereas much of the boutique guitar market seems to concentrate its efforts with exotic takes on early Gibson and Fender models, Campbell American guitars have altogether more character; the influences of the classics are there but these guitars are imbued with their own personality.

Although the Space Biscuit features a Fenderesque construction, the custom-built DiMarzio humbuckers take the sound in a very different direction. It's not a guitar that would suit every player, but for anyone after a versatile tone, distinctive looks, and the kind of craftsmanship the big names often fail to offer, the Space Biscuit is worth serious consideration. **TB**

Charvel Desolation
Star DST-3 FR 1Hs 2012

Type Solidbody electric
Body & neck Mahogany body, maple neck
Fingerboard Rosewood
Pick-ups Two EMG humbucker pick-ups

After its takeover by Fender in 2002, Charvel/Jackson gradually reintroduced some of its classic, hard-rock designs from the days of Randy Rhoads. The looks were nostalgic, but the prices took full account of the prevailing market conditions, which were arguably more competitive than ever before: the new wave of instruments were made in China, and were consequently more affordable than the originals.

Some hardcore metal enthusiasts disapproved of the company's abandonment of Superstrats, and guitars with lots of aggressive, pointy bits, in favor of softer-looking, Les Paul- and Mustang-style bodies, such as those that appear in Charvel's Desolation line. However, even the severest critics were mollified to some extent by the introduction in 2012 of the Soloist and the Star.

The Desolation Star is shaped rather like a Gibson Explorer: this has some attractions; there is no doubt that it makes the instrument slightly difficult to play sitting down. It has a through-body, a 25½ in.- (64.75 cm-) scale neck, with shark-tooth inlays on the fretboard that attractively complement the pointy bits of the body. (The transparent model has a flame maple top.)

Also included are a rosewood fingerboard, twenty-four jumbo frets, sealed, die-cast tuners, a recessed, Floyd Rose, double-locking tremolo, and black nickel hardware.

The Desolation Star has two pick-ups: a bright, responsive, EMG 81 humbucker at the bridge, and a warmer, EMG 85 at the neck.

On the debit side, there's no tone knob. But then, whoever uses one of those? **AJ**

Cort
GS Axe-2 2012

Type Solidbody electric bass
Body & neck Mahogany body, bolt-on maple neck
Fingerboard Rosewood
Pick-ups Two Mighty Mite MMPB-4 and MMJB-R pick-ups

When is an ax an ax? When it's the GS Axe-2, of course. The "GS" refers to Gene Simmons, the blood-spewing co-founder of kabuki-meets-flashpot rockers Kiss. As befits his "evil incarnate" stage persona, Simmons has wielded over the years ax-shaped basses from Kramer, Jackson, and luthier Steve Carr (credited with the first).

The GS Axe-2 features a mahogany body honed to a simulated ax edge where the treble bouts would be located on a more conventional instrument. South Korea-based Cort executed a night-black gloss finish that blends to silver at the edge, which has gnarly

> *"James Bond has a license to kill, rock stars have a license to be outrageous. Rock is about grabbing people's attention."*
>
> GENE SIMMONS

painted notches. The 34 in. (86 cm) longscale neck is cut from Canadian maple, and topped with a rosewood fingerboard housing twenty-one large frets. A black headstock features sealed diecast tuners and a screen-printed Gene Simmons signature. As far as hardware is concerned, the Axe-2 features an EB6 combined bridge and a pair of Mighty Mite pick-ups for plenty of grind. Volume and tone pots are topped by chrome knobs, while a three-way toggle offers pick-up switching. Cort followed the bass up with a six-string version, the GS Guitar Axe-2.

Cort took a big chance with the GS Guitar Axe-2, but the risk paid off handsomely. Given Simmons' fearsome reputation, one wonders if heads would have rolled otherwise. **DP**

◄ Gene Simmons of Kiss performing on stage with his signature guitar.

DBZ
Bolero AB Plus 2012

Type Solidbody electric
Body & neck Mahogany/maple body, mahogany neck
Fingerboard Rosewood
Pick-ups Two DBZB and DBZ5 custom-wound pick-ups

Few who recall the video that accompanied "Legs," the single from ZZ Top's album *Eliminator* (1983), will be surprised that Dean B. Zelinsky, creator of the spinning guitars featured therein, should have gone on to mastermind the Boleros, a series with mucho metal appeal. He did this under the auspices of DBZ, the company he founded with Jeff Diamant (of Diamond Amplification) and Terry Martin.

The list of the DB Plus's attractions is long. Starting with first impressions, the neck and body are made from mahogany, with a flame maple top and headstock. The binding is black, with abalone purfling. The hardware is nickel.

Moving on to technical details, it has Grover tuners, a Tune-o-matic bridge with an engraved Dean B. Zelinsky tailpiece, and a twenty-two fret, 24¾-in. (62.9-cm) scale set neck with a soft V-shape and Premier Series inlays. There are volume, tone, and three-way pick-up controls, and a coil tap.

In his review of the DBZ Bolero AB Plus, Iheartguitar blogger Peter Hodgson made special mention of the chunky, D-shaped neck, which, he wrote, "forces your thumb into the most ergonomic angle whether you're flattening your hand out to execute wide stretches on the thinner strings, or getting right up there to fret bass notes with your thumb over the top of the neck, Jimi style."

But you don't have to be Hendrix to get a lot out of this guitar. It offers every player comfort and potential for speed, and the warm, thick, clearly defined tones it produces are particularly well suited to all forms of rock, blues, and metal. **CR**

Farida JT-60 Sam Halliday 2012

Type Limited-edition signature solidbody electric
Body & neck Mahogany body, maple neck
Fingerboard Rosewood
Pick-ups Two P-90 and Alnico single-coil pick-ups

The artist-designed Farida JT-60 2DCC guitar is a signature model for Two Door Cinema Club's Sam Halliday. The Northern Irish indie rock band's lead guitarist was already a Farida fan. For this new instrument, he specified a unique, asymmetric body shape made of two pieces of African mahogany, for warmth of sound, and a bolt-on maple neck for additional brightness.

The JT60 has a chunky P-90 pick-up in the neck position, and, at the bridge, a single-coil made of Alnico (an iron alloy with aluminum, nickel, and cobalt). The most interesting aspect of the guitar, however, is undoubtedly its delay unit, which is built into the guitar's lower horn.

For all its innovations and modernity, this guitar still has a simple, retro feel. The unbound, white body is contrasted with a single-ply, black pickguard, a matching white reverse headstock, and a vintage-style tremolo bridge.

The overall impression is of an instrument that is neither too outlandish nor too conservative. Although this is a reasonably accurate reflection of Farina's corporate image, any perceived middle-of-the-roadness is outweighed by the quality of its products. Its reputation is growing, and it has recently developed new models for and on behalf of Frank Turner, ex-Million Dead, Steve Rothery of Marillion, and Matthew Murphy of The Wombats.

Only twenty-six of these Sam Halliday signature guitars were made; one for Sam himself, and the remainder—which were identical, and individually numbered—for sale to the public. **SH**

Fender Blacktop Jaguar 90 2012

Type Solidbody electric
Body & neck Alder with bolt-on maple neck
Fingerboard Rosewood
Pick-ups Two Fender single-coil pick-ups

The Blacktop series is part of Fender's continuing effort to maintain the broad scope of its classic models. Its variety of pick-up and finish options, with affordable midrange price points, means that there are Teles, Strats, Jags, and Jazzmasters to suit many different pockets and tastes.

The Mexican-made Blacktops are positioned in the marketplace between the Squier and the Mexican Standard, Classic, and Road Worn series. The Jaguar 90 is the most idiosyncratic Blacktop, because it dispenses with the original's floating tremolo and dual circuit

> *"It's an alternative to P-90-loaded Gibson and Epiphone models ... a great success ... Fender has a guitar for everyone."*
> GUITARIST MAGAZINE, SUMMER 2012

switches; just about the only remaining links to its heritage are the shape and the 24-in. (60.9-cm) scale.

Such variations on the original theme dismayed purists, but they won round many players who had not previously been enamored by Jags. Among the new attractions were the pick-ups: on the earlier Blacktop Jaguar HH, they had been twin humbuckers; on the current model, they are P-90s like those used on the Jaguar's close relative, the Jazzmaster.

There is no doubt that this streamlined Jag divides opinion. However, it is generally agreed that the instrument is well suited to a variety of styles, especially alt rock. And it shows that Fender has continued to evolve, and widen the scope of 1960s designs for a broader modern customer base. **RL**

Flaxwood
Vasara 2012

Type Solidbody electric
Body & neck Synthetic flaxwood body and neck
Fingerboard Flaxwood
Pick-ups One humbucker and one DiMarzio pick-up

The flaxwood from which this Finnish company takes its name is created by mashing up organic spruce into a pulp, which is then injected into molds with an "acoustically sensitive" binding agent. This makes for cheap, lightweight instruments, but are they any good?

Absolutely, according to critics, one of whom judged the Vasara "a truly remarkable, boutique-quality instrument with a much more affordable price point. Great tone, great playability, great feel and look, and a consistency from guitar to guitar that was simply not possible before."

> *"It is almost as though Flaxwood has designed out the less desirable tonal qualities of wood."*
>
> GUITAR BUYER MAGAZINE

The guitars have no knots, no grain, and no inconsistencies. This gives an even response across all frequencies. They are not affected by humidity or age, and they are eco-friendly. The company calls flaxwood "wood that is engineered to be acoustically perfect."

The flaxwood material received many thumbs up from reviewers, but what about the rest of the guitar? It's clearly a heavy-rock instrument, with those two meaty DiMarzio humbuckers. It comes only in black, with matching black hardware, and the spec is good: Gotoh SG360 height-adjustable locking tuners, a self-lubricating Tune-X locking nut, and a Gotoh Tune-o-matic bridge. The "F" logo inlays on the fingerboard complete the distinctive look—but they are the only clue that this isn't a normal hardwood guitar. **SH**

Fleck
Electric 2012

Type Solidbody electric
Body & neck Ash body, mahogany neck
Fingerboard Rosewood
Pick-ups Customer choice

It looks like no other guitar in this book, and costs from $3,200. It is produced in Anchorage, Alaska.

Mike Fleck had been repairing and building custom-ordered instruments for twenty years before he came up with his own Fleck Electric guitar. Customers still get a huge choice of features, such as pick-ups (humbuckers, single-coils, or P-90s), but the basic shape and quality of the guitar are constant. It's not a high-tech showcase, or a clone of some other famous instrument, but it has been acclaimed by players and reviewers.

> *"There's a rich complexity heard in the sounds of this ax rarely heard in guitars at any price."*
>
> LOU ADAMS, STACKCATS GUITARIST

Most versions are sold with two coil-tapped Seymour Duncan humbuckers, which, like all the hardware, can be given an authentic antique finish. There's a one-piece, contoured, ash body, and a mahogany neck with thin V-shaped profile, but even these features can be customized by buyers. Fleck gives them plenty of other tonewoods to choose from.

Note the attention to detail in the guitar's construction: the pick-ups and output jack cavities are shielded with nickel, while the underside of the pickguard is shielded with aluminum; the final body finish can be semi-transparent nitrocellulose lacquer, and top-quality 500k CTS volume and tone pots are fitted. Buyers can even specify nut, strap buttons, and neck inlays made from fossilized walrus ivory. **SH**

Freshman Apollo Boutique Series 2012

Type Steel-string acoustic
Body & neck Various solid woods
Fingerboard Rosewood
Pick-ups One Fishman Sonitone System pick-ups

Freshman's four new models made decent, solid-wood, electroacoustic guitars available to beginners and players on a tight budget. They were grouped together as "The Apollo Boutique Series," which featured four different acoustic guitars, all with solid exotic woods, a Fishman EQ system, and a hard case, at a very affordable price of around $750.

They are named after the four seasons. The Spring guitar is a cutaway, electroacoustic, orchestra-sized guitar made of koa with a spruce top. The Summer guitar has a similar-sized Grand Auditorium koa body,

> *"It's so refreshing to find a series that has been thought through to the extent that is in evidence with the Boutiques."*

ACOUSTIC GUITAR MAGAZINE REVIEW

but no cutaway, and a solid cedar top. Autumn is all koa, with a cutaway, and finished with an aged sunburst effect. Winter is a classical nylon-strung guitar, with a parlor-sized body, and open tuning slots on the headstock. Its body is maple with a Sitka spruce top.

The dark-bodied Autumn guitar is the headturner, with abalone-inlay rosette and binding. The tuners are gold-plated Grovers, the Fishman preamp has controls hidden just inside the sound hole. This helps the sound because it doesn't disrupt the solid wood resonance of the sides where EQ systems are normally placed.

A reviewer for *Guitar Interactive* online concluded: "Very impressed. This is a really good quality guitar for modest money. I've played guitars that are three times the price of this that aren't as good." **SH**

Gibson
Firebird X 2012

Type Solidbody electric with built-in software
Body & neck Mahogany body, maple top, mahogany neck
Fingerboard Rosewood
Pick-ups Three mini humbucker pick-ups

Gibson's fascinating Robot range continues to evolve. Laden with all manner of buttons, knobs, and faders, the $5,000 Firebird X like its predecessors keeps itself in tune and provides plenty of capabilities for fine tonal editing. New, however, is the appearance of the Pure Analog Engine, essentially an onboard computer system, which also provides a huge range of onboard software effects. (In what may well be a dig at competitors such as Line 6, Gibson stresses that this is most definitely not a modeling system.) Unsurprisingly, this adds an additional level of complexity with which many guitarists will be unfamiliar. Of course, there are numerous presets that may well prove to be sufficient for the needs of many, but harnessing this impressive technology most effectively requires you to get your hands a little dirty ... and maybe also your head, since it isn't always an intuitive process.

For some guitarists, the sight of a Gibson "Robot" seems little different to a vampire faced with a crucifix, but wherever you sit on the many, varied arguments, there is a genuine concern that guitars relying on upgradable software may eventually suffer the same fate of obsolescence that keyboard players have always had to face. Yet for all of Gibson's investment in this path, we can only wonder whether in fifty years from now the Firebird X be remembered as a noteworthy milestone in the evolution of the guitar, or it turns out to have been the Vox Organ Guitar of the early twenty-first century. After all, Dick Denning, the inventor of that eccentric curio of the late 1960s, doubtless believed he was onto something really big—something that would change the very nature of the instrument. **TB**

Godin
Passion RG-3 2012

Type Solidbody electric
Body & neck Spruce/maple body
Fingerboard Rosewood
Pick-ups Two humbuckers and one under-saddle pick-up

Designed by Robert Godin, the Passion RG-3 looks like a fairly standard Superstrat-type guitar, but this instrument is full of innovative features. The body is made of Sitka spruce and features five tuned chambers inside, creating not only a lightweight guitar, but an extremely resonant instrument with wonderful sustain.

The body is topped with carved, highly flamed maple. The 12-in. (30.5-cm) radius "C"-shaped neck is cut from rock maple and has a twenty-two-fret rosewood fingerboard with dot inlays. The scale length is 25½ in. (64.75 cm), the same as that used on Fender guitars, and the neck joint has been reduced for easy access to the upper frets. Particularly attractive features include the inlaid pickguard and the use of hardwood backplates for the vibrato and control cavities.

The RG-3 is also very well appointed from a hardware perspective, including the Godin Tru-Loc 2 Point vibrato that allows the player to lock the arm position in place. Stainless steel saddles give it clarity and sustain.

Like many Godins, the RG-3 boasts impressive electronics. There is a pair of custom humbuckers, as well as a Graph Tech Shadow under-saddle pick-up with a thirteen-pin "synth" output for connection to a Roland RG-3 system, or similar, and a USB socket for direct connection to a computer.

There are single volume and tone controls, plus a "synth control," along with a five-way selector switch. There is also a three-way mini switch, which is for individual guitar and synth outputs, and for both together. All in all, the RG-3 is a versatile guitar, and an outstanding value for the money. **JB**

Harden Engineering
Broncobuster 2012

HeliArc
B-52 2012

Type Solidbody electric
Body & neck Customer choice
Fingerboard Various handmade Harden custom
Pick-ups Various custom hand-wound pick-ups

Type Electric resonator
Body & neck Aluminum body, maple neck
Fingerboard Rosewood
Pick-ups Two Lace Alumitone pick-ups

Chicago-based Harden Engineering build guitar amps, distortion effects . . . and custom guitars. Bill Harden's guitars are designed to re-create the golden age of American guitar making—which, according to him, was the 1950s and 1960s.

They are all made by hand and, unusually, use their own painstakingly crafted original parts. Even the pick-ups are custom hand-wound.

Prices start at $1,500, and each guitar takes around two months to build. Although customers are given a free choice of woods, shape, size, decoration, and electrics, all Harden products end up with a retro look.

The Broncobuster, for example, is a strange mix of early Telecaster and Les Paul, with a Bigsby tremolo arm, two hand-made humbucker-sized pick-ups, and bull's-eye inlays along the rosewood neck. The semi-hollow Excalibur is a mix of mahogany (body and neck) and aluminum (engraved top and back on the body). It features two "extra-hot" Harden humbuckers, cat's-eyes inlays, and a pau ferro fingerboard. **SH**

HeliArc Guitars are hand-built in California, often using extraordinarily exotic materials. The B-52 is certainly an odd-looking instrument, rather like, it has been said, a guitar with a paper plate embedded; in fact, it has an ES-335-style body with a built-in resonator. The body is manufactured from aircraft-grade aluminum, with the top given a "swirled" effect, and comes in an assortment of attractive colors.

The wooden cone ("plate") is set into the body, and works in a similar way to a resonator unit. There are two very small f-holes positioned near the central cone. An adjustable bridge and separate tailpiece are mounted onto the cone, creating a unique sound. The B-52 is equipped with two very versatile Lace Alumitone pick-ups, which produce a wide range of amplified acoustic sounds, including a very passable classic Dobro. There is a single volume and tone control, along with a three-way pick-up selector switch. There are many who regard this as a "must-have" guitar. **JB**

Richard Howell Standard 2012

Type Classical
Body & neck Cedar top, rosewood back/sides, cedar neck
Fingerboard Ebony
Other features Sloane tuning machines, French polished

British-born Richard Howell first established himself as a guitar maker in Australia in the early 1970s when making student model guitars for the Adelaide Spanish Guitar Centre. It was there that he had the opportunity to study instruments made by great masters like Fleta, Hauser, and Hernández y Aguado, among others. In 1981 he moved to Mornington, Victoria, and started making the guitars for which he is renowned. The powerful-sounding guitars of Ignacio Fleta became his main inspiration and still exert a very strong influence on his work, as can be seen in this example from 2012. Headstock, choice of woods, overall shape, design, and construction principles are very similar to those of the Spanish master. Sound properties, in terms of tone quality and projection, are very similar too.

Howell works on his own in a small workshop at the back of his house where he has hand-crafted over 400 guitars, using only traditional hand tools and finishes, eschewing machinery of any kind. **GD**

Ibanez Meshuggah 8-string 2012

Type Eight-string solidbody electric
Body & neck Bubinga/maple body and neck, alder wings
Fingerboard Rosewood
Pick-ups One Lindgren M8 pick-up

The M8M started off with Meshuggah guitarists Mårten Hagstrom and Fredrik Thordendal hooking up with Ibanez to discuss custom designs. It was built in small numbers in Japan, and officially launched in 2012 with a $7,999 list price that Ibanez said reflected "exacting standards by the highest-skilled luthiers."

Anyone familiar with the extreme metal of the Swedish-based band—especially their album *Nothing* (2002)—will not be surprised to learn that the M8M is a down-tuned eight-string, with a long, bass-like 29.4-in. (74.7-cm) scale length.

It's also of neck-through body construction, with a five-piece bubinga/maple laminate neck, and alder body wings. Yet, in spite of the hefty price tag, the black finish is far from classy and there is only one pick-up—a hand-made, purpose-built Lundgren Model M8—and a fixed Edge III-8 bridge.

Tuning? It's designed to be a standard six-string guitar tuned down a semitone (E# to E♭), with two additional bass strings: B♭ and F. **DB**

Ibanez
X Series XG307 2012

King Blossom
RGM 2 2012

Type Solidbody electric
Body & neck Mahogany body, three-piece maple neck
Fingerboard Rosewood
Pick-ups One AH37 and one AH47 humbucker pick-up

Type Solidbody electric
Body & neck Maple/mahogany body, mahogany neck
Fingerboard Rosewood
Pick-ups Riffbucker Aticulator 1-N, Articulator 2-N

The Ibanez X Series comprises heavy metal guitars with extreme body shapes. Each model is named after a medieval sword—Halberd, Falchion, Glaive, and Xiphos. The series has been endorsed by Slipknot's Mick Thomson, who has his own signature model with the word "Seven" inlaid along the fingerboard.

The XG307 has seven strings (an added B string below the bottom E of a six-string), neck-through construction, through-body stringing to aid sustain, a fast and slim "Wizard" neck with twenty-four jumbo frets and reverse headstock, a fixed Tune-o-matic bridge, and an optional tremolo system.

The essentials are simple: two humbuckers, with a three-position pick-up selector switch and a master volume and tone control.

The body is flat, and available only in "flat black," with no bindings or decoration. There's no pickguard or neck inlay, either, and all the hardware is black, too.

The balance causes "neck dive," which is remedied by the addition of weights in the body cavity. **SH**

Working in a shed on the family farm in New Hampshire, King Blossom's founder Jeff Figley took two years, off and on, to build his first guitar, which he kept for himself. He still works slowly, producing only between twelve and fifteen guitars a year, but construction cannot be hurried: as he puts it, "World-class tone is no accident."

King Blossoms are commissioned guitars, each customized to its owner. The RGM2 (Riffguy Signature #0002) is the culmination of a two-year collaboration between King Blossom and guitarist and reviewer Riffguy. Combining features from the SG, Strat, and Les Paul guitars, the RGM2 debuted at the 2011 Montreal Guitar Show. It has, according to Riffguy, "all the warmth of a Les Paul but with the clarity and edge of a Strat." Typical of King Blossom's attention to detail are the exquisitely scalloped fingerboard beneath oversized stainless-steel frets, and the antique walrus tusk nuts on its headstock, which you'll notice only if you can tear your eyes away from its gorgeous ocean blue color. **BS**

Lacey
Artist Special 2012

Lakewood Sungha
Jung Signature 2012

Type Hollow body electric
Body & neck Mahogany/maple body, mahogany neck
Fingerboard Ebony
Pick-ups Two humbucker pick-ups

Type Grand concert acoustic
Body & neck Spruce and rosewood body, mahogany neck
Fingerboard Ebony

Originally from Australia, but currently living in the United States, Mark Lacey studied instrument-making in London in the early 1970s, and is now well established as a maker of a wide range of exceptional guitars. The Artist is Lacey's take on two of his favorite guitars—the Gibson Les Paul and ES-335 models.

The 15-in. (38-cm) one-piece body is hollowed out from a single piece of mahogany and has a carved, figured maple top. F-holes add a "jazz" feel to the instrument, even though it is only 1⅝ in. (4.1 cm) thick at the edges. The one-piece mahogany neck has an ebony fingerboard and headstock veneer. There are some wonderful details on the Artist, including maple pick-up surrounds and a flamed koa pickguard. Sound is delivered via a pair of Gibson '57 Classic humbuckers. The bridge is a Tune-o-matic, with a stop tailpiece, Q-parts knobs, and Grover Rotomatic tuners. All the hardware is gold-plated. This is a beautiful hybrid guitar, perfectly suited to jazz, rock, and everything in between. **JB**

Martin Seeliger became an apprentice guitar maker at eighteen years of age, and learned his trade on classical and steel-stringed guitars and mandolins. After years spent repairing guitars and learning what musicians did and did not want, he founded Lakewood Guitars in 1986 with a desire to create instruments that their owners would not merely own, but treasure.

As the company grew, so did Seeliger's ambitions, and in 2007 he became aware of South Korean fingerstyle guitarist and Internet sensation Sungha Jung. Seeliger contacted Jung and asked if he could be of any help, and later that year designed him a small-bodied Auditorium acoustic. Lakewood began sponsoring Jung in 2009, and in 2012 crafted him the magnificent Grand Concert, with its European spruce top and sides of Macassar ebony and characterized, as are all Lakewoods, by pronounced arches in the top and back. "The arch," Seeliger explains, "allows me to have a lot of strength while using thinner woods." **BS**

Mike Lull
Jeff Ament Bass 2012

Type Solidbody electric bass
Body & neck Mahogany body and neck
Fingerboard Rosewood
Pick-ups Two Custom Mike Lull T-Bass pick-ups

Mike Lull's introduction.to the world of luthiery came through necessity: "I built my first bass guitar in ninth grade because my parents wouldn't let me buy one." He may have only fitted the neck from a broken Japanese bass onto a pre-existent body, but that was enough for him to be "completely bitten by the whole 'putting-your-stuff-together' thing." Nearly four decades later, Lull is one of the world's most highly regarded makers of bass guitars.

Based in his home town of Bellevue, Washington State, Lull cut his teeth working for a local guitar repair shop, and opened his own repair business in 1975. He quickly gained a reputation as both a repair man and a custom builder, aided by being a working bass player on the thriving nearby Seattle music scene. In 1995 he launched his own range of instruments. As part of an intentionally small-scale business, he and a team of three continue to undertake building and repair work, his high-profile clients including Bob Dylan, Nirvana, Pearl Jam, and The Foo Fighters.

Many of Lull's bass guitars are designed around classic styles, a particular favorite being the Gibson Thunderbird, whose sound he loved, but which he found "terrible ergonomically." So he set about designing something that combined the tone of the original with the playability and balance of a Fender. And this is at the heart of the model he conceived with Jeff Ament. The Pearl Jam bassist had wanted his signature model to have a 20 percent oversized body and a reverse headstock, and to feature a chromed aluminum pickguard with his own take on the iconic "T-Bird" symbol. **TB**

Pearl Jam's Jeff Ament performing with his signature bass. ➡

ODD Atom
3D Guitar 2012

Type Plastic-bodied electric
Body & neck Duraform PA/mahogany body, maple neck
Fingerboard Rosewood
Pick-ups Two Lancaster active or Seymour Duncan pick-ups

The first time you see a 3D printer in action, you can't fail to be amazed by the simple fact that this technology even exists, let alone that it's almost affordable. You design a three-dimensional object on your laptop, press "Command P" and there it is. In principle, the process is rather like inkjet printing, but successive layers of plastic (or metal powder) build up the shape and are molded together. It's a technology that has the potential to revolutionize the way we think about manufacturing.

One person to take this technology in an unexpected direction is Olaf Diegel, professor of mechatronics at Massey University in New Zealand. Using CAD software and an EOS 3D printer, as an experiment he designed and printed . . . an electric guitar! The results were, he claims, "so good that I decided to set up a business selling them." And thus ODD Guitars was born.

Modifying his original all-plastic design, the body on the Atom 3D model shown here is printed with a rear cavity into which a smaller mahogany "core" is fitted; a stock Warmoth neck is bolted to the body. The sound comes from a choice of Lancaster active pick-ups or Seymour Duncan '59s. The overall effect is quite disconcerting, but it really works.

So is this a template for the future? Will home 3D printing change our lives? For the time being, most of us would happily settle for a printer that could deal with the occasional sheet of A4 without running out of ink, suffering some arcane communication error, or simply breaking down altogether. But we can all dream of a brave new world. **TB**

Peavey
AT-200 2012

Type Solidbody electric
Body & neck Basswood body, maple neck
Fingerboard Rosewood
Pick-ups Two Peavey custom humbucker pick-ups

Developed by Peavey in conjunction with Antares—the company behind the famous ATR-1 auto-tune studio effect—and introduced in 2012, the AT-200 is the first guitar ever to use built-in software to tune its own output automatically.

At first sight, it appears unremarkable—a generic, Stratocaster-shaped rock guitar (in either black or candy apple), with a fast neck, a pair of humbucker pick-ups, and all-black hardware. A closer look, however, reveals something much more interesting and unusual: indeed, a technological breakthrough.

On the bass side of the neck pick-up surround is a green LED, which indicates auto-tune activity. Next to the output jack is a MIDI (Musical Instrument Digital Interface) socket. The auto-tune feature is activated by pressing down the tone control; at this point, the output is switched from normal pick-up operation and routed through the built-in software. The guitar will now tune itself perfectly, without the player needing to touch the strings. The system also monitors intonation as it is played higher up the neck, so that notes at the twenty-fourth fret are still completely accurate. In addition, the AT-200 supposedly has the ability to recognize normal string-bending techniques, and to leave them unaffected; however, the auto-tune tends to cancel out the more subtle finger tremolo.

Musicradar.com were given a test run on the prototype, and they loved what they saw. Their verdict was that "The AT-200's output proves scarily accurate, even if the real-world guitar is out of tune and badly intonated." **AJ**

Peavey
Marvel X-Men 2012

Type Solidbody electric
Body & neck Basswood body, maple neck
Fingerboard Rosewood
Pick-ups Single humbucker pick-up

The Peavey Marvel Rockmaster series of solidbody electrics all come with high-gloss, basswood bodies emblazoned with highly detailed Marvel superhero artwork on a cool-looking black background (and "Marvel Rockmaster" logo on the black headstock) to suit all tastes within the realm of Marveldom. Whether your affinity lies with The Amazing Spiderman, The Avengers, Captain America, The Incredible Hulk, or the Uncanny X-Men, the full-size Rockmasters—Peavey's "super" range of entry-level electric guitars—have the hero you're looking for and provide an exciting amalgam of music and fantasy.

Peavey has long been almost synonymous with value for money, and the company's Rockmaster Superheroes enhanced this reputation, with every guitar in the series coming complete with an adjustable bridge (no non-locking tremolos that constantly require correcting) and sealed tuner gears in a lightweight body that is ideal for students. The single humbucker pick-up is a straightforward affair, designed to keep costs down, and its single volume and tone controls, as well as the amp jack, are ideally positioned for beginners to grasp. Its narrow neck is also great for players with small hands, and its shortish length makes stretching to reach notes less demanding than it generally is on larger instruments. And bevels cut into the back of the body make it comfortable to hold.

Strumming with your favorite superhero can also be done with Peavey half-size acoustics and three-quarter-sized electrics; every one of these instruments comes with the bonus of matching superhero-embossed picks and straps. **BS**

Potvin
Korina 2012

Type Solidbody electric
Body & neck Korina body and neck
Fingerboard Rosewood
Pick-ups Two Lollar humbucker pick-ups

Korina (a.k.a. limba or afara) is a hardwood from tropical West Africa used in furniture making. In the guitar world, it's best known as the stuff that the legendary early versions of Gibson's Explorers and Flying Vs were made of—it's regarded as a "super-mahogany," with a similar grain but lighter, with a sweeter mid range. In spite of this, it's a relatively uncommon choice for guitar manufacturers. Although the wood is not actually endangered, it can be difficult to source reliably—you have to get it from

> *"Beauty comes in many forms... My goal is to craft a guitar that fits like a glove and inspires players to create."*
>
> **MIKE POTVIN**

Africa, it's difficult to find big bits without splits in it, and it's susceptible to the staining caused by infestations of fungus and bacteria that like eating it.

Potvin guitars are hand-made by Mike Potvin in Canada. The Mercury model, which he says "conjures up images of classic 1950s cars with tailfins and gleaming chrome," has a body shape very similar to that of the Billy Gibbons Jupiter Gretsch. The standard version is mahogany, and has TV Jones Classic pick-ups and Grover tuners. The Mercury Korina, which retails at $2,985, replaces these with Lollar humbuckers, and Gotoh Vintage tuners. There are two volume knobs, a tone knob, and a three-way pick-up selector. It's finished in hand-rubbed oil, which shows off the korina wood very nicely, and enables anyone to see that it's free of fungus and bacteria stains. **AJ**

PRS
P22 2012

Type Solidbody electric
Body & neck Mahogany/maple body, set neck
Fingerboard Rosewood with bird-shaped inlays
Pick-ups Two humbuckers and one piezo pick-up

The LR Baggs/PRS co-designed piezo system first appeared on hollow body and archtop guitars—the only ones large enough to accommodate the sizeable internal circuitry and dual outputs. It gave them a dual electric, and a more acoustic-like tonality.

In 2012, thanks to a redesign of the circuitry, a smaller unit was fitted into a solidbody, and the P22—"P" for piezo, "22" for the number of frets—was born.

Hybrid guitars such as this are not new—Parker popularized the concept with its modernistic Fly guitar—but the P22 combines all of PRS's legendary

"A high-line PRS electric solidbody with arguably the best sounding and functioning piezo system currently available. Faultless."
GUITARIST MAGAZINE

build quality with one of the best-sounding piezo systems available on any electric instrument. The magnetic pick-ups on this model are a continuation of the 57/08 series, named the 53/10—the warmest-sounding humbuckers in the range.

Around 2005, Paul Reed Smith created his "Twenty-one Rules of Tone" philosophy, which included numerous changes to the way PRS built its guitars in order to maximize their "acoustic" response. By 2012, these were all in place, and included a new V12 nitrocellulose/acrylic finish, new "pattern" neck shapes, and new Phase III tuners and nut material.

Like most PRS electrics, the P22 follows the original 1985 Custom outline, but benefits from the intervening twenty-seven years of production experience. **DB**

Sinuous
SD-22 2012

Type Solidbody electric
Body & neck Poplar body, maple neck
Fingerboard Rosewood or maple
Pick-ups Two Seymour Duncan humbucker pick-ups

Greg Opatik studied art and design before becoming a maker of fine furniture. He eventually combined his furniture-making skills with his lifelong love of playing guitar by establishing the Sinuous Guitar Company in Grand Rapids, Michigan.

Sinuous make high-end boutique amps and guitars that have all the visual appeal of expensive, hand-made pieces of furniture. There is only one guitar at present, the SD-22, and it was developed by Opatik with the expert assistance of Elliot Easton, lead guitarist of The Cars.

"Our guitars are designed for the … guitarist who demands authenticity, craftsmanship, and an instrument that is truly special."
GREG OPATIK

The SD-22 may look like part of a Charles and Ray Eames chair, with sweeping curves and finely finished wood, but it's a serious, quality instrument. It is available in a wide range of custom finishes, and costs around $2,000–$3,000.

Buyers are offered a choice of beautifully decorated maple or Santos Palisander as a top for the unusually contoured body. Fingerboards are optionally rosewood or maple. There are two Seymour Duncan humbucking pick-ups—Pearly Gates in the neck position, and SH-5 at the bridge. Other features include a coil tap system, a simple three-way selector switch, a Hipshot bridge and tuners, and a graphite nut. The customization options even extend to a choice of hardware style—black, chrome, or gold. **SH**

Squier Jim Root Telecaster 2012

Type Solidbody electric
Body & neck Mahogany body, maple neck
Fingerboard Rosewood
Pick-ups Two Fender humbucker pick-ups

Once Fender's original 2007 signature guitar for Slipknot's Jim Root had proved a hit and a viable Telecaster for metal styles, a cheaper option for his legions of younger fans was almost inevitable.

The Squier signature followed five years after its Fender brethren, but an affordable signature model was something Root had wanted to see from the start of his relationship with Fender. "When we started working on the Teles, I did everything in my power to design a guitar that was under $800, so that if you're a fourteen- or fifteen-year-old fan of my band and don't have a job, mom and dad won't be scared to go get you this guitar."

The main difference between the two models is the pick-ups: the Squier has own-brand humbuckers; the Fender has an active EMG 81 and 60 set.

Root himself was immediately impressed with the prototype Fender; testing it through his Orange Rockerverb amp, and jamming songs by his own guitar heroes, Metallica: "It sounded great," he noted. **RL**

Squier Vintage Modified Surf Strat 2012

Type Solidbody electric
Body & neck Basswood body, maple neck
Fingerboard Ebony
Pick-ups Three Seymour Duncan single-coil pick-ups

This one's a real winner from Fender's Squier diffusion line. The Vintage Modified Surf Stratocaster, appears to be an early-1960s-style Strat with the pick-ups replaced by Danelectro lipstick cases. And that's really not far off the mark. One fundamental difference comes in the controversial use of the basswood instead of the traditional ash or alder. But given that many high-end Ibanez models (such as the Jem range) also use basswood, Fender can hardly be accused of using cheap, inferior wood. Let's just say that it's different.

This model certainly doesn't sound like a normal Strat, though. The three Seymour Duncan single-coil pick-ups are clearly based on Nathan Daniel's original lipstick-case designs from the 1950s, but are given considerably more poke than the originals. To be honest, anyone interested in twangy surf guitar should probably give this one a go. And with a retail price of under $500 (not to mention a street price a good 20 percent less) it represents quite extraordinary value. **TB**

Tacchi
Cerulea 2012

Type Classical
Body & neck Spruce/cedar/rosewood body,
mahogany neck
Fingerboard Ebony

The 2012 Cerulea consolidates several exciting innovations into a work of exquisite craftsmanship worthy of standing alongside the great artistic heritage of luthier Andrea Tacchi's native Florence. First there is his "Cochlea" concept, in which the front and back of the guitar are perfectly domed. Then there is the "Thucea" concept of the top itself, with an inner segment of spruce—personally sourced from the Italian Alps, to capture the initial string vibrations through the bridge, and provide the instrument's primary tone colors—and outer segments of cedar, which is very efficient in distributing sound to the outer edges of the top. Then there is the bracing system, in which four fan braces—tallest just below the bridge, and tapered at the ends—are positioned above a small, thin X-brace. Last, but not least, is the strikingly abstract rosette—a collage of perfectly duplicated samples from rosettes by some of the great guitar makers who have inspired Tacchi—Torres, Simplicio, and Bouchet, among others. The guitar shown here was made for a Chinese buyer. **GD**

Teuffel
Antonio 2012

Type Solidbody electric
Body & neck Mahogany
Fingerboard Rosewood
Pick-ups Custom-built neck pick-up

At first glimpse, what strikes you about Ulrich Teuffel's Antonio model is the shocking realization that compared to his earlier instruments—like the Bird Fish and Tesla—this looks remarkably like… a conventional guitar. It's still a characteristically beautiful piece of sculpture, but what we have here is essentially a classic narrow-waisted figure-of-eight body shape with a single Florentine cutaway. Indeed, this sees Teuffel looking back over the history of the instrument that he, as much as any other luthier working today, has taken into the twenty-first century. Accordingly, the naming of this guitar is no coincidence: "I decided my next model would have a name drawn from history; Antonio is the first name of both Antonio Torres and Antonio Stradivari." But it's far from an average electric guitar: the body is cut from Honduran mahogany and features an invisible chamber, as well as six smaller "tone chambers" at the rear behind the bridge; other features include carbon fiber neck reinforcement and a neck pick-up featuring "hand-weakened" Alnico magnets. **TB**

Teye Guitars Electric Gypsy La India 2012

Township Guitars Classic Pro 2012

Type Electric bass guitar
Body & neck Mahogany body (korina optional), walnut neck
Fingerboard Ebony
Pick-ups Two Carey Nordstrand MM humbucker pick-ups

Type Hollow body electric
Body & neck "Oil can" body, maple neck
Fingerboard Rosewood
Pick-ups Two single-coil pick-ups

Guitarist and luthier "Teye" was born in the Netherlands, eventually ending up in the United States, having been granted a Green Card as an "alien with extraordinary abilities in the arts." His website indicates a man happy to wear his heart on his sleeve; the most telling entry is headed "Bitching," and is a hand-scrawled list of the gripes he has with existing electric guitars, which he intends to address on his new Electric Gypsy design.

One look at this range of guitars and basses shows the very clear inspiration of Tony Zemaitis. The first six-stringed Electric Gypsy models emerged from his workshop in Austin, Texas, in 2005, with the bass guitars appearing some time later. This "La India" model is a medium-scale, 32-in. (81 cm) bass guitar featuring two humbucking pick-ups mounted side by side, and is capable of producing a wide variety of sounds. Visually it is, of course, quite stunning, the Zemaitis-style central pickguard surrounded by an intricately laid mother-of-pearl mosaic. In every way, this is an extraordinary piece of craftsmanship. **TB**

The "oil can" guitar evolved from the four-string ramkiekie, developed in the nineteenth century by the Khoi people in southern Africa after they came into contact with early European settlers.

Township Guitars are based in Cape Town, South Africa. These instruments first appeared in 2000, the work of the late Graeme Wells, a skilled luthier who recycled empty Castrol GTX oil cans for the body of his own electric guitars, which were later sold in limited quantities under the Afri-Can brand name. The oil can provides a unique tonal color—perhaps reminiscent of a metal-bodied resonator with a fitted pick-up.

Township Guitars now produce two different models, the single-coil Classic Pro (shown here) and the twin-coil Humbucker Pro. The bodies of the current range are made from Castrol Armaclean or generic olive-oil cans, which are left either in their original state or covered with a decal of the South African flag. They have been played by such eminent names as Brian May, Mark Knopfler, and David Gilmour. **TB**

Washburn
HB36 Vintage 2012

Type Hollow body electric
Body & neck Maple/spruce body, maple neck
Fingerboard Ebony
Pick-ups Two humbucker pick-ups

Washburn introduced the HB36 Vintage in 2012 as a deluxe version of its HB35. These guitars are mid-price copies of the classic Gibson ES-335, but still have a reputation for a good standard of craftsmanship and attention to detail. The "Vintage" name presumably refers not only to the design, but also to the aged quality of the finish—the gold hardware is distressed to make it look like worn brass, and it goes nicely with the patina of the multi-laminate binding on the tobacco sunburst.

The warmth of the humbucker pick-ups, and the mellow sound of the hollow body (the "HB" in the model name) suggest that this instrument might be a good choice if you wanted to play some cool 1950s jazz, or maybe a bit of blues—certainly, this instrument looks as if it would be more effective when played in those styles than on, for example, thrash metal or skate punk. It would also be a shame to put stickers all over the spruce top, or to write on it with a marker pen. **AJ**

Washburn
PS2012 2012

Type Solidbody electric
Body & neck Mahogany body and neck
Fingerboard Ebony
Pick-ups Two mini-humbucker pick-ups

You can have any color as long as it's black . . . or white. The latest addition to Washburn's Paul Stanley signature series is the PS2012—a top-end signature instrument from the Kiss guitarist.

Although it has a limited color scheme, and no binding on the body, the PS2012 has a high spec that includes a custom Paul Stanley tailpiece machined from a solid block of aluminum, mirrored pickguard and truss rod cover, and a Tune-o-matic bridge.

The mahogany body with raised central section and set neck produces warm, sustaining rock tones, which are collected by two Seymour Duncan mini-humbuckers. Versatility comes from the three-way selector, with two volume and two tone controls.

Like all contemporary U.S.-built Washburn guitars, the PS2012 uses the Buzz Fieten tuning system, which is basically an accurately compensated nut and saddle to correct the inherent intonation problems. The PS2012 was launched with a recommended retail price of around $4,000. **SH**

Carvin Brian Bromberg B24P 2013

Dean Dave Mustaine Zero 2013

Type Electric bass
Body & neck Alder body, flame maple top, maple neck
Fingerboard Ebony
Pick-ups Two RJ2 Alnico single-coils and one piezo pick-up

Type Solidbody electric
Body & neck Mahogany body and neck
Fingerboard Ebony or rosewood
Pick-ups Two Dave Mustaine Duncan Live Wire pick-ups

The Carvin brand pursues a niche line here with the B24P, a signature model for a musician who is highly regarded in his own field but little-known to the outside world. Brian Bromberg first hit the jazz scene as a teenager, playing in the Stan Getz Quintet, and has since carved a reputation playing with the likes of Herbie Hancock, Dizzy Gillespie, and Bill Evans.

With its flame maple top, the B24P is an attractively contoured bass that shares many characteristics with high-end boutique instruments, such as a neck-through design, active electrics including a wealth of on-board tonal control, and a piezo system embedded beneath the bridge, which provides a pretty decent simulation of an acoustic bass.

Overall, this is very smooth-sounding bass, and retailing at around $1,300 has the looks, construction, and performance of many instruments more than twice its price. It's perhaps not a bass for every player, however, being more suited to jazz, blues, and funk styles than heavy rock. **TB**

The Dean company has been working tirelessly to keep heavy metal supplied with angular guitars since 1976. Of all the notable metal guitarists who play its instruments—Michael Schenker (UFO), Leslie West (Mountain), Michael Angelo Batio (Holland), and many others—Dave Mustaine of Megadeth (and Metallica, before the other band members threw him out for being too uncompromisingly rock 'n' roll) is possibly the most prestigious.

His latest signature model is the Dave Mustaine Zero, which currently has four variant forms: the Zero itself; the Classic Black; the "In Deth We Trust"—this one has an eye-catching finish that looks like a distressed "Zero Dollar" bill, with a picture of whichever U.S. president it was who wore mirror shades and had no skin on his face—and the Angel of Deth II, which is pictured above. Two of them have bodies inspired by the Gibson Explorer, and the double-neck looks rather like two Flying Vs that entered the world as conjoined twins. **AJ**

Dean
Rusty Cooley 2013

Type Seven-string electric
Body & neck Alder body, maple neck
Fingerboard Ebony
Pick-ups Two EMG 707 active humbucker pick-ups

"This is the Lamborghini of seven-strings," says Rusty Cooley about his Dean signature Superstrat. Cooley plays in the band Outworld, and is one of the fastest of the new breed of super-fast metal shredders.

The acclaimed Texan is a Dean endorsee, and this special-edition guitar features "the thinnest neck on the planet," with tall frets, deep cutaways, and two active humbucker pick-ups, one of which is set at an angle to the strings. The low-profile tremolo is licensed by Floyd Rose. The bolt-on maple neck has an ebony fingerboard, and Grover tuners.

Most versions of the guitar have decorations on the body and fingerboard in the form of a "Xenocide" graphic inspired by a sci-fi novel of the same name. However, the guitar is also available in plain metallic black or white, or in natural mahogany finishes. Dean has also released an eight-string version with a fanned fret system.

The Cooley is a top-end guitar, with a price tag approaching £3,000. **SH**

Deimel
Firestar 2013

Type Solidbody electric
Body & neck Red alder body, rock maple neck
Fingerboard Rosewood
Pick-ups Selection of four Novak pick-ups possible

Berlin-based luthier Frank Deimel's Firestar is a fabulous collision of classic early-1960s styles—think Jaguar meets Non-Reverse Firebird. But although it could be described as a pastiche, it all comes together to produce something with a character of its own— not to mention some rather nice luxury touches, such as an ebony fingerboard and bone nut. As a custom instrument, there is plenty of scope for personalization, although who would seriously want to veer away from the magnificent metallic "Saturn Lavender" finish on this model? There are also options as far as the pick-ups go, and on show here we have a combination of Novak P-90 single-coil at the bridge and a Novak humbucker at the neck, giving a nice selection of Fender/Gibson crossover possibilities. The three on/ off switches beneath the front pick-up are also worth noting: the first is a bass cut; the second a series/ parallel switch for the humbucker; and the third, interestingly, engages a piezo pick-up fitted into the wood of the body. **TB**

Epiphone Tommy Thayer Spaceman 2013

Type Solidbody electric
Body & neck Mahogany body and neck
Fingerboard Rosewood
Pick-ups Two Gibson 498T humbucker pick-ups

For those who only recall Kiss in their glam heyday, the name Tommy Thayer won't mean a thing. He started out in Black 'n' Blue, two of whose albums—*Nasty Nasty* (1986), and *In Heat* (1988)—were produced by Gene Simmons, who subsequently hired Thayer, first to clean his house, then as a Kiss video producer, and later to help guitarist Ace Frehley re-learn long-forgotten riffs and solos from the 1970s! When Frehley left Kiss in 2003, Thayer was promoted to full-time guitarist, taking over the "Spaceman" persona in the band.

> *"This guitar is an exact version of my Gibson sparkle Custom Shop Standard that I've played onstage with KISS for years now."*
>
> **TOMMY THAYER**

On stage, Thayer plays a "silver sparkle" Gibson Custom Shop Les Paul Standard. What we have here is a Chinese-built Epiphone replica, called the Spaceman. On the surface, it does have all of the hallmarks of a "fan" guitar, including the special silver case, a studded silver leather strap just like Tommy's, and a signed certificate of authenticity that comes in a wallet holding a photograph of the man himself. And yet this is a fine piece of kit, well up alongside Epiphone's Elitist models. When first announced, it became one the brand's most eagerly anticipated models, with Thayer himself stoking interest by telling the world it had the same 498T pick-ups used on his Gibson. If you want a Les Paul but don't fancy Gibson prices—and are OK with sparkly guitars—then check this one out. Seriously. **TB**

Ernie Ball MusicMan
Armada 2013

Type Solidbody electric
Body & neck Mahogany/maple body, mahogany neck
Fingerboard Rosewood
Pick-ups Two MusicMan humbucker pick-ups

As far as heritage goes, the MusicMan brand emerged from illustrious roots: it was founded in the early 1970s by Fender's Forrest White and Tom Walker, who then installed the great man himself—Leo Fender—as company president. By the time Leo left to form G&L, and before MusicMan had been bought by Ernie Ball, the company had a well-established reputation for producing top-quality guitars based around the founders' classic designs.

This background makes the appearance of the Armada all the more surprising, in that there are a number of rather uncharacteristic Gibson overtones in evidence here. First there is the fabulously retro shape—which harks back more than a little to Gibson's Ray Dietrich/automobile styles of the early 1960s, with a rather angular Les Paul-ish single cutaway, and an arched top with an elevated, figured-maple panel reminiscent of a reverse Flying V. And then we have the scale length, which switches from Fender's 25½ in. (64.75 cm) to Gibson's 24¾ in. (62.9 cm). Finally, there is a pair of PAF-like MusicMan humbuckers. The neck design is also unusual for the brand, with a straight-through construction, and the neck and center of the body cut from a single piece of mahogany. This may not be regular Gibson fare—excepting the original Firebird/Thunderbird range—but it is a "quality" manufacturing technique that is difficult and costly to produce, and widely thought to increase sustain and improve tone.

The Armada may not be a Les Paul-killer, but it does have all the makings of a modern classic. Only time will tell. **TB**

ESP
SLAYER-2013 2013

Type Solidbody electric
Body & neck Alder body, maple neck
Fingerboard Ebony
Pick-ups Two EMG humbucking pick-ups

In 2011, ESP celebrated the twenty-fifth anniversary of Slayer's *Reign In Blood* (1986), a benchmark album in 1980s metal. The SLAYER-2011 featured a custom-graphic finish that drew from elements of the album cover artwork. Prepared in collaboration with Tom Araya and the late Jeff Hanneman of the band, the limited run of 250 proved to be popular among hardcore fan… so much so, in fact, that a year later ESP paid tribute to a second Slayer album, *South Of Heaven* (1986) with the SLAYER-2012. ESP seem to have now turned this into a tradition, with the appearance of the SLAYER-2013, which features the skull and crucifix artwork from the band's fifth album, *Seasons In The Abyss* (1990). (The graphics work on this guitar rather better than on the previous two versions.)

This is a thoroughly decent high-performance rock guitar, with an extra-slim twenty-four-fret bolt-on neck with some wonderful inlays on the ebony fingerboard—the Slayer logo on the twelfth fret, with skulls below the octave and crucifixes above. The pick-ups are active, with an EMG 81 on the bridge and an 86 on the neck. Controls are pretty basic, with one volume, one tone, and a three-way selector switch. There's a fully adjustable TOM bridge and no tailpiece, the strings threaded through the body in fine Telecaster style. All in all this is a very playable guitar with a great range of sounds, but it does beg the question as to who might buy an instrument like this. Would any serious, self-respecting metal guitarist want to be seen make such an overt declaration of admiration for another band? Fans might, more likely, want to buy the guitar in tribute to Jeff Hanneman, who passed away on May 2, 2013. **TB**

Fender
Mando-Strat 2013

Type Solidbody electric four-string mandolin
Body & neck Alder body, maple neck
Fingerboard Rosewood
Pick-ups One Fender single-coil pick-up

The Mando-Strat is a cross between the Fender Stratocaster six-string and a mandolin. It has only four strings, unlike most mandolins, which have eight, and is designed to re-create the sound, feel, and look of Fender mandolins of fifty years ago.

The bolt-on neck is maple with twenty-four frets and a C-shaped profile, but only a 13.78-in. (35-cm) scale. The alder double cutaway body features a specially designed Fender single-coil pick-up with a volume and tone control set into the tortoiseshell pickguard. Vintage-style tuners with white buttons sit on a Stratocaster-style headstock, and the body has a Strat-like, three-color sunburst finish. The vintage bridge with brass saddles may look familiar, too—it's made on the original machinery used to produce Fender's mandolin parts in the mid-twentieth century.

With four strings (G, D, A and E), the Mando-Strat produces a sound that is bright but which lacks the ringing of an eight-string instrument. The four-string Mando-Strat is built in Indonesia, where Fender's quality control is famously rigorous.

Jazzmando.com rates the Mando-Strat higher than the old and now discontinued Epiphone Mandobird to which it bears a passing resemblance. According to their online review, the pick-up on the Fender is better balanced, and the single coil, though by no means top-quality, is more than acceptable on an instrument that retails for only $399 in the United States and around £250 in the United Kingdom.

A future classic, the Fender Mando-Strat is currently endorsed by New England folk-rock band Rocket To The Moon. **SH**

Fender
Pro Newporter 2013

Type Acoustic six-string orchestra shape
Body & neck Mahogany body, maple neck
Fingerboard Rosewood
Pick-ups One Fishman sound hole pick-up

This limited-edition Custom Shop acoustic from Fender aims to recreate the appeal of the best of the company's acoustics from the 1960s. The original Newporter was marketed as a "pick-up-and-go" acoustic for strumming in the park or on the beach.

Only 150 of this top-end re-creation were made in the New Hartford workshop, and they all feature a high level of detail, including an all-solid mahogany body, gold pickguard, and Stratocaster-style headstock with six-on-a-side tuners. The Viking-style rosewood bridge, lacquered finish, and Fishman

"An all-solid mahogany orchestra-shape body tone machine that will have you reminiscing about fun-and-sun 1960s Fender acoustics."

FENDER SALES PROMOTION

sound hole pick-up, with volume and tone control inside the guitar body, complete the headline spec.

Design details include a neat "checkerboard" rosette, a "C"-shaped neck profile, and simple dot position markers on the 9-in. (22.9-cm) radius fingerboard. The tuners are nickel, while the nut, saddle, and bridge pins are all made of bone.

The Pro Newporter produces an impressive sound: the mahogany gives it a deep, warm tone, the maple neck adds brightness, and the Fishman system amplifies with accuracy and clarity.

With such attention to detail and premium features, it is no surprise that the Newporter costs $3,100. But the price tag has not deterred Avril Lavigne and The Kinks' Ray Davies. **SH**

Fender Vince Ray
Voodoo Bucket 300CE 2013

Type Electroacoustic
Body & neck Spruce/mahogany body, nato neck
Fingerboard Ebony/rosewood
Pick-ups One Fishman Isys III pick-up

The Fender T-Bucket 300CE electroacoustic has been around since 2009. Based on the Martin "Dreadnought" design, it features a compact preamp system with a versatile built-in tuner.

The 2013 Voodoo Bucket edition is covered with graphics by Vince Ray. Born Vincenzo Raymondo, Ray is a British artist, author, and tattooist who has also been lead singer and guitarist with The Vincent Razorbacks and, more recently, Vince Ray And The Boneshakers. By his own account, his early influences were "*Tales From The Crypt*, Batman, Emma Peel in *The Avengers*, and the U.S. rock 'n' roll subculture." He is also evidently a devotee of the sort of 1950s psychobilly and 1960s kitsch that make bands like The Cramps and The Meteors spring to mind.

The illustrations on the front and back of the Voodoo Bucket feature such trashy iconographia as snakes, Satan with a top hat, and a go-go dancer playing a pair of maracas while sitting by a gravestone with a snake wrapped round her—all rendered in black, red, and yellow against a natural wood background on the front and against black on the back. In addition, there is a little motif inlaid on the twelfth fret.

Ray has also designed the packaging for a range of "Fleline"-brand guitar strings, including his own signature set, the "Screaming Zombies." Lest anyone should doubt their originality, Ray explains how they were made: "We dug up a thousand coffins, stole the nails, and melted them down in the very pits of hell," and a "legion of zombie brains were distilled into green goo-goo slime and added to each individual string for extra lubrication." **AJ**

G&L Tom Hamilton
Signature Model 2013

Type Solidbody electric bass
Body & neck Pine body, maple neck
Fingerboard Ebony/rosewood
Pick-ups Two humbucker pick-ups

G&L's ASAT Bass has pretty much the same internal workings as its L-2000 model, but occupies a body that looks more like an unusually sparkly Telecaster than a Fender Precision. The MFD (magnetic field design) humbuckers have a ceramic bar magnet underneath each coil with adjustable pole pieces that let the player change the output of each string individually. For the Tom Hamilton signature model of the ASAT, G&L engineer Paul Gagon apparently listened to lots of Aerosmith records and fine-tuned the pick-ups so that they had exactly the right

> *"The new bass you built for Tom is fantastic, and he started tracking with it like twenty minutes after it arrived."*
>
> AIDEN MULLEN, HAMILTON'S GUITAR TECH

resonant peak to suit Hamilton's playing. Hence the "Hamiltone" nomenclature and G&L's tag line: "Putting the punch in the Aerosmith sound."

The Western sugar pine body and relatively compact size make the instrument easy on the player's back, and it's available in red, blue, or turquoise metal flake with silver-flake double binding.

According to G&L, "Tom Hamilton has been playing G&L ASAT Basses for nearly twenty years since he bought his first blue metal flake ASAT Bass at 48th Street Custom Guitars in New York City." Which is true, as far as it goes, but Hamilton has also been seen playing a Fender Precision, a MusicMan, a Gibson Thunderbird, a Gibson Les Paul bass, a Höfner Violin bass, and various Parker and Sadowsky basses. **AJ**

Gibson Joe Perry
1959 Les Paul 2013

Type Solidbody electric
Body & neck Mahogany/maple body, mahogany neck
Fingerboard Rosewood
Pick-ups Two Custombucker humbucker pick-ups

The 1959 Standard is one of the most sought-after Les Pauls, and among that year's guitars the one owned by Aerosmith's Joe Perry is often considered the very best. His old instrument—serial number 9-0663—is well worn by countless gigs and studio sessions, not only in his hands but also in those of the numerous other guitarists to whom it belonged down the years, including Slash, Billy Loosigian, and Eric Johnson. "It's got all the natural sustain and warmth, and when you turn it up it growls," says Perry, who would never have parted with it had it not been for the ups and downs in his band's fortunes.

Recognizing the pedigree of Perry's guitar, Gibson set about producing a limited-run copy of it. The re-creation started with a solid, one-piece, lightweight mahogany body with a maple top finished in "Tobacco Burst," just like the original. It even has aging that authentically matches the playing wear on the original.

The neck is carved from a single piece of quartersawn mahogany profiled from precise measurements of Joe's guitar. A set of Kluson tuners, lightweight aluminum tailpiece, cream binding, gold control knobs, and a cream plastic pickguard complete the vintage looks.

And this Les Paul sounds as close to Perry's original as possible, thanks to a pair of Custombucker humbucking pick-ups designed to match the original PAFs. The spec is awesome, but so, too, is the price—more than $10,000 (around £6,325). However, for the money you will get a period-faithful modern reproduction of an all-time great. **SH**

Gretsch Panther 2013

Type Solidbody electric
Body & neck Maple body and neck
Fingerboard Rosewood
Pick-ups Two Filter'Tron pick-ups

Gretsch introduced the Panther in 2013 to celebrate the company's 130th year of making instruments. At first glance, the Panther looks like many of the company's other models, but it seems genuinely aimed at modern players and can be used in "high gain" situations as well as having the clean tones normally associated with Gretsch instruments. It is available in black or white, and is easily recognizable by the outlined panther on the silver pickguard. The "CB" in the number (G6137TCB) denotes "Center Block" and refers to the spruce block set inside the slim, 1¾ in. (4.4 cm)- deep body. Beside reducing weight, this also helps to eliminate feedback. The hardware includes a Gretsch Bigsby vibrato, an adjustable bridge, and Grover "Stay-Tight" tuners. The pick-ups are high-sensitive Filter'Trons with a three-way selector switch and a master volume and tone control; there are also separate volume controls for each pick-up. Following in a fine tradition, the Panther looks set to become another classic. **JB**

Ibanez JS2410 Joe Satriani 2013

Type Solidbody electric
Body & neck Alder body, maple and bubinga neck
Fingerboard Rosewood
Pick-ups Two DiMarzio pick-ups

Joe Satriani taught Steve Vai, and played lead guitar on Mick Jagger's first solo tour in 1985. He has been playing his own signature Ibanez guitars since 1988, when the JS1 replaced the Ibanez 540 Radius model that he had previously been endorsing. The JS2410 is the latest in a long line of JS models and prototypes with a variety of custom features and paintwork.

One of the most consistent features is the Ibanez original "Edge" double-locking tremolo bridge, which is again present here, and the pick-ups are Joe Satriani signature DiMarzio humbuckers—the neck has a "Satch Track," and the bridge has a "Mo'Joe."

The "24" in the name refers to twenty-four frets—this is the first Joe Satriani model to be thus equipped. Unlike most guitars in the JS series, the JS2410 is made mostly of alder instead of basswood. There's a three-way pick-up selector with a master tone control that can be pulled to turn the humbuckers into single coils, and the master volume knob also operates as a high-pass filter switch. **AJ**

Ibanez
TAM100 2013

Type Eight-string solidbody electric
Body & neck Basswood/maple body, bubinga/wenge neck
Fingerboard Wenge
Pick-ups Three DiMarzio pick-ups

There's no question that Ibanez makes some pretty serious kit. This eight-string monster—a signature model for Tosin Abasi, of instrumental prog metal band Animals As Leaders—is as luxurious as you would expect from a guitar set to dent your bank balance to the tune of $5,000.

Visually, the TAM100 is pure Ibanez, with the characteristic body and headstock shape. The basswood body—another brand favorite—is topped with quilted maple; the neck is a five-piece construction of bubinga and wenge. The fingerboard is also cut from wenge, and fitted with twenty-four jumbo frets. The pick-ups are configured in the now-classic Superstrat H-S-H format, here featuring three different DiMarzio Ionizer 8s, controlled by a five-way selector switch and a two-way coil tap.

Two "extra" strings sit below the bottom E, and are factory-tuned to "E" and "B." The gold-plated hardware includes an FX EDGE III-8 double-locking fixed bridge to handle the stress of the two bass strings. **TB**

Jackson Corey
Beaulieu 2013

Type Solidbody six- or seven- string electric
Body & neck Alder/maple body, maple neck
Fingerboard Ebony
Pick-ups Two humbucker pick-ups

Corey Beaulieu is one of the twin lead guitarists of American metal band Trivium. He has long been a user of Jackson V guitars, and so it was no surprise when the company produced a signature model.

This special Jackson V model was designed by Corey himself and comes in either six- or seven-string versions. The electronics are simple: a three-way pick-up selector and a volume control. The pick-ups are two Seymour Duncan Blackout active humbuckers, extended for use with seven-string guitars.

Construction-wise, it's fairly standard—a through-neck design with twenty-four frets and a compound fingerboard radius altering the curve as you climb higher up the neck.

The details include pearloid shark-fin inlays, a pointy reverse headstock, ebony fingerboard, locking nut, black hardware, Jackson tuners and a Floyd Rose locking tremolo. The flame maple top is not hidden by any pickguard or binding. Such details account for the retail price, which is currently in excess of $3,500. **SH**

Kramer
B3 Baretta 2013

Type Solidbody electric
Body & neck Maple body and neck
Fingerboard Rosewood
Pick-ups One Seymour Duncan humbucker pick-up

The Kramer Barreta is a reissue of the original 1984 model made famous by Eddie Van Halen. It is difficult to describe the impact this guitar had on its first appearance—everything Van Halen did had such a vast influence, not only on guitarists but also on the global guitar-manufacturing industry. For a time, Kramer was one of the biggest guitar companies in the United States, in no small part because of the original Baretta. Indeed, even Gibson and Fender were forced to produce competing instruments, although with little success.

So how does this reissue compare to the original? They look identical, but there is a difference between a guitar built in New Jersey and one built in Korea. The Barreta has basically a Strat-style body, with a single pick-up, a Floyd Rose vibrato, and the characteristic "banana" headstock. Unlike the original, which was available only in white, black, or cream, the 2013 model comes in an assortment of finishes, including "bull's-eye" graphics. The body and neck are both maple and the fingerboard is rosewood. The angle of the headstock differs from that of the original, and is less "intense." Also, significantly, the neck is varnished, unlike the original, which was oiled. It does have the same neck profile, though, with a 12-in. (30.5-cm) radius and 14:1 ratio tuners. It is fitted with a licensed Floyd Rose and a single Seymour Duncan humbucker pick-up, with a coil-tap built into the single volume control. The overall look and feel are very close to the originals—which, as a former Kramer endorsee, I have owned. At $700, this is a very good guitar that does justice to its illustrious predecessor. **JB**

Loog
II 2013

Type Short-scale three-string nylon-string acoustic
Body & neck Basswood body, maple neck
Fingerboard Rosewood

Uruguayan Rafael Atijas conceived the Loog Guitar while writing his master's thesis at New York University; the first production run was paid for through the Kickstarter funding website. His idea was to produce a short-scale—20½ in. (52 cm)—three-stringed guitar intended for children aged six and above. His rationale was simple: "Three strings really makes it easier for kids to tune, play, and listen to the notes they are playing, offering a stimulating (and less overwhelming) experience that allows children to play music right from the start." It may not be an approach for music

> "I wanted to make a children's guitar that wasn't just a smaller guitar; I wanted to offer a real benefit that would make it fun to play."
>
> RAFAEL ATIJAS, INVENTOR OF THE LOOG

education purists, but is the perfect way of maintaining motivation in the very young. Children like to see immediate results, and the Loog gives them just that. Through tuning to the suggested open A (A-E-A), the player can play major chords with an index finger alone, changing them by moving up and down the fingerboard. Above all, it's brilliant fun.

What's more, in the age-old tradition of the cigar-box guitar, the three different Loog designs ("II" is shown here) have to be assembled. The kit takes around fifteen minutes to put together and requires no more than a screwdriver. And, as anyone who has built a guitar will tell you, the bond with an instrument you have made yourself is much stronger than that with one you have simply bought. **TB**

Reverend
Tricky Gomez 2013

Schecter Johnny
Christ Bass 2013

Type Semi-hollow body semi-acoustic
Body & neck Korina/maple, korina neck
Fingerboard Rosewood
Pick-ups Two Revtron pick-ups

Type Solidbody electric bass
Body & neck Ash body, maple neck
Fingerboard Ebony
Pick-ups Two EMG Active MMCS and 81 pick-ups

With its Revtron pick-ups, semi-hollow body, f-hole, and Bigsby tremolo, the Tricky Gomez from Reverend combines a retro vibe with modern build quality. It was designed for players who are attracted to old-style instruments, but who want something sturdy, stable, and reliable too.

It's clearly based on the company's Manta Ray guitar, but with added vintage mojo. The semi-hollow resonant korina (white limba) body, with two acoustic chambers on either side of a central korina core, gives a rich sound, and the custom-made Reverend pick-ups add punch. The latter are based on Gretsch's 1959 Filter'Trons, but wound a little hotter for a strong midrange presence.

Modern details include a satin finish, graphite nut, dual-action truss rod, roller bridge, and Reverend's "Pin-lock" tuners.

Controls include volume, tone, and Reverend's "bass contour" device, which allows players to vary between single-coil and humbucker sounds. **SH**

Some fans of Avenged Sevenfold feared that Johnny Christ's decision to abandon the MusicMan Stingray bass in favor of this Schecter signature model would rob him of the cutting edge he needed to compete with the guitars of fellow band members, Zacky Vengeance and Synyster Gates. On past performance, they were right to worry—Schecter basses had a reputation for being more effective at the bottom end of the frequency spectrum. But the makers responded effectively by fitting this bass with an EMG 81 pick-up—usually associated with lead guitars—in addition to the MM Bass humbucker at the bridge.

This bass also features Grover "MINI" machine heads, an ebony fretboard, and a three-piece maple neck. There are master volume and blend controls, and an active two-band EQ. The gold hardware looks pretty against the obligatory black body. There's an inlay of Avenged Sevenfold's "Skullbat" logo at the twelfth fret, and the inlaid fret markers are upside-down gold crucifixes. **AJ**

Schecter Nikki Sixx "Schecter Sixx" 2013

The Loar LH-319 2013

Type Solidbody electric bass
Body & neck Walnut and maple "through-neck" design
Fingerboard Rosewood
Pick-ups Two EMG active pick-ups

Type Archtop semi-acoustic
Body & neck Maple/spruce body, mahogany neck
Fingerboard Rosewood
Pick-ups Two Loar P-90 pick-ups

Nikki Sixx, the Mötley Crüe bass man, is well known for his long-standing use of the Gibson Thunderbird. So much so, in fact, that, in 2000, Gibson produced the Blackbird—a black Thunderbird, no less—in his honor. A few years later, Sixx gave his name to an uncharacteristic, rather beautiful, Ovation electroacoustic bass. And finally, at the NAMM trade show in January 2013, the Schecter Sixx was unleashed.

On paper, the instrument may not seem all that remarkable—the satin black finish is nothing new, and, of course, it is not the first Thunderbird-shaped bass. Nevertheless, this is a very special guitar. Schecter Guitar Research has come up with a multi-laminate, maple-and-walnut, "through-neck" design, powered by a flexible, EMG active pick-up system, which guarantees a clean and punchy midrange and a very warm low end. And an RRP of $1,399 is a pretty reasonable deal for an instrument of this quality. But let's leave the last word to Mr. Sixx himself: "Simply said, this bass rocks!" **TB**

Construction of the Loar LH-319 starts with the hand carving of a solid piece of fine spruce for the arched top, which is then married to select maple for the back and sides.

The neck is a traditional V-profile piece of mahogany, and the two custom Loar P-90 pick-ups complete the vintage vibe. Spot also the open-backed Grover Butterbean tuners, and the floating, trapeze-style tailpiece.

The build quality of the new LH-319 is high: you'll find details like an ivory-bound rosewood fretboard, an inlaid fleur-de-lis in the headstock, a standard bone nut, and a compensated ebony bridge. There's a simple three-way pick-up selector, plus a single volume and tone control. Loar have found the two best spots to place the two pick-ups for optimum tone and versatility.

The result is an attempt to revisit the golden age of archtop guitars, but with modern expertise, and a reasonable price tag of around $600. **SH**

Vigier Ron "Bumblefoot" Thal 2013

Type Double-neck electric
Body & neck Mahogany body, carbon-reinforced neck
Fingerboard One rosewood, one "delta metal"
Pick-ups Two DiMarzio Chopper/Tone Zone pick-ups

The website of Patrice Vigier guitars carries what amounts to a manifesto of a guitar maker devoted to excellence and experimentation swimming against a tide of the marketing-led mediocrity of the industry's big guns. "Nothing is ever perfect. Nothing is ever complete or final," he claims, before quoting Japanese luthier K. Yairi: "It is a crime against nature to manufacture instruments of poor quality."

For such lofty ideals to be anything more than bluster, Vigier's guitars need to be outstandingly good. Vigier's intention is to produce his instruments in France, using woods grown in French forests; over a thirty-year career, he has largely achieved this aim. And there's an important technological dimension: his guitars are well known for the "10/90" system of carbon reinforcement bars built into their necks. These replace the conventional truss rods, and offer, he believes, far greater stability.

Vigier previewed one of his most curious designs at NAMM 2013—a double-neck signature model for Ron "Bumblefoot" Thal of Guns N' Roses. Thal is one of a small number of guitarists to make extensive use of Vigier's fretless metal-fingerboard instruments, which have, perhaps surprisingly, been in production since 1979. Thal's signature model, unlike most instruments of this type, comprises two six-string necks, one conventional, the other fretless, thus combining his two favorite Vigiers in a single instrument.

Ron "Bumblefoot" Thal's fretless Vigier work can be heard to good effect on "all those drudging slurs . . . and weird soars" on Guns N' Roses' 2006 album *Chinese Democracy*. **TB**

Ron "Bumblefoot" Thal performing on stage with his signature Vigier. →

Index of Guitars by Model

Contributors

Owen Bailey (OB) is a writer and amateur musician. He has written for *Total Guitar* magazine, MusicRadar, Guitar Techniques, and Backbeat Books, and has been a regular contributor to *Guitarist* magazine since 2005.

Jim Barber (JB) has worked as guitar technician, and as a guitarist he has played on close to 200 albums. As a writer, he has contributed to many notable guitar books. He currently leads his own band, The Barberians.

John M. Bowers (JMB) is a musician, researcher, hacker, and instrument-builder, and plays both in the post-drone improv band Tonesucker.

Chris Bryans (CB) has written for *Time Out Singapore*, *Radio Times*, *Record Collector*, and the *Observer*. The first song he played on guitar was "New Rose" by the Damned.

Dave Burluck (DB) is one of the UK's most experienced guitar journalists. He's a performer, songwriter, and producer and is the gear reviews editor of *Guitarist* and *Total Guitar*.

Terry Burrows (TB) has written almost seventy books. A multi-instrumentalist, he's played on over fifty commercial releases, including co-founding a band recently listed in a national European magazine as the "twenty-third most underrated" of all time.

Paul Day (PD) has enjoyed an involvement with the guitar that spans over fifty years: as a player, professional performer, consultant, keen collector, historian, and author. He has written for numerous magazines and contributed to more than 300 books.

Michael Dregni (MD) has written for *Vintage Guitar*, *L'Express*, *Guitar Aficionado*, *Guitar Player*, *The Fretboard Journal*, and other magazines.

Gilberto Dusman (GD) is a classical guitarist, musicologist, author, and dramatist. He specializes in the Classical and Romantic periods.

Dave Gregory (DG) joined XTC in 1979 as guitarist and remained with them for nineteen years. He has toured and played on numerous recordings for other artists, and today is a member of both Big Big Train and Tin Spirits.

Simon Heptinstall (SH) is a writer and guitarist who describes his guitar style as "blues flamenco funk." He plays lead guitar in original roots rock band Billy in the Lowground.

Alan Jenkins (AJ) has played guitar on dozens of albums over the last thirty-four years. He is also the author of *How to be in a Pop Group* and is an award-winning trombonist.

Bruno MacDonald (BM) wrote *Air Guitar: A User's Guide*. He co-edited *1001 Songs You Must Hear Before You Die*, and his *Pink Floyd: Through The Eyes Of…* still remains in print in the United States after fifteen years.

Joel McIver (JM) is the author of twenty-four books on rock music and is the editor of *Bass Guitar* magazine. He regularly appears on radio and TV.

Ed Mitchell (EM) worked in guitar retail for eighteen years before joining *Total Guitar* in 2003. He now contributes to *Total Guitar* and *Guitarist* and is editor of *Classic Rock Presents The Blues*.

Dennis Pernu (DP) is gear editor at *Vintage Guitar* magazine and senior acquisitions editor at Voyageur Press.

Edward Pitt (EP) is a writer and guitar historian who has written for *Vintage Guitar* magazine and the *Blue Book of Electric Guitars*, as well as his own web site, JunkGuitars.com.

Rachel Price (RP) is a journalist who has written for newspapers and magazines including the *Daily Telegraph*, *Sky*, *Blockbuster*, and Gurgle. She was once in a band called Jody and the Creams.

Pooch Purtil (PP) was guitarist for punk band Discharge, and later went on to form NWOBHM band Hells Belles. He now works as a photographer.

Chris Riley (CR) has written music, pop culture, and lifestyle features for a variety of newspapers and magazines including the *New Statesman*, the *Guardian* and the *Daily Telegraph*. He is currently at *The Times*.

Barry Stone (BS) is an internationally published author of numerous general history titles, who, in his alter ego as a travel writer, spends far too much time plotting future destinations.

Ivan Symaeys (IS), a.k.a. lordbizarre, describes himself as an "electrotech" guitar collector and curator of Lordbizarre's Electric Guitar and Amplifier Museum.

Doug Tulloch (DT) is the author of *Neptune Bound… The Ultimate Danelectro Guitar Guide*, described by guitar guru George Gruhn as "a monumental task".

Picture Credits

Every effort has been made to credit the copyright holders of the images used in this book. We apologize for any unintentional omissions or errors and will insert the appropriate acknowledgment to any companies or individuals in subsequent editions of the work.

24 Paris, Musée Jacquemart-André – Institut de France © Musée Jacquemart-André- Culturespaces **25** Outline Press Ltd. **26** © Ashmolean Museum, University of Oxford. **27** De Agostini Picture Library/G. Dagli Orti/The Bridgeman Art Library **28** Edinburgh University **29** © Ashmolean Museum, University of Oxford. **30l** © Ashmolean Museum, University of Oxford. **30r** Outline Press Ltd. **31l** The Metropolitan Museum of Art **31r** The Metropolitan Museum of Art **32** Outline Press Ltd. **33** Outline Press Ltd. **34** Outline Press Ltd. **35** Courtesy of Gregg Miner **36** Outline Press Ltd. **37** Outline Press Ltd. **38** Outline Press Ltd. **39** The Metropolitan Museum of Art **40** Outline Press Ltd. **41** Outline Press Ltd. **42** Outline Press Ltd. **43** Pictorial Press Ltd/Alamy **44** Outline Press Ltd. **45** Outline Press Ltd. **46** Outline Press Ltd. **47l** Outline Press Ltd. **47r** Outline Press Ltd. **48** Outline Press Ltd. **49** Outline Press Ltd. **50** Outline Press Ltd. **51** Outline Press Ltd. **52** Getty Images **53** Outline Press Ltd. **54** Outline Press Ltd. **55** Outline Press Ltd. **56** Outline Press Ltd. **57** Outline Press Ltd. **58** Outline Press Ltd. **59** Outline Press Ltd. **60l** Outline Press Ltd. **60r** Outline Press Ltd. **61l** Outline Press Ltd. **61r** Outline Press Ltd. **62** Outline Press Ltd. **63** Getty Images **64** Outline Press Ltd. **65** Outline Press Ltd. **66** Outline Press Ltd. **67** Outline Press Ltd. **68** Outline Press Ltd. **69** Outline Press Ltd. **70** Outline Press Ltd. **71** Outline Press Ltd. **72** Outline Press Ltd. **73** Outline Press Ltd. **74** Outline Press Ltd. **75** Outline Press Ltd. **76** Outline Press Ltd. **77l** Outline Press Ltd. **77r** Outline Press Ltd. **78** Outline Press Ltd. **79** Outline Press Ltd. **80** Outline Press Ltd. **81** Outline Press Ltd. **82** Getty Images **83** Outline Press Ltd. **84** Outline Press Ltd. **85** Outline Press Ltd. **86** Courtesy of Michael Dregni **87** Michael Ochs Archives/ Getty Images **94** Outline Press Ltd. **95** Outline Press Ltd. **96** Outline Press Ltd. **97** Outline Press Ltd. **98** Outline Press Ltd. **99** Outline Press Ltd. **100** Getty Images **101** Outline Press Ltd. **102** Outline Press Ltd. **103** Outline Press Ltd. **104** Outline Press Ltd. **105** Getty Images **106l** Outline Press Ltd. **106r** Outline Press Ltd. **107l** Outline Press Ltd. **107r** Courtesy of Michael Dregni **108** Getty Images **109** The Metropolitan Museum of Art **110** Courtesy of Michael Dregni **111** William P. Gottlieb Collection (Library of Congress) **112** Outline Press Ltd. **113** Courtesy EMP Museum, Seattle, WA. **114** Outline Press Ltd. **115** Outline Press Ltd. **116** Outline Press Ltd. **117** Getty Images **118** Outline Press Ltd. **119** Outline Press Ltd. **120l** Outline Press Ltd. **120r** Courtesy of Marc Louthon **121l** Outline Press Ltd. **121r** Outline Press Ltd. **122** Outline Press Ltd. **123** Outline Press Ltd. **124l** Outline Press Ltd. **124r** Outline Press Ltd. **125l** Outline Press Ltd. **125r** Outline Press Ltd. **126** Outline Press Ltd. **127** Outline Press Ltd. **128** Outline Press Ltd. **129** Outline Press Ltd. **130** Redferns **131** Outline Press Ltd. **135** Courtesy of Deke Dickerson Photo Archive **136** Courtesy of Sotheby's Picture Library **137** Courtesy of Michael Dregni **138** Outline Press Ltd. **139** Michael Ochs Archives/Getty Images **140** Redferns **141** Outline Press Ltd. **142** Outline Press Ltd. **143** Outline Press Ltd. **144** Outline Press Ltd. **145** Outline Press Ltd. **146** Outline Press Ltd. **147** Outline Press Ltd. **148** Michael Ochs Archives/Getty Images **149** Outline Press Ltd. **150l** Outline Press Ltd. **150r** Outline Press Ltd. **151l** Outline Press Ltd. **151r** Outline Press Ltd. **152** Outline Press Ltd. **153** Michael Ochs Archives/Getty Images **154** Redferns **155** Outline Press Ltd. **156** Outline Press Ltd. **157** Outline Press Ltd. **158** Outline Press Ltd. **159** Redferns **160l** Outline Press Ltd. **160r** Outline Press Ltd. **161l** Outline Press Ltd. **161r** Outline Press Ltd. **162** Outline Press Ltd. **163** Outline Press Ltd. **164l** Outline Press Ltd. **164r** Outline Press Ltd. **165l** Outline Press Ltd. **165r** Outline Press Ltd. **166** Outline Press Ltd. **167** Redferns **168** Michael Ochs Archives/Getty Images **169** Outline Press Ltd. **170** Outline Press Ltd. **171l** Outline Press Ltd. **171r** Outline Press Ltd. **172** Outline Press Ltd. **173** Outline Press Ltd. **174l** Outline Press Ltd. **174r** Outline Press Ltd. **175l** Outline Press Ltd. **175r** Outline Press Ltd. **176** Outline Press Ltd. **177** Outline Press Ltd. **178** Outline Press Ltd. **179** Redferns **180l** Outline Press Ltd. **181l** Outline Press Ltd. **181r** Outline Press Ltd. **183** Getty Images **184** Outline Press Ltd. **185** Outline Press Ltd. **186l** Outline Press Ltd. **186r** Outline Press Ltd. **187l** Outline Press Ltd. **187r** Outline Press Ltd. **188** Outline Press Ltd. **189** Outline Press Ltd. **191** Outline Press Ltd. **192** Outline Press Ltd. **193** Redferns **194** Outline Press Ltd. **195** Laurence Berne **196** Outline Press Ltd. **197** NBC via Getty Images **198** Outline Press Ltd. **199** Getty Images **200** Outline Press Ltd. **201** Getty Images **202** Outline Press Ltd. **203** Getty Images **204** Getty Images **205** Outline Press Ltd. **206** Outline Press Ltd. **207** Outline Press Ltd. **208** Outline Press Ltd. **209** Redferns **210** Outline Press Ltd. **211** Outline Press Ltd. **212** Redferns **213** Outline Press Ltd. **215l** Outline Press Ltd. **217** Outline Press Ltd. **219** Redferns **220** Redferns **221** Outline Press Ltd. **223** Michael Ochs Archives/Getty Images **226** Outline Press Ltd. **231l** Outline Press Ltd. **231r** Outline Press Ltd. **232** Redferns **234** Outline Press Ltd. **235** Outline Press Ltd. **236l** Courtesy of Edward Pitt **236r** Outline Press Ltd. **237l** Courtesy of Edward Pitt **237r** Outline Press Ltd. **241** Outline Press Ltd. **242** Outline Press Ltd. **243** FilmMagic **244l** Outline Press Ltd. **244r** Outline Press Ltd. **245l** Outline Press Ltd. **247** Michael Ochs Archives/Getty Images **248** Paris Match via Getty Images **249** Outline Press Ltd. **250r** Outline Press Ltd. **252** Outline Press Ltd. **254** Outline Press Ltd. **256** Redferns **257** Outline Press Ltd. **258** Outline Press Ltd. **261l** Outline Press Ltd. **261r** Outline Press Ltd. **262** Outline Press Ltd. **263** ITV/Rex Features **264** Outline Press Ltd. **266** Outline Press Ltd. **269l** Outline Press Ltd. **269r** Outline Press Ltd. **270** Outline Press Ltd. **271** Outline Press Ltd. **273** Outline Press Ltd. **274l** Outline Press Ltd. **274r** Outline Press Ltd. **277** Getty Images **280l** Outline Press Ltd. **280r** Outline Press Ltd. **282** Outline Press Ltd. **284** Outline Press Ltd. **285** Outline Press Ltd. **286** Outline Press Ltd. **287** Outline Press Ltd. **288** Outline Press Ltd. **289** Redferns **290l** Terry Burrows **291r** Courtesy of Edward Pitt **292l** Outline Press Ltd. **292r** Doug Tulloch **293** Outline Press Ltd. **296** Redferns **297** Outline Press Ltd. **299** Redferns **300** Outline Press Ltd. **301** Outline Press Ltd. **302l** Outline Press Ltd. **302r** Outline Press Ltd. **303l** Outline Press Ltd. **305** Courtesy of Edward Pitt **306** WireImage **309** Redferns **312l** Outline Press Ltd. **313l** Outline Press Ltd. **314** Outline Press Ltd. **315** Getty Images **316l** Courtesy of Edward Pitt **316r** Outline Press Ltd. **317l** Outline Press Ltd. **319** Outline Press Ltd. **320** Outline Press Ltd. **321** Michael Ochs Archives/Getty Images **322** Outline Press Ltd. **323** Outline Press Ltd. **324l** Outline Press Ltd. **325l** Outline Press Ltd. **325r** Outline Press Ltd. **326** Outline Press Ltd. **329** Terry Burrows **330** Outline Press Ltd. **331** Laurence Berne **333** Outline Press Ltd. **335l** Outline Press Ltd. **335r** Courtesy of Michael Dregni **336** Outline Press Ltd. **337** Redferns **338l** Outline Press Ltd. **339l** Outline Press Ltd. **340** Outline Press Ltd. **342** FilmMagic **344** Gretsch Musical Instruments **348r** Outline Press Ltd. **349l** Outline Press Ltd. **349r** C. F. Martin & Co. **350l** Outline Press Ltd. **350r** Outline Press Ltd. **352** Outline Press Ltd. **355r** Outline Press Ltd. **356** Outline Press Ltd. **357** Outline Press Ltd. **358** Outline Press Ltd. **360** Outline Press Ltd. **361l** Outline Press Ltd. **361r** Courtesy of Edward Pitt **362l** KMC Music **362r** Outline Press Ltd. **363l** Outline Press Ltd. **363r** Outline Press Ltd. **364** Courtesy of Edward Pitt **365** Outline Press Ltd. **366** Outline Press Ltd. **367** Outline Press Ltd. **368** Outline Press Ltd. **370r** Outline Press Ltd. **371l** Doug Tulloch **371r** Outline Press Ltd. **372** Redferns **373** Courtesy of Sotheby's Picture Library **375** Redferns **376** Outline Press Ltd. **377** Outline Press Ltd. **378** Outline Press Ltd. **379** Outline Press Ltd. **380** Outline Press Ltd. **381** Outline Press Ltd. **382** Outline Press Ltd. **383** Outline Press Ltd. **384** Outline Press Ltd. **385** Courtesy of Edward Pitt **387**

739 Courtesy of Marc Louthon 740 Photo © Christie's Images 741 Mobius Megatar Ltd. 742 Paul Reed Smith Guitars 743 Outline Press Ltd. 744l Outline Press Ltd. 744r Outline Press Ltd. 745l Outline Press Ltd. 745r Outline Press Ltd. 746 Outline Press Ltd. 747 Outline Press Ltd. 748 Gibson Guitar Corporation 749 Redferns 750l Courtesy of Marc Louthon 750r MotorAve Guitars 751l Outline Press Ltd. 751r Outline Press Ltd. 752l Washburn/ US Music Corporation 752r Washburn/ US Music Corporation 753l Outline Press Ltd. 753r Outline Press Ltd. 754 Jens Ritter 755 Jens Ritter 756 Crafter Guitars 757 Gibson Guitar Corporation 758l Låg Tremontaine 758r McIlroy Guitars 759l Modulus Guitars 759r KMC Music 760 Taylor Guitars 761 Ulrich Teuffel 762 Washburn/ US Music Corporation 763 WireImage 764 Blackmachine 765 Daisy Rock Guitars 766r Outline Press Ltd. 767l Outline Press Ltd. 767r Outline Press Ltd. 768 Paul Reed Smith Guitars 769 Paul Reed Smith Guitars 770l RainSong Guitars 770r Warmoth Guitar Products 771l Warr Guitars Inc. 771r Art & Lutherie/Godin Guitars 772 Ayers Music Co. Ltd. 773 Outline Press Ltd. 774 Outline Press Ltd. 775 Ibanez Guitars 776 Yamaha Corporation 777 Outline Press Ltd. 778 C.F. Martin & Co. 779 Redferns 780l Rayco Resophonics 780r Santa Cruz Guitar Company 781l Outline Press Ltd. 781r Status Graphite 782 Getty Images 783 Taylor Guitars 784 Taylor Guitars 785 Alberto E. Rodriguez/Getty Images for Global Philanthropy Group 786 Ulrich Teuffel 787 Cole Clark 788 Photo © Christie's Images 789 Fender Musical Instruments Corporation 790 Gibson Guitar Corporation 791 Getty Images 792l Outline Press Ltd. 793l KMC Music 793r Paul Reed Smith Guitars 794 Jackson Guitars 795 Kremona USA 796 J.K. Lado & Co. 797 Luna Guitars 798 KMC Music 799 Outline Press Ltd. 800l Jens Ritter 800r Fender Musical Instruments Corporation 801l J.S. Technologies Inc. 801r Taylor Guitars 802 Washburn/ US Music Corporation 803 WireImage 804 Getty Images 805 Dean Campbell 806 Campbell American 807 Gibson Guitar Corporation 808l Gibson Guitar Corporation 808r Gibson Guitar Corporation 809l Ibanez Guitars 809r Fender Musical Instruments Corporation 810 Lakland Guitars LLC 811 WireImage 812 Redferns 813 Paul Reed Smith Guitars 814 Dean Guitars 815 Getty Images 816 The Evaline Guitar Company 817 Fender Musical Instruments Corporation 818 Gibson Guitar Corporation 819 Outline Press Ltd. 820 Paul Reed Smith Guitars 821 Ruokangas 822l Fender Musical Instruments Corporation 822r Taylor Guitars 823l Guitarras Almansa 823r Blindworm Guitars 824l Tom Cutler 824r Dean Guitars 825l Duesenberg USA Inc. 825r Outline Press Ltd. 826 Fernandes Guitars 827 Gibson Guitar Corporation 828l Godin Guitars 828r Ibanez Guitars 829l Ibanez Guitars 829r Ibanez Guitars 830 Manson Guitars 831 FilmMagic 832 Peerless Guitars 833 Paul Reed Smith Guitars 834 Samick Music Corporation 835 Fender Musical Instruments Corporation 836l Thomas V. Jones 836r John Hornby Skewes & Co. Ltd. 837l Vox Amplification Ltd. 837r Warwick/ US Music Corporation 838l Caparison Guitars 838r Collings Guitars 839l Duesenberg USA Inc. 839r Gibson Guitar Corporation 840 Outline Press Ltd. 841 ESP Guitar Company 842 Outline Press Ltd. 843 Ray Gander/ Gander Guitars 844 Outline Press Ltd. 845 Gibson Guitar Corporation 846 Gibson Guitar Corporation 847 Destroy All Guitars 848l Courtesy of Adam Jay 848r Guerilla Guitars 849l Indie Guitar Company 849r John Hornby Skewes & Co Ltd. 850 John Letts 851 M.V. Pedulla Guitars Inc. 852 Paul Reed Smith Guitars 853 Paul Reed Smith Guitars 854 Outline Press Ltd. 856 Schecter Guitars Research 857 Getty Images 858 Ernie Ball/MusicMan 859 Ernie Ball/MusicMan 860 B.C. Rich 861 Photo by Kevin Nixon/Classic Rock Magazine via Getty Images 862l Brazen Guitars 862r Dave Bunker 863l Outline Press Ltd. 863r Collings Guitars 864 Daemoness Guitars 865 Eastwood Guitars 866l Gibson Guitar Corporation 866r ESP Guitar Company 867l First Act Guitars 867r Woodview Enterprises Ltd. 868l Giannini Musical Instruments and Strings 868r Givson Musical Industry 869l Genuine Musical Products Inc. 869r Godin Guitars 870l Hagstrom/ US Music Corporation 870r Halo 871l Hoyer/ Ritter USA LLC 871r Patrick Hufschmid 872 John Hornby Skewes & Co Ltd. 873 Jay Turser/US Music Corporation 874 Jean Larrivée Guitars Inc. 875 Line 6 Inc. 876 George Lowden Guitars Ltd. 877 Brian Moore 878 Ernie Ball/MusicMan 879 Photo by Kevin Nixon/Classic Rock Magazine via Getty Images 880 Ernie Ball/MusicMan 881 Arne Jacobsen 882l KMC Music 882r Paul Reed Smith Guitars 883l Destroy All Guitars 883r Schecter Guitars Research 884l Starr Labs 884r Traben Company 885l Cort Guitars 885r Decibel Guitars 886 Redferns 887 Fender Musical Instruments Corporation 888 Fender Musical Instruments Corporation 889 Gibson Guitar Corporation 890 Gibson Guitar Corporation 891 GMW Guitarworks/Lee Garver 892 Ibanez Guitars 893 WireImage 894l Mayones Guitars and Basses 894r Michael Kelly Guitar Co. 895l Sadowsky Guitars Ltd. 895r Viktorian Musical Instrument Co. 896l Waterstone Guitars 896r Amfisound 897l Aristides Instruments 897r Babicz Guitars 898 B.C. Rich 899 FilmMagic 900 B.C. Rich 901 Courtesy of Laurence Berne Dean Campbell 903 Fender Musical Instruments Corporation 904 NBC via Getty Images 905 Cort Guitars 906 DBZ Guitars LLC 907 Farida Guitars 908 Fender Musical Instruments Corporation 909 Flaxwood 910 Mike Fleck 911 Freshman Guitars 912 Gibson Guitar Corporation 913 Godin Guitars 914l Destroy All Guitars 914r HeliArc 915l Richard Howell 915r Ibanez Guitars 916l Ibanez Guitars 916r Jeff Figley 917l Lacey Guitars 917r Lakewood Guitars GmbH & Co. KG 918 Mike Lull Custom Guitars 919 Getty Images 920 Olaf Diegel 921 Peavey Electronics 922 Peavey Electronics 923 Mike Potvin 924 Paul Reed Smith Guitars 925 Greg Opatik 926l Fender Musical Instruments Corporation 926r Fender Musical Instruments Corporation 927l Andrea Tacchi 927r Destroy All Guitars 928l Courtesy of Adam Jay 928r Courtesy of Nicci Strauss 929l Washburn/ US Music Corporation 929r Washburn/ US Music Corporation 930l Carvin Guitars 930r Dean Guitars 931l Dean Guitars 931r Deimel Guitarworks 932 Gibson Guitar Corporation 933 Ernie Ball/ MusicMan 934 ESP Guitar Company 935 Fender Musical Instruments Corporation 936 Fender Musical Instruments Corporation 937 Fender Musical Instruments Corporation 938 G&L Musical Instruments 939 Gibson Guitar Corporation 940l Fender Musical Instruments Corporation 940r Ibanez Guitars 941l Ibanez Guitars 941r Fender Musical Instruments Corporation 942 Gibson Guitar Corporation 943 Rafael Atijas 944l Reverend Guitars 944r Schecter Guitars Research 945l Schecter Guitars Research 945r The Loar 946 Vigier Guitars 947 Getty Images

Acknowledgments

Terry Burrows (terryburrows.com) would like to thank: all of the contributing writers for their most excellent efforts; Dave Gregory and Guy Mackenzie for allowing their mighty guitar collections to be photographed and to Pooch Purtil for taking the pictures (Guy's fabulous collection is online at theguitarcollection.org.uk); Nigel Osborne for providing images from his extensive library; Sergey Engel (cheesyguitars.com) for his invaluable help in sourcing Soviet-era guitars; Edward Pitt (junkguitars.com), Michael Dregni, Tom Cutler, Dan (odysseyguitars.ca), Andrew Mannering (shergold.co.uk), and Doug Tulloch for providing photographs of their own personal guitars; and Gregg Miner (harpguitars.net) for the use of images. And enormous thanks also to the following guitar builders/organizations who provided instruments, invaluable information, or images: Rafael Atijas of Loog Guitars, Laurene Berne, Dean Campbell (Campbell American), Olivier Carlón, Wayne Charvel, Cliff and Travis Cultreri of Destroy All Guitars, Prof. Olaf Diegel, Mark and Tom Erlewine, Jason Farrell, Mike Fleck, Paul Fischer, Ray Gander, Brian Godding, John Hornby Skewes, Arne Jacobsen, Adam Jay, Michael Judd, Marcus Nevin, Martin Howells, Patrick Hufschmid, Tom "TV" Jones, Joe Kovacic, Marc Louthon, Greg Opatik, Mike Potvin, Dale Rumbold, Paul Schuster of Mike Lull Custom Guitars, Andrea Tacchi, Nicolene Strauss at Township Guitars, Fred Stuart, Mark Warr, and Louis Burrows for additional picture research. And finally to everyone at Quintessence who helped to make it happen.